Sustainable Entrepreneurship and Social Innovation

Sustainable entrepreneurship has attracted growing attention in both scholarly and practitioner circles. Focusing on generating social, environmental and business value, the notion has been raised more recently to address the contribution of entrepreneurial activities to sustainable economic and social development.

Sustainable Entrepreneurship and Social Innovation builds on a theoretical framework that addresses related topics via a combination of insights from sustainability, policy, managerial, strategic, innovation and institutional perspectives. Providing empirical casework as well as a conceptual and theoretical framework, the book takes a global, interdisciplinary approach to the emergent field of sustainable entrepreneurship. The book highlights elements of sustainable entrepreneurship which have a societal impact as well as regional relevance and related aspects of innovation are also presented. Definitional issues are further elaborated in order to encompass the main interconnected fields of study, sustainable entrepreneurship and social innovation.

This book is an important resource for academic researchers, and postgraduate and advanced undergraduate students in the fields of entrepreneurship, innovation and sustainability.

Katerina Nicolopoulou is a Senior Lecturer at the Hunter Centre for Entrepreneurship, Strathclyde Business School, UK.

Mine Karatas-Ozkan is a Professor of Strategy and Entrepreneurship at the University of Southampton, UK.

Frank Janssen is full Professor of Entrepreneurship at the Louvain School of Management, Université catholique de Louvain, Belgium.

John Jermier is Professor of Sustainable Enterprise Research at the University of South Florida, USA.

Routledge Research in Sustainability and Business

Environmental Certification for Organisations and Products
Management approaches and operational tools
Edited by Tiberio Daddi, Fabio Iraldo and Francesco Testa

Energy Law and the Sustainable Company
Innovation and corporate social responsibility
Patricia Park and Duncan Park

Corporate Social Responsibility and Natural Resource Conflict
Kylie McKenna

Corporate Responsibility and Sustainable Development
Exploring the nexus of private and public interests
Edited by Lez Rayman-Bacchus and Philip R. Walsh

Sustainable Entrepreneurship and Social Innovation
Edited by Katerina Nicolopoulou, Mine Karatas-Ozkan, Frank Janssen and John Jermier

Sustainable Entrepreneurship and Social Innovation

Edited by Katerina Nicolopoulou, Mine Karatas-Ozkan, Frank Janssen and John Jermier

LONDON AND NEW YORK

from Routledge

First published 2017
by Routledge
2 Park Square, Milton Park, Abingdon, Oxon OX14 4RN

and by Routledge
711 Third Avenue, New York, NY 10017

First issued in paperback 2018

Routledge is an imprint of the Taylor & Francis Group, an informa business

© 2017 selection and editorial matter, Katerina Nicolopoulou, Mine Karatas-Ozkan, Frank Janssen and John Jermier; individual chapters, the contributors

The right of the editors to be identified as the authors of the editorial matter, and of the authors for their individual chapters, has been asserted in accordance with sections 77 and 78 of the Copyright, Designs and Patents Act 1988.

All rights reserved. No part of this book may be reprinted or reproduced or utilised in any form or by any electronic, mechanical, or other means, now known or hereafter invented, including photocopying and recording, or in any information storage or retrieval system, without permission in writing from the publishers.

Trademark notice: Product or corporate names may be trademarks or registered trademarks, and are used only for identification and explanation without intent to infringe.

British Library Cataloguing-in-Publication Data
A catalogue record for this book is available from the British Library

Library of Congress Cataloging in Publication Data
Names: Nicolopoulou, Katerina, editor. | Karataðs-èOzkan, Mine editor. | Janssen, Frank, (Professor of entrepreneurship) editor.
Title: Sustainable entrepreneurship and social innovation / edited by Katerina Nicolopoulou, Mine Karatas-Ozkan, Frank Janssen, John Jermier.
Description: New York : Routledge, 2016.
Identifiers: LCCN 2016023534| ISBN 9781138812666 (hb) | ISBN 9781315748665 (ebook)
Subjects: LCSH: Entrepreneurship. | Sustainable development. | Organizational change–Management. | Social change.
Classification: LCC HB615 .S9827 2016 | DDC 658.4/08–dc23
LC record available at https://lccn.loc.gov/2016023534

ISBN 13: 978-1-138-62577-8 (pbk)
ISBN 13: 978-1-138-81266-6 (hbk)

Typeset in Goudy
by Wearset Ltd, Boldon, Tyne and Wear

Contents

List of figures viii
List of tables x
Notes on contributors xii

Introduction: sustainable entrepreneurship 1
KATERINA NICOLOPOULOU, MINE KARATAS-OZKAN, FRANK
JANSSEN AND JOHN JERMIER

PART I
A theoretical framework for sustainable entrepreneurship 11

1 Sustainable entrepreneurship and eternal beginnings 13
PIERRE KLETZ AND ERIC CORNUEL

2 Addressing sustainability challenges through state-led social
innovation: the Singapore story 25
AZAD SINGH BALI, PETER McKIERNAN, CHRISTOPHER VAS
AND PETER WARING

3 Eco-socio innovation: underpinning sustainable
entrepreneurship and social innovation 40
JONATHAN M. SCOTT, PATRICK DAWSON AND
JOHN L. THOMPSON

4 Embeddedness as a facilitator for sustainable
entrepreneurship 57
FRÉDÉRIC DUFAYS

5 Sustainable at home – sustainable at work? The impact of
pro-environmental life-work spillover effects on sustainable
intra- or entrepreneurship 73
FRANZISKA DITTMER AND SUSANNE BLAZEJEWKSI

6 The application of the 'ambidexterity' theoretical
perspective to sustainable entrepreneurship: balancing the
sustainability-development equilibrium over time 101
LAURA A. COSTANZO

7 Sustainability entrepreneurship in marine protected areas 124
SIMON R. BUSH, MARISKA BOTTEMA, JAN JORIS MIDAVAINE
AND ELEANOR CARTER

PART II
Empirical insights from case studies – regional and sectoral
perspective 141

8 Lessons from sustainable entrepreneurship towards social
innovation in healthcare: how green buildings can promote
health and wellbeing 143
SHARON JACKSON, JOHN MALEGANOS AND KLEOPATRA
ALAMANTARIOTOU

9 Innovation in the face of tension: lessons from a sustainable
social enterprise 170
AASTHA MALHOTRA

10 'When the river ran purple': reframing Indigenous economics
in a global city 187
BILLIE LYTHBERG, CHRISTINE WOODS AND
MĀNUKA HĒNARE

11 Sustainable entrepreneurship, opportunity creation: a
corporate political activity view 210
XUANWEI CAO AND DORIS FISCHER

12 Innovation in sustainable entrepreneurship education in
Africa: strategy and social impact 228
SHIV K. TRIPATHI, UMESH MUKHI, MARIO MOLTENI AND
BENEDETTO CANNATELLI

13 Sustainable innovation and entrepreneurship in agriculture:
    empirical insights into the SME ecosystem   244
    RENAN TUNALIOGLU, MINE KARATAS-OZKAN,
    CAGLA YAVUZ, TOLGA BEKTAS, FERIT COBANOGLU,
    JEREMY HOWELLS AND AYSE DEMET KARAMAN

14 Sustainable entrepreneurship in maritime tourism:
    theoretical considerations and empirical evidence   272
    MARIA LEKAKOU, EVANGELIA STEFANIDAKI AND
    IOANNIS THEOTOKAS

PART III
Policy and institutional perspectives   287

15 Sustainable development and entrepreneurship: mapping
    definitions, determinants, actors and processes   289
    EMMANUEL RAUFFLET, LUC BRÈS, SOFIANE BABA AND
    LOUIS JACQUES FILION

16 Public-private partnerships in Kazakhstan and Russia: the
    interplay between social value, entrepreneurship and sustainability 306
    NIKOLAI MOURAVIEV AND NADA K. KAKABADSE

17 The everyday experiences of a sustainable entrepreneur:
    brokering for social innovation at the intersection of
    networks of practice   320
    EEVA HOUTBECKERS

18 Employee energy cooperatives: employee entrepreneurial
    activities towards a more sustainable future   338
    ANJA SHADABI AND CARSTEN HERBES

19 Building sustainable social enterprises: combining multiple
    institutional logics   352
    OLIVIA KYRIAKIDOU

20 Social entrepreneurship in an INGO: exploring the
    challenges of innovation and hybridization   369
    JAMIE NEWTH

    Index   391

Figures

2.1 Distribution of 215 firms surveyed across industrial subsectors 30
2.2 Firms' reliance on foreign labour 32
2.3 Firms and foreign labour 33
2.4 Extent of dependence on government policy and capital
access to invest in technology 33
2.5 To what extent is the following true for your firm 35
2.6 Extent to which firms were influenced by government policy
and schemes 36
2.7 Firm-level considerations 37
3.1 E-V-R congruence 46
3.2 Congruence restated: PAVing the way to success 47
3.3 Integrating ESI and EVR 47
4.1 Model of embedded sustainable entrepreneurship 61
5.1 Types of sustainable intra- and entrepreneurs 78
7.1 Map of three case studies and all other recorded EMPAs 125
7.2 Dynamic framework for understanding the development of
area based entrepreneurial conservation 127
8.1 Three spheres of sustainability 147
8.2 Model for open innovation, for social change and social
innovation 162
8.3 Sustainable building as a vehicle for TBL innovation in the
healthcare sector 163
9.1 Two distinct collaborations forming the bases of a mutually
beneficial relationship 177
10.1 Dead and discoloured eel at Oruarangi 188
10.2 He Korunga o Ngā Tikanga 193
10.3 Takarangi 195
10.4 Oruarangi Industry Pollution Prevention Programme
Pamphlet, page 2 199
10.5 The doughnut economics model 201
11.1 The role of CPA in the transformation of entrepreneurship 213
11.2 Sustainable entrepreneurship, opportunity creation and CPA 215

11.3	Critical juncture and actions taken by sustainable entrepreneur of T Group	222
12.1	Knowledge-practice interface in management	231
12.2	Participants in a collaboratory	232
12.3	Strategic framework for research process management	234
12.4	Conceptual framework for sustainable entrepreneurship education	236
13.1	SME approaches to strategic sustainability and innovation	246
17.1	The circulation of clothing	323
17.2	The combination of networks of practice	334

Tables

2.1	Industrial subsector and SSIC classification codes	29
3.1	Some examples of eco-socially innovative organizations and applicability and relevance of ESI and environment, resources and values to each example	49
5.1	Types of sustainable intra- and entrepreneurs	75
5.2	List of interviewees	80
5.3	Types of intra- and entrepreneurial spillover effects	94
7.1	Comparison of exploitation, consolidation and durability of three entrepreneurial marine protected areas	134
8.1	The TBL benefits of a green building	159
9.1	Summary of data sources	173
9.2	Summary of programmes run by SCOPE Plus till 2010	174
11.1	The quick development of T Group in the developing solar PV business	219
11.2	Mr. Liu's political appointment	220
11.3	Mr. Liu's honorary titles awarded from government, industry and society	220
13.1	Detailed inventory of data sources	250
13.2	Key findings pertaining to institutional involvement of government	258
13.3	Examples of key findings pertaining to the institutional involvement of universities and university-industry collaboration	260
A13.1	Detailed inventory of data sources	263
A13.2	Key findings pertaining to institutional involvement of government	265
A13.3	Examples of key findings pertaining to the institutional involvement of universities and university-industry collaboration	267
14.1	Summary of the main sustainability practices applied by cruise companies	280
15.1	Mapping definitions	290
15.2	Ecopreneur and sustainable entrepreneur: major differences	292

15.3	Typologies of sustainable entrepreneurs	296
17.1	Research data	324
17.2	Illustrative quotes	326
17.3	Work in the emerging networks of practice	330
18.1	Description of EEC1 and EEC2	343
20.1	Organizational templates	370
20.2	WVNZ interpretation of the future of development	377
20.3	Applying sustainable entrepreneurship to World Vision	379
20.4	Comparing extant/previous social logic versus required hybridized social entrepreneurship logic	381
A20.1	Representative data of extant institutional logic	386

Contributors

Katerina Nicolopoulou is a Senior Lecturer at the Hunter Centre for Entrepreneurship, Strathclyde Business School, UK. She has published in the areas of social, sustainable and diversity aspects of entrepreneurship, and on the concept of cosmopolitanism as a disposition for developing entrepreneurship as well as strategies for sustainability. As a resident Strathclyde academic in the United Arab Emirates (Dubai), she also researches different aspects of entrepreneurial ecosystems in the context of emerging economies.

Mine Karatas-Ozkan is a Professor of Strategy and Entrepreneurship at the University of Southampton, UK. Her research focuses on social and diversity dimensions of entrepreneurship. She has published several books and articles in these areas.

Frank Janssen is full Professor of Entrepreneurship at the Louvain School of Management, Université catholique de Louvain, Belgium, where he is also the President for the Louvain School of Management Research Institute and the academic director of the interdisciplinary programme in entrepreneurship (CPME). His research interests and recent publications are in the fields of firm growth, social entrepreneurship, entrepreneurial motivations, as well as entrepreneurial pedagogy.

John Jermier is Professor of Sustainable Enterprise Research at the University of South Florida, USA. He teaches graduate and undergraduate courses in organizational behaviour, corporate environmentalism and environmental policy, and the measurement of organizational effectiveness.

Pierre Kletz is a Professor at Ben-Gurion University of the Negev, Israel. He is the founding Director of the Mandel Social Leadership MBA. He served as Vice-President of the Mandel Foundation – Israel (2009–2014). He received his doctorate from HEC Paris. He holds an accreditation to supervise research from the Sorbonne.

Eric Cornuel has been the Director General and CEO of EFMD (European Foundation for Management Development) in Brussels since 2000. Eric's key qualifications are in the areas of strategy, international management and entrepreneurship and he is a regular contributor to the Emerald Management Journals.

Azad Singh Bali is a Research Fellow at Murdoch University's Singapore campus. He studies productivity in the Singapore economy as it restructures to cope with the economic and socio-political challenges of an affluent but rapidly ageing economy. His academic training is in economics and public policy and he works broadly on comparative social policy and social security in Asia.

Peter McKiernan is a Professor at the University of Strathclyde, Scotland. Peter is a prize-winning and active researcher engaged in cutting-edge analysis of changing political, economic and social trends, their impact on strategic formulation and implementation for businesses. He has authored books, including the international best seller *Sharpbenders* (Blackwell).

Christopher Vas is Associate Professor and Director of the Singapore Centre for Research in Innovation, Productivity and Technology (SCRIPT) at Murdoch University's Singapore campus. He was Commissioner in the Second Murdoch Commission on Food Security, Trade and Partnerships. His research has been published in leading journals such as *R&D Management* and *Journal of Comparative Policy Analysis: Research and Practice*.

Peter Waring is Murdoch University's Singapore Dean. A qualified lawyer, Peter also holds degrees in Commerce and Management. He is the co-author of four books on employment relations. His research and teaching interests span the business and law fields of employment relations, human resource management, corporate governance and labour law.

Jonathan M. Scott is a Reader in Entrepreneurship at Teesside University Business School, Middlesbrough, UK. His research interests include entrepreneurial finance, business support and social entrepreneurship.

Patrick Dawson is an Emeritus Professor of Management at the University of Aberdeen, Scotland and a Professorial Fellow at the University of Wollongong, Australia. He has an extensive publication list of over 60 refereed journal articles, 12 books and 50 book chapters. In 2005, he was made a Distinguished Member of the Australian and New Zealand Academy of Management and he has held Visiting Professorships at Lund University, Roskilde University and the Danish Technical University.

John L. Thompson is Professor of Social Entrepreneurship at Anglia Ruskin University and Emeritus Professor of Entrepreneurship at the University of Huddersfield, UK. His research is focused on the attributes of social entrepreneurs and also entrepreneurship enabling, including elements of entrepreneurship education. He has been a Visiting Professor in Australia, New Zealand and Finland.

Frédéric Dufays is a postdoctoral researcher and the coordinator of the Knowledge Centre for Cooperative Entrepreneurship at KU Leuven (Belgium). He holds a PhD in Economics and Management Sciences from HEC Liege, Management School of the University of Liege. His research interests include nascent social/sustainable entrepreneurship and the emergence of hybrid organizations, including cooperatives, and collective dynamics (teams and networks) in entrepreneurship.

Franziska Dittmer has an MA in Sustainability Economics and Management and is a research associate at the Chair for Sustainable Organization and Work Design at Alanus University, Germany. Her research focus and PhD project is on green identity work, sustainability tensions of employees and green employee involvement.

Susanne Blazejewski is Professor for Sustainable Organization and Work Design at Alanus University, Germany. Her research focuses on identity work, conflicts, paths and the role of arts in sustainable organizational development, particularly in 'greening' multinational corporations. Her work has been published in the *Journal of World Business*, *Competition and Change*, among others. She has coordinated the EGOS standing working group on 'MNC as social actors' since 2012.

Laura A. Costanzo, PhD, is Associate Professor of Strategy and Innovation at the Southampton Business School, University of Southampton, UK, where she lectures in the subject areas of strategic decision-making and global entrepreneurship. She researches and supervises a number of doctoral students in the areas of social entrepreneurship, sustainability and decision-making from a processual perspective. She is the main editor of the *Handbook of Research on Strategy and Foresight* (Edward Elgar) and has contributed to the relevant theoretical debate by publishing a number of book chapters and papers in top-ranked peers journals such as *Regional Development and Entrepreneurship*, *Journal of Small Business Management and British Journal of Management* amongst others. She is currently an Associate Editor of the *European Management Review* and also serves on the Editorial Board of the *British Journal of Management*, whilst being a referee for a number of other peer reviewed journals and funding bodies. Her work received a number of prestigious international awards by the British Academy of Management/Strategic Foresight SIG, the Emerald Literati Network Awards for Excellence, and the Top 10 Strategic Management Society/McKinsey Best Papers Award.

Simon R. Bush is Professor of Environmental Policy at Wageningen University, the Netherlands. His research focuses on the interaction between private and public environmental governance arrangements promoting the sustainable and equitable production, use and consumption of marine resources, including aquaculture and fisheries.

Mariska Bottema is a PhD candidate at the Environmental Policy Group of Wageningen University, the Netherlands. She has a background in coastal development and marine conservation. Her research focuses on the sustainable management of tropical coastal areas and resources. She has experience in the Caribbean and South East Asia.

Jan Joris Midavaine is a freelance researcher with a wide interest in marine conservation. He is currently working as an educational programme assistant for secondary school students with the *Wylde Swan*, the world's largest two-masted top sail schooner, leading a programme on increased collaboration with external actors to increase participant ocean literacy.

Eleanor Carter is the Director of Sustainable Solutions International Consulting. Her work has focused on the on-ground management of marine and coastal ecosystems, particularly the establishment and effective management of MPAs, for more than 20 years. Her geographic areas of focus are East Africa and the Asia-Pacific region.

Sharon Jackson is the Founder of the European Sustainability Academy (ESA) in Crete. She has developed experiential sustainable enterprise learning programmes in Europe, Australia, China and India. She is also a member of the Associate Faculty at the Cranfield School of Management, UK; an Associate Scholar at the University of Cumbria (IFLAS), UK; and a Visiting Research Fellow at the Athens University of Economics and Business (AUEB). Her Doctoral research explores disconnection between organizational sustainability intentions and actions in daily operations.

John Maleganos is an environmental economist (MSc) whose experience includes being an internal auditor and business consultant with Ernst & Young, and Director of the 'Business and Industry Engagement Program' with World Wide Fund for Nature (WWF) Greece. Later roles include business development manager, European Sustainability Academy (ESA), Crete, and independent business sustainability advisor on corporate sustainability strategy and reporting.

Kleopatra Alamantariotou is a PhD candidate in 'Innovation Health and Mobile Application', Trinity College Dublin. She graduated in 2008 from City University of London, UK with an MSc in Health Informatics. Previously she studied the art of Midwifery in Athens, Greece and received an MSc from Middlesex University in Midwifery in 2007.

Aastha Malhotra is a Research Fellow at the University of Southern Queensland. Her research and teaching interests include social innovation, non-profit strategy and sustainability and social entrepreneurship. She has published and reviewed academic publications and brings ten years of practitioner and consulting experience in India, Canada and Australia.

Billie Lythberg is a Senior Research Fellow at the University of Auckland Business School, New Zealand and an Affiliated Researcher at Cambridge

University Museum of Archaeology and Anthropology, UK. Billie works at the junction of economics, anthropology and art history, specializing in ethnographic studies and object-centric research.

Christine Woods' interest in entrepreneurship was sparked after working in Malawi as a small business advisor where she became 'hooked' on the passion and energy that entrepreneurs bring to what they do. She is an Associate Professor in Entrepreneurship and Innovation in the Faculty of Business & Economics at the University of Auckland, New Zealand.

Mānuka Hēnare is Associate Professor in Māori Business Development in the Department of Management and International Business and the foundation Director of the Mira Szászy Research Centre for Māori and Pacific Economic Development, New Zealand and leads a number of multidisciplinary research project teams.

Xuanwei Cao is a Senior Lecturer at the International Business School of Xi'an Jiaotong–Liverpool University (XJTLU). He is active in the areas of strategy management, entrepreneurship and leadership. As a key member of the United Nations endorsed Principles for Responsible Management Education, he is active in promoting CSR principles and sustainability values throughout all aspects of XJTLU's programmes.

Doris Fischer is Chair Professor of China Business and Economics at the University of Würzburg, Germany.

Shiv K. Tripathi, Ph.D. is Vice Chancellor at Mahatma Gandhi University, Meghalaya, India. Shiv is also a member in UN Principles for Responsible Management Education Working Group on 'Anti-Corruption in Management Curricula' and 'Poverty as a challenge for management education'.

Umesh Mukhi is a PhD student at Audencia Nantes School of Management, his research focuses on how business schools can embrace responsible management education.

Mario Molteni is Full Professor of Business Administration and Corporate Strategy at Università Cattolica del Sacro Cuore (UCSC), Milan. He founded ALTIS, the Graduate School Business & Society at UCSC. Now he is the CEO of E4Impact Foundation, a spin-off of the University which offers impact entrepreneurship MBAs in partnership with African Universities.

Benedetto Cannatelli is Assistant Professor in Entrepreneurship and Strategy at Università Cattolica del Sacro Cuore, Milan, Italy. He is actively involved as researcher at ALTIS, the Graduate School of Business and Society at the same University. His main research interests are Entrepreneurship, Social Entrepreneurship and Strategic Management.

Renan Tunalioglu is an Associate Professor in the Agricultural Policy subdivision at the Faculty of Agriculture at Adnan Menderes University in Aydın, Turkey. Prior to working at the University, she worked at the

Republic of Turkey Ministry of Food, Agriculture and Livestock. She has undertaken several funded research projects in the area of agricultural management and academy–industry partnership.

Cagla Yavuz is a doctoral researcher at the Southampton Business School at the University of Southampton, UK. Her research explores how organizational distinctiveness (habitus) is influential in the ways that organizational members interpret, make sense and respond to institutional complexities in the field of higher education in Turkish, Canadian and UK contexts. She has published her work in books and journals.

Tolga Bektas is Professor of Logistics Management at the University of Southampton, UK. He holds a PhD degree in Industrial Engineering from Bilkent University, Turkey. His research interests are in mathematical modelling and optimization of a variety of problems arising in freight logistics, including network design, 'green' transportation and vehicle routing.

Ferit Cobanoglu is an agricultural economist whose research has focused on agricultural and rural development issues, including rural finance, farm management, agricultural entrepreneurship and agricultural business. Currently, he is an Associate Professor at the Department of Agricultural Management in the Department of Agricultural Economics, Faculty of Agriculture, Adnan Menderes University, Turkey.

Jeremy Howells is a professor and an internationally renowned social scientist in the field of management and economic geography. His portfolio of highly influential research encompasses innovation, entrepreneurship, knowledge exchange and public policy. His work includes open innovation, tacit knowledge, innovation intermediaries, university and industry links and regional innovation systems.

Ayse Demet Karaman has been working at the Faculty of Agriculture, Department of Dairy Technology at Adnan Menderes University, Turkey since 2008. She has worked as a visiting scientist in the Department of Food Science and Technology at Ohio State University, USA on food quality and technology. She has many articles and projects on dairy technology, food safety and quality management systems.

Maria Lekakou is Associate Professor in Maritime Economics and Policy in the Department of Shipping, Trade and Transport at the University of the Aegean. She has research experience and published papers in the areas of passenger shipping, island transports, industrial organization of shipping and maritime competition.

Evangelia Stefanidaki is a Research Fellow in Research in the Shipping and Ports Laboratory in the Department of Shipping, Trade and Transport of the University of the Aegean. Her research interests are in maritime policies and especially in cruise destination development, short sea shipping, blue growth and entrepreneurship.

Ioannis Theotokas is Professor in Shipping and Human Resource Management in the Department of Shipping, Trade and Transport at the University of the Aegean and he currently serves as Secretary General in the Ministry of Shipping. His research interests are in shipping management, organizational behaviour and human resources management in shipping.

Emmanuel Raufflet is an Associate Professor in the Department of Management, HEC Montréal. Emmanuel is interested in social innovation, cross-sectoral partnerships, sustainable development and corporate social responsibility. His work has been published in journals such as the *Journal of Business Ethics*, the *Journal of Cleaner Production* and the *Journal of Management Studies*.

Luc Brès is an Assistant Professor in the Faculty of Business Administration at Laval University, Canada. Luc is interested in CSR standards, tools and markets' dynamics. His work has been published in journals such as *Human Relations*, the *Journal of Cleaner Production* and the *Journal of Business Ethics and Economics*.

Sofiane Baba is a PhD Candidate at HEC Montréal. His research focuses on corporate social responsibility, corporate-community relations and stakeholder engagement. Sofiane has published several articles, case studies and book chapters on these research topics.

Louis Jacques Filion is a Professor in the Department of Entrepreneurship and Innovation and the Rogers-J.-A. Bombardier Chair of Entrepreneurship at HEC Montréal. He has more than 100 publications including 15 books. His research is concerned with the activity systems of entrepreneurs and the visionary process.

Nikolai Mouraviev is a Senior Lecturer at Dundee Business School, Abertay University, Scotland. Previously he has held teaching positions at KIMEP University, Kazakhstan, Wayne State University, USA and Viterbo University, USA. His research focuses on public-private partnership management in Kazakhstan and Russia and he has published extensively in this area.

Nada K. Kakabadse is Professor of Policy, Governance and Ethics at Henley Business School, University of Reading, UK. She has co-authored 21 books and has published over 190 scholarly articles. She is an elected member of the European Academy of Science and Arts and a consultant to numerous global corporations, NGOs and governments.

Eeva Houtbeckers (M.Sc. Econ.) is a doctoral candidate at Aalto University School of Business, Department of Management Studies, Finland. Her PhD dissertation focuses on mundane social entrepreneurship in Finland and the work of microentrepreneurs in emerging sectors. Her postdoctoral research interests relate to post-growth work practices in the global North.

Anja Shadabi is a Research Assistant at Nuertingen-Geislingen University, Germany and a PhD candidate at Louvain School of Management, Belgium. Her research interests include individual and organizational identity, tensions in corporate sustainability and organizational theory. She is currently working on her dissertation in the field of corporate greening, where she looks into barriers to voluntary employee green behaviour.

Carsten Herbes is a Professor at Nuertingen-Geislingen University (NGU), Germany, and Director of the Institute for International Research on Sustainable Management and Renewable Energy. His research interests include marketing and acceptance of renewable energies as well as RE cooperatives. Before joining NGU he worked as a management consultant and board member of a bioenergy company.

Olivia Kyriakidou is an Assistant Professor in Organizational Behaviour at Athens University of Economics and Business. Her research areas turn around the wider field of organization studies and critical management studies. Her current research interests mainly focus on alternative forms of organizing, social enterprises and social movements, and diversity management.

Jamie Newth is based at the University of Auckland Business School where he teaches and innovation and entrepreneurship and conducts research focused on social innovation and entrepreneurship and hybrid organization. He sits on a number of social venture boards and regularly provides advisory and consulting services to entrepreneurial start-ups, SMEs and NGOs.

Introduction

Sustainable entrepreneurship

*Katerina Nicolopoulou, Mine Karatas-Ozkan,
Frank Janssen and John Jermier*

Sustainable entrepreneurship has attracted a growing attention in both scholarly and practitioner domains. It focuses on generating social, environmental and business value, which also is termed as shared value. There are several terms and definitions that encompass its attributes and dimensions. Shepherd and Patzelt (2011) have been expanding the remit of social entrepreneurship into 'sustainable' entrepreneurship, as a new interdisciplinary field, which 'explore(s) the role of entrepreneurial action as a mechanism for sustaining nature and eco-systems whilst providing economic and non-economic gains for investors, entrepreneurs and societies' (p. 138). Sustainability and sustainable development are imperative for the future of economies and societies. They are not only about the longer-term well-being of the environments and organizations but also about humanity.

Sustainable development meets at the juncture of three constituent parts – environmental sustainability, economic sustainability and socio-political sustainability (Bell and Stellingwerf, 2012). These form the foundations of an emerging relatively new field of entrepreneurship – sustainable entrepreneurship. This entails a holistic approach to venture development taking into account multiple bottom lines, i.e. environmental, economic and social sustainability dimensions. The notion of sustainable entrepreneurship has been raised more recently to address the contribution of entrepreneurial activities to sustainable economic and social development, which entails substantial sustainability innovations (Schaltegger and Wagner, 2011).

Drawing on this positioning, this edited volume has gathered the state-of-the-art in terms of conceptual frameworks of analysis, empirical insights and related policy discussions pertaining to sustainable entrepreneurship and social innovation.

Taking on board this composite perspective, the book highlights elements of sustainable entrepreneurship, which, additionally, have a societal impact as well as regional relevance. Related aspects of innovation are also presented, and definitional issues are further elucidated, so as to scope the relevant inter-connected fields of study, mainly sustainable entrepreneurship and social innovation.

In order to meet the future challenges of sustainability, organizations need to undertake transformational instead of incremental change. Transformational change towards sustainability involves fundamental change in cultural values and collective consciousness of a society that enables sustainability-driven values to flourish and embed (Ehrenfeld and Hoffman, 2013; Schaefer *et al.*, 2015). Entrepreneurship and social innovation are processes that can contribute to this transformation. Social and environmental value creation that foster sustainability can be achieved through sustainable entrepreneurship and social innovation.

Overview of chapters

In their chapter 'Sustainable entrepreneurship and eternal beginnings', **Kletz and Cornuel** challenge the very notion of sustainable entrepreneurship. Looking at the etymology of both words, they show that, whereas entrepreneurship is related to the notion of 'start', sustainability, on the other hand, is related to long-lastingness, which could be seen as the opposite of entrepreneurship. They overcome this apparent antagonism by looking at the links between social entrepreneurship and sustainable entrepreneurship – the latter stemming from the former. They assert that sustainable entrepreneurship adds meaning to classical entrepreneurship because the notion of sustainability is related to both the long-term consequences of activities and to environmental considerations.

In their chapter, **Bali, McKiernan, Vas and Waring** contextualize sustainability through a state-led innovation in Singapore. They provide substantial evidence as to the context of Singapore and how the Singapore Government has set ambitious sustainable development goals for its economy, which it hopes to achieve through boosting resource efficiency, creating a better urban environment, building new capabilities and fostering community action. Drawing on insights from 215 manufacturing firms, the authors demonstrate in their chapter that by nominating the public sector to act first and setting an example for rest of the economy, the Government's efforts have yielded positive results. Following significant investments in infrastructure, development of industry awareness programmes, capability-building initiatives and delivering policy incentives, it has started to make headway into achieving some of its objectives. The authors draw policy conclusions such as empowering firms to take leadership and ownership of furthering sustainability agenda. In other words, the Singapore Government must empower firms to demonstrate leadership and sustain innovation particularly within their own sectors. They note that while the leadership and vision from the Government is necessary to meet long-term sustainability goals, it is not a sufficient condition for success. Going beyond the manufacturing sector, the Singapore Government must catalyse further action across multiple sectors to achieve its sustainability agenda. At the firm level this may very well require a blended approach of sustainable entrepreneurial action, one that is able to sustain innovative practices and also blend with it the objectives of social innovation. The authors also highlight limitations of the top-down approach and set directions for future research and policy. They argue for a value co-creation or co-production approach between firms. They argue that this value co-creation approach needs to take shape between government policy and societal action.

The chapter by **Scott, Dawson and Thompson**, 'Eco-socio innovation: underpinning sustainable entrepreneurship and social innovation', represents scholarly work intended to move theory beyond dualisms in representing how social innovations are related to sustainable entrepreneurship. In this and other publications, they advance the novel concept of eco-socio innovation and use it to help structure thinking about exemplary organizations – those that achieve model performance outcomes in three domains: environmental, social and economic. Although analytically distinct, the authors see these three domains of performance as inseparable in high congruency organizational configurations. They argue prescriptively that the linkages and interrelationships among the three domains of performance should be strong and not easily broken. The contrast between this conceptualization and traditional triple-bottom-line thinking is noteworthy and leads to memorable illustrations of six high congruence firms from a variety of sectors and nation-states.

Dufays' conceptual chapter makes the case for a strong embeddedness at all stages of sustainable entrepreneurship – opportunity identification and/or creation, evaluation and exploitation. He argues that this strong embeddedness drives entrepreneurs towards sustainability through the set-up of long-term social contracts with multiple stakeholders. Building upon extant literature on sustainable, social and environmental entrepreneurship and the framework of stakeholder theory, as well as the embeddedness argument, this chapter contributes to the edited volume by developing a model demonstrating that sustainable entrepreneurship is strongly embedded, and that this strong embeddedness contributes to its sustainable character. This forms its theoretical contribution. The core argument is that different stages of sustainable entrepreneurship take place in interrelated contexts, which in turn influence sustainability. He stresses that sustainable entrepreneurship requires shared commitment in the long run by the establishment of social contracts between the entrepreneur and stakeholders. Theoretically, it implies that sustainable entrepreneurship is relying on mutual expectations towards what is perceived as sustainable, both by the entrepreneur and a large range of stakeholders. The importance of actors' perceptions is further reinforced by the elaboration of social contracts by the entrepreneur with non-existing counterparts, i.e. future stakeholders. In addition to this, the model highlights the importance of the multiplicity of long-term social contracts that are set up. This plurality is likely to be a source of conflict as perceptions of what is sustainable and stakeholders' interests do not necessarily align. Therefore, the overall conclusion of the chapter is that sustainable entrepreneurship can also be understood as lying in a nexus of social contracts, which need to be managed and maintained by the entrepreneur in such a way that it allows a long-term perspective for stakeholders.

In their chapter, **Dittmer and Blazejewski** explore life-work spillover effects of pro-environmental behaviour and their potential impact on sustainable intra- or entrepreneurship behaviour. Drawing on 25 qualitative interviews with citizens who are publicly or privately active in environmental or sustainability issues, they demonstrate that the forms of private or public pro-environmental behaviours (PEB) that imply a high degree of personal involvement can pave the way for sustainable intra- and entrepreneurship. This chapter highlights the capabilities, particularly of publicly engaged citizens, for creating sustainability-oriented start-ups or promoting bottom-up sustainability initiatives in organizations. The chapter makes a significant contribution by developing a typology of spillover processes and putting forward different ways of dealing with organizational barriers that generate tensions and hinder intrapreneurial activities inside existing organizations as well as strategies that employees use to overcome them. This chapter advances the research on sustainable entrepreneurship by focusing on private and public sphere PEBs as 'learned' behavioural strategies, which can serve as a source for innovative forms of PEB at work or for sustainable intra- and entrepreneurship. This implies strategies for practitioners as well. Employers are encouraged to discover and understand the private and public engagement of environmentally conscious employees in order to release the motivational potential of their work force for the sustainable transition in their organizations.

In her chapter entitled 'The application of the "ambidexterity" theoretical perspective to sustainable entrepreneurship: balancing the sustainability-development equilibrium over time', **Laura A. Costanzo** also starts from a tension, i.e. the one between sustainability and development, to see how this tension can be balanced over time. In order to do so, she uses the theoretical lens of ambidexterity to examine how the sustainability-development equilibrium can be reached within an entrepreneurial-oriented posture. According to her, sustainability could be jeopardized if the entrepreneurial act focuses on adaptation activities in the pursuit of business opportunities. Costanzo further elaborates the concept of contextual ambidexterity that requires supportive leadership values (such as sensitivity to environmental, communal and societal values, as well as altruism) and intra-firm mechanisms of knowledge integration and exchanges.

Bush, Bottema, Midavaine and Carter's contribution to the volume is based on a cross-case comparison of entrepreneurial marine protected areas (EMPA) in Tanzania, Indonesia and Belize. The ecological issues that are germane to their study range from biodiversity loss and species extinction to preservation of marine ecosystems and coastal resources. In previous research, the authors published case studies of initiatives in these three regions. The case studies form the groundwork for the present study which is aimed at determining what conditions and actions lead private actors to success in marine conservation. They show how patterns of *exploitation* (problem identification and opportunity identification), *consolidation* (institutional arrangement, formal status and international recognition) and *durability* (legal assurance, community support and political support) characterize these successful initiatives. Importantly, Bush *et al.* contend that state involvement is fundamental to building sustainable EMPAs, a theme often overlooked in entrepreneurship research.

Jackson, Maleganos and Alamantariotou demonstrate what the healthcare sector can learn from sustainable entrepreneurship and social innovation drawing on a literature review and a case study. Their findings indicate links between 'sustainable entrepreneurship' (notably the impact of ecological buildings on people) and 'social innovation' in the context of improving performance, enhancing quality of service and well-being for stakeholders in the healthcare sector. This chapter offers suggestions on combined social and eco-innovation towards enhanced performance and improved quality of service in the healthcare sector, and aims to give insight into how sustainable entrepreneurship mechanisms such as green-building design can impact positively on the health and well-being of stakeholder groups and also improve performance. They argue that green buildings and a holistic approach to 'eco-innovation' can bring about positive impacts on people in both internal and external stakeholder groups. Future research implications include further research on the positive impact of green buildings on people (society) and how they would be valuable in terms of understanding what specific areas of funding could make the greatest positive impact in the healthcare sector.

Malhotra's chapter focuses on the sustainability dimensions of SMEs and the ways in which relevant tensions can be resolved. The chapter outlines a single in-depth case, focused on the Program Nav Kria, run by SCOPE plus, a non-profit based in India. The adoption of innovation was a practice that the organization under study adopted, in order to deal with conflicting sustainability dimensions. The chapter adopts the 'connecter difference' social innovation theory in order to contextualize its findings, which can be clustered under dimensions of sustainability, tensions experienced in pursuing sustainability and practices used to resolve tensions. The chapter contributes to theory through the complex framework developed in terms of conflicting and inter-dependent aspects of sustainable social enterprises and the application of a practice-led aspect of social innovation theory.

In the chapter '"When the river ran purple": reframing Indigenous *economics* in a global city', **Lythberg, Woods and Hēnare** look at issues related to sustainable entrepreneurship through a Maori philosophy lens that sees humankind as a part of a network of life. They ask what the network requires to adapt and flourish. This Indigenous approach is used alongside another global framework, called the doughnut model. They apply it to the case of a river in metropolitan Auckland polluted by an industrial accident.

In their chapter 'Sustainable entrepreneurship, opportunity creation: a corporate political activity view', **Cao and Fischer** also highlight the important role played by the state in sustainable entrepreneurship. They begin by introducing the idea that some entrepreneurs act on Confucian values and even ideology in identifying and expanding on opportunities to create economic wealth and social welfare. Through a case study approach, they sketch political actions of a single entrepreneur (and his firm) in the Chinese solar energy industry. This research is an effort to shed light on the micro-foundations of environmental innovation while linking micro-phenomena to the broader institutional environment. By focusing on corporate political activity aimed at both the communist party and numerous other stakeholders, Cao and Fischer suggest how a firm and its leaders can successfully open up and expand a new line of green business without diminishing their more traditional business (food and aquatic products).

Tripathi, Mukhi, Molteni and Cannatelli's chapter highlights education as a critical component in the value chain of sustainable entrepreneurship development. The chapter builds upon the case of ALTIS (Alta Scuola Impresa e Società) offering a masters' in global sustainability and entrepreneurship; in order to do so, the chapter highlights in depth the profiles of five graduate entrepreneurs which showcase the impact creation of a context-tailored education programme on sustainable development. In addition to theoretical problematization in terms of the bottom lines involved in sustainable entrepreneurship, in particular when this is contextualized in developing countries to help them attain growth, the chapter focuses on the role of business schools as the nexus of the business, government and social sector; this unique positioning helps support the skillset of sustainability-driven entrepreneurship. The chapter focuses on addressing relevant questions in terms of ways in which this support can be rendered most effectively.

Tunalioglu, Karatas-Ozkan, Yavuz, Bektas, Cobanoglu, Howells and Karaman's chapter positions sustainable entrepreneurship as the engagement of SMEs in the entrepreneurial process in ways that not only minimize negative environmental, economic and social impact, but also that improve quality of life through the employment of innovative practices. The field of study of their chapter is sustainable entrepreneurship in emerging market contexts. The authors undertook the study as part of a research project under the auspices of the British Council's UK–Turkey Higher Education Partnership Programme implemented by Southampton University and Adnan Menderes University. The study employed a qualitative perspective and collected data from different sources, including documentary, focus group, semi-structured interviews as a dissemination workshop. Originally focused on exploring aspects of management capacity, entrepreneurial development of SMEs and their environmental and sustainability strategies, the study adopted an institutional theory perspective in order to highlight the role of institutional vehicles (government agencies, policies, intermediary organizations) in supporting entrepreneurs and SME owner managers in terms of innovative, sustainability-driven activities. Taking an entrepreneurial ecosystem approach, the chapter highlights the role of local universities, outreach activities and collaboration with international organizations towards supporting the sustainable development of rural communities and the enhancement of their reputation.

Lekakou, Stefanidaki and Theotokas' chapter focuses on a presentation and evaluation of maritime and coastal tourism in terms of sustainability. They look, in particular, to cruise shipping, as one branch of the industry with potentially high environmental impact, particularly when sailing into ports with fragile ecosystems. The chapter identifies wastewater treatment, air emissions and solid waste as the main contemporary industry challenges, and looks at the role of companies in terms of self-regulation of the market, as well as exploration of opportunities for enactment of entrepreneurship and innovation via the adoption and development of appropriate technologies, with positive impact on the maintenance of ecosystems, natural resources as well as economic gains for local communities. The chapter is innovative in terms of its contribution, i.e. approaching the cruise industry from a sustainable business perspective and to exploring the parameters that can determine the nature of sustainable entrepreneurship in the cruise industry.

Raufflet, Brès, Baba and Filion's chapter 'Sustainable development and entrepreneurship: mapping definitions, determinants, actors and processes' is a literature review based on 135 articles published between 1992 and 2012 on sustainable development and entrepreneurship. Like Kletz and Cornuel, they stress that, at first glance, entrepreneurship, seen as individualistic, materialistic and opportunistic, and sustainability, seen as long-term oriented, collective and social, could be understood as antagonistic. However, they show that there has been a growing number of studies linking both concepts since the early 1990s, meaning that the apparent antagonism offers fertile ground for research. They conclude with some avenues for future research, as well as implications for management research.

Mouraviev and Kakabadse explore why and how public-private partnerships (PPPs) are associated with elements of social value creation. Due to its long-term significance to society, the PPP capacity to create social value outweighs PPP costs and provides strong justification for accelerated PPP development by advancing sustainable entrepreneurship. In the context of Kazakhstan and Russia, PPS are new; however, governments are actively pursuing PPP deployment in transportation, urban infrastructure and the social sector. In bridging the conceptual gap between PPPs' low value for money and efforts aimed at extensive partnership implementation, the government needs to promote PPP social value. This entails creation of competitive and sustainable entrepreneurial environment that serves PPP supply chain, smaller government sector's scope and greater environmental sustainability. The contributions of the chapter are multiple. First, it contributes to the sustainable entrepreneurship research field by incorporating a new research sub-field that focuses on public-private collaboration and the government role in supporting PPP as a distinct form of entrepreneurial action. Second, by connecting the two streams of literature – sustainability literature with the PPP literature – the chapter offers a new framework that emphasizes the PPPs' ability to create social value, i.e. economic and non-economic gains to society. From the government perspective, the PPPs' capacity to create social value has proven more significant than each partnership's value for money. The reason for this stems from how a PPP generates, via its supply chain, a competitive and sustainable entrepreneurial environment. Third, another theoretical implication is that whilst PPPs are often associated with monopolization of public services and ability to manipulate the price for a monopolized service, which serves as a strong factor against PPP deployment, a newly developed theoretical framework permits to re-assess this criticism. The application of a different theoretical conceptual model that focuses on the PPP impact on sustainability and entrepreneurship permits to more fully capture PPP social value. The authors argue that through the prism of PPP social value, transaction cost economics and value for money as decision tools for PPP deployment need to be revisited. Whilst both tools have been extensively discussed in the academic literature and have a certain degree of practical usefulness in decision-making, a new framework calls for leveraging theoretical underpinnings and identifying robust conceptual foundations on which PPPs can be deployed. PPP social value, created by partnerships' engagement in sustainable entrepreneurship, may effectively serve as the core of a new set of PPP assessment criteria at the time of deployment and also at the time of performance evaluation.

Houtbeckers focuses on the values, holistic worldview and actions of a single entrepreneur. In an in-depth case study of various aspects of the clothing industry in Finland (2010–2014), she takes a process approach to understand the emergence of sustainable entrepreneurship and the ways in which the key actor both fit in and stood out in various networks of practice. One of the strengths of this research is the close study Houtbeckers made of the actual work of an emerging sustainable entrepreneur and the everyday actions taken by that entrepreneur as a broker spanning multiple networks of practice, through time, to generate social innovation. Her attention to the methodological details of narrative analysis is noteworthy as is her immersion in a toxic industry where sustainable entrepreneurship and social innovation are difficult to enact and difficult to infuse more broadly. In answering calls to shed light on the everydayness of entrepreneurship, this study provides guidance for scholars who seek to move beyond dichotomous images of entrepreneurs as heroes or villains.

The chapter 'Employee energy cooperatives: employee entrepreneurial activities towards a more sustainable future' by **Shadabi and Herbes** studies a case of sustainable entrepreneurship, i.e. employee energy cooperatives (EECs). These are independent businesses managed by employees that produce green electricity on their company's premises. Their qualitative study looks at the factors influencing the emergence of employee-driven entrepreneurial action and asks if something can be learned from these. They also show that the organizational context, the employee's motivations, as well as privately gained knowledge and experiences are important for that kind of initiative to emerge, and that employees use established teams or governance structures to promote their idea. They find that EECs increase sustainability in companies because these can become a role model for other sustainable entrepreneurial actions.

Kyriakidou and Salavou's chapter theoretically highlights aspects of sustainability in terms of social entrepreneurship as dependent on the ability of the social venture to incorporate elements from different institutional logics. The chapter draws upon an inductive study that highlights processes and strategies that reconcile such different logics and organizational goals, and focuses, in particular, upon: a) reconstructing profit as a means of increasing the sustainability of social value creation; b) performing social impact judgements regarding the costs and benefits of entrepreneurial value creation; c) reframing social entrepreneurship as a research and development lab; and d) balancing innovation and scale through complex networks.

The chapter contributes to the theory of social entrepreneurship by asserting the influence of social enterprises in the creation of agency, through their ability to work around institutional constraints. By following a paradox view on sustainability in terms of social enterprises, the chapter tackles the theoretically dominant separation-oriented prescriptions of social enterprise literature. The chapter thus contributes to the evidence base that legitimizes the use of paradoxical perspectives in highlighting a response to fundamental challenges of conceptualization and operation of social enterprises.

Newth's chapter, 'Social entrepreneurship in an INGO: exploring the challenges of innovation and hybridization', is based on 24 months of full-time work as a social enterprise consultant ('embedded actor') in an international non-governmental organization in New Zealand. In this role, he participated in social entrepreneurship initiatives in line with the organization's international mission to address extreme poverty and social injustice. This study extends research in social entrepreneurship to settings previously given little consideration – international humanitarian non-governmental organizations and aid agencies. Using institutional theory and the theme of competing institutional logics, Newth argues for the desirability of promoting hybrid organizations (those that blend and otherwise combine institutional logics) and new forms of social entrepreneurship. His study also identifies and illustrates constraints on hybridizing logics in traditional INGOs with a strongly embedded core institutional logic. The study is instructive in the way it explains how challenging social innovation is in fields with long histories of success achieved by appealing to donors using simple, emotional, humanitarian images. For example, 'saving a child's life' through 'sponsorship' of that child is so seemingly complete and compelling to both donors and employees that it inhibits the development of more sophisticated models that measure impact.

References

Bell, J. and Stellingwerf, J. J. (2012) 'Sustainable entrepreneurship: the motivations & challenges of sustainable entrepreneurs in the renewable energy industry', Jonkoping International Business School, Master's Thesis in Strategic Entrepreneurship.

Ehrenfeld, J. R. and Hoffman, A. J. (2013) *Flourishing: A Frank Conversation about Sustainability*. Stanford, CA: Stanford University Press.

Schaefer, K., Doyle Corner, P. and Kearins, K. (2015) 'Social, environmental and sustainable entrepreneurship research: what is needed for sustainability-as-flourishing?', *Organization and Environment*, pp. 1–20.

Schaltegger, S. and Wagner, M. (2011) 'Sustainable entrepreneurship and sustainability innovation: categories and interactions', *Business Strategy and Environment*, 20, pp. 222–237.

Shepherd, D. A. and Patzelt, H. (2011) 'The new field of sustainable entrepreneurship: studying entrepreneurial action linking what is to be sustained with what is to be developed?', *Entrepreneurship Theory and Practice*, 35, pp. 137–163.

Part I

A theoretical framework for sustainable entrepreneurship

1 Sustainable entrepreneurship and eternal beginnings

Pierre Kletz and Eric Cornuel

Sustainable entrepreneurship is drawing considerable interest from both scholars and practitioners. The first words of the title of the seminal article by Shepherd and Patzelt (2011) can help us to understand the reason for this interest: "The New Field of Sustainable Entrepreneurship." Since this feeling of novelty is shared by many other works (Lans *et al.*, 2014; Pinkse and Groot, 2015; Poldner *et al.*, 2015), it is interesting to analyze its source.

Since the earliest works by Richard Cantillon and Adam Smith in the late seventeenth and early eighteenth centuries, entrepreneurship has long been the subject of wide discussion. However, it is only in the last few years that it has become associated with sustainability: "Sustainable entrepreneurship is focused on the preservation of nature, life support and community in the pursuit of perceived opportunities to bring into existence future products, processes and services for gain" (Shepherd and Patzelt, 2011, 137).

Sustainable entrepreneurship is still about developing products and services in order to obtain a profit but restraint is required in order not to deplete the environment. Sustainable entrepreneurship must bring about externalities that constitute non-economic gains.

That is why sustainable entrepreneurship is understood as a new concept; it adds to classical entrepreneurship a dimension of sustainability that is related to a new approach to both the long-term consequences of activities and concerns about the environment.

Because sustainable entrepreneurship seeks social improvement, it stems from a distinctive origin – social entrepreneurship, which is dedicated to projects aimed at social progress. Unlike "classic" for-profit entrepreneurship, economic considerations are seen as a constraint that must be coped with.

To sum up, while classic entrepreneurship is focused on economic gain and social entrepreneurship on non-economic gain, sustainable entrepreneurship concentrates on both. Unlike many works that compare sustainable entrepreneurship with for-profit entrepreneurship, this chapter analyzes it in comparison to social entrepreneurship and asks not only what new perspectives allow sustainable entrepreneurship but also how our knowledge of social entrepreneurship can improve the practice of sustainable entrepreneurship.

Social entrepreneurship, the "other" origin of sustainable entrepreneurship

The call for chapters for this book referred to a field of broad reflection "building upon a framework that addresses sustainability, entrepreneurship and social innovation." However, the proposed perspective represents a radical change compared to the classical approach of entrepreneurship. In effect, this is an explicit reference to the work of Shepherd and Patzelt, who present sustainable entrepreneurship as being focused on "the pursuit of perceived opportunities to bring into existence future products, processes and services for gain" but "where gain is broadly construed to include economic and non-economic gains to individuals, the economy and society" (2011, 137).

Thus, this involves an approach in which it is possible to forge an alliance between economic profit and social progress in a large complex that can be called sustainable entrepreneurship.

Still, this new notion of sustainable entrepreneurship did not appear *ex-nihilo*. The reflection on the conditions in which entrepreneurship can generate both economic and social gains was primarily developed in the field of social entrepreneurship. Social entrepreneurship referred to a conceptual field that was much more limited in the sense that it was concerned first and foremost with creating "social value." However, the idea that profit-oriented entrepreneurship could also respond to social needs found support.

In a seminal article, Greg Dees (2001, 64) presented a definition of social entrepreneurship in which he argued that social entrepreneurship could be implemented in businesses as well as in the nonprofit sector:

> Social entrepreneurship is the process of pursuing innovative solutions to social problems. More specifically, social entrepreneurs adopt a mission to create and sustain social value. They draw upon appropriate thinking in both the business and nonprofit worlds and operate in a variety of organizations: large and small; new and old; religious and secular; nonprofit, for-profit and hybrid.

According to this definition, it is clear that the main thrust is the creation of social value and that it is possible to place the activity in the category of either a for-profit enterprise or a nonprofit one.

Dees, an authority on social entrepreneurship beginning in the 1990s (he died in 2013), included in the category of social entrepreneurship any project or organization whose goal or mission is to solve a social problem. According to this approach, this can occur even within the context of a for-profit enterprise, on the condition that the *raison d'être* of the enterprise includes a genuine concern for advancement in the field of social progress.

The approach proposed in this book, which clearly reflects the influence of the work of Shepherd and Patzelt, is much more global. Sustainable entrepreneurship can be (and usually is) motivated by a profit motive as long as there is a determination to create "economic and non-economic gains to individuals, the economy and society" (2011, 137). The prime motivation of the resolution of "social problems" is abandoned in favor of an approach that assumes, on the one hand, a possible convergence of the interests of individuals, the economy and society and, on the other, the coexistence of economic and non-economic gain. Obviously, the notion of "sustainable entrepreneurship" and the previously existing one of "social entrepreneurship" include major differences. In particular:

- Social entrepreneurship is generally engendered by a quest for social improvement. The focus was primarily on nonprofit organizations until it was realized that for-profits could also be associated with the search for this objective. In contrast to this, the notion of sustainable entrepreneurship derives from of the field of business administration. It was preceded by the realization that not only does social gain not obstruct economic profit, it can facilitate it.
- Social entrepreneurship was constructed to respond to the same challenges as sustainable entrepreneurship. It comes primarily from an attempt to bypass philanthropy as a more efficient way of addressing societal issues, introducing an economic rationale to improve society. Unlike the case of sustainable entrepreneurship, the question of value creation came at a later stage.

Beyond these differences, the reflection that was developed about social entrepreneurship offers interesting insights that can provide a solid basis for the notion of "sustainable entrepreneurship."

Breaking the dichotomy between economic and social gains

Social entrepreneurship is primarily motivated by the objective of "doing good"; "changing" social conditions constitutes a first priority. Therefore, when a given situation appears unacceptable, social entrepreneurship often focuses more on the processes of changing than on the results of change. Consequently, the planning is much more oriented on how to "escape the present reality" than on the outcomes to be obtained. Many articles and books have stressed the weak points of such an approach: poor planning, vague strategy and difficulty in evaluation.

The new approach of sustainable entrepreneurship, which considers social achievements to be "non-economic gains," is likely to give a relevant answer to these challenges: such an approach might have positive consequences especially for evaluation processes.

It remains true that the development and implementation of social entrepreneurship have revealed merits and made accomplishments possible. In particular, they have demonstrated the importance of social commitment. The social entrepreneur is often personally committed and this increases the relevance and realizations of the projects that are developed (Hemmati and Kia, 2013).

That the distance induced by an approach based on the notion of gains may cause the loss of some social commitment is a risk that must be taken into account. Beyond this, social entrepreneurship has attributed a central role to the concept of "intention." The social entrepreneur has "good intentions" and these intentions serve as a powerful driver for the endeavors s/he leads. The question of intention appears to be even more essential for sustainable entrepreneurship because, according to this approach, the intention is not unilateral. The intention focuses on the economic motivation along with the desire to cause no harm to the environment. Sustainable entrepreneurship is satisfied with the intention "not to do" but social entrepreneurship has stressed the importance of also having an intention "to do."

In historical terms, social entrepreneurship started developing in the seventeenth century, when societies started to promote structural reforms that gave many citizens the opportunity to become entrepreneurs.

> The changes began in Europe after centuries of Crown monopolies, the Church and feudal lords, and the guilds had restricted commercial activity, discouraged innovation. ... The first social entrepreneurs were called visionaries, humanitarians, philanthropists, reformers, saints or simply great leaders. Attention was paid to their courage, compassion and vision, but rarely to the practical aspects of their accomplishments.
>
> (Bornstein and Davis, 2010, 2)

If this historical trend provides us with the context for the development of social entrepreneurship, today's social entrepreneurship refers to different ways of developing action as it converges into a broad spectrum of definitions and perceptions. All these advances point to directions for the development of sustainable entrepreneurship while they also place a much greater stress on its social vocation than on its economic role.

Curiously, for some authors the main challenge of social entrepreneurship consists of offering a social dimension for the economic rationale. Dees, for example, comes up with an approach that is close to the dominant one nowadays by defining sustainable entrepreneurship even if it remains distinct. He draws on the works of the economists Say and Schumpeter, who claim that the entrepreneurs improve the productive capacity of society and provide "creative destruction" that promotes economic change.

Dees argues that social entrepreneurship works for the same purpose in the social field by combining people and resources that significantly improve society's ability to identify its problems. He explains that social entrepreneurs create social values, pursue new opportunities, act courageously to leverage resources and present a degree of accountability. In other words, social entrepreneurs are those that serve as "agents of change of the social sector" (Bornstein and Davis, 2010, 38) in parallel with economic development.

In this way, a similitude is drawn between economic and social developments although the perspective is one of a dichotomy. This similitude comes from acknowledging that "creative destruction" constitutes a powerful framework in order to recognize that a new situation has appeared and that it will require new ways to deal with it, in both the economic and social spheres.

However, unlike the approach of sustainable entrepreneurship, this similitude is related only to structures and modes of developments that are similar. It does not refer to the possibility of moving forward through the same entrepreneurial endeavors and economic and social achievements. The common interpretation of the term "entrepreneur" describes a person that establishes a new business but this interpretation is very limited. Bornstein and Davis (2010, 1) define social entrepreneurship as "a process in which citizens build or transform institutions to advance social solutions to social problems such as poverty, disease, illiteracy, environmental destruction, human rights abuses and corruption in order to make life better for many."

The new notion of sustainable entrepreneurship breaks with this dichotomy and takes the view that economic and social development can essentially coexist in the same organization. It goes far beyond the broad definitions of social entrepreneurship and the emphasis on their sociality is generic and includes both entrepreneurship and social – but not economic –aspects. In the end, along a broad spectrum, "social entrepreneurship" is considered a phenomenon in which social organizations become more market-driven, client-driven, self-sufficient, commercial or businesslike although, in practice, activity that is linked with "social entrepreneurship" usually includes revenue-source diversification, fee-for-service developments, private-sector partnerships and social-purpose business (Dart, 2004). That said, this does not imply that they perceive social reality through the notion of gain.

If social entrepreneurship has introduced an economic approach, it is included in the development of the mission. It can be said that social entrepreneurship and the organizations involved in it differ deeply from traditional non-profit organizations. For a traditional non-profit, the social mission is clear and unambiguous. All income is raised through donations and there is no earned-income enterprise. The typical nonprofit is either a charity or a foundation. Advantages include elimination of any conflict between the venture and social objectives, and the fact that donors receive a tax deduction for donations that go directly to fulfill the social mission. The primary disadvantage is that a traditional nonprofit is dependent on fundraising to operate (Fritz, 2014).

Social entrepreneurship is essentially different from traditional nonprofit activity in terms of strategy, forms of action, norms and values as it creates extreme innovation in the social sector world (Dart, 2004). This era of innovation blurs the boundaries between the traditional nonprofit and business sectors thus enhancing the potential for the independence of the social sector (Dees and Anderson, 2003).

Sustainable entrepreneurship vs. social entrepreneurship: what are the benefits of effects on externalities?

Switching from the notion of social entrepreneurship to that of sustainable entrepreneurship has many implications for the concept of social progress. According to the classical approach of social entrepreneurship, the first step consists of defining the social challenge that needs to be dealt with. The projects developed by social entrepreneurship are aimed at responding to this challenge. This has consequences for how to consider the concept of intention, which here is focused on a particular social challenge. Subsequently, the evaluation of the projects and their impact will be appraised in terms of this challenge.

In contrast to this, the process followed by sustainable entrepreneurship is multidimensional and social improvement is but one of many gains that may not all necessarily be social. Moreover, it stands to reason that when an approach such as this is involved, economic gain is usually the first motivation, at least from a chronological point of view if not in terms of the priority attributed to it when launching a project. After a project is launched, some social goals can be developed to share the essence of the project. In such a case, sustainable entrepreneurship will include many goals seeking out both economic and social gains; contributing to social progress is one motivation among others.

Two other major aspects of sustainable entrepreneurship can result from such an approach:

- A contribution to social progress can be generated by the effect on the externalities of a project. This does not imply anything about the quality and the size of such a contribution. But this impact will be intentional in the sense that the intention is to do good. However, it might be unintentional in the sense that there is very little control and focus on a particular goal because it was first planned with other objectives in mind.

- Sustainable entrepreneurship tends towards incremental social processes in which social contribution is decided on during the time projects are implemented. To a certain extent, a social orientation can be seen as a mindset or a paradigm that has a place in any sustainable entrepreneurship project. At the core is a benevolent attitude motivated by a deep need to give to others, although it goes beyond this. Many charities in the world have a similar benevolent perspective but sustainable entrepreneurship following a breakthrough initiated by social entrepreneurs bridges a gap not addressed by any other group. As Bill Drayton told one interviewer, social entrepreneurs want to transform entire systems: "You give people fish, that's good. Help them to learn to fish, that's a little better. But changing the fishing industry, now that's where the real leverage is … that's where entrepreneurs come in" (Drayton, 2009). Obviously, the partial social view induced by sustainable entrepreneurship, which is also oriented toward economic motivation, makes it hard to conceive of "changing the fishing industry."

But, on the other hand, it is also likely to scale social projects in a decisive way, a concept that is analyzed below.

Sustainable entrepreneurship is likely to provide greater efficiency for the management of social projects and to scale the dimension of these projects in a new way.

Joel L. Fleishman, in his book *The Foundation: A Great American Secret* (2007, 2009), predicts that social entrepreneurship and venture philanthropy (and any instance of social activity that generate incomes) will come to dominate philanthropy and social activities in the twenty-first century because these models for organizing and financing social change "significantly overachieve in impact the dollars spent the old fashioned way. However, one significant limitation of venture philanthropy is that, unlike startup businesses, social organizations don't generate profits when they are successful" (2009, 354). It seems that the model of sustainable entrepreneurship, which does generate income, meets the same conditions as defined by Fleishman in regard to social entrepreneurship; it creates the conditions for scaling and duplication because it is less dependent on external sources of financing.

The dangers of sustainable entrepreneurship

Shepherd and Patzelt (2011, 137) have extended the notion of social leadership to that of "sustainable entrepreneurship" – "where gain is broadly construed to include economic and non-economic gains to individuals, the economy and society."

In this chapter we have presented how such a perspective can contribute to overcoming approaches that include a dichotomy between economic and social benefits that has the potential for social conflicts.

But if this new perspective is attractive, the very notion of sustainable entrepreneurship also poses some dangers. Sustainable entrepreneurship appears to be a more highly focused concept than social entrepreneurship, of which Boschee notes, "it seems that everybody has a different definition of what it means" (2006, 28). The question of a definition is particularly elusive when it comes to differentiating social entrepreneurship from the traditional nonprofit activity that preceded it, and also from sustainable entrepreneurship. Several key theoreticians in the field of social activity have addressed this issue.

One of the most commonly quoted definitions of social entrepreneurship is that phrased by Dees. As he puts it, social entrepreneurs become agents of change in the social sector by adopting a mission to create and sustain social value; recognizing and relentlessly pursuing new opportunities to serve that mission; engaging in a process of continuous innovation, adaptation and learning; acting boldly without being limited by resources currently in hand; and exhibiting heightened accountability to the constituencies served and for the outcomes created (Dees, 1998). By this, Dees points to three main characteristics taken from this definition that are assumed by sustainable entrepreneurship:

the use of resources; the nature of change achieved (or aspired to); and the identification of opportunities.

The advent of social leadership has been characterized by the use of resources. As opposed to traditional nonprofit-sector organizations, social entrepreneurs use all available resource options, including the commercial methods of the business sector (Dees, 1998). They are not bound by sector definitions and are often not even considered nonprofit organizations (Defourny and Marthe, 2008). Some theoreticians even see the resource issue as the key differentiating factor. Boschee (2006), for instance, criticizes Dees for not putting enough emphasis on financial self-reliance. He claims that what differentiates social entrepreneurs from other social activists is the importance of their commitment to become financially sustainable or self-sufficient by relying on earned income. This is because earned income is what makes the entrepreneur truly independent of donors and governmental agencies.

But other researchers disagree with this approach. Light (2009) claims that not all entrepreneurial organizations should seek profit and that some of them have no chance of doing so. This view is consistent with Dees' notion that what differentiates social entrepreneurship from business entrepreneurship is that the value it creates is social rather than financial.

In conclusion, the option of earned income and commercial methods is an important component of social entrepreneurship but it is neither necessary nor sufficient. Light's objection is obviously a strong one: some social challenges, by definition, cannot bring in financial resources or in the terms used by Shepherd and Patzelt they cannot bring economic gains. Since it appears that profit is a key factor for sustainable entrepreneurship, these kinds of challenges will not be taken on by it. So, relying exclusively on it might lead to the neglect of entire sections of social problems that need to be addressed. Sustainable entrepreneurship should apparently be conceived as something that has to be coordinated with other activities in ways that still need to be defined for the benefit of social progress.

The second characteristic, and possibly the most critical factor in regard to which social entrepreneurship creates difficulties for sustainable entrepreneurship, is the creation of systemic social change. As Dees claims, social entrepreneurship attacks the underlying cause of a social problem not just its symptoms. This is the social parallel of Schumpeter's "creative-destructive" process of capitalism – the function of entrepreneurs is to reform or revolutionize the way things are done but do it with a social mission in mind (Dees, 1998).

Martin and Osberg (2007) claim that this is what basically distinguishes social entrepreneurship from other social services. Whereas social service suppliers act within a given equilibrium and only aspire to improve its outcomes, the social entrepreneur takes direct action to generate a new, superior and sustained equilibrium. In their view, ambitious aspiration is not enough – the motivation for a radical change has to be reflected in the design of the venture. In other words, the social entrepreneurship venture has to be designed to achieve large-scale change or have a large impact by enabling replications.

Since sustainable entrepreneurship is in essence focused on a single endeavor, a single project of a single corporation, the question of systemic social change is cardinal.

The third significant aspect that social entrepreneurship prompts us to address is its persistent pursuit of new opportunities. This characteristic, drawing mainly from Drucker's work in the field of business entrepreneurship, specifies the method entrepreneurs use to create a new equilibrium through a ceaseless search of the way to challenge it (Dees, 1998). Light points out that the seizing of opportunities is an important component of the ecosystem of social entrepreneurship (2009). It combines both of the two previous aspects since it is relevant both to financing opportunities and opportunities related to mission, e.g., social atmosphere, political shifts, etc.

Entrepreneurs see beyond the limits of the current needs and try to fit reality to their vision (Dees, 1998). Obviously, we are referring here to social vision, as a foundation for action. In this concept, action is preceded by vision-building. Sustainable entrepreneurship does not necessarily result from a global social vision. But many projects become a patchwork, with no unity of vision on which they are established.

Conclusion: abandoning the regulation approach

Comparing sustainable entrepreneurship to social entrepreneurship makes it possible to show how this perspective seeks to go beyond the classical approach, which generally views these themes from two angles:

1   The "restorative" perspective, which is founded on the proposition that economic developments, the quest for profit, production, trade activities and so on create social problems. The role of social entrepreneurship is therefore to identify and address these problems in order to make society more livable and to avoid social clashes. The approach adopted here is clearly regulatory and is primarily concerned with the question of permitting the system to continue functioning. Social entrepreneurship is an aggregate of initiatives aimed at solving social problems.
2   The perspective of sustainability is essentially the adoption of modes of economic development that cause relatively little or no damage. The theme of social responsibility is a good example of this approach, where one attempts to ensure that the present does not inflict damage on the future but instead paves the way for it.

Sustainable entrepreneurship generates both economic development and social progress. This new approach is rich and innovative but also creates a number of theoretical difficulties.

1   *The combining of economic development and social progress represents:*
    a   Positive potential: The pursuit of goals that are both financial and

social by means of the same entrepreneurial activities avoids a dichotomous approach that separates development activities from engagement with social problems. By joining these two spheres of activity, sustainable entrepreneurship constitutes a call for greater responsibility. It avoids becoming a constraint (as can be seen in the conduct of entrepreneurs upon whom social or behavioral norms are imposed). In this case, sustainability and activities are one and the same.

b   A risk: This approach presents the risk of scientism. It can easily lead one to assume that development in itself and progress per se can provide a sense of action. One risks therefore the abandonment of any critical perspective as to whether the action indeed justifies itself. Environmental disasters, the excessive exploitation of the work force, etc. have in the past been the expression of such a risk and one must do everything to avoid risks of this sort resurfacing.

2   *The very notion of sustainable entrepreneurship is deserving of careful examination.* In this respect, the etymology of the word entrepreneur is interesting because it comes from the Latin *in prehendere*, which means "to seize something with one's hand," and has entered the language of the global community through the French verb *entreprendre*, which means to begin or launch something. Now that it has entered the global community's language, we must ask ourselves what we mean when we talk about a beginning that is sustained or an action that begins in order to endure. These notions introduce us to a dialectic that literature and philosophy can find a place for.

a   The link between entrepreneurship and the necessity of believing in the long term (which the literature often terms immortality) for the development of a moral, constructive action is often encountered beyond the parameters of the management sciences. Dostoyevsky has one of his characters say: "if you were to destroy in mankind the belief in immortality, not only love but every living force maintaining the world would at once be dried up." In the same passage from his novel *The Brothers Karamazov*, he explains that human beings never embark on important projects if their time is limited because they are conscious that a limited time frame cannot guarantee that there will be a response to their positive or negative actions.

b   Inversely, other currents in the humanities have made us cautious with regard to risk, where the accent on durability and sustainability might run the risk of immobility (which is inconsistent with the image of the entrepreneur). However, first and foremost, the notion of sustainability exposes us to the quasi-existentialist question: What does entrepreneurship mean if we are talking about the long term? Can one undertake something, launch a beginning that will remain a beginning for a long time? What is a beginning that is of a long duration?

Heidegger wrote "The end … does not signify, in human reality, a being who is moving toward the end or being finished; rather it designates a being who lives for the end" (1962, 34).

If one also admits that the end, the very term itself, gives meaning to the action of the entrepreneur, does not the emphasis on sustainability risk removing from entrepreneurship its end, its goal? Does durability give meaning to the act of undertaking something?

References

Bornstein, D. and Davis, S. (2010). *Social Entrepreneurship: What Everyone Needs to Know*. Oxford: Oxford University Press.

Boschee, J. (2006). Social entrepreneurship: The promise and the perils. In A. Nicholls (ed.) *Social Entrepreneurship: New Models of Sustainable Social Change*, 356–390. Oxford: Oxford University Press.

Dart, R. (2004). The legitimacy of social entrepreneurship. *Nonprofit Management & Leadership*, 14(4), 411–424.

Dees, J. G. (1998). *The Meaning of Social Entrepreneurship*. Retrieved from www.fuqua.duke.edu/centers/case/documents/dees_SE.pdf.

Dees, J. G. (2001). Mastering the art of innovation. In J. G. Dees, J. Emerson and P. Economy (eds) *Enterprising Nonprofits: A Toolkit for Social Entrepreneurs*. New York: John Wiley & Sons.

Dees, J. G. and Anderson, B. B. (2003). Sector-bending: Blurring lines between non-profit and for-profit. *Society*, 40(4), 16–27.

Defourny, J. and Marthe, N. (2008). Conceptions of social enterprise in Europe and the United States: Convergences and divergences. Draft presented at the International Conference for the International Society for Third Sector Research.

Drayton, B. (2009, October 9). Interview on Bloomberg TV.

Fleishman, J. (2007). *The Foundation: A Great American Secret – How Private Wealth is Changing the World*. New York: Public Affairs.

Fleishman, J. (2009). *The Foundation: A Great American Secret – How Private Wealth is Changing the World*. New York: Public Affairs, paperback edition.

Fritz, J. (2014). Before starting a nonprofit, consider other business structures. *About Money*. Retrieved from http://goo.gl/PBm7vp.

Heidegger, M. (1962). *Being and Time* (trans. by John Macquarrie and Edward Robinson). London: SCM Press.

Hemmati, Y. and Kia, S. (2013). A study on the relationship between social entrepreneurship and organizational commitment. *Management Science Letters*, 3(8), 2241–2244.

Lans, T., Blok, V. and Wesselink, R. (2014). Learning apart and together: Towards an integrated competence framework for sustainable entrepreneurship in higher education. *Journal of Cleaner Production*, 62(1), 37–47.

Light, P. C. (2009). *The Search for Social Entrepreneurship*. Washington, DC: Brookings Institution Press.

Martin, R. and Osberg, S. (2007). Social entrepreneurship: The case for definition. *Stanford Social Innovation Review*, Spring, 28–39.

Pinkse, J. and Groot, K. (2015). Sustainable entrepreneurship and corporate political activity: Overcoming market barriers in the clean energy sector. *Entrepreneurship Theory and Practice*, 39(3), 633–654.

Poldner, K., Shrivastava, P. and Branzei, O. (2015). Embodied multi-discursivity: An aesthetic process approach to sustainable entrepreneurship. *Business & Society*, 1–39.

Shepherd, D. A. and Patzelt, H. (2011). The new field of sustainable entrepreneurship: studying entrepreneurial action linking "What is to be sustained" with "What is to be developed." *Entrepreneurship Theory and Practice*, Special Issue: Future of Entrepreneurship, 35(1), January, 137–163.

2 Addressing sustainability challenges through state-led social innovation

The Singapore story

Azad Singh Bali, Peter McKiernan, Christopher Vas and Peter Waring

Introduction

Governments, historically, were looked upon as a means to either organize society or a means to an innovation end, i.e. providing resources to boost development. Many decades later, as the New Public Management discourse showcases, governments were strained to emulate private sector practices in embracing innovation to design and deliver services. Efficiency was the key focus. Today, in the face of growing resource constraints, governments across the world have to do more with less. They must catalyse an ecosystem with new social innovations that result in far superior outcomes that could not have been achieved simply by market or philanthropic means (Moulaert *et al.*, 2013). The focus is not just on efficiency and effectiveness but also to meet long-term sustainability objectives. This chapter discusses this development in Singapore particularly in arguing that a top-down State-led social innovation approach is necessary but not a sufficient condition to achieve goals of sustainable development, particularly those relating to sustainable innovation. As a catalyst, the Singapore Government endeavours to stimulate creative thinking through collaboration amongst key actors in the hope that solutions derived will be 'effective, efficient and sustainable' (Phills *et al.*, 2008; Sorensen and Torfing, 2014).

Singapore's top-down governance approach has seen the country grow from a low middle-income economy to a high-income country in a short period of about five decades. Its economic progress is evident by the steep increase in its GDP per capita, growing from $24,898 in 1991 to $63,050 in 2011 (World Bank, 2013). Nevertheless, its growth and development strategy has given rise to perennial manpower shortages, which it has filled by relying on foreign labour at both ends of the skill spectrum. The growth of foreign labour, which now stands at 40 per cent of the labour force, has produced concerns over congestion externalities, particularly in transport, housing and recreational facilities; and competition for positional goods such as cars, housing and education have become an integral part of political and social discourse in Singapore (Low and

Vadaketh, 2014). This debate surfaced at the General Election in 2011 and focused on the perceived social problems created through an influx of foreign workers. Singapore's low annualized productivity growth over the past decade, particularly in industrial subsectors that relied heavily on foreign manpower at the lower end of the skills spectrum, accelerated the need for appropriate policy responses to ensure continued economic prosperity. The government has adopted a multi-faceted approach in responding to these challenges: it has introduced specific measures that aim to lower the influx of foreign workers and Singapore's reliance on foreign workers and placed renewed emphasis on improving productivity, fostering innovation and creating a *sustainable* Singapore.

The Sustainable Singapore Blueprint (SSB) 2009 outlines a four-pronged strategy – *boosting resource efficiency, enhancing urban environment, building new capabilities and fostering community action* – through which the Government aims to harness enough action from individuals and companies to achieve its vision (Ministry of Environment and Water Resources (MEWR), 2014). For instance, it is leading efforts to restructure the economy by encouraging SMEs to reduce their reliance on foreign labour and to raise productivity through multiple initiatives. The Government has also introduced a radical set of incentives and policy settings to address a confluence of these economic and political challenges. Many of these innovative policies are directed at encouraging firms to assess internal practices, to develop a culture of innovation, to invest in new capabilities and to heighten investment in human capital development. What is unique about the set of policy tools and incentives is that they are targeted across the spectrum of business activities in Singapore and not to any particular sector.

Taking this macro perspective, *this chapter will assess whether the Singapore Government's policy innovation efforts align with how firms and businesses view the catalytic role of Government, its top-down governance arrangements and are likely to sustain innovative practices.* Unlike the social innovation literature that relies primarily on businesses displaying innovation characteristics and meeting social outcomes amidst a business agenda, this chapter also looks at the role of government as a *social innovation catalyst.* Consequently, the central argument in this chapter is that while innovation can be catalysed, social innovation objectives cannot be achieved solely using a top-down State-driven approach. It requires the firm to sustain innovative practices.

The rest of this chapter is organized as follows. The next section discusses sustainability in Singapore and is followed by a discussion of the research methodology and research findings. The final section offers concluding remarks.

The sustainability paradigm in Singapore

For many decades, Singapore has been a source of inspiration for many cities in Asia. It has embraced the lack of natural resources as an opportunity to innovate and a source of competitive advantage. Singapore defines sustainable development to 'encompass the twin goals of growing the economy and protecting the environment' and its achievement in a balanced way (MEWR, 2009). In acknowledging constraints, through investment in technologies and knowledge Singapore wants to create new capabilities by which it improves environmental performance and drives economic growth (MEWR, 2009). It wants to achieve this aspiration and looks to collaborate with other countries to build sustainable cities around the world.

In 2008, Singapore set up the Inter-Ministerial Committee on Sustainable Development (IMCSD) to help create a national strategy for its sustainable growth. It produced a blueprint 'A Lively and Liveable Singapore: Strategies for Sustainable Growth' which was released in 2009. Boosting resource efficiency, enhancing Singapore's urban environment, building capabilities and fostering community action were the four key strategies that emerged. These strategies are intended to help Singapore achieve many of its energy-related goals. The ultimate objective relates to the building of 'capability and expertise' that will develop Singapore into an 'outstanding knowledge hub in the latest technology and services' (MEWR, 2009). Working towards these aspirations of sustainable growth, Singapore hopes to spur community action along the way. This will encourage society to participate in making Singapore clean, green and resource-efficient and, over time, the responsibility of sustainable growth will be shared in the way Singaporeans live, work, play and commute.

To execute this plan, the IMCSD identified specific measures including promoting industrial efficiency through productivity improvements; improving information for decision making; promoting new investment in processes and adopting new technologies; investing in research and development; building capabilities and means by which to share knowledge; and, most importantly, ensuring that the public sector sets the pace of action in industry and the community (MEWR, 2009). For instance, the role for Singapore's Economic Development Board (EDB) in nurturing new research and development opportunities to enable the creation of a vibrant research ecosystem is one such action. In addition to developing suitable incentive frameworks and policies for firms, the Government set aside $680 million to build new capabilities through research and the testing of programmes (MEWR, 2009). The Research, Innovation and Enterprise (RIE) 2020 plan released in January 2016 by the Government has attached priority to urban solutions and sustainability as being one of the four key areas to be further developed and by committing almost $1 billion to relevant programmes and initiatives.

The Singapore Government has also continued to develop its manpower by creating centres of excellence. Advancement of human capital in Singapore is expected to drive international collaboration, facilitate the transfer of know-how and promote better collaboration between industry, government and research institutions – all of which will enable businesses in Singapore to internationalise and further position Singapore as a 'sustainable development hub' (MEWR, 2009).

Some of the successes Singapore has achieved since the first blueprint in 2009 are noteworthy, particularly transformations that have taken place at the industry level ranging from awareness raising and capability building. For instance, over 200 firms have become part of the Energy Efficiency National Partnership, an initiative for inter-company sharing of best practices and over 1200 candidates received Singapore's Certified Energy Manager (SCEM) grants (MEWR, 2015:10–13). Singapore's agency that supports SME activities, the Standards, Productivity and Innovation Board (SPRING), introduced the SME Energy Efficiency Initiative. Many firms have utilized SPRING's Innovation and Capability Voucher (ICV) scheme. They use the ICV to undertake firm-level audits and identify areas for improvement. Furthermore, firms can tap into SPRING's Capability Development Grants programme, to defray some of the project costs involved with implementing new initiatives and adhering to best practices and quality standards (MEWR, 2015:55–56). Through such policy efforts, Singapore continues to build its sustainability agenda.

Research methodology

At the behest of SPRING Singapore, the Singapore Innovation and Productivity Institute (SiPi) commissioned a year-long study into productivity and innovation (P and I) practices among SMEs in Singapore's manufacturing sector. With the aim of creating a benchmark index, the research focused on key drivers of total factor productivity and examined firm-level performance by collecting primary data from the SMEs in identified subsectors.

The research adopted a three-pronged approach. First, a systematic literature review of the academic and extant literature on the macro and micro determinants of productivity was conducted. Second, 20 semi-structured interviews with SME leaders and entrepreneurs were completed to better understand the Singapore context. Third, a Delphi study – a structured iterative communication technique to engage with multiple experts on a topic with a view to achieving convergence – was completed, where views of global and local experts and thought leaders were sought on the drivers of productivity and innovation in SMEs.[1]

This triangulated approach produced six thematic determinants of productivity in SMEs:

1   Technology & Capital Utilisation;
2   Pay & Performance Management;
3   Training, Development & Organisational Learning;
4   Innovation Culture;
5   Government Policy, Markets And Regulation; and
6   Leadership and Management Quality.

Data from these sources was collected, coded, compared and analysed. Common data from all three sources were categorized by theme following a systematic process described by Miles and Huberman (1984) in the following terms:

From the beginning of data collection the qualitative analyst is beginning to decide what things mean, noting regularities, patterns, explanations, possible configurations, causal flows and propositions. The competent researcher holds these conclusions lightly maintaining openness and scepticism, but the conclusions are still there, inchoate and vague at first then increasingly explicit and grounded.

As common data was added to each analytical category, the evidence for each of the key drivers became stronger and reinforced the criticality of the driver as a 'prime mover' of total factor productivity. A survey instrument containing 41 multiple-choice questions across these six themes was designed. A stratified random sample of firms based on the share of economic output to the manufacturing sector was drawn from the Accounting and Corporate Regulatory Authority of Singapore. These subsectors (listed in Table 2.1) account for more than 80 per cent of manufacturing output in Singapore.

The number of firms surveyed across subsectors is illustrated in Figure 2.1. The survey data, with 215 firms, was collected in-person with the person 'most familiar with productivity and innovation issues' in the firm – usually the CEO or a senior manager. The survey took about one hour to complete, and data were captured on a tablet computer and uploaded to a cloud-based survey administrator in real time. To improve the response rate, this approach was complemented with a 'snow-balling' approach inviting SME firms that completed the survey to provide an introduction to other SMEs within their network. The research methodology and survey instrument received ethics clearance from Murdoch University.

The triangulated research design, incorporating quantitative data and in-depth qualitative interviews, strengthens the validity of the arguments presented in the subsequent section. This chapter however does not report the findings of the benchmarking study – but discusses qualitative data from the survey instrument, interviews with SME leaders, Delphi study as well as select descriptive statistics of two relevant themes, namely: *innovation culture* and *government, markets and regulation*.

Table 2.1 Industrial subsector and SSIC classification codes

Industrial subsector	SSIC classification – two-digit level
Chemicals and chemical products	C20
Pharmaceuticals and biological products	C21
Computer, electronic and optical products	C26
Fabricated metal products	C25
Foods and beverage	C10; C11
Machinery and equipment	C28
Other transport/manufacturing/engineering	C30

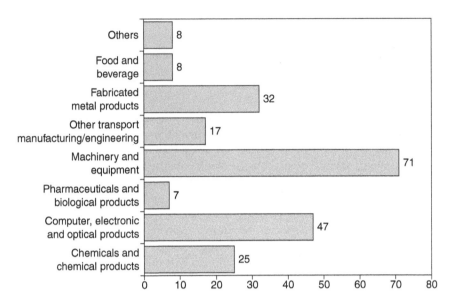

Figure 2.1 Distribution of 215 firms surveyed across industrial subsectors.

Research findings and discussion

The chapter assesses whether the efforts of the Singapore Government – to lead sustainable development through social innovation – align with how firms view the catalytic role of Government and its top-down governance arrangements. It is important to discuss these findings in the aforementioned socio-political context of Singapore. Three such contextual dimensions are discussed here: *foreign labour practices*, *expectations from Government* and *drivers of P and I* because they are important. These results of the Delphi study helped underscore some key messages here.

In the context of the role of government policies and incentives, one Delphi expert reflected on the common notions of 'newness' that is propagated by governments and researchers, suggesting:

> What is commonly forgotten by governments and academics as they grandly pronounce on 'innovation' is that everything cannot change at the same time; more important, it is a mistake to attempt to sponsor initiatives that do that. Doing existing things better requires a stable background against which changes (even small ones) can be judged for their effectiveness (and ultimate contribution to raising productivity). Thus, while government officials ramble on about the driving force of innovation, they should be reflecting not only on the need for change but on how much change can the economy (and society) efficiently absorb. It is this latter aspect of 'innovation' and 'productivity' studies that gets short shrift. That, in my view, is a big mistake.

Two important aspects emerge here. One, is the importance of producing new products and the need to do existing things in an improved and effective manner. Two, acknowledging that change for SMEs can only come about incrementally as opposed to a radical transformation. These two aspects have formed part of the Singapore Government's strategy and how it seeks to encourage firms to embrace the goals of sustainable development.

In building new capabilities, the Singapore Government has looked to encourage the internationalization of firms such that global interconnectedness and knowledge transfer across geographical boundaries is achievable and results in new economic opportunities. Creating conditions through which firms can participate in open and contestable markets is tied strongly to building innovation capabilities. A Delphi expert claimed that one of the key factors constraining innovation was that

> productivity and innovation only happen when management are committed to making it happen and have the skills and capacity to make it happen. That in turn depends on the incentives they face (in particular, competition) and their capacity to respond to those incentives (their own abilities and those of their employees), and the extent to which public policy blunts or distorts incentives, inhibits managements' capacity to respond to those incentives, and which adds to the stock of knowledge on which managements can draw.

This statement points to an important insight; that government policy regimes alone are *insufficient* to drive productivity and innovation – rather, and in addition, it is the capacity of the management of the firm to respond in a timely and effective manner to cost pressures, create value for customers, and ultimately ensure business sustainability through continuous change. Alongside this combined effort between organizations and governments to achieve resource efficiency is the need to invest further in new capacities and spur community action. It is no surprise why these aspects have formed part of the Sustainable Singapore strategy.

The findings from the Delphi study were supported strongly by the large-scale survey of 215 SMEs. Recall the earlier emphasis of Singapore's dilemma in the over-reliance on foreign labour coupled with declining productivity rates, plus the need for increased innovation and technological investment. SMEs were asked to describe the extent to which their firm relied on foreign labour.

The research findings, depicted in Figure 2.2, show that overall 70 per cent of firms show a moderate to large dependency on foreign labour. About 40 per cent indicate having a large reliance on foreign labour.

When asked about the criticality of such dependence and how firms were responding, 38 per cent of the firms acknowledge that the Government was sending signals on the need to reduce such over-reliance and firms intended to take action towards this end. Over 70 per cent of firms agreed that foreign labour was critical to their operations and about 55 per cent agreed that they would not be able to survive without foreign labour. About 48 per cent of the firms agreed that they were trying to reduce reliance on foreign labour, while only 28 per cent were able to reduce reliance to a 'small extent' or have no need for foreign labour at all.

While a small percentage (27 per cent) of firms agreed that easy access to foreign labour made it difficult for them to become more productive, about half of the surveyed firms did not think this was true. This suggests that beyond access to cheap foreign labour there are other competitive factors that require consideration.

To ascertain if other competitive pressures had any role in such over-reliance on foreign labour, SME firms were asked to consider the extent to which each of the following statements (in Figure 2.4) were true for their firms.

The vast majority of firms (almost 83 per cent) agreed with the statement that 'Competition drives productivity and innovation in our markets'. The majority of firms (55 per cent) believe the small size of the Singapore market acts as a natural restraint on the capacity of firms to improve. Market domination or market abuse by a small number of large providers is known to reduce competition but at the same time it can heighten the need to adopt P and I initiatives in order to compete and survive. Over 45 per cent of firms agreed that the market power of larger firms restricted SMEs from becoming more productive and innovative by agreeing to the statement 'Market domination by a few large players restricts our productivity and innovation'.

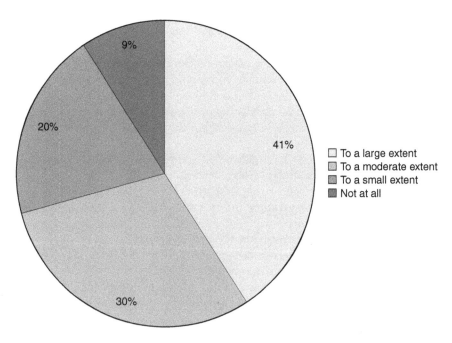

Figure 2.2 Firms' reliance on foreign labour.

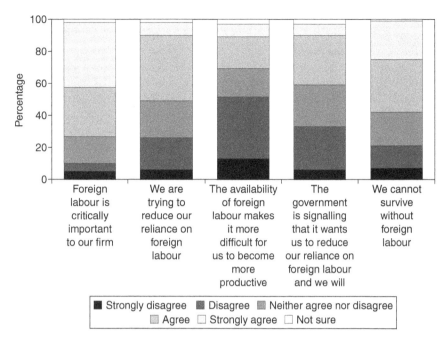

Figure 2.3 Firms and foreign labour.

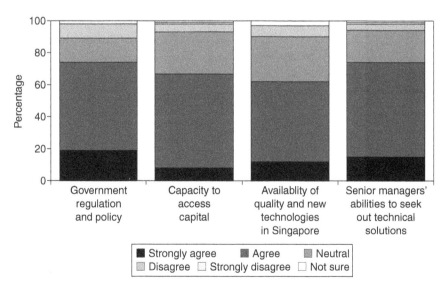

Figure 2.4 Extent of dependence on government policy and capital access to invest in technology.

Government as a catalyst can influence or drive industry action when it determines the need to do so. This premise was tested in the survey. A majority of firms (73 per cent) indicated that productivity could be raised if the Government assisted SMEs to enter into new markets (Figure 2.4). The overwhelming support to the statement that the Government can improve productivity through its buying decisions provides a sense of responsibility that firms associate with the Government at large. The proportion of firms (48 per cent) that are trying to reduce reliance on foreign labour at the behest of Government, signals the belief that the latter has an important role to play in productivity improvements by virtue of its buying decisions (62 per cent), Free Trade Agreement activity (60 per cent) and supportive policy action in opening up new markets (73 per cent). This evidence suggests that firms consider the Singapore Government as having an important catalytic role and a responsible authority that can drive firm-level action. This is evidence that greater economies of scale and exposure to market opportunity can be used as levers to drive productivity and innovation.

The next set of findings discusses insights that help us understand the extent to which the Singapore Government has been able to influence internal firm behaviour and action. SME firms were asked to determine the extent to which some of the statements (see Figure 2.5) were relevant to their firm.

Over 70 per cent of firms agreed that government regulation and policy was an important contributory factor in the context of new technology investment. Similarly, 66 per cent of firms agreed that the capacity of the firm to access capital was important, if the firm has to invest in new technology in a sustainable manner. The Government's ability to create a supportive policy framework under which firms can access resources to invest in new infrastructure is essential to lift P and I measures.

In addition to an enabling policy framework, what is useful for SMEs is the sector-wide environment within which they function. For instance, 62 per cent of firms agreed that the availability of quality and new technologies in Singapore contributed to SMEs considering the need to invest more in new technological infrastructure. This agreement resonated strongly, wherein 74 per cent of firms agreed that it was important for the firm's senior managers to seek out new solutions for investment.

These findings go to the heart of the Government's sustainability strategy of progressing action amongst its SMEs, while ensuring significant focus on advancing human capital practices and knowledge development efforts. The Government's role is essential in enabling sustainable thinking among SMEs. The study investigated this aspect, government's influence, in further detail.

Firms in the survey were also asked to consider to what extent government policy and schemes influenced their firm's approach along five factors: productivity improvement; building a culture of innovation; investing in new technology; developing new and better production techniques; and expanding the business (Figure 2.6).

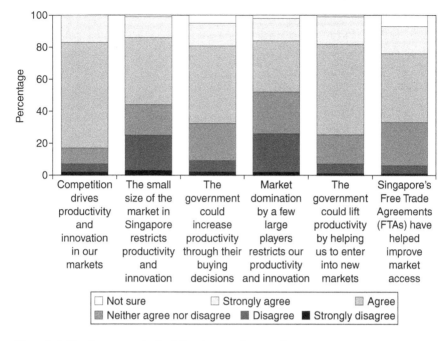

Figure 2.5 To what extent is the following true for your firm.

Of importance here is that over 75 per cent of firms agreed that government policy and schemes had a level of influence varying between 'some', 'strong' to 'very strong' where productivity improvements were concerned. This level of influence was also evidenced with 76 per cent of firms confirming that government policy has had an influence where investment in new technology was concerned. Despite this level of influence where productivity improvement and new investment were concerned, only 62 per cent of firms saw government having 'some', 'strong' to 'very strong' influence where building a culture of innovation was concerned. This finding suggests that beyond government's influence, firms were responsible in creating a culture of innovation. This supports the tenet that the Singapore Government, alone, cannot drive sustainable development action holistically. This effort has to be matched at the firm level as well as by the broader industry.

Delphi experts confirm that sustainable improvement in process innovation and production techniques is as important as the development of new products and services. It is no surprise that only 68 per cent of firms saw government as having 'some', 'strong' and 'very strong' level of influence when it comes to developing new and better production techniques. As far as business expansion was concerned, an overwhelming majority of firms (71 per cent) believed that government had an influence and a role to play in supporting firm expansion.

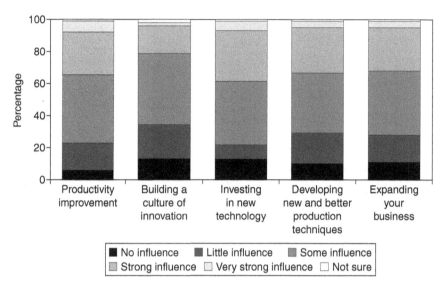

Figure 2.6 Extent to which firms were influenced by government policy and schemes.

The survey further delved into finding out the extent to which firms had accessed government schemes and incentives to improve productivity and drive innovation within the firm (Figure 2.7).

From Figure 2.7, it is evident that a large percentage of firms (85 per cent) accessed government programs, such as the Productivity and Innovation Credit scheme. A similar percentage discussed the need for productivity improvements internally. This aligns with findings in Figure 2.6, wherein over a quarter of the surveyed firms (29 per cent) of SMEs were in agreement, and saw 'no' or 'little' influence from government when it came to informing production techniques. Perhaps this is more an internal firm responsibility. The research shows that a smaller percentage (74 per cent) discussed the need to create a culture of innovation.

In relation to meeting the objectives of Sustainable Singapore, it is clear that while the efforts of the Government are a necessary condition, it is not a sufficient means by which objectives can be achieved.

To better understand the transition paths embarked upon by firms, particularly at the SME level, this study highlights the importance of the resource efficiency and capabilities building strategy – pillars identified in the Sustainable Singapore blueprint. In achieving the objectives of resource efficiency, progress is dependent on a number of issues. First, firms have to consider how internal resource efficiency can be achieved through cost management, process management and better human capital management practices. Only a sustained effort will enable effective and efficient resource usage that will create space for newer investments such as those in renewable infrastructure and energy usage, technologies and infrastructure. This

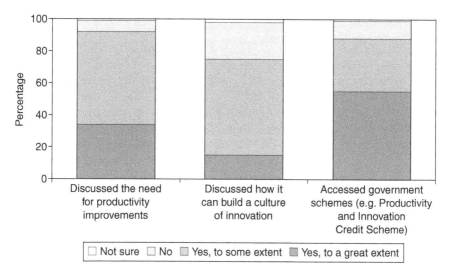

Figure 2.7 Firm-level considerations.

can have a positive impact on firm-level productivity. Without such building blocks, the expectation for firms to radically transform into smarter users of renewal sources of energy, to achieve better resource efficiency and subsequently long-term sustainable goals, can be futile.

For this reason, while firms should respond to government policy action and continuously work towards lifting their productivity and innovation more needs to be done by firms to sustain innovative practices. In this manner, they become efficient at resource utilization and are able to embrace new means of technological investment, human capital development and international connectedness, all of which are ambitions of a Sustainable Singapore.

Conclusion

The Singapore Government has set ambitious sustainable development goals for its economy, which it hopes to achieve through boosting resource efficiency, creating a better urban environment, building new capabilities and fostering community action. By nominating the public sector to act first and setting an example for rest of the economy, the Government's efforts have yielded positive results. Following significant investments in infrastructure, development of industry awareness programmes, capability-building initiatives and delivering policy incentives, it has started to make headway into achieving some of its objectives. However, further progress requires well-designed policy initiatives together with sustained action from the firms and the broader industry. In order to achieve the goals of a sustainability agenda, the Singapore Government must empower firms to demonstrate leadership and sustain innovation particularly within their own sectors.

Singapore must acknowledge that the top-down approach has limited efficacy. What is needed, and where future research can be directed, is towards a value co-creation or a co-production approach that we see between firms. For a State-led social innovation approach to be successful dialogue, connection and commitment is important (Randall *et al.*, 2011). This value co-creation approach needs to take shape between government policy and societal action. While the leadership and vision from the Government is necessary to meet long-term sustainability goals, it is not a sufficient condition for success. This chapter has gathered insights from the experience of 215 manufacturing firms to support this argument. Going beyond the manufacturing sector, the Singapore Government must catalyse further action across multiple sectors to achieve its sustainability agenda. At the firm level this may very well require a blended approach of sustainable entrepreneurial action, one that is able to sustain innovative practices and also blend with it the objectives of social innovation.

Note

1 See Hsu and Sandford (2007) for a review of the Delphi technique.

References

Hsu, C.-C. and Sandford, B.A. (2007) The Delphi technique: making sense of consensus. *Practical Assessment, Research & Evaluation*, 12(10), 1–8.

Low, D. and Vadaketh, S.T. (2014) *Hard Choices: Challenging the Singapore Consensus.* National University of Singapore Press, Singapore.

Miles, M. B. and Huberman, A. M. (1984) *Qualitative Data Analysis: A Sourcebook of New Methods.* SAGE, California.

Ministry of Environment and Water Resources (MEWR). (2009) *A Lively and Livable Singapore: Strategies for Sustainable Growth.* Available online at https://www.nccs.gov.sg/sites/nccs/files/Sustainable_Spore_Blueprint.pdf.

Ministry of Environment and Water Resources (MEWR). (2014) *Sustainable Singapore: A Lively and Livable City.* Singapore Government. Available online at http://app.mewr.gov.sg/web/Contents/ContentsSSS.aspx?ContId=1034.

Ministry of Environment and Water Resources (MEWR). (2015) *Sustainable Singapore Blueprint.* Singapore Government. Available online at http://app.mewr.gov.sg/web/ssb/index.html.

Moulaert, F., MacCallum, D., Mehmood, A. and Hamdouch, A. (2013) General introduction: the return of social innovation as a scientific concept and a social practice. In Moulaert, F., MacCallum, D., Mehmood, A. and Hamdouch, A. (eds). *The International Handbook on Social Innovation: Collective Action, Social Learning and Transdisciplinary Research.* Edward Elgar, Cheltenham, UK.

Phills, J.A., Deiglmeier, K. and Miller, D.T. (2008) Rediscovering social innovation. *Stanford Social Innovation Review*, 6(4), 34–43.

Ramirez, C.D. and Tan, L.H. (2003) *Singapore, Inc. Versus the Private Sector: Are Government-Linked Companies Different?* International Monetary Fund, Washington, DC.

Randall, W.S., Gravier, M.J. and Prubutok, V.R. (2011) Connection, trust and commitment: dimensions of co-creation. *Journal of Strategic Marketing*, 19(1), 3–24.

Sorensen, E. and Torfing, J. (2014) Enhancing social innovation by rethinking collaboration, leadership and public governance. *Social Frontiers: The next edge of social innovation research.* Available online at http://rudar.ruc.dk//bitstream/1800/13187/1/191799289_Enhancing_Social_Innovation_by_Rethinking_Collaboration_Leadership_and_Public_Governance.pdf.

World Bank. (2013) *World Development Indicators*, CD-ROM.

3 Eco-socio innovation

Underpinning sustainable entrepreneurship and social innovation

Jonathan M. Scott, Patrick Dawson and John L. Thompson

Introduction

Since the turn of the century, there has been a growing interest in both 'environmental' (e.g. Kirkwood and Walton 2010a, 2010b; Walley *et al.* 2010) and 'sustainable' entrepreneurship (Cohen and Winn 2007; Dean and McMullen 2007; Hall *et al.* 2010; Pacheco *et al.* 2010). Although the topic remains under-theorized and is largely disconnected from other mainstream literatures, public and practitioner attention, concern and relevance remains high. There is a need to address both the lack of empirical evidence that currently exists and the general absence of conceptual developments in this field of study (Thompson and Scott 2010). Within the market economy, and especially in relation to financial incentives, there has been less governmental interest and influence than one might expect given the growing public attention given to these issues.

Sustainable entrepreneurship is sourced from eco-regulatory changes, new knowledge, changes in perceptions and through the discovery and exploitation of what Drucker (1985a, 1985b) terms an ecological niche. The motivation to grasp such opportunities (in a desire to 'improve the world') arises from the actions of the inventor, entrepreneur and/or groups of environmentalists. Whilst environmentalists may be motivated by changes that create a greener and more sustainable world, the inventor and entrepreneur may also look towards the commercial possibilities of new innovations. It is not uncommon for opportunistic and committed environmental entrepreneurs to spot and exploit opportunities both to gain competitive advantage and deliver critical outcomes by focusing on green issues. Importantly, the outcomes can be the same but with the latter there may be longer-term opportunities for further development and expansion. Whilst 'both entrepreneurship and environmentalism are founded on a perception of value' (Anderson 1998, 135), sustainable entrepreneurs have distinct ecological values from other entrepreneurs who are primarily driven by commercial gain (Dixon and Clifford 2007; Libecap 2009; Linnanen 2005).

In further developing our understanding of these issues and the inter-relationship between sustainability, entrepreneurship and social innovation we develop and introduce the novel concept of eco-socio innovation (ESI). We theorize the role of social innovations in sustainable entrepreneurship (new venture creation associated with sustainable development) through building on Thompson's environment-values-resources (EVR) framework (Thompson 1999; Thompson *et al.* 2014). The chapter's novel contribution is in combining the concepts of sustainable entrepreneurship and social innovation into one over-arching meta-concept that acknowledges, first, the interplay with EVR and, second, the cascade effect of sustainable entrepreneurs' innovative ecological impacts upon social outcomes. In so doing, the chapter illuminates how the key components of ESI comprise an enacted and collective process that addresses both social and ecological objectives.

Our starting point, therefore, rests on a conceptualization of eco-socio innova-tions in relation to: the Environment (E), where changing public opinion, societal values and forms of legislation all influence the speed, direction and shape of eco-socio innovations; Values (V), with respect to the views and norms that reside within a particular organization; and Resources (R), which refers to activities in terms of impact, sustainability and wider indirect social outcomes. We argue that in order for changes to be truly sustainable, *values* must be affected although, in the short term, *environmental* driven change can have impacts. In the longer term, however, sustainability requires a shift towards positive customer perceptions of the changes and their environmental implications; for example, in the general public acceptance of the wider social good of purchasing Fairtrade goods or organic foodstuffs. The focus is on sustainable entrepreneurship – seen as new venture cre-ation associated with sustainable development – that provides a lens through which we can examine these processes in developing our concept of eco-socio innovation. This concept is used not only to generate further insight into the process by which sustainability-driven innovations that are enacted by sustainable entrepreneurs have direct positive ecological impacts that then cascade into indi-rect social outcomes, but also to shed light on the practical barriers and opportun-ities for change as well as advancing theory in this developing field of inquiry.

In the section that follows we discuss sustainable entrepreneurship drawing attention to the economic and ecological aspects that need greater recognition in managing capital in a sustainable way. We then turn to the concept of social innovation and highlight the development and use of this concept in the dis-covery and exploitation of innovations that improve the well-being of people in society. Our concept of eco-socio innovation is then developed and discussed in relation to a number of illustrative business scenarios. We conclude by calling not only for the need for further research but, perhaps more importantly, for greater business and governmental awareness, discussion and investment into this important area for sustainable business development.

Sustainable entrepreneurship

Although sustainable (environmental) entrepreneurship has acquired a huge body of research literature, the entrepreneurial dimension of green business remains largely unexplored (Schaper 2005, 4).[1] The concept of *ecopreneurship* has been reviewed (Schaper 2002a, 2002b, 2005), having emerged in the 1970s (Schaper 2005), but this nascent field has only gained traction more recently (Cohen and Winn 2007; Kirkwood and Walton 2010a; Schaper 2005). The focus of much of the previous research has been on environmental improvements in companies and specifically in existing small businesses. Schaper (2005, 3) has identified that the main gaps in the literature included definitions (though see Holt 2011), typologies, barriers, triggers, case versus quantitative research, and policies. Thus whilst Corporate Social Responsibility (CSR) and sustainability have been extensively researched and theorized (e.g. Bansal and Roth 2000), the main emphasis has been on sustainable entrepreneurship in terms of: organization design and business models (Birkin *et al.* 2009; Lewis 2004); motivations (Kirkwood and Walton 2010a); internationalized supply chain management (Kirkwood and Walton 2010b); and other aspects (see Cohen and Winn 2007).

A predominant qualitative focus drives much of the literature that attempts to provide in-depth understanding of the motivations, processes and outcomes of sustainable entrepreneurial activities. The findings of these studies have been used in various ways in developing typologies of environmental entrepreneurs (Isaak 2005). Whilst this research has been useful in clarifying and debating the range and type of environmental entrepreneurs that can be identified, there are other avenues of inquiry that may be more fruitful in a broader discussion of sustainability, entrepreneurship and social innovation. For example, the performance and growth of sustainable enterprises, which has been a rather neglected area given the difficulties of balancing the twin innovation goals of market and environmental sustainability (see Berchicci 2009), or some of the research that examines the importance of stakeholder links in building sustainable enterprises (see Bradford and Fraser 2008; Retolaza *et al.* 2009). Measuring the number of sustainable entrepreneurs is certainly a challenge, since some non-environmental firms may diversify into lines of business that have environmental aims (Hendrickson and Tuttle 1997). But this depends on how we define them, for example whether our definitions are based upon Standard Industrial Classification (SIC) codes or some other understanding of the particular industry they are involved in (Eastwood *et al.* 2006). Although it is possible to provide economic models of firms identified (Kotchen 2009), research attention needs to be given to questions such as: what are the main factors that are likely to influence performance and longer-term sustainability? How useful are the performance measures identified and used for existing SMEs (Hitchens *et al.* 2006; Simpson *et al.* 2004)? Studies on market leadership (Petersen 2005, 2006, 2010), firm failure (Holt 2011) and those that have examined the acquisition of firms and the potential of serial 'environmental' entrepreneurship (Kearins and Collins 2012), all offer avenues for consideration in a fuller examination of sustainable entrepreneurship. We contend that one way of starting to explore performance and outcomes more explicitly would be to link sustainability (in the context of environmental entrepreneurship) to social innovation and hence to our novel concept of eco-socio innovation.

Social innovation

Social innovation, as an emergent concept, has been distinguished from the more established technological innovations which align with the commercialization of inventions (Tidd and Bessant 2009; Tushman and Anderson 2004). Given the way in which the technology and market push-pull models have not taken into account social processes, a more nuanced definition of innovation is a 'multi-stage process whereby organizations transform ideas into new/improved products, service or processes, in order to advance, compete and differentiate themselves successfully in [the] marketplace' (Baregheh *et al.* 2009, 1334). Whilst innovation (like entrepreneurship) studies largely focus upon this commercialist paradigm, social (and environmental) outcomes of innovation have been largely overlooked. The main social focus has been on the various social barriers, such as norms, values, cultures that can impede innovation and act as determinants of successful change (Furglsang and Sundbo 2002). However, these social initiatives are receiving far more attention within the global media with the success and public engagement of social entrepreneurs like Mohammad Yunus and his development and support of a number of social business initiatives, such as, building a system for microcredit in Bangladesh (see Yunus 2007) – and in winning the Nobel Peace Prize.

Whilst social entrepreneurship has been around for a long time, it is a growing area of public and academic interest (see Bornstein 2003) and generally is used to refer to an individual who utilizes his or her commercial skills in managing ventures that bring about well-being for others in the pursuit of social change, embracing economic and technological interventions as necessary to achieve their goals (Dawson *et al.* 2010, 3). Within the mainstream innovation literature, 'economic' and 'technical' imperatives have long been assumed as the main triggers for innovations aimed at providing social benefit. These are now being questioned with the growing emergence of social issues that are being recognized as drivers of change accompanied by a growing interest in the links between social innovation and social entrepreneurship (Leadbeater 2007). This more recent and growing interest in socially based innovations marks a shift in emphasis, from the previous focus on technical imperatives and the profitability of new business ventures, toward socially responsible innovations and outcomes that can improve the well-being of people in society. Given that this is a new and emerging area of research and public concern, it is perhaps not surprising that there is still considerable ambiguity around the meaning of social innovation. Dawson and Daniel (2010) contend that – whilst there is much that can be drawn from existing studies that examine social processes in the development and application of innovation – the starting point for social innovation is, in fact, fundamentally different. They argue that, in order to develop a sound understanding of social innovation, there needs to be a synthesis in knowledge domains which embraces the social side as well as the innovation (creative) side of the process. To achieve this intellectual synthesis, they offer a framework which integrates both the perspective of the social challenge and that of the innovative goal into a four-component model of recursive negotiation between:

- the people involved;
- the shared challenge they face;
- the negotiation process in finding a suitable resolution; and
- the goal of improved well-being if a successful resolution is accomplished.

This simple and logical framework offers a fundamental model for both theoretical comparison and practical analysis of process and outcomes of social innovation:

> We argue that consideration of the knowledge domains of business innovation with social awareness highlights the importance of social meaning, interpretation, group discussion and social reflection ... Although science and technology can provide the materiality of change, dynamic social processes shape our understanding and evaluation of the social worth of change. As we have shown, much of the conceptual debate gets caught up in promoting a certain divide between either the technical and social or the commercial and social, with a focus on dualism ... We seek to sidestep this diversion in considering the concept of social innovation as an innovation that brings about social benefits but that may also secure certain commercial, technological, organizational or scientific aims – and the conditions that promote social innovation in the organization, community or society. We suggest that adopting a more critically reflective approach could go some way to opening up our minds to interpretive possibilities in the generation of new ideas and their application to innovations that meet social goals.
>
> (Dawson and Daniel 2010, 19)

While the debate on social innovation continues, it is more widely agreed that social innovation refers to innovations that aim to improve the welfare of groups and communities through initiatives that enhance the well-being of people in society (Ellis 2010). They are not driven by commercial or profit motives – though Saul (2011) points out that in making lasting solutions to social problems they have to be commercially sustainable – but by social goals, such as enabling low income communities access to banking facilities, providing health and educational support for remote and socially isolated communities, identifying and implementing solutions to ongoing community problems, or to introducing changes that improve the social conditions at work (Dawson and Daniel 2010). This push for more socially oriented innovations marks a growing interest in business practices that are environmentally sustainable (Benn *et al.* 2014), in using entrepreneurial principles (social entrepreneurship) to tackle pressing social problems (Goldsmith *et al.* 2010) and in the development of social business (Yunus 2007).

Eco-socio innovation and the role of environment, values and resources

In building on the work we have discussed above, this section sets out to define the novel concept of eco-socio innovation by theorizing the real and potential role of social innovations in sustainable entrepreneurship. In developing this concept, we present a number of examples and conceptual business scenarios against which we assess the relevance and applicability of ESI in relation to Dawson and Daniel's (2010) four-component model and Thompson's (1999) environment-values-resources framework. Whilst some of our examples and scenarios feature social innovations, others do not. We argue for the need to persuade organizations to consider changing their business models and to factor in sustainability criteria to a far greater extent in moving towards a more balanced ESI framework in managing change and innovation.

Our concept of eco-socio innovation extends Dawson and Daniel's (2010, 16) definition of social innovation through incorporating agency around sustainable entrepreneurial activities in the push for ecological solutions to social challenges that not only achieve social innovations but also commercial economic goals. In so doing, we propose the following extended definition of ESI (Dawson and Daniel 2010, 16):

> **Eco**-socio innovation refers to the **sustainable-entrepreneurially enacted** process of collective idea generation, selection and implementation by people who participate collaboratively to meet **ecological and** social challenges. These ideas are owned by people who work **(or, very often, venture)** together in pursuing **ecological and** social goals that may – but need not – service other organizational, technical, commercial or scientific goals.
>
> [extended/amended text in **bold**]

Extending ESI to incorporate EVR

Thompson (1999) developed the EVR (environment-values-resources) framework to capture the key elements of organizational success (see also Thompson *et al.* 2014). Environment (E) embraces various external factors and includes customers and investors as well as regulations. Resources (R) covers factors that are internal to the organization and thus includes activities and operations as well as clearly tangible resources. Values (V) represents culture and leadership elements as well as (commonly held) values and beliefs, and is seen as the driving force behind decisions that bring together (or not, as the case may be) external and internal factors. EVR, in effect, explores how and why organizations deal with their perceived opportunities and threats in relation to their strengths and weaknesses.

Diagrammatically, it can be represented as three overlapping circles as shown in Figure 3.1; the linkages should be strong and not easily broken. Strong

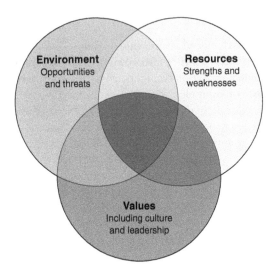

Figure 3.1 E-V-R congruence.

overlap of the three is classed as congruence – incongruency can thus take a number of forms. Where E and R overlap but V is isolated, the organization is unconsciously congruent. It is successful, it is satisfying the needs and expectations of stakeholders, but it is not clear why. This is a fragile position; circumstances can change quickly. Where E and V overlap but R is isolated, the organization is consciously incongruent. It knows there are resource weaknesses and that actions are required. The issue is: what is it going to do? Where V and R overlap but E is isolated, there has been strategic drift. The 'world has changed' in some way and the organization has failed to respond. Congruency has been lost.

It is straightforward to supplement this basic framework with the themes of sustainability. The desire to be more sustainable can begin with stakeholders within an organization. Key decision makers embrace the theme and are determined that the organization will behave in a different way. Equally, it can be external and driven by either legislation or public opinion – accepting that these are frequently intertwined. Here the positive element of motivation would be to see this constraint as an opportunity and seek ways to benefit from compliance. For true long-term impact, the hearts and minds of people within the organization will need to be affected – implying employees are persuaded by the external pressures or buy-in to the cause-driven values of the strategic leader. Common themes such as green energy and Fairtrade can thus easily carry different meanings in different organizations. To this end, EVR might be re-stated along the lines of Figure 3.2, while Figure 3.3 further integrates ESI and EVR as the underpinning 'context'. This third figure shows idea generation, idea selection and idea implementation being influenced by the four ESI themes: the

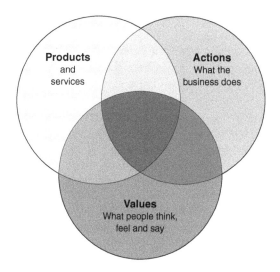

Figure 3.2 Congruence restated: PAVing the way to success.

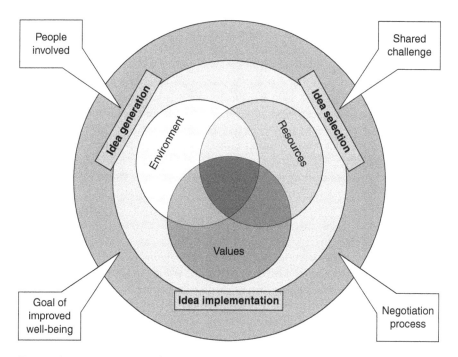

Figure 3.3 Integrating ESI and EVR.

people involved, the shared challenge, the negotiation process and the goal of improved well-being. The test of effectiveness is EVR Congruence which is, therefore, placed in the centre of the figure.

Established examples of Eco-Socially Innovative enterprises include those in Table 3.1. Each of these exemplar organizations have their own very different concepts and are often based on a quite different business model.

In each of these examples, commitment towards social and community values rates highly on the personal agendas of key stakeholders. However, it is the innovatory routes towards clearly specified aims following the identification of a need, problem or opportunity that engages entrepreneurs and stimulates action and decision-making. Whether using existing methods, technologies and techniques in novel ways or in unfamiliar contexts, or through rethinking and repositioning new and emerging ideas in creative ways, these successful ESI-oriented businesses engage using resources within environments that support their ideas and make their objectives a realizable and sustainable outcome. Interestingly, the examples also highlight how commercial success can generate wider business interest resulting in the acquisition of successful social enterprises into larger business conglomerates.

In order to more fully illustrate our concept of ESI, it is useful to conceptualize a number of business scenarios and discuss how these might enable or constrain developments along this path. To briefly reiterate, our concept of eco-socio innovation is used to theorize the role of social innovations in sustainable entrepreneurship through building on the EVR framework and drawing attention to: the way ESI-driven innovations enacted by agencies of sustainable entrepreneurship can produce positive ecological outcomes that improve the well-being of people in society, whilst also elevating opportunities for further sustainable developments over the longer term. There are a range of challenging situations that entrepreneurial business organizations often find themselves facing during their potential journey from initial set-up, maturity and longer-term development, with many enterprises falling by the wayside during the early stages of change. As well as new and developing organizations, existing companies and venture capitalists may also turn their attention to ESI agendas in seeking to make a wider social contribution to society. There are an infinite number of possibilities, drivers and barriers – contextual situations – that firms may find themselves in over time. For example, an organization that is acknowledged to be either sustainable, behaving sustainably or operating with sustainability in mind, might have started out with this agenda or started behaving this way because the person behind the organization spotted a real opportunity to 'do good' and to bring benefits to various stakeholders. Alternatively, the key decision makers within an organization may have been driven by industry-wide regulations resulting from legislation or public opinion or both; in this latter case the organizational decision makers might not like the constraints but simply accept them. These trends and similarities in the movements of organizations is usefully highlighted by institutional theory (Lawrence and Suddaby 2012) that also draws attention to the high levels of differentiation and contextual

Table 3.1 Some examples of eco-socially innovative organizations and applicability and relevance of ESI and environment, resources and values to each example

Organization	Description	Relevance to this chapter
Divine Chocolate	A UK-based manufacturer and distributor, supported by a Dutch social investor and working closely with a farmers' co-operative in Ghana.	A Fairtrade organization (values) that comprises a network of related interests. These interested parties must (and do) work collaboratively towards a shared goal.
Green and Black's	Another UK-based and Fairtrade chocolate producer; acquired by Cadbury and now owned by Kraft. First UK product to feature the Fairtrade kite mark.	Originally established by US 'social entrepreneur' Craig Sams, who was committed to organic foods. Begun 'by chance' after he struck an agreement with Mayan Indian farmers in Belize to buy their cocoa. Sams was not naturally a businessman and G&B did not sustain EVR Congruency. Challenge now is (re)aligning E and R with Sams' original values given the corporate ownership, multiple stakeholders and potential conflicting interests.
Innocent Smoothies	Very successful business with a range of smoothies and related products. Started by three partners but later sold in tranches to Coca-Cola.	A profit-seeking business with three co-leaders who shared values and principles. Committed to donating 10 per cent of annual profits to environmental causes. Promote the products as healthy as well as a convenient way of consuming '5 a day'. Values (and donations) retained with new ownership because of strength of brand association.
The One Foundation	Originally 'One Water' but now a range of products – all marketed as revenue generators for specific third world causes.	Effectively a set of partner associations between products and causes. Clear purpose shared by all involved. Operates as a social enterprise because of surplus distribution. Successful because each product involved has some competitive strengths.
Sole Rebels	An Ethiopian business that makes shoes from recycled products (which are hard to dispose of) and provides employment to local people. Started by a young female entrepreneur, who remains at the helm. Shoes available worldwide mainly via electronic commerce.	Largely driven by a social need-local employment. But values driven business (recycling) that has succeeding in finding overseas markets. EVR congruent.
Freitag	Swiss-based manufacturer of hard-wearing but fashionable bags. Again a recycler.	Similar principles to Sole Rebels but effectively an environmental business with a profit goal. Driven by a need its two joint founders had – attractive bags that cyclists can use and that can withstand adverse weather. Each bag is unique in some way and therefore individual. This creates a particular customer-company relationship.

Source: developed by authors.

uniqueness that can occur in the factors that shape these processes of innovation and change.

In the case of ESI, the personal drive and motivation to do some form of social good can often over-ride commercial concerns and even financial losses may not deter enthusiasm for change but ultimately a pathway needs to be established for securing longer-term social aims that are environmentally sustainable. Although key decision makers in socially driven organizations may not put a heavy emphasis on financial performance, an enterprise that suffers continuous financial loss will need to address economic issues and consider their trajectory if they wish to secure sustainable entrepreneurship and social innovation. As there are clearly a number of situations in which we can locate ESI activities, for our purposes in this chapter we conceptualize a categorization of businesses along four broad dimensions:

- *Successful and sustainable ESI businesses*: These are often characterized as 'model performers' in the circumstances that they find themselves in. These circumstances, however, can vary significantly and hence considerable differences may be in evidence. For example, some organizations driven by purely social objectives may identify unique pathways to success; other organizations may take more of a commercial orientation assessing that 'there's money in sustainability' (in this case, the primary driver is not social objectives); whilst yet other organizations may seek to exploit changes in the regulatory environment and see these as presenting opportunities (for a range of reasons, for example, in bringing about much needed social change, for broadening market opportunities and so forth).
- *Financially sustainable ESI businesses*: This refers to a business that is strong on various measures and indices, generally driven by individually identified opportunities with good financial business acumen. Those behind the organization may be driven by a strong sense of social and community value but recognize the importance of economic factors and may advocate 'the need to do well to do good'.
- *Under-achieving ESI businesses*: Whether driven by opportunities in the market, social values or a combination of eco-socio elements, these are business that are not achieving their aims; that is, they are under-achieving either against sustainability or social value themes, financially or a combination of these. It might be that they simply need to change their priorities to improve; but there is a need for a more critically reflective evaluation in the generation of new ideas and their application to innovations that meet eco-socio objectives in a more sustainable manner. This category also includes organizations that champion sustainability causes and 'talk well' but achieve little in practice.
- *Unsuccessful and unsustainable ESI businesses*: Whatever the driving motivations and expertise of key stakeholders, without a change in behaviours to remedy this shortfall, these ESI businesses are likely to fail and disappear altogether.

These possible scenarios highlight some of the possible pathways and the enabling and constraining factors that are likely to shape the speed and direction of change for new and developing ESI businesses. In each of these scenarios, it is possible to argue that motive is less important than outcomes. The overall situation can be changed (improved) with two broad approaches. One route is to look for ways to persuade organizations to change their business models and factor in sustainability to a greater extent; this might well involve various forms of innovation. The other route is to strengthen regulation. But at the same time, pressures can force behaviours in an alternative direction. It is arguable that when circumstances are generally favourable – say, during an economic upswing or when an organization faces only modest competition – sustainability objectives can feature strongly alongside financial measures. But what happens when competition for business is more intense and there is real pressure to reduce costs? We might then ask: 'how sustainable is sustainability?' Of course, these are exactly the circumstances where sustainability-driven innovation might prove very beneficial as it can give a business a distinctive edge.

Conclusion: policy implications and future research agenda

In proposing the concept of eco-socio innovation, we have attempted to develop a more integrated understanding of sustainable entrepreneurship and social innovation. The novel contribution of this chapter is that we combine the concepts of sustainable entrepreneurship and social innovation into one overarching meta-concept that acknowledges, first, the interplay with EVR and, second, the cascade effect of sustainable entrepreneurs' innovative ecological impacts upon social outcomes. In so doing, the chapter illuminates how the key components of ESI comprise an enacted and collective process that addresses both social and ecological objectives. Our concept of eco-socio innovation extends Dawson and Daniel's (2010, 16) definition of social innovation through incorporating agency around sustainable entrepreneurial activities in the push for ecological solutions to social challenges that not only achieve social innovations but may also service other organizational, technical, commercial or scientific goals.

The growing public interest in sustainable entrepreneurship has drawn attention to the challenges of uncovering innovative solutions to policies and practices that are ultimately unsustainable. Motivations for change can be in response to regulatory drivers from new legislation requiring organizations to comply with a prescribed set of environmental criteria or through the values and actions of entrepreneurs or environmentalists. For entrepreneurs pushing for social innovations that are sustainable in the longer term, there is an economic need to ensure that funding is available for reinvestment and for sustaining opportunities for further expansion and development. The context of change in relation to the environment, the values and norms that influence decision-making (for example, changes in public opinion and the culture and values adhered to by organizations and communities of practice), as well as the resources available externally and internally within organizations, all shape the way key stakeholders and entrepreneurs may respond to their perception of the opportunities for embarking on a process of eco-socio innovation in the development of sustainable enterprise. As we state in the main body of the text: eco-socio innovation refers to the sustainable-entrepreneurially enacted process of collective idea generation, selection and implementation by people who participate collaboratively to meet ecological and social challenges. These ideas are owned by people who work (or, very often, venture) together in pursuing ecological and social goals. The sustainable ESI business is often able to accommodate both the social (exhibits a high premium of values towards doing social good) and economic (financial competency and awareness of commercial needs) dimensions to business in developing sustainable policies and practices for both operational and longer-term trajectories. However, there are also considerable tensions in pursuing such trajectories that are clearly in evidence in the contradictions and paradoxes among social, environmental and financial criteria and their evaluative place in the drive for sustainable entrepreneurship and social innovation. Although this field is currently marked by a lack of fully refined concepts and an absence of empirical studies, with the growing public and political attention given to these issues there is a need for further research, as well as greater business and governmental debate and critical discussion on this key area for sustainable business development.

Chief among some of the key implications for policy makers is the need for eco-socio innovation policies that promote these collective processes in steering business organizations towards ecological goals that achieve sustainability through entrepreneurial activities. As such, policy discussions should not simply centre on a conceptual division between social and commercial strategies that results in attempts to draw after-the-fact links across separate pieces of policy but rather, open up wider business engagement and governmental commitment to integrative eco-socio innovation. We argue that widening entrepreneurial interest and appeal is more likely to be achieved through the development of policies and advice that draw out the close inter-twining that needs to occur in securing sound financial performance linked to social innovations in the drive for environmental sustainability. The choice should not be couched in terms of one or the other as the ultimate aim is to achieve recognition that there is not just one binary type of sustainable/environmental/social entrepreneuring. This recognition can emerge from directives and publicity that generate greater business knowledge about how eco-socio innovation enables, through the four components of Dawson and Daniel's (2010) original framework of social innovation, the collective generation, selection and implementation of ideas within organizations that have optimality and congruence with their environment, values and resources. Organizations that can be encouraged by policy makers to take this route will be able to address ecological aspects and socially innovative outcomes whilst also being aware of financial considerations. From the outset, the conceptualized ESI process recognizes the processual interplay of ESI with the stakeholders involved, the shared challenge they face, the negotiation process they must embark upon in finding suitable resolutions, with the concomitant goal of improved well-being if a successful resolution is accomplished (Dawson and Daniel 2010).

We advocate that a good starting point would be policy developments that promote and support ESI business that is able to combine a strong value-based commitment to social innovation with good financial business acumen. Greater business awareness about these processes and practices should be publicised by government in conjunction with policies and industry-wide regulations that require business to direct attention to issues of sustainability. Whilst external contextual factors, such as governmental regulations and public opinion can enhance awareness and steer business towards more sustainable trajectories, internal commitment and recognition of the value of pursuing such initiatives is also essential. Once again this highlights the importance of clarifying the insep-arability of the social and economic in the development of sustainable ESI business.

In considering the implications for future research, there are two important areas that we recommend require further investigation. First, greater empirical engagement in longitudinal case studies that are able to collect data on the iter-ative processes during the dynamics of social innovation and social enterprise as they occur in practice and over time. The complex interactions in the building of collective knowledge and experience from a range of formal and informal processes, as well as the collective sensemaking that shapes understanding in the identification and translation of new ideas that are negotiated and either accepted or not, should all be carefully examined. Attention could also be given to decision-making processes and agency and change in the uptake and integra-tion of new innovative processes.

Second, that attention is given to a theoretical consideration of the concepts of sustainable entrepreneurship and social innovation. Whilst we advocate the value of the concept of eco-socio innovation there remains the need for further work on terms and concepts that are able to embrace the complexity and dynamics of processes that are continually constituted and reconstituted over time and shaped by the culture and context of routine and emerging practices that both constrain and enable agency in the negotiated and shared understand-ing of realisable trajectories that are truly sustainable. To offset the tendency for binary divides – whilst maintaining a commitment to theorization that is prac-tice relevant – requires a pragmatist ontology that is not bounded by an episte-mological perspective that limits boundary crossing. Philosophies that limit theorization and understanding through implicit structures of incommensur-ability close off rather than open space for creativity and innovation in breaking traditional divides that dominate knowledge expertise and acceptable ways of thinking. The unique, novel, routine and emergent are all enacted in a present that is constrained by a history of how it is and a future of how it should be and yet, what is remains open for continual reconsideration and reconstitution, especially if we are able to move beyond established pre-existing boundaries that constrain our thinking. The socially sustainable enterprise benefits from commercial acumen and good financial management, but it also needs a set of values and motivations that go beyond an orientation of profits for the few (a shareholder executive view) to distribution to the many (breaking down wealth inequalities: see Piketty 2014) and yet our use of concepts, especially when bounded to the social or economic, are often placed at two ends of a continuum that masks or detracts attention from the importance of moving beyond dualisms in an interlacing co-constituting dynamic in the pursuit of eco-socio innovation.

Note

1 Conversely, Schaper (2002c) argues that the entrepreneurship field rarely addresses sustainability.

References

Anderson A. R. (1998) "Cultivating the Garden of Eden: Environmental entrepreneuring" *Journal of Organizational Change Management*, 11(2) 135–144.

Bansal P. and Roth K. (2000) "Why companies go green: A model of ecological responsiveness" *Academy of Management Journal*, 43(4) 717–736.

Baregheh A. Rowley J. and Sambrook S. (2009) "Towards a multidisciplinary definition of innovation" *Management Decision*, 47(8) 1323–1339.

Benn S. Dunphy D. and Griffiths A. (2014) *Organizational Change for Corporate Sustainability* Routledge, London.

Berchicci L. (2009) *Innovation and Sustainability: Green Entrepreneurship in Personal Mobility* Routledge, Abingdon.

Birkin F. Polesie T. and Lewis L. (2009) "A new business model for sustainable development: An exploratory study using the theory of constraints in Nordic organizations" *Business Strategy and the Environment*, 18(5) 277–290.

Bornstein D. (2003) *How to Change the World: Social Entrepreneurs and the Power of New Ideas* Oxford University Press, Oxford.

Bradford J. and Fraser E. D. G. (2008) "Local authorities, climate change and small and medium enterprises: Identifying effective policy instruments to reduce energy use and carbon emissions" *Corporate Social Responsibility and Environmental Management*, 15(3) 324–336.

Cohen B. and Winn M. (2007) "Market imperfections, opportunity and sustainable entrepreneurship" *Journal of Business Venturing*, 22(1) 29–49.

Dawson P. and Daniel L. (2010) "Understanding social innovation: A provisional framework" *International Journal of Technology Management*, 51(1) 9–21.

Dawson P. Daniel L. and Farmer J. (2010) "Editorial: Social innovation" *International Journal of Technology Management*, 51(1) 1–8.

Dean T. J. and McMullen J. (2007) "Toward a theory of sustainable entrepreneurship: Reducing environmental degradation through environmental action" *Journal of Business Venturing*, 22(1) 50–76.

Dixon S. and Clifford A. (2007) "Ecopreneurship – a new approach to managing the triple bottom line" *Journal of Organizational Change Management*, 20(3) 326–345.

Drucker P. F. (1985a) *Innovation and Entrepreneurship: Practice and Principles* HarperCollins, New York.

Drucker P. F. (1985b) "The discipline of innovation" *Harvard Business Review*, 63(3) 67–72.

Eastwood D. Eaton M. Monds F. and Stark T. (2006) "Northern Ireland's green economy: An examination of environmentally based employment opportunities" *European Environment*, 5(5) 134–144.

Ellis T. (2010) *The New Pioneers: Sustainable Business Success through Social Innovation and Social Entrepreneurship* Wiley, London.

Furglsang L. and Sundbo J. eds (2002) *Innovation as Strategic Reflexivity* Routledge, London.

Goldsmith S. Georges G. and Glynn B. T. (2010) *The Power of Social Innovation: How Civic Entrepreneurs Ignite Community Networks for Good* Wiley, London.

Hall J. K. Daneke G. A. and Lenox M. J. (2010) "Sustainable development and entrepreneurship: Past contributions and future directions" *Journal of Business Venturing*, 25(5) 439–448.

Hendrickson L. U. and Tuttle D. (1997) "Dynamic management of the environmental enterprise: A qualitative analysis" *Journal of Organisational Change Management*, 10(4) 363–382.

Hitchens D. Clausen J. Trainor M. Keil M. and Thankappan S. (2006) "Competitiveness, environmental performance and management of SMEs" in Schaltegger S. and Wagner M. eds, *Managing the Business Case for Sustainability* Greenleaf, Sheffield 274–290.

Holt D. (2011) "Where are they now? Tracking the longitudinal evolution of environmental businesses from the 1990s" *Business Strategy & the Environment*, 20(4) 238–250.

Isaak R. (2005) "The making of the ecopreneur" in Schaper M. ed., *Making Ecopreneurs: Developing Sustainable Entrepreneurship* Ashgate, Aldershot 13–26.

Kearins K. and Collins E. (2012) "Making sense of ecopreneurs' decisions to sell up" *Business Strategy & the Environment*, 21(2) 71–85.

Kirkwood J. and Walton S. (2010a) "What motivates ecopreneurs to start businesses?" *International Journal of Entrepreneurial Behaviour and Research*, 16(3) 204–228.

Kirkwood J. and Walton S. (2010b) "How ecopreneurs' green values affect their international engagement in supply chain management" *Journal of International Entrepreneurship*, 8(2) 200–217.

Kotchen M. J. (2009) "Some microeconomics of eco-entrepreneurship" in Libecap G. C. ed., *Frontiers in Eco-Entrepreneurship Research*, Advances in the Study of Entrepreneurship, Innovation & Economic Growth, 20 ix–xx.

Lawrence T. B. and Suddaby R. (2012) "Institutions and institutional work" in Greenwood R. Oliver C. Sahlin K. and Suddaby R. eds, *Institutional Theory in Organization Studies Vol. V* Sage, London 61–123.

Leadbeater C. (2007) *Social Enterprise and Social Innovation: Strategies for the Next Ten Years* Cabinet Office, Office of the Third Sector, London.

Lewis G. J. (2004) "Uncertainty and equivocality in the commercial and natural environments: The implications for organizational design" *Corporate Social Responsibility and Environmental Management*, 11(3) 167–177.

Libecap G. C. (2009) "Introduction" in Libecap G. C. ed., *Frontiers in Eco-Entrepreneurship Research*, Advances in the Study of Entrepreneurship, Innovation & Economic Growth 20 ix–xx.

Linnanen L. (2005) "An insider's experience with environmental entrepreneurship" in Schaper M. ed., *Making Ecopreneurs: Developing Sustainable Entrepreneurship* Ashgate, Aldershot 72–88.

Pacheco D. Dean T. and Payne D. (2010) "Escaping the green prison: Entrepreneurship and the creation of opportunities for sustainable development" *Journal of Business Venturing*, 25(5) 464–480.

Petersen H. (2005) "The competitive strategies of ecopreneurs: Striving for market leadership by promoting sustainability" in Schaper M. ed., *Making Ecopreneurs: Developing Sustainable Entrepreneurship* Ashgate, Aldershot 174–190.

Petersen H. (2006) "Ecopreneurship and competitive strategies: striving for market leadership by promoting sustainability" in Schaltegger S. and Wagner M. eds, *Managing the Business Case for Sustainability: The Integration of Social, Environmental and Economic Performance* Greenleaf, Sheffield 398–411.

Petersen H. (2010) "The competitive strategies of ecopreneurs: striving for market leadership by promoting sustainability" in Schaper M. ed., *Making Ecopreneurs: Developing Sustainable Entrepreneurship* Ashgate, Aldershot 223–238.

Piketty T. (2014) *Capital in the Twenty-first Century* (A. Goldhammer, Trans.) Belknap Press, Cambridge, MA.

Retolaza J. L. Ruiz M. and San-Jose L. (2009) "CSR in business start-ups: An application method for stakeholder engagement" *Corporate Social Responsibility and Environmental Management*, 16(6) 324–336.

Saul J. (2011) *Social Innovation, Inc.: 5 Strategies for Driving Business Growth through Social Change* Wiley, London.

Schaper M. (2002a) "The essence of ecopreneurship" *Greener Management International*, 38(Summer) 26–30.

Schaper M. (2002b) "Small firms and environmental management: Predictors of green purchasing in Western Australian pharmacies" *International Small Business Journal*, 20(3) 235–251.

Schaper M. (2002c) "The challenge of environmental responsibility and sustainable development: Implications for SME and entrepreneurship academics" in Füglistaller U. Pleitner H. J. Volery T. and Weber W. eds, *Radical Changes in the World: Will SMEs Soar or Crash?* eRecontres de St Gallen, St Gallen, Switzerland 541–553.

Schaper M. (2005) "Understanding the green entrepreneur" in Schaper M. ed., *Making Ecopreneurs: Developing Sustainable Entrepreneurship* Ashgate, Aldershot 3–12.

Simpson M. Taylor N. and Barker K. (2004) "Environmental responsibility in SMEs: Does it deliver competitive advantage?" *Business Strategy and the Environment*, 13(3) 156–171.

Thompson J. L. (1999) "A strategic perspective of entrepreneurship" *International Journal of Entrepreneurial Behaviour and Research*, 5(6) 279–296.

Thompson J. L. and Scott J. M. (2010) "Environmental entrepreneurship: The sustainability challenge", Institute for Small Business and Entrepreneurship (ISBE) conference, London, November.

Thompson J. L. Scott J. M. and Martin F. (2014) *Strategic Management: Awareness and Change* Cengage, Andover.

Tidd J. and Bessant J. (2009) *Managing Innovation: Integrating Technological Market and Organisational Change* Wiley, Chichester.

Tushman M. L. and Anderson P. eds (2004) *Managing Strategic Innovation and Change: A Collection of Readings* Oxford University Press, Oxford.

Walley E. E. Taylor D. W. and Greig K. (2010) "Beyond the visionary champion: Testing a typology of green entrepreneurs" in Schaper M. ed., *Making Ecopreneurs: Developing Sustainable Entrepreneurship (2nd edition)* London, Gower 59–74.

Yunus M. (2007) *Creating a World Without Poverty: Social Business and the Future of Capitalism* Public Affairs, New York.

4 Embeddedness as a facilitator for sustainable entrepreneurship

Frédéric Dufays

Introduction

It is widely acknowledged that economic phenomena do not occur in a vacuum and are embedded in social relations (Granovetter 1985). Sustainable entrepreneurship, defined here as the pursuit of opportunities focusing on the preservation of nature, life support and community for the creation of economic and non-economic gains (Shepherd and Patzelt 2011), is no exception to this. Indeed, by its very nature and aim, sustainable entrepreneurship is likely to be strongly embedded as it intends to act sustainably with regard to its (social) environment.

This conceptual chapter makes the case for a strong embeddedness at all stages of sustainable entrepreneurship: opportunity identification and/or creation, opportunity evaluation and opportunity exploitation (Shane and Venkataraman 2000; Alvarez and Barney 2007). Using stakeholder theory (Mitchell *et al.* 1997; Parmar *et al.* 2010), this strong embeddedness is argued here to be an important incentive for sustainability, because it involves entering into long-term relationships with multiple stakeholders, which put pressure on the entrepreneur to respect the triple bottom line.

Overall, this chapter aims to shift from the '*What* is to be sustained/developed' (Shepherd and Patzelt 2011) to the '*How*' questions by addressing the following research problem: *How does embeddedness of entrepreneurship facilitate sustainability?* More precisely, drawing on extant literature, it develops a model showing (1) that sustainable entrepreneurship is strongly embedded, and (2) that this strong embeddedness contributes to its sustainable[1] character. Thereby, it contributes to theory by highlighting that the different stages of sustainable entrepreneurship take place in interrelated contexts, which in turn influence sustainability.

The remainder of the chapter is organized as follows. First, the literature on embeddedness and stakeholder theory is reviewed against the backdrop of sustainable entrepreneurship and related notions of environmental entrepreneurship – sometimes also called eco or green entrepreneurship (for a review of the use of these terms, see Levinsohn 2013) – and social entrepreneurship (Tilley and Young 2009; De Hoe and Janssen 2014). Next, a model is developed and propositions are articulated. Finally, the model and its implications, as well as the contributions of this chapter, are discussed.

Literature review

Embeddedness

Paving the way for a tradition in economic sociology, Granovetter (1985) has popularized the concept of embeddedness in his attempt to go beyond under- and over-socialized conceptions of human action. He argues that "actors do not behave or decide as atoms outside a social context, nor do they adhere slavishly to a script written for them by the particular intersection of social categories that they happen to occupy" (487). Instead, Granovetter describes how actors' (economic) actions are embedded in systems of social interactions, i.e. in social networks. Literature based on this premise of organizations' and entrepreneurship embeddedness is abundant (e.g. Dacin *et al.* 1999; Granovetter 2000; Jack and Anderson 2002). It shows that entrepreneurs and organizations operate in a specific social, political, cultural and economic context and that their actions have to be understood in relationship with their environment and other actors evolving in this environment (Dacin *et al.* 1999), including the norms and values carried by their social structure (Granovetter 2000).

Besides sources and mechanisms of embeddedness, the organizational outcomes of embeddedness are granted some attention in the literature (Dacin *et al.* 1999; Granovetter 2005). Embeddedness has been shown to play a role in, for instance, organizational survival (Baum and Oliver 1992), access to resources (Uzzi 1999) or innovation (Burt 2004). During the entrepreneurial process, embeddedness influences the opportunity recognition and evaluation phases (Jack and Anderson 2002), but also the entrepreneurial performance (Aarstad 2012) and the likelihood to succeed in setting up hybrid organizations (Almandoz 2012; Dufays and Huybrechts 2016). However, so far, no study to our knowledge has theoretically or empirically addressed the issue of sustainable development as an outcome of embeddedness.

In a literature review on sustainable entrepreneurship, Levinsohn (2013) points at the failure of existing studies to consider sustainable development as an embedded concept. He highlights the tendency of scholars to define sustainable development in universal terms, and hence to disregard the local development priorities of communities. Besides contextualizing the entrepreneurial process (Welter 2011), scholars therefore also need to consider the embeddedness of its objectives and outcomes. Other scholars have highlighted sustainable entrepreneurship's embeddedness in political, social, environmental, regulatory systems (Dixon and Clifford 2007; Gray *et al.* 2014), as well as in cultural norms (O'Neill *et al.* 2006).

With regard to the related notion of environmental entrepreneurship, Meek *et al.* (2010) show that entrepreneurial intentions are influenced by formal and informal institutions. In particular, they find that high levels of family interdependence norms increase the level of founding of environmental ventures, probably because such social norms push individuals to think of future generations' environment healthiness. Besides, social entrepreneurship has been shown to display high levels of embeddedness (Dufays and Huybrechts 2014). Hence, it must be understood in relationship with its (local) social environment (Mair and Martí 2006; Khavul and Bruton 2013). Social entrepreneurship has been shown to differ from conventional entrepreneurship in the embeddedness in the local networks of the community (Shaw and Carter 2007), among others to identify local social needs and to try to develop solutions to fulfil these needs (Haugh 2007).

Overall, as embeddedness shapes economic activities and behaviour, sustainable entrepreneurship should be studied with consideration to its broader environment and the social interactions it is engaged in. Although empirical studies do not abound in the field yet, it seems clear that social norms and values have a strong influence on sustainable entrepreneurship. These norms and values imposed on an organization have been argued to be associated with the network of stakeholders an organization is related to (Rowley 1997). The next section therefore turns to stakeholder theory.

Stakeholder theory

Stakeholder theory was first introduced by Freeman (1984), with the fundamental premise that organizations may be conceived of as a set of relationships among groups that have a stake in the organization's activities. Bearing this understanding in mind, stakeholder theory attempts to describe how stakeholders interact to create and trade value, address the problem of the ethics of capitalism, and think about the managerial mind-set to adopt with regard thereto (Parmar *et al.* 2010). Over time, stakeholder theory has been applied to different settings, giving rise to many substantial developments (for a review, see Parmar *et al.* 2010). Among those, the evaluation of the influence stakeholders have on the organization and its strategy appears useful to highlight in the framework of this chapter. Indeed, stakeholder management has been described as a two-way relationship between a focal organization and its stakeholders. Such an understanding frames stakeholder theory in a contractarian business ethics approach (Dunfee and Donaldson 1995). The influence of stakeholders is shown to be a function among others of the network structure in which the entrepreneur is embedded (Rowley 1997) and of behavioural motives (Hahn 2015).

The issue of sustainability has also been touched upon through stakeholder theory by many scholars (Parmar *et al.* 2010; Hörisch *et al.* 2014). Indeed, many similarities are found between the two approaches, among others in the way the purpose of the enterprise (Pedersen *et al.* 2013), as well as the link between business and ethics (Hörisch *et al.* 2014), are perceived. Besides, stakeholders have been found to have an influence on the sustainability practices of businesses, especially with regard to the issues an enterprise focuses on (Sharma and

Henriques 2005). However, stakeholder theory differs from sustainability management in the longer-term orientation of the latter and the willingness to
bridge social, environmental and economic objectives (Anderson *et al.* 2012).

With regard to sustainable entrepreneurship precisely, Schlange (2006) suggests that the objective of meeting the triple bottom line implies interacting
with more stakeholder groups, and hence conducts to higher complexity in the
entrepreneurial process. He adds that sustainable entrepreneurs are future-
oriented in the sense that "they are grounded on the principle of meeting the
needs of present stakeholders without compromising the ability to meet the
needs of future stakeholders" (22). This relationship is somewhat nuanced
through the principles of organization design. Indeed, sustainable entrepreneurs
have been shown to give preference to some stakeholders, which they evaluate
more rewarding, be it in monetary or non-monetary terms (Parrish 2010).

The literature using stakeholder theory in studying environmental entrepreneurship has mainly dealt with the question of whether the environment or the
planet ought to be considered as a stakeholder. Some authors argue that managers should take into account the organizational impact on the environment
for moral and ethical reasons but should not consider it as a stakeholder because
of its non-human character (Phillips and Reichart 2000). Others consider the
natural environment as a primary and primordial stakeholder because of its
proximity to the firm (Starik 1995; Driscoll and Starik 2004). Stakeholder
theory has also largely been applied in the social enterprise literature (e.g.
Campi *et al.* 2006; Huybrechts *et al.* 2014). The most important observations
with regard to social entrepreneurship lie in the facts a) that there is probably a
larger diversity of stakeholders to the social entrepreneurial process as compared
to a conventional entrepreneurial process (Austin *et al.* 2006); and b) that these
stakeholders are often included in the entrepreneurial process and sometimes
take an active role in the governance of the nascent organization (Huybrechts
et al. 2014).

Bearing in mind this strong embeddedness of sustainable entrepreneurship in
a network of stakeholders and the reciprocal relationships it maintains with
each of these stakeholders, the following section develops a conceptual model
to describe embeddedness as a facilitator of sustainability.

Model development

The embeddedness of the sustainable entrepreneurship process

Sustainable entrepreneurship is often described in terms of value creation with
regard to a triple bottom line, i.e. profit, people and planet (e.g. Dixon and Clifford 2007). Therefore, sustainable entrepreneurship is embedded in an economic context, a social context and an environmental context, as depicted in
the upper left part of Figure 4.1. It has been argued that sustainable entrepreneurship builds on the relationship with the great variety of stakeholders which
embody the different bottom lines (Parrish 2010). The present subsection

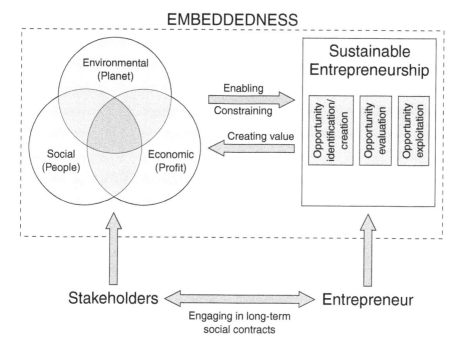

Figure 4.1 Model of embedded sustainable entrepreneurship.

reviews the different phases of the entrepreneurial process with regard to sustainable entrepreneurship's embeddedness in networks of stakeholders.

a Opportunity discovery and/or creation

Traditionally, the opportunity discovery and/or creation phase of sustainable entrepreneurship has been described in terms of failures – governmental, market and non-profit – (Cohen and Winn 2007; Dean and McMullen 2007) or of positive externalities (e.g. Santos 2012). At the micro-level, Patzelt and Shepherd (2011) demonstrate that sustainable entrepreneurs need to be knowledgeable about market disequilibrium as well as changes in the natural environment and community in which they live to discover opportunities. Thereby, they show that sustainable entrepreneurship opportunity discovery is highly embedded.

York and Venkataraman (2010) identify four incentives to address environmental degradation through entrepreneurial action: governmental regulations, activism from stakeholders, ethical motivation and competitive advantage. They argue that the two former motivations, which derive from entrepreneurs' embeddedness, are usually tied to opportunities for environmental action that have a higher impact. In an original analysis using game theory, Pacheco *et al.*

(2010) show that sustainable entrepreneurs can create opportunities by overcoming suboptimal market incentives. To escape what they term the 'green prison' – this is, the trade-off between collective incentives for environmental cooperation and individual short-term costs of cooperation – sustainable entrepreneurs need to engage in collective action to change or create institutions (Battilana *et al.* 2009). They can do so, among others, by partnering with stakeholders, be it competitors, other actors in the supply chain or with the broader community (Pacheco *et al.* 2010).

b Opportunity evaluation

During the opportunity evaluation phase, sustainable entrepreneurs analyse whether they are likely to create enough value to be economically viable in the long run, but also if they create social and environmental value to meet the triple bottom line. As mentioned above, the definition of sustainability they compare the opportunity against, is embedded (Levinsohn 2013). In other words, what an entrepreneur might consider as sustainable in a particular situation, in a given space-time context, is likely to be different in another context, due among others to the variation in needs and in cultural understandings.

In a resource-based view, this phase can be understood as "envisioning the future – specifically the wealth generating resource combinations to be controlled by the entrepreneur post-exploitation" (Haynie *et al.* 2009, 338). This type of cognitive process is strongly embedded in the entrepreneurial context. In other words, the resources that are deemed to be accessible to an entrepreneur, among others through their network of relationships, have a significant role in the opportunity evaluation process (Haynie *et al.* 2009; Shepherd *et al.* 2013). This is presumably especially the case for sustainable entrepreneurship, which is often characterized by a resource scarcity. Hence, opportunity evaluation is likely to include an assessment of the alignment to stakeholders' claims.

Besides, entrepreneurs also evaluate the adequacy of the opportunity they want to exploit with their own identity and the values they carry (Shepherd *et al.* 2013). Indeed, individuals having an identity that value sustainable development goals are argued to be likely to evaluate the opportunities with regard to what being an entrepreneur means to them – this is, creating value beyond economic wealth. The desirability of the creation of non-economic value is likely to be reinforced by the entrepreneurs' social network (Wry and York 2012).

c Opportunity exploitation

While empirical studies on sustainable entrepreneurship remain scarce, extant literature on related concepts such as social entrepreneurship (e.g. Campi *et al.* 2006), community entrepreneurship (e.g. Haugh 2007) and eco-entrepreneurship (e.g. Larsson 2012) demonstrates the embeddedness of the entrepreneur with regard to multiple stakeholders in exploiting opportunity. Often operating in scarce-resource environments, the success of these types of entrepreneurship depends even more on the ability to mobilize key stakeholders by responding to their claims and gaining legitimacy to their eyes (Schlange 2006).

Indeed, in a single case study, Gray *et al.* (2014) show the necessity of creating networks of local and global stakeholders to secure resources to exploit an opportunity as characteristic to sustainable entrepreneurship. This is achieved in a strategic way, with an instrumental aim, as sustainable entrepreneurs devote more attention to those stakeholders they perceive as more worthy for their organization (Parrish 2010). De Clercq and Voronov (2011) underline that the legitimacy that sustainable entrepreneurs acquire from adhering to profitability and sustainability logics results from the interaction between field-level expectations regarding the relative importance of each logic – probably influenced by dominant actors in the field – and individual agency. They further argue that the legitimacy sustainable entrepreneurs derive from this balance will reflect "their embeddedness in a web of expectations" (334).

It results from this discussion that the structure is both enabling and constraining (Giddens 1984) because, for instance, opportunities for sustainable entrepreneurship arise from the relationship with stakeholders but are limited by the access to resources and legitimacy provided by these stakeholders. Hence, it is suggested:

> Proposition 1a: Sustainable entrepreneurship is embedded in a network of stakeholders representing the broader economic, social and environmental context.

> Proposition 1b: Sustainable entrepreneurship embeddedness both enables and constrains opportunity creation and/or identification, evaluation and exploitation.

As the embeddedness argument navigates between over-and under-socialized views by acknowledging the mutual influence of the structure and the agent, the following subsection examines this interaction for sustainable entrepreneurship.

Embeddedness as a facilitator of sustainability

The embeddedness of entrepreneurship implies that entrepreneurs and their context, in particular their network of stakeholders, influence each other. This influence can be observed among others in terms of behaviour, of norms and values, and of opportunities (Jack and Anderson 2002). Hence, transactions exist between entrepreneurs and their environment. Such transactions can be viewed as going beyond the legal view of reciprocal rights and duties between parties by encompassing norms and values in considering a much broader relationship (Key 1999). These so-called social contracts presume "an implicit contract between the members of society and businesses in which the members of society grant businesses the right to exist in return for certain specified benefits" (Hasnas 1998, 29). These contracts can be viewed as operating both at a macro-level, i.e. that organization has a social contract with society, and at a micro-level (Wempe 2004), which this chapter focuses on.

For sustainable entrepreneurs, an aspect of these transactions lies in their attempt to create value – both monetary and non-monetary – for stakeholders (Anderson 1998; Shepherd and Patzelt 2011). The process of value creation without value capture is indeed considered by some scholars as the essence of how sustainable entrepreneurs have a positive impact on their environment (Santos 2012). In exchange for this value, stakeholders provide legitimacy to operate and resources (Hahn 2015). Prior to this value creation, sustainable entrepreneurs also need to exchange information with the whole set of stakeholders in order to perceive what creates value for them and what is likely to cause them harm. Because this engagement of stakeholders is voluntary (Bridoux and Stoelhorst 2014), entrepreneurs have to persuade their stakeholders to enter the transaction. This may be achieved by setting a social contract between them. This contract entails an exchange of (future) value creation by the entrepreneur against some kind of feedback by stakeholders about their claims, norms and values (Donaldson and Dunfee 1994; Dunfee and Donaldson 1995).

A specificity of sustainable entrepreneurship lies in its time focus. This is because sustainable entrepreneurship targets sustainability and durability in the broad sense – for the organization and for society at large (Schlange 2006) – it is concerned with both present and future (Thompson *et al.* 2011). As a consequence, sustainable entrepreneurs tend to engage in enduring relationships with their networks of stakeholders to meet both their current and future claims, as well as taking into account the claims of future stakeholders (Hörisch *et al.* 2014). Hence, it can be argued that the social contracts in which they engage are long-term, as depicted in the lower part of Figure 4.1.

Through the multitude of these long-term social contracts in which they engage with their network of present and future stakeholders, sustainable entrepreneurs acquire knowledge about what is expected by stakeholders towards sustainability, resources in order to act accordingly, as well as legitimacy to operate:

Proposition 2: In order to meet their commitment for sustainability, sustainable entrepreneurs engage in long-term social contracts with both current and future stakeholders to acquire:

- *a) information about what they ought to do to act sustainably;*
- *b) resources that are necessary to act sustainably; and*
- *c) the legitimacy that is necessary to conduct the entrepreneurial process.*

It may however happen that stakeholders' claims are conflicting, and eventually inhibit sustainability in favour of profitability (De Clercq and Voronov 2011). Indeed, sustainable entrepreneurs are embedded in a capitalist setting, which tends to be characterized by networks of actors that focus on short-term economic profitability as the sole criterion of performance. The latter actors often disregard social and environmental long-term consequences of their demands and, because of their long-standing presence in the market, tend to display strong inertia forces, which sustainable entrepreneurs have to counter in their aim to change perceptions of how problems can be solved (Dacin *et al.* 2010). This is especially applicable to the insurgent sustainable entrepreneurs identified by Muñoz and Dimov (2015), which emerge in the case of a lack of support from the social context. Insurgents are characterized as 'change agents', in contrast to the conformists that are 'sustainability conveyors'. Insurgents often make breakthroughs by disregarding strategic return. Instead, they pay attention to the long-run socio-economic changes they can induce through entrepreneurial action. This highlights the importance of the entrepreneur's commitment to sustainability and the need to adapt their strategy depending on their network of stakeholders to achieve their aim.

The question of how sustainable entrepreneurs react to these conflicting demands may also be explored through the framework of institutional theory. When individuals are facing conflicting logics in their network of stakeholders, they may opt for one or several of the following strategies: ignorance, compliance, defiance, compartmentalization and combination. More precisely, ignorance indicates no reaction of the individual to the prescription of one logic; compliance refers to a full adhesion to one logic's prescribed norms, values and practices; and defiance means in contrast the rejection of these norms, values and practices. Through compartmentalization, the individual aims at segmenting across time and/or space compliance and ignorance/defiance strategies with competing logics to find consistency in the prescribed values, norms and practices. Finally, a combination – or hybridization – strategy indicates the individual's attempt at bringing together some of the norms, values and practices of the competing logics (Pache and Santos 2013).

According to Rowley (1997), higher density of the network of stakeholders will impose more constraints on the focal organization. The high embeddedness of sustainable entrepreneurship makes a broad and dense network of current stakeholders very probable. Hence, sustainable entrepreneurs are likely to adopt a compromising strategy – which may be associated to the combining strategy identified above – in order to manage the conflictual demands and meet the claims of their stakeholders. However, the fact that future stakeholders are also taken into account by sustainable entrepreneurs may provide them with some room for agency with regards to claims on what is sustainable. Indeed, they have the opportunity to rest on their own perceptions of who are their future stakeholders and their socio-ecological needs to define their present action on sustainability (Parrish 2007).

Based on these observations, it is suggested that the entrepreneur's response will depend on the temporal dimension surrounding the demands that are conflicting, in particular because of the social contract set with future stakeholders:

*Proposition 3a: Given their commitment to sustainability, sustainable entre-
preneurs are likely to adopt hybridization strategies when faced with conflicting
social, economic and environmental long-term demands.*

*Proposition 3b: Given their commitment to sustainability, sustainable entre-
preneurs are likely to adopt ignorance and/or defiance strategies when faced with
conflicting social, economic and environmental short-term demands.*

Discussion

This chapter makes a few contributions to the literature and, despite some limitations, has several theoretical as well as practical implications. First, this
chapter makes clear that sustainable entrepreneurship is strongly embedded in a
network of stakeholders, as well as in a broader social, economic and environmental context. The designed model especially highlights that the different
stages of the sustainable entrepreneurship process – opportunity identification,
opportunity evaluation and opportunity evaluation – take place in these interrelated contexts. Thereby, it contributes to setting the grounds of the nascent
field of sustainable entrepreneurship by emphasizing the need to look at the
process both holistically (in contexts) and dynamically (in interactions).

Further, by integrating stakeholder theory and the embeddedness argument, the
developed model contributes answering the call to shift research from the *What* to
the *How* questions on sustainable entrepreneurship (Shepherd and Patzelt 2011),
as well as calls for research on the outcomes of embeddedness and on reciprocal
embeddedness (Dacin *et al.* 1999; Jack and Anderson 2002). Indeed, this chapter
goes beyond the mere recognition of the high level of embeddedness as a feature of
sustainable entrepreneurship (Dufays and Huybrechts 2014) by highlighting the
role of embeddedness and of the long-term social contracts the entrepreneur is
engaged in with stakeholders in order to achieve sustainable development objectives. Embeddedness, translated into multiple social contracts with a range of stakeholders, may therefore be considered as a facilitator of sustainability.

Third, it contributes to the sustainable entrepreneurship literature by
exploring alternative theoretical lenses. As Dacin *et al.* (2010) noted for social
entrepreneurship research, existing theoretical frameworks should first be
applied to such new phenomena, in order to uncover the need for new theory.
Here, it is suggested that a contractarian approach to stakeholder management,
which is an inherent activity of (sustainable) entrepreneurship, helps to understand how the sustainable character of entrepreneurship is formed.

Consequently, as a first theoretical implication, it confirms the importance of
studying sustainable entrepreneurship in a contextualized way (Welter 2011). It

also implies that sustainable entrepreneurship needs to be understood through the relationships the entrepreneur maintains with other actors, including future ones. In other words, it calls for a holistic and interactional, hence dynamic, understanding of the sustainable entrepreneurship process.

The model and the alongside propositions also stress that sustainable entrepreneurship entails shared commitment in the long-run by the establishment of social contracts between the entrepreneur and stakeholders. Theoretically, it implies that sustainable entrepreneurship is relying on mutual expectations towards what is perceived as sustainable, both by the entrepreneur and a large range of stakeholders. The importance of actors' perceptions is further reinforced by the elaboration of social contracts by the entrepreneur with non-existing counterparts, i.e. future stakeholders. Indeed, what is good for future generations can only be based on perceptions of current actors (both the entrepreneur and stakeholders) and is shaped by the information available nowadays as well as by these actors' norms and values.

A last theoretical implication of the model lies in the multiplicity of long-term social contracts that are set up. This plurality is likely to be a source of conflict as perceptions of what is sustainable and stakeholders' interests do not necessarily align. The potential for conflict is strengthened by the fact that the social contracts between entrepreneurs and stakeholders are tacitly negotiated and accepted. Hence, sustainable entrepreneurship can also be understood as lying in a nexus of social contracts, which need to be managed and maintained by the entrepreneur in such a way that it allows a long-term perspective for stakeholders.

That being said, such a deductive and theoretically derived model has some inherent limitations. First, it simplifies the relationships between structure and agents, as well as interactions between agents, and therefore fails to reflect the many shades that can be empirically observed. Second, due to the lack of empirical studies on sustainable entrepreneurship, this chapter builds mainly on the related concepts of social entrepreneurship and environmental entrepreneurship by assuming that similar mechanisms are at work (De Hoe and Janssen 2014). Another limitation resides in the inertia that characterizes institutions and actors that is barely taken into account in the model, although such forces potentially give entrepreneurship's embeddedness an inhibiting character with regard to sustainability. Hence, stakeholders' expectations may be driving the sustainable entrepreneur away from their objective of sustainability, especially if their demands are oriented on short-term expectations.

Consequently, this model and the alongside propositions pave the way for future research on the factors favouring sustainability in entrepreneurship. Among others, it calls for longitudinal studies assessing empirically to what extent the sustainable character of sustainable entrepreneurship may be attributed to embeddedness, in contrast to individual values and motivations of the entrepreneur. Indeed, the latter are left out of the analysis in this chapter for the sake of model simplification, even though they have been shown to play a significant role in the sustainable character of the entrepreneurial process (Kuckertz and Wagner 2010; Wry and York 2012). Further, the reciprocal influence of sustainable entrepreneurs and their stakeholders should be investigated more in-depth to understand the content of the long-term moral contract established between them. Finally, the relationship between the salience of some types of stakeholders and their contribution to sustainability objectives appears interesting to investigate further, using for instance social network analysis tools.

Practical implications may also be derived for policy-makers and for sustainable entrepreneurs by making the point that sustainable entrepreneurs differ from their conventional counterparts in the fact that they have to take their stakeholders and their broader environment into account by entering into long-term social contracts. First, in the context of environmental crises such as global warming, policy-makers tend to encourage all initiatives aiming at contributing to sustainable development, among which is sustainable entrepreneurship. In order to favour such entrepreneurial action, policy-makers should strive for helping entrepreneurs to establish long-term relationships with other actors in society. This is achieved, among others, in setting transparent expectations towards entrepreneurs and a clear sustainable development policy. Finally, this chapter suggests that having an idea that contributes to sustainable development is not sufficient for entrepreneuring sustainably. Sustainable entrepreneurs should pay attention to their broader environment and to their social relationships if they want to meet the triple bottom line in an enduring way, even though this may result in redefining their project in function of the balance between the three objectives. Integrating the perspective of multiple social contracts with their network of both current and future stakeholders may help the entrepreneur to ensure sustaining the flow of resources, including legitimacy, and to contribute to the sustainable development of society.

Conclusion

Overall, this chapter addresses the issue of how sustainability is imbued throughout the sustainable entrepreneurship process by highlighting the importance of embeddedness. It offers a conceptual model illuminating the interactions that take place between social entrepreneurs and a large range of stakeholders, including future – i.e. not existing yet – stakeholders, during the different stages of sustainable entrepreneurship process. It suggests looking at embeddedness in terms of multiple long-term social contracts with this large range of stakeholders, which drive the entrepreneur towards sustainability by answering today's needs without hampering fulfilment of future generations' needs.

Acknowledgement

This research was carried out within the framework of an Interuniversity Attraction Pole funded by the Belgian Science Policy Office under the title 'If Not for Profit, for What and How?'.

Note

1 In this chapter, 'sustainable' and 'sustainability' are understood in the sense of the sustainable development concept (Hall *et al.* 2010) rather than in the sense of sustaining a venture over time, unless otherwise specified.

References

Aarstad J. 2012 "Do structural holes and network connectivity really affect entrepreneurial performance?" *The Journal of Entrepreneurship, 21* 253–268.

Almandoz J. 2012 "Arriving at the starting line: The impact of community and financial logics on new banking ventures" *Academy of Management Journal, 55* 1381–1406.

Alvarez S. A. and Barney J. B. 2007 "Discovery and creation: Alternative theories of entrepreneurial action" *Strategic Entrepreneurship Journal, 1* 11–26.

Anderson A. R. 1998 "Cultivating the Garden of Eden: Environmental entrepreneuring" *Journal of Organizational Change Management, 11* 135–144.

Anderson M. W., Teisl M. and Noblet C. 2012 "Giving voice to the future in sustainability: Retrospective assessment to learn prospective stakeholder engagement" *Ecological Economics, 84* 1–6.

Austin J., Stevenson H. and Wei-Skillern J. 2006 "Social and commercial entrepreneurship: Same, different, or both?" *Entrepreneurship Theory and Practice 30* 1–22.

Battilana J., Leca B. and Boxenbaum E. 2009. "How actors change institutions: Towards a theory of institutional entrepreneurship" *Academy of Management Annals, 3* 65–107.

Baum J. A. C. and Oliver C. 1992 "Institutional embeddedness and the dynamics of organizational populations" *American Sociological Review, 57* 540–559.

Bridoux F. and Stoelhorst J. W. 2014 "Microfoundations for stakeholder theory: Managing stakeholders with heterogeneous motives" *Strategic Management Journal, 35* 107–125.

Burt R. S. 2004 "Structural holes and good ideas" *American Journal of Sociology, 110* 349–399.

Campi S., Defourny J. and Grégoire O. 2006 "Work integration social enterprises: Are they multiple-goal and multi-stakeholder organizations?" in Nyssens M. ed., *Social enterprise: At the crossroads of market, public policies and civil society* Routledge, London 29–49.

Cohen B. and Winn M. I. 2007 "Market imperfections, opportunity and sustainable entrepreneurship" *Journal of Business Venturing, 22* 29–49.

Dacin M. T., Beal B. D. and Ventresca M. J. 1999 "The embeddedness of organizations: Dialogue & directions" *Journal of Management, 25,* 317–356.

Dacin P. A., Dacin M. T. and Matear M. 2010 "Social entrepreneurship: Why we don't need a new theory and how we move forward from here" *Academy of Management Perspectives, 24,* 37–57.

De Clercq D. and Voronov M. 2011 "Sustainability in entrepreneurship: A tale of two logics" *International Small Business Journal, 29,* 322–344.

De Hoe R. and Janssen F. 2014 "L'entrepreneuriat social et l'entrepreneuriat durable sont-ils liés" [Are social entrepreneurship and sustainable entrepreneurship linked?] in Guillouzo R. ed., *Entreprenariat, développement durable et territoires: Approches contextualisées* Hachette, Paris 61–86.

Dean T. J. and McMullen J. S. 2007 "Toward a theory of sustainable entrepreneurship: Reducing environmental degradation through entrepreneurial action" *Journal of Business Venturing, 22,* 50–76.

Dixon S. E. A. and Clifford A. 2007 "Ecopreneurship – a new approach to managing the triple bottom line" *Journal of Organizational Change Management, 20* 326–345.

Donaldson T. and Dunfee T. W. 1994 "Toward a unified conception of business ethics: integrative social contracts theory" *Academy of Management Review, 19* 252–284.

Driscoll C. and Starik M. 2004 "The primordial stakeholder: Advancing the conceptual consideration of stakeholder status for the natural environment" *Journal of Business Ethics, 49* 55–73.

Dufays F. and Huybrechts B. 2014 "Connecting the dots for social value: A review on social networks and social entrepreneurship" *Journal of Social Entrepreneurship, 5,* 214–237.

Dufays F. and Huybrechts B. 2016 "Where do hybrids come from? Entrepreneurial team heterogeneity as an avenue for the emergence of hybrid organizations" *International Small Business Journal, 34,* 777–796.

Dunfee T. W. and Donaldson T. 1995 "Contractarian business ethics: Current status and next steps" *Business Ethics Quarterly, 5* 173–186.

Freeman R. E. 1984 *Strategic management: A stakeholder approach* Pitman Books Limited, London.

Giddens A. 1984 *The constitution of society: Outline of the theory of structuration* Polity Press, Oxford.

Granovetter M. 1985 "Economic action and social structure: The problem of embeddedness" *American Journal of Sociology, 91* 481–510.

Granovetter M. 2000 "The economic sociology of firms and entrepreneurs" in Swedberg R. ed., *Entrepreneurship: A social science view* Oxford University Press, Oxford, New York 244–275.

Granovetter M. 2005 "The impact of social structure on economic outcomes" *Journal of Economic Perspectives, 19,* 35–50.

Gray B. J., Duncan S., Kirkwood J. and Walton S. 2014 "Encouraging sustainable entrepreneurship in climate-threatened communities: A Samoan case study" *Entrepreneurship & Regional Development, 26,* 401–430.

Hahn T. 2015 "Reciprocal stakeholder behavior: A motive-based approach to the implementation of normative stakeholder demands" *Business & Society, 54,* 9–51.

Hall J. K., Daneke G. A. and Lenox, M. J. 2010 "Sustainable development and entrepreneurship: Past contributions and future directions" *Journal of Business Venturing, 25* 439–448.

Hasnas J. 1998 "The normative theories of business ethics: A guide for the perplexed" *Business Ethics Quarterly, 8* 19–42.

Haugh H. 2007 "Community-led social venture creation" *Entrepreneurship Theory and Practice, 31* 161–182.

Haynie J. M., Shepherd D. A. and McMullen J. S. 2009 "An opportunity for me? The role of resources in opportunity evaluation decisions" *Journal of Management Studies, 46* 337–361.

Hörisch J., Freeman R. E. and Schaltegger S. 2014 "Applying stakeholder theory in sustainability management: Links, similarities, dissimilarities, and a conceptual framework" *Organization & Environment, 27* 328–346.

Huybrechts B., Mertens S. and Rijpens J. 2014 "Explaining stakeholder involvement in social enterprise governance through resources and legitimacy" in Defourny J., Hulgård L. and Pestoff V. eds, *Social enterprise and the Third Sector: Changing European landscapes in a comparative perspective* Routledge, New York 157–176.

Jack S. L. and Anderson A. R. 2002 "The effects of embeddedness on the entrepreneurial process" *Journal of Business Venturing, 17* 467–487.

Key S. 1999 "Toward a new theory of the firm: A critique of stakeholder 'theory'" *Management Decision*, 37, 317–328.

Khavul S. and Bruton G. D. 2013 "Harnessing innovation for change: sustainability and poverty in developing countries" *Journal of Management Studies*, 50 285–306.

Kuckertz A. and Wagner M. 2010 "The influence of sustainability orientation on entrepreneurial intentions – Investigating the role of business experience" *Journal of Business Venturing*, 25, 524–539.

Larsson M. 2012 "Environmental entrepreneurship in organic agriculture in Järna, Sweden" *Journal of Sustainable Agriculture*, 36 153–179.

Levinsohn D. 2013 "Disembedded and beheaded? A critical review of the emerging field of sustainability entrepreneurship" *International Journal of Entrepreneurship and Small Business*, 19 190–211.

Mair J. and Martí I. 2006 "Social entrepreneurship research: A source of explanation, prediction, and delight" *Journal of World Business*, 41 36–44.

Meek W. R., Pacheco D. F. and York J. G. 2010 "The impact of social norms on entrepreneurial action: Evidence from the environmental entrepreneurship context" *Journal of Business Venturing*, 25 493–509.

Mitchell R. K., Agle B. R. and Wood D. J. 1997 "Toward a theory of stakeholder identification and salience: Defining the principle of who and what really counts" *Academy of Management Review*, 22 853–886.

Muñoz P. and Dimov D. 2015 "The call of the whole in understanding the development of sustainable ventures" *Journal of Business Venturing*, 30 632–654.

O'Neill G. D., Hershauer J. C. and Golden J. S. 2006 "The cultural context of sustainability entrepreneurship" *Greener Management International*, 55 33–46.

Pache A.-C. and Santos F. 2013 "Embedded in hybrid contexts: How individuals in organizations respond to competing institutional logics" in Lounsbury M. and Boxenbaum E. eds, *Institutional logics in action, Part B* Emerald Group Publishing Limited, Bingley 3–35.

Pacheco D. F., Dean T. J. and Payne D. S. 2010 "Escaping the green prison: Entrepreneurship and the creation of opportunities for sustainable development" *Journal of Business Venturing*, 25 464–480.

Parmar B. L., Freeman R. E., Harrison J. S., Wicks A. C., Purnell L. and de Colle S. 2010 "Stakeholder theory: The state of the art" *Academy of Management Annals*, 4, 403–445.

Parrish B. D. 2007 "Designing the sustainable enterprise" *Futures*, 39, 846–860.

Parrish B. D. 2010 "Sustainability-driven entrepreneurship: Principles of organization design" *Journal of Business Venturing*, 25 510–523.

Patzelt H. and Shepherd D. A. 2011 "Recognizing opportunities for sustainable development" *Entrepreneurship Theory and Practice*, 35 631–652.

Pedersen E. R. G., Henriksen M. H., Frier C., Søby J. and Jennings V. 2013 "Stakeholder thinking in sustainability management: the case of Novozymes" *Social Responsibility Journal*, 9 500–515.

Phillips R. A. and Reichart J. 2000 "The environment as a stakeholder? A fairness-based approach" *Journal of Business Ethics*, 23 185–197.

Rowley T. J. 1997 "Moving beyond dyadic ties: A network theory of stakeholder influences" *Academy of Management Review*, 22 887–910.

Santos F. M. 2012 "A positive theory of social entrepreneurship" *Journal of Business Ethics*, 111, 335–351.

Schlange L. E. 2006 "Stakeholder identification in sustainability entrepreneurship" *Greener Management International*, 55 13–32.

Shane S. A. and Venkataraman S. 2000 "The promise of entrepreneurship as a field of research" *Academy of Management Review*, 25 217–228.

Sharma S. and Henriques I. 2005 "Stakeholder influences on sustainability practices in the Canadian forest products industry" *Strategic Management Journal*, 26 159–180.

Shaw E. and Carter S. 2007 "Social entrepreneurship: Theoretical antecedents and empirical analysis of entrepreneurial processes and outcomes" *Journal of Small Business and Enterprise Development*, 14 418–434.

Shepherd D., Patzelt H. and Baron R. 2013 "'I care about nature, but…': Disengaging values in assessing opportunities that cause harm" *Academy of Management Journal*, 56 1251–1273.

Shepherd D. A. and Patzelt H. 2011 "The new field of sustainable entrepreneurship: Studying entrepreneurial action linking 'What is to be sustained' with 'What is to be developed'" *Entrepreneurship Theory and Practice*, 35 137–163.

Starik M. 1995 "Should trees have managerial standing? Toward stakeholder status for non-human nature" *Journal of Business Ethics*, 14 207–217.

Thompson N., Kiefer K. and York J. G. 2011 "Distinctions not dichotomies: Exploring social, sustainable, and environmental entrepreneurship" in Lumpkin G. T. and Katz J. A. eds, *Social and Sustainable Entrepreneurship*. Emerald Group Publishing Limited, Bingley 201–229.

Tilley F. and Young W. 2009 "Sustainability entrepreneurs: Could they be the true wealth generators of the future?" *Greener Management International*, 55 79–92.

Uzzi B. 1999 "Embeddedness in the making of financial capital: How social relations and networks benefit firms seeking financing" *American Sociological Review*, 64 481–505.

Welter F. 2011 "Contextualizing entrepreneurship – Conceptual challenges and ways forward" *Entrepreneurship Theory and Practice*, 35 165–184.

Wempe B. 2004 "On the use of the social contract model in business ethics" *Business Ethics: A European Review*, 13 332–341.

Wry T. and York J. G. 2012 "For love and money: The role of the self in new venture creation" *SSRN Working papers series*. Retrieved on 11 August 2014, from http://ssrn.com/abstract=2173308.

York J. G. and Venkataraman S. 2010 "The entrepreneur–environment nexus: Uncertainty, innovation, and allocation" *Journal of Business Venturing*, 25, 449–463.

5 Sustainable at home – sustainable at work?

The impact of pro-environmental life-work spillover effects on sustainable intra- or entrepreneurship

Franziska Dittmer and Susanne Blazejewski

Introduction

The perspective of environmental psychology is particularly valuable for understanding why individuals create new organizations that pursue sustainability targets (*sustainable entrepreneurship*) (Shepherd & Patzelt, 2011) or renew existing organizations and business models (*sustainable intrapreneurship*). In this chapter, we explore how individuals negotiate and align their private sustainability concerns with their working roles and if this leads to sustainable intra- or entrepreneurship, or to other types of pro-environmental behavior (PEB) at work. In this respect, we focus on spillovers of PEB between private and public spheres to the working sphere as a source for sustainable intra- and entrepreneurship.

Spillovers occur when one PEB has a positive or negative effect on a person's subsequent PEBs (Thøgersen, 1999; Truelove, Carrico, Weber, Raimi & Vandenbergh, 2014). Based on in-depth interviews with 25 individuals, we explore spillover effects from private and public sphere PEBs to work sphere PEBs (life-work spillover effects) with a specific focus on sustainable intra- and entrepreneurial activities: Do individuals who installed a photovoltaic system at home (private PEB) in their role as employees also seek to introduce renewable energies at their companies? Is a member of a non-governmental organization for environmental protection (public PEB) more likely to establish a new sustainability-oriented business than somebody who has no public commitment to sustainability issues? Our overall research question is: Is there a potential in the life-work spillover of private and public sustainability involvement for sustainable entre- or intrapreneurship at work?

On the basis of our qualitative study, we develop a typology of spillover processes and show that sustainable intra- and entrepreneurship, as well as other forms of PEB at work, is influenced by individuals' environmental activities in private and public spheres. We show that people who are characterized by a relatively high degree of personal involvement in sustainability issues are more likely to engage in sustainable intra- and entrepreneurship than people with a relatively low degree of personal involvement. Those individuals who show the highest degree of involvement at work are also strongly engaged in public PEB and/or driven by the motivation to make their contribution to sustainability. Individuals who are largely driven by the motivation to save money are more focused on technologically oriented PEB in the private and work sphere (e.g., using technologies for increasing energy efficiency) and are not active in public PEB. We further explore different ways of dealing with organizational barriers that generate tensions and hinder intrapreneurial activities inside existing organizations as well as strategies that employees use to overcome them.

The next section provides an introduction to the literature on sustainable intra- and entrepreneurship and life-work spillover of PEB. In the following section, we report results from qualitative research on 25 individuals and their ways to align their pro-environmental and sustainability behavior at home and at work. Our research enables us to identify different types of PEB spillover effects that are connected with behavioral strategies and motivational orientations towards sustainable entre- or intrapreneurship. In this way, we extend research on sustainable entrepreneurship by focusing on private and public sphere PEBs as "learned" behavioral strategies which can serve as a source for innovative forms of PEB at work or for sustainable intra- and entrepreneurship. On the basis of our findings, employers are encouraged to discover and understand the private and public engagement of environmentally conscious employees in order to release the motivational potential of their work force for the energy transition in their companies.

The spillover of private pro-environmental behavior to the work context as a source for sustainable intra- and entrepreneurship

Sustainable intra- and entrepreneurship

There is a wide range of definitions that conceptualize sustainable entrepreneurship (Schaltegger & Wagner, 2011). Considering the various organizational contexts of sustainable entrepreneurial action, we distinguish between:

1   *Sustainable entrepreneurship* that can be defined in its narrow sense as innovative company start-ups with a business model that is based upon generating a positive social and/or environmental impact (Pichel, 2008; Schaltegger & Wagner, 2011).[1]

2   *Sustainable intrapreneurship* covers individuals or groups within an existing organization that aim at generating sustainable ideas and turning them into profitable products and services, analogous to the concept of environmental intrapreneurship of Hostager, Neil, Decker and Lorentz (1998). Schrader and Harrach (2013) augment this focus on products and services and define the "sustainable intrapreneur" as an individual who (i) works in a corporation or organization and develops and promotes practical solutions for environmental

or social challenges, (ii) pushes and pulls colleagues and supervisors towards the solutions and (iii) is characterized by a sustainable lifestyle and willing and able to transfer the private sustainability conviction to the workplace and use it as a resource for intrapreneurial activities (Schrader & Harrach, 2013, p. 185f.). Hence, the authors explicitly draw attention to life-work spillover as a source of sustainable intrapreneurship.

While there are diverse studies that characterize different types of eco- or sustainability entrepreneurs (e.g., Isaak, 2002; Linnanen, 2002; Schaltegger, 2002; Walley & Taylor, 2002), eco- or sustainability intrapreneurs and related activities have not yet been systematically described. Similar to the concept of intrapreneurship, Wright, Nyberg and Grant (2012) describe different types of sustainable change agents who seek for a sustainable organizational change. They focus on the organizational transition process rather than on product development. In contrast, Ramus (2001) describes employees' activities as eco-innovators, that comprise, e.g., the development of new environmentally friendly products. Based on main characterizations of sustainable entre- and intrapreneurs in the literature, we suggest a cluster with four categories: (i) change-oriented; (ii) financially oriented; (iii) ethically oriented; and (iv) innovation-oriented sustainable entre- and intrapreneurs (see Table 5.1).

The first type encompasses entre- and intrapreneurs with a transformative sustainability orientation. They primarily focus upon a sustainability change by

Table 5.1 Types of sustainable intra- and entrepreneurs

Focus	Sustainable entrepreneurs	Sustainable intrapreneurs
Change-oriented	"visionary champions" (Walley & Taylor, 2002) "successful idealist" (Linnanen, 2002) Isaak's (2002) "ideal type of ecopreneur"	"green change agent" (Wright et al., 2012)
Financially oriented	"innovative opportunist"/"ad hoc enviropreneur" (Walley & Taylor, 2002) ecopreneur (Schaltegger, 2002) "opportunist" (Linnanen, 2002)	"rational manager" (Wright et al., 2012)
Ethically oriented	"ethical maverick" (Walley & Taylor, 2002) "alternative actors" (Schaltegger, 2002) "self-employer" (Linnanen, 2002)	"committed activist" (Wright et al., 2012)
Innovation-oriented	"bioneers" (Schaltegger, 2002)	"employees as eco-innovators" (Ramus, 2001)

Source: Author.

"improving the world" or creating markets (Isaak, 2002; Linnanen, 2002; Walley & Taylor, 2002). Others show strong change agency for embedding environmental sustainability within the organization as well as in professional networks and at home (Wright et al., 2012).

The second type is mainly driven by economic considerations. These entrepreneurs act very strategically by exploring green market niches. They also aim at a growing market share with their environmentally friendly products and are usually focused on environmental technologies (Linnanen, 2002; Schaltegger, 2002; Walley & Taylor, 2002). Close to these decriptions, Wright et al. (2012) characterize "the rational manager" as a sustainability intrapreneur who is linked to traditional business concerns, yet deals with sustainability through discourses of efficiency, profitability, reputational risks and provides new opportunities for value creation.

The third type, ethically focused sustainable entrepreneurs, usually own small businesses, are satisfied with a turnover that enables a reasonable standard of living and distance themselves from growth and the capitalistic economic system. They are value-driven, generate alterative business styles and create a counterculture to the conventional economy (Linnanen, 2002; Schaltegger, 2002; Walley & Taylor, 2002). Likewise, "committed activists" as change agents within organizations are strongly driven by their personal values and oftentimes actively engaged in volunteer work as members of the sustainability community outside the working context (Wright et al., 2012).

The fourth type, innovation-oriented "bioneers," concentrate on attractive, medium-sized market niches with customer-focused eco-products and sustainability innovations. They are usually strongly shaped by a company owner or family authority. Ramus (2001) describes a similar type of employee who acts as an eco-innovator inside organizations. By bringing in their pro-environmental intrinsic motivation as well as related skills and values, they are able to develop eco-innovations.

However, these types characterize positions that are not fixed: sustainable entre- and intrapreneurs rather have mixed motivations, combining green, ethical and social aspects. These motivations are often difficult to separate (Walley & Taylor, 2002) and can also lead to tensions between personal ideals and economic challenges that are handled by sustainable entrepreneurs in a creative manner (Schaltegger, 2002). Our research focuses on this aspect: the enrichment and tensions between sustainability agendas and behaviors in different life domains as well as the related potential for sustainable entre- or intrapreneurship of individuals.

We argue that many innovative business activities of sustainable entrepreneurs and intrapreneurs arise from social and environmental grassroots initiatives (public, social and environmental behavior) such as the fair trade movement (Hockerts, 2006), organic food (Thiers, 2002) and renewable energies (Hargreaves, Hielscher, Seyfang & Smith, 2013; Hielscher, Seyfang & Smith, 2013; Wüstenhagen, 2000). Ethically and change-oriented sustainable entre- and intrapreneurs show close connections to or are even actively involved in environmental and social movements, networks and groups. Hence, there are relationships and spillover effects between private and public engagement and sustainable activities at work. Furthermore, sustainability activities in the private sphere, e.g., bottom-up processes of sustainable collaborative consumption and production, can lead to new consumer roles that are (e.g., as lead users) involved in the development of sustainable products (Blättel-Mink, 2014). This argument is in line with Markusson (2010) who maintains that the alignment of private life environmental concerns with the working life is an underlying motivation for environmental champions in companies. In the following, we briefly introduce literature about such life-work spillover effects and discuss potential insights for sustainable intra- and entrepreneurship.

The spillover of private and public PEB to the work context

The literature on environmental psychology concentrates on two spheres of pro-environmental behavior (PEB) and behavioral spillovers:

1 *Public sphere PEB*, that includes more active forms (environmental activism) such as involvement in environmental protection organizations or environmental demonstration, and more passive forms (environmental citizenship) like financial contributions to environmental organizations or supporting environmental petitions (Dietz, Stern & Guagnano, 1998; Kashima, Paladino & Margetts, 2014; Stern, 2000; Stern, Dietz, Abel, Guagnano & Kalof, 1999).
2 *Private sphere PEB* comprises behaviors at home which aim at saving water, energy, and resources concerning products (e.g., recycling, reuse), mobility (e.g., riding a bike), technologies (e.g., installing energy-efficient light bulbs) and consumption (e.g., buying organic food) that can be performed as single actions or add up in a pro-environmental lifestyle (mundane environmentalism) (Kashima et al., 2014).

These types of behavior can be transferred between different life spheres as well as inside, e.g., the private domain. Positive examples for PEB spillovers can be found in a number of studies (see Figure 5.1): Berger's study (1997) about PEBs of Canadian households identifies correlations between recycling, energy and water conservation, composting, buying recycled paper and reusing shopping bags. In a survey of 300 Danish consumers, Thøgersen (2004) reports positive correlations between buying organic food and recycling. Van der Werff, Steg and Keizer (2013) show that fuel-efficient driving influences environmental self-identity, which in turn encourages the intention to reduce meat consumption. In a study about the effects of the installation of solar systems, Hondo and Baba (2009) demonstrate that household members who are self-conscious about their installed solar systems tend to also increase their energy-saving behavior at home.

Due to our research focus, we examine spillovers of PEB in private and public spheres that might induce sustainable intra- and entrepreneurship or related forms of change agency in the work sphere. In this respect, Kashima et al. (2014) propose that *environmental activism* and related strivings lead to a broader spectrum of PEB than mundane environmentalism. This is closely related to the argument above according to which initial PEB enhances people's environmental self-identity. This in turn can serve as a gateway for more challenging PEBs (Van der Werff et al., 2013). According to Van der Werff, Steg and Keizer (2014), the more challenging, difficult or unique the PEB shown, the stronger is the person's pro-environmental identity. Thus, environmental identity serves as a mediator for positive spillover effects of PEB (Truelove et al., 2014).

So far, spillover processes of PEB are mainly analyzed in the private and public domain (Thøgersen, 1999, 2004; Thøgersen & Crompton, 2009; Thøgersen & Ölander, 2003; Van der Werff et al., 2013), in the field of recycling and energy behavior (see above), and more recently, for the influence of PEB at work on PEB at home (Muster & Schrader, 2011; Rashid & Mohammad, 2011, 2012). Despite many studies focusing on spillover effects between PEBs within the private sphere, empirical research of behavioral spillover across spheres, and more specifically from the private to the work sphere, has received little attention. Studies that focus on life-work spillover effects of PEB only cover a limited range of behaviors, such as energy use or recycling (Andersson, Eriksson & von Borgstede, 2012; Lee, De Young & Marans, 1995; Littleford, Ryley & Firth, 2014). Thus, there is a research gap regarding spillovers of PEB concerning more demanding forms of behavior. Especially PEBs that imply a high personal involvement (e.g., being an active member of an environmental group) and possible spillover effects to equally demanding forms of PEB at work (like, e.g., introducing renewable energies at work) have been scarcely explored yet. We therefore propose that environmental strivings and environmental identity constitute a crucial motivational basis for life-work spillover of related intra- or entrepreneurial behaviors.

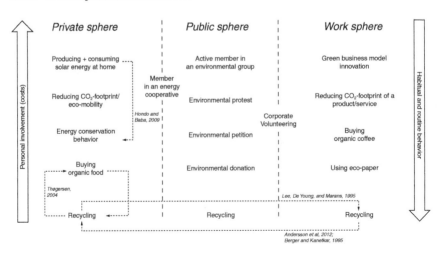

Figure 5.1 Types of sustainable intra- and entrepreneurs.

Research design

Our study focuses on self-employed persons as well as employees who show pro-environmental behavior in the private, public or work sphere. All interviewees exhibit considerable private or public pro-environmental commitment such as green activism, community energy projects or a private solar roof. The first respondents were identified via internet research, e.g., some of the interviewees are part of a list of regional "climate-mentors." These "climate mentors" promote the use of renewable and energy-efficient technologies and open their houses for demonstrating these technologies to interested people. Other interviewees were identified via snowballing, by asking either the first interviewees or professional acquaintances to name people whom they know for being involved in sustainable intra- or entrepreneurship. This resulted in a sample of 26 individuals with 8 self-employed persons or owners of small businesses, 15 company employees and 3 employees of non-profit/public organizations (see Table 5.2 for further details). The length of the interviews ranged from 49 up to 98 minutes. All interviews were tape-recorded and professionally transcribed.

Interviewees were asked to freely elaborate on their private, public and work pro-environmental behavior, their motivation for and experiences with PEB, as well as potentially supporting and/or hindering factors for PEB in their work context. The aim of the interview was to create an atmosphere in which interviewees would provide narratives about their behavior, motivations, perceptions about PEB at work as well as their activities in the private and public domain.

For data analysis we used established forms of content analysis (Mayring & Fenzl, 2014) by coding the private and public engagement of our interviewees, including their concrete environmental activities (and as far as given the environmental organizations they are involved in) as well as the motivation for their engagement. As far as the empirical material provides, we also coded self-characterizations and interview passages in which the interviewees negotiated conflicts or compatibilities and spillovers of their PEB at work and at home. For the work context, we coded their profession and employment status (self-employed, CEO, employee, etc.), their career stages, job satisfaction and attempts of job change, as well as environmental or sustainability activities at work including sustainable intra- and entrepreneurship behavior. Lastly, we inductively identified different forms of perceived organizational barriers for PEB at work and sustainable intrapreneurship, such as colleagues, supervisors, as well as corporate culture, strategies, policies, infrastructures, financial resources for environmental projects and innovations and job-related demands that hindered the interviewees from pursuing their sustainability engagement at work. Through this iterative and deliberately open process we sought to better understand and identify patterns of behavioral and identity work strategies employed by pro-environmentally engaged individuals in negotiating their roles and self-conceptualizations between public, private and working domains. The research is exploratory in kind. In line with our research goals, we therefore predominantly concentrated on identifying concepts, understandings and relationships between concepts that arose from the data.

Table 5.2 List of interviewees

Name[a]	Job	Employee/self-employed
Alex	Electric engineer/consultant	Self-employed/formerly: company employee
Ben	Hotelier	Self-employed
Craig	Ceramist	Self-employed
Daniel	Salesman of photovoltaic systems	Self-employed
Eric	Environmental and geological consultant	Self-employed
Gary	Developer of wind power projects	Self-employed/formerly: company employee
Greg	Owner of a company for office equipment	Self-employed
Jerry	Farming consultant	Company employee
Keith	Business economist	Company employee
Lucy	Sociologist	Public sector employee
Luke	Agricultural engineer	Employee in an association
Megan	Sustainability manager	Company employee
Nell	Environmental manager	Company employee
Patrick	Engineer	Self-employed/formerly: company employee
Paul	Employee in the telecom sector	Company employee
Rachel	Employee for geographic services	Company employee
Rebecca	Employee in a financial institute	Company employee
Richard	Engineer and project manager	Company employee
Sandra	Employee in corporate development	Company employee
Sara	Employee in process management and IT	Company employee
Scott	Environmental manager	Company employee
Sean	Employee in transformation management	Company employee
Susan	Member of the management	Company employee
Taylor	Employee in a state ministry	Public sector employee
Thomas	Product manager in a technology company	Company employee/today: retiree
William	Controller in an automotive company	Company employee

Source: author.

Note

a All names are pseudonyms.

Results

We identified five types of sustainable intra- or entrepreneurship and of PEB at work as well as respective spillover orientations. We clustered the entrepreneurial behaviors into (i) thrifty and (ii) politically oriented sustainable entrepreneurship, depending on the type of PEB and motives. The PEBs of employees are clustered as follows: (iii) sustainable intrapreneurship, change-oriented activities and suggesting sustainability or eco-initiatives at work; (iv) green activities and green positioning of employees; (v) task-related or no PEB at work. We describe each PEB and spillover orientation in detail below.

Thrifty sustainable entrepreneurship

Four of the interviewed entrepreneurs emphasized economic prudence or savings as underlying motivation for their pro-environmental entrepreneurial activities both at home and at work. They argue that the concentration on energy and resource efficiency is a means to save money. Their work-related activities are limited to using and promoting resource and energy efficiency technologies. Their business model is not necessarily based on sustainability in an ecological sense. However, the entrepreneurs strive for using the latest environmental technologies that are available on the market. Still, they are very skeptical about new technologies that are not yet profitable in their eyes, such as photovoltaic systems, because the return of investment of solar energy is too low in Germany.

> No, with me it's always about the money, [laughs] to put it plainly.... For me, the energy question is strictly a business thing.
>
> (Ben)

The issue of energy efficiency is not limited to their work. In all cases, we observed spillover effects of efficiency-oriented PEB between the private, public and work sphere as stated by Eric.

> I can't decouple private and business matters from one another that way, I can't just say, I made that experience there and now I would pretend that I have no idea of that in private life.
>
> (Eric)

However, the spillover is limited to energy-related behavior and using energy-efficient technologies at home, but not to other PEBs like consuming ecological food or using eco-friendly mobility modes. Some interviewees even emphasized that they are quite unecological in the private sphere by driving a big car, traveling by plane very often and rarely buying ecological food. So the spillover is limited to PEBs that are based on using new, efficient technologies, but not to change the standard of living due to environmentally oriented motives. The interviewees were very self-confident and openly talked about their environmentally harmful lifestyle.

> I drive a car, and I, somehow, drive such a gigantic ride, that is actually completely unecological, so I, let's say, actually don't belong to the group of ecologically thinking people, to be honest.
>
> (Eric)

I am quite comfort-bound, I drive a lot by car in my job, flew by plane a lot, have never consciously refrained from doing something like that for ecological reasons.

(Ben)

Political sustainable entrepreneurship

Four of the interviewed entrepreneurs are more politically oriented. They are active in the public sphere in driving forward the energy transition and focus on green electricity that is produced by solar and wind energy – like the following four stories show: Craig is a self-employed ceramist. He is politically active in the anti-nuclear movement in his municipality and strives for producing his ceramics with green electricity. Daniel is also self-employed and sells photovoltaic systems. Besides he is very active in the anti-nuclear movement of his home town and privately owns six photovoltaic systems that he runs on the roofs of municipalities and schools. Gary, formerly a company employee, became interested in the upcoming wind turbine technology and decided to become self-employed for projecting and realizing wind energy projects.

Yes, my heart is set on wind power. Well, also on community projects, but I have decided on wind power professionally and now I have had my own planning bureau for two years, for project development and realization of wind projects.

(Gary)

Patrick, an engineer, was very active in the early years of the anti-nuclear movement and then worked for over ten years at a large power supply company. There, he tried to introduce a green energy product line (sustainable intrapreneurship) but failed due to a lack of supervisory support and no organizational willingness to change the established nuclear- and coal-based energy production. As a consequence, he decided to establish a green electricity company that provides direct marketing for renewable energy projects. With his own business, he finally got the chance and the freedom to do everything in the "right way" like he had had it in mind for a long time.

And then that was a new energy supplier on a greenfield site. And then there I had the freedom to do everything in a way like I've had it in my mind for a long time. That you'd do it the right way. There was no moron who would dictate something to me …

(Patrick)

The motivations in this group are clearly political and encompass involvement in climate and environmental protection, regional value creation, anti-nuclear activism and civic engagement for the energy transition. One interviewee describes that he started his engagement after the Fukushima nuclear disaster:

2011 was the accident in Fukushima, right? ... March 2011. Yes. There I started. Before that, I was unpolitical you could say ... Not at all active ... and there we have made right after the accident ... protests, Monday-protests, over nine weeks.... in consequence the citizen initiative under this name has formed to also promote the energy transition in [my home town].

(Craig)

Interviewees in the group of politically oriented entrepreneurs exhibit spillover of their PEB to different life spheres. This implies, for example, the abandonment of their own car (by two interviewees), using a bike for short distances, consuming regional and ecological products, and reducing meat consumption.

Yes, well, my flat is well equipped in a very energy saving way. I have no car. I do everything by bike and train. And ... I would say, shopping in the organic food store 70 percent.... Well, meat and vegetables in any case ... well meat very little anyways, but if, then in the organic store. And all of the vegetables.... Milk most of the time.... Yes. So this way about 70 percent, I would say.

(Daniel)

All politically oriented sustainable entrepreneurs are actively working toward a societal and political energy transition and are actively involved in public sphere projects (public PEB) to pursue that goal. Their activities usually started in public sphere activism and spilled over to their jobs as the market for renewable energies in Germany has been established in the last ten years.

Sustainable intrapreneurship and change-oriented pro-environmental behavior at work

Six interviewees, who reported about sustainable intrapreneurship activities, regard the working sphere as an important domain for pushing forward sustainability issues. Four of them are in-role (employees in the environmental or sustainability division or working in a sustainability-oriented sector), one is a member of the management, and one has a position in the strategic management department.

Among the employees, we interviewed several very proactive intrapreneurs who tried to initiate sustainability projects – some with and some without success. For example Susan, who is working in the management of a manufacturing company, initiated the change to a green energy supplier and improved the environmental performance of her company. Based on her management position, she was able to sign the contracts with the electricity provider although the change implied additional costs for the company. In order to protect herself against opposition or unwanted questioning, she did not disclose the change to the organization and her colleagues.

And, so there are only few electricity suppliers that provide really ecological power ... The amount it costs more, that is so small ... that is, I think,
300 Euro a year that it costs more, such a small amount that is. And then I
thought, well now come on? ... It will be done now. And I also won't talk
about it. I'm just doing it. I can sign the contracts and no one really knows
actually. I just do that.

(Susan)

Suggestions and initiatives that improve the environmental and climate performance of the organization are often refused due to budgetary constraints and too long
payback periods. Hence, the sustainability intrapreneurs hardly get organizational
approval and many very proactive green change agents struggle with that challenge.
Especially those who tried to create new green(er) products: such as Patrick who
tried to introduce a new green energy product in his company (see the last subsection), or Sean who still tries to improve the resource efficiency in the mobile sector
by decoupling mobile phone contracts from the automatic offer of a new smartphone. These employees who suggested such projects often develop a business case
and try to emphasize the overall benefit for the organization to get their environmental suggestions realized. However, they fail with their eco-intrapreneurship
activities due to too low returns on investments and/or a lack of supervisory support.
The lack of supervisory support was a barrier that was reported by all of those interviewees whom we classified as sustainable intrapreneurs. Sean stated that supervisors are often afraid to promote unconventional sustainability-oriented ideas.
They would rather do nothing because they fear putting their career at risk.

No, I always run against closed doors. That is not welcomed, ... In such a
big company, you can only lose if you go out on a limb. If you don't do anything, you don't do something wrong! ... or as a head of marketing. That is
really difficult, if you do it as a big bold move and that is going completely
wrong, you're out.

(Sean)

William tried to convince managing directors to install a photovoltaic system
on the roof of the production facilities of the company but he failed due to a too
low return on investment and the resulting lack of top management support.
Nell, who tried to improve the environmental performance of the company's
car pool, failed the same way. However, she did not get discouraged.

But it's always a question of returns ... [Company X] or generally all major
corporations invest only if the investment is returned within four years.
And that just ain't the case with renewable energies ...

(William)

Yes, I have proposed ... to take a look at our car pool somehow, if you could
use it with electric vehicles, or gas vehicles. Now, what they thought was

"mhm" [affirming].... And then please evaluate this economically, if that pays for us.... No, it does not pay so well for us, because: It is still a bit too expensive. But I have already promised that I will bug them with it again ... [laughs]. So there, I won't let up.

(Nell)

Beyond a lack of supervisory support and too low returns, some intrapreneurs state that the corporate culture and mindsets are opposed to eco-initiatives and prevent intrapreneurial activities in companies.

But they are all people. They have a completely different way of thinking. They also treat this subject in a completely different way.... Also they talk, for example, about the environmental conservation act, ... and make it completely ridiculous. And you sit there and think to yourself: "something's wrong here" ... Well that is, you learn that other people are wired differently.... At some point, you just simply tell yourself: "Okay, they are just different from me, they think in a different way," and you have to cope with that somehow.

(Nell)

Without exception, all sustainable intrapreneurs talked about life-work PEB spillover effects. Susan, who secretly introduced green energy in her company, is also an active member in an environmental association. Keith, who introduced green energy and tried to green the vehicle fleet, was one of the first changers to a green electricity provider, concerning his private consumption. Because he works in a company that produces and sells solar technology, his pro-environmental spillover attempts are supported in his company. Furthermore, he purchases organic products, invests his money in renewable energies and solar funds, is a supporting member of an environmental association, and tries to convince others to change to a green electricity provider. Other sustainable intrapreneurs refrain from owning and using a car, consume green electricity at home, are vegetarians with an ecological motivation, and buy a smartphone with minimal negative social and ecological impact. However, we observed that two intrapreneurs are very active in the public sphere while three of them mainly concentrate on their job-related sustainability activities as they perceive this as having more impact than with public sphere activism. In comparison to public sphere activism, Megan and Sean see the work sphere as a context where they can make a greater impact on sustainable development. Consequently, their personal focus is on activities in the working sphere.

Well ... some say then: You work for [company X]? Yes? And sustainability? M'hm! Then I always say: Yes, sure, there exactly you can move something. I don't have to be in the citizens' initiative.... Have to sit in the headquarters.

(Megan)

> Well I say, privately, when I place myself on the streets and hold up a poster: "Don't waste mobiles!" they would say: What does he want from me? But assuming I do [my initiatives at work] another five years and that has some influence, ... that those are billions, where you could save billions of dollars, where you could basically save waste with that. And that is, with such a huge corporation, an enormous lever, if it works.
>
> (Sean)

Similar to the politically oriented entrepreneurs, the motives for the engagement of intrapreneurs are societal and ecologically oriented. They encompass, for example, engagement to recognize "the limits to growth" and against nuclear energy (as a result of the Chernobyl and Fukushima nuclear disasters).

> I am ... I am since 1986 ... so since Chernobyl I realized, that it can't go on like that, yes. My son was three years old then ...
>
> (William)

When interviewees pursue life-work integration they also seek to employ their work-related competences for the benefit of their private or public pro-environmental engagement. One interviewee uses her financial skills at work to organize the financial administration of her local environmental group. Like Susan, some interviewees experience personal conflicts as their sustainability initiatives are blocked or the business model of their employer was perceived as incompatible with the sustainability values and behaviors in the private and public sphere.

> Our main customers are food processing companies, mainly meat and fish-processing.... And that naturally does not go well with my way of thinking. And part of that is disgusting. And so I ask myself sometimes if I am in the right place.... Because that is not what I live for.
>
> (Susan)

Where conflicts between the work context and private and/or public contexts occurred, interviewees employed different strategies in order to cope with the intra- and interpersonal tensions around their PEB orientation. The interview data discloses behavioral strategies for coping with organizational barriers. Four interviewees talked about their resilience which describes the fact of receiving a setback without giving up, staying on task and developing frustration tolerance. One interviewee stated that her ecological lifestyle meets with refusal from her colleagues. However, she decided that she will stay true to herself.

> And in the end you somehow have to reflect on it and then – some people might think: That is arrogant – but you have to have, somehow, enough self-esteem to say to yourself: "No, the way I am, is completely alright." And you don't have to conform. And why should I conform?
>
> (Nell)

Overcoming organizational barriers was a big issue for the sustainable intrapreneurs. For example, Scott talked about the ways in which he tries to implement sustainability activities in his company. He has been working in a large-scale enterprise for over 20 years and developed different strategies to overcome organizational barriers. He waits for a window of opportunity, searches for supervisors and colleagues who are interested in sustainability issues, attempts to create factual constraints in favor of his agenda, and searches for informal and unconventional ways to implement sustainability projects.

> Yes, now it wasn't that I permanently pushed that, but I have always observed when it would fit in, when does a window open, right, where you can go in again. And before all, does my superior enjoy that or does it disturb him, right. That was the main topic actually.
>
> (Scott)

Due to the organizational barriers, many intrapreneurs talked about exit strategies such as changing jobs, leaving the company or starting a new business (sustainable entrepreneurship) when their core values were disturbed or their sustainability initiatives were hindered in the long run.

> And I am not the type who conforms to the circumstances, no, then I rather leave. Well there is this: Love it, leave it, or change it. Exactly, when you, I think, wear yourself out in this change effort, then it is somehow time to leave.
>
> (Megan)

As discussed above, this exit option was employed by Patrick, who founded a new green energy company (sustainable entrepreneurship), after ten years of trying to foster his intrapreneurial ideas in a conventional energy business. Likewise, the example of Scott, who privately runs a small business for electric bicycles as a side job, shows that a lack of supervisory support for sustainable intrapreneurship can lead to enhanced involvement in entrepreneurial activities.

> So there are developments, that now, well my boss has also contributed to that, that I do that here and, so to say, am engaged in private.
>
> (Scott)

These examples show that continuously restraining an employee's sustainability engagement bears the risk of losing innovative employees.

Green activities and green positioning of employees

In comparison to the change-oriented sustainable intrapreneurs, seven employees reported about their green activities at work as representing their personal values and lifestyles. Rather than aiming at the green transformation of the organization or its product and service portfolio, they concentrate on their public sphere engagement. As fundraiser for environmental and social projects, or as chairpersons of renewable energy cooperatives, some interviewees put a lot of personal involvement and free time into their civic engagement. At work they exhibit and promote their green lifestyle, attitudes and behaviors among their colleagues.

For instance, a manager in a large enterprise providing services and technical solutions also for the nuclear industry nevertheless cycles to work with an anti-nuclear sticker on his bike. Moreover, he rejects managing nuclear-power related projects. Contrary to what might be expected, his behaviors are accepted by both his colleagues and his supervisor.

> Back when I started to work for [my company], I have done support for a lot of nuclear power plants, had no problem with that at all. And that became a problem for me only as time went by.... Meanwhile I have no inhibitions at all anymore to carry a "Nuclear Power – no thanks!" sticker on my bike, ... but also that is no problem there.... Well, but we do support for nuclear power plants and that gradually did become more and more of a problem for me.... I have been asked if I wouldn't do it, as project supervisor, but I declined that with thanks. Also that has been accepted ...
>
> (Richard)

When green-minded employees feel unable to transfer their convictions to colleagues and to achieve pro-environmental change at work through dialogue, some tend to withdraw their involvement and focus on their public and private sphere PEB. Two employees reduced their working time in favor of their environmental engagement. One of them devoted her time to fundraising for victims of the Fukushima nuclear disaster. She was close to a burnout because her job together with her engagement was too demanding. So she decided to reduce her working time by 50 percent. Likewise, Rachel reduced her working time by 20 percent to devote more time to her private beekeeping activities. For her, work is for earning money and completely separated from her private environmental activities.

> I've reduced my working hours a bit, because I think, that is my strategy ... Well, so I've made my peace with it and work is for ..., yes to earn money, ... But yes I believe I've shifted a lot of my engagement towards my private life. Yes, it's like two worlds, right? The one is for business, and how I live my private life, is just very different.
>
> (Rachel)

These interviewees spill over their green lifestyle and convictions to the workplace, but do not strive for a more fundamental sustainability change in their organization, nor do they initiate any intrapreneurial activities. They focus primarily on social, civic and health issues in their public sphere activities (e.g., help for orphans). However all of them have a very ecologically oriented life-style (private PEB) by being vegetarians (or even vegans) for ecological reasons, consuming green electricity and using ecological means of transportation. When they transfer their private PEB to the work sphere, some colleagues and super-visors accept and support that behavior, but others are rather annoyed.

> … one of my superiors is completely with me, really…. but the one above him, his superior, … we were having a meal together. And there he heard that I am a vegetarian. And that, I think, has somehow really shaken him. He just couldn't understand that people are vegetarian. And that he himself knows one now.
>
> (Richard)

Similar to some intrapreneurs who thought about their exit strategy, five green-minded employees tried to find a job with an environmental or sustainability focus. Hence, they seek for a change from extra-role to in-role PEB. Two of them gave up due to very low salary offers. Two others invested a lot of time and effort in advanced vocational training programs for green jobs. One of them is just finishing an MBA in Corporate Social Responsibility, and another one took part in a competence development program for managing energy coopera-tives which was a stepping stone for her new job.

> What I really have difficulty with, that occupy myself with IT, Customer Relationship Management, with pharmaceutics four days a week and then on the fifth day I'm supposed to switch, … And thus I am currently trying again to apply, and to find a different job somewhere else, …, I want that idea, to somewhere be more sustainable or to be on the way for social responsibility for some company.
>
> (Sara)

Green-minded employees are characterized by a spillover of their private PEB, like riding the bike to work, eating vegan, taking care of recycling and resource saving behavior (e.g., double-sided printing, turning off the heating when the window is open). In addition, some of them have shown attempts at extending their green behavior at work by, e.g., asking for a CO_2-compensation of their job-related travels. But unlike sustainable intrapreneurs, they are not very resil-ient in upholding their questioning and early-stage initiatives. They discuss with colleagues and ask critical questions, but if the questions remain unanswered they neither keep trying nor do they start initiatives or intensify their engagement.

> I remember well that many years ago I handed in a proposal for an improve-ment, that every office should be equipped with such a switchable plug bar, so that in the end of the day, the computer and printer and so on are

disconnected from the grid. The reaction to this was *so absolutely* negative and devastating that I've become very cautious concerning the handing in of suggestions.

(Taylor)

Especially those who work in large companies often have tight time and task requirements that are incompatible with any environmental and sustainability extra-role engagement. However, we observed two subgroups of dealing with the organizational barriers: Some interviewees tried very actively to get sustainability-related jobs and positions (e.g., through self-paid professional development) in which they can harmonize their green convictions and activities with their jobs (see above). Employees, who failed to get a new job within or outside their company, tend to reduce their working time in order to have more free time for their private and public sphere PEB – a phenomenon which was also observed with one of the sustainable intrapreneurs. Others see their current job as an important financial basis for their public sphere PEB (see the quote of Rachel above) and can thus reconcile their PEB engagement with their job.

Task-oriented pro-environmental behavior

We interviewed three employees who did not report on any PEBs at work which go beyond switching off the lights and the computer before going home in the evening. However, they actively support energy transition projects in private and public domains (e.g., by living in a passive house or being a "climate mentor"). At work, they see other departments in the organization as being responsible for environmental issues. According to them, experts from the energy or facility management are confronted with such issues every day and thus are the ones who will develop respective technical solutions. The tenor of the interviewees was that they are ordinary employees with no competences or opportunities to influence such issues.

Well, when I put that to my employers, I can't tell them a thing, they know that ten times better than me. So ... we aren't a takeaway, I'd say, it's professionals that sit there, ... that think about this anew every day, how they can solve the energy problem and there I can't help them. So I'd say, concerning my employer.... zero, I can't exert any influence there.

(Jerry)

However, all of them are very keen to use energy efficient technologies or renewable energies at home. One employee even tried to make his home completely energy autonomous.

Yeah well, the motivation is to be completely independent, energy-wise. Completely. So now this goal motivated me tremendously. Tremendously. I want to be away from oil heating.... I play with the thought of buying an electric car and generally to shift everything to wind power and photovoltaics.

(Jerry)

The two others were more interested in saving money and gaining more comfort by living in a house of high quality. As they do not report on PEB at work, they do not spill over their private, more energy-related PEB to the work sphere. The statements and motivations for PEB in the private sphere were very close to the thrifty sustainability entrepreneurs because the interviewees emphasized financial motives for their PEB and separate themselves from being ecologically oriented idealists. Furthermore, they also focus on energy efficiency and technological solutions rather than sufficiency-orientated forms of PEB.

Well, to come back to your original question, I am quite a ... Concerning energy saving, quite yes ... That does have to pay, right? So I am not such an idealist and ideologist who does this because he finds joy in doing it or from a save-the-planet-attitude ... But in the end it has to pay.

(Paul)

Discussion and conclusion

Based on our empirical data, we are able to identify distinctive types of sustainable intra- and entrepreneurship as well as types of PEB at work that are characterized by different kinds of life-work spillovers.

The interviewees who show business-case oriented, *thrifty sustainability entrepreneurship* focus on economic gains and energy efficiency as a motivational basis such as the "opportunist" described by Linnanen (2002). Unlike the "innovative opportunist," described by Walley and Taylor (2002), they clearly focus on thriftiness rather than on exploring new green niches with their entrepreneurial activities. They make a contribution to sustainability goals by being efficient and business-driven but clearly separate themselves from being idealists or sustainability-driven and even point out their unecological lifestyle in the interviews. As so-called "climate mentors" they are willing to show other interested persons the energy-efficient technologies they implemented at home, when they receive a request. Their spillover between private and work sphere PEB is restricted to using energy-efficient technologies (see Table 5.3). The demonstration of their environmentally harmful lifestyle and the aspect that they are registered as "climate mentors" to advise other people in the use of energy-efficient technologies, is not perceived as a tension. Although all four entrepreneurs are registered as "climate mentors," they do not mention this aspect in the interviews. It does not seem to be relevant for their life and their self-concept.

All interviewees who engage in politically oriented sustainable entrepreneurship show life-work spillovers of PEB that originate from and are reinforced by their environmental involvement in the public sphere. In all four cases, the public sphere PEB for bringing forward the energy transition serves as a basis for their business activities in this field (see Table 5.3). Thus, their self-reported behavior supports the proposition that environmental identity constitutes a motivational basis for life-work spillover that leads to sustainable entrepreneurship. Interviewees who show *political sustainable entrepreneurship* resemble Isaak's ideal type of an ecopreneur, who is mainly driven by making a contribution to improving the world (Isaak, 2002). Three politically driven sustainable entrepreneurs run a one-man company, present themselves as being a "self-employer," and are satisfied with an income that sustains their standard of living (Linnanen, 2002). One runs a small enterprise and seeks to occupy a medium-sized market niche, such as the "bioneers" described by Schaltegger (2002). He is akin to the "visionary champions" of Walley and Taylor (2002) who seeks for a societal transformation through structural changes. The other three did not present themselves as being very outgoing or visionary. Instead, they use close, local networks to run their business and are engaged in the public sphere to bring forward the energy transition like the "ethical maverick" described by Walley and Taylor (2002).

The findings for sustainable intrapreneurs are mixed. We found that *three sustainable intrapreneurs* clearly concentrate on their working activities as they perceive them to have the highest positive impact on sustainability. These individuals are sufficiency-oriented in their private PEB (e.g., being vegetarians, etc.) and show a limited degree of public PEB. They concentrate on their engagement at work and put all their efforts into it, because they perceive to have a greater impact with their working sphere activities than they could achieve with public engagement. They are similar to the "green change agent" who "promote[s] environmental sustainability both within their organization and outside of work through professional networks, as well as in their family life and home" (Wright et al., 2012, p. 1461). Like the "green change agent" (Wright et al., 2012), the three interviewees concentrate on the process and the aspect of being a mediator and initiator. They aim at changing employee perceptions and behavior and try to induce cultural changes on the organizational level. *The remaining three sustainable intrapreneurs*, who are additionally engaged in the public sphere as active members of environmental associations, are more rebellious and venturesome than the "green change agents." Their focus lies on the result rather than on the process as in the case of the "committed activist" (Wright et al., 2012). If the scope of action for their engagement at work is limited due to organizational barriers, they shift their focus to their private and public sphere eco-activities. Due to the more venturesome character, this type is closer to the environmentally oriented "eco-innovator" (Ramus, 2001) and also can become a sustainable entrepreneur, if the opportunity arises. This connection between sustainable intra- and entrepreneurship is illustrated by the activities of one interviewee who privately runs a small business for eco-mobility, in addition to his full-time job and eco-initiatives at work. Concerning sustainability intrapreneurship, we found personal strategies such as developing resilience to setbacks, waiting for windows of opportunity, or searching for unconventional procedures to bypass formal organizational structures and barriers. These strategies enable the intrapreneurs to uphold their engagement, even when they face strong organizational barriers.

Employees that show *green activities and green positioning* at work are very interested in sustainability issues but have not (yet) found the proper position and role to follow their private interests at work. They concentrate on environmentally friendly ways to accomplish their immediate work tasks. Helping and influencing others is a second type of behavior that these interviewees report. In contrast to the intrapreneurs, once they realize that the communicative strategies do not take root at their workplaces they tend to withdraw their workplace engagement. Some attempt to exit the corporation, to switch to a sustainability-related job more in line with their pro-environmental private identity, or reduce their working time to focus on their private and public PEB. Similar to the intrapreneurs, green-minded employees are characterized by a spillover of private sufficiency-oriented PEB (see Table 5.3). Due to their strong civic engagement in the public sphere, that already requires a high degree of personal involvement, their power to initiate intrapreneurial activities at work is limited.

Employees who show no or only *task-oriented PEB* at work are close to the "thrifty" business-case oriented entrepreneur as they focus on energy efficiency, technological solutions and profitability considerations. Their private sphere PEBs are also of a similar kind (e.g., energy-efficient lights; see Table 5.3). They share many characteristics with the "rational manager" (Wright et al., 2012) who supports sustainability activities as long as they are profitable or save money. They have an attitude of being rational and objective and clearly distinguish themselves from the "idealists" and "saviors of the world." The business case is a clear boundary for them to consider an involvement in sustainability activities both at work and at home. In their companies, they reported no PEB activities beyond switching off the light and the computer when they go home in the evening. Personally, they see no scope of influence for PEB at work. They concentrate on their job and take the view that other departments in the company are responsible for energy and sustainability issues.

Limitations of our spillover perspective lie in the possibility that employees' environmental citizenship activities and initiatives are exploited by the employer to benefit corporate agendas (Nyberg, Spicer & Wright, 2013). We realize that there is a fine line between enabling employee engagement and the exploitation (or regulation) of employees' private interests and skills. This fine line is shaped by the freedom that employees have to integrate their "private" interests and identities, or to keep them separate. Thus, employers should open up the opportunity for intrapreneurial PEB and eco-initiatives but refrain from forcing or manipulating employees by applying pressures towards the inclusion or exclusion of their environmental and sustainability commitment at work.

On the basis of our interview data, we conclude that a life-work spillover of pro-environmental and sustainability behavior can lead to sustainable entre- and intrapreneurship, but it is dependent on several factors. Concerning sustainable

Table 5.3 Types of intra- and entrepreneurial spillover effects

Type	Private sphere	Public sphere	Work sphere	Spillover
Thrifty sustainable entrepreneurship	Applying energy-efficient technologies	Sporadically advising interested others in the use of energy-efficient technologies as "climate mentors"	Applying energy-efficient technologies	The spillover is restricted to the use of energy-efficient technologies
Political sustainable entrepreneurship	Pro-environmental lifestyle, e.g., green electricity, organic food, (abandonment of their own car in two cases)	Environmental demonstrations, public activities for the energy transition, mostly active in the anti-nuclear movement, and membership in environmentally oriented NGOs or parties	Focus on markets for renewable energies and green electricity, changing to green electricity provider for pottery production	Activities for the energy transition usually started in the public sphere and spilled over to self-employed work, e.g., as market shares for renewable energies grew in the last years
Sustainable intrapreneurship	Pro-environmental lifestyle, e.g., green electricity, organic and vegetarian food, green mobility modes (bike, etc.)	Partly members of environmental associations, donations to environmental associations	Occupation as sustainability/ environmental managers or in the upper management, introducing green electricity, attempts of introducing products, attempts of greening the company (car pool, etc.)	Life-work spillover, but interviewees concentrate on one sphere (mostly the work sphere) for their involvement. The focus can change when the work context limits the scope of action for sustainability initiatives.

Green activities and positioning	Pro-environmental lifestyle, e.g., green electricity, organic and vegetarian/vegan food, biking, beekeeping	Social and civic engagement (e.g., help for orphans), chairperson of/engagement in renewable energy cooperatives	Riding the bike to work, discussing sustainability issues with colleagues, positioning as green employees	Spillover of private PEB and environmental conviction (e.g., anti-nuclear sticker, eating vegan, etc.), some apply for green jobs/or participate in advanced educational training for green jobs
Task-oriented pro-environmental behavior	Using energy-efficient technologies and renewable energies at home (in one case: living in a passive house); no further activities	Sporadically advising interested others in the use of energy-efficient technologies as "climate mentors"	No activities that go beyond switching off the computer and the lights, when leaving the office	No spillover

Source: author.

entrepreneurship, our data show several cases, in which individuals who are (and were) involved in public PEB to bring forward the energy transition in Germany, later founded their own business in this field, as the market conditions for renewable energies improved. As sustainable entrepreneurs are dependent on the development of green markets, sustainability intrapreneurs are dependent on the supportive and enabling context of the organization they are working in. They need a broad scope of action as their activities do not fit the dominant conventional business practices and management systems. For realizing their ideas they need supervisory support or a position with decision-making power, such as Susan who, based on her formal role, was able to sign the contract with the green electricity provider. Intrapreneurs therefore actively search for the "right" position to support greening processes in the organization, or to be able to initiate ecological improvements of products and processes. Those intrapreneurs, who are also engaged in the public sphere, can sidestep to other "niches" (e.g., in projects and initiatives in their environmental associations) when organizational barriers hinder their green engagement at work. For intrapreneurs, it is important to be a driver for the sustainability transition and to be at the "right" place to have an impact on that goal. As long as they perceive to have an impact, they have the resilience to endure setbacks and barriers. For the respective organizations and its members, it may be difficult to handle those sustainable intrapreneurs who are very demanding, provoke with their behavior and disregard given conventions. However, this "sustainability avant-garde" can be an innovative and creative driver of change for the development of sustainable products (Blättel-Mink, 2014) and business practices.

Like the sustainable intrapreneurs, green-minded employees seek for an integration of their green behavior and identity at work, and struggle to be accepted by colleagues and supervisors. By openly demonstrating their green position and behavior, they provoke some colleagues and supervisors who clearly distance themselves from that behavior. Although they do not directly try to induce "green" changes in the organization, they create small green niches that might eventually affect the organization at large. Although most of the green-minded employees are relatively happy inside their green niches, some still show a low job satisfaction and apply for green jobs or for jobs in organizations with greener business practices. Others extend their private green identities and behavior and reduce their working time. This enhancement of green private sphere activities can be seen as a strategy to compensate the limited opportunities for green activities at work. Those green-minded employees search for and sometimes extend their green niches – either at work or in their private activities. Thus, they are valuable for organizations that seek to expand the green behavior of their employees or try to establish a green organizational culture. Comparable with the "ethical mavericks" (Walley & Taylor, 2002) and "alternative actors" (Schaltegger, 2002), green-minded employees are relatively satisfied with small scopes of action that enable them to follow their sustainability convictions and spill over their green lifestyle to the workplace. They do not intend to have a large impact on the organization. They just want to be acknowledged with their green behavior at work and have the freedom to interact with colleagues or customers that share their values and enable them to follow their identity preferences.

Our empirical results have implications for the concept of "sustainable intrapreneurship": In our view, "sustainable intrapreneurship" goes beyond sustainable product and service innovations (Hostager et al., 1998) or practical solutions for environmental and social challenges (Schrader & Harrach, 2013). While Hostager et al. (1998) point at innovations for customers and the society, we emphasize that the challenges "sustainable intrapreneurs" are faced with lie *inside* their organizations, such as challenging and changing the direct unsustainable working environment, business practices and organizational culture. Concerning the definition of Schrader and Harrach (2013), who also focus on the organizational perspective, another related question remains unanswered: What are the effects on the organizational system when employees act visibly as a green role model thus inspiring their colleagues by setting an example, or seeking to persuade their colleagues to share their "green cause," as proposed by Schrader and Harrach (2013)? Following this argumentation those of the interviewees who show green behavior and positioning at work would have to be considered sustainable intrapreneurs. We do, however, not follow this extended definition, because our respondents do not strive for having an impact on the organization. They just spill over their private sustainability behavior and convictions to the work sphere, may act as a role model for direct colleagues, but do not show any initiatives for sustainable innovations at the organizational level. On the other hand, do "sustainable intrapreneurs" need to create sustainable and profitable products and services, as proposed by Hostager et al. (1998)? In this case, none of our "sustainable intrapreneurs" would actually fall into this category, because they failed with their initiatives – like Sean who tried to decouple mobile phone contracts from the automatic offer of a new smartphone to save resources. The argument of the successful creation of profitable and sustainable products or services implies that "sustainable intrapreneurs" already have supervisory and organizational support to realize their ideas and initiatives. Those employees who still struggle to get this support are perceived as "troublemakers," because they run against social expectations in their organizations and against closed doors of their supervisors. Consequently, they would not be considered intrapreneurs. We propose instead that "sustainable intrapreneurs" are those who go beyond being a role model, idea generator or product developer. They are the ones who (try to) implement sustainable innovations inside their organizations, even if this needs considerable personal involvement and does not always turn out to be successful. To fulfill this demand, "sustainable intrapreneurs" require to integrate their "private identities" and "work roles" in a creative manner, combining sustainable ideas with contextual knowledge about how to deal with given business practices and barriers in their organization. Here, more empirical research is needed to identify the personal competences and characteristics that are needed to accomplish these tasks.

Pro-environmental and sustainability behaviors that imply a high personal involvement and possible spillover effects to equally demanding forms of PEB at work have been scarcely explored so far. However, they bear a high potential for an organizational sustainability transition from the bottom up that is currently largely undisclosed and underexplored by researchers. Concerning practical implications, employers are encouraged to recognize employees' motivational orientations and spillover attempts as potentially powerful drivers in a transition process. Organizations and corporations need to overcome the view that sustainability is solely an expert task and have to create open spaces, enabling structures and a sustainability culture that welcomes employees' contributions regardless of their position. By enhancing their instruments for active employee participation, organizations can tap employee-driven innovations and allow sustainability initiatives to unfold.

Note

1 In a wide definition of sustainable entrepreneurship, intrapreneurs are taken into account as a subgroup of sustainable entrepreneurs (Schaltegger & Wagner, 2011).

References

Andersson, M., Eriksson, O. & von Borgstede, C. (2012). The effects of environmental management systems on source separation in the work and home settings. *Sustainability*, 4(6), 1292–1308.

Berger, I. E. (1997). The demographics of recycling and the structure of environmental behavior. *Environment and Behavior*, 29(4), 515–531.

Berger, I., &. Kanetkar, V. (1995). Increasing environmental sensitivity via workplace experiences. *Journal of Public Policy & Marketing*, 14(2), 205–215.

Blättel-Mink, B. (2014). Active consumership as a driver towards sustainability? GAIA-*Ecological Perspectives for Science and Society*, 23(Supplement 1), 158–165.

Dietz, T., Stern, P. C. & Guagnano, G. A. (1998). Social structural and social psychological bases of environmental concern. *Environment and Behavior*, 30(4), 450–471.

Hargreaves, T., Hielscher, S., Seyfang, G. & Smith, A. (2013). Grassroots innovations in community energy: The role of intermediaries in niche development. *Global Environmental Change*, 23(5), 868–880.

Hielscher, S., Seyfang, G. & Smith, A. (2013). Grassroots innovations for sustainable energy: Exploring niche-development processes among community-energy initiatives. In M. Cohen, H. Brown & P. Vergragt (Eds.), *Innovations in sustainable consumption: New economics, socio-technical transitions and social practices* (pp. 133–158). Cheltenham, UK: Edward Elgar.

Hockerts, K. (2006). CafeDirect: Fair trade as social entrepreneurship. In F. Perrini (Ed.), *What awaits social entrepreneurial ventures?* (pp. 192–209). Cheltenham, UK: Edward Elgar.

Hondo, H., & Baba, K. (2009). Socio-psychological impacts of the introduction of energy technologies: Change in environmental behavior of households with photovoltaic systems. *Applied Energy*, 87(1), 229–235.

Hostager, T. J., Neil, T. C., Decker, R. L. & Lorentz, R. D. (1998). Seeing environmental opportunities: Effects of intrapreneurial ability, efficacy, motivation and desirability. *Journal of Organizational Change Management*, 11(1), 11–25.

Isaak, R. (2002). The making of the ecopreneur. *Greener Management International*, 2002(38), 81–91.

Kashima, Y., Paladino, A. & Margetts, E. A. (2014). Environmentalist identity and environmental striving. *Journal of Environmental Psychology*, 38(0), 64–75.

Lee, Y.-J., De Young, R. & Marans, R. W. (1995). Factors influencing individual recycling behavior in office settings: A study of office workers in Taiwan. *Environment and Behavior*, 27(3), 380–403.

Linnanen, L. (2002). An insider's experiences with environmental entrepreneurship. *Greener Management International*, 2002(38), 71–80.

Littleford, C., Ryley, T. J. & Firth, S. K. (2014). Context, control and the spillover of energy use behaviours between office and home settings. *Journal of Environmental Psychology*, 40, 157–166.

Markusson, N. (2010). The championing of environmental improvements in technology investment projects. *Journal of Cleaner Production*, 18(8), 777–783.

Mayring, P., & Fenzl, T. (2014). *Qualitative inhaltsanalyse*. Wiesbaden: Springer Fachmedien.

Muster, V., & Schrader, U. (2011). Green work-life balance: A new perspective for green HRM. *German Journal of Research in Human Resource Management*, 25(2), 140–156.

Nyberg, D., Spicer, A. & Wright, C. (2013). Incorporating citizens: Corporate political engagement with climate change in Australia. *Organization*, 20(3), 433–453.

Pichel, K. (2008). Enhancing ecopreneurship through an environmental management system: A longitudinal analysis for factors leading to proactive environmental behavior. In R. Wüstenhagen, J. Hamschmidt, S. Sharma & M. Starik (Eds.), *Advances on research in corporate sustainability* (pp. 141–196). Cheltenham, UK; Northampton, MA, USA: Edward Elgar.

Ramus, C. A. (2001). Organizational support for employees: Encouraging creative ideas for environmental sustainability. *California Management Review*, 43(3), 85.

Rashid, N., & Mohammad, N. (2011). Spillover of environmentally friendly behaviour phenomenon: The mediating effect of employee organizational identification. *OIDA International Journal of Sustainable Development*, 2(12), 29–42.

Rashid, N. R. N. A. & Mohammad, N. (2012). A discussion of underlying theories explaining the spillover of environmentally friendly behavior phenomenon. *Procedia-Social and Behavioral Sciences*, 50, 1061–1072.

Schaltegger, S. (2002). A framework for ecopreneurship. *Greener Management International*, 2002(38), 45–58.

Schaltegger, S., & Wagner, M. (2011). Sustainable entrepreneurship and sustainability innovation: Categories and interactions. *Business Strategy and the Environment*, 20(4), 222–237.

Schrader, U., & Harrach, C. (2013). Empowering responsible consumers to be sustainable intrapreneurs. In U. Schrader & C. Harrach (Eds.), *Enabling responsible living* (pp. 181–192). Berlin Heidelberg: Springer.

Shepherd, D. A., & Patzelt, H. (2011). The new field of sustainable entrepreneurship: Studying entrepreneurial action linking "what is to be sustained" with "what is to be developed." *Entrepreneurship Theory and Practice*, 35(1), 137–163.

Stern, P. (2000). Towards a coherent theory of environmentally significant behavior. *Journal of Social Issues*, 56(3), 322–348.

Stern, P. C., Dietz, T., Abel, T., Guagnano, G. A. & Kalof, L. (1999). A value-belief-norm theory of support for social movements: The case of environmentalism. *Human Ecology Review*, 6(2), 81–98.

Thiers, P. (2002). From grassroots movement to state-coordinated market strategy: The transformation of organic agriculture in China. *Environment and Planning C: Government and Policy, 20*(3), 357–373.

Thøgersen, J. (1999). Spillover processes in the development of a sustainable consumption pattern. *Journal of Economic Psychology, 20*(1), 53–81.

Thøgersen, J. (2004). A cognitive dissonance interpretation of consistencies and inconsistencies in environmentally responsible behavior. *Journal of Environmental Psychology, 24*(1), 93–103.

Thøgersen, J., & Crompton, T. (2009). Simple and painless? The limitations of spillover in environmental campaigning. *Journal of Consumer Policy, 32*(2), 141–163.

Thøgersen, J., & Ölander, F. (2003). Spillover of environment-friendly consumer behaviour. *Journal of Environmental Psychology, 23*(3), 225–236.

Truelove, H. B., Carrico, A. R., Weber, E. U., Raimi, K. T. & Vandenbergh, M. P. (2014). Positive and negative spillover of pro-environmental behavior: An integrative review and theoretical framework. *Global Environmental Change, 29*(0), 127–138.

Van der Werff, E., Steg, L. & Keizer, K. (2013). I am what I am, by looking past the present: The influence of biospheric values and past behavior on environmental self-identity. *Environment and Behavior, 46*(5), 626–657.

Van der Werff, E., Steg, L. & Keizer, K. (2014). Follow the signal: When past pro-environmental actions signal who you are. *Journal of Environmental Psychology, 40*(0), 273–282.

Walley, E., & Taylor, D. W. (2002). Opportunists, champions, mavericks...? *Greener Management International, 2002*(38), 31–43.

Wright, C., Nyberg, D. & Grant, D. (2012). "Hippies on the third floor": Climate change, narrative identity and the micro-politics of corporate environmentalism. *Organization Studies, 33*(11), 1451–1475.

Wüstenhagen, R. (2000). *Ökostrom-von der nische zum massenmarkt: Entwicklungsperspektiven und marketingstrategien für eine zukunftsfähige elektrizitätsbranche* (Vol. 2). St Galen: vdf Hochschulverlag AG.

6 The application of the 'ambidexterity' theoretical perspective to sustainable entrepreneurship

Balancing the sustainability-development equilibrium over time

Laura A. Costanzo

Introduction

Sustainable development has emerged as an influential concept for business and policy makers. There is a growing awareness of pressing environmental issues such as ecosystem degradation and global climate change and the significance of entrepreneurship as the medium to bring great transformation to entire industries for the provision of more sustainable products, services and processes. Sustainability has become a common denominator in many firms' corporate strategies since most large firms now have explicit public sustainability policy statements and claim to apply a "triple bottom line" that considers a firm's financial, environmental, and social performance (Hall *et al.* 2010). Yet, the theory of entrepreneurship is still unclear on the definition of sustainable entrepreneurship. From a theoretical point of view scholars have mostly used the word 'sustainability' to refer to three pillars of a sustainable society, sustainable environment and sustainable economy (Zaman and Goschin 2010). Early literature on sustainable entrepreneurship has addressed these pillars separately and fewer scholars have explored sustainability within the entrepreneurial-orientation debate.

This chapter contributes to the current scholarly debate on sustainability and entrepreneurship by drawing on Shepherd and Patzelt's (2011) definition of sustainable entrepreneurship where the focus is on the *role of the entrepreneurial action linked to the concept of opportunity recognition* in the pursuit of sustainability and development. We augment theoretical knowledge of this phenomenon by positioning the concept of *sustainable entrepreneurship* within the debate of the firm's *entrepreneurial orientation* (EO) and argue that the balancing of *sustainability* with *development*, which is intrinsic in Shepherd and Patzelt's (2011) definition, depends on the organisational and environmental contexts and needs to be addressed simultaneously over time. Hence, this chapter aims to theoretically understand how the aspects of 'sustainability' and 'development' can be achieved over time. To this effect it applies the theoretical lens of ambidexterity largely used in studies of innovation. By doing so we respond to Shepherd and Patzelt's (2011, 136) call for the need of "sustainable entrepreneurship research to explore the role of entrepreneurial action as a mechanism for sustaining nature and eco-systems while providing economic and non-economic gains for investors, entre-preneurs, and societies".

In the next sections, first definitional issues and context and temporal expects of sustainable entrepreneurship are discussed; this is then followed by the con-ceptualisation of sustainable entrepreneurship within the firm's entrepreneurial-orientation literature. Subsequently, building on this literature, we further elaborate our conceptual framework by referring to the ambidexterity theoret-ical perspective. Finally, we apply the contextual ambidexterity perspective to the case of SMEs pursuing a sustainable entrepreneurship posture.

Sustainable entrepreneurship: definitional issues, context and temporal aspects

Scholars have mostly used the word 'sustainability' to refer to three pillars of a sustainable society, sustainable environment and sustainable economy (Zaman and Goschin 2010). Early literature on sustainable entrepreneurship has addressed these pillars separately. For instance, they have been primarily focused on environmental issues (Isaak 1999; Keogh and Polonsky 1998; Kuckertz and Wagner 2010; Linnanen 2002; Pastakia 1998; Schaltegger 2002; Schaper 2002; Walley and Taylor 2002) and the role of entrepreneurs, the so-called enviro-capitalists, who are aimed at the preservation of the space, development of wild-life habitat, the preservation of endangered species, and overall improvement of environmental quality by the utilisation of business and management practices (Anderson and Leal 1997, 3).

Subsequent contributions to the field have focused on social issues primarily on the social aspect of sustainable entrepreneurship (Borzaga and Defourny 2001; Bright et al. 2006; Brinckerhoff 2000; Desa and Kotha 2006; Mair and Martì 2006; Milstein et al. 2006; Nicolls 2006; Prahalad 2005, 2006; Prahalad and Hammond 2002). Studies on social issues have focused on innovations that make goods and/or services more accessible to specific deprived market segments (Desa and Kotha 2006), particularly in the context of bottom-of-the-pyramid (Prahalad 2005, 2006). The social focus of sustainable entrepreneurship over-laps with the concept of social entrepreneurship (Austin et al. 2006; Dacin et al. 2010; Dees and Battle Anderson 2006; Defourny and Nyssens 2010) which "encompasses the activities and processes undertaken to discover, define, and exploit opportunities in order to enhance social wealth by creating new ven-tures or managing existing organizations in an innovative manner" (Zahra et al. 2009, 519). Hence, the social entrepreneurship literature has mainly been con-cerned with case studies of successful non-profit social ventures (e.g. Desa and Kotha 2006; Perrini 2006; Perrini et al. 2010) and the effect of globalisation on opportunities for social entrepreneurship (Zahra et al. 2008). A considerable number of social entrepreneurship case studies have developed particularly to address management and policy issues driven by the pursuit of conflicting missions, socio versus economic goals (Costanzo *et al*. 2014; Smith *et al*. 2010).

The social entrepreneurship literature remains focused on the development of economic and social gains for individuals or societies, but it does not include the environmental aspects, the planet, in terms of sustaining current states of nature, sources of life support, and community. Hence, whilst sustainable entrepreneurship incorporates a focus on the three Ps (profit, people and planet) these elements have not been focused simultaneously. With this in mind, some scholars (Spence *et al*. 2008) have referred to sustainable entrepreneurship as an *entrepreneurial phenomenon* which incorporates the strategic dimension of corporate social responsibility, in that the entrepreneur would demonstrate the ability to achieve viable, liveable and equitable development through the integration and management of natural and human resources in business. Within these studies there have been also distinctions between the incumbent firms that become incrementally more environmentally focused (Isaak 1999) as a necessity to respond and adapt to environmental changes and concerns from the new entrants that offer environmentally oriented products and services by using environmentally friendly processes from the inception of their business operations. However, in these studies we note the absence of the dimension of innovativeness (e.g. radical versus incremental or original versus imitation) which seems to be of considerable relevance in the entrepreneurship literature, for entrepreneurial rents' reasons and as well as *opportunity* pursuit (Linnanen 2002; Walley and Taylor 2002).

A comprehensive definition of sustainable entrepreneurship has recently been offered by Shepherd and Patzelt (2011, 142) where the focus is on the role of the *entrepreneurial action* as a mechanism for sustaining nature and ecosystems while providing economic and non-economic gains for investors, entrepreneurs and societies. Particularly, in Shepherd and Patzelt's words (2011, 142)

> sustainable entrepreneurship is focused on the preservation of nature, life support, and community in the pursuit of perceived opportunities to bring into existence future products, processes, and services for gain, where gain is broadly construed to include economic and non-economic gains to individuals, the economy, and society.

In Shepherd and Patzelt's (2011) definition there is an emphasis on '*what has to be sustained*' and '*what has to be developed*', precisely nature, life support systems and community have to be sustained whilst individuals, the economy and society have to be developed. Furthermore, the two facets of '*development*' and '*sustainability*' should be addressed *simultaneously*. Shepherd and Patzelt (2011) argue that entrepreneurship that addresses sustainability without development (or vice versa) is not sustainable entrepreneurship. At the same time, research that simultaneously addresses the two facets of sustainability and development cannot be defined as sustainable entrepreneurship if the link between sustainability and development does not involve the discovery, creation or exploitation of future goods, processes or services. In sum, in the conceptualisation of sustainable entrepreneurship the *role of the entrepreneurial action linked to the concept of opportunity recognition* is fundamental in the pursuit of *sustainability* and *development*.

The recent literature on sustainable entrepreneurship has consequently attempted to integrate environmental and social aspects (Cohen 2006; Kyrö 2001; Larson 2000), and simultaneously links the *process of entrepreneurship* (Bhave 1997) to the concept of *opportunity recognition*. For instance, building on Venkataraman's (1997) definition, Cohen and Winn (2007, 35) define sustainable entrepreneurship as the investigation of "how opportunities to bring into existence 'future' goods and services are discovered, created, and exploited, by whom, and with what economic, psychological, social, and environmental consequences". Dean and McMullen (2007) take up a similar position; however, they highlight the necessity of adopting a process perspective (Brazeal and Herbert 1999) with their definition of sustainable entrepreneurship as "the process of discovering, evaluating, and numerous respects closely related to exploiting economic opportunities that are present in market failures which detract from sustainability, including those that are environmentally relevant" (Dean and McMullen 2007, 58). Pinkse and Groot (2015, 634) define sustainable entrepreneurship as "the discovery, creation, and exploitation of entrepreneurial opportunities that contribute to sustainability by generating social and environmental gains for others in society (Hockerts and Wüstenhagen 2010; Pacheco *et al.* 2010; Shepherd and Patzelt 2011)". By developing new technologies and business models, sustainable entrepreneurs contribute to resolving environmental degradation and increasing the quality of life to the benefit of consumers, communities and the natural environment (Larson 2000; Schaltegger and Wagner 2011; Shepherd and Patzelt 2011). In these more recent studies of sustainable entrepreneurship there is an increasing alignment of the concept of sustainable entrepreneurship with the pursuit and exploitation of opportunities, thus we argue that the concept of sustainable entrepreneurship cannot be discussed outside the *entrepreneurial-orientation* (EO) debate. Within the latter, the focus is on business management processes to exploit entrepreneurial opportunities that address the triple bottom line.

Furthermore, studies of sustainable entrepreneurship have become concerned with *temporal* and *context* issues and firm size. Gray *et al.* (2014) argue that sustainable entrepreneurship is focused on *enduring* social, economic and environmental benefits. Although sustainable entrepreneurship focuses on the exploitation of opportunities to bring future innovations (Cohen and Winn 2007; Shepherd and Patzelt 2011) for economic, social and environmental gains, the focus is on long-term innovations that represent solutions to environmental, social and/or economic problems. Since natural systems are limiting entrepreneurial actions aimed at improving human well-being must be undertaken within those environmental limits (Hall *et al.* 2010). Yet, the sustainability and development constructs should not neglect the environmental context peculiarities. For instance, Gray *et al.* (2014) questioned whether sustainability is a realistic goal in the context of climate-threatened communities. In contexts, where climate change and biodiversity loss might have moved beyond threshold points, perhaps resilience (Whiteman *et al.* 2013) which focuses on adaptation of the system to exogenous shocks might be a more realistic construct than sustainability. Resilience is "the capacity of a system, enterprise or a person to maintain its core purpose and integrity in the face of dramatically changed circumstances" (Zolli and Healy 2012, 18). Resilience which also resonates with the entrepreneurial concepts of bricolage, effectuation and improvisation (Daniel *et al.* 2015; Di Domenico *et al.* 2010; Fisher 2012) could offer more pragmatic innovative solutions to those economic contexts, i.e. small nations, where response to environmental and ecological change might be difficult because of limitation of high-intensive capital investment programmes.

Hence we conclude that *temporal* and *contextual* attributes disserve careful considerations in sustainable entrepreneurship research. Sustainability and development are constructs that carry a temporal dimension that cannot be confined to cases of single acts of entrepreneurship, i.e. new entrant that through an innovative solution (green innovations) fixes an environmental/ social problem. The outcomes of the entrepreneurial act have to be durable and sustained over a considerable period of time. In the next paragraph, we better frame the concept of sustainable entrepreneurship within the entrepreneurial-oriented (EO) debate by having regard to the temporal and contextual issues.

Sustainable entrepreneurship within the EO debate

Miller's (1983) seminal work is central to the entrepreneurial-orientation debate. Essentially a firm is perceived to be entrepreneurial-oriented if it is innovative, proactive and risk-taking (Lumpkin and Dess 1996). Under Lumpkin and Dess's (1996) concept of entrepreneurship, an EO can exist at different levels: (1) individual because it is often associated with the introduction of a new business concept by an individual (the entrepreneur); (2) small-business firms which are thought to be responsible for job creation and economic growth; (3) corporate level as a means of growth and strategic renewal of existing larger firms.

In recent research by Anderson *et al.* (2015) the EO definition emphasis is placed on the three dimensions of innovativeness, proactiveness and risk-taking (Covin and Slevin 1989, 1991). Precisely entrepreneurial-oriented firms are innovative because they are able to introduce new products, processes and business models; proactive because they are actively entering new product/market spaces and seeking market leadership positions; and they are risk-taking because they demonstrate a willingness among strategic decision makers to contribute resources to projects with uncertain outcomes (Anderson *et al.* 2009). In the analysis of Anderson *et al.* (2015) the focus is on 'entrepreneurial behaviour' which collapses the two components of innovativeness and proactiveness that are inextricably confounded: innovation is a necessary condition for entrepreneurship, yet it is not sufficient, nor is it meaningfully independent from proactiveness (Rosenbusch *et al.* 2011).

The sustainability-development equilibrium within the EO literature

According to Anderson *et al.* (2015) entrepreneurial behaviour ranges in a continuum from a more conservative to a more entrepreneurial one, with the entrepreneurial end of the spectrum evidenced by innovativeness, proactiveness and risk-taking (Covin and Slevin 1989, 1991). Equally sustainable entrepreneurship which is a manifestation of the entrepreneurial orientation of firms that address the triple Ps (profit, people and the planet) can have an entrepreneurial behaviour that ranges in a continuum from a more conservative to a more entrepreneurial one which depends on the dimensions of innovativeness, proactiveness and risk-taking. We argue that innovativeness is about the introduction of innovative solutions that address issues of sustainability and gain for the individual, economy and society, whilst proactiveness is about the creation of new market space that might have an impact on the development of the local economy, individuals and society at large whilst ensuring that nature, environment and communities are sustained. We argue that in this continuum from a more conservative to a more entrepreneurial behaviour, the issue of sustainability and development might be differently focused. For instance, under a more conservative entrepreneurial behaviour the issue of sustainability might be prioritised over the issue of development; whereas under a situation of more entrepreneurial behaviour the issue of development may be prioritised over the issue of sustainability.

We argue that the balancing of sustainability with development, which is intrinsic in Shepherd and Patzelt's (2011) definition, depends on the organisational and environmental contexts and needs to be addressed simultaneously over time. As mentioned earlier, entrepreneurial behaviour is not a perfect correlate of the strategic decision maker's propensity towards risk (Anderson *et al.* 2015). Hence, while the acts of innovation, i.e. new market entry, carry a degree of risk, the antecedents that encourage the undertaking of those specific strategic actions are organisational and/or environmental context-driven that might represent a driver of a firm's entrepreneurial orientation. Furthermore, a sustainable entrepreneurship posture consistent with EO has to be observed over a period of time (Covin and Slevin 1991), in the sense that firms must engage in entrepreneurial behaviours with some reasonable consistency across time (Covin and Lumpkin 2011). It is argued that prior entrepreneurial action reinforces the disposition to engage in future entrepreneurial action (Haynie *et al.*, 2010). From a temporal point of view, the entrepreneur's experience and prior knowledge, found in the subjectivist theory of entrepreneurship (Kor *et al.* 2007), are salient because they can affect the entrepreneurs' perceptions of opportunity (Kor *et al.* 2007) and, therefore, their decision-making in regard to the pursuit of specific acts of entrepreneurships at certain points. This can explain why some firms exhibit higher levels of EO than others despite they might be facing similar contextual opportunities, such as changes in the external environment that resolve in new technological knowledge available or availability of skilled labour. Similarly sustainable entrepreneurship within the entrepreneurial-orientation debate poses temporal considerations: the innovative solutions to environmental concerns cannot resolve in isolated acts of entrepreneurship, but have to be consistent over a prolonged period of time. Hence, there is a need to understand how the aspects of 'sustainability' and 'development' can be achieved over time. To this effect, in the next paragraphs we draw our analysis on the theoretical lens of ambidexterity that has been extensively used in studies of innovation to address the exploitation-exploration relationship.

Ambidexterity in innovation studies

When facing challenging external contexts characterised by technological, regulatory and environmental changes, entrepreneurial-oriented firms are compelled to manage the tension between streamlining their current activities and developing new lines of business (Dougherty 2008; Fauchart and Keilbach 2009; Ford and Ford 1994; Tushman *et al.* 1997). Streamlining the current activities is about alignment which involves efficiency of the current business activities ensuring that existing customers are retained via the undertaking of incremental innovations; whereas developing new business lines is about adaptability which involves a substantial re-arrangement of the business activities that is usually attained with radical innovation (De Clercq *et al.* 2014; De Visser *et al.* 2010; Gibson and Birkinshaw 2004; Raisch and Birkinshaw 2008). In the latter case, entrepreneurial-oriented firms should decide about the commitments of resources to the development of new products or services, to strategies of entry into new market segments or industries and/or new geographical markets.

Mainstream innovation studies have emphasised the need for firms to simultaneously pursue exploitation and exploration activities in relation to the attainment of both incremental and radical innovations, respectively in the short and long term (Andriopoulous and Lewis 2010). In March's (1991) view the basic challenge confronting an organisation was to engage in sufficient exploitation of existing assets and capabilities to ensure its current viability and, at the same time, to devote enough energy to exploration to ensure its future viability (Andriopolous and Lewis 2009; Tushman and O'Reilly 1996). Exploitation activities entail continuous improvement of existing products, services and processes to address the short-term requirements of efficiency and discipline; by contrast, exploration activities entail experimenting with new ideas and innovations in terms of new products, services and processes to address the long-term requirements of flexibility, risk-taking, less formal systems and control (O'Reilly and Tushman 2008). Thus exploitation requirements are in tension with exploration requirements as they involve conflicting tasks demands (Raisch 2006; Raisch and Birkinshaw 2008) and competing firm designs (March 1991; Tushman and O'Reilly 1996). It is argued that in order to survive, innovate and manage these tensions firms should be *ambidextrous* (Duncan 1976), that is the capability of simultaneously addressing the conflicting requirements of exploitation and exploration. A number of quantitative and qualitative empirical studies have investigated the ambidexterity construct in regard to its impact on firm's performance in the short and long term, means to achieve ambidexterity and under what conditions ambidexterity is most useful (O'Reilly and Tushman 2013).

Empirical studies on the antecedents of ambidexterity suggest that under conditions of technological and market uncertainty, ambidexterity is most beneficial and when sufficient resources are available, which is often the case with larger firms than smaller firms, although variations of these effects exist across industries. For instance, Junni *et al.*'s (2013) study found that ambidexterity had stronger effects for the technological firms than for the manufacturing firms. A number of qualitative in-depth case studies has also shown evidence of how ambidexterity plays out over time during the attempts of firms' adaptation to changes in the external environment. O'Reilly and Tushman (2013) in their review concluded that, as suggested by March (1991), either overestimation or underestimation of ambidexterity comes at a cost, whereby firms in order to address the issue of sustainability in the short and long term should achieve a balanced dimension of ambidexterity.

Ambidexterity solutions to manage the exploitation-exploration tensions

Scholars have proposed organisational solutions to manage the exploitation-exploration induced tensions (Raisch and Birkinshaw 2008); these solutions can vary between *architectural ambidexterity* (Gupta *et al.* 2006) and *contextual ambidexterity* (Birkinshaw and Gibson 2004). Proponents of the *architectural ambidexterity* solutions have suggested the spatial separation of the exploitative and explorative activities in separate business units. The separate business units pursuing exploration are smaller, more decentralised and flexible than the business units pursuing exploitation. This differentiation enables ambidextrous organisations to address inconsistent demands arising from emerging and mainstream business opportunities (Gilbert 2005). However, O'Reilly and Tushman (2008) noticed that architectural ambidexterity does not just involve structural separation via different business units, but also different competencies, culture, systems, incentives and processes, each internally aligned. Hence, the separation should be coordinated by targeted integration mechanisms to leverage shared assets (Jansen *et al.* 2006; Raisch and Birkinshaw 2008). These linking mechanisms are largely dependent on the internal organisational context, whereby they are unique to each firm.

Recent contributions have also emphasised that such structural separation might not be necessary when the *organisational context* is characterised by conditions that are complementary to both types of innovative activities (Gibson and Birkinshaw 2004) so that conflicts between opposing demands are balanced.

An organisational context that is characterised by overarching vision, cultural values and flexibility creates internal conditions that facilitate ambidexterity (O'Reilly and Tushman 2008). For instance, Gibson and Birkinshaw (2004) argue that the internal conditions of cooperation, autonomy and rewards are the typical dimensions of *contextual ambidexterity* that occurs at the invidual level. Contextual ambidexterity is "the behavioural capacity to simultaneously demonstrate alignment and adaptability across an entire business unit" (Gibson and Birkinshaw 2004, 209). In other words the balance between exploitation and exploration is an individual task and depends on a supportive organisational context characterised by interaction of stretch, discipline and trust (Gibson and Birkinshaw 2004). Discipline is regarded as an outcome of clear performance standards, expectations, feedback and control mechanisms (Bartlett and Ghosal 1994). Stretch, on the other hand, refers to an organisational context where employees voluntarily push their own standards and expectations to higher levels (Bartlett and Ghosal 1994). Trust is thought to be influenced by perceptions of equity within the organisation, the competence of organisational leaders and level of involvement offered to employees within the organisations (Bartlett and Ghosal 1994). In other words, contextual ambidexterity is focused on the individuals rather than the organisational unit and it enables individuals to make their own judgement as to how divide their time between the conflicting demands of exploitation and exploration (Gibson and Birkinshaw 2004). These individuals are ambidextrous as they are "aligned and efficient in their management of today's business demands while also adaptive to change enough in the environment that they will still be around tomorrow" (Gibson and Birkinshaw 2004, 209).

The concept of contextual ambidexterity suggests that ambidexterity does not require physical separation of the exploration and exploitation activities; rather it can be achieved within the same unit. However, it has been argued (Papachroni *et al.* 2015) that although the concept of contextual ambidexterity does not involve a spatial separation, it often involves a temporal separation between the exploitation and exploration activities at the individual level. In other words contextual ambidexterity occurs when individuals make decisions on exploitation over exploration activities (and vice versa) at different times, depending on the specific circumstances that they face at certain times.

The individual focus of ambidexterity studies has also led to considering personal attributes of ambidextrous managers (Gibson and Birkinshaw 2004; Smith and Tushman 2005) alongside their diverse exposure to knowledge flows (Cohen and Levinthal 1990; Mom *et al.* 2007), social integration (Jansen *et al.* 2008) and senior teams' behavioural integration (Lubatkin *et al.* 2006; O'Reilly and Tushman 2008) as antecedents of ambidexterity. In other words, drawing on Tushman and O'Reilly's (1996) contribution, scholars (Lubatkin *et al.* 2006; Mom *et al.* 2009) have emphasised the critical role deployed by leaders in the ambidextrous coordination of exploitative and explorative innovative activities. Jansen *et al.* (2009) argue for the social integration of the senior team as a means of facilitating, coordinating and managing conflicting demands of structurally separated business units. Similarly, Lubatkin *et al.* (2006) have suggested that behavioural integration of the top management team described by collaborative behaviour, information exchange and joint decision making enhances ambidexterity and firm performance. Fundamentally, top management team processes can enable ambi-dexterity provided that the organisational context is supportive (Carmeli and Halevi 2009).

According to O'Reilly and Tushman (2013) ultimately the key to ambidex-terity is a superior leadership capable of sensing and seizing new opportunities through simultaneous exploitation and exploration and this is the task of leader-ship rather than structural separation. Nevertheless, studies of ambidexterity have also emphasised the role of middle-managers in enabling contextual ambi-dexterity (Mom *et al.* 2007, 2009). Given their position within the organisa-tion, they can enable both top-down and bottom-up and horizontal knowledge inflows that are fundamental to the enactment of exploitation and exploration activities. Ultimately ambidextrous managers are multitaskers, able to deal with tensions and adapt and renew their knowledge and expertise in a flexible and efficient manner (Eisenhardt *et al.* 2010).

Theoretical and empirical gaps in ambidexterity studies

It is noticed that architectural, contextual and leadership solutions to ambi-dexterity to better manage tensions, when dealing with opposing requirements induced by different types of demands, all present overlapping conditions (Chang and Hughes 2012). It is argued that our understanding of ambidex-terity is incomplete until we consider how these conditions come together (Chang and Hughes 2012). Furthermore, it is argued that organisational solu-tions to ambidexterity are static: firms, particularly the existing ones, become ambidextrous by adopting an ideal state of structures and systems at a certain point in time (Raisch *et al.* 2009), thus leading to the concept of *sequential ambidexterity*, the temporal sequence of exploitation and exploration (Venkat-ram *et al.* 2007). This contrasts with the emphasised simultaneity of address-ing exploitation and exploration (Raisch and Birkinshaw 2008); Raisch (2008) argues that these static organisational configurations are inadequate to deal with the range of boundary conditions that an organisation faces over time. Thus, ambidexterity might be the case of dynamic rather than static alignment (Westerman *et al.* 2006), whereby the adoption of time might become an important lens to explore the dynamic emergence of ambidexterity (Raisch *et al.* 2009). On a similar line of reasoning, Papachroni *et al.* (2015) have argued that organisational ambidexterity literature conceptualises exploration and exploitation as conflicting activities, and proposes separation-oriented approaches to accomplish ambidexterity; namely, structural and tem-poral separation. They argue for the need to move beyond such separation-oriented prescriptions toward synthesis or transcendence of dual poles of the phenomenon and as well as toward longitudinal explorations of how tensions dynamically interrelate over time. In this way, the conceptual repertoire of ambidexterity theory is enriched and empirical research can more closely and pragmatically track practice.

Furthermore, it is noticed that studies on ambidexterity, either theoretical or empirical, are largely referred to large firms, i.e. MNEs. Forms of structural ambidexterity require duplication of efforts and might not be a viable option for each firm (Raisch *et al.* 2009); rather resource constraints in SMEs require employees to focus their energies and resources simultaneously on both exploitative and explorative activities concurrently (Lubatkin *et al.* 2006). It is suggested that SMEs are likely to pursue ambidexterity by creating a behavioural context that requires the integration of different activities at the lower level (Andriopoulos and Lewis 2009; Mom *et al.* 2009). Contextual ambidexterity is also identified as a 'harmonic' view of ambidexterity. However, little empirical research has been carried out to explore conditions of contextual ambidexterity, particularly in regard to SMEs (Patel *et al.* 2013).

Apart from a few studies (Chang and Hughes 2012; Lubatkin *et al.* 2006; Voss and Voss 2013) ambidexterity to manage tensions between exploration and exploitation activities is not explored within the context of SMEs, which understandably present issues that are different from those of large organisations, hence prescriptions on how to achieve ambidexterity, generally elaborated for large companies, cannot be easily applied to SMEs. For instance, it is noticed that SMEs are resource-constrained with limited access to specific internal and external resources; particularly, they are limited in the access to human and financial capital and managerial expertise (Forbes and Milliken 1999). These contextual constraints limit their capabilities of managing change in relation to the requirements of simultaneous alignment and adaptation. At the same time, SMEs are less bureaucratic than large organisations; they have fewer formalities, procedures, systems and planning activities than their larger counterparts. On the one hand, such organisational characteristics can represent a driver of innovation activities as informal structures are conducive to an internal environment which favours innovation in general; on the other hand, they can also represent a hindrance to innovation in contexts where tensions between conflicting demands have to be managed. As Andriopoulos and Lewis (2009) stated in their study of small firms in the design/consultancy industry, SMEs face more challenges in managing contradictions, conflicts and tensions associated with both exploitative and explorative innovations. Drawing on Cao *et al.* (2009), Chang and Hughes (2012) argue that a 'balanced dimension' of ambidexterity that accounts for architectural, context and leadership dimensions at the same time is more suitable to manage tensions within SMEs.

Given such theoretical developments in the domain of ambidexterity and entrepreneurship, we argue that the field of sustainable entrepreneurship represents a fertile terrain for the application and the extension of the ambidexterity theoretical lens. In the next section we explore this potential by focusing our analysis on sustainable entrepreneurship positioned within the entrepreneurial-orientation debate. In doing so, we also fill a gap in current studies of ambidexterity which seem to have overlooked the internal frictions that might result from adopting an ambidextrous posture (Raisch and Birkinshaw 2008).

The application of the ambidexterity lens to the management of tensions within sustainable entrepreneurship

Studies on the management of exploitation-exploration tensions have historically been dominant in the profit sector. To the best of our knowledge, neither conceptual nor empirical research has investigated the application of the ambidexterity perspective to the field of sustainable entrepreneurship. This chapter attempts to address this gap and, in doing so, we particularly draw on Shepherd and Patzelt's (2011) conceptualisation which captures the two fundamental and interrelated constructs of SE, that are 'what has to be sustained' and 'what has to be developed', precisely nature, life support systems and community have to be sustained whilst individuals, the economy and society have to be developed. We particularly focus our analysis on the SMEs that in the pursuit of sustainable entrepreneurship initiatives are not immune from the tensions that exist between alignment and adaptation. These firms are committed to the continuous improvement of existing products, services and processes which bring gain to individuals, economy and society whilst sustaining nature, life support systems and community; yet, they also face dynamic environments where issues of growth and profitability compel firms to adapt their activities. Such adaptation can take place via entry strategies in new markets or existing ones with new products and services. In these contexts, it is the managing of the exploitation-exploration activities and their relationships in terms of resource commitment that can potentially arm the 'sustainability-development' equilibrium relationship. As noticed earlier, entrepreneurial behaviours range along a continuum from more conservative (i.e. exploitation activities) to more entrepreneurial (i.e. exploration activities); at the same time, entrepreneurial decisions range along a continuum from 'sustainability' to 'development', which respectively represent the two poles of tension. The 'sustainability-development' equilibrium, which is intrinsic in Shepherd and Patzelt's (2011) conceptualisation, can be undermined if decisions and subsequent entrepreneurial acts linked to opportunity recognition are mainly concerned with exploration activities; in other words, their focus is predominately on 'development' issues thus neglecting considerations of 'sustainability'.

The issue of managing tensions between conflicting demands has already been addressed by studies on social entrepreneurship. Smith et al.'s (2012) findings suggested that the 'temporal' element had an influence on the degree of tension between the economic and social components of social enterprises' (SEs) mission statements. For instance, SEs at birth seemed to experience fewer tensions as the social service and business identities were often more fully integrated. The timing of multiple identities also directly affected the type of management responses to address such tensions (Smith et al. 2012). Particularly, during the development stage it was found that the management approaches of compartmentalisation, deletion and integration were used when one existing identity (social service) preceded the introduction of another identity (business identity). In contrast with this, when an organisation began with a hybrid identity, the identity tension was often managed through integration and the establishment of a meta-identity. Costanzo *et al.*'s (2014) cross-sectional qualitative study of dual mission management of a group of established UK social firms found that approaches to dual mission management varied along a continuum ranging from the dimension of high compartmentalisation to the dimension of high integration. In sum, studies on managing tensions in social enterprises suggest different approaches to attending to competing demands, including temporal or spatial separation and seeking synergies though integration of competing demands. Some social enterprises alternated their focus over time between social concerns and business purposes, illustrating temporal separation (Jay 2013). Others created boundaries between their business ventures and social missions illustrating spatial separation (Battilana *et al.* 2012; Battilana *et al.* 2015). Other social enterprises developed novel structures that integrated social with business ventures (Smith *et al.* 2007; Smith *et al.* 2010). In line with most ambidexterity studies in other sectors, social enterprises seem to have opted for models of architectural ambidexterity and/or contextual ambidexterity. In some cases (Costanzo *et al.* 2014) specific contextual processes such as strategic planning, tailored production processes and blended governance and management structures seemed to be critical key drivers of integration approaches to dual mission management.

In the spirit of Shepherd and Patzelt's (2011) conceptualisation, we argue that the 'sustainability-development' equilibrium is incompatible with mechanisms of 'spatial' and 'temporal' separations found in social entrepreneurship. Since sustainability and development have to be simultaneously addressed, their relationship is more compatible with solutions of contextual ambidexterity that move beyond separation-oriented prescriptions toward synthesis of the two poles of the phenomenon. Particularly, we propose that contextual ambidexterity supporting alignment-adaptation strategic initiatives alongside the sustainability-development equilibrium requires specific contextual mechanisms: leadership values and intra-firm mechanisms of knowledge integration and exchanges. In the next section we discuss these mechanisms.

Contextual ambidexterity in sustainable entrepreneurship

Entrepreneurial decisions of exploration activities require long-term commitment and investments that can pose conflicting demands on the economic, social and environmental mission components. Thus the tension between exploitation and exploration activities, which is common to any type of enterprise, further aggravates the persistent conflicting demands that a triple-bottom-line posture poses to firms embracing sustainable entrepreneurship. Specifically, firms with such posture face a number of tensions in regard to:

investment decisions in highly profitable unrelated business activities versus alignment of existing activities that maintain a steady status of the environment, community and society; the attraction and hiring of highly talented and skilled staff with a strong business mind-set versus socially disadvantaged staff and/or employees who have more sensitivity towards the environment, community and altruism; stakeholders' expectations of achieving high economic value towards social and environmental values.

Scholars have also indicated four primary drivers of business decisions regarding sustaining the natural environment: values, economic opportunities, legislation and stakeholder pressures (Bansal and Roth 2000). Sometimes, these drivers can bring divergence between 'sustainability' and 'development'. For instance, the attractiveness of growing more profitable markets might shift leaders' decision focus from the issues of environmental sustainability towards more the pursuit of economic values. On the other hand, it has been found that top managers' personal values can influence decisions that impact the natural environment (Agle *et al.* 1999; Lawrence and Morrell 1995). Shepherd *et al.* (2013) argue that entrepreneurs' assessments of the attractiveness of opportunities that harm the natural environment depend on the simultaneous impact of values and personal agency. In their study of 83 business founders they found that under specific circumstances, decision makers cognitively disengage from their pro-environmental values, and perceive opportunities that harm the environment as highly attractive. Particularly, the extent of founders' disengagement of their pro-environmental values was stronger when they had high, rather than low, entrepreneurial self-efficacy, and stronger when industry munificence was perceived as low rather than high.

Leaders' strategic entrepreneurial decisions are also influenced by their dominant logic (Bettis and Prahalad 1995; Meyer and Heppard 2000) which reflects top management beliefs, attitudes and philosophies regarding the value and advisability of entrepreneurial actions. Such dominant logic is shaped by their previous experience and knowledge of environmental issues as well (Patzelt and Shepherd 2011). For instance, Patzelt and Shepherd (2011) indicated that opportunity recognition, based on the solo entrepreneurial knowledge and economic motivation, are insufficient to explain the recognition of opportunities for sustainable development. Patzelt and Shepherd's (2011) research suggests that entrepreneurs are more likely to discover sustainable development opportunities the greater their knowledge of natural and communal environments becomes, the more they perceive that the natural and communal environment in which they live is threatened, and the greater their altruism toward others becomes. These relationships are strengthened when the individuals possess prior entrepreneurial knowledge (Shane 2000). In other words, there is a complementary relationship between entrepreneurial knowledge and knowledge of the natural/communal environment, perceptions of threat and motivation of altruism. Entrepreneurial knowledge is a mechanism that facilitates the transformation of the environmental knowledge into the recognition of sustainable development opportunities (Patzelt and Shepherd 2011).

Furthermore, knowledge exchanges within firms are an important mechanism for ambidextrous firms in order to ensure a balancing between alignment and adaptability activities (De Clercq *et al.* 2014). In regard to a sustainable entrepreneurship posture, internal flows of knowledge exchanged between managers who are responsible for different functional activities, have a direct impact on how ambidexterity benefits the entire firm (Gibson and Birkinshaw 2004). Contextual ambidexterity requires managers who hold different function-specific knowledge to recognise how they can draw from and use one another's current knowledge domains in order to incrementally refine and improve their existing activities (He and Wong 2004; Lubatkin *et al.* 2006). At the same time individual managers have the flexibility to develop radically new knowledge on the basis of the differences that exist between their own knowledge domain and that of colleagues specialising in other areas (Lane and Lubatkin 1998; March 1991). Thus, individual managers in ambidextrous firms tend to refine both their own and others' current practices and develop new strategic lenses in the course of the interactions they have with one another (Dougherty 2008). Under conditions of strong internal rivalry, managers may be reluctant to share knowledge with 'competing' functional areas, which prevents them from gaining access to new knowledge or integrating their own knowledge with that of others (De Clercq *et al.* 2014). By contrast, high levels of external rivalry and associated perceptions of external threats to the firm may bring managers together, across the firm's ranks, such that these conditions motivate them to openly share knowledge with one another, with the ultimate goal of defending the firm as a whole against outside threats (Lahiri *et al.* 2008). SMEs adopting a sustainable entrepreneurship posture need to consider the competitive context surrounding their intrafirm knowledge exchange. When these ambidextrous firms are marked by high levels of internal rivalry for resource allocation, exchanges between entrepreneurial and environmental knowledge may reduce and disruptive power games may unfold, thus undermining the sustainability-development equilibrium. Yet, under low managerial perception of external threats to the environment, community and society, there is a limited perception of the need to combine and integrate different knowledges. Hence, in SMEs high individual awareness of external threats combined with reduced internal rivalry among managers for resource allocation can facilitate an ambidextrous posture for the attainment of the sustainability-development equilibrium over time.

Conclusions

Building on Shepherd and Patzelt's (2011) concept of sustainable entrepreneurship, this chapter applied the theoretical lens of ambidexterity to shed light on how SMEs can achieve the sustainability-development equilibrium over time within an entrepreneurial-oriented posture. We particularly addressed the issue of the 'sustainability-development' equilibrium that can be undermined if entrepreneurial acts are predominately focused on adaptation activities in the pursuit of attractive business opportunities, thus jeopardising the aspect of 'sustainability'.

Drawing on previous studies of ambidexterity, we further elaborated the concept of contextual ambidexterity as an appropriate theoretical lens that enables leaders to address the tension between the two poles of 'sustainability' and 'development'. We proposed that contextual ambidexterity requires (1) supportive leadership values such as a sensitivity to environmental, communal and societal values alongside altruism and (2) intra-firm mechanisms of knowledge integration and exchanges.

Our discussion has mainly focused on the concept of contextual ambidexterity since ambidexterity approaches based on spatial and temporal separations are incompatible with the sustainability-development relationship. Furthermore, since the tensions between the two poles of sustainable entrepreneurship are permanent, we propose that the ambidexterity construct can be enriched by the consideration of the paradox lens (Costanzo and Di Domenico 2015; Papachroni *et al.* 2015) in order to move beyond a static view of ambidexterity towards a synthesis of paradoxical poles. The latter can be achieved via longitudinal explorations of how the paradoxical poles of 'sustainability' and 'development' interact dynamically over time. These longitudinal explorations would enrich the ambidexterity theoretical perspective which has been largely constrained by cross-sectional studies and spatial and temporal separation prescriptions. They would also enrich the sustainable entrepreneurship and entrepreneurial-oriented debates by having regard to leaders' dominant logic (Bettis and Prahalad 1995), their shared beliefs and entrepreneurial motivation (Shane *et al.* 2003) as antecedents of acts of sustainable entrepreneurship.

Empirical research of sustainable entrepreneurship could also investigate the EO-performance relationship in different regional contexts since the latter can differently affect the sustainability-development dynamics. Studies have extensively emphasised the positive effect of an entrepreneurial orientation on firm's performance (Wang 2008) in different regional contexts, i.e. developed versus developing economies (Puumalainen *et al.* 2015; Rodrigues and Raposo 2011; Tang and Tang 2012; Tang *et al.* 2008; Yusuf 2002), different industries, such as manufacturing (Jantunen *et al.* 2005) and services industries. The EO-performance relationship is context specific and the dimensions of EO may vary independently of each other in a given context. Hence, while the acts of innovation, i.e. new market entry, carry a degree of risk, the antecedents that encourage the undertaking of those specific strategic actions are organisational and/or environmental context-driven. This has also policy implications. Regional governmental policies often provide economic incentives to motivate entrepreneurs to pursue and exploit opportunities that sustain the natural and communal environments while generating social gains (e.g. Lewis and Wiser 2007). However, empirical research is needed to verify the effectiveness of such programmes by having regard to the EO-performance relationship and its inherent impact on the sustainability and development dynamics, which are both context specific. The empirical results of the EO-performance relationship investigations may shed new knowledge on the salient variables affecting this relationship by having regard to the issue of sustainability and development that have to be simultaneously addressed. Policy makers should also be cognisant of the nuanced interplay between the entrepreneurial start-ups and incumbents, which are often driven by different motivations in the pursuit of sustainability, and design policies that favour cooperation amongst different players, which ultimately can result in the transformation of entire industries into rich sustainable systems rather than isolated environmental interventions.

Management implications include the important role of leaders whose degree of prior exposure and sensitivity to environmental issues and altruism would impact on strategies of sustainable entrepreneurship and integration between entrepreneurial and environmental knowledge. At the same time leaders should support cultural contexts that minimise internal rivalry for knowledge sharing and maximise internal co-operation in the face of external threats to both 'sustainability' and 'development'. These management aspects should be echoed by the development of comprehensive interdisciplinary management education programmes that are closer to the field of sustainable entrepreneurship, and are drawn on theories of entrepreneurship, strategic management and environmental sciences and technology.

References

Agle B.R., Mitchell R.K. and Sonnenfeld J.A. (1999) "Who matters to CEOs? An investigation of stakeholder attributes and salience, corporate performance, and CEO values" *Academy of Management Journal, 42* 507–525.

Anderson B.S., Covin J.G. and Slevin D.P. (2009) "Understanding the relationship between entrepreneurial orientation and strategic learning: An empirical investigation" *Strategic Entrepreneurship Journal, 3* 219–241.

Anderson B.S., Kreiser P.M., Kuratko D.F., Hornsby J.S. and Yoshihiro E. (2015) "Reconceptualizing entrepreneurial orientation" *Strategic Management Journal 36* 1579–1596.

Anderson T.L. and Leal D.R. (1997) "The rise of the enviro-capitalists" *Wall Street Journal – Eastern Edition, 230* A16.

Andriopoulous C. and Lewis M.W. (2009) "Exploitation-exploration tensions and organizational ambidexterity: Managing paradoxes of innovation" *Organization Science, 20* 696–717.

Andriopoulous C. and Lewis M.W. (2010) "Managing innovation paradoxes: Ambidexterity lessons from leading product design companies" *Long Range Planning, 43* 104–122.

Austin J., Stevenson H. and Wei-Skillern J. (2006) "Social and commercial entrepreneurship: Same, different or both?" *Entrepreneurship Theory and Practice, 30* 1–22.

Bansal P. and Roth K. (2000) "Why companies go green: A model of ecological responsiveness" *Academy of Management Journal, 43* 717–736.

Bartlett C.A. and Ghosal S. (1994) *Managing across borders* Harvard Business School Press, Boston.

Battilana J., Lee M., Walker J. and Dorsey C. (2012) "In search of the hybrid ideal" *Stanford Social Innovation Review, 10* 50–55.

Battilana J., Singul M., Pache A.C. and Model J. (2015) "Harnessing productive tensions in hybrid organizations: The case of work integration social enterprises" *Academy of Management Journal, 58* 1658–1685.

Bettis R.A. and Prahalad C.K. (1995) "The dominant logic: Retrospective and extension" *Strategic Management Journal, 16* 5–14.

Bhave M.P. (1997) "A process model of entrepreneurial venture creation" *Journal of Business Venturing, 9* 223–242.

Birkinshaw K. and Gibson C. (2004) "Building ambidexterity into an organization" *MIT Sloan Management Review, 45* 46–55.

Brazeal D.V. and Herbert T.T. (1999) "The genesis of entrepreneurship" *Entrepreneurship Theory & Practice, 23* 29–45.

Bright D.S., Fry R. and Cooperrider D.L. (2006) "Transformative innovations for mutual benefit in business, society and environment" *Academy of Management Meeting*, Atlanta, GA.

Borzaga C. and Defourny J. (2001) "Conclusions: Social enterprises in Europe: A diversity of initiatives and prospects" in Borzaga C. and Defourny J. (Eds) *The emergence of social enterprise*, 350–371, Routledge, London.

Brinckerhoff P.C. (2000) *Social entrepreneurship: The art of mission-based venture development* John Wiley & Sons, New York.

Cao Q., Gedajlovic, E. and Zhang H. (2009) "Unpacking organizational ambidexterity: Dimensions, contingencies, and synergistic effects" *Organization Science, 20* 781–796.

Carmeli A. and Halevi M.Y. (2009) "How top management team behavioral integration and behavioral complexity enable organizational ambidexterity: The moderating role of contextual ambidexterity" *Leadership Quarterly, 20* 207–218.

Chang Y.Y. and Hughes M. (2012) "Drivers of innovation ambidexterity in small- to medium-sized firms" *European Management Journal, 30* 1–17.

Cohen B. (2006) "Sustainable valley entrepreneurial ecosystems" *Business Strategy and the Environment, 15* 1–14.

Cohen B. and Winn M.L. (2007) "Market imperfections, opportunity and sustainable entrepreneurship" *Journal of Business Venturing, 22* 29–49.

Cohen W.M. and Levinthal D.A. (1990) "Absorptive capacity: A new perspective on learning and innovation" *Administrative Science Quarterly, 35* 128–152.

Costanzo L.A. and Di Domenico M.L. (2015) "A multi-level dialectical-paradox lens for top management team strategic decision-making in a corporate venture" *British Journal of Management, 26* 484–506.

Costanzo L.A., Vurro C., Foster D., Servato F. and Perrini F. (2014) "Dual-mission management in social entrepreneurship: Qualitative evidence from social firms in the UK" *Journal of Small Business Management, 52* 655–677.

Covin J.G. and Lumpkin G.T. (2011) "Entrepreneurial orientation theory and research: Reflections on a needed construct" *Entrepreneurship Theory & Practice, 35* 855–872.

Covin J.G and Slevin D.P. (1989) "Strategic management of small firms in hostile and benign environments" *Strategic Management Journal, 10* 75–87.

Covin J.G. and Slevin D.P. (1991) "A conceptual model of entrepreneurship as firm behaviour" *Entrepreneurship Theory & Practice, 16* 7–24.

Dacin P.A., Dacin M.T. and Matear M. (2010) "Social entrepreneurship: Why we don't need a new theory and how we move forward from here" *Academy of Management Perspective, 24* 37–57.

Daniel E.M., Di Domenico M.L. and Sharma S. (2015) "Effectuation and home-based online business entrepreneurs" *International Small Business Journal, 33* 799–823.

Dean T.J. and McMullen J.S. (2007) "Toward a theory of sustainable entrepreneurship: Reducing environmental degradation through entrepreneurial action" *Journal of Business Venturing, 22* 50–76.

De Clercq D., Thongpapanl N. and Dimov D. (2014) "Contextual ambidexterity in SMEs: The roles of internal and external rivalry" *Small Business Economics, 42* 191–205.

Dees G. and Battle Anderson B. (2006) "Framing a theory of social entrepreneurship: Building on two schools of practice and thought" ARNOVA *Occasional Paper Series, 1* 39–66.

Defourny J. and Nyssens M. (2010) "Conceptions of social enterprise and social entrepreneurship in Europe and United States: Convergences and divergences" *Journal of Social Entrepreneurship, 1* 32–53.

Desa G. and Kotha S. (2006) "Ownership mission and environment: An exploratory analysis into the evolution of a technology social venture" in Mair J., Robertson J. and Hockerts K. (Eds) *Social entrepreneurship* Palgrave Macmillan, New York.

De Visser M., de Weerd-Nederhof P., Faems D., Song M., van Looy B. and Visscher K. (2010) "Structural ambidexterity in NPD processes: A firm-level assessment of the impact of differential structures on innovation performance" *Technovation, 30* 291–299.

Di Domenico M.L., Haugh H. and Tracey, P. (2010) "Social bricolage: Theorizing social value creation in social enterprises" *Entrepreneurship: Theory & Practice, 34* 681–703.

Dougherty D. (2008) "Bridging social constraint and social action to design organizations for innovation" *Organization Science, 29* 415–434.

Duncan R.B. (1976) "The ambidextrous organization: Designing dual structures for innovation" in Kilmann R.H., Pondy L.R. and Slevin D. (Eds) *The management of organization design: Strategies and implementation,* 167–188, North Holland, New York.

Eisenhardt K.M., Furr N.R. and Bingham C.B. (2010) "Microfoundations of performance: Balancing efficiency and flexibility in dynamic environments" *Organization Science, 21*(6) 1263–1273.

Fauchart E. and Keilbach M. (2009) "Testing a model of exploration and exploitation as innovation strategies" *Small Business Economics, 33* 257–272.

Fisher G. (2012) "Effectuation, causation and bricolage: A behavioural comparison of emerging theories in entrepreneurship research" *Entrepreneurship Theory and Practice* 36 1019–1051.

Forbes D.P. and Milliken F.J. (1999) "Cognition and corporate governance: Understanding boards of directors as strategic decision-making groups" *Academy of Management Review, 24* 489–505.

Ford J.D. and Ford L.W. (1994) "Logics of identity, contradiction, and attraction in change" *Academy of Management Review, 19* 756–795.

Gibson C. and Birkinshaw J. (2004) "The antecedents, consequences, and mediating role of organizational ambidexterity" *Academy of Management Journal, 47* 209–226.

Gilbert C. (2005) "Unbundling the structure of inertia: Resource versus routine rigidity" *Academy of Management Journal, 48* 741–763.

Gray B.J., Duncan S., Kirkwood J. and Walton S. (2014) "Encouraging sustainable entrepreneurship in climate-threatened communities: A Samoan case study" *Entrepreneurship Theory & Practice, 26* 401–430.

Gupta A.K., Smith K.G. and Shalley C.E. (2006). "The interplay between exploration and exploitation" *Academy Management Journal, 4* 693–706.

Hall J.K., Daneke G.A. and Lenox M.J. (2010) "Sustainable development and entrepreneurship: Past contributions and future directions" *Journal of Business Venturing, 25* 439–448.

Haynie J.M., Shepherd D., Mosakowski E. and Earley P.C. (2010) "A situated metacognitive model of the entrepreneurial mindset" *Journal of Business Venturing, 25* 217–229.

He Z. and Wong P. (2004) "Exploration vs. exploitation: An empirical test of the ambidexterity hypothesis" *Organization Science, 15* 481–494.

Hockerts K. and Wüstenhagen R. (2010) "Greening Goliaths versus emerging Davids – Theorizing about the role of incumbents and new entrants in sustainable entrepreneurship" *Journal of Business Venturing, 25* 481–492.

Isaak R. (1999) *Green logic: Ecopreneurship, theory and ethics* Kumarian, West Hartford, CT.

Jansen J.P., van den Bosch F.A. and Volberda H.W. (2006) "Exploratory innovation, exploitative innovation and performance effects: Effects of organizational antecedents and environmental moderators" *Management Science, 52* 1661–1674.

Jansen J.J.P., George G., van den Bosch F.A.J. and Volberda H.W. (2008) "Senior team attributes and organizational ambidexterity: The moderating role of transformational leadership" *Journal of Management Studies, 45* 982–1007.

Jansen J.J.P., Tempelaar M.P., van den Bosch F.A.J. and Volberda H.W. (2009) "Structural differentiation and ambidexterity: The mediating role of integration mechanisms" *Organization Science, 20* 797–811.

Jantunen A., Puumalainen K., Saarenketo S. and Kyläheiko K. (2005) "Entrepreneurial orientation, dynamic capabilities and international performance" *Journal of International Entrepreneurship, 3* 223–243.

Jay J. (2013) "Navigating paradox as a mechanism of change and innovation in hybrid organizations" *Academy of Management Journal, 56*(1) 137–159.

Junni P., Sarala R.M., Taras V. and Tarba S.Y. (2013) "Organizational ambidexterity and performance: A meta-analysis" *Academy of Management Perspectives, 27* 299–312.

Keogh P.D. and Polonsky M.J. (1998) "Environmental commitment: A basis for environmental entrepreneurship?" *Journal of Organizational Change Management, 11* 38–49.

Kor Y., Mahoney J.T. and Michael S.C. (2007) "Resources, capabilities and entrepreneurial perceptions" *Journal of Management Studies, 44* 1187–1212.

Kuckertz A. and Wagner M. (2010) "The influence of sustainability orientation on entrepreneurial intentions: Investigating the role of business experience" *Journal of Business Venturing, 25* 524–539.

Kyrö P. (2001) "To grow or not to grow? Entrepreneurship and sustainable development" *International Journal of Sustainable Development and World Ecology, 8* 15–28.

Lahiri S., Perez-Nordtvedt L. and Renn R.W. (2008) "Will the new competitive landscape cause your firm's decline? It depends on your mindset" *Business Horizons, 51* 311–320.

Lane P.J. and Lubatkin M. (1998) "Relative absorptive capacity and interorganizational learning" *Strategic Management Journal, 19* 461–477.

Larson A.L. (2000) Sustainable innovation through an entrepreneurship lens" *Business Strategy and the Environment, 9* 304–317.

Lawrence A. and Morrell D. (1995) "Leading-edge environmental management" in Post J. (Ed.) *Research in corporate social performance and policy*, 99–126, JAI, Greenwich, CT.

Lewis J.I. and Wiser R.H. (2007) "Fostering a renewable energy technology industry: An international comparison of wind industry policy support mechanisms" *Energy Policy, 35* 1844–1857.

Linnanen L. (2002) "An insider's experiences with environmental entrepreneurship" *Greener Management International, 38* 71–80.

Lubatkin M.H., Simsek Z., Ling Y. and Veiga J.F. (2006) "Ambidexterity and performance in small-to-medium-sized firms: The pivotal role of top management team behavioural integration" *Journal of Management, 32* 646–672.

Lumpkin G.T. and Dess G.G. (1996) "Clarifying the entrepreneurial orientation construct and linking it to performance" *Academy of Management Review, 21* 135–172.

Mair J. and Martì I. (2006) "Social entrepreneurship research: A source of explanation, prediction, and delight" *Journal of World Business, 41* 36–44.

March J.G. (1991) "Exploration and exploitation in organizational learning" *Organization Science, 2* 71–87.

Meyer G.D. and Heppard K.A. (2000) *Entrepreneurship as strategy: Competing on the entrepreneurial edge* Sage, Thousand Oaks, CA.

Miller D. (1983) "The correlates of entrepreneurship in three types of firms" *Management Science, 29* 770–791.

Milstein M.B., London T. and Hart, S. (2006) "Capturing the opportunity of creating a more inclusive capitalism" *Academy of Management Meeting*, Atlanta, GA.

Mom T.J., van den Bosch F.A. and Volberda H.W. (2007) 'Investigating managers' exploration and exploitation activities: The influence of top-down, bottom-up, and horizontal knowledge inflows" *Journal of Management Studies, 44* 910–931.

Mom T.J., van den Bosch F.A.J. and Volberda H.W. (2009) "Understanding variation in managers' ambidexterity: Investigating direct and interaction effects of formal structural and personal coordination mechanisms" *Organization Science, 20* 812–828.

Nicholls A. (2006) *Social entrepreneurship: New models of sustainable social change* Oxford University Press, Oxford.

O'Reilly III C.A. and Tushman M.L. (2008) "Ambidexterity as a dynamic capability: Resolving the innovator's dilemma" *Research on Organizational Behaviour, 28* 185–206.

O'Reilly III C.A. and Tushman M.L. (2013) "Organizational ambidexterity: Past, present, and future" *Academy of Management Perspectives, 27* 324–338.

Pacheco D.F., Dean T.J. and Payne D.S. (2010) "Escaping the green prison: Entrepreneurship and the creation of opportunities for sustainable development" *Journal of Business Venturing, 25* 464–480.

Papachroni A., Heracleous L. and Paroutis S. (2015) "Organizational ambidexterity through the lens of paradox theory: Building a novel research agenda" *Journal of Applied Behavioral Science, 51* 71–93.

Pastakia A. (1998) "Grassroots ecopreneurs: Change agents for a sustainable society" *Journal of Organizational Change Management, 11* 157–174.

Patel P., Ankaj C., Messersmith J.G and Lepak D.P. (2013) "Walking the tightrope: An assessment of the relationship between high-performance work systems and organizational ambidexterity" *Academy of Management Journal, 56* 1420–1442.

Patzelt H. and Shepherd D.A. (2011) "Recognizing opportunities for sustainable development" *Entrepreneurship Theory & Practice, 35* 631–652.

Perrini F. (2006) *The new social entrepreneurship: What awaits social entrepreneurial ventures?* Edward Elgar, Cheltenham, UK.

Perrini F., Vurro C. and Costanzo L.A. (2010) "A process-based view of social entrepreneurship: From opportunity identification to scaling-up social change in the case of San Patrignano" *Entrepreneurship and Regional Development, 5.*

Pinkse J. and Groot K. (2015) "Sustainable entrepreneurship and corporate political activity: Overcoming market barriers in the clean energy sector" *Entrepreneurship Theory & Practice, 39* 633–654.

Puumalainen K., Sjögrén H., Syrjä P. and Barraket J. (2015) "Comparing social entrepreneurship across nations: An exploratory study of institutional effects" *Canadian Journal of Administrative Sciences, 32* 276–287.

Prahalad C.K. (2005) *The fortune at the bottom of the pyramid* Wharton School Publishers, Pennsylvania, NJ.

Prahalad C.K. (2006) "The innovation sandbox" *Strategy + Business, 44* 1–10.

Prahalad C.K. and Hammond A. (2002) "Serving the world's poor profitably" *Harvard Business Review, 80* 48–57.

Raisch S. (2006) "Exploration vs. exploitation: A metaparadigm view of the ambidextrous organisational forms" *Annual Meeting of the Academy of Management,* Atlanta, GA.

Raisch S. (2008) "Balanced structures: Designing organizations for profitable growth" *Long Range Planning, 41* 483–508.

Raisch S. and Birkinshaw J. (2008) "Organizational ambidexterity: Antecedents, outcomes, and moderators" *Journal of Management, 34* 375–409.

Raisch S., Birkinshaw J., Probst G. and Tushman M.L. (2009) "Organizational ambidexterity: Balancing exploitation and exploration for sustained performance" *Organization Science, 20* 685–695.

Rodrigues R.G. and Raposo M. (2011) "Entrepreneurial orientation, human resources information management, and firm performance in SMEs" *Canadian Journal of Administrative Sciences, 28* 143–153.

Rosenbusch N., Brinckmann J. and Bausch A. (2011) "Is innovation always beneficial? A meta-analysis of the relationship between innovation and performance in SMEs" *Journal of Business Venturing, 26* 441–457.

Schaltegger S. (2002) "A framework for ecopreneurship" *Greener Management International, 38* 45–59.

Schaltegger S. and Wagner M. (2011) "Sustainable entrepreneurship and sustainability innovation: Categories and interactions" *Business Strategy and the Environment, 20* 222–237.

Schaper M. (2002) "The essence of ecopreneurship" *Greener Management International, 38* 26–30.

Shane S. (2000) "Prior knowledge and the discovery of entrepreneurial opportunities" *Organization Science 11* 448–469.

Shane S., Locke E.A. and Collins C.J. (2003) "Entrepreneurial motivation" *Human Resource Management Review, 13*(2) 257–280.

Shepherd D.A. and Patzelt H. (2011) "The new field of sustainable entrepreneurship: Studying entrepreneurial action linking 'what is to be sustained' with 'what is to be developed'" *Entrepreneurship Theory & Practice, 35* 137–163.

Shepherd D.A., Patzelt H. and Baron R.A. (2013) "'I care about nature, but…': Disengaging values in assessing opportunities that cause harm" *Academy of Management Journal, 56* 1251–1273.

Smith B.R, Knapp J., Barr T.F, Stevens C.E. and Cannatelli B.L. (2010) "Social enterprises and the timing of conception: Organizational identity tension, management and marketing" *Journal of Nonprofit & Public Sector Marketing, 22,* 108–134.

Smith W. and Tushman M.L. (2005) "Managing strategic contradictions: A top management model for managing innovation stream" *Organization Science, 16* 522–536.

Smith W.K., Leonard H. and Epstein M. (2007) *Digital divide data: A social enterprise in action* Harvard Business School Case Study.

Smith W.K., Besharov M.L., Wessels A.K. and Chertok M. (2012) "A paradoxical leadership model for social entrepreneurs: Challenges, leadership skills, and pedagogical tools for managing social and commercial demands" *Academy of Management Learning & Education, 11* 463–478.

Spence M., Boubaker Gherib J.B. and Ondoua Biwole V. (2008) "A framework of SME's strategic involvement in sustainable development" in Starik M., Wustenhagen R., Hamschmidt J. and Sharma S. (Eds) *Advances on research in corporate sustainability* Edward Elgar, Boston.

Tang J., Tang Z., Marino L.D., Zhang Y. and Li Q. (2008) "Exploring an inverted U-shape relationship between entrepreneurial orientation and performance in Chinese ventures" *Entrepreneurship: Theory & Practice, 32* 219–239.

Tang Z. and Tang J. (2012) "Entrepreneurial orientation and SME performance in China's changing environment: The moderating effects of strategies" *Asia Pacific Journal of Management, 29* 409–431.

Tushman M.L. and O'Reilly C. (1996) "The ambidextrous organisation: Managing evolutionary and revolutionary change" *California Management Review, 38* 1–23.

Tushman M.L., Anderson P.C. and O'Reilly C. (1997) "Technology cycles, innovation streams, and ambidextrous organizations: Organization renewal through innovation streams and strategic change" in Tushman M.L. and Anderson P. (Eds) *Managing strategic innovation and change: A collection of reading* Oxford University Press, Oxford.

Venkataraman S. (1997) "The distinctive domain of entrepreneurship research: An editors' perspective" in Katz J. and Brockhaus J. (Eds) *Advances in entrepreneurship, firm emergence and growth* Springer, New York.

Venkatram N., Lee C.H. and Iyer B. (2007) *Strategic ambidexterity and sales growth: A longitudinal test in the software sector* Boston University.

Voss G.B. and Voss Z.G. (2013) "Strategic ambidexterity in small and medium-sized enterprises: Implementing exploration and exploitation in product and market domains" *Organization Science, 24* 1459–1477.

Walley E.E and Taylor D.W. (2002) "Opportunists, champions, mavericks…?"*Greener Management International, 38* 31–43.

Wang C.L. (2008) "Entrepreneurial orientation, learning orientation, and firm performance" *Entrepreneurship: Theory & Practice, 32* 635–657.

Westerman G., McFarlan F.W. and Iansiti M. (2006) "Organization design and effectiveness over the innovation life cycle" *Organization Science, 17* 230–238.

Whiteman G., Walker B. and Perego P. (2013) "Plenatary boundaries: Ecological foundations for corporate sustainability" *Journal of Management Studies, 50* 307–336.

Yusuf A. (2002) "Environmental uncertainty, the entrepreneurial orientation of business ventures and performance" *International Journal of Commerce & Management, 12* 83–103.

Zahra S.A., Gedajlovic E., Neubaum D.O. and Shulman J.M. (2009) "A typology of social entrepreneurs: Motives, search processes and ethical challenges" *Journal of Business Venturing, 24* 519–532.

Zahra S.A., Rawhouser H.N., Bhawe N., Neubaum D.O and Hayton J.C. (2008) "Globalization of social entrepreneurship opportunities" *Strategic Entrepreneurship Journal, 2* 117–131.

Zaman G. and Goschin Z. (2010) "Multidisciplinary, interdisciplinary and transdisciplinary: Theoretical approaches and implications for the strategy of post-crisis sustainable development" *Theoretical & Applied Economics 17* 5–20.

Zolli A. and Healy A.M. (2012) *Resilience* Headline, London.

7 Sustainability entrepreneurship in marine protected areas

Simon R. Bush, Mariska Bottema, Jan Joris Midavaine and Eleanor Carter

Introduction

The involvement of private actors in marine conservation has steadily increased in recent decades as the need for sustainable funding models has become apparent (Dixon *et al.*, 1993; Colwell, 1998; Balmford *et al.*, 2004; Christie and White, 2007). In these so-called 'entrepreneurial marine protected areas' (EMPAs) (Colwell, 1997), private-actors seek business opportunities that fund a combination of conservation activities and local livelihood (Colwell, 1998; de Groot and Bush, 2010; Bottema and Bush, 2012). Building on the emerging perspective of Shepherd and Patzelt (2011), these EMPAs appear to characterize the role of entrepreneurial action as a catalyst for sustaining or protecting ecosystems by "providing economic and non-economic gains for investors, entrepreneurs and societies" (p. 138).

The type of entrepreneurial intervention in EMPAs ranges from collecting diver fees that directly fund park management (Dixon *et al.*, 1993; Tongson and Dygico, 2004; de Groot and Bush, 2010), to designing and implementing co-management arrangements in state designated parks (Teh *et al.*, 2008), and to private tenure over spatially delimited marine habitat (Svensson *et al.*, 2010). While the specific drivers for private sector involvement differ per case, one constant challenge they face is maintaining a requisite level of legitimacy and authority to practise conservation. We argue (based on earlier work, see Bottema and Bush, 2012) that the long-term 'durability' of their entrepreneurial activity, including the institutions they establish around the EMPAs, is dependent on continued support of both states actors and local communities.

Based on our earlier work in three EMPAs in South-East Asia, Central America and Africa (see Figure 7.1), this chapter explores how diverse entrepreneurial approaches have identified and exploited opportunities for spatially delimited, or 'territorial', private conservation of marine resources. In doing so we provide a meta-analysis of the cases to identify a generalizable set of conditions under which sustainability entrepreneurs are able to identify and exploit opportunities for generating individual and communal benefits, as well as consolidate their activities into long-term conservation activities.

The following section provides an overview of entrepreneurialism and marine conservation where we outline key conditions for exploitation, consolidation

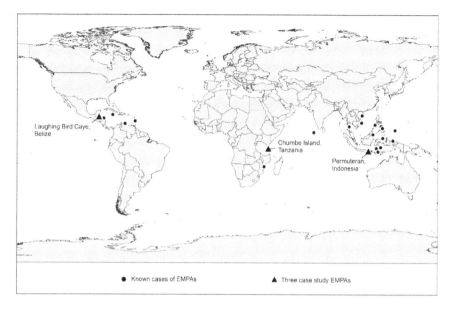

Figure 7.1 Map of three case studies and all other recorded EMPAs

and durability of conservation-related entrepreneurial activity. We then detail three diverse case studies of EMPAs in Indonesia, Belize and Tanzania using a mix of primary and secondary data (recent studies by the authors include Bottema and Bush, 2012; Nordlund *et al.*, 2013; Midavaine, 2014). Based on this cross-case comparison we then discuss the challenges of entrepreneurs to maintain private authority for long-term conservation.

Marine sustainability entrepreneurialism

The emergence of EMPAs

Reflecting the slow progress made towards a establishing a global network of MPAs, the Convention on Biodiversity recently shifted its ambition of 10 per cent coverage of the world's oceans from 2012 to 2020 (see Rife *et al.*, 2013). The effectiveness of established parks has been questioned, with many labelled as 'paper parks'. At local scales demands for coastal resources often exceed the capacity of those habitats to maintain a requisite level of biodiversity (Selig and Bruno, 2010). As variously argued (e.g. Selig and Bruno, 2010; Mascia *et al.*, 2010; Chuenpagdee *et al.*, 2013), meeting the national and global demands for MPA establishment remains firmly linked to the local contexts within which conservation activities are embedded.

Although a more recent phenomenon than terrestrial-based private-led conservation (Norton, 2000), the role and scope of EMPAs has increased and diversified since being first introduced. Colwell's (1997) initial description involved networks of small-scale protected areas managed by partnerships between local communities and private operators which "have a vested economic interest in promoting abundant marine life" (p. 110). He indicated that these discrete pockets of protected habitat can be developed within or in combination with state-led MPAs. Private-sector involvement is therefore seen as: (1) a short-term intervention that can stimulate the development of state-led protected areas by raising local awareness and building local capacity (Colwell, 1998); (2) a way of providing alternative sources of income to local communities, thereby reducing extractive pressure on marine resources (Dixon *et al.*, 1993; Christie and White, 2007); and/or (3) a long-term means of establishing economic activities around marine conservation that can provide a durable source of funding (Bottema and Bush, 2012).

The small number of studies of EMPA-like conservation initiatives have analysed the role of hotels in establishing no-take areas (e.g. Svensson *et al.*, 2009), dive shop operated reef conservation (e.g. de Groot and Bush, 2010), public-private partnerships (e.g. Teh *et al.*, 2008) and user fee systems (e.g. Dixon *et al.*, 1993; Tongson and Dygico, 2004; Uyarra *et al.*, 2010). While the majority of these studies have focused on ecological issues, co-management and the economics of private intervention, there is a dearth of sociological analysis on the role entrepreneurs play in marine conservation.

Entrepreneurial exploitation, consolidation and durability

Applied to sustainability, entrepreneurship refers to a process through which individuals discover and exploit individual business opportunities that are oriented towards changing the consumption or management of the natural and/or communal environment, which in turn provides development gains for others (Patzelt and Shepherd, 2011; Schaltegger and Wagner, 2011). Here we propose a framework to evaluate the dynamic process of entrepreneurial interventions in territorial based conservation such as EMPAs (see Figure 7.2) by dividing sustainability entrepreneurialism into three analytical phases – exploitation, consolidation and durability.

The *exploitation* of any opportunity for sustainability entrepreneurship begins with a 'problem' defined by any combination of environmental and social factors. For example, a problem related to environmental issues might be characterized by a decline in an ecological dimension such as biodiversity, or an increase in material flows such as effluent. However, underlying these declines or inputs are often institutional or market failures; such that environmental problems result from weak regulation or adverse allocation of resources (Cohen and Winn, 2007). Whether an entrepreneur responds to these problems is dependent on the extent to which they can identify and exploit an opportunity to create new approaches for reaching a sustainability goal. Following Eckhardt and Shane (2003), these opportunities are often related to the introduction of new goods, services or markets or organizational methods as means to the ends

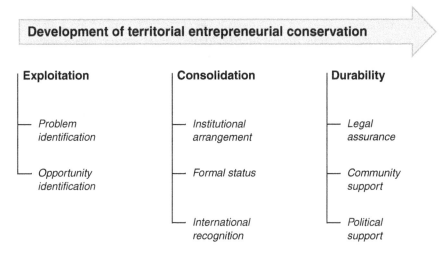

Figure 7.2 Dynamic framework for understanding the development of area based entrepreneurial conservation

of improved sustainability. By examining the emergence of EMPAs, we compare the conditions that enable entrepreneurs to exploit conservation opportunities.

Once established, the *consolidation* of a conservation-based entrepreneurial activity also depends on the extent to which it can be institutionally embedded. Consolidation in this sense refers to the type of institutional arrangement, including the degree of support received from the state or communities, for creating varying degrees of exclusion to habitat or biological resources within that habitat (Pacheco *et al.*, 2010; Bennett and Dearden, 2014). The extent of exclusion may vary from full enclosure of a habitat with state support, to partial or seasonal exclusion established through usufruct rights. Formal recognition from the state, in customary tenure arrangements and/or in co-management arrangements all contribute to the legitimacy of entrepreneurial activity and therefore the degree to which entrepreneurs can establish conservation rights (e.g. Lambooy and Levashova, 2011; Lamers *et al.*, 2014). In addition, entrepreneurial activity can be further consolidated if an entrepreneur receives international recognition and support, ranging from intergovernmental funding or status to professional accreditation (e.g. through scuba diving associations).

Finally, *durability* refers to the conditions that allow sustainability entrepreneurs to persist in a given social and institutional setting, and their capacity to create and shape change towards environmental conservation (Busenitz *et al.*, 2003). Given its relational nature the private authority of entrepreneurs is largely determined by their capacity to set new norms and practices for environmental conservation, which is in turn bound to their ability to (re)produce the trust of other societal and state actors (Partzsch and Ziegler, 2011; Green, 2013). Direct state support through legal assurance of an entrepreneur's status, and conversely legal compliance, is the most direct and durable means of establishing and maintaining trust in their activities. However, without a clear legal status entrepreneurial activities can also be supported through either explicit or tacit community support (Smith and McElwee, 2013). Entrepreneurs may be able to gain political support for their activities, allowing them to persist with activities even if their legal status remains ambiguous.

In the rest of this chapter we apply the above framework to the experiences of three EMPAs embedded in different natural, social and political settings. In doing so we identify the conditions under which private actors are able to identify, exploit and exercise sustainability entrepreneurship.

Comparative experiences with EMPAs

Chumbe Island Coral Park, Tanzania

Chumbe is a 22 hectare coral island located 12 km off the south-west coast of Zanzibar in Tanzania. In 1990 an expatriate consultant worked on the Zanzibar Integrated Land and Environmental Management Project which proposed immediate action on environmental education for communities who depended on marine resources and for staff of the Department of Environment (Rojas-Laserna, 2011). However, government support for both marine protection and environmental education in Zanzibar was limited. Instead, responding to the release of state coastal leases for tourism development, the entrepreneur saw an opportunity to *exploit* a link between education and conservation through a self-funded eco-lodge. The result was Chumbe Island Coral Park Ltd (CHICOP), gazetted by the Government of Zanzibar in 1994 as the first private-led MPA established in Tanzania.

The *consolidation* of CHICOP took place over a number of years and required ongoing high level political support (Nordlund *et al.*, 2013). Although the opportunity came partly from government policy aimed at promoting tourism development on Zanzibar, the proposal to establish a privately run MPA initially faced resistance from local fishers and some local government officials. In response the entrepreneur approached the Prime Minister's office on the importance of education and conservation, and successfully gained support for the lease (Rojas-Laserna, 2011). This support was further strengthened when the park was listed as a gazetted park and again when classified as a Category II protected area by the International Union for the Conservation of Nature (Nordlund *et al.*, 2013).

Despite growing recognition of the EMPA, private tenure over the island and protection of the surrounding waters remains vulnerable given that leases issued under the 1986 Investment Protection Act can be revoked by the State "with relative ease" (Riedmiller, 2003). Difficulties in re-negotiating leases for the island and adjacent marine area, every 33 and 10 years respectively, reflects this challenge (Riedmiller and Carter, 2001b). As private tenure of public resources has been questioned CHICOP has stressed the link between effective protection of marine resources as a condition for the growth and sustainability of quality tourism (Rojas-Laserna, 2011). CHICOP has also actively developed a range of local and national social and political relations, with the express intent of further strengthening long-term tenure over the EMPA.

A range of strategies have been adopted to strengthen the relations which grant CHICOP the ongoing legitimacy and authority to operate (see Riedmiller and Carter, 2001a; Riedmiller, 2003; Nordlund *et al.*, 2013). An advisory committee including nine representatives from adjacent villages, research and government departments is held twice a year. In addition, CHICOP releases regular activity reports and a biannual newsletter. Institutional links are also made to local and foreign research institutes. Relations with surrounding communities have also been strengthened through regular consultation meetings, fisher association support (including provision of an in-water rescue service for fishers in distress) and the proactive employment of local community members in the project. Building on the education goals of the entrepreneur, the programme funds and manages visits from schools throughout Zanzibar, has established school environment clubs, and fisher associations. Finally, a historic lighthouse functions as an important maritime navigation system, managed by CHICOP staff in co-operation with the Harbour Authority.

The wider legitimacy of CHICOP was also consolidated through investment in the environmental credentials of the park – including the development of eco-touristic activities, the use of eco-architecture and eco-technologies in lodge design and construction. The park has also received considerable international recognition as an exceptional example of private sector led marine conservation by the Nature Conservancy and the European Union, and has received awards from groups including the United Nations and National Geographic.

Despite its success there remain a series of threats to the ongoing *durability* of CHICOP. The entrepreneur herself argues that the long-term prospect of the EMPA depends on the ongoing willingness of the government to extend the management agreements (Reidmiller, 2008). CHICOP has no legal assurance that a renewal of its leases will occur, and it is also made vulnerable by the Zanzibar Investment Act of 1986 which affords no protection against expropriation by the government (Nordlund *et al.*, 2013). Management agreements and tenure arrangements are held through two key lease agreements: A Closed Forest Reserve Agreement (33 years renewable, currently valid to 2027), and a Reef Sanctuary Agreement (10 years renewable, currently valid to 2024). While the relations established with government and the local community puts CHICOP in a strong position to renew the leases, a change in government or political will leave the future of the EMPA open to a new round of discussion.

Pemuteran, Indonesia

Pemuteran is a small fishing village in the north-west of Bali, Indonesia's most popular island tourism destination. Pemuteran's tourism industry developed in the early 1990s (Piskurek, 2001; Goreau *et al.*, 2008). Illegal dynamite and cyanide fishing methods were still being employed by local fishermen. Recognizing the resulting reef degradation, two entrepreneurs, a Balinese hotelier and an expat who established Pemuteran's first dive shop, began communicating to fishermen about the consequences of their activities. Recognizing both a problem and opportunity to *exploit* for entrepreneurial activity, the expat incorporated coral repair into dives he offered his clients. Influenced by the awareness raised by the entrepreneurs, in 1995 the village community declared a local ban on illegal fishing methods, appointed beach guards to enforce this, and declared a No Take Zone (NTZ) of 1 hectare for which an entry fee was charged to tourists.

In 1998 the Asian economic crisis resulted in many displaced Indonesian workers turning to fishing, bringing illegal fishing practices back to Pemuteran. Recognizing the need to conserve coral suffering from both bleaching and overfishing a Balinese entrepreneur decided to invest in Biorock, a coral restoration technology developed by the Global Coral Reef Alliance (GCRA) (Goreau *et al.*, 2008). In 2000 numerous hotels invested in Biorock coral nurseries, involving the local community in their construction. Management and maintenance of these nurseries was consolidated under the NGO *Yayasan Karang Lestari*. The community subsequently appointed a traditional community-based security unit to reinforce the national ban on destructive fishing practices and to protect the newly established NTZ where the coral nurseries were located. Fishermen were said to not be sufficiently included in the decision-making process leading to creation of this NTZ, so this development initially faced more resistance than the previously appointed NTZ. Eventually however, the fishermen came to accept this new protected area.

Marine conservation institutions in Pemuteran are in place largely due to efforts of a few independently acting entrepreneurs. The *consolidation* of the EMPA comprises several informal institutions which work toward common goals, but appear to operate individually. The dive sector is also not formally organized, without structural communication and no formalized price agreement. However, the dive shops cater to different niches. It appears that competitive behaviour, which can lead to overuse and degradation of reefs (e.g. Roman *et al.*, 2007), has thus been avoided.

The private sector gained legitimacy through financial and non-financial investments in the local community. Some dive shops pay fishermen for using their area, some supply the fishermen with fish aggregating devices. The private sector has also invested in cultural assets and activities such as funding restoration of temples, which has been important for building support amongst the local community. Gaining support of the village's religious leaders and employing locals has been beneficial in exercising social control over the community in terms of resource use. It can be argued that Biorock technology has also played a role in legitimating entrepreneurial conservation activities. Its presence produces tangible proof of private sector investments in conservation, provides local employment and educates local inhabitants and tourists about the need for marine conservation.

The reefs have largely remained common property as there has only been minimal enclosure of areas. As a result the private sector has been able to exercise marine conservation without marginalizing original resource users. However, norms and rules established by the private sector have not been formalized into government regulation, or into du jure rights over these areas. Pemuteran is designated as a Daerah Parawisata Laut (Sea Tourism Area) by provincial law; regency law states that the area has to exercise a conservation effort but does not state specifically how. In Pemuteran's village decree it is stated that the area designated for tourism can only be used for tourism, which indirectly supports designation of the NTZ, but grants the area no official protected area status. The private sector has formed two informal semi-voluntary agreements with fishermen in cooperation with the village: a local agreement to enforce a national ban on destructive fishing practices and the creation of a de facto NTZ. The collapse of the previous equally informal agreements in 1998 due to effects of the economic crisis leads one to question the long-term *durability* of this EMPA as it currently stands.

The private sector's relations with the original resource owners – Pemuteran village and fishermen – appear to be based on mutual cooperation largely due to initial efforts of the two initial individual entrepreneurs to build trust. These two entrepreneurs remain key individuals for management of the EMPA due to their leadership function and their connecting role in relations with local stakeholder groups. This brings with it a risk of overdependence and consequently leads one to question the EMPA's long-term durability even further.

Laughing Bird Caye, Belize

Since the 1980s, Placencia has grown to become one of the fastest growing tourism destinations in Belize. Tourism activity began with tours to the surrounding cayes (islands) by local fishermen. Most tourists were brought to Laughing Bird Caye (LBC), a long and narrow island of 0.57 hectares 11 miles of the coast of Placencia. In 1990 fishermen and pioneering tour guides found out LBC was being surveyed to be sold and developed. Recognizing the impact that this development would have on tourism and fishing in the area, a resident expat owner of a local hotel, fishermen and other concerned community members established the Friends of Laughing Bird Caye Committee. The Committee was a means for the entrepreneur to engage and *exploit* an opportunity for tourism and conservation. With a successful petition among the inhabitants of Placencia the Committee established a voluntary ban on fishing in the surrounding waters and camping on the caye. Significant lobbying further resulted in protection of LBC as a national park under the 1981 National Park System Act of the Forest Department in 1991 (Wildtracks, 2010). National parks (NP) in Belize are strictly non-extractive reserves "for the protection and preservation of natural and scenic values of national significance for the benefit and enjoyment of the general public" (Government of Belize, 2000, p. 6).

At the national level an integrated coastal zone management approach for the protection of Belize's reefs was envisioned. A Coastal Zone Management Unit was established under the Fisheries Department in 1990 and followed up with the UNDP/GEF funded Coastal Zone Management Project in 1993. The Committee received funding from this project to develop a management plan for LBCNP.

In 1996 the national park was expanded as part of the Belize Barrier Reef Reserve System, a collective UNESCO World Heritage Site. As a result the entire Laughing Bird Caye Faro, an elongated ridge of reef covering approximately 12 square nautical miles was *consolidated* by gaining a formal national legal status (Vellos, 2003). This development was welcomed by the inhabitants of Placencia undergoing a transition toward becoming more tourism oriented. Despite the involvement of the Forest Department, there was insufficient capacity from the government and the Committee to adequately deal with day-to-day management. Instead responsibility was given to the newly formed NGO Friends of Laughing Bird Caye, which took on the development of the management plan, as well as ongoing monitoring and enforcement. The management of the EMPA was further consolidated with an agreement signed with the Forest Department in 2001, receiving de jure rights and official recognition as a co-manager of LBCNP. Soon after external funds from UNDP, GEF, World Wide Fund for Nature (WWF) and The Nature Conservancy (TNC) allowed those business owners originally involved in the Committee to step aside and be replaced by a professional reserve manager and ranger who were made special constables of the state police force (Vellos, 2003).

The *durability* of the MPA has been facilitated by the co-management arrangement, given that the private sector has been able to maintain an active role in the management and maintenance of the MPA as a tourism destination. This caused the NGO, now known as the Southern Environmental Association, to function as a platform to negotiate the link between tourism and conservation. It allowed the private sector to maintain influence and build facilities like picnic tables and a barbeque, though restricted to develop exclusive rights. Similar to the Pemuteran case, the no-take status of LBCNP appeared to provide a suitable investment environment for a coral restoration initiative. This initiative, known as Fragments of Hope, is run by a resident expat marine biologist and is funded by among others WWF and the World Bank (Bowden-Kerby and Carne, 2012).

Historically co-management appeared to be a successful concept to solve government departments' lack of capacity and channel funding from international conservation organizations (Young and Horwich, 2007). However, with over 94 protected areas, accounting for 36 per cent of Belize's national territory in 2005, legislation, mandates, roles and responsibilities started to get unclear (Meerman, 2005). In response to this, policies were revised and (re-) formulated leading to the establishment of the National Protected Areas System Plan (NPASP) in 2005, demanding co-management organizations sign a new co-management agreement in November 2012. Signing the agreement increases state control and limits NGO autonomy, and in particular risks alteration of arrangements made between co-management organizations and the private sector. Refusing to sign makes activities carried out by co-management organizations illegal. With some exceptions most co-management organizations still refused to sign by 2013.

Discussion

The three cases present diverse but comparable experiences on how entrepreneurs establish and consolidate EMPAs based on exploitation, consolidation and durability. In summary we see that: (1) entrepreneurs exploit business opportunities that are wholly dependent on conservation outcomes; (2) they consolidate institutional arrangements by gaining recognition by states and/or local communities; and (3) the long-term durability of EMPAs is dependent on maintaining social relations with civil society groups, state actors and local communities. Seen as such EMPAs do not fill short-term 'gaps', but can provide long-term strategies that states might be able to coordinate for wider communal returns. Based on these observations and linking the work of Lambooy and Levashova (2011) and Lamers *et al.* (2014), we now compare the three cases (see Table 7.1) and discuss the conditions required for entrepreneurs to establish the legitimacy and ultimately authority necessary to persist with the conservation of public resources over the long term.

Overall, the three cases show strong variation in how entrepreneurs identified and exploited opportunities to develop their EMPA. But common to all cases, entrepreneurial exploitation of conservation opportunities requires changes in politics, policy and/or regulation for redistributing value to support improved (privately led) environmental stewardship (following Shepherd and Patzelt, 2011). While in Pemuteran there was a clear link between reef degradation and restoration, the problems identified in the other two cases were in response to perceived 'institutional failures' (Dean and McMullen, 2007). In Chumbe, there was a lack of awareness around marine protected areas and in Laughing Bird Caye the entrepreneurial action was a form of resistance against externally driven uncontrolled tourism development. By exploiting opportunities to establish territorial control over these areas, entrepreneurs were able to generate individual and communal benefits. However, the cases also demonstrate that the overall effectiveness of these territorial approaches to conservation required substantial efforts to create and consolidate their position with both the state and local communities.

The approach and extent to which entrepreneurs can establish EMPAs that receive state and/or international support, differ substantially. Both CHICOP and Laughing Bird Caye have received recognition from national government by establishing entrepreneur-led co-management arrangements (cf. von Heland *et al.*, 2014). In the case of CHICOP this was done by inviting government and local community representatives to join its advisory committee. Reflecting a multi-level strategy for sustainable entrepreneurialism (Dyerson and Preuss,

Table 7.1 Comparison of exploitation, consolidation and durability of three entrepreneurial marine protected areas

Conditions		Chumbe Island, Tanzania	Permuteran, Bali, Indonesia	Laughing Bird Caye, Belize
Exploitation	Problem identification	• Lack of environmental education and lack of marine conservation areas	• Reef degradation through illegal fishing methods and coral bleaching events	• Coordinated opposition to privatization
	Opportunity identification	• Opportunity for establishment of marine conservation area to support education, self-financed through resort development established through tourism and investment legislation	• Opportunity to re-establish 'no take area' around Biorock structures for dive tourism	• Opportunity for establishing no take area and dive operation on the coast of Placencia
Consolidation	Institutional embedding	• Formal lease; advisory committee with input from communities and state	• Minimal enclosure leading to ongoing cooperation with local communities	• Co-management arrangement established with the forest department
	Formal status	• Gazetted as nationally listed marine protected area	• Designated by provincial law as Daerah Parawisata Laut (Sea Tourism Area). Village decree states areas which can only be used for tourism purposes	• Gazetted as national park • Part of Belize MPA network
	International recognition	• International funding and awards • IUCN listed protected area	• Known as largest Biorock reef	• International funding • One of seven MPAs of Belize Barrier Reef World Heritage Site
Durability	Legal assurance	• No legal assurance of lease renewal	• No legal assurance of access and investment	• Weak assurance; national level renegotiation of co-management agreements
	Community support	• Medium to high community support	• Variable community support	• Strong community support
	Political support	• Renewal of lease vulnerable to national and local political change	• Recognition through visits of various government officials	• The MPA and its management should comply with guidelines prescribed in the National Protected Areas Policy and System Plan

2012), CHICOP has also consolidated political support by receiving formal listing as a national MPA in addition to international level recognition from IUCN. Similarly, in Laughing Bird Caye legitimacy has been established with both the community and government through a formally recognized co-management agreement with the forest department. In contrast, the case of Pemuteran demonstrates that in the absence of national recognition, informal agreements with the local community and only limited international support can also enable entrepreneurs to consolidate their conservation activities. However, the consequence appears to be less rigid territorial control, which may benefit communities, but also result in trade-offs in terms of conservation.

Finally, these findings also point to how the durability of 'entrepreneurial authority' (Green, 2013) takes shape and is challenged. All three cases demonstrate that the long-term durability of entrepreneurial activity to overcome implementation and enforcement failures is dependent on their perceived legitimacy by both the state, which grants formal tenure, and the communities, which grant usufruct rights over habitats and biological resources. As the cases show, where state support is highly institutionalized, the durability of the EMPAs is subject to changes in national level support for private marine tenure; CHICOP's lease remains vulnerable to political change and Laughing Bird Caye is vulnerable to a turn to more centralized state control after a long period of devolved conservation. While the theme of private authority is taken up in international environmental governance (e.g. Pattberg, 2007; Green, 2013), more research is needed in the context of sustainable entrepreneurship – especially around territorial forms of conservation.

How effective these EMPAs are as territorial conservation approaches in the long term also appears to be dependent on the timing and source of entrepreneurial action. In both Pemuteran and Chumbe relations with communities are characterized by ongoing friction over the usufruct rights they have granted to the entrepreneurs. In both cases the impetus for creating an EMPA was to change endogenous negative impacts of local fishing practices by limiting access to habitat and resources in return for alternative income streams and (potential) increases in fish yields from effectively managed exclusion areas. In contrast, Laughing Bird Caye was developed in response to the exogenous threat of dredging and only subsequently led to the exclusion of fishers; a process which the fishers themselves initiated. In this case the legitimacy of a conservation intervention was established prior to the entrepreneurs establishing authority over this intervention. In the other cases there was no agreed basis from which the entrepreneurial intervention could draw their legitimacy. As reflected in other resource sectors (e.g. Gritten and Saastamoinen, 2010; Gedajlovic *et al.*, 2013), gaining acceptability and support and ultimately legitimacy through the relations entrepreneurs build with different actors especially is even more essential when there is a degree of resource enclosure.

Overall, the results support claims that in conserving common or open access resources entrepreneurial activity relies on changing access and use rights and establishing new industry norms to shape the behaviour of resource users (Dean and McMullen, 2007; Pacheco *et al.*, 2010). The long-term success of a sustainability entrepreneur in such area-based arrangements is therefore not only related to their capacity to identify and exploit opportunities, but also the extent to which they can consolidate their activities and create durable long-term institutional change. Such observations extend the literature on sustainability entrepreneurialism by opening up the challenges of territorially based entrepreneurial activity and making links to other studies of locally embedded private conservation (Rosen and Olsson, 2013; Van Wijk *et al.*, 2015). Building on Green (2013), these observations also point to the need for further research on the under-explored notion of entrepreneurial authority, and in doing so offer an opportunity to extend the literature on sustainable entrepreneurialism.

Conclusion

The future of sustainability entrepreneurship in the establishment of MPAs is dependent on not only the capacity of entrepreneurs to seek and exploit opportunities, but also on their capacity to consolidate private institutions over the long term. The cases analysed in this chapter demonstrate that the 'durability' of their entrepreneurial activity is dependent on the support they are able to gain and sustain from the state and local communities. Entrepreneurial activity in marine conservation, involving spatial demarcation of conservation activities, is therefore a highly relational and dynamic process of legitimating private authority. The more institutionalized an arrangement becomes the more secure the economic and environmental individual and communal payoffs may be, yet concurrently flexibility remains an essential component of entrepreneurialism and innovation. Balancing these juxtaposing elements is a challenge all EMPAs face.

Furthermore, the results show that private control over marine conservation is not independent of the state. On the contrary, state involvement is fundamental in providing the 'action space' for entrepreneurs to exploit and consolidate opportunities, while also ensuring they are able to contribute to the stewardship of public habitat and resources. Without a clear framework for state collaboration and support these private sustainability entrepreneurs are unlikely to be able to establish durable spatially delimited institutions around the conservation of marine resources over the long term. Nevertheless, the durability of these conservation areas also remains dependent on the flexibility and efficiency of entrepreneurial activity. Future research can further our understanding of how EMPAs can contribute to wider-scale marine and coastal planning either by connecting wider network of small conservation areas, or stimulating state marine protected areas that promote resilience through coastal linkages with EMPAs. However, in doing so, questions need to be asked about how both private and public interests can be flexibly and efficiently met.

References

Balmford, A., P. Gravestock, N. Hockley, C. J. McClean and C. M. Roberts (2004) "The worldwide costs of marine protected areas" *Proceedings of the National Academy of Sciences of the United States of America*, 101 9694–9697.

Bennett, N. J. and P. Dearden (2014) "From measuring outcomes to providing inputs: Governance, management, and local development for more effective marine protected areas" *Marine Policy*, 50 96–110.

Bottema, M. J. M. and S. R. Bush (2012) "The durability of private sector-led marine conservation: A case study of two entrepreneurial marine protected areas in Indonesia" *Ocean and Coastal Management*, 61 38–48.

Bowden-Kerby, A. and L. Carne (2012) "Thermal tolerance as a factor in Caribbean Acropora restoration", in *Proceedings of the 12th International Coral Reef Symposium*. James Cook University, Cairns, 1–5.

Busenitz, L. W., G. P. West, D. Shepherd, T. Nelson, G. N. Chandler and A. Zacharakis (2003) "Entrepreneurship research in emergence: Past trends and future directions" *Journal of Management*, 29 285–308.

Christie, P. and A. T. White (2007) "Best practices for improved governance of coral reef marine protected areas" *Coral Reefs*, 26 1047–1056.

Chuenpagdee, R., J. J. Pascual-Fernandez, E. Szelianszky, J. L. Alegret, J. Fraga and S. Jentoft (2013) "Marine protected areas: Re-thinking their inception" *Marine Policy*, 39 234–240.

Cohen, B. and M. I. Winn (2007) "Market imperfections, opportunity and sustainable entrepreneurship" *Journal of Business Venturing*, 22 29–49.

Colwell, S. (1997) "Entrepreneurial marine protected areas: Small-scale, commercially supported coral reef protected areas", in M. E. Hatziolos, A. J. Hooten and M. Fodor (eds) *Coral Reefs: Challenges and Opportunities for Sustainable Management*. World Bank, Washington DC, 110–114.

Colwell, S. (1998) "Dive-tourism and private stewardship of small-scale coral reef marine protected areas" in I. Dight, R. Kenchington and B. J. Townsville (eds) *Proceedings: International Tropical Marine Ecosystems Management Symposium (ITMEMS)*. Great Barrier Reef Marine Park Authority, Australia, 217–221.

De Groot, J. and S. R. Bush (2010) "The potential for dive tourism led entrepreneurial marine protected areas in Curacao" *Marine Policy*, 34 1051–1059.

Dean, T. J. and J. S. McMullen (2007) "Toward a theory of sustainable entrepreneurship: Reducing environmental degradation through entrepreneurial action" *Journal of Business Venturing*, 22 50–76.

Dixon, J. A., L. Fallon Scura and T. Van't Hof (1993) "Meeting ecological and economic goals: Marine parks in the Caribbean" *Ambio*, 22 117–125.

Dyerson, R. and L. Preuss (2012) "The nexus of innovation, entrepreneurship and sustainability: Making the case for a multi-level approach" in M. Wagner (ed.) *Entrepreneurship, Innovation and Sustainability*, Greenleaf Publishing in association with GSE Research, Sheffield, 11–31.

Eckhardt, J. T. and S. A. Shane (2003) "Opportunities and entrepreneurship" *Journal of Management*, 29 333–349.

Gedajlovic, E., B. Honig, C. B. Moore, G. T. Payne and M. Wright (2013) "Social capital and entrepreneurship: A schema and research agenda" *Entrepreneurship Theory and Practice* 37(3) 455–478.

Goreau, T., W. Hilbertz and R. France (2008) "Bottom-up community based coral reef and fisheries restoration in Indonesia, Panama, and Palau" in R. L. France (ed.) *Handbook of Regenerative Landscape Design*, CRC Press, Boca Raton, FL, 143–159.

Government of Belize (2000) *The Substantive Laws of Belize*. Revised Edition. Chapter 215. National Park System Act, Belize, Government of Belize.

Green, J. F. (2013) *Rethinking Private Authority: Agents and Entrepreneurs in Global Environmental Governance*. Princeton University Press, Princeton, NJ.

Gritten, D. and O. Saastamoinen (2010) "The roles of legitimacy in environmental conflict: An Indonesian case study" *Society and Natural Resources*, 24 49–64.

Lambooy, T. and Y. Levashova (2011) "Opportunities and challenges for private sector entrepreneurship and investment in biodiversity, ecosystem services and nature conservation" *International Journal of Biodiversity Science, Ecosystem Services and Management*, 7 301–318.

Lamers, M., R. van der Duim, J. van Wijk, R. Nthiga and I. J. Visseren-Hamakers (2014) "Governing conservation tourism partnerships in Kenya" *Annals of Tourism Research*, 48 250–265.

Mascia, M. B., C. Claus and R. Naidoo (2010) "Impacts of marine protected areas on fishing communities" *Conservation Biology*, 24 1424–1429.

Meerman, J. C. (2005) *Belize Protected Areas Policy and System Plan*. Result 2: Protected Area System Assessment and Analysis Belize, Public Draft, Government of Belize.

Midavaine, J. J. (2014) *Co-management and entrepreneurship: An analysis of the relation between co-management and the opportunities for commercial entities to invest in biodiversity conservation in Belize's marine protected areas*. Wageningen, Wageningen University, MSc [online] http://library.wur.nl/WebQuery/clc/2058918.

Nordlund, L. M., U. Kloiber, E. Carter and S. Riedmiller (2013) "Chumbe Island Coral Park: Governance analysis" *Marine Policy*, 41 110–117.

Norton, D. A. (2000) "Conservation biology and private land: Shifting the focus" *Conservation Biology*, 14 1221–1223.

Pacheco, D. F., T. J. Dean and D. S. Payne (2010) "Escaping the green prison: Entrepreneurship and the creation of opportunities for sustainable development" *Journal of Business Venturing*, 25 464–480.

Partzsch, L. and R. Ziegler (2011) "Social entrepreneurs as change agents: A case study on power and authority in the water sector" *International Environmental Agreements: Politics, Law and Economics*, 11 63–83.

Pattberg, P. H. (2007) *Private Institutions and Global Governance: The New Politics of Environmental Sustainability*. Edward Elgar, London.

Patzelt, H. and D. A. Shepherd (2011) "Recognizing opportunities for sustainable development" *Entrepreneurship Theory and Practice*, 35 631–652.

Piskurek, N. (2001) "Dive tourism in coral reefs – impacts and conditions for sustainability: A case study from Desa Pemuteran (Bali/Indonesia)" *ACP-EU Fisheries Research Report* 10 57–65.

Riedmiller, S. (2003) *Private Sector Investment in Marine Protected Areas – Experiences of the Chumbe Island Coral Park in Zanzibar/Tanzania*. Vth World Parks Congress: Sustainable Finance Stream, September 2003, Durban, South Africa.

Reidmiller, S. (2008) *Chumbe Island Coral Park: Helping Save the Coral Reefs of Tanzania*. A Private Sector Approach – Conservation Agreements in support of Marine Protection, 16–19 June 2008, Seattle, WA, The Nature Conservancy, Conservation International, and Conservation and Community Investment Forum.

Riedmiller, S. and E. Carter (2001a) "Ecotourism in a private Marine Protected Area: Chumbe Island, Tanzania" *ACP–EU Fisheries Research Report*, 10 45.

Riedmiller, S. and E. Carter (2001b) "The political challenge of private sector management of Marine Protected Areas: The Chumbe Island Case Tanzania" *ACP-EU Fisheries Research Report*, 10 141–153.

Rife, A. N., B. Erisman, A. Sanchez and O. Aburto-Oropeza (2013) "When good intentions are not enough … Insights on networks of 'paper park' Marine Protected Areas" *Conservation Letters*, 6 200–212.

Rojas-Laserna, M. (2011) *Entrepreneurialism in Marine Protected Areas governance: The case of Chumbe Island Coral Park in Zanzibar, Tanzania*, Wageningen, Wageningen University. MSc [online] http://library.wur.nl/WebQuery/clc/1970933.

Roman, G. S., P. Dearden and R. Rollins (2007) "Application of zoning and 'limits of acceptable change' to manage snorkelling tourism" *Environmental Management*, 39 819–830.

Rosen, F. and P. Olsson (2013) "Institutional entrepreneurs, global networks, and the emergence of international institutions for ecosystem-based management: The Coral Triangle Initiative" *Marine Policy*, 38 195–204.

Schaltegger, S. and M. Wagner (2011) "Sustainable entrepreneurship and sustainability innovation: Categories and interactions" *Business Strategy and the Environment*, 20 222–237.

Selig, E. R. and J. F. Bruno (2010) "A global analysis of the effectiveness of Marine Protected Areas in preventing coral loss" *PLoS ONE*, 5 e9278.

Shepherd, D. A. and H. Patzelt (2011) "The new field of sustainable entrepreneurship: Studying entrepreneurial action linking 'what is to be sustained' with 'what is to be developed'" *Entrepreneurship Theory and Practice*, 35 137–163.

Smith, R. and G. McElwee (2013) "Confronting social constructions of rural criminality: A case story on 'illegal pluriactivity' in the farming community" *Sociologia Ruralis*, 53 112–134.

Svensson, P., L. D. Rodwell and M. J. Attrill (2009) "Privately managed Marine Reserves as a mechanism for the conservation of coral reef ecosystems: A case study from Vietnam" *Ambio*, 38 72–78.

Svensson, P., L. D. Rodwell and M. J. Attrill (2010) "The perceptions of local fishermen towards a hotel managed marine reserve in Vietnam" *Ocean and Coastal Management*, 53 114–122.

Teh, L. C. L., L. S. L. Teh and F. C. Chung (2008) "A private management approach to coral reef conservation in Sabah, Malaysia" *Biodiversity and Conservation*, 17 3061–3077.

Tongson, E. and M. Dygico (2004) "User fee system for marine ecotourism: The Tubbataha Reef experience" *Coastal Management*, 32 17–23.

Uyarra, M. C., J. A. Gill and I. M. Cote (2010) "Charging for nature: Marine park fees and management from a user perspective" *Ambio*, 39 515–523.

Van Wijk, J., R. Van der Duim, M. Lamers and D. Sumba (2015) "The emergence of institutional innovations in tourism: The evolution of the African Wildlife Foundation's tourism conservation enterprises" *Journal of Sustainable Tourism*, 23 104–125.

Vellos, A. (2003) *Co-management of Laughing Bird Caye National Park*, in Proceedings of the 54th GCFI and Caribbean MPA Symposium 2001, 702–708.

Von Heland, F., J. Clifton and P. Olsson (2014) "Improving stewardship of marine resources: Linking strategy to opportunity" *Sustainability*, 6 4470–4496.

Wildtracks (2010) *Laughing Bird Caye National Park Management Plan 2011–2016*. Placencia Village, Belize, SEA Belize National Office.

Young, C. and R. Horwich (2007) "History of protected area designation, co-management and community participation in Belize", in S. Balboni (ed.) *Taking Stock: Belize at 25 Years of Independence*, Cubola Productions, Belize, 123–145.

Part II

Empirical insights from case studies – regional and sectoral perspective

8 Lessons from sustainable entrepreneurship towards social innovation in healthcare

How green buildings can promote health and wellbeing

Sharon Jackson, John Maleganos and Kleopatra Alamantariotou

Introduction

There is a growing body of evidence to suggest a connection between the competitiveness of an organization and the health of the communities in which it operates. These communities consist of 'stakeholder groups' (Freeman, 1984), both inside and outside the organization, with the term 'stakeholder' being broadly defined as anyone who affects or is affected by an organization (Clarkson, 1995; Freeman, 1984; Mitchell *et al.*, 1997).

Where the organization is seen to be operating in the positive interest of local society and the natural environment, studies have shown that creative and innovative solutions to everyday 'internal' organizational challenges can often come from external 'secondary stakeholder groups' and people in the local community (Beleno and Andres, 2014; Howaldt *et al.*, 2014).

Green building design is becoming a popular area of sustainability innovation for minimizing impacts on the natural environment and improving human health through improved working conditions indoors. Environmental health studies suggest that people spend 90 per cent of their time indoors and therefore the 'health' of the indoor environment has a direct impact on human health and holistic wellbeing (Allen *et al.*, 2015). However, most studies rely on people's perceptions of comfort and aesthetics of 'green buildings' and there is conflicting debate about the real impact of 'green building' on improved human health (Paul and Taylor, 2007).

The issue of 'innovation' towards sustainable development of improved performance and enhanced quality of service in healthcare is an ongoing international challenge (EURAM, 2012). Some studies have developed 'health performance indicators' which suggest the benefits of green building hospitals include faster patient recovery, improved staff performance and reduced infection rates (Allen *et al.*, 2015).

With this in mind, this chapter addresses the following questions, through a literature review and a single case study approach.

- What can the healthcare sector learn from sustainable entrepreneurship and social innovation?
- Can ecological buildings and 'sustainable spaces' positively impact on the performance and quality of services provided by healthcare organizations, for the benefit of stakeholder groups, including clients, patients and employees?

A literature review revealed studies of eco-building in the healthcare sector from a perspective of examining the physical aspects and cost reduction benefits of environmental management such as waste, water, air quality issues. However, this chapter considers a broader holistic impact of eco-buildings and nature based design on primary stakeholder groups, namely the people giving and receiving the service provided (healthcare), as well as the impact on the overall processes of workplace innovation itself (Smith, 2010).

The case study examines 'The European Sustainability Academy (ESA)' in Crete, Greece (www.eurosustainability.org). ESA is a purpose designed, innovative centre for experiential, sustainable leadership and management training, hosted in a fully ecological building with bioclimatic properties. ESA is an exemplary application of an off-grid, sun-powered, sustainable construction, using natural materials which integrates aspects of biomimicry. This example of sustainable entrepreneurship adopts congruent, sustainable daily operational processes in full cooperation with the local community and in alignment with the surrounding natural environment. This holistic and innovative approach has been shown to make a positive impact on people's learning through triggering heightened and enhanced cognitive sensemaking (Weick, 1995) around enacting sustainability in organizations (Jackson, 2009) whilst simultaneously contributing to a sense of enhanced wellbeing and positive psychology (Seligman, 2003). This approach can contribute to breaking down cognitive barriers to innovation and enacting positive change. In the context of ESA's objectives to teach sustainability leadership and management skills, the positive impact of the ecological characteristics of the construction and the congruent sustainable activities of the enterprise appear to create an enhanced sense of well-being for the clients which can stimulate 'triggers' (Jackson, 2009) for stimulating positive attitudes, enhancing thinking capacity and broadening perception. There is emerging practitioner based evidence to suggest that the positive impact of an ecological building can enhance the learning experience and become an 'anchor' for carrying new sustainability thinking and new skills into daily behaviours.

Social cohesion is a critical component of sustainability (Elkington, 1997; Grayson and Hodges, 2002, 2004) and the example of ESA as a sustainable, entrepreneurial enterprise as an enabler for positive change through social innovation, can be replicated in other business sectors and organizational schemes. Using the example of ESA, this chapter aims to demonstrate how fundamental elements of sustainable business (ecological construction and practices) can be applied specifically to the healthcare sector as an effective tool for social innovation.

This chapter aims to show how the replicability of the ESA 'sustainable entrepreneurship' paradigm could become a 'trigger' towards the creation of social innovation which can lead to enhanced wellbeing of stakeholders which in turn contributes to improved quality of service and performance in the healthcare sector. The ESA case study suggests that the characteristics of an ecological, sustainable building can contribute towards the enhancement of an organization's reputation in the eyes of its stakeholders due to perceived health benefits. Using natural construction materials and avoiding the use of toxic materials during building construction and building maintenance materials, contributes positively to the 'health' of buildings. In healthcare services this has been shown to impact on improved patient healing, boosting employee satisfaction and long term operational efficiencies for the benefit of a wide range of stakeholders including patients, workers, visitors and the local community in which the healthcare facility operates.

New practical research suggests that nature based designed buildings can improve psychological wellbeing to people and economic benefits in the healthcare sector (Witherspoon, 2014). The ESA building was designed and built with the objective of creating a holistic sustainability teaching experience, however an unexpected consequence has been the notable positive impact of mood, health and wellbeing of people using the eco-building and its outdoor spaces. Visitors' words used to describe their experience of the ESA building have included 'uplifting', 'recovery', 'healing', 'sanctuary', 'shrine' and 'balance'.

This suggests transferrable observations between the ESA eco-building and the potential benefits of green buildings in the healthcare sector which can contribute to addressing the gap in knowledge and broader understanding about the positive potential of green building design on humanity. Beyond hospitals, the ESA example could contribute new understanding towards improving old age facilities, palliative care facilities, children's nurseries, community centres and other similar facilities where social wellbeing is a central concern.

This chapter explores this notion further and considers the gap in consensus about the positive impact of green buildings (Paul and Taylor, 2007) by discussing the transferable benefits of the impacts of a green building in a learning context with the impact of a green building in the healthcare context. In particular, the emerging field of 'biophilia' (William, 1984; Kellert *et al.*, 2008) appears to bring new insight and practical examples to the debate.

The next section gives an introduction to the key terms used, and the relationship between them in the context of this chapter.

Can sustainable entrepreneurship be an enabler of social innovation?

The aim of 'social innovation' is broadly considered to be the development of new ideas, which lead to the enactment of enhanced products and services (Drucker, 1985) which contribute to improved human wellbeing in both individual and social situations. The concept of 'sustainable entrepreneurship' and more broadly 'sustainability', consider the financial long term health of the enterprise to be inextricably linked with the present and future health and wellbeing of the society and natural environment in which that enterprise operates (Ram et al., 2009). The concept of 'sustainability' includes the health and wellbeing of society as one of its three core pillars of 'performance' measurement known as 'triple bottom line' (TBL).

The next section explains 'sustainability' and TBL in more detail.

Sustainability explained

The concept of 'sustainability' can have numerous different meanings (Bass and Dalal-Clayton, 2012) and interpretations that differ according to who is using the term and in what context (Pezzey, 1992). From an abstract, macroscopic point of view, the word 'sustainability' refers to the ability to 'sustain' in the sense of keeping 'something' constant over a period of time. For example, health and wellbeing of society (Weitzman, 2003).

In the context of 'sustainable entrepreneurship' the 'something' is about the sustainability of the enterprise itself. This can be measured through the TBL principles of accountability and measuring sustainable business (Elkington, 1997). The phrase 'triple bottom line' was first coined in 1994 by John Elkington (Norman and MacDonald, 2004), the founder of SustainAbility, a UK-based consultancy (The Economist, 2009). The term had significant public outreach with the 1997 publication of Elkington's book *Cannibals With Forks: The Triple Bottom Line of 21st Century Business*.

TBL is now globally recognized as a framework for measuring an enterprise's success beyond the usual single bottom line of economic performance, to three distinct bottom lines of social, environmental and economic performance (Willard, 2002; Norman and MacDonald, 2004). This is also referred to as the '3 Ps' – people, planet, profits – a term also coined by Elkington and later adopted by several organizations as a core framework for reporting their public sustainability disclosure. The idea is that for a business entity to be sustainable in the long run, being profitable in the conventional sense is a necessary but not sufficient condition. Businesses must also be socially responsible both internally and externally, i.e. towards their own employees and the communities/societies in which they exist and operate (Savitz and Weber, 2006).

In this chapter, the term 'sustainability' will be consistently used in the notion of TBL, i.e. financial viability, environmental friendliness, social responsibility (see Figure 8.1).

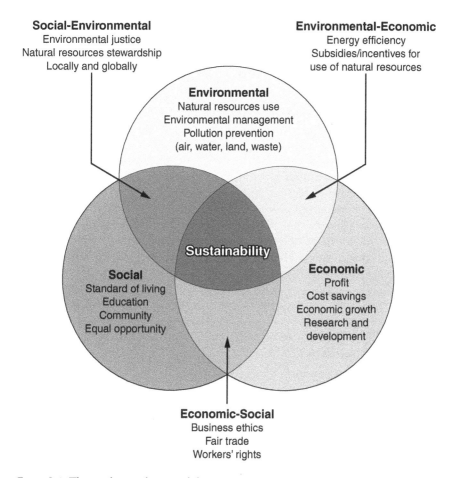

Social-Environmental
Environmental justice
Natural resources stewardship
Locally and globally

Environmental-Economic
Energy efficiency
Subsidies/incentives for
use of natural resources

Environmental
Natural resources use
Environmental management
Pollution prevention
(air, water, land, waste)

Sustainability

Social
Standard of living
Education
Community
Equal opportunity

Economic
Profit
Cost savings
Economic growth
Research and
development

Economic-Social
Business ethics
Fair trade
Workers' rights

Figure 8.1 Three spheres of sustainability.
Source: Vanderbilt University website, 2015. www.vanderbilt.edu.

The primary question in this chapter is how sustainability, enacted through sustainable entrepreneurship, overlaps and contributes to social innovation in the healthcare sector. Addressing this question requires a specific understanding of 'social entrepreneurship' as a core pillar of sustainability. To develop this understanding, we reviewed the literature on 'social entrepreneurship', which suggests that one of the seminal definitions (Dees, 1998) of the role of the 'social entrepreneur' is a person who plays the role of change agent in the society by:

- adopting a mission to create and sustain social value;
- recognizing and relentlessly pursuing new opportunities to serve that mission;

- engaging in a process of continuous innovation, adaptation and learning;
- acting boldly without being limited by resources currently at hand; and
- exhibiting a heightened sense of accountability to the constituencies served and for the outcomes created.

A broad overview of 'social entrepreneurship' conducted by Praszkzier and Nowak (2012) found other definitions which include the targeting of neglected or highly disadvantaged populations and aiming at large scale transformational benefits for society or a 'section' of society (Martin and Osberg, 2007). The same overview suggests social entrepreneurs are generally highly creative, ethical problem solvers who exhibit commitment to their ideas of social change.

The TBL framework suggests there are clear, compelling overlaps between sustainable entrepreneurship and social entrepreneurship. Social entrepreneurship is a core component of manifesting the concept of sustainability into practice through enterprise models that create shared value for the environment and the community as a whole. The World Economic Forum (2013) describes 'social innovation' as 'the application of innovative, practical, sustainable, business-like approaches that achieve positive social and/or environmental change'. This suggests that sustainable business, social innovation and managing environmental impacts go hand in hand.

In the next sections, the terms 'social innovation' and the processes of social innovation are discussed.

Social innovation explained

Social innovation can be defined as the development and implementation of new ideas (products, services and models) which are motivated by the goal of meeting social needs and creating new social relationships or collaborations. Social innovations are for the 'social good', with a fundamental aim towards improving human wellbeing in both an individual and collective capacity. The social innovation 'movement' is a response to social demands and relies on the collective inventiveness of citizens, civil society organizations, local communities, business and public servants and services (Europe 2020 Strategy, 2003; Mulgan, 2006b).

Stimulating entrepreneurship is fundamental to social innovation. This presents an opportunity for the public sector and for the private sector 'markets', to develop products and services that provide more 'meaningful' satisfaction for individuals and collective societal benefits (Mulgan, 2006b).

Current articles in this field suggest that 'social innovation' is a more useful term than 'social entrepreneurship' and 'social enterprise'. Social innovation can be enacted across the traditional boundaries separating not-for-profit organizations, governments and for-profit businesses. There is evidence of new emergence of cross-sector co-creation and collaboration and free flowing of transferrable ideas, relationships and access to alternative forms of finance for driving contemporary social innovation. This suggests that 'social innovation' can be an effective mechanism for creating sustainable positive impact which combines society and the natural environment (Phills *et al.*, 2008).

The Stanford Social Innovation Review, from the 'Center for Social Innovation' at the Stanford Graduate School of Business, defined social innovation as 'the process of inventing, securing support for, and implementing novel solutions to social needs and problems' (Phills *et al.*, 2008).

And: 'dissolving boundaries and brokering a dialogue between the public, private, and nonprofit sectors'.

Phills *et al.* (2008) suggest the need to dismantle barriers between sectors to 'unleash new and lasting solutions to the most vexing social problems of our times'.

Michael Young was widely seen from the 1960s to the 1990s as one of the world's most effective social entrepreneurs. The Young Foundation has helped to create dozens of new institutions which include the Open University and similar initiatives around the world to support social innovators with the support of funding through the Economic and Social Research Council (ESRC). In specific relevance to this chapter are new innovative institutions in healthcare which have pioneered new social models such as phone based health diagnoses and patient led healthcare. The Young Foundation continues to promote and offer training for the enactment of the intentions of social innovation in practical organizational daily operations. This work is cross-sectoral and includes cities, governments and companies (Mulgan, 2006a).

The process of social innovation

There are many interpretations of social innovation. Most discussions about social innovation generally adopt one of two main lenses for understanding:

- How social change happens, with social change portrayed as being driven by a small number of 'heroic, energetic and impatient individuals'. Some of these names are well known, such as Muhammad Yunus, the founder of Grameen Bank and the concept of microcredit, and Kenyan Nobel Prize winner Wangari Maathai (Mulgan, 2006a).
- The second lens takes the view of understanding 'who drives social innovation'. This view considers individuals as the temporary 'carriers' of ideas of innovation rather than the originators.

In examples of social innovations with long lasting impact over the past half century, the role of specific individuals is soon forgotten, including movements of change such as environmentalism. These movements involve millions of people, intellectuals and organizational leaders, many of whom realize they are following and 'carrying' change in service to the needs of public demands. 'Some of the most effective methods for cultivating social innovation start from the presumption that people are competent interpreters of their own lives and competent solvers of their own problems' (Mulgan, 2006a, p. 150).

Workplace innovation (green buildings)

In some countries, particularly in Northern Europe, the term 'social innovation' is used to describe 'workplace innovation'. Businesses can be supported by European Regional Development Funding (ERDF) to finance workplace innovations which help management and employees to explore and develop more productive and healthy ways of working.

The focus of workplace innovation is to improve all aspects of work in organizations, including enhanced management techniques and involving employees at all levels in daily business decision making and workplace improvements. Workplaces with flatter hierarchies tend to be more open to addressing both social and technological challenges and this creates more possibilities for employees to contribute creative suggestions about workplace enhancements which have been shown to lead to more productivity in the workplace. Well known examples include Google, which allows employees to spend 20 per cent of their time on their own projects, and IKEA which enables innovative practices including 'stand-up round-table meetings' that empower employees to address problems in the workplace in a self-directed manner with minimum interference from the management team.

Workplace innovation also includes 'eco-innovation' and the growing movement towards 'green buildings' and green office spaces. The increase in green building and design, and green retrofit, has evolved from the recognition that buildings can have both negative and positive impacts on people and the environment (Allen *et al.*, 2015). Using Google again as an example, it has 'green classrooms' for employee and management in-house training which have been shown to enhance learning. From an external stakeholder perspective, it has been shown that green buildings can enhance reputation of organizations which increases employee attractiveness (EPA, 2007).

Over the past 20 years there has been a growing interest about how 'eco-innovation' and the 'designed environment' can provide a vital role in improving performance in the health and wellness sector. Emerging practical research suggests that investing in nature based designed buildings can improve psychological wellbeing and economic benefits (Witherspoon, 2014). This interest is underpinned by the notion of 'biophilia', which means design and construction to bring buildings to life in a way to connect human beings with nature and ecological systems (Kellert *et al.*, 2008).

The fundamental principle of biophilia is that humans have a biological need for connection with nature. A growing body of research suggests that biophilic 'design' can have an overwhelmingly positive effect on people, physically, mentally and socially. Therefore, the design industry is shifting towards introducing 'biophilia' elements relating to humans' basic need to connect with nature, especially in healthcare, as a way to improve patient and employee wellness (Lamin art, 2014).

Small scale biophilic elements can have positive effects in reducing stress in hospitals for patients and staff. In a study conducted at a Swedish university hospital in 1990, scenes of nature in artwork and murals were shown to reduce anxiety and discomfort in patients recovering from open heart surgery. The study showed a reduction in post-operative anxiety for patients looking at pictures of natural scenes that included water, compared with pictures of abstract art, a control picture or no picture at all (Ulrich and Lunden, 1990).

Examples of biophilic applications in hospitals include:

- nature based 'art';
- use of nature based colours to promote the feeling of comfort and wellness in patients, including beiges and other neutral colours with accents of warm woods, ochres, blues and greens;
- architectural surfaces made of natural fibres, jute textiles and both real and printed wood designs;
- adding biophilic elements such as increased daylight, water, plants, trees and non-threatening animals is found to reduce patient and staff anxiety.

(Witherspoon, 2014)

Canadian studies investigating the long term benefits in health and cost of green buildings find that the energy cost savings of green buildings is generally agreed upon, however there is disparity between practitioner and researcher perception with respect to the benefits to health and increased productivity as an impact of green buildings (Issa *et al.*, 2010).

There is further evidence that green buildings benefit society beyond physical health such as reduction in asthma and allergies (Allen *et al.*, 2015) and also improve mental health, clarity of thinking, productivity and overall wellbeing (Allen *et al.*, 2015; University of Exeter, 2014).

In support of the assertions of the 'biophilia' movement, studies conducted by Cardiff University and the University of Exeter indicate how even a small 'greening' change in the workplace, such as including plants and foliage as an integral part of the interior decoration, can boost productivity. Lead researcher Marlon Nieuwenhuis, from Cardiff University's School of Psychology, said:

> Our research suggests that investing in landscaping the office with plants will pay off through an increase in office workers' quality of life and productivity. Although previous laboratory research pointed in this direction, our research is, to our knowledge, the first to examine this in real offices, showing benefits over the long term. It directly challenges the widely accepted business philosophy that a lean office with clean desks is more productive.

Co-author Dr Craig Knight, of Psychology at the University of Exeter, added:

> Psychologically manipulating real workplaces and real jobs adds new depth to our understanding of what is right and what is wrong with existing workspace design and management. We are now developing a template for a genuinely smart office.

(University of Exeter, 2014)

If a number of plants on the inside of the workplace can boost positive energy, increase a sense of wellbeing and thus enhance productivity, this suggests that a holistic green, sustainable building can trigger a much more potent mix of social good and potentially aid healing in both physical and mental conditions (Issa *et al.*, 2010).

In the context of healthcare, the benefits of green buildings have been shown to include:

- enhanced patient healing as a consequence of more natural light;
- improved health of the building through reduced chemicals and toxic building materials;
- long term enhanced operational efficiency for patients, workers and visitors;
- improved employee satisfaction.

(EPA, 2007)

Other studies which use Indoor Environmental Quality (IEQ) metrics to compare the impacts of green hospital buildings and conventional buildings found a 19 per cent decrease in mortality, 70 per cent decrease in blood stream infections, a general increase in quality of patient care and increase in employee satisfaction in the green facilities (Allen *et al.*, 2015).

With a more broad view of society, research based evidence suggests that people living in cities are generally more overactive and stressed than those in rural areas (Tracada and Caperna, 2012) with evidence to suggest the benefits of nature on human health. The WHO Expert Committee on Environmental Health in Urban Development noted that the health of city dwellers is strongly influenced by physical, social, economic, political and cultural factors in the urban environment. These factors interact with synergy between each other to impact on human health (WHO, 1991, p. 11). This is supported by a 2011 study conducted at the University of Oregon which revealed that 10 per cent of employee absences could be attributed to building and architectural structures that are unconnected with nature. The study found that a person's view had a primary impact on absenteeism. When asked to rate scenes according to their preference, people using the building significantly preferred views of greenery and vegetation over the urban views. The study showed that employees with natural landscape views took an average of 57 hours of sick leave per year compared to the 68 hours taken by employees with no view at all (Elzeyadi, 2011).

The next section makes the links between social innovation (workplace innovation) and healthcare.

Social innovation in healthcare

Social innovation in healthcare can be viewed as the development of new partnerships and collaborations of networks between:

- healthcare organizations;

- healthcare professionals;
- social capital and patient relations.

A social innovation perspective of the healthcare system could increase knowledge and insightful know-how with regards to the knowledge based decision making processes in management systems for quality and integrity control (EURAM, 2012). Social innovation in healthcare can help many areas such as organizational networks, quality, performance and productivity of healthcare services, strategic collaborations of health policy and governance, as well as health management and entrepreneurship (Smith, 2010).

Social innovation at its core consists of new ideas and solutions aiming at resolving social needs and problems. The term 'social innovation' covers a diverse range of initiatives and actions including: local currencies, new models of healthcare, eco-commuting initiatives, co-housing schemes and online platforms for eco-innovation. There are many definitions of the term and central to the concept is the involvement and empowerment of citizens to enable society's capacity to act for change (Caulier-Grice *et al.*, 2012).

There are overlaps of data between frameworks, tools and theoretical approaches towards social innovation in the environmental and healthcare sectors with practical recommendations for the evolution of social and eco-innovation. This includes diverse community groups, NGOs, charities, governments, businesses, industries, academics, philanthropists or combinations of these (Biggs *et al.*, 2010).

Social innovation in health systems contributes to maximizing performance and assists public and private efforts in delivering improved services and ultimately promote health at both individual and community levels. Social innovation is a socio-political concept which existed before 'technological innovation' (Howaldt *et al.*, 2014). Technological advancements in healthcare include new drugs, devices, diagnostics, vaccines as well as new ways to organize human resources, information, and decision making in health systems (Gardner *et al.*, 2007).

Societal trends are increasingly perceived as opportunities for innovation with trends in demography, communities, social media, environment, health and wellbeing all being drivers of growing markets (Grayson and Hodges, 2002, 2004). In particular, health is an important sector of the economy and one of the faster growing sectors. In general, these trends tend to be community oriented. In Finland, for instance, there are many examples of social innovation combined with technological advancements, which bring together public services and private industries for the improved benefit of end-user groups and other key stakeholders (European Commission, 2013).

This is an exciting time for social innovation in the environmental and health sectors with a growing number of initiatives, hubs and incubator clusters to co-create and develop a body of new research and knowledge (Gardner *et al.*, 2007). It is important to understand how social innovation happens, including those initiatives being driven by a small number of 'energized and impatient individuals' (Mulgan, 2006a; Science communication unit, 2014), such as changes for ageing populations, enhanced healthcare and enhanced urban planning. There is a growing diversity of issues in countries and cities which drives the need for innovative, creative and holistic ways of organizing schooling, housing and healthcare (Grayson and Hodges, 2002).

Moreover, there is a rise in chronic diseases and mental/psychological problems related to modern lifestyles, including arthritis and depression, thus illustrating the need for social innovation towards better health and overall improved quality of life. This rising occurrence of chronic diseases will not be resolved solely by conventional medical treatments, but a combination of social and scientific innovations (Mulgan, 2006a). In the future, improvements in human health and life expectancy can be brought about as the combined result of improved, well targeted diagnostic methods and treatments, attention to environment and innovative ways of empowering patients, both individually and as groups.

The starting point of innovation is an idea of how to meet a need that has not yet been addressed. Creativity is stimulated by people's thinking processes which then becomes a contribution to social innovation. However, creativity, new ideas and social innovation require support and nourishment and in some societies there is no source of funding or sufficient knowledge about social innovation. Thus, social innovation is much more likely to happen within appropriate, favourable conditions and environments with sufficient supporting resources (Mulgan, 2006b; EURAM, 2012; European Commission, 2013).

The next section discusses the relationship between social innovation, healthcare and the natural environment.

How is the concept of social innovation used in research into health innovation and the environment?

Social innovation can be understood as a 'starting point for creating social dynamics behind technological innovations' (BEPA, 2010, p. 8), as something that arises as a result of constant changes by inventive and imitating actors (Tarde, 2009, p. 67). There are many examples of social innovation from well known organizations such as: Wikipedia, NHS Direct, Open University. It is said that 'social innovation' is a key to making public services smarter and more efficient for the benefit of the society (Mulgan, 2006b).

If we look at the history of movements seeking 'sustainable change', such as the environment, we can see how these activities have been influenced by different stakeholders. In the nineteenth century, we can trace social movements for the protections of forests and nature in general which shifted in the twentieth century to more sophisticated movements to protect biodiversity and ecosystems from unsustainable economic activity (Mulgan, 2006a). In the twenty first century, many social-eco innovations exist such as community recycling as part of the broader schemes of urban protection. The success of social innovation 'movements' requires multiple skills including process management, change management, relationship and collaboration network skills and a balance of actors from both public and the private sectors (Lappi *et al.*, 2014).

In regards to the private sector, mounting evidence indicates that the competitiveness of an organization and the health of communities close to its operations are strongly interconnected. Quite often, innovative solutions in communities are being generated by ordinary people in their own localities in response to challenges stemming from local business activities (Beleno and Andres, 2014; Howaldt *et al.*, 2014). Such innovations are generally focused on people's need for improved healthcare, quality of life, overall wellbeing, education, and prosperity at their local level (Howaldt *et al.*, 2014).

As well as organizations and local communities, nation-states also need transformational change. The indicators for this suggestion include the ongoing economic crises in many parts of the world, income inequality and escalating environmental degradation, which are triggers for the creation of systemic change at national and sectoral levels in the private and social economy (Primorac and Jovancai, 2014). Social innovation for sustainable development is necessary on all fronts: economic, social, political and cultural (Beleno and Andres, 2014).

According to Van den Hazel (2010), the main challenge of environmental protection and human health is not due to the lack of scientific evidence, but rather the ability to effectively communicate, share and integrate existing knowledge into respective policy making processes. This suggests that thinking in a collectively, socially innovative way, could contribute to addressing environmental degradation, investment in human capital and new skills necessary to promote the efficiency, distribute resources equitably and ensure diversification and pluralism (Lopez, 2008). From a research perspective this indicates a need for a broader number of studies combining IEQ metrics and qualitative user perception of the health and wellbeing benefits of eco-innovation.

Many countries in the top competitiveness rankings of the World Economic Forum (including Finland, Sweden, Denmark and Singapore) are becoming exemplary social innovation paradigms. The importance of social innovation needs to become more deeply recognized and sufficiently understood by political and business leaders, in order for governance structures, policies and procedures to be transformed and updated to meet contemporary world challenges. This phenomenon will have increasing importance in the future as governments struggle to deliver the demands of increased public services with fewer financial resources (Mulgan, 2006a).

Methodology

The approach for this chapter was a single case study and literature review. We conducted a literature review for research studies which explored the impact of green building on human health, wellbeing, comfort and enhanced productivity. Each paper was read and reviewed for inclusion by at least two of the three authors. Because of the contemporary nature of this study topic, we also conducted internet searches for 'grey' literature such as government reports. Data collection was conducted in an evolving, naturally occurring ad-hoc way during the 3 years (2012–2015) of the green building (ESA) operation. This is explained in the fifth section. Visitors' comments about their perceptions and experiences of the green building were captured through a visitor satisfaction survey, using a 1–5 Likert scale. Following this study, a second page of questions, with a focus on the aspects of the green building, were added (see Appendix 8.1). Other responses were selected from free flowing, qualitative written comments in the ESA visitor book. Comments from both data collection tools which relate directly to the health and wellbeing 'experience' of green building were selected for inclusion in this chapter. Other comments such as about the event operations or catering arrangements were not included.

The next section explains the observed impact of an ecological design building on the health and wellbeing of people using the facility.

Case study – sustainable entrepreneurism – green building (The European Sustainability Academy – ESA, Crete, Greece)

A literature review on the relationship between green buildings and health found a relatively small number of articles, but increasing by year. Fifteen core published studies are discussed extensively by Allen et al. (2015, p. 253). We found other studies examining the impact of green buildings on comfort, productivity and health in housing and offices (Jacobs et al., 2009; Kim et al., 2013; Wolf and Robbins, 2015) and for education (Paul and Taylor, 2007). Others also evaluate the long term cost benefits of green building in the context of improved health and improved productivity (Issa et al., 2010). The findings between the studies are variable, sometimes conflicting and 'biased', for example, users' impression of the 'beauty' of a building can significantly impact on their short and long term sensemaking (Weick, 1995) and perception about the comfort and health benefits of the building (Paul and Taylor, 2007). However, we noticed overlaps and synergy in the studies in respect to the experiences and perceptions of the users, notably the studies which focus on the human need for connection with nature in living and working spaces and the growing body of enquiry around biophilic design (Kellert et al., 2008).

In this chapter we are inspired by the notion of the transferability of understanding about the green building impacts on people in the different user groups of teaching and healthcare and also the understanding of social innovation emergence from invention and imitation (BEPA, 2010, p. 8). Therefore, we are taking a cross sector perspective (education and healthcare) in terms of the benefits of green buildings for transient, visiting populations. A common factor between healthcare and teaching environments is the temporary communities of public visitors from diverse backgrounds who use the facilities and the services offered inside the building.

ESA background and synchronization with the Greek socio-economic turbulence

The European Sustainability Academy (ESA) was built during 2011 in the village of Drapanos, Crete and opened in 2012. The core aim of ESA is to provide 'leadership for positive impact' through holistic and authentic sustainability learning processes. The serendipity of building this sustainable enterprise, which provides experiential teaching services on sustainable leadership and sustainable business management, came into fruition co-incidentally at the same time that Greece was undergoing a deep recession and fiscal adjustment due to chronic political, leadership and structural shortfalls of previous years. The health of Greek society was affected by increased chronic stress, depression and suicide rates.

The Greek sovereign debt crisis of 2010 revealed the lack of leadership in multiple layers of the country's administration and management in politics, public administration and private sector. This leadership deficit created an unsustainable operating model that eventually brought the country to the brink of economic collapse. These macro conditions can create challenges and opportunities for a social and eco-entrepreneurial initiative like ESA, but above all, make ESA very relevant and current in terms of contemporary socio-economic need.

About ESA ecological and biomimicry elements

The ESA training academy was designed as an innovative, fully ecological bio-climatic construction, with the core purpose of providing teaching programmes on sustainable leadership to business and organizational leaders, and university students (www.eurosustainability.org). The ESA teaching philosophy is one of 'applied sustainability' which involves combining academic research with practical action. With a strong emphasis on action learning, ESA management and leadership programmes are designed to be highly stimulating for participants, via the experiential learning approach at the heart of ESA.

ESA client quote, September 2013:

> ... this building is fabulous. I feel very honoured that you gave me this wonderful opportunity to visit one of the most beautiful and special ecological buildings I have ever visited in the world. I especially love the amazing ecological aura and powerful atmosphere for learning. I very much look forward to returning.

Crete was chosen as the location for ESA because of its ancient history of philosophical and ethical debate and unique natural landscape. The design of the building is essential to effectively blend ESA's unique 'user-experience' teaching approach with the beautiful surroundings and maximize the benefits for all stakeholders. It is one of the Academy's founding principles that the benefits of teaching sustainable leadership, management and innovation can only be maximized when taking place in a sustainable, bioclimatic building located in a remote, natural setting which creates numerous positive enablers.

ESA client quote, October 2012:

> ... it was a very interesting experience on different levels. The building you've made is really unique for its environment and its unique elements. It is a true innovation. Thank you.

Harnessing the principles of biomimicry, the ESA building was literally raised from the ground using local natural materials (wood, earth, straw and stone) in a similar way that ants or birds create their nests using available materials from the local area. The building draws energy exclusively from the sun via photovoltaic panels and operates to achieve zero emissions and generate zero waste ending up in local landfills. The underpinning objective of ESA is to be a low environmental impact building for conducting low environmental impact business activity, resulting in a TBL, net positive contribution to the market, the environment and community. It is noteworthy that during ESA's first two years of operation, the enterprise contributed approximately €100,000 to the local, rural communities of the rural, hilltop, Apokoronas region in Crete and provided much needed local employment.

ESA client quote, October 2012:

> I wasn't quite sure what to expect, but ESA exceeded my expectations in every way as an exceptional place for learning...

During the ESA construction period, action learning workshops about sustainable construction and community stakeholder involvement were the beginning of ESA's unique experiential teaching process and skills development. People from across Europe participated in workshops to learn how to manage sustainable construction projects. This objective has been at the forefront of ESA's strategy right from its inception.

'Sustainability', however, in ESA's context not only pertains to its low environmental impact and related operational efficiency gains, but also to the holistically positive effect that sustainable buildings have on visitors, clients, employees and the local community.

ESA client quote, September 2013:

> ... congrats on developing such an inspiring space and community for learning. I look forward to returning and watching the centre evolve straw by straw and fingerprint by fingerprint.

Research over 40 years indicates that people spend 90 per cent of their time inside their houses or work buildings. Green building design can influence human health in two different ways. First for the individual by providing better working

Table 8.1 The TBL benefits of a green building

Environmental benefits	Economic benefits	Social benefits
• Enhance and protect biodiversity and ecosystems • Improve air and water quality • Reduce waste streams • Conserve and restore natural resources	• Reduce operating costs • Create, expand and shape markets for green product and services • Improve occupant productivity • Optimize life-cycle economic performance	• Enhance occupant comfort and health • Heighten aesthetic qualities • Minimize strain on local infrastructure

Source: EPA (2009), www.epa.gov/greenbuilding/pubs/gbstats.pdf.

and living indoor environments, and second indirectly on the broader population through reductions in energy use and air pollution. A growing body of evidence is developing to bring new insights into how building related factors impact profoundly on health, wellbeing, quality of life and productivity (Allen *et al.*, 2015).

All of the input efficiencies explained above contribute significant positive impacts on human health, both physical and mental. According to the US Environmental Protection Agency (EPA), the benefits of green building, from a TBL perspective, can be summed up in Table 8.1.

ESA in alignment with the natural landscape

ESA's bioclimatic architectural design is an example of biophilic design discussed earlier in this chapter. The construction is built around existing trees and rock formations which directly connects the building with nature and creates an overlap of indoor and outdoor spaces. The design takes into account the climate and environmental conditions of its specific locus, seeking cohesion between the building and its functions and natural elements (biodiversity, sun, wind, rain). This leads to an optimization of resources and makes the Academy a low maintenance facility, which, in turn, means fewer resources to operate, clean, maintain, expand, restore or repair the building. In general, green bioclimatic structures minimize or completely abolish indoor pollutants and eliminate hazardous materials which are damaging to the environment and have been linked with cancer and respiratory diseases. The eco and natural materials of an eco-building such as ESA reduce negative impact on human health by eradicating damaging substances: 'coming primarily from combustion sources, building materials and furnishings, household cleaning, maintenance, personal care, or hobby products; central heating and cooling systems and humidification devices; and outdoor sources such as radon, pesticides, and outdoor air pollution' (EPA, 2009).

ESA guest quote, 2013:

> The openness to my [new] ideas in such an inspirational venue is deeply fulfilling. Thank you.

Studies have found that nature promotes and increases human performance, by improving workplace satisfaction (Wolf and Robbins, 2015). Also, productivity levels improve when people moved from conventional buildings to green buildings, and in the case of educational facilities, an increase of daylight in learning rooms improves student performance by 9–20 per cent. In cases of long term use of green building education facilities there has been indications of a decrease in incidents of allergies and asthma (Issa *et al.* 2010).

Furthermore, this unique, innovative, fully ecological, experiential learning facility in a stunning natural Cretan location amplifies the effectiveness of the teaching process by 'disconnecting' participants from their hectic daily rhythms, thus making them more receptive to new knowledge, information, ideas and attitudes towards the sustainability challenge and the crucial role of the business world in meeting that challenge.

The ESA approach to sustainable business is a systemic learning process to integrate sustainability actions into organizational operations. In summary, ESA teaches managers and business leaders how to build in sustainability as opposed to bolt on sustainability.

ESA client quote, May 2014:

> This place is made of magic. So peaceful. So connected with nature. So healing. So conducive to learning. Thank you for everything.

Conclusion

The aim of this chapter is to explore the debate about social innovation and the real impact of 'green building design' on improved human health (Paul and Taylor, 2007) and to provide new insight and practical observation to contribute to that debate. Health performance indicators do suggest that patients recover faster in hospitals with eco-design and connectivity with nature (Allen *et al.*, 2015) and both patient recovery and staff morale and performance are improved by the adoption of biophilic design to connect people to nature and bring buildings to life (Kellert *et al.*, 2008). More broadly there is evidence of a sense of improved health and wellbeing in communities that are connected with nature (Tracada and Caperna, 2012).

The ESA building, discussed in the case study, was designed and built with the objective of creating a holistic sustainability teaching experience, however an unexpected consequence has been the notable positive impact of mood, health and wellbeing of people using the eco-building and its outdoor spaces. This suggests transferrable observations between eco-buildings used by the public and the potential benefits of green buildings on human health including and over and beyond hospitals.

With a view to exploring the question *'What can the healthcare sector learn from sustainable entrepreneurship and social innovation?'*, the overarching themes from exploring the impact of sustainable entrepreneurship suggest there is a positive impact on the quality of life, health and sense of wellbeing of people (society) that can be gained from living and working in 'green buildings'. The design of 'healthier' spaces and eco-buildings which connect people with nature has been shown to create better productivity gains through a process of meeting people's deep need to connect with nature (Van den Hazel, 2010; Howaldt *et al.*, 2014). However, when considering the main question 'Are green buildings healthier buildings?' many of the indicators of better health in green buildings are 'perceived' self-reported health outcomes (Allen *et al.*, 2015) and conflicting. The growing movement towards 'biophilic' design in healthcare provides the opportunity for more study to gain more knowledge about the validity of this perception.

When considering the second question posed at the start of this chapter '*Can ecological buildings and "sustainable spaces" positively impact on the performance and quality of services provided by healthcare organizations, for the benefit of stakeholder groups, including clients, patients and employees?*' the studies of biophilic design (Kellert *et al.*, 2008; Witherspoon, 2014) with the responses from ESA visitors and users suggest that there is a positive impact on the health and wellbeing of stakeholder groups. This exploration found detailed IEQ and productivity KPI evidence to suggest that green buildings can and do contribute to enhanced physical human health as well as improved mental health, clarity of thinking, productivity and overall wellbeing (Issa *et al.*, 2010; University of Exeter, 2014; Allen *et al.*, 2015).

The ESA ecological building described previously is a relatively new (three years) bespoke, green building which has been designed and built specifically as a teaching facility which also provides enhanced health and productivity (learning) outputs. From the new information arising from this study and with enhanced data collection and IEQ metrics, ESA can become a longitudinal practical research study to bring new insight into the most impactful, positive aspects of green building on people and to the general public and the transference of this insight to other 'transient communities of users' such as healthcare environments.

More broadly, focusing on developing solutions in social innovation, sustainable entrepreneurship and sustainable healthcare can bring new insight and practical positive impacts which can contribute to greater social effectiveness of governments, industries, universities and individuals. To achieve such levels of sustainability and social innovation on the scale of national development requires a strategic approach (Bass and Dalal-Clayton, 2012). For this to happen it is important to create partnerships through an open innovation model between community, government, industry, universities and individuals (see Figure 8.2) and enhance understanding and effective communication about the positive and negative impacts of environmental protection and health for inclusion in policy making processes (Van den Hazel, 2010).

The small sample of comments from users of the purpose built green building, ESA, described in the case study section of this chapter support studies that suggest that green *buildings* can positively affect people's mood, energy, sense of wellbeing and productivity. In the case of ESA-Crete, this is manifested as more

Quadruple helix innovation

Government, academia, industry and citizens collaborating together to drive structural changes far beyond the scope of any one organization could achieve on its own

Figure 8.2 Model for open innovation, for social change and social innovation.

Source: Open innovation 2.0 conference: Sustainable economy, society, stability, jobs, prosperity, Dublin, Ireland, 20–21 May 2013. www.slideshare.net/DCSF/open-innovation-20-martin-curley-opening-final.

effective teaching programmes and happier, more engaged and relaxed learners who become more receptive to new information, knowledge, mindsets and attitudes. Perhaps this sense of enhanced wellbeing can be transferred to greater co-creativity and collaboration in cross sectoral social innovation.

Sustainable construction, as an integral part of sustainable enterprise, not only reduces negative environmental and social impacts but also enables enhanced cognitive and behavioural processes that strengthen the broader social entrepreneurial cause. In the case of ESA, sustainable construction in a natural setting becomes an enabler of better services provided (teaching) by breaking down cognitive barriers by enhancing positive 'psychology' thus facilitating improved learning procedures and outcomes.

Overlapping studies suggest that ecological, sustainable constructions can improve the quality of learning environments in education and also enhance the quality of services in healthcare. IEQ measured benefits in green buildings can be transposed to better self-reported health and wellbeing indicators (Allen *et al.*, 2015) in multiple sectors. More research using mixed methods of quantitative IEQ metrics and qualitative user narratives is necessary for gaining deeper understanding about the longer term impact of green buildings on human (individual and collective) physical and mental health and overall sense of well-being.

As discussed in this chapter, the lessons from sustainable entrepreneurship in the teaching and training sector can be applied to the healthcare services through social innovation and eco-innovation processes. In the same way that the influence of a sustainable construction can break down learning and teaching barriers, emerging evidence suggests that 'connection with nature' can break down barriers to healing and positively contribute to enhanced states speedy recovery for people. Sustainable buildings as social innovation in the healthcare sector can create happier employees, patients and visitors and ultimately generate a product of higher quality and better performance in healthcare and contribute to healthcare organizations becoming sustainable organizations (Eccles *et al.*, 2012).

ESA client quote, September 2014:

> Dear ESA team, it has been an amazing week of important insights, conversations with extraordinary people, in the most uplifting and wonderful place with delicious food and rich nature experiences. Thank you so much. PS. I don't want to go home – not just yet.

The green building concept of ESA in Crete can be seen as a practical manifestation of sustainability principles and social innovation as shown in Figure 8.3.

The contribution of this chapter is a starting point, from a small sample, which provides some practical validation of existing research studies on the positive impact of green buildings on health and health care. The sample of user comments from this publicly used green building in the education sector supports findings of the perceived positive impact of green buildings, particularly in healthcare (hospitals) (Allen *et al.*, 2015).

The limitations of this study include only one case study and a small number of respondents over a short time of three years. The data collection methodology has relied on people's perceptions.

The outcomes of this preliminary study suggest the need for enhanced data collection and analysis methodology for a further study. To that end, Appendix 8.1 illustrates a revised data collection tool.

The literature review revealed a consistent theme that most studies on the topic of the impact of green buildings on health do not provide clear evidence that green buildings are healthier buildings. This seems to be due to relying on 'perceptions' of comfort, health and wellbeing, rather than on the more objective framework of 'Health Performance Indicators'.

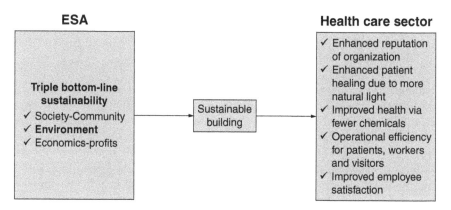

Figure 8.3 Sustainable building as a vehicle for TBL innovation in the healthcare sector.
Source: ESA Crete.

Further research suggestions

It is essential to teach and educate local and global communities about the benefits of eco-innovation and to equip people with the necessary skills and knowledge in order to achieve environmental and community sustainability. It is important to create environments where collaboration and a collective 'sense of sustainability' can be developed with the purpose of driving positive social change.

There is a need for national and global investment via diverse forms of 'funding' to support the 'creative economy' of social innovation and eco-innovation (through sustainability entrepreneurism) in many sectors, including education and healthcare. More case studies and longitudinal studies which focus on the more holistic positive impact of sustainable, eco-innovation could bring new insight and new practical solutions for enhanced performance in education and healthcare. More research about the positive impact of green buildings on people (society) would be valuable in terms of understanding what specific areas of funding could make the greatest positive impact to different stakeholder groups. The data and information from such research can be applied to transforming healthcare systems through social innovation.

More specifically, this exploratory narrative suggests that there is fertile ground for further research in two interlinked fronts:

How sustainable buildings affect an organisation in terms of its operations as part of the triple bottom line (TBL) sustainable business framework. There appear to be links and synergies that require further elucidation in order to be exploited as a promotional tool for sustainable buildings and also for driving sound policy recommendations. Tapping in to the insights of the ESA case study, further focus could be given to the positive knock-on effects of sustainable constructions on organizations which provide teaching/mentoring/coaching programmes and related services. This can be especially interesting to understand how a sustainable eco-construction can contribute to an enhanced learning process through the positive impact of enabling mechanisms which trigger participants and clients to relax, feel safe and positively altering the sense-making and cognitive learning processes. A second stage of this research could be application to other sectors including healthcare.

There is a need for further exploration of the impact of holistic sustainable buildings as an integral part of the healthcare sector processes, with a clear focus on how this affects healthcare sector employees, surrounding communities and especially the psychological state and healing process of the patients. There seem to be clear, positive impacts on the end-user of services provided by the healthcare sector. This requires further elucidation for the healthcare industry to increase adaptation of sustainable construction as standard practice. Clarifying the links between sustainable buildings and improved healthcare can be a contribution to policy making instruments that might promote sustainable building and make eco-innovation processes mandatory in specific sectors.

Appendix 8.1: visitor satisfaction survey

Event:..
Date:...
Name (optional):...

Please scale the following aspects on a 1–5 basis where 5 signifies 'yes, agree strongly' and 1 signifies 'No, disagree strongly'	5	4	3	2	1	N/A

Did the event match your needs?
Did you gain relevant knowledge and information?
Will you be able to apply such knowledge and
  information in your work?
Did you find the presentation of the sessions interesting?
Were you satisfied with the registration procedure?
Were you satisfied with your accommodation?
Were you satisfied with the transfers?
Were you satisfied with the venue location?
Did you feel the venue was suitable for the event?
Were you satisfied with the meal arrangements?
Were you satisfied with the equipment provided?
Were you satisfied with the interpretation?
Overall were you satisfied by the event?

Other comments

Thank you for your time. This feedback is important to us in our aim to maintain the delivery of high quality programmes that meet client expectations.

Eco-building

We are interested about understanding the impact of the features of green buildings on people's experiences. We would greatly appreciate your feedback about your experience of the ESA building.

Please rate the ESA building by ticking the box on the scale of 1–5 basis where 3 is the middle point.

	5	4	3	2	1	
Beautiful	5	4	3	2	1	Ugly
Relaxed	5	4	3	2	1	Tense
Colourful	5	4	3	2	1	Dull
Too bright	5	4	3	2	1	Too dim
Glare	5	4	3	2	1	No glare
Draughty	5	4	3	2	1	Still
Too hot	5	4	3	2	1	Too cold
Too noisy	5	4	3	2	1	Too quiet
Too dry	5	4	3	2	1	Too humid
Too sunny	5	4	3	2	1	Not enough sun
Poor working environment	5	4	3	2	1	Excellent working environment

Overall how did you feel during your time at ESA?

About you

How would you describe your work?

1   Administration/Clerical
2   Professional
3   Managerial
4   Other...

What is your age?

1   20 or under
2   21–30
3   31–40
4   41–50
5   51–60
6   Over 60

What is your gender?

1   Female
2   Male

References

Allen, J.G., MacNaughton, P., Laurent, J.G.C., Flanigan, S.S., Eitland, E.S. and Speng-ler, J.D. (2015). 'Green buildings and health'. *Current Environment Health Report*, Vol 2. pp. 250–258. Springer. DOI 10.1007/s40572-015-0063-y.

Bass, S. and Dalal-Clayton, B. (2012). *Sustainable Development Strategies: A Resource Book*. Routledge, London.

Beleno, M. and Andres, C. (2014). 'About challenges of the modern world: Health, environment and social development America Latina case'. *Megatrend Review*, Vol. 11, No. 3, p. 135.

BEPA (Bureau of European Policy Advisers) (2010). *Empowering People, Driving Change: Social Innovation in the European Union*. Publication Office of the European Union, Luxembourg.

Biggs, R., Westley, F.R. and Carpenter, S.R. (2010). 'Navigating the back loop: Fostering social innovation and transformation in ecosystem'. *Management, Ecology and Society*, Vol. 15, No. 2, p. 9.

Caulier-Grice, J., Davies, A., Patrick, R. and Norman, W. (2012). *Defining Social Innovation. Part One of Social Innovation Overview: A deliverable of the project:* 'The theoretical, empirical and policy foundations for building social innovation in Europe' (TEPSIE), European Commission – 7th Framework Programme, European Commission, DG Research, Brussels. Available online at: http://siresearch.eu/sites/default/files/1.1%20 Part%201%20-%20defining%20social%20innovation_0.pdf Accessed on 8th May 2015.

Clarkson, M.B.E. (1995). 'A stakeholder framework for analyzing and evaluating corporate social performance', *Academy of Management Review*, Vol. 24, pp. 92–117.

Dees, J.G. (1998) *The Meaning of Social Entrepreneurship*. Kauffman Center for Entrepreneurial Leadership. Available online at: www.technologycouncil.ca/files/documents/The%20meaning%20of%20social%20Entrepreneurism.pdf. Accessed on 8th May 2015.

Drucker, P.F. (1985). *Innovation and Entrepreneurship*. Harper & Row, New York.

Eccles, R.G., Miller-Perkins, K. and Serafeim, G. (2012). 'How to become a sustainable company'. *MIT Sloan Management Review*, Vol. 53, No. 4.

Economist, The (2009). 'Idea: Triple Bottom Line'. 17th November. Available online at: www.economist.com/node/14301663 Accessed on 8th May 2015.

Elkington, J. (1997). *Cannibals with Forks: The Triple Bottom Line of 21st Century Business*. Capstone, Oxford.

Elzeyadi, I.M. (2011). *Daylighting Bias and Biophilia: Quantifying the Impact of Daylighting on Occupants' Health*. Greenbuild 2011 Proceedings, USGBC Press.

EPA (2007). *Building Healthy Hospitals: Case Studies Overview*. Available online at: www. epa.gov/region9/waste/p2/pdf/overview-factsheet-final-071126.pdf Accessed on 8th May 2015.

EPA (2009). *Buildings and their Impact on the Environment: A Statistical Summary*. Available online at: www.epa.gov/greenbuilding/pubs/gbstats.pdf Accessed on 8th May 2015.

EURAM (2012). 'Social innovation for competitiveness organizational performance and human excellence'. Available online at: http://euram2012.nl/r/default.asp?iId=FEJEEK. Accessed on 9th May 2015.

Europe 2020 Strategy (2003). *Guide to Social Innovation*. Available online at: http://ec.europa.eu/regional_policy/sources/docgener/presenta/social_innovation/social_innovation_2013.pdf Accessed on 21st April 2015.

European Commission (2013). *Guide to Social Innovation*. Available online at: http://ec.europa.eu/regional_policy/sources/docgener/presenta/social_innovation/social_innovation_2013.pdf. Accessed on 1st March 2015.

European Sustainability Academy Crete: www.EuroSustainability.org.

Freeman, R.E. (1984). *Strategic Management: A Stakeholder Approach*. Pitman, Boston.

Gardner, A.C., Acharya, T. and Yach, D. (2007). 'Technological and social innovation: A unifying new paradigm for global health'. *Health Affairs*, Vol. 26, No. 4 pp. 1052–1061. Available online at: http://content.healthaffairs.org/content/26/4/1052. full.pdf Accessed on 9th May 2015.

Grayson, D.R. and Hodges, A. (2002). *Everybody's Business*. Dorling Kindersley, London.

Grayson, D.R. and Hodges, A. (2004). *Corporate Social Opportunity*. Greenleaf, London.

Howaldt, J., Butzin, A., Domanski, D. and Kaletka, C. (2014). 'Theoretical approaches to social innovation – a critical literature review'. A deliverable of the project: 'Social Innovation: Driving Force of Social Change' (SI-DRIVE). Sozialforschungsstelle, Dortmund. Available online at: www.iat.eu/aktuell/veroeff/2014/literature-review.pdf Accessed on 9th May 2015.

Issa, M.H., Rankin J.H. and Christian, A.J (2010). 'Canadian practitioners' perception of research work investigating the cost premiums, long-term costs and health and productivity benefits of green buildings'. *Building and Environment*, Vol. 45, pp. 1698–1711.

Jackson, S.M. (2009). 'Exploration into the relationship between managers' sensemaking and CSR outcomes', unpublished MSc thesis, Cranfield University.

Jacobs, D.E., Wilson, J., Dixon, S.L., Smith, J. and Evans, A. (2009). 'The relationship of housing and population health: A 30-year retrospective analysis'. *Environmental Health Perspectives*, Vol. 117, No. 4, pp. 597–604.

Kellert, S.R., Heerwagen, J. and Mador, M. (2008). *Biophilic Design: The Theory, Science and Practice of Bringing Buildings to Life*. John Wiley & Sons, Hoboken, NJ.

Kim, M.J., Oh, M.W and Kim, J.T. (2013). 'A method for evaluating the performance of green buildings with a focus on user experience'. *Energy and Buildings*, Vol. 6, pp. 203–210.

Lamin art (2014). *Designing with Nature in Mind*. Available online at: www.healthcaredesignmagazine.com/sites/healthcaredesignmagazine.com/files/whitepapers/Lamin-Art_Whitepaper042913.pdf Accessed on 11th January 2016.

Lappi, M., Hirvasniemi, R., Pekkarinen, S., Kiuru, E., Perälä-Heape, M. *et al.* (2014). 'Open innovation in health and social services'. *Interdisciplinary Studies Journal*, Vol. 4, pp. 269–281.

Lopez, O. (2008). 'La sustentabilidad urbana: una aproximacion a la Gestion ambiental en la ciudad. Cali-Colombia: Programa Editorial Universidaddel Valle'. Available online at: http://dialnet.unirioja.es/descarga/articulo/4735067.pdf Accessed on 9th May 2015.

Martin, R.L. and Osberg, S. (2007). 'Social entrepreneurship: The case for definition'. *Stanford Social Innovation Review*, Spring, pp. 29–39.

Mitchell, R.K., Agle, B.R. and Wood, D.J. (1997). 'Toward a theory of stakeholder identification and salience: Defining the principle of who and what really counts'. *Academy of Management Review*, Vol. 11, No. 4, pp. 815–828.

Mulgan, G. (2006a). 'The process of social innovation'. *Innovations: Technology, Governance, Globalization*, Vol. 1, No. 2, pp. 145–162. MIT Press.

Mulgan, G. (2006b). 'Society: Extreme makeover: From health to housing, social innovation is the key to making public services smarter and more efficient. It's time to take it more seriously'. Available online at: http://search.proquest.com/docview/246460457?accountid=36196 Accessed on 9th May 2015.

Norman, W. and MacDonald, C. (2004). 'Getting to the bottom of triple bottom line'. *Business Ethics Quarterly*, Vol. 14, No. 2, pp. 243–262.

Paul, W.L. and Taylor, P.A (2007). 'A comparison of occupant comfort and satisfaction between a green building and a conventional building'. *Science Direct*, Vol. 43, pp. 1858–1870.

Pezzey, J. (1992). 'Sustainable development concepts: An economic analysis'. *World Bank Environment Paper no. 2*, World Bank, Washington, DC.

Phills, J.A. Jr, Deiglmeier, K. and Miller, D.T. (2008). *Rediscovering Social Innovation*. Available online at: www.ssireview.org/articles/entry/rediscovering_social_innovation Accessed on 27th March 2015.

Praszkzier, R. and A. Nowak (2012) *Social Entrepreneurship: Theory and Practice*. Cambridge University Press, Cambridge, UK.

Primorac, D. and Jovancai, A. (2014). 'Economic and social development'. 5th International Scientific conference. Varazdin development and entrepreneurship Agency Megatrend.

Ram, N., Prahalad, C.K. and Rangaswami, M.R. (2009). 'Why sustainability is now the key driver of innovation'. *Harvard Business Review*, Vol. 87, No. 9, pp. 57–64.

Savitz, A.W. and Weber, K. (2006). *The Triple Bottom Line: How Today's Best-Run Companies Are Achieving Economic, Social and Environmental Success – and How You Can Too*. Jossey-Bass, San Francisco, CA.

Science communication unit, University of the West of England, Bristol (2014). 'Science for the environment, Policy in depth report. Social innovation and the environment report'. Produced for the European Commission Environment, February 2014. Available online at: http://ec.europa.eu/science-environment-policy Accessed on 5th March 2015.

Seligman, M.E.P. (2003). *Authentic Happiness*, Nicholas Brealey, London.

Smith, R.W. (2010). *Understanding and Linking Sustainability for Healthcare*. Healthcare Johnson Controls, Inc., Milwaukee, WI.

Tarde, G. (2009). *Monadologie und Soziologie*. Taschenbuch publications, Suhrkamp, Frankfurt a.M.

Tracada, E. and Caperna, A. (2012). *Biourbanism for a Healthy City: Biophilia and Sustainable Urban Theories and Practices*. Vol. 4: Biotechnology/Textile Technology/Fashion Technology of the International Convention on Innovations in Engineering and Technology for Sustainable Development, 3–5 September 2012, in Bannari Amman Institute of Technology, Erode District, Tamil Nadu, India.

Ulrich, R.S. and Lunden, O. (1990). 'Effects of nature and abstract pictures on patients recovering from open heart surgery'. In International Congress of Behavioral Medicine, Uppsala, Sweden, June.

University of Exeter (2014). 'Why plants in the office make us more productive'. Available online at: www.exeter.ac.uk/news/featurednews/title_409094_en.html Accessed 8th October 2015.

Van den Hazel, P., Keune, H., Randall, S., Yang, A., Ludlow, D. and Bartonova, A. (2010). 'The challenge of social networking in the field of environment and health'. *Environmental Health*, Vol. 11 (Supp. 1), No. 15. Available online at: www.ehjournal.net/content/pdf/1476-069X-11-S1-S15.pdf Accessed on 9th May 2015.

Weick, K.E. (1995). *Sensemaking in Organizations*, Sage, Thousand Oaks, CA.

Weitzman, M. (2003). *Income, Wealth and the Maximum Principle*. Harvard University Press, Cambridge, MA and London.

WHO, Environmental Health in Urban Development (1991). Report of Who Expert Committee, World Health Organization.

Willard, B. (2002). *The Sustainability Advantage: Seven Business Case Benefits of a Triple Bottom Line*. New Society Publishers, British Columbia, Canada.

William, E.O. (1984). *Biophilia*, Harvard University Press, Cambridge, MA.

Witherspoon, B. (2014). *Benefits of Biophilic Design*. Available online at: http://humanspaces.com/2014/12/19/benefits-of-biophilic-design/ Accessed on 11th January 2016.

Wolf, K.L. and Robbins, A.S. (2015). 'Metro nature, environmental health, and economic value'. *Environmental Health Perspectives*, Vol. 123, No. 5, pp. 390–398.

World Economic Forum (2013). http://reports.weforum.org/social-innovation-2013/how-to-read-this-report Accessed on 7th July 2015.

9 Innovation in the face of tension

Lessons from a sustainable social enterprise

Aastha Malhotra

Introduction

Informed by literature on sustainable development, entrepreneurship, ecopreneurship and social entrepreneurship, recently the notion of sustainable entrepreneurship has emerged as a tool to deliver social and environmental benefits through long-term and sustainable solutions (Dean and McMullen 2007; Gibbs 2009; Parrish 2010; Shepherd and Patzelt 2011). While promising, the field is characterised by competing views, a lack of consensus and conceptual limitations (Sharpley 2000; Seghezzo 2009; Shepherd and Patzelt 2011). Criticisms include omission of industry-specific and geographical contextual factors, acknowledgement of the conflicting nature of sustainability dimensions (for example, social, economic and environmental) and how these are pursued (Seghezzo 2009; Shepherd and Patzelt 2011). The concept of sustainability entrepreneurship is currently a "black box", and acknowledging the combination of economic, social and environmental goals in organisations' practices does not explain how they are pursued or met (Gibbs 2009: 65).

Addressing the above and adding to the growing body of knowledge that seeks to examine and inform the afore-mentioned criticisms and ambiguity (cf. Cohen and Musson 2000; Shepherd and Patzelt 2011), this study aims to *explore the sustainability dimensions relevant to small social enterprises* and *the tensions that arise in their pursuit* as well as *practices used to resolve them* in the context of the Indian nonprofit and social enterprise landscape. It makes two distinct contributions: contributing to theory by offering a more nuanced understanding of sustainable entrepreneurship by capturing sustainability dimensions relevant to sustainable social enterprises and drawing attention to their conflicting yet inter-dependent nature. It contributes to practice by identifying areas where an organisation may experience tensions (as a result of the conflicting priorities) and offers insights into how the tensions can be managed. In particular it highlights the value of social innovation as a mitigator of tensions as well as a facilitator of sustainable entrepreneurship. A practice-led social innovation theory – "connecter difference" (Mulgan *et al.* 2007) is used to contextualise the findings and delineate lessons for other organisations that are, or are planning to, engage in sustainable entrepreneurship.

The chapter sets the context for this study with a brief theoretical background followed by a summary of the research context and methodology. Using the research objectives as a guide, the findings are broadly categorised using the following lenses: Dimensions of Sustainability, Tensions (experienced while pursuing them) and Practices (used to resolve them). The final section discusses the findings in the light of social innovation literature and suggests directions for future research.

Theoretical background

Sustainable entrepreneurship and multiple dimensions of sustainability

The field of sustainable entrepreneurship is characterised by ambiguity and inconsistency (Sharpley 2000; Seghezzo 2009; Shepherd and Patzelt, 2011). While some allude to the "triple bottom line" combination of environmental, economic and social dimensions as the key characteristic (Elkington 1998; Young and Tilley 2006; Parrish 2010), others include cultural and political dimensions (Brown 1991; Shepherd and Patzelt 2011). Still others argue that the dimensions noted above need to take into account industry-specific and geographical contextual factors, characteristics and even individual views. For example, Seghezzo (2009) offers an alternative conceptual framework for environmental development that includes 'Place', 'Permanence' and 'Persons' (the new three Ps) while Mair and Marti (2006) note that depending on personal and cultural backgrounds, the social dimension can mean different things to different people. In recent years, this breadth has been captured by scholars who have tried to synthesise and review the field (cf. Schaltegger 2002; Hall *et al.* 2010; Shepherd and Patzelt 2011). Shepherd and Patzelt (2011) embrace the multi-disciplinary nature of the field by allowing inclusion of multiple and often diverse theoretical perspectives. They note that while their work brings some consensus to the field, it is but "an important step in [the field's] continued development" (2011: 138).

The link between sustainable and social entrepreneurship and navigating intrinsic tensions

Inherent to sustainable entrepreneurship is an emphasis on social outcomes that draws parallels with the field of social entrepreneurship. Social entrepreneurship itself involves innovative use and combination of resources to address social needs in sustainable ways (Dees and Elias 1998; Zahra *et al.* 2009; Wilson and Post 2013). The potential overlap between the two fields is well-recognised (Dean and McMullen 2007; Patzelt and Shepherd 2011; Shepherd and Patzelt 2011; Thompson *et al.* 2011). It is supported by scholars who view social entrepreneurship as a vehicle that can solve the world's social and environmental problems in a sustainable way through innovative activities (Haugh 2006; Perrini and Vurro 2006; Seelos and Mair 2007).

Common to both fields is the presence and pursuit of multiple and often conflicting goals. Scholars within the sustainable entrepreneurship domain have recognised the conflicting nature of dimensions and its negative impact on organisations. Examples include ethical dilemmas and complications in management decision-making owing to competing stakeholder needs (Lahdesmaki 2005); and incoherent identities as organisations attempt to reconcile economic and environmental goals (Cohen and Musson 2000; Gibbs 2009). The social enterprise literature is rife with concerns about organisations balancing social value with financial sustainability (Austin *et al.* 2006; Zahra *et al.* 2009; Santos 2012; Doherty *et al.* 2014). These goals, traditionally considered paradoxical, have been linked to enforced trade-offs (Austin *et al.* 2006; Zahra *et al.* 2009; Battilana and Dorado 2010).

One promising area of enquiry that seeks to mitigate these conflicts is that of social innovation. It involves creation of new or reconfiguration of existing ideas, products, services, programmes, networks and collaborations to fulfil social needs and fight against societal problems (Austin *et al.* 2006; Hull and Lio 2006). While the majority of research enquiry within this field has occurred in the last decade and lacks an explicit understanding, coherent theory and empirically driven frameworks (Mulgan *et al.* 2007; Crutchfield and Grant 2008; Nicholls and Murdock 2011); advocates argue that it can lead to positive outcomes such as balancing multiple stakeholder demands (McDonald 2007; Bridgstock *et al.* 2010) and dealing with resource constraints (Eirikur and Lio 2006; Hull and Lio 2006). This study examines a practice-led theory of social innovation, "connected difference" (Mulgan *et al.* 2007) within the context of an Indian nonprofit that aims to pursue multiple sustainability dimensions.

Research context and method

India, with an annual GDP growth of over 7 per cent since 2003, is one of the fastest growing economies in the world – this growth, reflected in the significant gap between the 'rich' and the 'poor', is far from inclusive (Flavin and Aeck 2004; Pruthi 2012). The social sector within this context serves as a crucial medium to support the disadvantaged (Baviskar 2001; Ghosh 2009; Pastakia 2010). Self-reliant social enterprises, in particular, have been heralded as innovative solutions that can improve livelihoods, provide employment outcomes and create inclusive and sustainable growth (Sheth 2010; AFI Dasra 2012; Pruthi 2012).

This chapter provides an in-depth case study of Program Nav Kria run by SCOPE Plus, a nonprofit based in New Delhi, India. The researcher had personal and professional involvement with the organisation until 2006. However, the awareness that SCOPE Plus's approach to balancing multiple dimensions of sustainability could serve as a valuable case study was only cemented in recent years as the researcher undertook extensive academic study and research (from 2007 to 2013) in the area of nonprofit and social enterprise management. As a result, the researcher decided to approach the organisation again for the purpose of conducting this study.

A qualitative case study approach was used to allow the researcher to account for context, integrate diverse perspectives and delve into 'how' and 'why' questions related to the multiple dimensions and practices adopted by the organisation (Eisenhardt 1989; Creswell 2009; Yin 2011). Drawing on the principles of triangulation to enhance rigour and reduce researcher subjectivity and bias this study incorporated three distinct data sources (Eisenhardt 1989; Yin 2011). These included interviews with organisational members, interviews with collaborators and organisational documents (Table 9.1).

The interviews followed a semi-structured format and included questions about the individual's role, nature of their relationship with the organisation including motivations and challenges, involvement with the specific programme reported in this study and broader activities of partner organisations. The interviewees were identified by the founder and selected on the basis of their involvement with the income generation programme. All interviews (each between 35 and 50 minutes) except one were conducted over the phone with help from a Scope Plus volunteer. One participant asked to be interviewed by email but then agreed to a follow-up phone conversation. Interviews were recorded subject to consent of the interviewee and transcribed. The primary language of the interviews was English but there was some code switching to Hindi when interviewees tried to explain ideas. These were translated into English by the researcher during transcription.

The analysis process adopted the view that research may be guided by but not limited by theory (Eisenhardt 1989; Yin 2011). While the theoretical

Table 9.1 Summary of data sources

Semi-structured interviews	
Founder-CEO (Mrs Seema Malhotra)	IntA
Program Coordinator (Mrs Shashi Paul)	IntB
Collaborator Representative (Corporate – Ms Deepa Menon, PVR Cinemas Nest (www.pvrnest.org))	IntC
Collaborator Representative (Academic Institution – Mrs Sunita (Retired Teacher) Public School in New Delhi)	IntD

Organisational documents	
Program Nav Kria brief	Ext 1.1
Program Nav Kria flyer	Ext 1.2
SCOPE Plus Decade-Report	Ext 1.3
SCOPE Plus Decade-Newsletter	Ext 1.4
SCOPE Plus Annual Report 2006	Ext 1.5
SCOPE Plus Annual Report 2007	Ext 1.6
SCOPE Plus Annual Report 2008	Ext 1.7
SCOPE Plus Annual Report 2009	Ext 1.8
Industry Report prepared by SCOPE Plus	Ext 1.9
Raddi Exchange Flyer	Ext 1.10
MOU with Academic Institution	Ext 1.11
Annual Report – Collaborator	Ext 1.12

background and research aims served as a guide, the researcher used the data in three stages to develop a coherent story. The first stage involved detailed reading of interview transcripts, notes and documents. Principles of content coding were used to delineate data relevant to each of the research aims, namely different dimensions of sustainability and their nature, the issues and tensions experienced while pursuing them and ways and means used to resolve the issues and tensions. In the second stage a relatively rich case summary was written up (the founder was reapproached at this stage to verify the facts). The third stage involved identification of the appropriate theoretical lens to frame and explain findings through a literature and expert review. The process was iterative with the researcher alternating between data, description and theory.

Case summary and findings

SCOPE Plus, a registered nonprofit established in 1996, aims to empower those living in difficult circumstances. Its founder-CEO is a qualified social worker with ten years of experience in education and literacy prior to starting the organisation. While the organisation in recent years has repositioned itself to deliver training programmes in the area of education and awareness, its portfolio in the past included numerous social programmes. These are summarised in Table 9.2. The main reasons for this transition were the illness of the founder-CEO in 2010 and shifting local needs.

Program Nav Kria

An income generation initiative, Program Nav (new) Kria (activity or action) operated using a social enterprise model. The programme was formalised in 1998 and was extremely active until 2010. It focused on teaching disadvantaged people to manufacture hand-made environmentally friendly products such as reusable jute and cloth bags, stationery items from recycled paper and other gift items. The revenue from product sales was directed into social programmes. Operating out of a storage room in the CEO's own house, Nav Kria in its early days was informal and catered to any disadvantaged person who wanted to earn some money, "*it was adhoc on the side kind of our education programme, we first made 100 petticoats and then we made some paper bags, people were paid per piece*" (*IntA*) but later moved its operations to working with undertrial inmates at an Indian prison with a wider product range.

Table 9.2 Summary of programmes run by SCOPE Plus till 2010

Education programmes for under-privileged youth and children
Computer Education programmes for under-privileged youth and children
Manufacturing and Income Generation programmes
Gender Awareness and Sensitisation programmes
Youth awareness and Mobilisation

Dimensions of sustainability

The programme was designed to create sustainability across multiple dimensions as can be seen in the programme brief, *"Nav Kria generates awareness about eco-friendly products and practices and provides skills for long-term work to under privileged people of our society to (1) keep them occupied (2) make them self-sufficient by learning a long-term vocational skill (3) generate income for them and the organisation"* (Ext 1.1). Unpacking this brief reveals the three integral programme dimensions:

1   environmental – visible in the organisation offering customers environmentally friendly products and raising awareness about using them.
2   social – linked to the mission of the organisation – *empowering the powerless* (Ext 1.3). This is reflected by the desire to provide long-term skills as opportunities for self-employment.
3   sustainability – reflected in the desire to achieve economic sustainability in two areas – for beneficiaries who can earn a living and for the organisation to deliver its own social programmes.

Two additional characteristics stand out. The first is that dimensions were inter-related. For example, environmental and social dimensions of the products served as a unique selling point that attracted customers, *"We also wanted to assist the [prison] inmates in having an income generation programme that would not only support them financially but also help increase their confidence and outlook towards life"* (IntC), thus helping the organisation pursue its economic goal. Similarly, economic sustainability was inherently linked to the social dimension – empowering of beneficiaries, *"SCOPE Plus is committed towards skill development and income generation activities as part of its empowerment programme"* (Ext 1.8).

The second aspect is the conflicting nature of the dimensions which is reflected in the tensions experienced by the organisation.

Tensions

Access to resources

The programme required human, infrastructure and financial resources to fulfil manufacturing and selling processes, and in turn the economic dimension. The inherent social dimension of the organisation had significant implications for the procurement of these resources. Rather than actively seeking out employees with the necessary manufacturing skills and/or qualifications, the focus was on working with disadvantaged individuals. Many of these were women and while dedicated, they posed concerns such as irregular work hours and complicated social dynamics. The CEO shared a story of a woman beaten by her husband and restrained from working (even after extensive intervention from SCOPE Plus), as he felt that she was spending too much time in the manufacturing unit and not looking after the house, *"it gave them self-esteem and some pocket money, they would forego housework"* (IntA).

Similarly the philanthropic roots meant that SCOPE Plus relied heavily on the contribution of volunteers and donations and prioritised the needs of the beneficiaries. As such, not only did the organisation have limited resources, they were directed towards mostly the social programmes, *"even the refreshments and prizes for other programs, the money came from the income generation program"* (IntA). While this approach worked in initial years, it became a problem as the programme began to grow. For example, an increase in sales underlined the need for more reliable manufacturers as well as additional investment into raw material and physical space, *"I could not keep on getting bags and folders made and keep them in my house . . . I could not afford it"* (IntA).

Developing programme capacity

The dearth of resources meant that the organisation was unable to invest in people who had the right skills and knowledge to run the programme, *"I interviewed managers, they wanted [more money] which I did not have"* (IntA). This was compounded by another aspect that reflects the social dimension – the expertise available within the organisation. According to the CEO, she was a social worker and did not have adequate knowledge about running a small business, *"I should have stayed a social worker . . . and someone else should have handled the programme"* (IntA). As a result, there was little emphasis on raising capital, developing appropriate costing models or operational planning, *"I had production problems as I did not have any knowledge"* (IntA). These tensions contributed to an unending cycle of problems that adversely impacted the day-to-day running of the programme as well as expansion efforts.

Lacking marketing and promotion channels led to erratic sales, *"my workers were sitting idle, without work"* (IntA). Periods of none or very low sales had an unfavourable impact on beneficiary and organisational income. In contrast, periods of higher sales increased pressure on the workers, infrastructure and resources (for example, extra storage space and more investment in raw materials).

Stakeholder priorities

Stakeholders in the case of Nav Kria included customers and the manufacturers (or beneficiaries). The programme also had to keep in mind the environmental dimension. Customers wanted competitive prices, a wide range of products and in some cases higher number of products for events; fulfilling these demands was integral to the economic dimension. The beneficiaries however wanted to manufacture within their homes without having to purchase expensive equipment, *"they were asking for work within their hut, within their one-room house . . . we would give them work, they would take raw material, make it and we would pay them per piece"* (IntA). The social dimension required prioritisation of skill-building and empowerment of these beneficiaries. The production there-fore emphasised 'hand-made' rather than 'machine-made' processes. The environmental dimension prioritised the use of environmentally friendly raw material such as jute and recycled paper.

The hand-made processes, while beneficiary-focused, were time-consuming and compromised the quality of the product, *"some inconsistencies were always there, they were made by hand"* (IntB) and inhibited large-scale production, *"there were only so many pieces that we could make when we were cutting everything with scissors"* (IntB). Adding to this, the environmentally friendly raw material was almost 30 per cent more expensive than alternatives and also restrictive. For example, jute was not as durable or waterproof as synthetic materials. These attributes compromised the competitiveness of the products and impacted the economic dimension.

Practices

Pivotal in mitigating these tensions and allowing SCOPE Plus to continue pur-suing the three dimensions are two distinct collaborations which form the basis of a symbiotic and mutually beneficial relationship. This is best illustrated in Figure 9.1.

Collaboration with a prison complex

During the early 1990s, the founder-CEO was involved in running an educa-tional programme in an Indian prison as a part of its reform and rehabilitation initiatives. These initiatives which continue include drug de-addiction centres, counselling services, adult education and computer and vocational training courses run with support from local nonprofits. It is important to note here, the context of the prison environment in India which has been replete with prob-lems such as mismanagement, overcrowding, unhygienic conditions and poor medical facilities, particularly in previous decades (Roy 2003). This environment

Figure 9.1 Two distinct collaborations forming the bases of a mutually beneficial relationship.

is challenging for inmates who are awaiting trial (undertrials) and account for nearly 70 per cent of the prison population (NHRC 2002). Some of these individuals serve extended sentences because of a slow judicial system and/or inability to pay bail money; this impacts the mental health of the individual, exposes them to other criminals, drug abuse and allows them to engage in unproductive activities (Dhanuka 2013; UHRF 2012).

The CEO's involvement with reform and rehabilitation activities and some comments from the undertrial inmates themselves made her realise that there was a possibility of a collaboration where the inmates could learn a skill set and earn a living, *"boys only told me, ma'am why don't you start something, bring us work" (IntA)*. She initiated conversations with the prison authorities for setting up a production unit where the undertrial male inmates (referred to from here on as inmates) would be responsible for manufacturing products and be renumerated 'per piece'. A formal collaboration was set up in 1998. Prison authorities supported the programme by helping in the identification of inmates who could work within the unit (for example, conducting background checks), providing the infrastructure (for example, secure rooms where the inmates could work, products could be stored and other programme employees could meet with potential customers) and additional resources (for example, electricity and water).

SCOPE Plus was responsible for training the individuals, procuring raw material, providing product specifications, supervising the manufacturing process and paying the inmates, *"we were given two rooms inside to work in, we kept all our machines and raw material there, we also had one room outside where we kept the finished products" (IntB)*. The initial work was all done by hand and SCOPE Plus purchased raw material such as scissors, threads, jute and cloth from local wholesalers. In subsequent months, some local community groups encouraged by the possibility of rehabilitating inmates donated resources, *"people donated sewing and cutting machinery, people donated raw material" (IntA)*.

This collaboration helped SCOPE Plus resolve the tensions mentioned in the previous section and in turn pursue the different dimensions of sustainability. The infrastructure and material resources provided by the prison authorities along with donations from other groups assisted in subsidising the product cost and enabled SCOPE Plus to use environmentally friendly raw materials and still offer price-competitive products. Surplus funds were directed towards building programme capacity, for example, purchase of a computer to maintain stock and creation of a product catalogue. The manufacturers were also more reliable – they had a schedule and had a place to come and work every day. While some irregularities remained, *"if they had a court hearing they would not come for work and if they got bail then they would leave" (IntB)*, the overall work environment was more organised, *"there was no problem, we had set timings and they would even open the prison early if we had urgent orders" (IntB)*. These changes helped in streamlining processes, meeting deadlines and manufacturing larger product quantities. By catering to the needs of the customers Nav Kria achieved its economic and environmental goals.

The social dimension was fulfilled with inmates developing vocational skills for self-employment and earning money for personal use, *"the earning that they had they would send to their families, and they would also use it to buy extra cups of tea" (IntA)*. It also kept them engaged and facilitated positive mental health, *"it enables them to pass time, by indulging in such activities their minds are diverted from the sorrows" (Ext 1.9)*.

This collaboration reinforced the reform and rehabilitation activities as numerous other organisations continue to engage with inmates, *"lots of other organisations even some religious ones are still working, some companies are even hiring people from there now" (IntB)*. While the entire credit of these developments cannot be given to SCOPE Plus, its success lent credence to the potential of such collaborations.

Collaboration with academic institutions and corporates

The second collaboration involved academic institutions and corporates. This study focuses on their role in the 'raddi' or waste-exchange project (explained next) and hence groups them together for ease of analysis. Raddi or waste includes used newspapers, cardboard, plastic and glass which can be recycled. In India, these products are collected and then sold to local raddi-wallas (or waste agents), a practice that encourages recycling and re-use of products. The collaboration required the academic institutions and corporates to collect raddi and give it to SCOPE Plus instead of donations, *"Don't give me donation ... I don't want donation because today you will give tomorrow you will not, I cannot afford that I need running money" (IntA)*. SCOPE Plus would sell the waste and retain the income, but provide the products manufactured in the prison in return, *"Around 100 kgs of our office's waste paper is passed on to SCOPE Plus through a 'Raddi Exchange Programme'. This waste is sold by SCOPE Plus and the money generated is utilised towards the vocational training of Tihar inmates" (IntC)*.

The raddi-exchange project became extremely successful and, by 2008, SCOPE Plus had numerous formal and informal collaborations through this project. Some collaborators were even engaged in long-term, *"We are few rupees short ... does not matter we will adjust it next time" (IntD)* and large-scale transactions, *"we used to take a whole bus full of newspapers to the SCOPE Plus Office" (IntD)*. The products were used as prizes and gifts during events, *"We stopped by buying presents or gifts for our visitors or guests, we used to give them folders and jute bags" (IntD)* and in some cases personalized, *"We have got the products customised with our logo" (IntC)*.

These collaborations even helped SCOPE Plus cope with tensions and pursue the different dimensions of sustainability. The steady source of orders facilitated purchase of raw material and cash flow planning. It gave the inmates recurrent work and assisted in anticipating future orders thus contributing to the economic and social dimensions. The most significant advantage was felt in the environmental dimension as the raddi-exchange programme served three purposes – offering environmentally friendly products, generating environmental awareness, "*We made the children aware not to waste a single bit of paper, earlier we used to get newspapers, we still do and they used to make airplanes, swords and just play around*" (*IntD*) and promoting recycling, "*The paper generally used to be put in the regular dustbins. To counter this, we created specially marked boxes installed in strategic locations in the office*" (*IntC*).

This collaboration also served as a pathway for other benefits. For example, academic institutions embraced environmentally friendly alternatives in other products, "*I used to encourage my teachers not to use the normal paper for covering their papers and register, we used to get recycled paper from SCOPE*" (*IntD*). Furthermore, according to the CEO, PVR Cinemas continues to support the educational programme delivered by SCOPE Plus and recently organised a free screening of a film for over 150 disadvantaged children, "*because of the waste exchange relationship which was very active earlier today in 2014 they invited our 150 kids to see a movie and even gave free refreshments*" (*IntA*).

Discussion, implications and some lessons

This study examined the Nav Kria, an income generation programme run by SCOPE Plus, an Indian nonprofit using the following lenses: Dimensions of Sustainability, Resulting Tensions and Practices used to resolve them.

Taking the first lens, Dimensions of Sustainability, the three sustainability dimensions relevant to Nav Kria were economic, social and environmental. These dimensions resonate closely with the triple bottom-line views of sustainability (Elkington 1998). The three dimensions while contradictory in nature are also inter-dependent, that is they are integral to the fulfilment of another. For example, the economic dimension is buoyed by the environmental and social dimensions that served as differentiators, helping Nav Kria to attract customers keen on buying socially motivated and environmentally friendly products. In contrast to observations where sustainable and social entrepreneurship initiatives focus on creating social and environmental value with economic value as a by-product only necessary to ensure financial self-sufficiency (Clifford and Dixon 2006; Mair and Martı 2006); or caveats where social objectives are sacrificed to achieve financial sustainability (Eikenberry and Kluver 2004; Zahra et al. 2009; Santos 2012); the findings lend credence to an alternate view – one where the creation of social and environmental benefits is integral to the successful achievement of economic outcomes and vice versa (Dacin et al. 2011; Wilson and Post 2013).

The second linked lens recognises the conflicting nature of the dimensions and the tensions that arise in their simultaneous pursuit. Three distinct areas were identified: access to resources; developing programme capacity; and stakeholder priorities where organisations may experience tensions. While the majority of the tensions arose from the competing nature of economic and social priorities, the environmental dimension further complicated the operations. This study builds on the work of scholars who have recognised and examined the tensions arising as a result of competing goals and highlighted issues of compromise and stakeholder dissonance (Battilana and Dorado 2010; Pache and Santos 2010; Doherty *et al.* 2014). It also provides knowledge about social enterprise dynamics in a developing country and Indian context, which is an under-researched area (Ghosh 2009; Pruthi 2012).

New ground is then covered under the third lens by identifying practices used to mitigate these tensions and achieve sustainability across all three dimensions. Instrumental to this were the two collaborations mentioned earlier in the chapter. When viewed together (Figure 9.1), the findings show Nav Kria is not just collaborating but serving as a 'connection' that brings together different organisations into a symbiotic and mutually beneficial relationship. In other words, they point towards a novel solution where existing ideas and services are reconfigured to fulfil social, environmental and economic goals. These characteristics reflect the concepts of social innovation discussed earlier in the chapter and resonate closely with a promising practice-led theory of social innovation termed, "connected difference" (Mulgan *et al.* 2007).

"Connected difference" highlights the role of connectors or those who "link together people, ideas, money and power" in a social innovation system and deem them critical to social development (Mulgan *et al.*, 2007: 35). This connector or bridging role, where organisations position themselves between other actors in society or attempt to bring them together in an innovative way to work on development problems and facilitate social change in a long-term and viable way have also been observed by others, albeit without explicitly linking it to social innovation (Brown 1991; Westley and Vredenburg 1991; Selsky and Parker 2005; Hulme and Edwards 2013). This study lends credence to these views but extends them further by illustrating that the role of 'connectors' and social innovation may mitigate the tensions that come with conflicting sustainability dimensions and enable successful sustainable entrepreneurship. This is the key take-away from this study.

However, some questions remain. The literature shows that social innovation is an embryonic area of enquiry and lacks an explicit understanding and coherent frameworks. If such knowledge is limited then how do we know that Nav Kria is indeed social innovation in action? How can the study go beyond describing one sustainable social enterprise and instead contribute to our understanding of pursuing sustainable entrepreneurship? More importantly, how can the findings be used to elicit learnings for others who are in the process of, or want to, engage in sustainable entrepreneurship? To redress these queries, the study uses the three main characteristics emphasised by the 'connected difference theory', and juxtaposes them against insights from the study and other relevant literature, to frame some lessons (from Nav Kria's experience) for organisations that may want to embrace social innovation and the role of 'connectors' while engaging in sustainable entrepreneurship.

The first characteristic is that "social innovations are usually new combinations or hybrids of existing elements, rather than being wholly new in themselves" (Mulgan *et al.* 2007: 34). The relationships developed under Nav Kria are not new – not for the organisation and not for the sector. The novelty lies in the way that they have been combined. This is visible in the shift from a one-to-one relationship (for example, receiving a grant from a corporate) towards a multi-partner approach resembling a symbiotic web or network of partnerships which facilitate the balancing of multiple sustainability goals and deliver mutual benefit (Gnyawali and Madhavan 2001; Clifford and Dixon 2006). The first lesson is to 'Embrace out-of-the box thinking and deliver mutual benefit'.

The second characteristic is that social innovation "involves cutting across organisational, sectoral or disciplinary boundaries (and often tapping into new sources of value by arbitraging ideas and knowledge)" (Mulgan et al. 2007: 34). It is similar to integrative (Austin 2000) and longer-term engagement focused cross-sector partnerships (Selsky and Parker 2005) that draw in each partner's resources and skills to address social issues and causes. Nav Kria's collaborations spanned across and sought participation from academic and corporate sectors, cutting across sector boundaries and diverse areas of work. Rather than asking for donations or developing grant-based projects, Nav Kria adopted a hybrid approach. It still obtained resources but leveraged its own, re-purposed the ones the collaborators already had access to and offered something tangible in return. The second lesson is to, 'Leverage and barter existing resources through cross-sector relationships to maximise impact'.

The third characteristic is that social innovations "leave behind compelling new social relationships between previously separate individuals and groups" (Mulgan et al. 2007: 35). This in turn "opens up the possibility of further innovations" and promotes continued combat of sustainability-related issues (Mulgan et al. 2007: 35). Nav Kria reinforced other activities, for example, the free screening of a film for over 150 children and recruitment of inmates by corporates. The enormity of tackling sustainability-related issues could greatly benefit from this snowball effect. The third lesson is to 'Consider your initiative as a platform through which other linkages can be formed, preserved and/or expanded'.

Limitations, conclusions and directions for future research

Sustainable development is a complex issue, as is the practice of sustainable entrepreneurship. Problems, whether small (for example, local unemployment) or big (for example, global warming) cannot be solved without the active involvement of multiple sectors and organisations. Social innovation can facilitate sustainable solutions. Some limitations exist such as dependence on interviewees' past reflections owing to the organisation's changed focus in recent years, an inherent language barrier and most significantly the single–case approach.

Such an approach can lead to a narrow scope and restricted generalisibility. The single case, however, is ideal for accessing unusual research contexts and informing broader and more complex studies (Patton 1990; Siggelkow 2007; Yin 2011). It also allows for exploring and gathering rich insights into a revelatory phenomenon that is distinct to what other organisations can provide (Patton

1990; Siggelkow 2007; Yin 2011). The exploratory nature of this study, emergent nature of sustainable entrepreneurship (cf. Gibbs 2009; Shepherd and Patzelt 2011), the Indian social enterprise body of knowledge (cf. Ghosh 2009; Pruthi 2012) and the novel ways the organisation managed tensions and facilitated sustainable entrepreneurship make the use of single case not only axiomatic but also serves as an exciting platform for future work. The study opens the door to the possibility where people and organisations engaging in sustainable entrepreneurship look to social innovation and embrace being 'connectors'. As connectors, they are able to promote a convergence of sectors, integrate ideas and even repurpose and leverage already scarce resources in order to address and solve sustainability-related issues. This study, drawing on the work of Siggelkow (2007: 21), fulfils one of the main uses of research based on a single case that is "as inspiration for new ideas" and highlights the need for more broad yet sensitively designed studies. Two research directions are worth mentioning.

A multi-case approach can be used to shed insight on the intricate links between sustainable entrepreneurship and innovative strategies and in particular between sustainable entrepreneurship and connectors. Comparing and contrasting findings across multiple cases can refine the concept of social innovation and develop 'connecters' into an innovative strategic tool that can be especially valuable for early stage sustainable entrepreneurship ventures and those operating in resource-scarce and uncertain environments. A longitudinal approach can capture how the 'connector roles' commence, evolve and in some cases even terminate in other industries (for example, landscaping or hospitality). This helps to understand potential external and internal barriers to survival, for example, entry of competitors, value clashes, power inequalities and long-term consequences identified in other forms of collaborations (cf. Westley and Vredenburg 1991; Selsky and Parker 2005) and context-specific operational constraints, resource needs and legislative frameworks. Consider the following. A catering-focused social enterprise providing employment for people with a physical disability may find it difficult to collaborate as potential partners may not have infrastructure in place. Similarly, a landscaping social business may be more susceptible to an economic downturn and lose customers as a result of factors outside their control. Researchers must be sensitive to such nuances and build them into the research design to gain understanding of how organisations can fulfil the role of 'connectors' in the long run. Such research addresses the important knowledge gap around processes of social innovation and unpacks the 'black box' of sustainable entrepreneurship.

References

AFI Dasra, 2012, *Growing Social Innovation: Leveraging Technology and the Government: Action for India.* www.actionforindia.org/wp-content/uploads/2012/03/AFI_Dasra.pdf.

Austin, J.E. 2000, 'Strategic collaboration between nonprofits and business', *Nonprofit and Voluntary Sector Quarterly*, vol. 29, no. 1, pp. 69–97.

Austin, J.E., Stevenson, H. and Wei-Skillern, J. 2006, 'Social and commercial entrepreneurship: Same, different, or both?' *Entrepreneurship Theory and Practice*, vol. 30, no. 1, pp. 1–22.

Battilana, J. and Dorado, S. 2010, 'Building sustainable hybrid organizations: The case of commercial microfinance organizations', *Academy of Management Journal*, vol. 53, no. 6, pp. 1419–1440.

Baviskar, B.S. 2001, 'NGOs and civil society in India', *Sociological Bulletin*, vol. 50, no. 1, pp. 3–15.

Bridgstock, R.S., Lettice, F.M. and Ozbilgin, T.A 2010, 'Diversity management for innovation in social enterprises in the UK', *Entrepreneurship and Regional Development*, vol. 22, no. 6, pp. 557–574.

Brown, L.D. 1991, 'Bridging organizations and sustainable development', *Human Relations*, vol. 44, no. 8, pp. 807–831.

Clifford, A. and Dixon, S.E. 2006, 'Green-Works: A model for combining social and ecological entrepreneurship', in Mair, J., Robinson, J. and Hockerts, K. (eds), *Social Entrepreneurship*, Palgrave Macmillan, New York, pp. 214–234.

Cohen, L. and Musson, G. 2000, 'Entrepreneurial identities: Reflections from two case studies', *Organization*, vol. 71, no. 1, pp. 31–48.

Creswell, J.W. 2009, *Research Design: Qualitative, Quantitative, and Mixed Methods Approaches*, 4th edn, Sage Publications, Thousand Oaks, California.

Crutchfield, L.R. and Grant, H.M. 2008, *Forces for Good, Revised and Updated: The Six Practices of High-impact Nonprofits*, Jossey-Bass, San Francisco.

Dacin, T.M., Dacin, P.A. and Tracey, P. 2011, 'Social entrepreneurship: A critique and future directions', *Organization Science*, vol. 22, no. 5, pp. 1203–1213.

Dean, T. and McMullen, J. 2007, 'Towards a theory of sustainable entrepreneurship: Reducing environmental degradation through entrepreneurial action', *Journal of Business Venturing*, vol. 22, no. 1, pp. 50–76.

Dees, J.G. and Elias, J. 1998, 'The challenges of combining social and commercial enterprise', *Business Ethics Quarterly*, vol. 8, no. 1, pp. 165–178.

Dhanuka, M. 2013, 'The great divide: Theory and practice of criminal defence laws in India', *Criminal Justice Matters*, vol. 92, no. 1, pp. 22–23.

Doherty, B., Haugh, H. and Lyon, F. 2014, 'Social enterprises as hybrid organizations: A review and research agenda', *International Journal of Management Reviews*, vol. 16, no. 4, pp. 417–436.

Eikenberry, A.M. and Kluver, J.D. 2004, 'The marketization of the nonprofit sector: Civil society at risk?', *Public Adminstration Review*, vol. 64, pp. 132–140.

Eirikur, C. and Lio, B.H. 2006, 'Innovation in non-profit and for-profit organizations: Visionary, strategic, and financial considerations', *Journal of Change Management*, vol. 6, no. 1, pp. 53–65.

Eisenhardt, K.M. 1989, 'Building theories from case study research', *The Academy of Management Review*, vol. 14, no. 4, pp. 532–540.

Elkington, J. 1998. 'Partnerships from cannibals with forks: The triple bottom line of 21st-century business', *Environmental Quality Management*, vol. 8, no. 1, pp. 37–51.

Flavin, C. and Aeck, M.H. 2004, 'Energy for development: The potential role of renewable energy in meeting the millennium development goals', REN21 Network, The Worldwatch Institute,Washington, DC.

Ghosh, B. 2009, 'NGOs, civil society, and social reconstruction in contemporary India', *Journal of Developing Societies*, vol. 25, no. 2, pp. 229–252.

Gibbs, D. 2009, 'Sustainability entrepreneurs, ecopreneurs and the development of a sustainable economy', *Greener Management International*, vol. 55, pp. 63–78.

Gnyawali, D.R. and Madhavan, R. 2001, 'Cooperative networks and competitive dynamics: A structural embeddedness perspective', *Academy of Management Review*, vol. 26, no. 3, pp. 431–445.

Hall, J.K., Daneke, G.A. and Lenox, M.J. 2010, 'Sustainable development and entrepreneurship: Past contributions and future directions', *Journal of Business Venturing*, vol. 25, no. 5, pp. 439–448.

Haugh, H. 2006, 'Social enterprise: Beyond economic outcomes and individual returns', in Mair, J., Robinson, J. and Hockerts, K. (eds), *Social Entrepreneurship*, Palgrave Macmillan, New York, pp. 180–205.

Hull, C.E. and Lio, B.H. 2006, 'Innovation in non-profit and for-profit organizations: Visionary, strategic, and financial considerations', *Journal of Change Management*, vol. 6, no. 1, pp. 53–65.

Hulme, D. and Edwards, M. 2013, *Making a Difference: NGO's and Development in a Changing World*, Routledge, London.

Lahdesmaki, M. 2005, 'When ethics matters: Interpreting the ethical discourse of small nature-based entrepreneurs', *Journal of Business Ethics*, vol. 61, pp. 55–68.

Mair, J. and Martı, I. 2006, 'Social entrepreneurship research: A source of explanation, prediction, and delight', *Journal of World Business*, vol. 41, pp. 36–44.

McDonald, R.E. 2007, 'An investigation of innovation in nonprofit organizations: The role of organizational mission', *Nonprofit and Voluntary Sector Quarterly*, vol. 36, no. 2, pp. 256–281.

Mulgan, G., Tucker, S., Ali, R. and Sanders, B. 2007, 'Social innovation: What it is, why it matters and how it can be accelerated', Skoll Centre for Social Entrepreneurship, University of Oxford. http://eureka.bodleian.ox.ac.uk/761/.

National Human Rights Commission (NHRC) 2002, *Annual report 2001*, New Delhi, India.

Nicholls, A. and Murdock, A. 2011, *Social Innovation: Blurring Boundaries to Reconfigure Markets*, Palgrave Macmillan, Hampshire, United Kingdom.

Pache, A.C. and Santos, F. 2010, 'When worlds collided: The internal dynamics of organizational responses to conflicting institutional demands', *Academy of Management Review*, vol. 35, no. 3, pp. 455–476.

Parrish, B.D. 2010, 'Sustainability-driven entrepreneurship: Principles of organization design', *Journal of Business Venturing*, vol. 25, no. 5, pp. 510–523.

Pastakia, A. 2010, 'Ecopreneurship in India: A review of key drivers and policy environment', in Michael, S. (ed.), *Ecopreneurs: Developing Sustainable Entrepreneurship*, Ashgate Publishing Ltd, Farnham.

Patton, M. 1990. *Qualitative Evaluation and Research Methods* (2nd edn), Sage Publications, Newbury Park, California.

Patzelt, H. and Shepherd, D.A. 2011, 'Recognizing opportunities for sustainable development', *Entrepreneurship: Theory & Practice*, vol. 35, no. 4, pp. 631–652.

Perrini, F. and Vurro, C. 2006, 'Social entrepreneurship: Innovation and social change across theory and practice', in in Mair, J., Robinson, J. and Hockerts, K. (eds), *Social Entrepreneurship*, Palgrave Macmillan, London, pp. 57–85.

Pruthi, S. 2012, 'Process of social entrepreneurship in India: The case of Goonj', in Underwood, S., Blundel, R., Lyon, F. and Schaefer, A. (eds), *Contemporary Issues in Entrepreneurship Research*, vol. 2, Emerald Group Publishing Limited, Bingley, UK, pp. 1–23.

Roy, S. 2003, 'Jail reforms in India: A review', *Criminology and Social Integration*, vol. 11, no. 1, pp. 33–40.

Schaltegger, S. 2002, 'A framework for ecopreneurship: Leading bioneers and environmental managers to ecopreneurship', *Greener Management International*, vol. 38, pp. 45–58.

Santos, F.M. 2012, 'A positive theory of social entrepreneurship', *Journal of Business Ethics*, vol. 111, no. 3, pp. 335–351.

Seelos, C. and Mair, J. 2007, 'Profitable business models and market creation in the context of deep poverty: A strategic view', *The Academy of Management Perspectives*, vol. 21, no. 4, pp. 49–63.

Seghezzo, L. 2009, 'The five dimensions of sustainability', *Environmental Politics*, vol. 18, no. 4, pp. 539–556.

Selsky, J.W. and Parker, B. 2005, 'Cross-sector partnerships to address social issues: Challenges to theory and practice', *Journal of Management*, vol. 31, no. 6, pp. 849–873.

Sharpley, R. 2000, 'Tourism and sustainable development: Exploring the theoretical divide', *Journal of Sustainable Tourism*, vol. 8, no. 1, pp. 1–19.

Shepherd, D.A. and Patzelt, H. 2011, 'The new field of sustainable entrepreneurship: Studying entrepreneurial action linking "what is to be sustained" with "what is to be developed"', *Entrepreneurship Theory and Practice*, vol. 35, no. 1, pp. 137–163.

Sheth, A. 2010, *An Overview of Philanthropy in India*, Bain & Company. www.bain.com/Images/India_Sheth_Speech.pdf.

Siggelkow, N. 2007, 'Persuasion with case studies', *Academy of Management Journal*, vol. 50, no. 1, pp. 20–24.

Thompson, N., Kiefer, K. and York, J.G. 2011, 'Distinctions not dichotomies: Exploring social, sustainable, and environmental entrepreneurship', in Katz, J. and Corbett, A.C. (eds), *Advances in Entrepreneurship, Firm Emergence and Growth*, vol. 13, Emerald Group Publishing Limited, Bingley, UK, pp. 201–229.

United Human Rights Federation (UHRF) 2012, *The Under Trial Prisoners in Overcrowded Indian Jails*, United Human Rights Federation, New Delhi.

Westley, F. and Vredenburg, H. 1991, 'Strategic bridging: The collaboration between environmentalists and business in the marketing of green products', *Journal of Applied Behavioral Science*, vol. 27, no. 2, pp. 65–90.

Wilson, F. and Post, J.E. 2013, 'Business models for people, planet (& profits): Exploring the phenomena of social business, a market-based approach to social value creation', *Small Business Economics*, vol. 40, no. 3, pp. 715–737.

Yin, R.K. 2011, *Qualitative Research from Start to Finish*, Guilford, New York.

Young, W. and Tilley, F. 2006, 'Can businesses move beyond efficiency? The shift toward effectiveness and equity in the corporate sustainability debate', *Business Strategy and the Environment*, vol. 15, no. 6, pp. 402–415.

Zahra, S.A., Gedajlovic, E., Neubaum, D.O. and Shulman, J.M. 2009, 'A typology of social entrepreneurs: Motives, search processes and ethical challenges', *Journal of Business Venturing*, vol. 24, pp. 519–532.

10 'When the river ran purple'

Reframing Indigenous *economics* in a global city

Billie Lythberg, Christine Woods and Mānuka Hēnare

Dedicated to Maryanne Rapata (Te Ahiwaru, Waiohua, Te Akitai), 1959–2015

Background

Aotearoa-New Zealand's largest city, Auckland, is more properly called Tāmaki-Makaurau, 'Tāmaki of a hundred lovers'. The Indigenous metaphor evokes the many migrations to this region, and battles fought by Māori because of its beauty and rich resources. At its narrowest, Tāmaki-Makaurau is just 2 km wide, a land bridge and portage between the harbours known as Manukau and Waitematā, and the Tasman Sea and Pacific Ocean they open into. The names of both harbours also recall the desirability of this area: Manukau refers to the many migratory birds who settle there each year (Taonui 2012) while Waitematā refers to the beauty of shimmering 'obsidian waters', because its calm sea was thought to resemble the glassy surface of volcanic obsidian rock.[1] Close to the portage between the harbours is Māngere, named for its 'lazy winds' (ngā hau māngere) that create a nurturing microclimate. Fertile soils and abundant seafood have nourished people here for more than 800 years; this is not a place in which to be merely sustained, but in which to flourish.

Today, Māngere is home to Aotearoa-New Zealand's busiest airport and to thriving business and industrial estates, the international award-winning Villa Maria Vineyards, and suburban settlements. This global city is also home to Ihumatao, Auckland's longest continually occupied Māori settlement, nestled next to the ancestral river, Oruarangi. 'Ko au te awa, Ko te awa ko au' – 'I am the river and the river is me' – say the people of Ihumatao, who for centuries have entered the river's waters and been fed by its many children. If sustainability can be measured by continuity of people and place over an extended timeframe, then Ihumatao is an example par excellence. Makaurau Marae is the community's tangible centre, comprising an open grass space, a large carved meeting house, a dining hall and commercial kitchen complex. Leaders of Makaurau Marae – including the late Maryanne Rapata, to whom this chapter is dedicated – have developed close working relationships with the businesses who are their neighbours, and with Auckland Council, initiating entrepreneurial activities and enterprises targeting the inseparable well-beings and sustainability of the people of Makaurau and their environment.

In July 2013, Oruarangi River ran purple. More than 1000 litres of toxic Methyl violet dye, spilled in an industrial incident, ran into the stormwater system, which drains into the river and out to Manukau Harbour.[2] Alerted by Villa Maria Vineyards, upstream from Makaurau Marae, Auckland Council reacted promptly to contain the spill, but 3.5 km of estuarine environment were polluted. The river lost most of its fish, shellfish and eels;[3] its people mourned.

In a report to Auckland Council, Makaurau Marae representative Paula Adams wrote:

> Like the pumping of blood through a vein,
> Your flow was cut off and so a source has died.
> We your people cry for you, for ourselves.
> You were our sustenance, our playground;
> We have survived 800 years on this land with you always there
> Glistening around us,
> The water flowing back and forth.

Spurred by this ecological crisis, Makaurau Marae seized the opportunity to partner with Auckland Council to develop an innovative Industry Pollution Prevention Programme to deliver to businesses in their area. Their aim was to

Figure 10.1 Dead and discoloured eel at Oruarangi.
Source: Auckland Council.

capture and communicate their approach to sustainable development within the boundaries of their local environment in order to protect their river, and by doing so, to protect and sustain all the waterways in the greater Māngere area.

Introduction

The Oruarangi Industry Pollution Prevention Programme is the anchor for this chapter, which identifies opportunities relevant to global issues of sustainable entrepreneurial activity and social innovation in perspectives and philosophies drawn from Māori economics. It considers and contextualises transformative innovation as it has emerged through the lens of a collaborative project between Auckland Council officers and their contractors, and a Māori kin-group acknowledged as mana whenua (having responsibility for, and occupation and usage rights to, land and sea; caretakers of the local ecosystem). In particular, we are interested in the project's innovative articulation between the knowledge systems of Māori, local government, ecological experts and local businesses, as they pertain to framing resource management and biodiversity sustainability for future generations.

In 2011 Shepherd and Patzelt broke new ground by positioning 'sustainable' entrepreneurship as a new interdisciplinary field. In their paper, the authors identified the value in "explor[ing] the role of entrepreneurial action as a mechanism for sustaining nature and ecosystems whilst providing economic and non-economic gains for investors, entrepreneurs and societies" (2011, 138). Here we are considering the Oruarangi Industry Pollution Prevention Programme as one such entrepreneurial action towards sustaining nature and ecosystems whilst supporting the economic goals of neighbouring businesses, and non-economic benefits for all parties concerned. We are especially interested in the *framing* of such opportunities in both the literature and in practice, beginning with our deliberate framing of a collaboration between Indigenous people and local government as an exemplar of social innovation for sustainability. Moreover, we are suggesting an epistemological shift in the framing of sustainability itself. Shepherd and Patzelt posed the question 'what is to be sustained?' They explored this question in relation to the 'life support' system that sustains humanity. In this chapter we are suggesting that this question could be productively reframed to ask instead, 'what **is it** to be sustained?', not as (human) benefactor of a (nature) life support system but as part of a dynamic, ever changing, ever turning world – known to Māori as Te Ao Hurihuri. Taking its point of departure from Shepherd and Patzelt, this chapter offers a case study not only of social innovation for sustainability from the perspective of what **is** to be sustained (Shepherd and Patzelt 2011), but also for reframing what **it is** to be sustained.

The concept of 'frames' and the processes and outcomes of 'reframing' deserve explication. Frames, McGrall (2013, 231–232) explains, citing Lakoff (2004), are models which act as deep 'mental structures' shaping the way we see the world (Lakoff, 2004). Lakoff (2004, xv) contends that "as a result, they shape the goals we seek, the plans we make, the way we act, and what counts as a good or bad outcome of our action".

Of particular relevance here, McGrall (2013, 232) has explored the application of frames and reframing in relation to foresight work and sustainable futures.

They are drawn on for new ways of making progress on 'stuck' problems: that is, breaking and overcoming complex 'sustainability impasses' (Jerneck and Olsson 2011). Jerneck and Olsson (2011, 258) define reframing as being a "process of shifting one's thinking into a different system and structure of concepts, language and cognitions". Reframing requires acknowledgement of the very different ways people engaged in environmental debates see the world and the range of legitimate perceptions and problem definitions that, consequently, must be engaged with (Dryzek 2005; Hulme 2009; Verweij *et al.* 2006).

The search for new ways to frame sustainable futures has been described by Loomis (2000) as a call for a 'new epistemology', a new theory of knowledge that might underpin sustainable development and business practice (Warren 1996; Senge *et al.* 2010). This call is being answered by international communities of scientists and economists who have prepared frameworks that illustrate, at the global level, the planetary boundaries for sustainable human societies and development (Rockström *et al.* 2009a, 2009b; Steffen *et al.* 2015) based on "expert assessment and synthesis of the scientific knowledge of intrinsic biophysical processes that regulate the stability of the Earth System" (Steffen *et al.* 2015, 8). Such scholars warn that some of these thresholds have already been breached and others are extremely vulnerable (Rockström *et al.* 2009a, 2009b), while their opposition draws on older research to maintain that the boundaries have not yet been overrun and that human innovation is sufficient to avoid this ever happening (see Boserup 1965; Ruttan 1977; Simon 1996; as cited by DeFries *et al.* 2012, 603). In the middle ground, others (DeFries *et al.* 2012, 604) argue for a reframing of planetary 'opportunities' to afford "the view that although Earth's life-support systems set the broad envelope for human survival, societies evolve, adapt to, and sometimes alter this broad envelope to overcome many biophysical constraints and to correct negative environmental consequences". In particular they position global scientific assessments and models as "necessary starting points" that are "insufficient unless they are coupled with finer-scale research to inform local needs and potential solutions". Dearing *et al.* (2014, 228) add that "traversing the scales to regional boundaries requires explicit attention to both the human drivers of change and social distributional issues, bringing new transdisciplinary, conceptual and ethical challenges to the planetary boundaries concept".

Academics working in the space of Māori sustainable innovation and entrepreneurship are acknowledging a similar need for wider recognition of their efforts to reinvigorate relational, community and co-operative organising, and (re)align these with traditional values and culture. Reflecting upon this challenge, the authors of this chapter have elsewhere (Hēnare *et al.* in press) posited that the new and sustainable economic epistemology being sought must not only be cognisant of the local but should also incorporate "a (re)discovery, (re) generation and (re)vitalisation of an age old holistic world view, deeply embedded within the traditional knowledge systems and ancient wisdom of Indigenous communities" (see Cajete as cited in Racette 2009; Hēnare and Lindsay 2000; Spiller *et al.* 2010; Suzuki *et al.* 1997). Specifically, and in collaboration with other colleagues, we have developed frameworks for Māori innovators and entrepreneurs in the areas of social innovation (Tapsell and Woods 2008a, 2008b, 2010), governance and entrepreneurship (Overall *et al.* 2010), family entrepreneurship (Nicholson *et al.* 2012), theoretical development (Kawharu *et al.* 2013), Māori enterprise teams (Hēnare *et al.* 2014) and the humanistic–spiritual tenets of temporality and intent that underpin Māori entrepreneurship and innovation (Hēnare *et al.* in press).

In this chapter we engage directly with the process of reframing prevailing models of, and work towards, sustainability by examining the underlying frameworks of an innovative Māori approach to sustainability at the micro and literally 'grass roots' level of Oruarangi River. We then take up the challenge to couple the approach taken to local needs by "human drivers of change" (Dearing *et al.* 2014, 228) and their opportunities for innovation, with the conceptual macro framework for global sustainability proposed by Kate Raworth's 'doughnut economics' (2012). Raworth's doughnut model marries nine biophysical thresholds with eleven basic human rights, "with an explicit focus on the social justice requirements underpinning sustainability" and has been scaled to define safe and just operating spaces at the regional level (Dearing *et al.* 2014, 228). Our case study is itself an exercise in reframing approaches to resource management and biodiversity sustainability to bring about an epistemological shift. Our contribution is to examine not only the similarities and differences between the Indigenous and global/regional science models of sustainability that are our focus, but also the very epistemological foundations of 'sustainability' itself.

We begin by locating Indigenous entrepreneurship and innovation in the literature, before expanding its remit into sustainable entrepreneurship. Then we widen our scope to consider Māori conceptualisations of the economy and its four well-being capitals: spiritual, ecological, economic and kinship. We introduce two generative and iterative models that utilise the koru (unfurling spiral) and takarangi (double spiral) to capture the interaction between these four well-beings, the actors responsible for their flourishing, and the motivators for Māori entrepreneurial behaviour. Predicated on the rhizomatic growth patterns of gourd plants, these models visualise Māori concepts of innovation and sustainability in recognisably Māori ways. With this foundation laid, we describe the Industry Pollution Prevention Programme and the particular innovations of the Oruarangi initiative. Finally, we return to Kate Raworth's doughnut economics model and consider it from a Māori world view.

Indigenous entrepreneurship, social innovation and a Māori world view

Indigenous entrepreneurship is a distinct disciplinary field emerging from mainstream entrepreneurship scholarship and indigenous development literature (Hindle and Moroz 2010; Peredo and Anderson 2006). Contributing to the distinction of this new field of research is the issue of "what matters and for whom-specifically" (Hindle and Moroz 2010, 361). Within mainstream discourse on entrepreneurship and the neo-liberal Anglo-Western mode of capitalist development, individual self-interest is paramount. What matters is a profitable outcome for the individuals involved in an entrepreneurial venture. In contrast, a key distinguishing feature of Indigenous entrepreneurship is the importance of a community that comprises a wider array of stakeholders and issues than those examined in the dominant discourse (Hindle and Moroz 2010), engaged in entrepreneurial activity emerging from community needs as well as contributing to community well-being. Social-interest rather than self-interest is central (Dey and Grant 2014; Marsden 2003); spiritual, cultural and social values are more important than purely economic values (Hēnare 2001); and well-being is created "along the way, rather than after creating wealth in financial terms" (Spiller *et al.* 2010, 166).

Māori have a long history of entrepreneurial activity (Petrie 2006; Tapsell and Woods 2008a); they are entrepreneurs and innovators who apply commercial strategies to maximise improvements in human and environmental well-being. Their social aims are primary, and profits are secondary. In the Māori world view, people and their environment are inseparable, and this is expressed in the term commonly used to describe Māori: tangata whenua, people of the land and sea. This is evinced by the social entrepreneurs and innovators of Makaurau under consideration here, whose enterprising activities focus on contributing positively to the well-being of their community without degrading the ecological well-being of their environment – in other words, sustaining the environment that sustains them as people.

In service of the sustaining of both people and their environs, Māori philosophy of the economy is inclusive and complex. It considers the well-being and priorities of spiritual and human ancestors, and descendants not yet born (Hēnare *et al.* 2014; Hēnare *et al.* in press), and prioritises holistic value creation over profit maximisation. Four key Māori well-beings can be useful for determining the overall well-being of Māori culture and society – known as Māoritanga – that Māori philosophy of the economy strives for. These can be expressed as spiritual well-being, ecological well-being, kinship well-being and economic well-being. In combination these well-beings – and thereby Māori economic thinking and practice – convey levels of partnership: of the spiritual with humanity; of humanity in ecological systems; of humans with other humans; and of economies embedded in the spiritual, ecological and human networks of their societies. The holistic well-being these partnerships describe transcends development indexes captured by GDP (Fleurbaey and Blanchet

2013) and is better visualised through the motifs central to ancient and contemporary Māori art: the generative and iterative models of the koru (the unfurling spiral, a symbol of new growth) and takarangi (the balanced double spiral with its emergence from and return to the primary source). We will now explore two such models that have been used to frame the interaction between the four key Māori well-beings, the actors responsible for their flourishing, and the motivators for Māori entrepreneurial behaviour.

He Korunga o Ngā Tikanga – a spiral or matrix of ethics

As conceptualised by Hēnare (1998, 2001, 2003, 2011a, 2011b), the framework He Korunga o Ngā Tikanga (see Figure 10.2) is a vitalistic spiral of constantly unfolding, interactive virtues that illustrate complementary counterpoints at the level of moral forces.

These are the moral forces from which the Māori entrepreneur or innovator emerges, and which shape their ethics and practices:

1 Tikanga te ao mārama: the ethic of wholeness, evolving, cosmos.
2 Tikanga te ao hurihuri: the ethic of change and tradition.
3 Tikanga tapu: the ethic of existence, being with potentiality, power, the sacred.
4 Tikanga mauri: the ethic of life essences, vitalism, reverence for life.
5 Tikanga mana: the ethic of power, authority and common good, actualisation of tapu (sacredness).

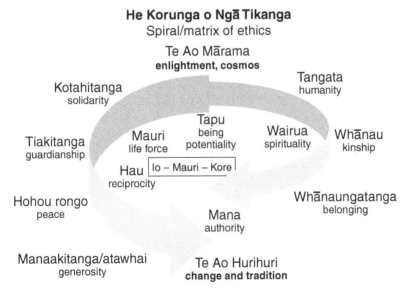

Figure 10.2 He Korunga o Ngā Tikanga.

Source: Mānuka Hēnare.

6   Tikanga hau: the ethic of the spiritual power of obligatory reciprocity in relationships with nature, life force and breath of life.
7   Tikanga wairua: the ethic of the spirit and spirituality.
8   Tikanga tika: the ethic of the distinctive nature of things, of the right way, of the quest for justice.
9   Tikanga whānau: the ethic of family and tangata – the human person.
10 Tikanga whānaungatanga: the ethic of belonging, reverence for the human person.
11 Tikanga tiakitanga: the ethic of guardianship of creation, land, seas, forests, environment.
12 Tikanga hohou rongo: the ethic of peace and reconciliation, restoration.
13 Tikanga kotahitanga: the ethic of solidarity with people and the natural world and common good.
14 Tikanga manaaki-atawhai: the ethic of love and honour, solidarity and reciprocity.

He Korunga o Ngā Tikanga is a Māori-Polynesian system of ethical pluralism (cf Sen 2000), and a contribution towards an Indigenous development ethics inclusive of a moral philosophy (Goulet 1974). Adherence to He Korunga o Ngā Tikanga generates and sustains the flourishing of the cosmos.

Takarangi – a double spiral of creativity/innovation

In a series of papers authored by Tapsell, Woods and colleagues (Hēnare *et al.* in press; Kawharu *et al.* 2013; Overall *et al.* 2010; Tapsell and Woods 2008a, 2008b, 2010) they suggest that Māori entrepreneurial activity is culturally and historically situated and they draw on the fundamental understanding that the Māori world "is viewed through a genealogical matrix of complementary but different counterpoints" (Tapsell and Woods 2010, 545). This is symbolically represented by the Takarangi framework, a double spiral of creativity/innovation whereby heritage can serve as a pathway for innovation.

This generative model depicts an entrepreneurial team inclusive of both ancestral wisdom and the responsibility for descendants yet to be born. It captures the interaction between entrepreneurial endeavour and traditional practices aligned with the four well-beings discussed above and He Korunga o Ngā Tikanga. This Māori-centred understanding of sustainable innovation allows both a redress of inequality and injustice as well as the achievement of human potential.

As we have explained elsewhere (Hēnare *et al.* in press):

> The He Korunga o Ngā Tikanga and Takarangi models encapsulate, respectively, the fundamental values and ethics that inspire and inform Māori innovation and entrepreneurship, and Māori entrepreneurial agents and agency, in a dynamic, ever-evolving world. Using the spiral frameworks, ancient wisdom and experience merge with the contemporary context to

Figure 10.3 Takarangi.
Source: adapted from Overall *et al.*; reproduced courtesy of Hēnare *et al.* 2015.

enable future possibilities. The name given by Māori to the 'Turning World' evident in both the koru and takarangi forms is Te Ao Hurihuri (Ao: world; Hurihuri: turning), a term in contemporary use to describe a world of change and stability, tradition and modernity. This dynamic capability of life is imbued in each Māori entrepreneurial team.

Weaving the whole 'turning' universe together is whakapapa (Marsden 2003): a network of relationships between everything spiritual, human, natural world and non-human; between the living, those who have lived before them, and those that will come after. Thus we see the full expression of, and commitment to, sustainability in the innovative and custodial activities of kin-groups like Makaurau Marae, who harness the opportunities of Te Ao Hurihuri – the phenomenon of tradition and change taking place simultaneously – in service of sustainable legacies.

The Oruarangi industry pollution prevention plan

To her people, Oruarangi is both an awa, a creek or river, and a tupuna, an ancestor, an integral part of the whakapapa network that is Te Ao Hurihuri. 'Oruarangi ka toto te Wairua' her people say, 'Her flowing waters nurture, sustain and give us strength.'[4] A literal translation of this saying describes Oruarangi as the mauri (life force) and hau (life force of reciprocity) that imbue the lifeblood (toto) of her people's spiritual well-being (wairua). Furthermore,

Oruarangi gives physical life through her abundance of fresh water and food sources. To be the river, and to know that the river is you, is to acknowledge not only ancestral connections through the vital networks of whakapapa but also to give perceptual and conceptual prominence to the stuff of physical nourishment, to the conversion of Oruarangi food sources into human flesh.

Recalling the day that Oruarangi ran purple, Maryanne Rapata explained, "It was like the air had been sucked out of my body, I couldn't breathe, only cry." Maryanne's statement would later become an important part of the Industry Pollution Prevention Programme (IPPP) pamphlet distributed in Māngere (Auckland Council 2014b). The desecration of Oruarangi impacted not only on the waterways it flowed into but also on the spiritual and physical well-being of its people; the people Oruarangi sustains. Besides the clean-up challenge its pollution presented, the people of Makaurau Marae recognised an opportunity to share their ancestral, spiritual and physical connections to Oruarangi, aiming to inspire greater care from their river's other neighbours. Though this case study describes a decidedly local problem, the management of the world's waterways is critical to global sustainable development. The role of water quality and quantity in sustaining cultural values is receiving burgeoning attention from the academy, especially within New Zealand and from Māori academic and traditional experts (Harmsworth 2002; Harmsworth *et al.* 2013; Harmsworth *et al.* 2014; Morgan 2003; Tipa and Tierney 2006; Townsend *et al.* 2004; Young *et al.* 2008), as is the role that Indigenous knowledge can play in water governance internationally (McGregor 2012, 2014). The IPPP provided the framework for Makaurau to engage their neighbours, local government and environmental scientists in such discussions at a grassroots level, and to explore Māori approaches to innovation and sustainability through the sharing of Oruarangi the river with people who had not yet been introduced to Oruarangi the ancestor.

The IPPP outline, written by Auckland Council Senior Environmental Programmes Advisor Tessa Chilala, describes the programme's particular approach:

> The purpose of the programme is primarily educational and aims to inform industry and business on the impacts that their activities may be having on local waterways if they are not managed well. The approach is proactive and non-regulatory, with an expert visiting each site, conducting a site inspection, talking to the business owners about potential issues and then following up with a report to the business if changes are needed.
>
> The benefit of this approach is that it seeks to educate the businesses about potential issues with the aim of preventing pollution at source. This approach is recommended in areas where there is a concentration of industry and business close to water bodies, including streams and harbours. The programme involves a GIS mapping exercise to ensure that commercial businesses understand the stormwater network connections in relation to local waterways. A key aspect of this programme is to build relationships with and an understanding of the local industrial sector in a Local Board area.
>
> (Auckland Council 2014a)

By September 2014 the programme had been implemented in eight catchment areas in Auckland, including Oruarangi, often in collaboration with local businesses and conservation volunteers. What distinguishes the Oruarangi IPPP is the innovative partnership that developed between the Council's Local Board and Makaurau Marae to co-develop and co-deliver a programme that would ensure their mana whenua perspective on sustainability, and what it is to be sustained, was communicated to local industry.

The programme was developed and delivered by representatives from each partnering group, which allowed the relationships and perspectives of the contributors to be quite personal. Makaurau appointed two women as its representatives; Council appointed the contractor who would work with them to develop their IPPP and deliver it via face-to-face meetings with local business owners and employees. A Geographic Information Systems (GIS) map was prepared illustrating the meshwork of stormwater drains and natural culverts that empty into Oruarangi and the Manukau Harbour; this would become the back page of the IPPP pamphlet. Site visits were made by the contractor and Makaurau representatives to introduce the programme and draw attention to the interconnectedness of business activities with the area's waterways and people.

Significantly, the programme is non-regulatory and participation is entirely voluntary. Where businesses agreed to participate their sites were audited, risks were identified, and practical solutions identified and recommended. Contractors and Makaurau Marae representatives visited 142 sites, wrote 66 reports, and delivered 24 spill kits and 39 'drains to sea' stencil kits for stormwater drains. They attended 17 pollution events and identified and prevented 70 potential pollution events. Throughout the development and delivery process the individuals learned from each other and reported back to the people and institutions they represented, and the mana whenua perspective was communicated and acknowledged. The difference this made to the IPPP process and relationships between Makaurau Marae and its neighbouring businesses is described in the programme feedback prepared by one of Council's contractors:

> I was pretty nervous when it was suggested that I work in collaboration with Makaurau Marae on this pollution prevention programme ... "Oh no, this will be a long, slow process. The companies will hate it. We'll get kicked off these industrial sites." My fears were proven completely wrong.
>
> We approached each company in a non-confrontational way. There was no benefit in pointing the finger of blame at these businesses and making them feel bad for past mistakes. We talked to them about the risks of spills on sites, and told the story of the dye spill to show them how easily things can go wrong. If they were interested, Fiona or Paula would explain in more detail how much the awa [river] meant to the people of [Makaurau Marae].
>
> In some cases companies were interested in how they could connect more with the marae. In many cases, people didn't even realise there was a settlement or a marae just across the river from them. Some companies

thought it would be a good idea to have a marae representative come and talk to their staff as part of their environmental/spill training.

(Wilkinson 2014)

The innovative contributions made to the IPPP by Makaurau are also borne out by differences between the pamphlet prepared for Oruarangi and an earlier IPPP pamphlet prepared for another polluted waterway in Auckland, Omaru. The latter is double-sided, with a GIS map of the area's stormwater lines on one side and a simple description of Omaru stream and its connection to the stormwater system on the other. It is illustrated with a photograph of the stream that shows a boardwalk running alongside it – suggesting human presence – and a computer generated illustration of a young boy wading in the stream with a small net, while a butterfly flutters overhead, a fish and a frog swim nearby, and a native marsh hen wades behind him. The need for the IPPP is conveyed by industrial pollution running into a stormwater drain, which then discharges into the stream. It is a simple and visually effective pamphlet, but somewhat generic and impersonal.

The pamphlet prepared for Oruarangi is twice as large. Like the Omaru pamphlet, the back page is a GIS map of the stormwater system. But the front page depicts a glorious sunset reflected in the Manukau Harbour, with a banner of small photographs of Makaurau Marae elders and children at the Marae itself and enjoying the waterways they care for and relate to in kinship terms. Inside, two photographs show the Oruarangi running purple, and two evocative quotes describe the relationship between Makaurau Marae and Oruarangi, their river and ancestor.

A further six images show the river and the harbour it discharges into, and the stormwater drains and culverts that flow into both. Simple text marries the significance of Oruarangi to Makaurau Marae with its importance in the Māngere ecosystem, explaining the interconnectedness of all businesses with Makaurau and Oruarangi and offering a helpline number should any incidents occur.

The IPPP captured the people of Oruarangi and their traditional knowledge alongside simple advice pertaining to the protection of the river. It pivoted on the opportunity for an exchange of knowledge between Makaurau Marae representatives and Council-contracted environmental experts, and the personalising (and perhaps personification) of the river. This 'river' of knowledge then flowed to the sea of businesses, through face-to-face meetings and via tailor-made pamphlets that foregrounded the significance and fragility of the river as a living entity and in relation to the people who have cared for it – sustaining it and being sustained by it – for 800 years. The collaborative model allowed differently situated knowledge systems to be acknowledged and reciprocated, influencing community dynamics, sustainable ecological well-being, and policy-making. An epistemological shift occurred when each group – Makaurau Marae representatives, Council officers, expert contractors and owners and employees of local business – was empowered to acknowledge the

The Oruarangi Creek is a tidal waterway with a catchment that includes farmland and the Airport Oaks business area. The creek flows past the Puketapapa papakāinga (settlement) into the Manukau Harbour adjacent to the Otuataua Stonefields.

The creek, or Awa, is of deep significance to the local Māori people. Historically, it was an important source of food, but this food source was taken away with the development of the Mangere sewage treatment ponds. In the decade since the treatment ponds were removed, the creek has been steadily recovering to the point that fish and shellfish could once again be harvested around the mouth of the creek.

One of the biggest potential sources of pollution entering the Manukau Harbour is from pollution incidents like spills on yards that get washed into stormwater drains, into streams and eventually into the harbour.

In 2013 there was an accidental spill of toxic dye into the Oruarangi Creek from a business in the Airport Oaks area. The spill killed much of the aquatic life in the creek, including fish and shellfish, and will cost the responsible party a large amount to clean up and remediate. This programme aims to help businesses to prevent incidents like this from happening.

"It was like the air had been sucked out of my body, I couldn't breathe only cry"
– Maryanne Rapata

3 MONTHS LATER

"Ko au te awa, ko te awa ko au"
I am the river and the river is me...

To help improve water quality in the Oruarangi Creek, the Mangere-Otahuhu Local Board is working with community groups and businesses to reduce water pollution.

Figure 10.4 Oruarangi Industry Pollution Prevention Programme pamphlet, page 2.
Source: Auckland Council and Makaurau Marae.

different ways other people engaged with Oruarangi and to see as legitimate their perceptions of the boundaries beyond which their activities would be defined as problems. The very personal connection of Makaurau Marae representatives to Oruarangi, and the long history of their relationship with what is both a waterway and an ancestor, became a powerful motivator for pollution prevention.

> When I saw tears well up in Paula's eyes as she talked about the dye spill, it inspired me to do as much as we could to protect the awa [river]. I knew that it would be valuable for local businesses to hear this story from a mana whenua perspective and it would be one more reason to stop pollution.
>
> (Wilkinson 2014)

In the Oruarangi IPPP we see the tangible results of sustainable innovation in response to a localised 'planetary opportunity' at the micro and literally grass-roots level. It offers a particularly successful model for cross-cultural and cross-institutional economics, formulated in accordance with Māori world view and conceptually underpinned by the generative and iterative spiral dynamics of the Takarangi and He Korunga models. Now we turn to consider what these models and the micro focus of the Oruarangi IPPP might offer to the macro 'planetary boundaries' framing of doughnut economics and its pursuit of sustainability.

Doughnut economics and Indigenous social innovation

Kate Raworth presented her 'doughnut economics' model to Oxfam in 2012, where she was an economist and researcher.[5] It depicts social and ecological challenges according to the planetary boundaries framework for sustainable human societies and development. Raworth's 'doughnut', a green torus, is a metaphor for the space in which every person has the resources they need to meet their human rights, balanced between the planetary and social boundaries for sustainability. To generate the model, Raworth selected 11 basic human rights from a list made by governments preparing for Rio +20 in 2012, which examined how economies have grown at the expense of natural resources and human capital since the last Earth Summit in Rio in 1992.[6] These radiate out from the middle of the doughnut hole: adequate income; effective healthcare; access to education; decent work; modern energy services; resilience to shocks; gender equality; social equity; a voice in democratic politics; food security; and clean water and good sanitation.

At the outer rim of the doughnut Raworth placed the nine planetary boundaries or biophysical thresholds that must be observed if humanity is to remain in the "safe operating space" of Holocene-like conditions we have enjoyed for the last 12,000 years, as identified by Johan Rockström of the Stockholm Resilience Centre, and 28 of his colleagues (Rockström *et al.* 2009a, 2009b). They are: climate change; ozone depletion; ocean acidification; particles in the atmosphere; nitrogen and phosphate use; freshwater use; changes in land

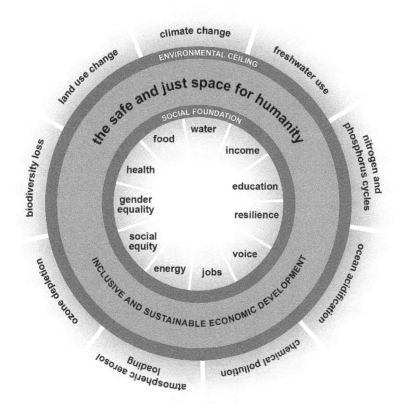

Figure 10.5 The doughnut economics model.
Source: Kate Raworth 2012.

use; biodiversity loss; and chemical pollution. The last five are directly relevant to our case study and interconnected with the other four.

Raworth describes the doughnut, poised between human deprivation and planetary exploitation, as the "safe and just space for humanity to *thrive* in" (2012, 4, our italics). Raworth's choice of words is significant: much as her model pivots on sustainability, her emphasis is not on stasis but on thriving. Here, Raworth echoes not only the Māori aspiration to flourish, evoked by Takarangi and He Korunga o Ngā Tikanga, but also the primary goal of the planetary boundaries scientists (Steffen *et al.* 2015, 1): to "define a safe operating space for human societies to develop and *thrive*" (our italics). Where the planetary boundaries framework has "significantly influenced the international discourse on global sustainability", the doughnut model "allows multi-metric 'compasses' to be elaborated for directing decision-making", especially at the regional level (Dearing *et al.* 2014, 228).

Beyond the doughnut's outer rim, resource use becomes unsustainable. At its centre, the doughnut hole represents the under-resourcing of social priorities. Deprivation within these areas often prompts the provision of social services, aid, and ever more frequently, the emergence of modes of entrepreneurship focused on the social and sustainable. Many mainstream social entrepreneurs respond to deficit-driven models that emerge from the failings of the market and an economy of exploitation; in Raworth's model, this is the doughnut hole. However, as we have demonstrated, Māori social entrepreneurship emerges from a concept of inclusive prosperity at the heart of an economy predicated on, and in service of, four well-beings located within Te Ao Hurihuri – the turning and ever changing world where tradition and change work simultaneously. Māori entrepreneurship is by its very nature sustainable and agile, and emerges from potential as opposed to deficit.

Raworth's model can be used to illustrate that – for example – at a global level we have already gone beyond the thresholds for climate change, biodiversity loss, and nitrogen and phosphate use, and we are not yet meeting any of the 11 basic needs of the world's human population. It is extremely effective as a snapshot of measurements, but is also proposed as a matrix that ought to be considered whenever decisions pertaining to resource use and social priorities are being negotiated: How might development look on the doughnut model? What social priorities are being served and what impact is this having on planetary boundaries? In addition, Raworth has argued that alongside considering the impact that humankind is having on planetary resources we must also reconsider the base economic model to make it inclusive of what for so long have been considered externalities. She retains the familiar basic circular flow of goods and money but adds in the complications of the biosphere; the huge contribution of unpaid work; social exchanges; and the inequality of households within this framework. This is the flow chart of an inclusive economy that underpins her model.

Makaurau Marae, an ancestral community centre, encompasses all of the complex activities detailed in Raworth's expanded flow chart. Makaurau Marae is not simply a consumer or supplier of capital, but both, and has formal and informal economic activities operating within, and inseparable from, its biosphere. To this we would also add an ethnosphere cognisant of both science and traditional knowledge systems. Canadian anthropologist Wade Davis, Explorer in Residence at the National Geographic Society, first introduced the concept of the ethnosphere (cited by Parsell 2002), and explained the value of multiple frames for sustainability:

> Just as there is a biological web of life, there is also a cultural and spiritual web of life: the 'ethnosphere'. It's really the sum total of all the thoughts, beliefs, myths, and institutions brought into being by the human imagination. It is humanity's greatest legacy, embodying everything we

have produced as a curious and amazingly adaptive species. The ethnosphere is as vital to our collective well-being as the biosphere. And just as the biosphere is being eroded, so is the ethnosphere – if anything, at a far greater rate. Some people say: "What does it matter if these cultures fade away." The answer is simple. When asked the meaning of being human, all the diverse cultures of the world respond with 10,000 different voices. Distinct cultures represent unique visions of life itself, morally inspired and inherently right. And those different voices become part of the overall repertoire of humanity for coping with challenges confronting us in the future.

Specific to the Māori ethnosphere and the frames it provides, it is critical to acknowledge that ancestors and descendants yet to be born are considered and consulted in all decision making, as illustrated by Takarangi. Ancestral directives are key drivers for enterprise activities on Makaurau Marae, and so is the planning ahead for future generations. This is in keeping with the key thrust of the Earth Summit in Rio in 1992 when the concept of 'sustainable development' was actively promoted as a way to meet "the needs of the present without compromising the ability of future generations to meet their own needs".[7]

Takarangi and He Korunga o Ngā Tikanga differ from the doughnut in many ways, but conceptually perhaps the biggest distinction is that the Māori models are primarily generative rather than measurement tools. Moreover, He Korunga o Ngā Tikanga describes not only the motivators for innovation but also a matrix of virtues as well-beings to aspire towards. This framework offers another lens onto what it is to be sustained in ways that are "morally inspired and inherently right" (Parsell 2002), and highlights what Māori would promote as social priorities that must be considered alongside those in the doughnut economics model. Furthermore, if the ancestral directives of He Korunga o Ngā Tikanga are observed, they balance the planetary boundaries; thus the framework has no need to model boundaries and thresholds as these are constantly within human awareness and under negotiation in Te Ao Hurihuri.

Conclusion

In our introduction we proposed a reframing of Shepherd and Patzelt's (2011) question 'what is to be sustained?' We suggested that this question might be productively reframed to ask instead, 'what **is it** to be sustained?' We explored this question through a Māori approach to sustenance and the economy that sees humankind as just one part of a (spiritual, ecological, kinship and economic) flourishing network of life, rather than the primary benefactor of a life support system. The case study of Oruarangi provided an opportunity to focus this.

Furthermore, it allowed a wider focus on 'sustainability' in order to overturn its implications of stasis; offering a Māori perspective and aspiration that aligns more closely with 'flourishing', known as te puāwaitangi, and with an ever evolving world, Te Ao Hurihuri (the turning world of tradition and change). Thus we have asked not only what **it is** to be sustained – that is, what does it mean to be part of a healthy, relational network – but also, what does the network require to adapt and flourish: what is it to *thrive*? The significance of this question emerged when we brought together Raworth's doughnut economics model with the Māori Takarangi and He Korunga o Ngā Tikanga models of innovation. Where the doughnut model aspires to thriving within limits, the Māori models capture visually the rhizomatic flourishing of gourd plants, and imply a reciprocation and constant unfurling between source and outcome, earth and plant, ancestors and descendants, heritage and innovation.

We believe that Takarangi and He Korunga o Ngā Tikanga, with their iterative unfurling in response to and support of Te Ao Hurihuri, the ever changing world, model achievable, local sustainability, or more correctly, flourishing. These Indigenous frameworks offer ways to frame the holistic nature and aspirational opportunities of our turning world within or alongside global frameworks like the doughnut model. Significantly, each approach represents a framework predicated on an understanding that "Earth is a single complex, integrated system" and that "the stable functioning of the Earth System is a prerequisite for thriving societies around the world" (Steffen *et al.* 2015, 7). When brought together they begin to illustrate the productive coupling of global scientific assessments with local, Indigenous approaches to – and concepts of – innovation and sustainability.

In February 2015, an Auckland company was fined more than NZ$100,000 for the spill that polluted Oruarangi. The IPPP with Makaurau won the Supreme Award at Auckland Council's Consultation and Engagement Awards in December 2014, evidence of the local government's recognition of both its innovation and the reciprocal knowledge exchange on which it was built.

As this chapter was in preparation, Maryanne Rapata died. At her tangi (funeral rites) an opportunity was recognised: 'Who will care for Oruarangi like Maryanne has?' A saying well-known in Aotearoa offers reassurance that the extraordinary work of this tupuna (ancestor) of Makaurau will be continued by her descendants, whilst it echoes the spiral dynamics so pivotal to our chapter:

Ka hinga atu ra he tete-kura. Ka hara mai he tete-kura
When one fern frond dies, one is born to take its place

Glossary

Māori	:	English
Aotearoa	:	land of the long white cloud' – Māori name for New Zealand
awa	:	river
hau	:	wind, air
katiaki	:	caretaker, custodian
koru	:	single spiral
mana whenua	:	customary authority exercised by a Māori kingroup in an identified area
Māori	:	Indigenous people of New Zealand
Māoritanga	:	Māori culture; Māori perspective
marae	:	meeting area, focal point of settlement
mauri	:	life principle
ngā hau māngere	:	lazy winds
takarangi	:	double spiral
tangata whenua	:	people of the land and sea; Indigenous Māori
Te Ao Hurihuri	:	the turning world
te puāwaitangi	:	flourishing
toto	:	blood
tupuna	:	ancestor
wairua	:	spirit

Notes

1 In Te Arawa tradition, the harbour was named by the ancestor Tamatekapua, when he placed a volcanic stone as a mauri (talisman) in its waters near Birkenhead. The Ngāpuhi people called it Te Wai-o-te-mate (the waters of death) – a reference to battles to control the Tāmaki isthmus (McClure 2012, 9).

2 Manukau is the second largest harbour of New Zealand (about 350 km) with a tidal range of up to 4.6 m; 60 per cent of the harbour is sand and mud flats; it is home to many sharks and is an important nursery area for fish; of the 16 bathing beaches tested during summer 2012/13, 83 per cent passed the recreational bacteria guidelines; and the harbour's water quality has been ranked as 'fair'.

3 Court documents would later detail the "'calamitous' effect on the awa, which had previously supported a 'healthy and abundant' freshwater fish and eel population, dominated by short-fin eels and inanga as well as some long-fin eel and banded kokopu" (Morton 2015). The species decimated included endangered and protected fish.

4 Attributed to Chris Whaanga, Oruarangi Sports and Whanau Development Trust, www.schoolground.co.nz/oruarangi_swdt.

5 In 2015, at the time of writing, Raworth was Senior Visiting Research Associate at Oxford University's Environmental Change Institute, where she teaches on the Masters in Environmental Change and Management, and Senior Associate of the Cambridge Institute for Sustainability Leadership.

6 www.un.org/en/sustainablefuture/about.shtml.

7 www.un.org/en/sustainablefuture/sustainability.shtml.

Bibliography

Adams, P. (2014), *Report to Auckland Council*, Oruarangi Industry Pollution Prevention Programme.

Auckland Council (2014a), *Industry Pollution Prevention Programme Report*, Senior Environmental Programmes Advisor Tessa Chilala.

Auckland Council (2014b), *Industry Pollution Prevention Programme*, Oruarangi Pamphlet.

Auckland Council (2014c), *Industry Pollution Prevention Programme*, Omaru Pamphlet.

Boserup, E. (1965), *The Conditions of Agricultural Growth: The Economics of Agrarian Change under Population Pressure*. Earthscan, London.

Dearing, J.A., R. Wang, K. Zhang, J.G. Dyke, H. Haberl, Md. Sarwar Hossain, P.G. Langdon, T.M. Lenton, K. Raworth, S. Brown, J. Carstensen, M.J. Cole, S.E. Cornell, T.P. Dawson, C.P. Doncaster, F. Eigenbrod, M. Flörke, E. Jeffers, A.W. Mackay, B. Nykvist and G.M. Poppy (2014), 'Safe and just operating spaces for regional social-ecological systems', *Global Environmental Change*, 28: 227–238.

DeFries, R.S., E.C. Ellis, F.S. Chapin III, P.A. Matson, B.L. Turner II, A. Agrawal, P.J. Crutzen, C. Field, P. Gleick, P.M. Kareiva, E. Lambin, D. Liverman, E. Ostrom, P.A. Sanchez and J. Syvitski (2012), 'Planetary opportunities: A social contract for global change science to contribute to a sustainable future', *BioScience*, 62(6): 603–606.

Dey, K. and S. Grant (2014), 'Māori communities as social enterprise', *Social Entrepreneurship and Enterprise*, 194–216.

Dryzek, J.S. (2005), *The Politics of the Earth: Environmental Discourses*, 2nd ed. Oxford University Press, New York, NY.

Fleurbaey, M. and D. Blanchet (2013), *Beyond GDP: Measuring Welfare and Assessing Sustainability*. Oxford University Press, New York, NY.

Goulet, D. (1974), *A New Moral Order. Development Ethics and Liberation Theology*. Orbis Books, Maryknoll, NY.

Harmsworth, G.R. (2002), 'Māori environmental performance indicators for wetland condition and trend. Coordinated Monitoring of New Zealand Wetlands, Phase 2, Goal 2.' Landcare Research Report LC 0102/099. Manaaki Whenua – Landcare Research, Palmerston North, NZ, 65 pp.

Harmsworth G.R., S. Awatere and C. Pauling (2013), 'Using mātauranga Māori to inform freshwater management.' Landcare Research Policy Brief. Integrated Valuation and Monitoring Framework for Improved Freshwater Outcomes (C09X1003). 5 pp.

Harmsworth, G., S. Awatere and J. Procter (2014), 'Meeting water quality and quantity standards to sustain cultural values.' Written for presentation at the 21st Century Watershed Technology Conference and Workshop, Improving Water Quality and the Environment, The University of Waikato, New Zealand, 3–7 November 2014.

Hēnare, M. (1998), 'Globalisation: An Indigenous religious/cultural perspective', in J. Camilleri and C. Muzaffar (eds), *Globalisation: The Perspectives and Experiences of the Religious Traditions of Asia Pacific*. International Movement for a Just World, Selangor, pp. 75–89.

Hēnare, M. (2001), 'Tapu, mana, mauri, hau, wairua. A Māori philosophy of vitalism and cosmos', in J.A. Grim (ed.), *Indigenous Traditions and Ecology: The Interbeing of Cosmology and Community*. Harvard University Press for the Centre for the Study of World Religions, Cambridge, UK, pp. 197–221.

Hēnare, M. (2003), 'Changing Images of Nineteenth Century Māori Society – From Tribes to Nation', Unpublished PhD thesis, Victoria University of Wellington, NZ.

Hēnare, M. (2011a), 'Lasting peace and the good life: Economic development and the "Te Ātanoho" principle of Te Tiriti o Waitangi', in V.M.H. Tawhai and K. Gray-Sharp (eds), *Always Speaking: The Treaty of Waitangi and Public Policy*. Huia, Wellington, pp. 261–275.

Hēnare, M. (2011b), *Rangatiratanga, Tohungatanga, Wairuatanga: The Good Life, People of the Metaphorical Mind, Māori Leadership*. Leadership Seminar Presentation. Ngāruawāhia: The University of Auckland Business School.

Hēnare, M. and V.J. Lindsay (2000), 'Traditional ethics and values of Indigenous peoples: Humanism in business and economy', Paper presented at the 3rd Conference on Ethics and Contemporary Human Resource Management, Imperial College Management School, London.

Hēnare, M., B. Lythberg and C. Woods (2014), 'Teaming with intent: Harmonising heritage, innovation and multiple generations within the Māori entrepreneurial team', *The Business and Management Review*. IMRA-ABRM Conference Proceedings, Cambridge University, UK, 23–24 June 2014.

Hēnare, M., B. Lythberg and C. Woods (in press), 'Te Ohu Umanga Māori: Temporality and intent in the Māori entrepreneurial team', *Research Handbook on Entrepreneurial Teams*, Edward Elgar.

Hindle, K. and P. Moroz (2010), 'Indigenous entrepreneurship as a research field: Developing a definitional framework from the emerging canon', *The International Entrepreneurship and Management Journal (IEMJ)*, 6: 357–385.

Hulme, M. (2009), *Why We Disagree about Climate Change: Understanding Controversy, Inaction Opportunity*. Cambridge University Press, Cambridge, UK.

Jerneck, A. and L. Olsson (2011), 'Breaking out of sustainability impasses: How to apply frame analysis, reframing and transition theory to global health challenges', *Environmental Innovation and Societal Transitions*, 1(2): 255–271.

Kawharu, M., P. Tapsell and C.R. Woods (2013), 'Resistance and challenge: The shaping of indigenous entrepreneurship, a Māori context', *ANZAM Conference*, Hobart, Australia, December 2013.

Lakoff, G. (2004), *Don't Think of an Elephant!: Know Your Values and Frame the Debate*, Chelsea Green, White River Junction, VT.

Loomis, T.M. (2000), 'Indigenous populations and sustainable development: Building on Indigenous approaches to holistic, self-determined development', *World Development*, 28(5): 893–910.

Marsden, M. (2003), 'The woven universe: Selected writings of the Rev. Māori Marsden', in T.A. Royal, *The Woven Universe: Selected Writings of the Rev. Māori Marsden*. Estate of M. Marsden, Otaki, NZ.

McClure, M. (2012), 'Auckland places – Waitematā Harbour', Te Ara – the Encyclopedia of New Zealand', updated 13 July 2012. www.TeAra.govt.nz/en/auckland-places/page-9 (accessed 15 December 2014).

McGrall, S. (2013), 'Framing and reframing the emerging "planetary crisis": A plea to avoid, and for increasing critique of, neoenvironmental determinism', *On the Horizon*, 21(3): 230–246.

McGregor, D. (2012), 'Traditional knowledge: Considerations for protecting water in Ontario' (Special issue on water and Indigenous peoples). *International Indigenous Policy Journal*, 3(3): article 11.

McGregor, D. (2014), 'Traditional knowledge and water governance: The ethic of responsibility', *Alternative*, 10(5): 493–507.

Morgan, K. (2003), 'The sustainable evaluation of the provision of urban infrastructure alternatives using the Tangata Whenua Mauri model within the smart growth sub-region.' Technical report. Mahi Maioro Professionals, Auckland, NZ.

Morton, J. (2015), 'Wildlife killed by purple dye spill', *New Zealand Herald*, 16 February 2015.

Nicholson, A., C.R. Woods and M. Hēnare (2012), 'Umanga whanaungatanga: Family business', *Journal of Australian Indigenous Issues*, 15(4): 36–50.

Overall, J., P. Tapsell and C.R. Woods (2010), 'Governance and indigenous social entrepreneurship: When context counts', *Social Enterprise Journal*, 6(2): 146–161.

Parsell, D. (2002), 'Explorer Wade Davis on vanishing cultures', *National Geographic News*, 28 June 2002. http://news.nationalgeographic.com/news/2002/06/0627_020628_wadedavis.html (accessed 30 December 2014).

Peredo, A.M. and R.B. Anderson (2006), 'Indigenous entrepreneurship research: Themes and variations', *International Research in the Business Disciplines*, 5, pp. 253–273.

Petrie, H. (2006), *Chiefs of Industry: Māori Tribal Enterprise in Early Colonial New Zealand.* Auckland University Press, Auckland, NZ.

Racette, P. (2009), 'Indigenous perspectives in GEOSS: An interview with Dr. Gregory Cajete'. www.earthzine.org/2009/04/06/indigenous-perspectives-in-geoss-an-interview-with-dr-gregory-cajete/ (accessed 30 April 2011).

Raworth, K. (2012), 'A safe and just space for humanity: Can we live within the doughnut?' Oxfam discussion paper, Oxfam International, Oxford. www.oxfam.org/en/research/safe-and-just-space-humanity (accessed 27 June 2016).

Rockström, J., W. Steffen, K. Noone, Å. Persson, F.S. Chapin III, E. Lambin, M. Lenton, M. Scheffer, C. Folke, H.J. Schellnhuber, B. Nykvist, C.A. de Wit, T. Hughes, S. van der Leeuw, H. Rodhe, S. Sörlin, K. Snyder, R. Constanza, U. Svedin, M. Falkenmark, L. Kalberg, V.J. Corell, J. Fabry, J. Hansen, B. Walker, D. Liverman, K. Richardson, P. Crutzen and J. Foley (2009a), 'Planetary boundaries: Exploring the safe operating space for humanity', *Ecol. Soc.*, 14: 32.

Rockström, J., W. Steffen, K. Noone, Å. Persson, F.S. Chapin III, E. Lambin, M. Lenton, M. Scheffer, C. Folke, H.J. Schellnhuber, B. Nykvist, C.A. de Wit, T. Hughes, S. van der Leeuw, H. Rodhe, S. Sörlin, K. Snyder, R. Constanza, U. Svedin, M. Falkenmark, L. Kalberg, V.J. Corell, J. Fabry, J. Hansen, B. Walker, D. Liverman, K. Richardson, P. Crutzen and J. Foley (2009b), 'A safe operating space for humanity', *Nature*, 461: 472–475.

Ruttan, V.W. (1977), 'Induced innovation and agricultural development', *Food Policy*, 2: 196–216.

Sen, A. (2000), *Development as Freedom.* Alfred A. Knopf, New York.

Senge, P., B. Smith, N. Kruschwitz, J. Laur and S. Schley (2010), *The Necessary Revolution.* Nicholas Brealey Publishing, London, UK.

Shepherd, D. and H. Patzelt. (2011), 'The new field of sustainable entrepreneurship: Studying entrepreneurial action linking "What is to be sustained" with "What is to be developed"', *Entrepreneurship Theory and Practice*, January: 137–163.

Simon, J.L. (1996), *The Ultimate Resource 2*, Princeton University Press, Princeton, NJ.

Spiller, C., L. Erakovic, M. Hēnare and E. Pio (2010), 'Relational well-being and wealth: Māori businesses and an ethic of care', *Journal of Business Ethics*, 98(1): 153–169.

Steffen, W., K. Richardson, J. Rockström, S.E. Cornell, I. Fetzer, E.M. Bennett, R. Biggs, S.R. Carpenter, W. de Vries, C.A. de Wit, C. Folke, D. Gerten, J. Heinke, G.M. Mace, L.M. Persson, V. Ramanathan, B. Reyers and S. Sörlin (2015), 'Planetary boundaries: Guiding human development on a changing planet', *Science*, 15 January, 10.1126. www.sciencemag.org/cgi/content/full/science.1259855/DCI (accessed 1 February 2015).

Suzuki, D., A. McConnell and A. Mason (1997), *The Sacred Balance*. Greystone Books, Vancouver, CA.

Taonui, R. (2012), 'Tāmaki tribes – Tribal history and places', Te Ara – the Encyclopedia of New Zealand, updated 15 November 2012. www.TeAra.govt.nz/en/photograph/1021/manukau-harbour (accessed 15 December 2014).

Tapsell, P. and C.R. Woods (2008a), 'Indigenous entrepreneurship in a Māori context', *Journal of Enterprising Communities: People and Places in the Global Economy*, 2(3): 192–203.

Tapsell, P. and C.R. Woods (2008b), 'A spiral of innovation framework for social entrepreneurship: Social innovation at the generational divide in an indigenous context', *Emergence*, 10(3): 25–34.

Tapsell, P. and C.R. Woods (2010), 'Social entrepreneurship and innovation: Self-organisation in an indigenous context', *Entrepreneurship and Regional Development*, 22(6): 535–556.

Tipa, G. and L. Tierney (2006), 'A Cultural Health Index for streams and waterways: A tool for nationwide use.' Final technical report. Ministry for Environment, Wellington, NZ, 72 pp.

Townsend, C.R., G. Tipa, L.D. Teirney and D.K. Niyogi (2004), 'Development of a tool to facilitate participation of Māori in the management of stream and river health', *Ecohealth*, 1: 184–195.

United Nations, 'What is sustainability?' www.un.org/en/sustainablefuture/sustainability.shtml (accessed 15 December 2014).

United Nations, 'What is Rio +20?' www.un.org/en/sustainablefuture/about.shtml (accessed 15 December 2014).

Verweij, M., M. Thompson and C. Englel (2006), 'Clumsy solutions', in M. Verqeij and M. Thompson (eds), *Clumsy Solutions for a Complex World: Governance, Politics, and Plural Perceptions*, Palgrave Macmillan, New York, NY.

Warren, R.C. (1996), 'FOCUS: Business as a community of purpose', *Business Ethics: A European Review*, 5(2): 87–96.

Whaanga, C., Oruarangi Sports and Whanau Development Trust, www.schoolground.co.nz/oruarangi_swdt (accessed 15 December 2014).

Wilkinson, S. (2014), *Contractor report to Auckland Council*, Oruarangi Industry Pollution prevention programme.

Young, R., G. Harmsworth., D. Walker and T. James (2008), 'Linkages between cultural and scientific indicators of river and stream health. Motueka Integrated Catchment Management Motueka ICM) Programme Report.' Prepared for Stakeholders of the Motueka Integrated Catchment Management Programme.

11 Sustainable entrepreneurship, opportunity creation

A corporate political activity view

Xuanwei Cao and Doris Fischer

Introduction

Entrepreneurs are becoming an important power in promoting a transformation to sustainable development through various ways (Schaltegger and Wagner, 2011). Some scholars even see entrepreneurship as panacea for many social and environmental concerns (Brugmann and Prahalad, 2007; Senge *et al.*, 2007). In previous studies discussing why firms engage in corporate sustainability activities, many authors followed organizational or industry level approaches, often drawing on social movements and institutional theory at the macro level (e.g., Campbell, 2006; Doh and Guay, 2006; Husted and Allen, 2006; Schneiberg *et al.*, 2008; Sine and Lee, 2009; Jackson and Apostolakou, 2010; Brammer *et al.*, 2012). Although they acknowledged that personal values of entrepreneurs can lead to specific entrepreneurial actions including sustainable entrepreneurship (Shepherd and Patzelt, 2011), it remains open what values are most influential among entrepreneurs when discovering or creating opportunities to both create personal economic and societal benefits. The question of how entrepreneurs discover and develop opportunities leading to emerging sustainable businesses has not been investigated so far. We believe it is important to understand to what extent and how entrepreneurs seek opportunities in the bottom-up processes of promoting the development of new industry (Walker *et al.*, 2014).

While entrepreneurs respond to challenges of social development with positive and legitimate participation in policymaking, scholars still lack explanations why entrepreneurs engage in social and public welfare and how entrepreneurs secure both personal economic and societal benefits through seeking social and/or sustainable opportunities. A recent study argues that cultural-dependent ideologies or values drive successful private-firm entrepreneurs' motivation to pursue political appointments for the sake of influencing policymaking and contribute to the greater good (Li and Liang, 2015). Li and Liang provide a good foundation to understand why private-firm entrepreneurs in a Confucian cultural context pursue pro-self and pro-social objectives through political engagement. However, they neither explored how private-firm entrepreneurs identify and create entrepreneurial opportunities to simultaneously realize pro-social welfare and business sustainability nor how entrepreneurial political appointments impact on institutional change. This latter aspect is relevant as political engagement of private-firm entrepreneurs had a notable increase in recent years at least in China.

In order to grasp the relation between private-firm entrepreneurs' ideology and the creation of opportunities for sustainable entrepreneurship, this study introduces a corporate political activity (CPA) perspective which allows bridging the aspect of entrepreneurial behavior at the micro level and the change of industry and institutions at the macro level.

Accordingly, we address the following research question: How do entrepreneurs create opportunities for sustainable entrepreneurship through engaging in CPA?

We answer our research question using a longitudinal case study of a private-firm entrepreneur in the solar PV industry in China from 2007 to 2014. Our study addresses the interrelationship between sustainable entrepreneurship and CPA. First, we argue that sustainable entrepreneurs' values influence how they identify and create opportunities and corporations' engagement in sustainable business. Second, sustainable entrepreneurs seek and create sustainable business opportunities through their CPAs with stakeholders in different issue areas. Third, sustainable business opportunities evolve dynamically with entrepreneurs' CPAs, thereby creating a positive impact on industrial and institutional change towards sustainability-orientation.

CPA and sustainable entrepreneurship

Sustainable entrepreneurship and CPA

Scholars from entrepreneurship, environment management, business ethics, strategy, innovation and other fields are increasingly exploring how entrepreneurship can address societal level issues such as sustainable development (Pacheco *et al.*, 2010; York and Venkataraman, 2010; Schaltegger and Wagner, 2011; Pinkse and Groot, 2015). While some scholars remain skeptical regarding the intention of entrepreneurship with regard to sustainability, claiming that "it remains an open question as to whether and, to what extent, entrepreneurs have the potential for creating sustainable economies" (Hall *et al.*, 2010, p. 440), others argue that entrepreneurship has an important role to play in transformation towards a more sustainable future (Belz and Binder, 2015). Entrepreneurs are expected to be able to balance the triple bottom line of economic, social and ecological goals (Schaltegger and Wagner, 2011) and to pursue simultaneously economic viability, social equity and environmental stability (Thompson *et al.*, 2011).

As our chapter aims at the process of entrepreneurial opportunity creation in developing solar energy business, we use the definition of sustainable entrepreneurship of Belz and Binder (2015). Sustainable entrepreneurship is understood as "the recognition, development and exploitation of opportunities by individuals to bring into existence future goods and services with economic, social and ecological gains." This definition acknowledges that some entrepreneurs, "unlike Schumpeterian entrepreneurs [may be] driven by a social instead of an economic motive" (Reinstaller, 2005, p. 1366). Such entrepreneurs do not only wish to capture economic value for themselves, but also want to find new avenues towards social improvement and to create social value. Sustainable entrepreneurs consider the sustainability of their business as well as the ethical and long-term impact of their business on society and the natural environment. They are not blindly pursuing short-term business profit. As a result, sustainable entrepreneurship has the potential to contribute solutions for environmental and social problems through sustainability innovations that aim at the mass market and provide benefit to the larger part of society (Schaltegger and Wagner, 2011).

Despite the growing interest in sustainable entrepreneurship, most research adopts an "outside-in" perspective to understand how external factors, regulations and policies could encourage investment in sustainable and socially responsible entrepreneurship. As an exception, a recent study of Belz and Binder (2015) offers a process model of recognizing, developing and exploiting opportunities for sustainable entrepreneurship. However, this study has not addressed the mind–heart nexus of entrepreneurship, i.e., the factors that affect entrepreneurs' personal values and sense of corporate purpose. For a comprehensive understanding of the behavior and actions of sustainable entrepreneurs, we need to consider the fundamental microfoundations (Zahra and Wright, 2011) that nurture their sustainability orientation. We therefore deem it relevant to investigate the ideologies, values and motives that underline entrepreneurs' political actions.

Recent studies on entrepreneurs' venturing on sustainability disclosed that sustainable entrepreneurs must sometimes become politically active to overcome market barriers (Pacheco et al., 2010; Pinkse and Groot, 2015). Although CPA can generally be understood as corporate attempts to shape government policy in ways favorable to the firm (Hillman and Hitt, 1999), previous studies have mainly focused on how firms use their strategic political resources and capabilities to improve their profitability (McWilliams et al., 2002) and have limited the analysis to enterprises in Western industrialized economies. In addition, some Western scholars equal CPAs in transition economies with corruption (Lawton et al., 2013) which produces harmful results and risks for corporations (Mantere et al., 2009). Other studies however argue that in the incomplete institutional environment of emerging economies, firms do not only have to adapt to institutional change but can actually develop considerable power to influence it (Dieleman and Boddewyn, 2012). Entrepreneurial actors are able not only to identify the institutional constraints constructed by the social, political and economic context within which entrepreneurs are embedded, but also to envision and alternate the institutional arrangement (Suddaby et al., 2015).

Most studies on entrepreneurial CPA have, however, focused on the economic motivation of CPAs, i.e., entrepreneurs' aim to employ CPAs to increase their firms' competitiveness by access to additional resources, capital or assets. However, Li and Liang (2015) argue that beyond this kind of "pro-self" motivation, private-firm entrepreneurs influenced by Confucian doctrine, also show "pro-social" motivation and engage politically in order to promote general social welfare. This obviously raises the question whether some entrepreneurs' sustainability orientation and related CPA are derived from specific ideologies and values of the entrepreneurs.

In one of the few studies that ask how sustainable entrepreneurship becomes successful in a specific institutional context through political activity, Pinkse and Groot (2015) analyzed the collective actions of entrepreneurs for overcoming market barriers, but left the question of how sustainable entrepreneurs identify, develop and seize opportunities unaddressed. Other scholars have suggested paying more attention to the purpose of organizations as well as the role of values and political ideologies of business leaders (Chin *et al.*, 2013; Briscoe *et al.*, 2014; Hollensbe *et al.*, 2014).

It is in this context that the Chinese example becomes relevant. Li and Liang (2015) argue that in the Confucian culture, successful entrepreneurs are more inclined to engage politically as a means to fulfill Confucian values and extend themselves to serve the larger community and to pursue societal harmony. This was, of course, not possible in the socialist economy of China before the reforms. Therefore, entrepreneurs in China in the 1980s and 1990s were preoccupied with rehabilitating entrepreneurship, earning money and accumulating wealth. Today, however, after more than 30 years of quick economic development, entrepreneurs in China are again changing their attitudes to wealth, and begin to rethink their roles in society. Some of the successful entrepreneurs are intending to develop their businesses cleanly and sustainably for the whole society instead of pursuing purely economic interests for themselves. These changes in value and purpose of those entrepreneurs allow their CPA to be public interests oriented. Figure 11.1 below illustrates the pulling role of CPA in the transformation of entrepreneurs towards sustainable entrepreneurship.

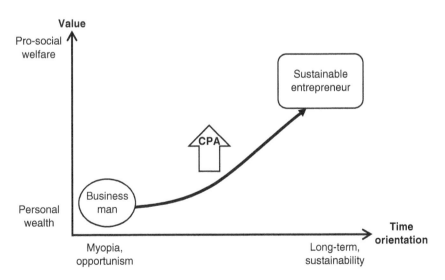

Figure 11.1 The role of CPA in the transformation of entrepreneurship.

CPA and entrepreneurial opportunities

Although it has been argued that firms pursuing CPA could benefit in terms of increased long-term sustainability (Hillman and Hitt, 1999), the potential role of the individual entrepreneur on exploring and creating sustainability opportunities through CPA is seldom discussed.

To answer the question of why and how individual entrepreneurs actively pursue sustainability opportunities, we have to look into the motivations that drive entrepreneurial activities. This refers to the microfoundation of entrepreneurs (Felin *et al.*, 2015) and implied to acknowledge noneconomic motives of entrepreneurs (Shepherd *et al.*, 2015). Haynie *et al.* (2010) have illustrated how the beliefs of entrepreneurs influence the cognition and impact their search for opportunities. Chin *et al.* (2013) illustrated that the political ideologies and other values of business leaders can be expected to influence their extra-firm associations, affiliations and public policies. They also found out that entrepreneurs' personal values have impact on firm initiatives such as corporate social responsibility. In addition, a study by Hond *et al.* (2014, p. 803) clarified that ideological differences among companies can cause institutional change. Business leaders' political ideologies reflect personal values and therefore "help[s] to explain why people do what they do (Jost, 2006: 653)." Thus, by introducing the lens of political ideology into the analysis of sustainable entrepreneurs' opportunity creation, we can attain a richer contextual understanding of entrepreneurs' behavior and decisions including the potential tradeoff between economic and noneconomic considerations in exploring opportunities.

The concept of ideology comprises an interconnected set of beliefs and attitudes related to problematic aspects of social and political topics that are shared and used by members of a group and that inform and justify choice and behavior (Hond and Bakker, 2007). In this line, ideological (value) factors influence how entrepreneurs interact with society and address the expectations and pressures coming from stakeholders. Recent calls for value-based business (Chandler, 2014) and indigenous management theory (Suddaby, 2014) require us to review the ideologies and values of entrepreneurs to understand their influence on business and on the entrepreneur's attitude with regard to solving societal problems. Ideologically motivated entrepreneurs create value-rational organizations, which reflect their belief in substantive principles rather than efficiency or profitability only (Weber, 1978: 24–26; DiMaggio and Anheier, 1990). Thus, we can expect that some ideologically motivated, pioneering entrepreneurs seek opportunities to create public goods such as sustainable development and CPAs accordingly.

Opportunities are created from the interactive process between entrepreneurs and stakeholders (Companys and McMullen, 2007). Thus, companies will take two types of CPAs to deal with stakeholders. One is direct CPA with government; another is indirect CPA with other stakeholders. The former may take various strategies, from visiting the government officials regularly to participating in the formulation of government policies and putting forward research reports from firms' own angle to government and industry organization and so on (Deng *et al.*, 2010); the latter are emerging more and more in the pattern of corporate social responsibility (CSR) as it is becoming a popularity in China. Through this kind of indirect CPA, corporations could strengthen their participation in formal and direct CPA. For example, corporations could make a demonstration project to increase support from stakeholders and further their legitimacy to push institutional change. The formal CPA would more be conducted by corporations, while the indirect CPA would more be presented through individual entrepreneurs.

Thus, in the process of interacting with key stakeholders, through taking the patterns of responsible lobbying (Lawton *et al.*, 2013), CSR (Deng *et al.*, 2010), political CSR (Scherer and Palazzo, 2011), corporations/entrepreneurs could intendedly take actions via various channels to reshape institutional and industry environment (Shepherd and Patzelt, 2011). In the process of environmental jots and institutional change, such as in the rapid development and evolution of new industries, entrepreneurs with pro-social values could explore and create opportunities through engaging in CPAs with various stakeholders and realize the transformation towards sustainable entrepreneurship.

Figure 11.2 below illustrates the conceptual model of the process of opportunity creation through sustainable entrepreneurs' engagement in CPAs. In this process, entrepreneurs' ideology and values could potentially impact sustainable entrepreneurs' identification of opportunities and correspondent CPAs. With the positive enabling power of sustainable entrepreneurs in engaging CPAs, favorable institutions for the development of sustainable business which benefits both private and public interests would be expected to be developed. Thus, successful private entrepreneurs could create and realize opportunities in pursuing sustainable business both in the meaning of business sustainability and for environmental and societal sustainable development.

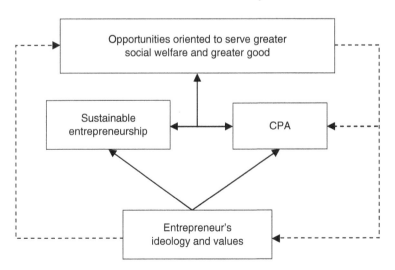

Figure 11.2 Sustainable entrepreneurship, opportunity creation and CPA.

Methodology

Many scholars have emphasized that the study of entrepreneurship demands a rich, detailed interpretive analysis of the particular context where it occurs (Berglund et al., 2015). Along the same lines it is argued that more emphasis should be put on longitudinal studies to better understand organizational phenomena and respective change both within a level over time and across level over time (Ployhart and Vandenberg, 2010). Longitudinal studies also allow following change in entrepreneurial opportunities and impact with regard to institutional change (Shepherd et al., 2015). Following these calls for in-depth qualitative research on the role of entrepreneurship in organizations, community and society (Suddaby et al., 2015) this chapter uses the method of historical case study with event driven explanation to analyze an individual corporate example (Van de Ven, 2007). As Siggelkow has argued with regard to case studies, "getting closer to constructs and being able to illustrate causal relationships more directly are among the key advantages of case research" (Siggelkow, 2007, p. 22). We track the historical development and use the historical event sequencing method to investigate the dynamic interaction between sustainable entrepreneurship and opportunity creation by observing the respective CPAs.

Research context

Among the industries related to sustainable development, we see the solar PV industry as an ideal case to examine the activities of Chinese entrepreneurs and their roles in the process of industry development. Different from previous popular stereotypes regarding entrepreneurs in transition economies, which depict entrepreneurs only relying on institutional voids to seek opportunities (Puffer et al., 2010), we have identified sustainable entrepreneurs in China who engage in promoting solar PV industry development and solar energy use based on personal values that go beyond pecuniary interests. We suppose that some Chinese entrepreneurs have played a significant role in the relevant institutional development. Unfortunately, past research on the Chinese PV sector development has hardly reflected this aspect.

The selection of context and the specific case was guided by the phenomenon and issues we address in this chapter. Specifically, we selected the solar PV industry as the research context for three reasons. First, the solar PV industry is a high-opportunity branch which experienced rapid development in recent years in China. This indicates that entrepreneurs who were able to create and seize opportunities could become "path defining" for the industry's development. Second, against the background of Chinese government policy to foster strategic emerging industries, the solar PV industry witnessed intensive interactions between entrepreneurs and policy makers. Thus, the solar PV industry offers a good example to show how micro-level political activities by entrepreneurs influence the transformation of the industry development and induce institutional change at the macro level. Third, the case company and the entrepreneur in this study had not been involved in the solar energy industry before 2006. The quick entrance of the case company into the solar PV industry and the influence since then exercised by the entrepreneur of the case company provide a good basis to observe and understand the development process of sustainable entrepreneurship.

Research data

A historical case study requires the collection of data from different channels in order to identify "events, activities and choices" over time and reveal who did what, when (Langley, 1999, p. 692). To understand the CPAs taken by the entrepreneur, the motivation behind these and their influence on the development of institutional change of the Chinese solar PV industry, this study relies on three levels of data gathered to illustrate the dynamic interactions between entrepreneurial ideology at the micro level of the individual entrepreneur and transformation of institutions at the macro level including firm, industry and institution. Entrepreneurial and firm-level data were collected from historians' accounts of the industry. Firm publications that focus on annual milestone events, reports by solar energy industry associations and official statistics were collected to get information about the development of the industry. Institutional-level data including industrial policies and policy proposals by entrepreneurs were collected from public information and reports disclosed by relevant government bodies.

Case: the solar PV industry of T Group

Background

Solar PV industry in China has developed quickly over the past decade and entrepreneurs have swarmed into the industry to gain from this development. In this process, some strongly motivated entrepreneurs participated in the important process of institutional building and reform in this industry. Hence, the industry is a good field to observe and analyze the behaviors and activities of entrepreneurs on seizing opportunities for sustainable business.

The case of T Group provides a good example to illustrate why and how the values and ideologies upheld by an entrepreneur influence his decision making towards sustainable entrepreneurship. From this case, we can observe the cross-level dynamic interactions among entrepreneurial ideology, CPA and entrepreneurial opportunity over time.

T Group – a leading private enterprise in the area of feed and aquatic products established in 1984 in Sichuan Province, Western China – had by 2006 grown to be the world's largest aquatic feed manufacturer as well as a major livestock and poultry feed producer. In February 2007, T Group entered the upstream of the solar PV industry value chain with huge investment in a chemical factory producing polyvinyl chloride (PVC) which is used as raw materials for the production of polycrystalline silicon, a major input material for PV modules. From then on, T Group expanded into the solar energy industry without neglecting the original business line, thereby, following a dual core business strategy. In the words of Mr. Liu, the founder and chairman of T Group, T Group is a company devoted to providing society with green power sources, with aquatic feed providing power that satisfies human beings' demand for food, and solar energy providing power that satisfies society's demand for energy.

Upon entering the PVC business, Mr. Liu actually planned to construct a comprehensive value chain in the PV power industry. Therefore, also in February 2007, T Group decided to also invest in polycrystalline silicon. Indicating a fast process from feasibility research to high-standard production, the first stage of the polycrystalline silicon project with 1,000 tons production capacity was successfully put into operation before 2008, when the outbreak of the global financial crisis hit the industry. While the successful project marked an important step on T Group's new path and the realization of Mr. Liu's ambitious dream to explore green gold from the new energy industry, the impact of the global financial crisis on the industry's development led T Group to a cautious expansion strategy of its solar energy business. Regionally, this expansion proceeded from southwest to northwest and northeast by establishing production facilities in many counties in China.

In 2013, T Group acquired a large solar cell maker and made huge investment to operate its new production base of polycrystalline silicon. Although T Group is not a pioneer of the Chinese PV industry, with Mr. Liu's firm commitment and determination into this field and his positive political activities to call for favorable PV sector related industrial policies, T Group has quickly developed into one of the largest PV producers and operators of PV power stations in China, with a very comprehensive industrial chain in the solar PV industry. With its own technologies and over 100 technical patents for producing polycrystalline silicon, T Group holds an important position in the Chinese market.

The great impact of T Group in China's solar industry development, however, was not only supported by its solar business as such, but also by the active political engagement of Mr. Liu, including the regular submission of policy proposals and research reports to related central government bodies.

Table 11.1 below illustrates the rapid development of T Group in the solar PV business.

Corporate political activity and solar PV business in T Group

Parallel to the T Group's growth and development, Mr. Liu, the founder and the Board Chairman of T Group's executive board, also accumulated political achievements with great success. Since 1994, Mr. Liu has turned himself from a successful businessman into an influential entrepreneur with significant political appointment in the Chinese political system. Since 1994, Mr. Liu has been a

Table 11.1 The quick development of T Group in the developing solar PV business

Year	Main activities in developing solar PV business
2006	Aimed at entering the solar PV industry cautiously.
2007	• Invested a chemical factory to produce PVC with a production capacity of 5,000 tons per year. PVC is the material for producing polycrystalline silicon. This marks the milestone of T Group making a decision to enter into the solar PV industry. • Donated 50 million RMB to construct 6 PV power stations in remote western rural areas with a total installed capacity of 1.355 MWp. • Increased investment to expand the production capacity of polycrystalline silicon to 9,000 tons per year
2008	• Showed in the 2008 Asian Solar PV Exhibition. • Realized quick returns of investment in producing polycrystalline silicon.
2010	• Increased investment further in its polycrystalline silicon project with 3,000 tons production capability.
2011	• Made investment expansion in Chengdu. • Investment in polycrystalline silicon production base in Jianwei county, with 46.2 billion RMB. • Reached strategic cooperation agreement with Xinjiang autonomous region government to develop 50,000 tons of polycrystalline silicon and 3GW silicon slices, with a total investment of 26 billion RMB.
2012	• Sichuan Provincial Government approves a demonstration project of 30MW solar PV with grid connection in Yanyuan County with a total installed capacity of 100MW.
2013	• Acquisition of solar PV company LDK and expanded investment of PV business in producing PV slice.
2014	• Decision to extend the industrial chain to the construction and operation of decentralized PV power stations. • Ranked as the largest PV slice producer in China.

Source: T Group's website.

member of the China Democratic National Construction Association (CDNCA), one of the eight democratic parties on the patriotic united front led by the Chinese Communist Party which are represented in the Chinese People's Political Consultative Conference (CPPCC). He was later elected a member of the Central Standing Committee of CDNCA as well as a member of the Standing Committee of the CPPCC and received numerous honors, awards and high appreciations from different levels of government as well as other social organizations and entities. In addition, as a model of successful private-firm entrepreneurship during the early times of reform, starting from local county in 1986, Mr. Liu has received honors and awards at increasingly higher levels.

Tables 11.2 and 11.3 show the main political appointments and honorary titles and awards of Mr. Liu.

With the accumulation of political appointments, Mr. Liu was able to submit policy proposals and suggestions to the CPPCC and other government institutions, and to receive feedback and confirmation whether his judgment regarding investments in new energy projects would be a rightful strategic

Table 11.2 Mr. Liu's political appointment

Year	Political appointment
1994	Member of China Democratic National Construction Association (CDNCA)
1998	• Member of Standing Committee of Sichuan CPPCC Committee • Member of the CPPCC National Committee • Member of Entrepreneurs Committee of CDNCA
2002	Standing member of the Central Committee of CNDCA
2008	Member of Standing Committee of the CPPCC National Committee

Source: T Group's website.

Table 11.3 Mr. Liu's honorary titles awarded from government, industry and society

Year	Honorary titles and awards
2009	• Member of New Energy Chamber of Commerce under the umbrella of All China Federation of Industry and Commerce • "Responsible Leadership Award" of the 1st China Corporate Social Responsibility Summit
2011	• Standing deputy director of New Energy Chamber of Commerce • "Global New Energy Business Leadership" Award
2012	• Recognized as "the No. 1 Figure in Solar PV Industry" by National Energy Administration • "Most Civil Responsible Chinese Entrepreneur" • "2012 Most Social Responsible Chinese Entrepreneur"
2013	• Listed among the "HuRun 100 Riches List of the Most Respected Entrepreneur" • Listed among "2013 Caijing List of Person with Impact"

Source: T Group's website.

decision. Therefore, it is Mr. Liu's political capital and his active engagement in CPAs, both individually and in cooperation with other entrepreneurs, that helped him make investments in the solar PV business at appropriate moments in time. We should not ignore, however, the internal motivations for Mr. Liu's firm devotion to push the development of the solar energy industry in China. With the imprinted Confucian values believing that business activities (based on profits) are only a part of the whole life and one ought to seek moral self-cultivation and the development of human virtues, Mr. Liu, like many other successful and impactful private-firm entrepreneurs, has transcended the pursuit of pro-self interests, utilizing successful business growth and development as a vehicle for personal growth. Based on his strong personal values on pursuing a larger purpose, i.e., pursuing the greater good for the public, with his well-balanced ambidexterity on conducing political activities and making strategic decisions in front of complex market competition, Mr. Liu could bring his group into exploring commercial opportunities in sustainable business. In this process, the conducting of CPA serves to facilitate to create and seize opportunities in sustainable business for realizing entrepreneurs' personal ideology and value. For example, in 2007, Mr. Liu donated 50 million RMB to construct 6 PV power stations in remote western rural areas with a total installed capacity of 1.355 MWp. That philanthropic project is a positive response to the initiative of CNDCA to eradicate poverty. On the one hand, the donation of six PV power stations solidified the political appointment of Mr. Liu as a member of the Central Standing Committee of CDNCA. On the other hand, these demonstration PV power stations showed the strategic posture of T Group on extending into the PV power business in near future.

The interactive dynamics between CPA and the creation of opportunities in T Group's pursuit on sustainable business is illustrated in Figure 11.3.

As indicated in this case, it should be kept in mind that the identification and creation of opportunities in this sustainable business field is rooted to a great extent in the close interlinkage and interactions between Mr. Liu's personal political appointments and activities and his reinforced commitment on developing the solar PV industry.

The case of T Group additionally indicates a strong relationship between the entrepreneur's political activities on the one hand and his engagement for the expansion of PV energy use. The T Group accompanied its expansion into the solar PV industry by financing public demonstration projects of photovoltaic power stations in remote western areas of China. In this way, it added to the positive reputation of T Group and received attention from relevant stakeholders. At the same time, while ensuring the success of those philanthropic demonstration projects, T Group also took additional CPAs under the leadership of Mr. Liu to create and form business opportunities through leveraging the support from both local and central government. For this purpose, T Group tried to influence the institutional environment individually and in cooperation with other solar industry stakeholders. For example, T Group supported collective efforts of other industry actors to push for a new energy subsidy policy in 2011, using Mr. Liu's seat in CPPCC and his honorary position as the standing deputy director of New Energy Commerce. In August 2011, the National Development and Reform Committee issued the expected subsidy policy for photovoltaic power producers. The founder and chairman of T Group, Mr. Liu, therefore represents a group of emerging powerful entrepreneurs in China. With deep rooted Confucian values in their ideologies, those ambitious entrepreneurs are exploring and developing new opportunities with their well-developed market-political ambidexterity for seeking long-term business success and contributing to the greater good. The development of recently defined new emerging strategic industries is very much supported by this type of sustainable entrepreneur, who aim at pursuing sustainable competitive advantage while at the same time promoting the institutional development to help solve a certain social issue.

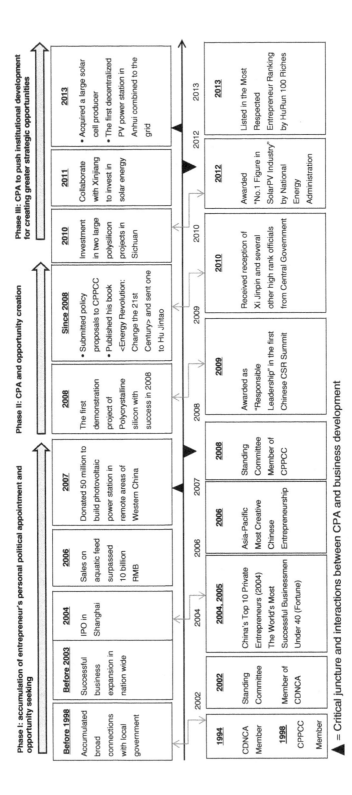

Phase I: accumulation of entrepreneur's personal political appointment and opportunity seeking

Phase II: CPA and opportunity creation

Phase III: CPA to push institutional development for creating greater strategic opportunities

Before 1998	Before 2003	2004	2006	2007
Accumulated broad connections with local government	Successful business expansion in nation wide	IPO in Shanghai	Sales on aquatic feed surpassed 10 billion RMB	Donated 50 million to build photovoltaic power station in remote areas of Western China

2008	Since 2008	2010	2011	2013
The first demonstration project of Polycrystalline silicon with success in 2008	• Submitted policy proposals to CPPCC • Published his book <Energy Revolution: Change the 21st Century> and sent one to Hu Jintao	Investment in two large polysilicon projects in Sichuan	Collaborate with Xinjiang to invest in solar energy	• Acquired a large solar cell producer • The first decentralized PV power station in Anhui combined to the grid

1994	2002	2004, 2005	2006	2008
CDNCA Member 1998 CPPCC Member	Standing Committee Member of CDNCA	China's Top 10 Private Entrepreneurs (2004) The World's Most Successful Businessmen Under 40 (Fortune)	Asia-Pacific Most Creative Chinese Entrepreneurship	Standing Committee Member of CPPCC

2009	2010	2012	2013
Awarded as "Responsible Leadership" in the first Chinese CSR Summit	Received reception of Xi Jinpin and several other high rank officials from Central Government	Awarded "No.1 Figure in SolarPV Industry" by National Energy Administration	Listed in the Most Respected Entrepreneur Ranking by HuRun 100 Riches

▶ = Critical juncture and interactions between CPA and business development

Figure 11.3 Critical juncture and actions taken by sustainable entrepreneur of T Group.

Conclusion

Our work contributes to the literatures in the following aspects. First, this study enriches the sustainable entrepreneurship literature through responding to the call for more contextualized entrepreneurship research (Welter, 2011) by looking into the example of the solar PV industry in China. The example of T Group and Mr. Liu highlights that successful entrepreneurs in China who pursue long-term economic and social goals are likely to do so by accepting political appointments and engaging in political activities. For some successful entrepreneurs, their personal attitudes regarding wealth and the purpose of business have changed in the process of 30 years of quick economic development. These entrepreneurs may feel a spiritual and moral call to action to serve the community and society at large. This resonates with the argument of Li and Liang that traditional Confucian values of transcending beyond selfhood and promoting the general social welfare are employed to find a way toward personal greatness (Li and Liang, 2015). In this case, engagement in CPA is a means to fulfill their personal ideology and values to contribute to social welfare. Thus, this chapter contributes insight to the argument that entrepreneurs in emerging economies conceive indigenous solutions to help solve specific social issues (Lewin, 2014).

The other contribution of this chapter is to investigate the interactions of corporate political activities and entrepreneurial opportunities through bringing entrepreneurs' ideology into the entrepreneurial process. Although previous studies have noticed the link between ideology and CPA, they positioned at an institutional level instead of at the individual level (Lux *et al.*, 2011). The presented longitudinal case of Mr. Liu and T Group illustrates how an ideologically motivated entrepreneur created opportunities by leveraging his political positions and engaging in institutional building. Driven by his strong internal commitment to improve economic development and people's welfare in inland regions, the successful entrepreneur was able to create a favorable institutional environment for the sustained development of his business. By analyzing the co-evolvement of the entrepreneur's political activities and the institution development, the case illustrates that the opportunity for solar PV industry development was created by the integration of individual and collective actions of entrepreneurs and multiple stakeholders.

Different from previous studies on CPA mostly in the US context, our study identifies the potential positive impact from sustainable entrepreneurs' political engagement and participating in CPAs in the context of a transition economy. Our study demonstrates how CPAs conducted by sustainable entrepreneurs could lead to institutional change favorable for the whole industry development instead of only for the benefits of individual entrepreneurs' enterprise. Our case provides a powerful example against the stereotype of entrepreneurs' utilization of institutional void to seek opportunities in transition economies (Puffer *et al.*, 2010). This study provides also a cross-level perspective to look at the individual entrepreneur's CPA and the consequent impacts on institutional change, namely a favorable industrial policy environment for the emerging new industry. CPA in the context of a transition economy therefore provides additional insight into the dynamic relationship between institutional work and entrepreneurial opportunity creation.

Although this study is far from enough to answer the question whether the emerging powerful private entrepreneurs can effectively form a politically influential class which has the potential to profoundly influence the progress of society (Tsai, 2007), we can still assume that entrepreneurs who care for sustainability could play an important role in promoting the transition. As the Chinese Communist Party and government has shown a tendency to encourage successful private-firm entrepreneurs to become involved in important political entities, ideologically motivated successful private-firm entrepreneurs may grasp the opportunity to become politically engaged for their purposes. In the near future, we may well expect to see more sustainable entrepreneurs engaging actively in politics for public benefit.

Limitation and future research

The use of qualitative case studies is appropriate to generate new insights and to build new theories. However we must acknowledge that the single case introduced in this chapter still lacks power to build an indigenous theory. To further the argument, more primary data regarding the intertwined dynamic process of entrepreneurs' CPA and opportunity creation, the role of personal values with regard to the entrepreneurs' motivation to engage for sustainability and societal goals will be necessary, and the impact of the institutional environment in transition or emerging economies on process and motivations would be necessary.

Our chapter suggests several lines of future inquiry. First, different groups of business leaders (such as CEOs of state owned enterprises in comparison to private owned enterprises) could be explored to better understand the impact of ideologies on entrepreneurs' opportunity creation strategies in emerging economies. Second, different cases of entrepreneurship in the solar energy industry could be compared to understand whether sustainable entrepreneurs in same institutional context share ideologies and follow similar approaches of opportunity creation and how they influence the institutional environment. Third, a qualitative comparative case study to examine how entrepreneurs' cognition and behavior of business sustainability is affected by different institutional and community contexts should be conducted. Fourth, to further enrich entrepreneurship research, theoretical lenses from other disciplinary fields, such as sociology and political theory, should be brought in to deepen our understanding on the societal impact of sustainable entrepreneurship.

References

Belz, F.M., Binder, J.K. (2015) "Sustainable entrepreneurship: A convergent process model," *Business Strategy and the Environment*, advance access.

Berglund, H., Jones, P., Higgins, D. (2015) "Between cognition and discourse: Phenomenology and the study of entrepreneurship," *International Journal of Entrepreneurial Behavior & Research*, advance access.

Brammer, S., Jackson, C., Matten, D. (2012) "Corporate social responsibility and institutional theory: New perspectives on private governance," *Social Economic Review*, 10(1): 3–28.

Briscoe, F., Chin, M.K., Hambrick, D.C. (2014) "CEO ideology as an element of the corporate opportunity structure for social activists," *Academy of Management Journal*, 57(6): 1786–1809.

Brugmann, J., Prahalad, C. (2007) "Cocreating business's new social compact," *Harvard Business Review*, 85(2): 80–90.

Campbell, J.L. (2006) "Institutional analysis and the paradox of corporate social responsibility," *American Behavioral Scientist*, 49(7): 925–938.

Chandler, D. (2014) "Book review: *Morals, Markets, and Value-Based Businesses,*" *Academy of Management Review*, 39(3): 396–406.

Chin, M.K., Hambrick, D.C., Treviño, L.K. (2013) "Political ideologies of CEOs: The influence of executives' values on corporate social responsibility," *Administrative Science Quarterly*, 58(2): 197–232.

Companys, Y.E., McMullen, J.S. (2007) "Strategic entrepreneurs at work: The nature, discovery, and exploitation of entrepreneurial opportunities," *Small Business Economics*, 28(4): 301–322.

Deng, X.M., Tian, Z.L., Abrar, M. (2010) "The corporate political strategy and its integration with market strategy in transitional China," *Journal of Public Affairs*, 10: 372–382.

Dieleman, D., Boddewyn, J.J. (2012) "Using organization structure to buffer political ties in emerging markets: A case study," *Organization Studies*, 33(1): 71–95.

DiMaggio, P.J., Anheier, H.K. (1990) "The sociology of nonprofit organizations and sectors," *Annual Review of Sociology*, 16: 137–159.

Doh, J, Guay, T. (2006) "Corporate social responsibility, public policy, and NGO activism in Europe and the United States: An institutional stakeholder perspective," *Journal of Management Studies*, 43(1): 47–73.

Felin, T., Foss, N.J., Ployhart, R.E. (2015) "The microfoundations movement in strategy and organization theory," *The Academy of Management Annals*, 9(1): 575–632.

Hall, J.K., Daneke, G.A., Lenox, M.J. (2010) "Sustainable development and entrepreneurship: Past contributions and future directions," *Journal of Business Venturing*, 25(5): 439–448.

Haynie, M.J., Shepherd, D., Mosakowski, E., Earley, P.C. (2010) "A situated metacognitive model of the entrepreneurial mindset," *Journal of Business Venturing*, 25(2): 217–229.

Hillman, A.J., Hitt, M.A. (1999) "Corporate political strategy formulation: A model of approach, participation, and strategy decisions," *Academy of Management Review*, 24(4): 825–842.

Hollensbe, E., Wookey, C., Hickey, L., George, G., Nichols, C.V. (2014) "Organization with purpose," *Academy of Management Journal*, 57(5): 1227–1234.

Hond, F.D., Bakker, F.G.A. de. (2007) "Ideologically motivated activism: How activist groups influence corporate social change activities," *Academy of Management Review*, 32(3): 901–924.

Hond, F., Rehbein, K.A., Bakker, F.G.A., Lankveld, H.K. (2014) 'Playing on two chessboards: Reputation effects between Corporate Social Responsibility (CSR) and Corporate Political Activity (CPA)," *Journal of Management Studies*, 51(5): 790–813.

Husted, B.W., Allen, D.B. (2006) "Corporate social responsibility in the multinational enterprise: Strategic and institutional approaches," *Journal of International Business Studies*, 37(6): 838–849.

Jackson, G., Apostolakou, A. (2010) "Corporate social responsibility in Western Europe: An institutional mirror or substitute?" *Journal of Business Ethics*, 94(3): 371–394.

Jost, J.T. (2006) "The end of the end of ideology," *American Psychologist*, 61: 651–670.

Langley, A. (1999) "Strategies for theorizing from process data," *Academy of Management Review*, 24(4): 691–710.

Lawton, T., McGuire, S., Rajwani, T. (2013) "Corporate political activity: A literature review and research agenda," *International Journal of Management Reviews*, 15(1): 86–105.

Lewin, A. (2014) "Emerging economies open unlimited opportunities for advancing management and organization scholarship," *Management and Organization Review*, 10(1): 1–5.

Li, X.H., Liang, X.Y. (2015) "A Confucian social model of political appointments among Chinese private-firm entrepreneurs," *Academy of Management Journal*, 58(2): 592–617.

Lux, S., Crook, T.R., Woehr, D.J. (2011) "Mixing business with politics: A meta-analysis of the antecedents and outcomes of corporate political activity," *Journal of Management*, 37(1): 223–247.

Mantere, S. Pajunen, K., Lamberg, J.A. (2009) "Vices and virtues of corporate political activity: The challenge of international business," *Business & Society*, 48(1): 105–132.

McWilliams, A., Van Fleet, D.D., Cory, K. (2002) "Raising rivals' costs through political strategy: An extension of the resource-based theory," *Journal of Management Studies*, 39: 707–723.

Pacheco, D.F., Dean, T.J., Payne, D.S. (2010) "Escaping the green prison: Entrepreneurship and the creation of opportunities for sustainable development," *Journal of Business Venturing*, 25(5): 464–480.

Pinkse, J., Groot, K. (2015) "Sustainable entrepreneurship and corporate political activity: Overcoming market barriers in the clean energy sector," *Entrepreneurship Theory and Practice*, 39(3): 633–654.

Ployhart, R.E., Vandenberg, R.J. (2010) "Longitudinal research: The theory, design, and analysis of change," *Journal of Management*, 36(1): 94–120.

Puffer, S.M., McCarthy, D.J., Boisot, M. (2010) "Entrepreneurship in Russia and China: The impact of formal institutional voids," *Entrepreneurship Theory and Practice*, 34(3): 441–467.

Reinstaller, A. (2005) "Policy entrepreneurship in the co-evolution of institutions, preferences, and technology: Comparing the diffusion of totally chlorine free pulp bleaching technologies in the US and Sweden," *Research Policy*, 34(9): 1366–1384.

Schaltegger, S., Wagner, M. (2011) "Sustainable entrepreneurship and sustainability innovation: Categories and interactions," *Business Strategy and Environment*, 20(4): 222–237.

Scherer, A.G., Palazzo, G. (2011) "The new political role of business in a globalized world: A review of a new perspective on CSR and its implications for the firm, governance, and democracy," *Journal of Management Studies*, 48(4): 899–931.

Schneiberg, M., King, M., Smith, T. (2008) "Social movements and organizational form: Cooperative alternatives to corporations in the American insurance, dairy, and grain industries," *American Sociological Review*, 73(4): 635–667.

Senge, P., Lichtenstein, B., Kaeufer, K., Bradbury, H., Carroll, J. (2007) "Collaborating for systemic change," *MIT Sloan Management Review*, 48(2): 44–53.

Shepherd, D.A., Patzelt, H. (2011) "The new field of sustainable entrepreneurship: Studying entrepreneurial action linking 'what is to be sustained' with 'what is to be developed'," *Entrepreneurship Theory and Practice*, 35(1): 137–163.

Shepherd, D., Williams, T.A., Patzelt, H. (2015) "Thinking about entrepreneurial decision making: Review and research agenda," *Journal of Management*, 41(1): 11–46.

Siggelkow, N. (2007) "Persuasion with case studies," *Academy of Management Journal*, 50(1): 20–24.

Sine, W.D., Lee, B.H. (2009) "Tilting at windmills? The environmental movement and the emergence of the U.S. wind energy sector," *Administrative Science Quarterly*, 54(1): 123–155.

Suddaby, R. (2014) "Indigenous management theory: Why management theory is under attack (and what we can do to fix it)," in J. Miles (ed.), *New Directions in Management and Organization Theory*, Newcastle, UK: Cambridge Scholars, pp. 457–468.

Suddaby, R., Bruton, G.D., Si, S.X. (2015) "Entrepreneurship through a qualitative lens: Insights on the construction and/or discovery of entrepreneurial opportunity," *Journal of Business Venturing*, 30(1): 1–10.

Thompson, N., Kiefer, K., York, J.G. (2011) "Distinctions not dichotomies: Exploring social, sustainable, and environmental entrepreneurship," *Advances in Entrepreneurship, Firm Emergence and Growth*, 13: 205–233.

Tsai, K.S. (2007) *Capitalism Without Democracy: The Private Sector in Contemporary China*. Ithaca, NY: Cornell University Press.

Van de Ven, A.H. (2007) *Engaged Scholarship: A Guide for Organizational and Social Research*. New York, NY: Oxford University Press.

Walker, K., Schlosser, F., Deephouse, D.L. (2014) "Organizational ingenuity and the paradox of embedded agency: The case of the embryonic Ontario solar energy industry," *Organization Studies*, 35(4): 613–634.

Weber, M. (1978) *Economy and Society: An Outline of Interpretive Sociology* (translated and edited by Guenther Roth and Claus Wittich). Berkeley: University of California Press.

Welter, F. (2011) "Contextualizing entrepreneurship – conceptual challenges and ways forward," *Entrepreneurship Theory and Practice*, 35(1): 165–184.

York, J.G., Venkataraman, S. (2010) "The entrepreneur–environment nexus: Uncertainty, innovation, and allocation," *Journal of Business Venturing*, 25(5), 449–463.

Zahra, S.A., Wright, M. (2011) "Entrepreneurship's next act," *Academy of Management Perspectives*, 25(4): 67–83.

12 Innovation in sustainable entrepreneurship education in Africa

Strategy and social impact

Shiv K. Tripathi, Umesh Mukhi, Mario Molteni and Benedetto Cannatelli

Introduction

Sustainable entrepreneurship has emerged as a responsible strategy to address the sustainability related issues through entrepreneurial action. Sustainable development is important for three fundamental reasons: first, there is limited availability of natural resources; second, there is exponential human population growth; and third, current and future generations have the right to fulfil their needs (CSCP, 2011, p. 9). Building on the sustainability concept (WCED, 1987), sustainability impact can be seen in triple bottom-line indicators: people, profit and planet. The sustainability impact and sustainability of the enterprise are closely interlinked and, therefore, sustainable entrepreneurship emphasizes a combination of social, environmental and economic sustainability (Hockerts and Wustenhagen, 2010). Sustainable enterprises positively impact the sustainability indicators in the context. It is quite evident that entrepreneurship can be sustainable only if it produces the desired impact and, therefore, it can be seen as proactive innovative business interventions for impacting on sustainability indicators in the context.

Sustainability driven entrepreneurs are creating wonderful impact across the globe (CSCP, 2011, pp. 15–25; Dorsey, 2015). Sustainable entrepreneurship is quite significant in emerging and low income countries due to the complex socio-economic problems. The concept of 'social or sustainable entrepreneurship' is of relatively recent origin and, thus, making the standardization of its meaning challenging. Despite some variations in the interpretations, stakeholders agree that with sustainability orientation, entrepreneurship cuts across the business, society and knowledge driven innovations. Sustainable entrepreneurs combine the triple bottom-line indicators through their entrepreneurial actions (Elkington, 1997; Nicolopoulou, 2014). This implies that like 'entrepreneurship', 'sustainable entrepreneurship' also needs multi-stakeholder focused orchestrated efforts for its effective and impactful development, however, with emphasis on triple bottom-line consideration.

Higher business and entrepreneurship education institutions are important stakeholders with potential to impact the sustainable entrepreneurship development process. Kuckertz and Wagner (2010) stress that for development of sustainable entrepreneurship, special focus should be on master's degree, executive and continuing education programmes, which will help in closing the gap apparently opened by business experience.

Business schools are uniquely positioned to foster sustainability driven entrepreneurship, as these institutions are at the nexus of business, government and social sector. The objective of sustainable entrepreneurship education should be to develop desired mindset and skill-sets in target groups. There are some important issues:

- What should be the approach for effective sustainable entrepreneurship education?
- Is the context tailored sustainable education effective in producing the sustainability impact?
- How should the education system contribute to the sustainable entrepreneurship development?

First, we touch upon the current scholarly thinking in entrepreneurship and management education by focusing on the need for changing the B-School[1] role in sustainable development. Next, we examine the role of innovation in entrepreneurship education with emphasis on the sustainable entrepreneurship education intervention in Africa by ALTIS. Finally, we examine the initial impact of the sustainable entrepreneurship cases, selected from the projects developed by the graduates of ALTIS Africa.

A critical examination of these enterprises on sustainability would help in understanding and analysing the role of entrepreneurship education in developing entrepreneurship with sustainability impact in the context. The analysis of the cases also helps in reviewing sustainable entrepreneurship models in practice in the African context. This would eventually facilitate understanding the role of multi-stakeholder driven interventions in promoting sustainable entrepreneurship education, particularly in the African context.

Can we develop sustainable entrepreneurs with conventional management education?

B-schools play an important role in society by training the managers and leaders of the future. However, during the last few decades, the role of business education has been questioned by a number of scholars on the grounds that it is contributing to stimulate greedy theories and, thereby, promoting the mindset of only reaping economic benefits (Clarke, 2008; Ghoshal, 2005). Other scholars (Starkey and Madan, 2001; Mintzberg, 2004) questioned the relevance of current management education model as it separates theory and the practice. Mintzberg (2004) challenged the conventional way of management education, as it only emphasizes the science of management. Amann *et al.* (2011) challenges the modern B-school education system and suggests bringing a more humanistic focus. Others shed light on new models, which B-schools can embrace to become socially responsible institutions (Martell, 2011; Nonet, 2013; Tripathi *et al.*, 2015). These scholars emphasize that the role of B-schools is not limited to training managers for companies, but also on training a league of managers who are able to connect the dots between complex social and economic issues and resolve it through their sustainable entrepreneurial mindset. Entrepreneurship development is deeply rooted in the management education framework; and needs adjustments according to the context in which the entrepreneurs act.

This implies that B-schools can't afford to focus on developing leadership skills for economic benefits alone. Educational institutions must develop capacity to train sustainable entrepreneurs. The question remains about the type of innovations required to make business and entrepreneurship education a catalyst to development of sustainable entrepreneurs. For example, in rural areas of Rajasthan (India) a school teaches illiterate women and men to become solar engineers, artisans, dentists and doctors in their own villages.[2] It's called the Barefoot College. It is not a conventional academic institution, but has brought innovation to trigger the potential of sustainable entrepreneurs in the region.

We focus our analysis on role of B-school innovations for promoting sustainable entrepreneurship for three reasons: first, the B-schools have the right experience and knowledge to deal with the sustainable entrepreneurship related managerial issues; second, the resources available at the B-schools are relevant to the need of sustainable entrepreneurship education; and finally, a number of B-schools have displayed promising interventions.

How to align entrepreneurship education for sustainable development?

In the recent past, a number of initiatives have focused on making business education more responsible; and aligned to sustainable development. The initiatives like UNGC[3] and PRME[4] are an important step. The 50+20 responsible management education framework (50+20 Report, 2012) rests on the foundation of creating responsible leaders who imbibe the dimensions of sustainability, responsibility and statesmanship; and suggests four inter-related dimensions of responsible leadership:

1   Sustainable entrepreneurship with visionary and long-term perspective.
2   Responsible leadership with ethical and inclusive perspective.
3   Enlightened statesmanship with societal and political perspective.
4   Reflective awareness with universal perspective as core to the above three.

Sustainable entrepreneurship remains a major dimension of the responsible leadership development chain. Holistic analytical and decision-making skill remains at the core of the responsible leadership development process (50+20 Report, 2012, p. 3):

Globally responsible leaders will need more cognitive sophistication to cope with the complexity of multidimensional responsibilities on a global level – as well as reflected awareness, critical thinking, multi-cultural and societal wisdom and the moral depth to weigh competing choices. These new dimensions complement existing known traits such as entrepreneurship and leadership competencies.

Sustainable entrepreneurs deal with business environment complexities. Tripathi (2007) suggested a framework to shift from a 'business environment' mindset to a 'business universe' mindset in managerial decision-making. Translating the concept into the sustainable entrepreneurship context, it implies that the sustainable entrepreneurs should have an understanding of the inter-linkages among individuals, institutions and the planet as a whole.

Sustainable entrepreneurship education requires an active approach linking teaching research and action based learning. Figure 12.1 conceptualizes the mechanism of knowledge development and dissemination in management

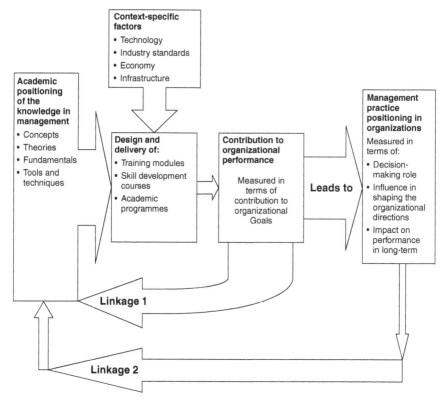

Figure 12.1 Knowledge-practice interface in management.
Source: Tripathi, 2012.

education (Tripathi, 2012); and the same can be extended to understand the process-dynamics of sustainable entrepreneurship education. The teaching and research needs to be closely aligned to generate the impact in the context to address relevance concerns by the scholars (Starkey and Madan, 2001; Mintzberg, 2004).

The 50+20 Report (2012, p. 6) suggests a management education framework with an enabling and engaging process embedded in it. The education process should focus on developing and encouraging new learning approaches like transformative learning; issues-centred learning; and reflective practice and fieldwork. In addition, the enabling dimension should focus on aligning relevant research and the engagement dimension should aim at encouraging multi-stakeholder engagements. This all combined would lead towards development of a 'collaboratory' and thus, giving space to stakeholder partnership based management and entrepreneurship education (Figure 12.2). Muff *et al.* (2013) observes:

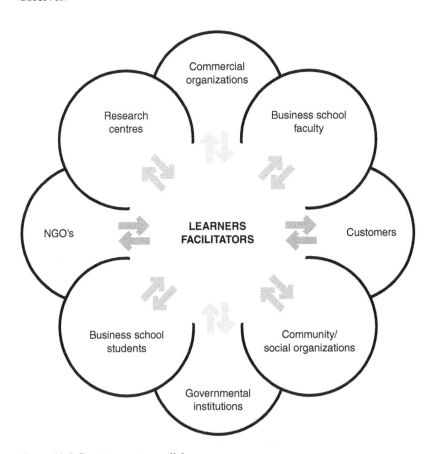

Figure 12.2 Participants in a collaboratory.

Source: Fernando D'Alessio from Muff *et al.*, 2013.

Collaboratories should always reflect a rich combination of stakeholders: coaches, business and management faculty, citizens, politicians, entrepreneurs, people from different regions and cultures, youth and elders.... In such a space, learning and research is organized around issues rather than disciplines or theory. Such issues include: hunger, energy, water, climate change, migration, democracy, capitalism, terrorism, disease, the financial crisis, transformation of economic systems and educational reform amongst other similarly pressing matters.

(Muff *et al.*, 2013, p. 62)

Developing a collaboration based education process is an effective solution to promote need based sustainable entrepreneurship education, focusing on the entire system value chain from content planning to post-delivery action. A conceptual framework (Tripathi, 2012) suggests the need for an active stakeholder participation in meeting the need based sustainable entrepreneurship education (Figure 12.3).

Important characteristics of an impact-oriented sustainable entrepreneurship education can be summarized as:

1   *Action-Driven:* Learning by doing or in other words applying the entrepreneurial knowledge and skills and learning from the action experiences.
2   *Collaborative:* Involving direct and indirect stakeholders and developing both need and solution together, i.e. moving from a supplier-customer approach to a 'development-partner' mindset.
3   *Humanistic:* The moment we shift priorities from profit-driven to human-driven, the entire paradigm of the education changes right from the learning objective to the content and the pedagogy. The education must be based on long-term humanistic considerations in the view of '*planetistic*' realities.
4   *Issue-Focused:* While developing sustainable entrepreneurship in the context, the education system must aim at addressing the context-specific issues and, thus, delivering a solution to the context-specific development problems.
5   *Synergistic:* The availability of the right kind of resources is one of the major challenges in the process of effective education delivery. Creating a synergistic participation of the stakeholders may result in a cost-effective education system with impact. Also the mutual benefit driven resource sharing would contribute to the development of a sense of ownership among the stakeholders.
6   *Transformative:* The educational outcomes should be tangible and focus on changes in the knowledge and skills, measured through the sustainability impact of the entrepreneurial actions delivered by the target potential entrepreneurs.

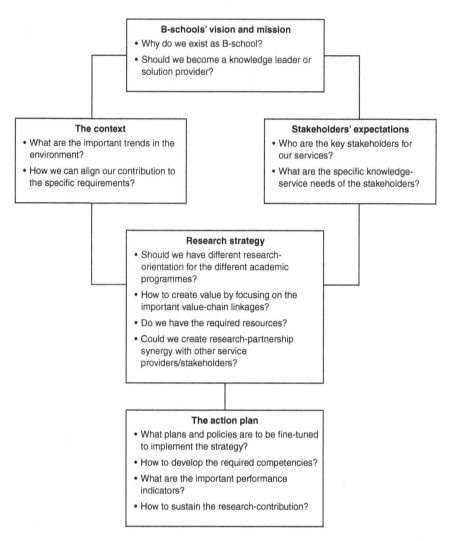

Figure 12.3 Strategic framework for research process management.
Source: Tripathi, 2012.

A conceptual framework for sustainable entrepreneurship education

Sustainable entrepreneurship can be considered as a behaviour combining entrepreneurial aspirations to sustainability mindset. Sustainable leadership focuses on a new mindset of leaders and entrepreneurs, their worldview and how they impact the society (Tideman *et al.*, 2013). Kuckertz and Wagner (2010, p. 526) observe: 'Sustainable behavior, or in short sustainability, is a paradigm that can function as a reference point for the development of solutions to today's environmental and societal challenges.'

A conflict arises when it comes to prioritize and balance the economic returns with desired sustainability impact and, thus, leading to a question of basic intentions of sustainable entrepreneurs. Building on Ajzen and Fishbein's (1977) findings that the intentions are the most important predictor of the actual behaviour, Kuckertz and Wagner (2010) suggest that educators and policy makers must look into this important dimension. Therefore, for sustainable entrepreneurship education, the focus should be on both assessing the intentions of the learners as well as making efforts to shape the intentions.

Emphasizing the nature of the sustainable business solutions, the CSCP (2011, p. 12) suggests:

- business solutions should be for one specific social and/or environmental problem;
- there should be clearly defined business models;
- the businesses should be scalable; and
- they should inspire others to contribute or trigger action among others to develop their own solutions.

We consider these desired venture characteristics as parameters to assess the initial impact of business ventures, created by the sustainability entrepreneurship programme learner.

The theory of organizational learning and the approach for business schools in learning novel pedagogical and teaching approaches could provide future research directions (Sobczak and Mukhi, 2015). Therefore, the direction and process of B-school efforts in shaping sustainable entrepreneurship education is also dynamic in nature, depending on a number of context-specific factors. Building on Russ-Eft and Preskill's (2001) input-process-output model of teaching learning, Ghina (2014) proposed a conceptual model to evaluate the entrepreneurship programme's effectiveness and desired higher educational institutional support in context of entrepreneurship education in Indonesia. In addition to the inputs, process and outputs, the model also incorporates variables like opportunity, ability and incentive to learn. Modifying the framework in the context of sustainable entrepreneurship education and combining the desired sustainable entrepreneurship education process characteristics, discussed in the previous section, a conceptual framework is presented (Figure 12.4).

The framework can be used to examine the impact of context-specific sustainable entrepreneurship education. These parameters can be tested, refined and updated by applying them across the different contexts.

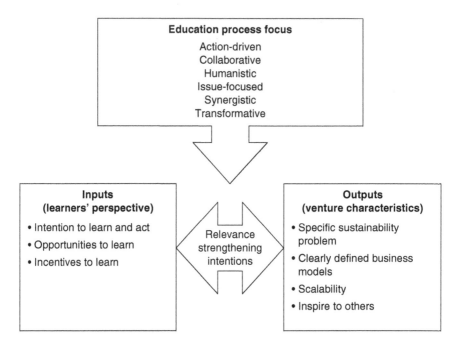

Figure 12.4 Conceptual framework for sustainable entrepreneurship education.

How does ALTIS aim at sustainable entrepreneurship development?

ALTIS brought an innovation in sustainable entrepreneurship education in selected African countries by focusing on context-specific issues. Its Master of Business Administration (MBA) programme in global sustainability and entrepreneurship programme is currently being offered in selected African countries: Kenya, Ghana and Sierra Leone. The programme is likely to be introduced in many other African countries soon. The programme aims to promotes innovation driven business models with inclusive development agenda in the given context. The programme modules are standard across different places within the African continent and, thus, facilitating the intra-region knowledge transfer from one country to another through the sharing of knowledge resources. However, in view of the varying local requirements, customized delivery is encouraged. In other words, this can be viewed as a combination of standardization and customization but standardization also aiming at specific Sub-Saharan African requirements.

Each programme cohort is divided into two components: a first phase of one year duration with module based knowledge and skill development; and the second phase of one year when perspective sustainable entrepreneurs implement their business ideas with the help of a dedicated business coach or mentor. The participants in the cohorts are selected on the basis of business idea competition. The industry and other stakeholders participate actively in business idea screening and the participant selection process. The module based learning is applied in nature and the focus is on only essential module-specific theory inputs with a large part of the module delivery and student performance assessment focusing on how well the students are developing solutions related to their specific business idea. For example, if one participant has a business idea of developing a local fruit processing network and is studying a module on marketing, the learning and assessment of the student will focus on how well the student has developed a marketing plan for the selected business idea. Therefore, by the end of the module based learning phase, the cohort participants are ready with the functional and strategic plans for their business ideas.

The second programme phase is also quite interesting when students with their respective 'ready to act plan' start the implementation of the business idea with the help of a business coach. The business coach is selected on the basis of their familiarity and expertise in dealing with the local entrepreneurial environment. They assist the participants in procedural and administrative issues related to the enterprise development. They also help participants in linking with the important stakeholders in the participants' business domain. Based on the initial implementation experiences, the participants present their refined business plans before they graduate.

In terms of the cost, the programme is highly subsidized as a number of venture capitalists and other sponsors have supported the programme financially by sponsoring a large part of the education cost of the potential sustainable entrepreneurs. The programme has also been successful in receiving funding from a number of international agencies and has been awarded the prestigious Ashoka Foundation award for its innovation driven impact in Africa. The programme has produced a considerable impact on sustainability dimensions in Africa through the sustainable enterprises developed by the graduates of this innovative and unique entrepreneurship programme.

How are ALTIS entrepreneurs performing?

In this section we focus on the selected five cases of the enterprises developed by the graduates of the programme. The brief stories of these ventures give a reflection on how a context-specific sustainable entrepreneurship programme can spark the entrepreneurial development process in the context with emphasis on issue based problem solving.

Case 1: NUCAFE, Uganda

Joseph Nkandu, one of the 2011–2012 cohort graduates, is Executive Director and Founder of the National Union of Coffee (NUCAFE), Uganda. Under his leadership, NUCAFE established a sustainable market driven system of coffee farming enterprise, empowered to increase farmers' household incomes through enhanced entrepreneurship and innovation in 19 districts of Uganda. The market which was earlier influenced with the intermediaries often acting to exploit the farmers' interests and depriving them of the due profit sharing for their efforts, has now been changed to a market with empowered farmers participating in the coffee value-chain in Uganda.

The interventions made by Joseph helped in increasing the membership base from 120 to 155 associations. The organization also witnessed increased volume of coffee marketed from 759 MT in 2011 to 1450 MT in 2013. The organization also influenced and contributed to the development of a National Coffee Policy and, thus, bringing the coffee farmers' interest in the national policy positively. The organizations also contributed to improving gender relations among coffee farming households. Based on the impact, Joseph was nominated Ashoka Fellow in 2013. The organization also contributed to establishment of a farmer owned coffee processing factory, which was part of Joseph's MBA business plan. The implementation of the Farmer Ownership Model, developed and implemented under Joseph's leadership, was selected among the European Union's CTA top 20 innovations that empower farmers. Based on its performance, the organization has received grants from a number of organizations. NUCAFE has also partnered in the establishment of a US$2 million agribusiness incubator with Makerere University and National Agricultural Research agency.

Case 2: Innovation Eye Center, Kenya

Jacqueline Kiage, one of the 2012–2013 cohort graduates, has co-founded the Innovation Eye Center Limited with Dr Kiage. The company is a healthcare focused social enterprise that offers high quality, affordable and accessible comprehensive world class eye care services to the community in the South Western Region of Kenya and beyond. The organization is the first eye hospital in the region of South Western Kenya. In just 15 months of existence, the organization has successfully served more than 20,000 patients including 1285 cataract surgeries.

In order to reach patients in remote areas, the organization has organized 85 community outreach programmes (eye camps), with more than 100 patients per session. As per the latest records, the organization has already served 10,421 patients through the outreach eye camps. The organization has a corrective eye care shop that serves more than 100 patients with eye glasses per month. The organization began with start up funding of US$300,000 from the Fiat Lux Foundation and activity based funding support from different organizations including US$200,000 support from the Hilton Foundation in collaboration with the Dana Centre and LAICO/Aravind Eye Care System, €36,000 from Right to Sight Ireland/Norway, €43,000 from the Brien Holden Vision Institute and €10,000 from the Eye Foundation. The organization is a good example of how an issue based enterprise can be developed by attracting support from different international partners.

Case 3: Starr Radio 103.5, Ghana

Bola Ray, one of the 2013–2014 cohort graduates, has founded Starr Radio 103.5, a Ghanaian urban lifestyle radio station that connects emotionally to every single individual by delivering audio and internet compelling programmes across multiple platforms including entertainment/lifestyle-led talk, educative programmes, music, etc. The organization has the mission of impacting positively on society and lifestyles and aims to be a radio station with a difference in terms of disseminating the right social and cultural values through its programmes. Bola's original business idea referred to an existing entertainment company but the ALTIS programme challenged him to get outside the comfort zone and establish a radio station with a focus on social values. He established a strategic partnership with UniBank in June 2014 to create Starr Radio.

The radio station went on-air in August 2014. Within three months of operations, Starr Radio has been able to secure major events (Hennessy Artistry, MTN Hit Maker and Alvin Slaughter's 'Thanks Giving' to name a few) and has attracted plenty of advertisers, hosts and stars. The Starr Radio website has been upranked in Ghana from 300,000 to 43 in just three months (over 6 per cent of its visitors are from the USA and UK) thus making it one of the fastest growing websites in Ghana with a good number of international audiences.

Case 4: Emigoh Ghana Limited, Ghana

Stephen Eku, one of the 2013–2014 cohort graduates, is Chief Executive Officer at Emogoh Ghana Limited, a food and nutrition company, specializing in dairy and juice processing. The company focuses on fighting malnutrition by providing healthy dairy products and fruit juices. The company has developed a network of 3000 retailers in the Greater Accra Region. Stephen Eku's training has helped the company to successfully scale-up the business in Kumasi (Asante region) and Takoradi (Western region), Ghana.

During the last year, the company has witnessed an increase in customer base of 15 per cent and an increase in revenues of 10 per cent. The scaling up of the business also resulted in an increase in number of employees. Stephen has managed to remove major bottlenecks in some of Emigoh's operations to improve on their capacity and efficiency. He has also developed a compact business plan to attract investment for further expansion.

Case 5: M-Farm Limited, Kenya

Susan Oguya, one of the 2013–2014 cohort graduates, is Chief Operating Officer and founder of M-Farm Limited, an organization with an aim to offer agribusiness software solutions that enable Kenyan farmers to get information on the retail price of their product and help them buy their farm inputs directly from manufacturers at favourable prices. It also assists in finding buyers for farmer products across Kenya. During the ALTIS programme, Susan received a grant funding of US$350,000 from major organizations such as Safaricom and USAID among others plus another US$100,000 as an equity contribution.

In a short period of time, the organization has scaled up operations in the three Kenyan counties. The organization has impacted 15,000 smallholder farming households. Susan was nominated by Forbes as among the 20 youngest most powerful women in Africa in 2014.

Is ALTIS impacting sustainable development?

It can be seen that the ALTIS education approach is gradually creating a multiplier effect in the sustainable development of the specific contexts where the ALTIS graduates are operating. It is too early to say conclusively about the scale of the impact, as the intervention is relatively new and the time-horizon is not sufficient to assess the impact. However, the initial signs of ALTIS' entrepreneurship development efforts indicate promise for potential sustainable development in the region through ALTIS trained entrepreneurs. We can also examine the ALTIS approach based on the suggested parameters for impact-driven sustainable entrepreneurship in Figure 12.4. Our focus in this chapter is to examine the initial impact of business ventures created by the ALTIS graduates. All these cases confirm that each of the ventures has clearly defined business models and the business solutions focused on a particular sustainability issue across the triple bottom-line indicators. In terms of scalability the initial results show the promising future and models are inspiring to others, as they have already been shown to have triggering effects of network action. The selected cases also show how ALTIS' approach confirms to desired education process characteristics for an effective sustainable entrepreneurship education.

All of these ventures reflect the action driven impact of the education with focus on specific issues. It can be seen that each of the selected enterprises has developed its business model on a particular sustainability linked issue. Most of these enterprises have attracted support from different sponsors, who also participate in the education value-chain and this shows the fit on the 'collaborative' and 'synergistic' dimension of the sustainable entrepreneurship education, if not completely, at least to a significant degree. In terms of 'humanistic' considerations with holistic vision, some of the enterprises like Nucafe, M-Farm and Innovation Eye Care appear to influence more. The ventures also indicate the transformation potential of the ALTIS model as most of the cases have added value to the development in specific domains through their respective interventions.

Conclusions

Sustainable entrepreneurship has been defined in a different ways. However, for the purpose of the analysis in this chapter we defined it as 'an entrepreneurial actions with focus on impacting the triple bottom-line sustainability parameters'. The literature review on responsible leadership and management education helped to develop a desired 'characteristics-set' for an effective and impact oriented sustainable entrepreneurship education approach. ALTIS has been a pioneer in brining context-specific sustainable entrepreneurship education intervention in Sub-Saharan Africa. Although it would be too early to conclude on the impact of the ALTIS approach to sustainable education, a brief analysis of the five selected ventures developed by ALTIS graduates indicate the education approach confirms to the desired characteristics of effective sustainability education. Bringing the spark of sustainable development in the developing region of Sub-Saharan Africa itself is a good sign of 'entrepreneurship for impact' or E4impact (as emphasized by ALTIS) through education. In future, further studies can be undertaken with the aim of measuring the longitudinal impact of such ventures. Also the future studies can be designed to assess the inter-relationships among the sustainable entrepreneurship education process dimensions.

Notes

1 The term B-school (Business School) is often interpreted as a system of education for developing managerial talents for businesses and, sometimes, being interpreted differently in the different contexts. We use B-school as an education system offering management and entrepreneurship education.
2 Refer to www.ted.com/talks/bunker_roy?language=en for details.
3 United Nations Global Compact (UNGC) is an organization established in 2000 by the United Nations with the support of private sector organizations to enhance private sector contribution to the sustainable development agenda.
4 Principles for Responsible Management Education (PRME) is an educational initiative of UNGC, focusing on developing responsible managers, leaders and entrepreneurs.

References

50+20 Report (2012). *The 50+20 Agenda: Management Education for the World*. Retrieved 9 January 2015 from http://50plus20.org/wp-content/uploads/2012/06/5020_AGENDA_PRINT_a4_English.pdf.

Ajzen, I. and Fishbein, M. (1977). Attitude behavior relations: a theoretical analysis and review of empirical research. *Psychological Bulletin*, 84, 888 (as cited in Kuckertz and Wagner, 2010, op. cit.).

Amann, W., Pirson, M., Dierksmeier, C., Kimakowitz, E. and Spitzeck. H. (2011). *Business Schools Under Fire: Humanistic Management Education as the Way Forward*. London: Palgrave Macmillan.

Clarke, T. (2008). The business schools: 50 years on. *Education + Training*, 50(1), 52–54.

CSCP (2011). Collaborating Centre on Sustainable Consumption and Production. Retrieved 14 December 2015 from www.scp-centre.org/fileadmin/content/files/6_Resources/1_Publications_pdfs/60_Creating_impact_full.pdf.

Dorsey, C. (2015). Africa's next-generation social entrepreneurs are ready. Are we? *Forbes*, 15 July. Retrieved 18 December 2015 from www.forbes.com/sites/echoinggreen/2015/07/20/africas-next-generation-social-entrepreneurs-are-ready-are-we/.

Elkington, J. (1997). *Cannibals with Forks: The Triple Bottom Line of 21st Century Business*. Gabriola Island, Canada: New Society Publishers (as cited in Kuckertz and Wagner, 2010, op. cit.).

Ghina, A. (2014). Effectiveness of entrepreneurship education in higher education institutions. Proceedings of The 5th Indonesia International Conference on Innovation, Entrepreneurship and Small Businesses (IICIES, 2013). *Procedia – Social and Behavioural Science*, 115(2014), 332–345. Retrieved 19 December 2015 from http://ac.els-cdn.com/S1877042814019880/1-s2.0-S1877042814019880-main.pdf?_tid=87d23490-ada6-11e5-9f7f-00000aab0f27&acdnat=1451336826_f9692bf9d5bf392ea182c3406c20a727.

Ghoshal, S. (2005). Bad management theories are destroying good management practices. *Academy of Management Learning & Education*, 4(1), 75–91.

Hockerts, K. and Wustenhagen, R. (2010). Greening Goliaths versus emerging Davids: theorizing about the role of incumbents and new entrants in sustainable entrepreneurship. *Journal of Business Venturing*, 25(5), 481–492.

Kuckertz, A. and Wagner, M. (2010). The influence of sustainability orientation on entrepreneurial intentions: investigating the role of business experience. *Journal of Business Venturing*, 25, 524–539. Retrieved 18 December 2015 from www.dge.ubi.pt/msilva/papers_mece/paper_4.pdf.

Martell, J. (2011). *Socially Responsible Business Schools: A Proposed Model*. 14 September. Retrieved from www.tesisenred.net/bitstream/handle/10803/51014/MARTELL_Tesis%20Doctoral_Versi%C3%B3n%20Defendida.pdf?sequence=1.

Mintzberg, H. (2004). *Managers Not MBAs: A Hard Look at the Soft Practice of Management and Management Development*. San Francisco: Berrett-Koehler Publishers.

Muff, K., Dyllick, T., Drewell, M., North, J., Shrivastava, P. and Haertle, J. (2013). PART 2: understanding the core of the vision. *European Business Review*. Retrieved from www.europeanbusinessreview.com/?p=1262.

Nicolopoulou, K. (2014). Social entrepreneurship between cross-currents: toward a framework for theoretical restructuring of the field. *Journal of Small Business Management*, 52(4), 678–702.

Nonet, G. (2013, September). *Responsible Management & Business Schools: Analysis of the Schools Strategy and the Education*. Université Montpellier 1.

Russ-Eft, D. and Preskill, H. (2001). *Evaluation in Organizations: A Systematic Approach to Enhancing Learning, Performance, and Change*. New York, NY: Basic Books (as cited in Ghina, 2014, op. cit.).

Sobczak, A. and Mukhi, U. (2015). The role of UN principles for responsible management education in stimulating organizational learning for global responsibility within business schools, an interview with Jonas Haertle. *Journal of Management Inquiry*, 1056492615618027.

Starkey, K. and Madan, P. (2001). Bridging the relevance gap: aligning stakeholders in the future of management research. *The British Journal of Management*, 12(1), S3–S26.

Tideman, S. G., Arts, M. C. and Zandee, D. P. (2013). Sustainable leadership: towards a workable definition. *Journal of Corporate Citizenship*, 49, 17–33. http://doi.org/10.9774/GLEAF.4700.2013.ma.00004.

Tripathi S. K. (2007). Managing business as a spiritual practice: the Bhagwadgita way to achieve excellence through perfection in action. In *Integrating Spirituality and Organizational Leadership* (Eds: Singh Sengupta, S. and Fields, D.). McMillan Advanced Research Series, New Delhi. Proceedings of International Conference on Integrating Spirituality and Organizational Leadership, February 2007.

Tripathi, S. (2012). Teaching-research synchronization in business schools: a conceptual framework for aligning the research value chain. In *New Perspectives on Management Education* (Eds: Amann, W., Kerretts-Makau, M., Fenton, P., Zackariasson, P. and Tripathi, S.). New Delhi: Excel Books.

Tripathi, S., Amann, W. and Kamuzora, F. R. (2015). Developing responsible managers for new generation organizations: why existing business education system needs humanistic shift? *3-D International Journal of Management and Leadership*, Indus Business Academy, Bangalore, India, Jan–Jul 2015.

WCED (1987). *World Commission on Environment and Development: Our Common Future.* Oxford: Oxford University Press.

13 Sustainable innovation and entrepreneurship in agriculture

Empirical insights into the SME ecosystem

Renan Tunalioglu, Mine Karatas-Ozkan, Cagla Yavuz, Tolga Bektas, Ferit Cobanoglu, Jeremy Howells and Ayse Demet Karaman

Introduction

Sustainable entrepreneurship has emerged as a new interdisciplinary subject domain. It offers the opportunity to study entrepreneurship holistically by viewing 'entrepreneurial action as a mechanism for sustaining nature and ecosystems whilst providing economic and non-economic gains for investors, entrepreneurs and societies' (Shepherd and Patzelt, 2011: 138). The focus of sustainable entrepreneurship is on blended value, which refers to organisations pursuing blends of financial, social and environmental values across different business models (Bugg-Levine and Emerson, 2011; Zahra *et al.*, 2014). They should develop distinct organisational capabilities to improve business processes for the global sustainable well-being and community development.

We take a broader view in this chapter and define sustainable entrepreneurship in agriculture as SMEs' engagement in the entrepreneurial process, which minimises negative environmental, economic and social impact and improves the quality of life of the local community through innovative practices. The relative cost of innovation is often more significant to SMEs than to large firms, due to limited resources (Laforet, 2013). Additionally, government policies are geared for clearer understanding of innovation outcomes and its consequences in SMEs to evaluate costs and benefits of innovation policies. As an industry sector, agriculture entails innovative production and business processes that remain viable over an infinitive period and do not degrade environment. It is an economic sector requiring a great degree of engagement and co-operation between the producer (farmer) and the seller, and the intermediary organisations. Partnerships and open dialogue that foster great alignment of the full spectrum of stakeholders with the goals of sustainable development (Moffat and Auer, 2006) are crucial for sustainable agriculture. Co-ordinated efforts of various organisations for sustainability are key to success (Jegantheesan *et al.*, 2009). This leads to the debate of the SME ecosystem in agriculture whereby key players often require a more holistic approach through the alignment of business practices of SMEs, policies and actions of intermediary organisations and government agencies.

In this chapter, we discuss sustainable entrepreneurship practices of SMEs in agriculture in emerging market settings. We suggest that strong motivational drive for sustainability and weak institutional settings characterise their practices. These weak institutional vehicles (such as government agencies, policies and ineffective intermediary organisations) may channel entrepreneurs and SME owner-managers away from innovative and sustainability-driven activities. Our research question is therefore the following: how do agricultural SMEs engage in sustainable entrepreneurship as a part of wider entrepreneurial ecosystem? How can policies encourage and support sustainable entrepreneurship in agriculture? We address these questions by applying institutional theory and drawing on empirical insights generated from a research study in the area of entrepreneurship, SME development and sustainability with a specific focus on agriculture as the sector. Our key findings indicate SME's concerted efforts for sustainability-driven production strategies, eradication of negative environmental impacts, more effective interactions with the local universities and outreach activities beyond the immediate regional context, sustainable development of rural communities and collaboration with international organisations to enhance worldwide reputation.

There is extant literature that includes studies focusing on sustainable entrepreneurship in other sectors such as tourism (e.g. Hall *et al.*, 2012; Crnogaj *et al.*, 2014), rubber and plastic industry (Bos-Brouwers, 2010), manufacturing (Baldwin *et al.*, 2005), coffee (Adams and Ghaly, 2007) and wine industry (Gabzdylova *et al.*, 2009). In agriculture, the focus of the scholarly debate has been reduced to agricultural innovation systems (e.g. Hounkonnou *et al.*, 2012; Hermans *et al.*, 2013). Our contribution to the field is two-fold: first, we generate empirical insights to sustainable entrepreneurship in agriculture by drawing on an empirical research project with 35 SMEs and 5 other stakeholders in the agricultural sector in an emerging market context, which is Turkey. Second, our findings indicate several policy and practice implications.

Sustainability-driven entrepreneurship and innovation in SMEs: key research issues

Increasingly, sustainability, defined in its broadest sense including social and environmental sustainability as well as business sustainability, has been recognised as a core dimension of strategy formation. A stream of research on sustainability oriented innovations and entrepreneurship with a broader focus on environmental, social and economic dimensions has evolved (see Hall, 2002; Rodgers, 2010; Schaltegger and Wagner, 2011; Klewitz and Hansen, 2014). How SMEs adapt such an approach and how the economic, social and environmental aspects of sustainability become integrated into the design of new products, processes, organisational structures and management approaches is an important research problem that warrants attention. This entails taking a holistic approach to sustainability. Adopting Dyllic and Hockerts' (2002) definition, in this chapter we conceptualise sustainability as systematic management efforts of enterprises to balance environmental and social goals with economic goals in order to minimise harm to, and increase benefits for, natural environments and communities. To what extent sustainability efforts can be systematic and effective in SMEs remains a question.

From an SME perspective, sustainable entrepreneurship is concerned with entrepreneurial businesses that develop and diffuse sustainability oriented innovation primarily in niche markets but subsequently also in mass markets (Schaltegger, 2002; Klewitz and Hansen 2014). Sustainable entrepreneurship is defined as examination of 'how opportunities to bring into existence future goods and services are discovered, created, and exploited, by whom, and with what economic, psychological, social, and environmental consequences' (Cohen and Winn, 2007: 35). An integrated framework is offered by Klewitz and Hansen (2014), who note that strategic sustainability behaviour can be classified into five approaches: resistant, reactive, anticipatory, innovation-based and sustainability-rooted. This shows the degree of sustainable innovation through a continuum of more incremental to more radical approaches. Figure 13.1 depicts these strategic outlooks.

Taking the innovation-based SMEs, which are those seeking innovative solutions to environmental and social challenges, and sustainability-rooted SMEs where the business model builds on the triad of the environmental, social and economic bottom lines in order to contribute to the sustainable development of markets and communities as exemplary models, we are particularly concerned with the level of interaction with external actors in this process.

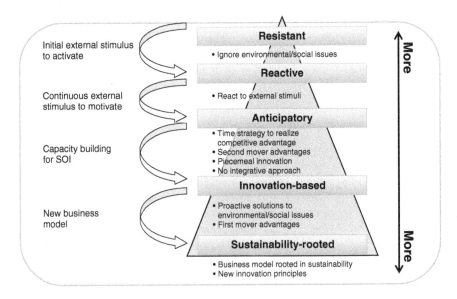

Figure 13.1 SME approaches to strategic sustainability and innovation.

Source: developed from Klewitz and Hansen, 2014, p. 69.

Collaboration is a key element for the SMEs' transition towards sustainable entrepreneurship and innovation (see Lozano, 2007; Klewitz and Hansen, 2014), particularly linked to Research and Development (R&D) support (see Kang and Park, 2013; Hottenrott and Lopes-Bento, 2014). Innovation is viewed as collaborative and thus contingent on the interaction between the internal and external orientation of a firm (Chesborough, 2011). This implies the open innovation model, which supports the premise that the network collaboration is an important external component within the innovation process in the context of resource-constrained SMEs (Corsten and Felde, 2005; McAdam *et al.*, 2014). Interaction with multiple actors helps SMEs remodel their innovation and entrepreneurial processes with a subsequent impact of more proactive sustainability strategies. This raises a host of questions: Who are these actors? What is the nature of collaboration? Which innovation models encapsulate such collaboration as the focal point?

Building on social network theory as one of the models, McAdam *et al.* (2014) explore horizontal collaborative networks for agri-food SMEs in the UK. Key areas of concern for the current study include kinds of institutional support and formal facilitation of collaboration; enhanced network to incorporate more external knowledge relating to new and emergent market changes; and a desire to discuss, share and learn from agricultural firms within the region. Institutional support mechanisms comprise government support for SME innovation and entrepreneurship. The aim of government support, in the form of targeted and quality business support including financial support, should be to establish a self-sustaining SME sector functioning effectively without financial aid (Doh and Kim, 2014).

Translating this to the open innovation model discourse, an outward-looking focus is required (Malik and Wei, 2011; Cheng and Huizingh, 2014). Institutional processes and activities are mainly in the form of outside-in activities, inside-out activities and coupled activities (Gassmann and Enkel, 2004). Outside-in activities refer to the ability to gain and explore knowledge from external partners, whereas inside-out activities include activities involved in the external exploitation of internal ideas; and coupled activities refer to collaborative activities between different actors in the innovation system and this combines outside-in and inside-out activities (Cheng and Huizingh, 2014). How these collaborations can be explained by illuminating the macro-institutional influences that facilitate or obstruct innovation and entrepreneurial processes in agricultural SMEs is the underlying question of the current research. We attempt to address this question by applying institutional theory.

Research setting: Turkish agricultural sector

Turkey presents a unique and interesting setting for research and policy development in this area. Turkey is the world's 18th largest economy (World Bank, 2013), with agriculture being one of the driving industry sectors. Turkey is ranked as 1st in Europe and 7th in the world in agricultural production, ranks among the world's top 5 in the production of over 20 crops, and exports more than 1,530 different agricultural produce to 177 countries (Report of MoFAL, 2014; Yesilada and Sanli, 2015). Turkey is a country that is able to feed its population of 76 million, along with the 35 million tourists who visit Turkey annually. The added value of the food sector is $62.0 billion per annum, representing one-fifth of the manufacturing sector's total output. There are about 60,000 companies that are active in the food and beverage sector in Turkey. Turkey's exports of agriculture and food products reached $17 billion in 2014; accounting for about 10 per cent of the country's total exports of $158 billion in 2014 (Yesilada and Sanli, 2015: 35).

In particular, Aydin, in which the Turkish partner, Adnan Menderes University, is based, is a city in south-western Turkey, located in the Aegean region. It makes a significant contribution to the Turkish economy through its key industry, i.e. agriculture. Aydin is Turkey's leading producer of figs and exports dried figs worldwide. Turkey's yearly production of dried figs is almost all from Aydin, which makes Turkey the leading world producer of figs. Other key agricultural products of economic importance are olive and chestnut, most of which are processed, packaged and domestically sold or exported by other cities in the Aegean and Marmara regions of Turkey due to dearth of a well-established SME sector in agriculture in Aydin.

Method

This study reports from a wider research project under the British Council's UK-TURKEY Higher Education Partnership Programme, which was developed as a result of the collaboration between two universities, namely University of Southampton (UK) and Adnan Menderes University (Turkey). In order to address the research objective, an exploratory qualitative study has been developed, which relies on multiple data sources including documentary data, focus group, semi-structured interviews and a dissemination workshop. Data were collected in multiple rounds during the period from May 2012 to February 2014. Table 13.1 presents detailed inventory of data sources from agricultural field from the Turkish context.

Documentary data including publicly available documents such as official reports of Ministry of Food Agriculture and Livestock, TUSIAD (Turkish Industry and Business Association), Egeli & Co (Yesilada and Sanli, 2015) (agricultural oriented venture capital company), ISPA (Ministry Investment Support and Promotion Agency) and TOBB (The Union of Chambers and Stock Markets of Turkey), as well as academic publications dealing with evaluation of agricultural sector in Turkish context, were reviewed. Fieldwork initiated with a focus group meeting with 15 key stakeholders including industry partners and intermediary organisations (including government agents) in the agricultural sector, in May 2012.

Data collection process was followed by 17 interviews during the period of March–April 2013 and 23 additional interviews in July 2014. Overall, this exploratory qualitative study draws on a sample of 40 participants, consisting of SME manager/owners and other stakeholders pertinent to the agriculture sector in Aydin region, Turkey. Interviews lasted a total of approximately 20 hours and 40 minutes, with each taking an average of 35 minutes.

Lastly, a knowledge exchange-dissemination workshop was held in February 2014 by the industry and academic partners. Overall, multiplicity of data sources enables us to gain in-depth insights about the ecosystem of agricultural SMEs in the Turkish context. All interviews and focus group meetings were tape-recorded, transcribed verbatim and coded according to themes identified through iterations with relevant literature.

Research findings

Major problems of the sector include lack of entrepreneurial approach to enterprise development and management and also challenges pertaining to environmental management and sustainability issues. Industry experts and academics highlight the significant potential of the city in key areas of growing importance to the EU and the rest of the world, such as organic agricultural production and food safety. Some of the SME owner-managers acknowledge the potential of expanding their business by pursuing new business opportunities and enhancing their organisational management capacity. However, they are deprived of a comprehensive and systematic knowledge base in the areas of sustainable entrepreneurship, enterprise management and environmental management. Most of the SMEs lack a long-term strategic orientation with a focus on day-to-day survival because of lack of innovation capabilities and an entrepreneurial outlook. Therefore, our study has particular import for sustainability-driven policy and practice development. We present our findings pertinent to the nature of interaction of agricultural SMEs with external stakeholders in practicing sustainable entrepreneurship in two sections, namely institutional involvement of government and university-industry relations.

Institutional involvement of government

The SME ecosystem in agriculture is characterised by weak institutional settings in Turkey. One important institutional actor in the SME innovation and entrepreneurship ecosystem is the government and associated institutions. Our findings reveal the importance of governmental monitoring mechanisms and effectiveness of governmental policies for the sustainable entrepreneurship practices of agricultural SMEs. While the lack of monitoring mechanisms facilitate informal economy and cause challenges in control of production system, ineffective governmental policies are manifested in misalignment between legislations and needs of industry, shortages in strategic agricultural planning, allocation of supports and incentives, as well as unstable legislations. The next section is devoted to discussion of the importance of these mechanisms and effective governmental policies for entrepreneurial development of agricultural SMEs.

Table 13.1 Detailed inventory of data sources

Sector	Enterprise activity	Family business	Age of enterprise	Duration of interviews
Olive industry	Exporting olive, olive oil and fig	No	7 years	8 hours
	Olive oil production	Yes	36 years	
	Olive and olive oil processing	Yes	36 years	
	Olive and olive oil processing and stocking	No	9 years	
	Olive and olive oil production	No	8 years	
	Olive production and marketing	No	5 years	
	Olive production and marketing (100% exportation oriented)	No	18 years	
	Exporting honey, olive and olive oil	No	14 years	
	Olive-pomace oil production	No	11 years	
	Processing domestic sales and exporting of olive and olive oil (mainly exportation oriented)	Yes	31 years	
	Production and marketing table olive (90% exporting)	Yes	19 years	
	Processing and exporting (98%) olive and pickle	Yes	34 years	
	Production and marketing olive oil, cotton gin, vegetable oil and cotton (domestic)	Yes	44 years	
	Olive oil production	Yes	57 years	
	Olive oil production	No	16 years	
Dried fruit processing/ exporting	Fig processing (domestic and exportation)	No	10 years	2 hours and 20 mins
	Fig processing	No	5 years	
	Fig production and packaging (domestic and exportation 20%)	Yes	9 years	
	Processing and exporting dried apricots and fig	Yes	42 years	
	Production and marketing of dried fruits, spices and honey	Yes	NK	

Category	Description		Years	Time
Milk and cheese production and marketing	Cheese production and marketing	Yes	92 years	1 hour
	Milk and cheese production	Yes	58 years	
	Production and marketing cheese	Yes	35 years	
Fruit and vegetable deserts processing and marketing	Fruit and vegetable deserts processing and marketing	No	7 years	5 hours
	Production and marketing olive, canned food, sauses, jams, halva (90% exporting)	NK	13 years	
	Processing sesame and processing/marketing tahina and halva	Yes	75 years	
	Production, packaging and exporting candy, drink powder and teas	Yes	39 years	
	Processing peanuts – domestic and export	Yes	27 years	
	Production and marketing popcorn (domestic: 100%)	No	30 years	
	Production and sales of dairy products	No	NK	
Livestock related business	Butcher	Yes	26 years	2 hours
	Livestock business (2)	NK	NK	
		No	14 years	
	Slaughterhouse	Yes	64 years	
Other stakeholders	Board member of the ATO (Aydin Chamber of Commerce)			2 hours and 20 minutes
	Chair of the Aydin Directorate of Provincial Food, Agriculture and Livestock			
	Director of the Small and Medium Enterprises Development Organisation (KOSGEB)			
	General Secretary of Aydin Commodity Exchange			
	Chair of the Board of Directors – Aydin Cooperative			

Monitoring mechanisms

As highlighted by our participants, the state should provide monitoring mechanisms to regulate the sector and also support producers and exports through funding, training and other opportunities. It has been also implied in the official reports that 'all stages from production to consumption are being controlled by using high levels of technology including use of satellite images for identification of agricultural lands on a basis of parcels; agricultural information system for efficient and correct use of agricultural supports' (Report of MoFAL, 2014, p. 34). However, still lack of monitoring mechanisms, which is mainly evident in the existence of the informal economy and shortages in control of overall production system, is one of the main issues that impact on sustainable entrepreneurship activities of SMEs. This has been highly emphasised by participants:

> There are now regulations but what matters is to enforce these regulations. It is not enough to have these regulations. Lack of monitoring mechanisms creates problems for the sector.
>
> (Int. 28)

Informal economy. The informal economy has been one of the most serious issues that harms the formal economy and prevents efficiency in the agriculture sector. It has been characterised by ineffective control system of unlicensed firms, leniency in punishment mechanisms and high cost of inputs. This challenge also has been highlighted in sectoral reports:

> Another problem is the coddling of the informal sector in the name of political populism and preserving employment, which in turn has been able to produce necessities at much lower cost and grow at the expense of the regulated and tax-paying establishments. The penalties for brand-copying and selling tainted foods are extremely low, acting as yet other disadvantages to the formal sector.
>
> (Yesilada and Sanli, 2015: 56)

Numerous participants also draw attention to the size of the informal economy in the agriculture sector:

> There are many unlicensed firms. Firstly, those firms should be shot down ... Government have to take responsibility and shoot down the firms, which don't have, for example, epoxy. This approach is important in ensuring total quality in the sector. There are approximately 1,500 unlicensed firms. This problem should have been solved by this time.
>
> (Int. 28)

> Government do not know how to punish. Only some of the big firms are punished, but not the SMEs. Smaller ones run away easily. For example,

there are two olive stock markets in Akhisar, and there are two hundred firms in total in this area. Locating in 100 meter-square area, these firms produce the same tins as we do, but in unsterile conditions. They hire uninsured employees and do not pay any tax.

(Int. 23)

One of our biggest challenge is the informal economy, which is also evident in every sector. Because costs are so high. Cost of the minimum wage, insured employee, fuel etc. is so high … Consider the cost of production of [Turkish] delight with an uninsured employee working for only 10–15 liras. It is not comparable with our cost.

(Int. 29)

Control of production process. Participants also mention lack of overall controls and checks over the production process. TUSIAD (2014) also reports need for establishment of a food security committee that would increase number and quality of controls.

Although legislations relating to health of food and livestock are brought into force in Turkey, the ones particularly relating to consumption and control of food have not achieved to its aim. As it is also underlined in the Progress Report of EU, transfer of EU food safety legislation to domestic law has not been practiced successfully yet.

(TUSIAD, 2014: 73)

These processes are mainly pertinent to control of pesticides which also provide challenges in exportation.

Products are not controlled utterly in the Turkish agricultural sector. For example, pesticides might be seen in exported olives, due to lack of overall control system.

(Int. 1)

Farmers are also responsible for product-quality checks. They need to work in collaboration with the Ministry of Agriculture; but it is not just complying with regulations, it has more to do with ensuring full control and checks over the production process beyond compliance.

(Int. 10)

Effectiveness of governmental policies

Since the agricultural industry in the Turkish context is seen as one of the leading engines of development, governmental resources are directed for the development of the sector (Yesilada and Sanli, 2015). As documented by Larson *et al.* (2015: 14) agricultural policies provide greater support for producers than

that provided by most OECD countries. In alignment with this, support programmes have been rearranged with the aim of allocation of more resources for
the sector. Importantly, the Rural Development Support Programme, which was
targeted only for support of small farmers and investors, was initiated in 2006,
along with other support schemes (ISPA, 2014). For example, within this scope,
5,450 new processing facilities have been constructed. While a 1.1 billion TL
grant has been given to the enterprises, a 1 billion TL grant support was provided for 262,000 machineries and equipments between 2007 and 2013. Additionally 2.1 billion TL were paid for the beneficiaries under the Rural
Development Support Programme for new facilities and machinery and equipment purchased by the farmers, as noted in the report of MoFAL (2014: 80).
An increasing amount of grants and incentives for the agricultural SMEs also
has been mentioned by numerous participants.

However, ineffective agricultural policies, which are particularly seen in mis-
alignments between legislations and needs of industry; shortages in strategic agricultural planning and production; misallocation of supports and incentives and
unstable policies, provide the main challenges for agricultural SMEs and put the
Turkish agricultural sector in a disadvantaged position in the global arena.

Misalignment between legislations and needs of industry. Alignment of legislations and real needs of the industry is critical for the effectiveness, innovativeness and competitiveness of the SMEs:

> Agricultural policy is far from reflecting upon needs of the future, and insuf-
> ficient in meeting today's needs. Unhappiness of employers in the agricul-
> tural sector is a result of the shortcomings of these policies. For example,
> previously, we were able to determine price of the products according to
> cost of all inputs and profit margin. But, today, if we calculate it in this way,
> prices remain high, compared to global prices, and we can't sell products
> due to the global price policies ... production and olive oil policies are com-
> pletely different today, compared to 20 years ago ... While stocking up was
> essential in the international olive oil trade 10–15 years ago, today,
> dishoarding [not stocking] is essential due to inventory cost. Over the years,
> production increased, production techniques changed, production costs
> decreased. However, we could not decrease production cost. We are not
> able to compete with global prices, owing to our agricultural policy.
>
> (Int. 2)

> We observe many problems in enforcement of laws. Adopting a top-down
> approach, these laws are made according to European Union laws, but
> without consideration of contextualised, real regional problems. Because
> law makers are not part of this decision.
>
> (Int. 13)

Shortages in strategic agricultural planning and production. Sustainable entrepreneurship must be achieved through strategic agricultural planning and production. In

this regard, key stakeholders have implied importance of the land consolidation problem, which should be sorted out for innovative techniques for modern farming, professionalisation of value chain system through, for example, well-established information systems among key stakeholders, clarity in strategic direction of production planning including kind of production (whether boutique or massive), the type of products as well as allocation of resources for privileged crops and activities. These main issues have been implied both in the official reports and by participants. More specifically, a land portioning problem in agricultural areas that prevents innovative techniques in agriculture, is reported:

> The most astonishing lack of innovation is the refusal of villagers to pool resources to buy farm machinery to work small parcels together, or organize into co-ops to do so officially. This would largely mitigate the small-parcel problem and allow most farmers to capitalize on modern farming techniques that would be too costly to access given the capital-intensive nature of the modern equipment such as tractors. The dilemma shows up in many forms. Farm experts report villages (and we can personally attest to this phenomenon) where every farmer boasts of brand-new tractors which lay idle 99% of the time, while the said person has difficulty making the loan payment on the equipment.
>
> (Yesilada and Sanli, 2015: 48)

The following quotes imply that ambiguities in production planning restrain effectiveness of SMEs.

> We have to deal with so many stakeholders including, for example, farmers. We have to send employees to each region in order to bargain, weigh and collect the crop. However, if another department could take this responsibility, if olives could be stocked in particular place, if amount of harvest [*rekolte*] detailing out its calibre was determined before,... and potential buyers buy from there.... This would help us a lot ... Governmental policies are wrong.... Government provided incentives for the Gemlik olive, and millions of trees were planted accordingly, yet this kind of olive is not favoured by exported countries.
>
> (Int. 28)

> If one product is profitable for one year, another year it is not profitable because of lack of planning. Almost all firms suffer. It has been mentioned at the meeting that same problem will occur this year as well.
>
> (Int. 31)

As noted earlier, strategic agricultural production planning should include sharpness in production methods (whether boutique or massive), distinction of privileged products as well as allocation of resources for production and marketing of these products.

There is no future in the olive-oil sector. Because we are not able to compete across the globe. On the one hand, we can't compete with industrial production, on the other hand, we also can't do boutique production or we are not able to make this image. We are stuck in the middle. We have to make our own path. Do we want to produce with best quality or are we eager to prefer industrial production? We have to determine our own strategy. Trouble within the sector is pertinent to lack of strategic direction.

(Int. 7)

Most basic inputs are imported. Turkey imports almost all of its hydrocarbons and mining inputs for fertilizers. Prior to the massive oil price shock, the price of inputs has risen faster than agricultural commodities putting Turkish farmers at a natural disadvantage, which has been only partially compensated by government deficiency and support payments.

(Yesilada and Sanli, 2015: 47)

Misallocation of supports and incentives. Especially, funding opportunities should be in alignment with strategic planning:

Firstly, incentives are crucial for implementation of projects. We have not received any support from Development Agencies ... We face various institutional challenges. For instance, if you exported before, then it is not allowed to benefit from incentives or credits [*hibe kredisi*]. We have to export with our own financing. Government does not provide financial support for exporting firms, but prefers to support for the ones which have not exported before. I think it is wrong. Benefitting from experience of exporting firms is important. Government should support the exporting firms, which have capacity for growth. Although my firm has a capacity for more exportation of apricot, I am not able to process and export more apricot, since I don't have the required machine for processing, which costs approximately 150–160 thousand euros. I have to buy ready, packageable apricot, rather than processing...

(Int. 10)

Incentives are provided for specific organic areas, rather than exporting firms. For instance, organic firms get financial support, even for uncultivated pastures in many regions of Anatolia. Those firms do not do anything, they do not contribute to the organic sector, but they benefit from supports. This policy is very wrong. Value-added projects should be supported, but not uncultivated pastures.

(Int. 17)

For example, fig should be supported well, since the fig only grows in Turkey. We know very well about processing of the fig.

(Int. 25)

In general, government directs all resources to particular areas, but not to important ones. Nowadays, there is no any support for fig. If fund could be created for the fig, if bad figs are withdrawn from sector, we will be able to produce better figs and contribute more to this sector. We are number one in the world.

(Int. 34)

Adoption of a flexible and contextualised approach in allocation of resources, rather than implementing EU laws entirely, is the another important issue. This requires interrogation of real needs of the sector in particular areas, which is pertinent to alignment of legislations and need of the industry, as aforementioned. This is emphasised in the reports and blogs of the international intermediary organisation, the World Bank:

In Turkey, much of the support targets specific crops that are politically or economically important. While in the EU, there is a trend to provide support to farmers that is de-linked from production. Adopting this more flexible approach may help Turkey continue a transformation of its agricultural sector that has been largely beneficial.... To start, Turkey could adapt a more flexible domestic support program for agriculture unilaterally, without implementing the EU CAP in its entirety. Turkey and the EU could also agree to fully incorporate agriculture into the Customs Union, especially if the dwindling set of irritants under the current CU can be resolved.

(Larson and McKenna, 2014)

Unstable legislations. Rapidly changing regulations in different directions with no consideration of the public interest or without satisfactory consultation with stakeholders has been implied in reports of TOBB (2013) and TUISAD (2014).

The agricultural field in the Turkish context is unstable, since agricultural policies change cyclically. This should be analysed from the perspective of 'economic regulation theory'.

(TUSIAD, 2014: 47)

The following quote also highlights this:

We assume that law makers dream, for example about olive, and make laws about it on another day. Suddenly, they say that let's make this law. But they are not thinking about what this law would mean, how it would affect producers. During the period that I was exporting strawberry powder and kinds of other sugared products with containers, laws changed all of a sudden, and then, we had to stop exporting ... While we do our best to obey the rules, on the other hand, laws are very shifty and unstable, since they serve for the benefit of the favoured stakeholders.

(Int. 29)

Table 13.2 presents additional illustrative examples to key findings pertaining to institutional involvement of government.

University-industry engagement

Collaboration with state and public organisations requires adapting different institutional logics for all institutional agents. University-industry collaboration, for instance, is key for an effective SME ecosystem. Universities' involvement as

Table 13.2 Key findings pertaining to institutional involvement of government

First-order theme	Second-order theme	Illustrative data
Government involvement and related policies	Monitoring mechanisms	*State should develop monitoring mechanisms; they should audit all SMEs equally. However, due to lack of these mechanisms, informal economy still exists in Turkey, particularly in olive processing and production.* (Int. 23) *There are now regulations but what matters is to enforce these regulations. It is not enough to have these regulations. Lack of monitoring mechanisms creates problems for the sector.* (Int. 28) *Farmers are also responsible for product-quality checks. They need to work in collaboration with the Ministry of Agriculture; but it is not just complying with regulations, it has more to do with ensuring full control and checks over the production process beyond compliance.* (Int. 10)
	Legislations and decision makers	*Who is making decisions, policies for us? The parliament. They are the ones who develop policies and legislations. When you look at the composition of the parliament and profile of MPs, there are very few people who understand about production in general, and agricultural production in particular.* (Int. 27) *The current legislation was introduced in 2006 and it defined the framework for agricultural policy. However, it doesn't do justice to our needs. There are two main reasons: external factors and internal factors. When we look at internal factors, current deficit, debts and our credibility are amongst many factors. Seasonal problems in agriculture, lack of effective government support mechanisms are some others. External factors on the other hand include the way in which WTO, EU, IMF and WB type of international institutions and their impact on our agricultural policy.* (Int. 9)

institutional actors is significant in terms of educated and trained business community, educating next generations of famers, producers, managers and entrepreneurs and engagements with industry in the form of consultancy, knowledge exchange and R&D efforts. Table 13.3 illustrates examples of empirical evidence to support these findings.

As can be viewed from Table 13.3, university-industry collaboration can take forms of consultancy, knowledge exchange and project management. It is often the case that SMEs do not have resources or capacity to engage in consultancy with the universities and other institutions. Deliberate management of economic, social and ecological aspects of the agricultural firm, and hence their integration into products, services and business models, puts another pressure on SMEs. These should be considered when building relationships with SMEs.

Discussion and conclusions

In this chapter we have aimed to address the research question of how agricultural SMEs engage in sustainable entrepreneurship and innovation as part of wider entrepreneurial ecosystem and hence what the policy implications are. We have found that a strong motivational drive for sustainable entrepreneurship and weak institutional settings characterise their engagement. By weak institutional settings, we refer to lack of effective government monitoring and support mechanisms; lack of strong inter-firm collaboration in the sector and problems associated with university-SME collaborations. These weak institutional vehicles divert SME owner-managers and entrepreneurs from innovation processes and sustainability-driven activities.

SMEs often lack knowledge and other resources about the broader innovation processes (Van Goolen *et al.*, 2014). By operating in an effective innovation and entrepreneurial ecosystem, they can develop capacity to anticipate the needs of the market and gain competitive advantage. Our findings demonstrate that SMEs have limited resources that they can allocate for consultancy and R&D. A close collaboration between government institutions, intermediary organisations, other firms and knowledge centres such as universities can yield creative ideas for SMEs (Van Goolen *et al.*, 2014). A collaborative meeting ground between universities and SMEs in agriculture is imperative for an effective SME ecosystem. The benefits of such collaboration are three-fold: first, it can help SMEs develop product, service and business model innovation and enhance entrepreneurial capacity. Second, SMEs can develop a more systematic approach for sustainability and innovation processes. Third, such collaboration can encourage policy makers and other potential collaborators to create an open innovation culture. Such open innovation cultures face conflicting institutional logics and require institutional actors to develop hybrid strategies and practices.

The SME ecosystem, which is characterised by involvement of a range of multiple actors, exemplifies hybrid organisational arrangements by spanning the boundaries of the private, public and non-profit sectors and by bridging the institutional fields (Tracey *et al.*, 2011; Doherty *et al.*, 2014). However, conflicting

Table 13.3 Examples of key findings pertaining to the institutional involvement of universities and university-industry collaboration

First order code	Second order code	Illustrative data
Involvement of universities	Educated and trained business community	We have talked to our university in this area: entrepreneurship courses should be a part of curriculum as optional. Such courses need to run in collaboration with organisations such as KOSGEB, who can jointly certify the award of the graduate. In this way, students will not only achieve their target credits for graduation but also contribute to their personal development as entrepreneurs and managers. (Int. 8) Universities are not educating well. There is lack of high-quality education in universities. It is not the number of universities that matter; it is the quality of education. (Int. 23)
	Workforce implications	Universities should identify workforce requirements of their locality and develop curriculum and new programmes accordingly. (Int. 23) We don't need more engineers in agriculture; but we do need more technical human resource who can fill the gap. (Int. 28)
	Student internships	Universities are coming to us with demands to place students for internship in our businesses. We support such initiatives and try to train students in all areas of their study, including theoretical and practical aspects. (Int. 14) When students complete their degree, they should have a sound practical knowledge and understanding of agricultural products. You cannot have graduates who cannot differentiate ocra and corn plants. Through internships and placements, applied aspects of education should be strengthened. (Int. 5) Our sector is open to student visits and internships. University should demand this. (Int. 18) Usually purpose of internships is to do justice to internship requirements of the degree. Rather than full engagement, students often are after completing the paperwork. (Int. 17) Instead of one-month or two-month internships, a student should have a year-long placement in a company. There They should be engaged in knowledge exchange with their professors as well as business managers. There should be an internship evaluation made by the company so that students' understanding and experience can be assessed. (Int. 27)
University-industry collaboration	Consultancy	Other than individual efforts of academics as consultants, there is not much collaboration in consultancy terms with universities. TUBITAK supports some consultancy projects but not every project gets accepted. They mainly support R&D but R&D is not an area where SMEs are prioritising efforts as it is not directly related to profitability. SME will make an investment, and TUBITAK will fund the project and an R&D lab will be established. . . . This is a long and complex process and our SMEs are not that advanced yet. There are many other management issues that need to be taken care of before this. (Int. 28)

Project management	When we form a project team, we involve a number of institutions, including public sector organisations, our university and representatives of industry. In the last few years, there is an increasing collaboration with universities. This doesn't only involve government-industry collaboration but a triple helix of university-industry-government collaboration is evident. I think this is a process and we are getting better in time. (Int. 9)
	Project management is a challenging task. When we look at SME management and entrepreneurship, project management approach has much relevance. There is lack of this approach in many of our institutions including SMEs. However, our students from the university are really successful in this area. (Int. 9)
Misalignment of goals and interests	There is a disconnect between academia and industry. On one hand, there are academics with sound research and knowledge base; on the other hand there are practitioners. They are so disconnected from each other as the knowledge and experience do not match and there is also a problem in transferring knowledge from one side to another. I think co-ordination should be provided by the government support. (Int. 7)
	There is such significant research and activities going on in the university; however investors or entrepreneurs are not aware of these. Our major problem as a sector is that SMEs have resource constraints and their objectives and interests do not align with the universities. (Int. 7)
Hybrid approaches and institutionalisation of relationship	In the recent years, universities are paying significant attention to university-industry collaboration. This is a pleasing development; however, it is not enough. Most of our SME managers are not sensitive or alert enough to knowledge or network flows from universities. We don't have much time or energy to devote to such things. However, it is very important to get some of your practices institutionalised and address multiple bottom lines and institutionalise activities and relationships. (Int. 13)
	For R&D, restructuring and renovation of enterprises, universities should pave the way. However, scientists cannot easily adapt to market conditions. At this juncture, applied research and implementation is critical. It is very challenging to bring together the science base and enterprises. Universities should focus on the problems and issues that SMEs face and tailor their research and related activities accordingly; and then they are tasked with the mission of informing government policy. University leadership is fundamental in achieving this. (Int. 27)

institutional logics (see Pache and Santos, 2013) prevail in such organisational ecosystems. Alignment of interests and approaches is imperative in achieving synergy out of collaboration in such ecosystems.

We make two important contributions to the field in this study. First, we generate empirical insights into the SME ecosystem in sustainable innovation and entrepreneurship in a key industrial sector, namely agriculture, by drawing on a rich empirical data set. Second, our findings indicate policy and practice implications for the institutional actors of this ecosystem. The research and out-reach activity underpinning this study has the overall objective of informing public policy and strategy development and related public service delivery in the area of agro-entrepreneurship and sustainable development of agricultural SMEs in Turkey. An important implication is that universities should be better connected with users within and outside the SME community and industry-informed research and curriculum should be prioritised. The value of inter-organisational alliances that spans across sectoral and national boundaries should be acknowledged by all institutions of the ecosystem.

Reassessment of SMEs' engagement in sustainable innovation and entrepre-neurship and related university-SME collaborations as changing institutional responses as a part of wider ecosystem in agriculture has implications for future research and practice. Research implications include evaluations of inter-national comparisons and further exploration of strategic alliances with different stakeholders such as local community and government engagement. There are managerial implications for university leaders, academics and SME owner-managers. It is crucial to understand the importance of multiple logics under-pinning institutional responses of each actor and hybrid approaches characterising networked collaborations. Governance of these networked rela-tionships, based on trust and mutual value creation, is crucial in sustaining an effective SME ecosystem.

Appendix

Table A13.1 Detailed inventory of data sources

Data type	Data source	Data specifics	Characteristics
Documentary data	Parliamentary reports: Ministry of Food Agriculture and Livestock (MoFAL)	Report of Ministry of Food Agriculture and Livestock: 'Structural changes and reforms in Turkish agriculture 2003–2014' (61 pages)	Provides basic economic and demographic indicators of the Turkish agriculture sector and governmental policy in agriculture, state intervention, regulation and private sector participation
	Egeli & Co (Yesilada and Sanli, 2015) (agriculture oriented venture capital company)	Report of Egeli & Co: 'Turkish Agriculture 2015 and beyond: Is there opportunity for FDI?' (98 pages)	
	TUSIAD (Turkish Industry and Business Association)	Report of TUSIAD: 'Gida, Tarim ve Hayvancilik Rekabet Gucu – Temel Bulgular (Competitiveness of Food, Agriculture and Livestock – Basic Findings – 2014)' (112 pages)	
	ISPA (Ministry Investment Support and Promotion Agency)	Report of ISPA: 'Food & Agriculture in Turkey, 2014' (55 pages)	
	TOBB (The Union of Chambers and Stock Markets of Turkey)	Report of TOBB: 'Turkiye Tarim Sektoru Raporu (Turkish Agricultural Sector Report), 2013' (98 pages)	
Focus group meeting	Focus group with 15 key stakeholders	Discussion with industry partners and intermediary organisations (including government agents) in agricultural sector (1 hour 30 mins)	Provides initial insights about opportunities, challenges and issues university-industry collaboration as well as entrepreneurial development of SMEs from the perspective of practitioners and policy makers

continued

Table A13.1 Continued

Data type	Data source	Data specifics	Characteristics
Semi-structured interviews	35 interviews with SME managers/owners	15 firms from olive industry (8 hours) 5 firms from dried fruit processing/exporting (2 hours 20 mins) 4 firms from milk and cheese production (1 hour) 7 firms from fruit and vegetable desserts processing and marketing (5 hours) 4 firms from livestock related business (2 hours)	Provides insights about main challenges and issues for entrepreneurial development of SMEs from the perspective of practitioners
	5 interviews with other stakeholders	Board member of the ATO (Aydin Chamber of Commerce) Chair of the Aydin Directorate of Provincial Food, Agriculture and Livestock Director of the Small and Medium Enterprises Development Organisation (KOSGEB) General Secretary of Aydin Commodity Exchange Chair of the Board of Directors – Aydin Cooperative (in total, 2 hours and 20 minutes)	Provides insights about main challenges and issues for entrepreneurial development of SMEs from the perspective of policy makers
Dissemination workshop	Knowledge exchange-dissemination workshop with approximately 50 industry and academic partners	Presentation of findings of the research and furthering discussion of findings industry and academic partners (one day)	Provides assessment of credibility of findings and make recommendations to facilitate uni-industry collaborations

Table A13.2 Key findings pertaining to institutional involvement of government

First and second order theme	Third order theme	Illustrative data
Government involvement and related policies Lack of monitoring mechanisms	Control in informal economy	'The state should develop monitoring mechanisms; they should audit all SMEs equally. However, due to lack of these mechanisms, informal economy still exists in Turkey, particularly in olive processing and production' (Int. 23) 'Governmental control should be done through field visits, not at the desk. Certificates are very crucial. In Turkey, the majority of the firms work without certificates, which should be an essential requirement' (Int. 25) 'A second example is the inability of hazelnut growers to subscribe to licensed warehouses. King's Paradox runs paramount in the Turkish hazelnut market. Farmers actually make more money in years where the crop is very poor, because they failed to pool resources or lobby the government to invest into an efficient licensed warehousing network which would store their output to be sold at better market conditions throughout the year, or in bad years' (Report of Egeli & Co, 2015: 49)
	Control of overall production process	'We do afro-toxin checks under purple light in dark rooms. Yet, provincial agricultural laboratories do not check samples under these conditions. Accordingly, the afro-toxin percentage that escapes from one's notice, escapes during the exportation process. Additionally, although we get reports of analysis from Turkey, analyses are also done in the other countries in Europe. Due to differences in technological conditions, we fail in afro-toxin examinations. This is not a problem of the Provincial Agricultural Directory, but there are overlooked methods of control' (Int. 10) 'The essential duty of the provincial agricultural directory is to control correctness of content of products. For instance, tahini is written on the products, but there is no information about the type of tahini, we do not know whether it is soya or sesame tahini' (Int. 28)
Ineffective agricultural policies	Misalignment between legislations and needs of industry	'Who is making decisions, policies for us? The parliament. They are the ones who develop policies and legislations. When you look at the composition of the parliament and profile of MPs, there are very few people who understand about production in general, and agricultural production in particular' (Int. 27) The current legislation was introduced in 2006 and it defined the framework for agricultural policy. However, it doesn't do justice to our needs. There are two main reasons: external factors and internal factors. When we look at internal factors, current deficit, debts and our credibility are amongst many factors. Seasonal problems in agriculture, lack of effective government support mechanisms are some others. External factors on the other hand include the way in which WTO, EU, IMF and WB type of international institutions and their impact on our agricultural policy. (Int. 9).

continued

Table A13.2 Continued

First and second order theme	Third order theme	Illustrative data
	Ineffective strategic agricultural planning and production	'Now, there is no agricultural planning in the region. All of a sudden, alfalfa has become very valuable. Aydin became even a country of strawberry, country of corn, or country of cotton. We have serious shortages in agricultural planning. All of a sudden, tomato was planted in every corner of Turkey, and then watermelon was planted without planning' (Int. 25)
		'Land consolidation is required for the region of Cine. Government should organise production. Specific products should be determined for specific areas to be planted. For instance, only corn will be planted in the region of Cine' (Int 33)
	Misallocation of supports and incentives	'High quality supports are required, that we mention in every meeting of Chamber of Commerce. There is no any support for the most important three products of this region, which are fig, olive and chestnut. Aydin is the city where the majority of the fig is produced in the world. Although we meet 60% of the world's fig need, there is not any support for the fig producers. We are number one in production of chestnut, however, it has not evaluated as an agricultural product yet. There is only support for olive oil. If we consider supports for other products, for example, it is uncertain whether cotton will be planted in the Soke district or not. In some years, corn is favoured more, rather than cotton' (Int. 5)
		'Governmental support for the agricultural sector is very much a debated topic. There are many supports, but these are not allocated for the main needy people. For example, there was a new popcorn firm, they applied for the supports of rural development, but the firm could not benefit from these supports. Other firms from the region where olive oil waste is very high, benefitted from the support for olive oil. As far as I'm concerned, the popcorn firm deserved this support more' (Int. 7)
	Unstable legislations	'Our main problem is that there is no stability. There is no guarantee for the standardised prices' (Int. 15)
		'Unfortunately, Turkey's membership process for the EU is very challenging, since there have been many shifty regulations, which are incredibly and unnecessarily detailed and difficult to implement. Accordingly, we suffer and are punished, when the product falls outside the scope of the legislation. Overall, these legislations should be quite general and doable' (Int. 29)

Table A13.3 Examples of key findings pertaining to the institutional involvement of universities and university-industry collaboration

First order code	Second order code	Illustrative data
Involvement of universities	Educated and trained business community	'We have talked to our university in this area: entrepreneurship courses should be a part of the curriculum as optional. Such courses need to run in collaboration with organisations such as KOSGEB, who can jointly certify the award of the graduate. In this way, students will not only achieve their target credits for graduation but also contribute to their personal development as entrepreneurs and managers' (Int. 8) 'Universities are not educating well. There is a lack of high-quality education in universities. It is not the number of universities that matter; it is the quality of education' (Int. 23)
	Workforce implications	'Universities should identify workforce requirements of their locality and develop curriculum and new programmes accordingly' (Int. 23) 'We don't need more engineers in agriculture; but we do need more technically able human resource who can fill the gap' (Int. 28)
	Student internships	'When students complete their degree, they should have a sound practical knowledge and understanding of agricultural products. You cannot have graduates who cannot differentiate between ocra and corn plants. Through internships and placements, applied aspects of education should be strengthened' (Int. 5) 'Usually purpose of internships is to do justice to internship requirements of the degree. Rather than full engagement, students often are after completing the paperwork' (Int. 17) 'Instead of one-month or two-month internships, a student should have a year-long placement in a company. They should be engaged in knowledge exchange with their professors as well as business managers. There should be an internship evaluation made by the company so that students' understanding and experience can be assessed' (Int. 27)
University-industry collaboration	Consultancy	'Other than individual efforts of academics as consultants, there is not much collaboration in consultancy terms with universities. TUBITAK supports some consultancy projects but not every project gets accepted. They mainly support R&D but R&D is not an area where SMEs are prioritising efforts as it is not directly related to profitability. SME will make an investment, and TUBITAK will fund the project and an R&D lab will be established ... This is a long and complex process and our SMEs are not that advanced yet. There are many other management issues that need to be taken care of before this' (Int. 28)

continued

Table A13.3 Continued

First order code	Second order code	Illustrative data
	Project management	'When we form a project team, we involve a number of institutions, including public sector organisations, our university and representatives of industry. In the last few years, there has been an increasing collaboration with universities. This doesn't only involve government-industry collaboration but a triple helix of university-industry-government collaboration is evident. I think this is a process and we are getting better in time ... Project management is a challenging task. When we look at SME management and entrepreneurship, the project management approach has much relevance. There is a lack of this approach in many of our institutions including SMEs. However, our students from the university are really successful in this area' (Int. 9)
	Misalignment of goals and interests	'There is a disconnect between academia and industry. On one hand, there are academics with sound research and knowledge base; on the other hand there are practitioners. They are so disconnected from each other as the knowledge and experience do not match and there is also a problem in transferring knowledge from one side to another. I think co-ordination should be provided by the government support ... There is such significant research and activities going on in the university; however investors or entrepreneurs are not aware of these. Our major problem as a sector is that SMEs have resource constraints and their objectives and interests do not align with the universities' (Int. 7)
	Hybrid approaches and institutionalisation of relationship	'In the recent years, universities are paying significant attention to university-industry collaboration. This is a pleasing development; however, it is not enough. Most of our SME managers are not sensitive or alert enough to knowledge or network flows from universities. We don't have much time or energy to devote to such things. However, it is very important to get some of your practices institutionalised and address multiple bottom lines and institutionalise activities and relationships' (Int. 13) 'For R&D, restructuring and renovation of enterprises, universities should pave the way. However, scientists cannot easily adapt to market conditions. At this juncture, applied research and implementation is critical. It is very challenging to bring together the science base and enterprises. Universities should focus on the problems and issues that SMEs face and tailor their research and related activities accordingly; and then they are tasked with the mission of informing government policy. University leadership is fundamental in achieving this' (Int. 27)

Acknowledgements

We would like to acknowledge the funding support granted by the British Council (Grant reference no: TR/012012/KP23) for the research project.

References

Adams, M. and Ghaly, A. E. (2007) Maximizing sustainability of the Costa Rican coffee industry, *Journal of Cleaner Production*, 15, pp. 1716–1729.

Baldwin, S. J., Allen, M. P., Winder, B. and Ridgway, K. (2005) Modelling manufacturing evolution: thoughts on sustainable industrial development, *Journal of Cleaner Production*, 13, pp. 887–902.

Bos-Brouwers, J. E. H. (2010) Corporate sustainability and innovation in SMEs: evidence of themes and activities in practice, *Business Strategy and the Environment*, 19, 7, pp. 417–435.

Bugg-Levine, A. and Emerson, J. (2011) *Impact Investing: Transforming How We Make Money While Making a Difference*. San Francisco: Jossey-Bass.

Cheng, C. J. and Huizingh, E. K. R. E. (2014) When is open innovation beneficial? The role of strategic orientation, *Journal of Product Innovation Management*, 31, 6, pp. 1235–1253.

Chesborough, H. W. (2011) *Management Innovation for the Future of Innovation*. Boston, MA: Harvard Business School Press.

Cohen, B. and Winn, M. I. (2007) Market imperfections, opportunity and sustainable entrepreneurship, *Journal of Business Venturing*, 22, pp. 29–49.

Corsten, D. and Felde, J. (2005) Exploring the performance effects of key-supplier collaboration: an empirical investigation into Swiss buyer-supplier relationships, *International Journal of Physical Distribution and Logistics Management*, 35, 6, pp. 445–461.

Crnogaj, K., Rebernik, M., Hojnik, B. and Gomezelj, D. O. (2014) Building a model of researching the sustainable entrepreneurship in the tourism sector, *Kybernetes*, 43, 3/4, pp. 377–393.

Doh, S. and Kim, B. (2014) Government support for SME innovations in the regional industries: the case of government financial support programme in South Korea, *Research Policy*, 43, 9, pp. 1557–1569.

Doherty, B., Haugh, H. and Lyon, F. (2014) Social enterprises as hybrid organisations: a review and research agenda, *International Journal of Management Reviews*, 16, pp. 417–436.

Dyllic, T. and Hockerts, K. (2002) Beyond the business case for corporate sustainability, *Business Strategy and Environment*, 11, 2, pp. 130–141.

Gabzdylova, B., Raffensperger, F. J. and Castka, P. (2009) Sustainability in the New Zealand wine industry: drivers, stakeholders and practices, *Journal of Cleaner Production*, 17, 982–998.

Gassmann, O. and Enkel, E. (2004) Towards a theory of open innovation: three core process archetypes. Proceedings of the R&D Management Conference, Lisbon, 6–9 July.

Hall, J. (2002) Sustainable development innovation: a research agenda for the next 10 years, *Journal of Cleaner Production*, 10, pp. 195–196.

Hall, J., Matos, S., Sheehan, L. and Silvestre, B. (2012) Entrepreneurship and innovation at the base of the pyramid: a recipe for inclusive growth or social exclusive, *Journal of Management Studies*, 49, pp. 785–809.

Hermans, F., Stuiver, M., Beers, P. J. and Kok, K. (2013) The distribution of roles and functions for upscaling and outscaling innovations in agricultural innovation systems, *Agricultural Systems*, 115, pp. 117–128.

Hottenrott, H. and Lopes-Bento, C. (2014) (International) R&D collaboration and SMEs: the effectiveness of targeted public R&D support schemes, *Research Policy*, 43, 6, pp. 1055–1066.

Hounkonnou, D., Kossou, D., Kuyper, T. W., Leeuwis, C., Nederlof, E. S., Roling, N., Sakyi-Dawson, O., Traore, M. and van Huis, A. (2012) An innovation system approach to institutional change: smallholder development in West Africa, *Agricultural Systems*, 108, pp. 74–83.

ISPA – Ministry Investment Support and Promotion Agency – (2014) Food & Agriculture in Turkey (www.invest.gov.tr/en…/FOOD.AND.AGRICULTURE.INDUSTRY).

Jegatheesan, V., Liow, J. L., Shu, L., Kim, S. H. and Visvanathan, C. (2009) The need for global coordination in sustainable development, *Journal of Cleaner Production*, 17, pp. 637–643.

Kang, K-N. and Park, H. (2013) Influence of government R&D support and inter-firm collaborations on innovation in Korean biotech SMEs, *Technovation*, 31, 1, pp. 68–78.

Klewitz, J. and Hansen, E. G. (2014) Sustainability-oriented innovation of SMEs: a systematic review, *Journal of Cleaner Production*, 65, pp. 57–75.

Laforet, S. 2013. Organisational innovation outcomes in SMEs: effects of age, size, and sector, *Journal of World Business*, 48, pp. 490–502.

Larson, D., Martin, M., Sahin, S. and Tsigas, M. (2015) Agricultural policies and trade paths in Turkey, *The World Economy*, doi: 10.1111/twec.12294.

Larson, F. D. and McKenna, M. (2014) Why it is time to take action on agriculture in Turkey. 10 December (http://blogs.worldbank.org/trade/why-it-time-take-action-agriculture-turkey).

Lozano, R. (2007) Collaboration as a pathway for sustainability, *Sustainable Development*, 15, pp. 370–381.

Malik, K. and Wei, J. (2011) How external partnering enhances innovation: evidence from Chinese tech-based SMEs, *Technology Analysis and Strategic Management*, 23, pp. 401–413.

McAdam, M., McAdam, R., Dunn, A. and McCall, C. (2014) Development of SME horizontal innovation networks: UK agri-food sector study, *International Small Business Journal*, 32, 7, pp. 830–853.

Moffat, A. and Auer, A. (2006) Corporate Environmental Innovation (CEI): a government initiative to support corporate sustainability leadership, *Journal of Cleaner Production*, 14, pp. 589–600.

Pache, A. and Santos, F. (2013) Inside the hybrid organisation: an organisational level view of responses to conflicting institutional demands, *Academy of Management Journal*, 56, 4, pp. 972–1001.

Report of Ministry of Food Agriculture and Livestock (MoFAL) (2014) Structural changes and reforms in Turkish agriculture 2003–2014. (www.tarim.gov.tr/SGB/Belgeler/Haberler/ING.12.11).

Rodgers, C. (2010) Sustainable entrepreneurship in SMEs: a case study analysis, *Corporate Social Responsibility Environmental Management*, 17, pp. 125–132.

Schaltegger, S. (2002) A framework for ecopreneurship-leading bioneers and environmental managers to ecopreneurship, *Greener Management International*, 38, pp. 45–58.

Schaltegger, S. and Wagner, M. (2011) Sustainable entrepreneurship and sustainability innovation: categories and interactions, *Business Strategy Environment*, 20, pp. 222–237.

Shepherd, D. A. and Patzelt, H. (2011) The new field of sustainable entrepreneurship: studying entrepreneurial action linking 'what is to be sustained' with 'what is to be developed', *Entrepreneurship Theory & Practice*, January, pp. 137–162.

TOBB – The Union of Chambers and Stock Markets of Turkey – (2013) Turkiye Tarim Sektoru Raporu (Turkish Agricultural Sector Report, ISBN: 978–605–137–388–1).

Tracey, P., Phillips, N. and Jarvis, O. (2011) Bridging institutional entrepreneurship and the creation of new organisational forms: a multilevel model, *Organization Science*, 22, pp. 60–80.

TUSIAD – Turkish Industry and Business Association – (2014) Gida, Tarim ve Hayvancilik Rekabet Gucu – Temel Bulgular (Competitiveness of Food, Agriculture and Livestock – Basic Findings, Publication No: TÜSIAD-T/2014–11/561).

Van Goolen, R., Evers, H. and Lammens, C. (2014) International Innovation Labs: an innovation meeting ground between SMEs and business schools, *Procedia Economics and Finance*, 12, pp. 184–190.

World Bank (2013) Turkey: country at a glance (www.worldbank.org/en/country/turkey).

Yesilada, A. and Sanli, G. A. (2015) Agriculture oriented venture capital company: Turkish Agriculture 2015 and beyond: is there opportunity for FDI? Agriculture-Agrobusiness Sector Report Series No. 2, Istanbul.

Zahra, S. A., Newey, L. R. and Li, Y. (2014) On the frontiers: the implications of social entrepreneurship for international entrepreneurship, *Entrepreneurship Theory & Practice*, January, pp. 137–158.

14 Sustainable entrepreneurship in maritime tourism

Theoretical considerations and empirical evidence

Maria Lekakou, Evangelia Stefanidaki and Ioannis Theotokas

Introduction

Maritime and coastal tourism is recognized as an economic activity with significant contribution to European economy and furthermore as "one of five focus areas for delivering sustainable growth and jobs in the blue economy" (COM (2014)86). Maritime tourism includes a wide range of activities, but cruise tourism and yachting are the largest segments under this umbrella term.

The cruise tourism sector is an interesting case of a globalized industry in an environment of international competition, capital mobility and labor migration (Douglas and Douglas, 2004; Wood, 2000). Wild and Dearing (2000) refer to the sector as a blend of transport, tourism and leisure. To that extent, there is a limited number of available definitions describing industry's structure, boundaries and markets, whilst the existed ones lack clarity and as such the activity stands at the margin of the tourism and shipping industry. Despite that, what has been widely accepted is that the sector, even being the fastest economic activity, recording since 1990 an average growth rate of 6.55 percent (Cruise Market Watch, 2015), lacks scientific attention and thus relevant research is fragmented (Papathanassis and Beckmann, 2011). The generated economic impact is at the center of current scientific research, while during the last few years there has been an increasing interest towards the study of the environmental effects; mostly on the marine and air environment. Nevertheless, the investigation of the sustainability of the sector requires the knowledge of the structural components and trends of the industry. In this context, cruise shipping is a diversified maritime activity with the operational characteristics of a typical maritime transport service, especially in terms of safety and security, whilst the primary motivation is not the transport of a passenger from one place to another but the luxury accommodation of visitors onboard (Stefanidaki and Lekakou, 2012a). The provision of high level services and the range of onboard activities are characteristic of the industry and as such cruise ships are often compared to shore based hotels.

The contemporary sector is characterized by three major trends: Gigantism, Oligopolization and Destinazation (GDO) (Stefanidaki and Lekakou, 2014).

Oligopolization refers to the domination of the market by a few companies. Carnival Corporation & PLC and Royal Caribbean International are the two major groups constituting more than 70 percent of the market (Cruise Market Watch, 2015). Concentration is observed in ownership resulting in the imbalanced distribution of the power among the various stakeholders involved and in itineraries, meaning that the actual cruise traffic is concentrated in certain cruise ports – both home ports and port of calls – in each geographic market.

Since 1970 ship size has been quintupled in terms of GT, and tripled in terms of passenger capacity. As cruise ships become larger, new services are added in order to satisfy the expectations and needs of diversified users (Lekakou *et al.*, 2014). Ship size is connected with economies of scales whilst increasing the potential of onboard revenues. To that extent, the ship is becoming the "destination" and core of the cruise experience, while the contribution of the destination to the overall experience is gradually decreased (Keynote, 2008).

In its beginning the activity was considered as an alternative type of tourism, which due to its limited clientele had almost zero side effects at destination level, whereas passengers' high income level produced significant economic effects at the calling port-cities. However, after the 1990s when a tremendous development was recorded, the profile of the industry gradually altered and currently the sector is characterized by massiveness. Both the cruise ships and the cruise passengers are considered sources of impacts. In this context, the sustainability of the cruise activity is frequently questioned mostly due to its routines at the calling destinations and the potential of negatively impacting the environment and the host societies. Based on the historical evolution of the cruise sector the core question to be investigated is to what extent can the business strategies currently adopted by the cruise industry to contribute to the maintenance and preservation of the natural resources while creating value for the local economies and enhance the sociocultural diversity of the port communities. So far the concept of sustainable entrepreneurship is lacking from the cruise tourism's literature, despite the fact that there are various authors who investigate the subcriteria of industry's sustainability both at regional and global level.

The objective of this chapter is to conduct an exploratory review of the business practices applied from the cruise industry in order to ascertain whether the companies' operations and practices are "compatible" with the concept of sustainable entrepreneurship. Specifically, based on Shepherd and Patzelt's (2011) triple bottom line approach, certain economic, societal and environmental parameters – preconditions of sustainable entrepreneurship – are examined. This section through a comprehensive review of the sustainability reports of the major groups and individual cruise companies aims at generating knowledge and to respond to the sustainability question concerning the international cruise sector.

How cruise shipping can affect the destination system

Economic effects

The way a cruise ship affects a destination is not a uniform process and depends both on the dominant trends in the international market and the structure of the regional system; however, the operations occurred at each destination do not present sufficient differences. The contribution of the sector to the national and local economy depends on the level of expenditure conducted by the "producers" and the "consumers" of the cruise itinerary, meaning operators, passengers and crew. Nevertheless, the type and size of the destination (mainland vs. island), the ports' character (home port vs. port of call) and the developmental stage differentiate the economic impact of the activity on a local basis (Stefanidaki and Lekakou, 2012b). The generated economic impact is anticipated to diverge in local and national level (Dwyer and Forsyth, 1998), implying that, at regional level, the cruise activity can evidence important effects, while, at national level, the contribution to the GNP may be negligible (Dwyer *et al.*, 2004).

Based on OECD data (2015), the average spending per cruise visit is estimated at $100 while the average economic contribution is estimated at $200. Nonetheless, it should be stressed that while averages can facilitate the understanding of the potential economic effects of the cruise industry, not all passengers become cruise visitors at every destination (Wilkinson, 1999) and as such the application of averages can be misleading.

As regards the economic effects, the Cruise Line International Association conducts every year an economic impact assessment and at the same time there is a number of regional economic studies, mostly for established destinations. However, the economic contribution of the industry to the various destinations is contested since this is concentrated into specific cities (countries) in which cruise companies or significant complementary service providers are located. This is the case of North America, Italy and Germany, etc. Concerning calling destinations there is a strong controversy about the net/actual benefits generated. It is argued that the model applied is similar to the "all inclusive" of shore based hotels and as such the impact is poor concerning only a limited number of economic activities like catering and transport. Johnson (2006) argues that it is typical for a cruise line to add profit margin of up to 60–100 percent to shore excursions generating significant economic leakages. Simultaneously, the practice of cruise ships to call at destinations for only a limited time – ranging from three to five hours – restricts excursion possibilities and thus the potential of passengers to spend more on local activities, while the passengers are unwilling to miss their onboard lunch which is already included into their vacation package and its cost.

Environmental concerns

A contemporary critique the sector receives is that this is not sustainable (Diedrich, 2010) due to the way regional sectors are expanded and developed, neglecting the social and environmental effects of the activity (Brida and Zapata Aguirre, 2010; Butt, 2007; Diedrich, 2010; Dodson and Gill, 2006; Klein, 2009). However, Sweeting and Wayne (2006) suggest that cruise shipping has minor environmental impacts compared to the entire shipping activity, but when a cruise ship calls at a port with a fragile ecosystem, such as Alaska or the Caribbean, the impacts can be considerable. The ascertainment of Saveriades (2000) a few decades ago about the "smokeless" nature of the tourism industry also has application to cruise tourism. Since 1990 there has been a raised awareness about the environmental effects of cruise ships' operation both at sea or ashore, a fact confirmed by Johnson (2006) who argues that almost 70 percent of the cruise destinations are found in places of high biodiversity.

Sweeting and Wayne (2006) argue that even if the activity is well regulated by the International Maritime Organization and national authorities, there is evidence that the cruise sector is not acting responsibly, since there are cruise companies which were fined for the violation of environmental regulations. Klein (2011) asserts that wastewater treatment, air emissions and solid wastes are the contemporary challenges the industry needs to address. Apart from ships' operation effects on the ecosystem, the interventions occurred at destination level are also affecting the quality of the natural environment. Butt (2007) suggests that significant pressures originate from the modifications taking place in the natural and built surrounding with the construction of new port infrastructures, the most common ones. Denature can also result from the exploitation of local energy resources (Johnson, 2002). Johnson (2002) asserts that a core problem for assessing the environmental effects of cruising is the difficulty of monetizing the impacts, in contrast to the economic ones which are more easily captured and perceived, and classifies them into infrastructural, operational (use of energy, water, air pollution), distributional (tourists' travels and logistics of the cruise ship supply chain), use impacts (during the cruise passengers' activities in a destination) and waste (related with IMO regulations)

Social concerns

Apart from the obvious interventions, there are also "invisible" social effects that are not immediately perceived and thus not properly addressed from current literature. This is due to the time needed to be evolved, before the alterations to the societal structure receive more permanent character. Burdge and Vanclay (1995, 59) suggest that social impacts

> include all social and cultural consequences on human populations by any public or private action that alters the ways in which people live, work, play, relate to one another, organize to meet their needs, and generally cope as members of society.

The development of the local cruise sector may have a variety of impacts for the host populations. One of the most important ones is the positive interaction between locals and passengers (Brida and Aquirre, 2008). In the case of Messina (Brida *et al.*, 2012) the host population recognizes that the cruise activity increased the level of public and private investments, as well as employment opportunities. On the other hand, regarding the cultural interaction, residents expressed the opinion that cruise shipping has a positive effect since they learn about other cultures. At the same time through this process, local tradition is valorized and tourism and commercial infrastructure is improved. It should be also stressed that the locals recognized that the outcomes from the activity were more for the external business parties than for the community.

Another research realized by the Center of Ecotourism and Sustainable Development for Belize revealed similar findings. Again investments, job opportunities and improvement of infrastructures were identified as major positive effects. Respectively, insufficient spending and antagonism with stayover tourists were referred to as the negative ones. In the field of social parameters, it was shown that cultural sharing and learning was the dominant perception. On the opposite side, the negative perceived effects focused on the increase of crime, violence and drug use, rise in land prices, traffic and congestion. Wilkinson (1999) studying the cruise tourism in the Caribbean set the dilemma whether this type of growth is an illusion or delusion and argues that economic effects are "minimal" and mostly related to "some jobs and income." In the same context, Sheridan and Teal (2006) argue that while cruise tourism is generally perceived as a generator of prosperity, it seems that this does not correspond to the needs of local societies. The same authors, in the case of Ensenada–Mexico, observed that the cruise operators add pressure the cruise operators add pressure on local authorities to improve infrastructures and services and this was passed on to the taxpayers. Among the benefits gained from the cruise industry, locals recognized employment and income, while the major impact was generated on the service and hospitality sector. Respectively, in the case of Cozumel, it was observed that from 1965 till 2003 the local population showed an increase of 2400 percent because of the development of the regional cruise sector. Also, during that period local business was replaced by outside competitors.

Klein (2005) highlights the congestion created in public places which leads to the disruption of residents' everyday life. High levels of concentrations creates pressures on the residents leading to the alteration of their daily routines. In the case of Santorini apart from the recognition of congestion and the intense use of community infrastructures, residents said that cruise tourism has contributed to the establishment of new professions not necessarily compatible with the identity of the island while the international clientele visiting the destination and the limited hours remaining lead to the need for fast and cheap products (Stefanidaki and Lekakou, 2015).

Restriction of space and competition for the same activities (such as transport means) are referred to as phenomena that affect host community routines and can lead to the adoption of different moral conducts (Zapata-Aguirre and Brida, 2008). Indicative is the fact that in some cases the ratio of cruise passengers/residents is very high (Espinal, 2005 cited in Zapata-Aguirre and Brida,

2008). Prevailing conditions also generate poor acceptability of the cruise industry and low support by the local societies. It is noted that residents of crowded destinations have more negative perception towards the touristic activity (Pizam, 1978), as happened in Venice recently, where activists protested against the big cruise ships.

Corporate strategies and cruise industry sustainability

In this context, the cruise industry recognizes the impacts generated at the environment and destinations and implements specific actions and activities in order to preserve natural resources, protect biodiversity and ensure its sustainability. In this section the strategies of the main companies are briefly presented and examined.

Carnival Corporation & PLC

"Cruising-Commitment-Community" is the message of Carnival Corporation & PLC.

Carnival has developed a holistic assessment of the environmental, social, governance and economic aspects of its operations. In this context, the company sets multiple environmental and social considerations for the day-to-day operations of its fleet which is not part of a Corporate Social Responsibility program but a strategic choice, as referred in its Sustainability Report (2013). The company's dedication to the objective of mitigating the negative externalities of its operations is seen in its decision to have environmental officers on board in order to ensure compliance and implementation of corporate procedures.

The group has established certain goals and corresponding activities in an effort to increase the efficiency of its operations and simultaneously to lessen the impact on natural resources. Currently, the main challenge of the shipping industry is to minimize its impact on air quality through reducing its contribution to the formulation of CO_2 emissions. International regulations set certain objectives concerning ship based emissions and determine sensitive areas as well the synthesis of fuels to be used in these areas. In this context, Carnival has set as a corporate target the reduction of CO_2 by 20 percent. To achieve this objective, 20 percent of the Carnival fleet is equipped with shore power connections. At the same time, the group monitors, reports and verifies the GHG emissions produced by its fleet in an effort to manage its impact on air environment and adjust its strategies to the prevailed conditions each time and set new targets. This evaluation takes place not only for the fleet's operation but also for the full supply chain. The group's R&D department aims at evaluating and establishing new technologies. The system applied is called ECO-Exhaust Gas Cleaning[1] and the company claims this is a pioneering approach as combining two methods for the reduction of exhaust emissions. Energy efficiency is another field in which the group invests, and as such has established a Corporate Energy Conservation aiming at reducing the overall energy consumption of the group. In this context, the group supports a number of initiatives that move beyond regulations and include various aspects from ship designing, to minimizing fuel consumption or energy saving initiatives, etc.

Water consumption is another aspect of the corporate strategy and the company and in this field has been able to produce 73 percent of potable water from sea water, while the rest is purchased from shore. In the field of waste management, the company apart from complying with the international regulations regarding waste disposal at sea, moves beyond applying a strategy based on recycling and packaging reducing. Food sourcing is another field which the group pays attention to. Carnival has set corporate standards with respect to the selection of appropriate food producers.

Royal Caribbean Cruises Ltd

Royal Caribbean Ltd is the second most important group of the cruise industry. The group represents 27 percent of the cruise market in terms of passengers and includes Azamara Club Cruises, Celebrity Cruises and Royal Caribbean International. The sustainability policy of the Royal Caribbean Ltd gives priority to the safeguarding of the oceans and destinations as well the health and well-being of its guests and crews.

The group shares the common view that destination stewardship is a responsibility shared among local government, tourism businesses, communities and guests. To that extent the group has developed since 2010 the Sustainable Shore Excursion Standard in order to facilitate companies when selecting operators that provide high quality of shore excursion and at the same time support local communities and preserve the environment. The core corporate principle is "Above and Beyond Compliance." Since 1992 the group has established the program "Save the Waves" in an effort to improve its environmental performance. Since then the program has been evolved representing the company's philosophy. In this context, the group has set various objectives ranging from reduction of the air emissions to provision of information to guests and key stakeholders about the group's environmental priorities and practices.

In the field of environmental management and responsibility the group is applying a variety of activities. The Ocean Fund supports financially the University of Miami's Rosenstie School of Marine and Atmospheric Science which operates two labs on board RCL fleet and specialized equipment for monitoring oceanographic and atmospheric data related to climate change. Concerning the reduction of air emissions the group is applying certain measures toward this objective, which as reported in its sustainability report has led to a reduction of 20.6 percent per available passenger-cruise day since 2005. In the majority of RCL's fleet the Advance Exhaust Purification Systems are tested.

Apart from the internal efforts made to ensure that corporate operations are satisfying the principles of sustainability, the RCL is making its guest a component of its sustainability strategy whilst this becomes part of their experience. To that extent, cruise visitors are informed about companies' efforts and moreover, some companies provide to their guests the opportunity to further support certain destinations through donations. This is the case of Celebrity Cruises which visits the Galapagos and gives the opportunity to its guests to donate to the Galapagos Fund, which the company together with the Virginia-based Galapagos Conservancy manages. RCL in order to promote its sustainable profile is supporting organizations through financing. Specifically, during 2013, $700,000 was awarded from the Ocean Fund. Complementary, 34 percent of shore excursions are offered from providers who have enrolled in a sustainable tourism education and verification program. Another significant initiative is the development and piloting of destination monitoring tool and the implementation of action projects.

RCL's corporate citizenship programs are aimed at strengthening and enhancing companies' relationships with the communities of the destinations at which their cruise ships call and support the progress of less privileged communities. In this context the group during 2013 was engaged in various activities toward this objective, like charities, disaster relief contribution, employees donations, wish at sea program, etc. As it is stated corporate actions focus on organizations that can benefit communities as a whole and more specifically support activities dealing with children and families, educational programs and marine environment conservation. United Way, Breast Cancer Research Foundation, The Miami Foundation and Make-A-Wish are some of the foundations currently cooperating.

Additionally, the group has established the "Get Involved Volunteer Everywhere" (GIVE) since 1997 as a way to motivate and mobilize its personnel while involving suppliers and other business partners to assist non-profit organizations working for the improvement of communities' conditions.

NCL

NCL recognizes the environment as "a core value" of its business and as such has developed the Eco-Smart cruising program for demonstrating this commitment. Alike, the company's main objectives include activities that minimize the environmental footprint of its operation through garbage disposal and wastes, recycling and re-use of materials, prevention of accidents, etc. Specifically, the company reports 30 percent recycling rates while all the ships of the company are equipped with advanced water waste treatment systems. Corporate reports make reference to the practice followed in the port of Miami, where cooking oil is delivered to a local farmer who converts it to bio-diesel fuel. Moreover, the company is using low sulfur fuels in sensitive regions and simultaneously applies several other activities such as low power lighting, automatic air conditioning systems, voyage routing optimization systems, etc., in order to reduce fuel consumption and consequently emissions. The company is initiating the Norwegian's Breakaway Plus class which as claimed will be the first cruise ship equipped with innovative scrubber technology and will be as eco-friendly as possible. Environmental officers are responsible for supervising the environmental performance and efficiency.

NCL is also collaborating with one of the largest producer of wind and solar power in North America and provides to its guests the opportunity, through a donation program, to contribute to the construction of renewable energy projects across the United States, by giving the amount of $10 per person per cruise. In addition the company has established an environmental educational program addressed to its guests in order to encourage participation in voluntary programs. Focus is given to young cruisers who can be educated through the Officer Snook Water Pollution program about the impacts of marine pollution and further can be involved in simulated beach cleanup.

Apart from the environment commitment, NCL also develops corporate giving activities that can benefit the community. In this context, the company supports the Make-A-Wish foundation, the Camillus House, an organization that supports poor and homeless persons, and the Virlanie foundation in the Philippines that provides protection for underprivileged children. Finally, NCL operates a donation program that supports various activities and foundations.

Table 14.1 summarizes the main sustainability practices applied by cruise companies.

Table 14.1 Summary of the main sustainability practices applied by cruise companies

Sustainability area	Industry's practices
Sources of life/environment	**Air pollution** • Innovative eco technology for the mitigation of air emissions • Use of cleaner fuels • Use of renewable sources of energy • Hull design optimization • Energy efficient equipment • Active involvement in research projects **Wastewater** • Advanced wastewater treatment systems • Oil filtering equipment **Wastes/garbage** • Recycling • Packaging reducing
Community	• Selection of food suppliers applying sustainable practices/standards • Sustainable Shore Excursions standards
Economic gain for the community	• Income generation from cruise companies' expenses, passengers' and crew spending • Selection of local suppliers, etc
Non-economic gains to the society	• Philanthropic activities through which the activities of the various NGOs and other foundations are supported • Volunteer initiatives involving cruise passengers and companies' staff

Conclusions

Cruise shipping is a prominent paradigm of globalized industry generating multiple effects both positive and negative – at destinations' systems. Cruise companies demonstrate acknowledge of their responsibility towards the protection and preservation of the natural resources while recognizing the impacts generated at the host populations due to their operations. To that extent, corporate sites illustrate the various policies and strategies currently applied by the companies addressing sustainability issues, whilst at the same time they inform the various stakeholders about corporate priorities and promote the companies' responsible image. The willingness of the industry to demonstrate its proactiveness has been further enforced by the recent Costa Concordia accident, which occurred near the Italian coast and received much publicity. However, the impacts reported at the various destinations compared to the activities illustrated at companies' sustainability reports leads to contradictory views.

The review of the sustainability reports of the major cruise groups shows that environmental protection is top priority across the industry and in this context the range of environmental activities and initiatives adopted are reported in a highly descriptive way. Air emissions have been a major concern for the shipping industry in general. IMO's International Convention for the Prevention of Pollution from Ships is the main regulative framework applied to all ships aiming at preventing the pollution of the marine environment. The Convention also regulates oil pollution, sewage, garbage and air pollution. It is clear that cruise ships are obliged to follow the rules in order to maintain their operations. However, cruise ships, mostly due to their size, produce large volumes of wastes, wastewater and emissions and this is a major reason for which cruise companies proclaim their beyond regulations philosophy in the context of the market's effort for self-regulation. In this context, the cruise industry's practices aim at minimizing the spillover effects of their routines and thus the sustainable character of the industry could be argued.

However, maintaining the quality of the ecosystems where cruise ships operate offers certain entrepreneurial opportunities/potentials. Specifically, as suggested by Johnson (2006) the coastal ecotourism experience which is currently lacking as an alternative shore excursion. The creation of this type of shore side activities in wide scale/across the industry could not only contribute to the maintenance of ecosystems and natural resources but also to the generation of economic gains for the local communities. Moreover, as noted by Klein (2011), the applied technological advances can only have limited effects and as such the development of appropriate technologies could become an opportunity of entrepreneurship and innovation.

Community engagement is another field of corporate responsibility. Companies focus on the economic impacts generated at local level, through the spending of companies, passengers and crew. However, corporate reporting on the economic impacts generated is poor and as noted there is no reference to specific initiatives addressing the economic gap in community level, while infrastructural interventions are the kind of activities mostly referred (Bonilla-Priego *et al.*, 2014). The most frequent criticism in the field of communities' economic gains is the uneven distribution of benefits and equitability (Klein, 2011). This could be considered as a failure of the local system and as such the establishment of standard communication channels can provide the companies with the necessary info about their impacts in regional level and further with sufficient solutions. This presupposes that cruise destinations dispose monitoring mechanisms and specialized indicators, meaning that potentially the communities should develop not only a reactive behavior in order to address cruise challenges but also a proactive conduct by generating the appropriate institutional framework that can ensure environmental preservation and social well-being (Vemuri and Constaza, 2006). Such an approach may enhance and further facilitate the development of sustainable entrepreneurship in regional level. The "No Navi Grandi" social initiative in Venice can be perceived as a forerunner of an institutional reform based on the community's activism and awareness. In fact, this movement has managed to result in certain changes in the way cruise ships operate in the Grand Canal and currently both local authorities and the industry are in pursuit of alternatives.

Corporate foundations are the mechanism through which grants are allocated to the various institutions and NGOs aiming at supporting research, community projects and other philanthropic activities. Moreover, responsibility is becoming part of the cruise experience, since cruise passengers are educated in sustainability issues while provided with the opportunity to support companies' sustainability programs. It is worth mentioning that the majority of the charities and donations are mostly directed to the countries where the cruise companies' headquarters are located. Bonilla-Priego *et al.* (2014) reviewing the sustainability reports of the cruise companies note that the majority of the companies do not report regularly on CSR but responsibility issues are addressed through corporate sites in the context of sustainability strategies. The same authors also suggest that the cruise industry is "in the early stages of accepting responsibility" justified by the small number of companies which report. Moreover, the companies provide info about soft indicators and few data are available about core business practices. This is not a surprising outcome when compared with the practices followed by other segments of the shipping industry. More specifically, based on CSR relevant research for shipping it was concluded that the industry is a CSR laggard despite the innovative character of the activity (Skovgaard, 2012). However, the direct interaction of the cruise industry with passengers and other stakeholders make the need to be sustainable more urgent than ever, mostly due to the diachronic trend of ships' gigantism and the increasing volumes of cruise passengers.

It becomes apparent that the industry is using a blend of activities to manage its sustainability. As in the case of cargo shipping, the question to be investigated is which are the responsibility boundaries of a cruise company, given the fact that the cruise activity is crossing the borders of a single country and responsibility spectrum varies from local to global. Aforementioned cruise companies are focusing much of their philanthropic efforts on North America and especially Miami, which is the location of many cruise companies' headquarters. From this perspective someone can claim that the industry is addressing the issue of economic value creation, job positions, etc. but gains have geographic limitations and concentration. On the other hand, there are calling destinations that receive limited benefits compared to the resources committed for serving the cruise ships. In this context, someone could question the sustainability of the industry, since there is an unbalanced distribution of the benefits not only among destinations but also among various regions of similar profile. Summarizing, it is concluded that the industry is promoting the adoption of best practices for the management of sustainability issues, beyond regulation standards, nevertheless the actual net impacts both on the environment, the economy and society are not well documented mostly due to the lack of diachronic research.

This has been a first attempt to approach the cruise industry from a business sustainable approach and to explore the parameters that can determine the nature of cruise sustainable entrepreneurship. Nevertheless, future research should address issues beyond the industry's sustainable profile and responsible image and explore whether and if the industry integrates the principles of the sustainable entrepreneurship into its day-to-day operations, the motives for the adoption of environmental friendly technologies, the practices and process adopted when initiating a new destination to their itineraries and the mechanism for resolving potential community conflicts as well the drivers for the creation of new cruise packages and services. In addition, it would be of high importance to investigate how the cruise industry can become the source of sustainable entrepreneurship and start-ups that can benefit the regional economic structure and maintain socio-cultural identity and moreover how the sector can enhance this type of businesses through using their products and services.

Note

1 The ECO-EGC system includes two major systems; the first one concerns the usage of filters that reduces particles matters emitted from the engines and the other the usage of seawater to remove sulfur compounds from the exhaust gases.

References

Bonilla-Priego M.J., Font X. and Pachero-Olivares M.D.R. (2014) "Corporate sustainability reporting index and baseline data for cruise industry" *Tourism Management* 44 149–160.

Brida J.G. and Zapata-Aguirre S. (2010) "Economic impacts of cruise tourism: The case of Costa Rica" *Anatolia: An International Journal of Tourism and Hospitality Research* 21(2) 322–338.

Brida J.G., Riano E.M. and Zapata-Aguirre S. (2012) "Residents' attitudes and perception toward cruise tourism development: A case study of Cartegena de Indias, Colombia" *Tourism and Hospitality Research* 11 181–196.

Burdge R. and Vanclay F. (1995) "Social impact assessment" in Vanclay F. and Bronstein D.A (eds.) *Environmental and Social Impact Assessment* Chichester, Wiley, 31–65.

Butt N. (2007) "The impact of cruise ship generated waste on home ports and ports of call: A study of Southampton" *Marine Policy* 31 591–598.

Carnival Corporation & PLC (2013) *Sustainability Report FY2013.*

COM (2014)86 "A European Strategy for More Growth and Jobs in Coastal and Maritime Tourism."

Cruise Market Watch (2015), *Growth of the Cruise Line Industry.* www.cruisemarketwatch.com/growth/.

Diedrich A. (2010) "Cruise ship tourism in Belize: The implications of developing cruise ship tourism in an ecotourism destination" *Ocean & Coastal Management* 3(5–6) 234–244.

Dodson S. and Gill A. (2006) "Environmental policy challenges for cruise industry: Case studies from Australia and the USA" in Ross K. Dowling (ed.) *Cruise Ship Tourism* CABI Publishing, London, 338–349.

Douglas N. and Douglas N. (2004) "Cruise ship passenger spending patterns in Pacific island ports" *International Journal of Tourism Research* 6 251–261.

Dwyer L. and Forsyth P. (1998) "Economic significance of tourism" *Annals of Tourism Research* 25 393–415.

Dwyer L., Forsyth P. and Spurr R. (2004) "Evaluating tourism's effects: New and old approaches" *Tourism Management* 25 307–317.

Johnson D. (2002) "Environmentally sustainable cruise tourism: A reality check" *Marine Policy* 26(4) 261–270.

Johnson D. (2006) "Providing ecotourism excursions for cruise passengers" *Journal of Sustainable Tourism* 14(1) 43–54.

Keynote (2008) *Cruise Market.* Keynote Limited.

Klein R. (2005) "Playing off the ports: BC and the cruise tourism industry" Canadian Center for Policy Alternatives, Halifax, Nova Scotia. www.cruisejunkie.com/ccpa3.pdf.

Klein R. (2009) "Cruising without a bruising: Cruise tourism and the maritimes" Canadian Center for Policy Alternatives, Halifax, Nova Scotia. www.cruisejunkie.com/ccpa4.pdf.

Klein R.A. (2011) "Responsible cruise tourism: Issues of cruise tourism and sustainability" *Journal of Hospitality and Tourism Management* 18 107–116.

Lekakou M., Stefanidaki E., Bras I. and Vintzilaios D. (2014) "Information-knowledge-experience: Heraklion: a *'brand new'* traditional cruise destination" paper presented at the 5th International Cruise Conference (ICC5), Bremerhaven, January, 24–26.

Papathanassis A. and Beckmann I. (2011) "Assessing the 'poverty of cruise theory' hypothesis" *Annals of Tourism Research* 38(1) 153–174.

Pizam A. (1978) "Tourism impacts: The social costs to the destination community as perceived by its residents" *Journal of Tourism Research* 16(4) 8–12.

OECD (2014) *The Competitiveness of Global Port-Cities,* OECD Publishing.

Royal Caribbean Cruise Ltd (2014) *Sustainability Report.*

Saveriades A. (2000) "Establishing the social tourism carrying capacity for the tourist resorts of the East Coast of the Republic of Cyprus" *Tourism Management* 21(2) 147–156.

Shepherd D.A. and Patzelt H. (2011) "The new field of sustainable entrepreneurship: Studying entrepreneurial action linking 'what is to be sustained' with 'what is to be developed" *Entrepreneurship Theory and Practice* 35 137–163.

Sheridan L. and Teal G. (2006) "Fantasy and reality: Tourist and local experiences of cruise ship tourism in Ensenada, Baja California, Mexico" in Ross K. Dowling (ed.) *Cruise Ship Tourism* CABI Publishing, London, 315–326.

Skovgaard, J. (2012) "Corporate social responsibility in the Danish shipping industry" paper presented at the DRUI Academy Conference, University of Cambridge, January 19–21.

Stefanidaki E. and Lekakou M. (2012a) "Liberalization assessment: The Greek cruise market" *Tourism* 60(1) 91–105.

Stefanidaki E. and Lekakou M. (2012b) "Generated economic impact to cruise destinations: The Piraeus case" in A. Papathanassis, T. Lucovic and M. Vogel (eds.) *Cruise Tourism and Society: A Socioeconomic Perspective* Springer-Verlag, Berlin Heidelberg, 69–84.

Stefanidaki E. and Lekakou M. (2014) "The cruise carrying capacity: A conceptual approach" *Research in Transport Business & Management* 13 43–52.

Sweeting J.E.N and Wayne S.L. (2006) "Shifting tide: Environmental challenges and cruise industry responses" in Ross K. Dowling (ed.) *Cruise Ship Tourism* CABI Publishing, London, 327–337.

Vemuri W.A. and Constaza R. (2006) "The role of human, social, built, and natural capital in explaining life satisfaction at the country level: Toward a National Well-Being Index (NWI)" *Ecological Economics* 58 119–133.

Wild P. and Dearing J. (2000) "Development of and prospects for cruising in Europe" *Maritime Policy and Management* 27(4) 315–337.

Wilkinson P. (1999) "Caribbean cruise tourism: Delusion? Illusion?" *Tourism Geographies* 1 261–282.

Wood R. (2000) "Caribbean cruise tourism: Globalization at sea" *Annals of Tourism Research* 345–370.

Zapata-Aguirre S. and Brida J.G. (2008) "The impacts of the cruise industry on tourism destinations" in V. Castellani and S. Sala (eds) *Sustainable Tourism as a Factor of Local Development*, Tangram Edizioni Scientifiche (Colla). Available at SSRN: http://ssrn.com/abstract=1298403.

Part III
Policy and institutional perspectives

15 Sustainable development and entrepreneurship

Mapping definitions, determinants, actors and processes

Emmanuel Raufflet, Luc Brès, Sofiane Baba and Louis Jacques Filion

Introduction

Researchers in the field of entrepreneurship have shown an increasing interest in sustainable development over the last two decades. This chapter, based on a review of 135 papers published between 1992 and 2014, maps the definitions, determinants, actors and processes of sustainable entrepreneurship, and the conclusion identifies some avenues for future research. It follows and improves a previous publication on this subject (Brès *et al.*, 2011).

Sustainable development and entrepreneurship: mapping definitions

Sustainable entrepreneurship has emerged only recently as a field of study (Richomme-Huet and De Freyman, 2011), and lies at the intersection of two other relatively new fields, namely sustainable development and entrepreneurship. The primary challenge faced by researchers is to define and conceptualize the key elements that characterize this interface between two fields (Hall *et al.*, 2010), and to consolidate past research (Shepherd and Patzelt, 2011) into three closely related formulations, namely sustainable entrepreneurship, eco-entrepreneurship and social entrepreneurship.

Researchers have coined several different terms for the overlapping concepts of environmental entrepreneur (Linnanen, 2002), green entrepreneur (Walley and Taylor, 2002; Berchicci, 2005), ecological entrepreneur (Marsden and Smith, 2005), ecopreneur (Pastakia, 1998; Isaak, 2002; Schaltegger, 2002; Dixon and Clifford, 2007) and sustainable entrepreneur (Cohen and Winn, 2007; Dean and McMullen, 2007; Katsikis and Kyrgidou, 2007; Choi and Gray, 2008a; Schaltegger and Wagner, 2011). Generally speaking, these three overlapping concepts refer to the same practices, but from different standpoints.

The 'field' that encompasses them – sustainable entrepreneurship – emerged and took shape gradually during the 1990s, in a somewhat confused process that fluctuated in intensity and peaked around the turn of the century (Schaper, 2005). Some key definitions drawn from papers published in scientific journals on this subject between 1998 and 2012 are listed in the table below:

Table 15.1 Mapping definitions

Definition	Examples
Ecopreneur	
'Individuals or institutions that attempt to popularise eco-friendly ideas and innovations either through the market or non-market routes may be referred to as ecopreneurs' (Pastakia, 1998)	Jerry Greenfield (Ben & Jerry's) Anita Roddick (Body Shop) Claus Hipp Hipp Co. (producers of baby food) Jambhekar (alternative fertilizers in India)
'A person who seeks to transform a sector of the economy towards sustainability by starting up a business in that sector with a green design, with green processes and with a life-long commitment to sustainability in everything that is said and done' (Isaak, 2002)	
'Actors and companies making environmental progress to their core business can be called ecopreneurs' (Schaltegger, 2002)	
'Entrepreneurs who found new businesses based on the principle of sustainability' (Kirkwood and Walton, 2010)	
Sustainable entrepreneur	
Uses Isaak's (2002) definition as a basis, and distinguishes this entrepreneur from a green entrepreneur using a comparison of green business and green green business: 'In this paper we have argued that the definition of green entrepreneurs should be wide, encompassing not only ecopreneurs (individuals who set up businesses founded on the principle of sustainability) but also opportunist entrepreneurs who happen to have found a green niche' (Walley and Taylor, 2002)	Jerry Greenfield (Ben & Jerry's) Anita Roddick (Body Shop) Hackett Electronics/Maxim Power Green Building Council (a group of industry members) Chios Gum Mastic, Greeks Growers (cooperative) Ray Anderson (Carpet interface)
'We define sustainable entrepreneurship as the examination of how opportunities to bring into existence future goods and services are discovered, created, and exploited, by whom, and with what economic, psychological, social, and environmental consequences' (Cohen and Winn, 2007)	
As many types of sustainable entrepreneurs as there are market failures: 'Coasian entrepreneurship, institutional entrepreneurship, market appropriating entrepreneurship, political entrepreneurship, producer focused informational (Austrian) entrepreneurship, customer focused informational entrepreneurship' (Dean and McMullen, 2007)	

'The teleological process aiming at the achievement of sustainable development, by discovering, evaluating and exploiting opportunities and creating value that produces economic prosperity, social cohesion and environmental protection' (Katsiskis and Kyrgidou, 2007)

'Entrepreneurs who create and build profitable companies that also pursue environmental or social causes' (Choi and Gray, 2008a)

'Actors and companies making environmental progress to their core business can be called sustainable entrepreneurs. They generate new products, services, techniques and organizational modes that substantially reduce environmental impacts and increase the quality of life. ... Sustainable entrepreneurs destroy existing conventional production methods, products, market structures and consumption patterns, and replace them with superior environmental and social products and services. They create the market dynamics of environmental and societal progress' (Schaltegger and Wagner, 2011)

'Sustainable entrepreneurship is focused on the preservation of nature, life support, and community in the pursuit of perceived opportunities to bring into existence future products, processes, and services for gain, where gain is broadly construed to include economic and non-economic gains to individuals, the economy, and society' (Shepherd and Patzelt, 2011)

This table clearly shows the diversity of terms used to refer to the notion of sustainable development and entrepreneurship, and hints at the problems this proliferation may cause. Until the early 2000s, these various terms tended to be employed interchangeably, and their definitions were fairly broad. Generally speaking, they referred to individuals who were concerned about the environment, and sometimes about the social impacts of their activities (Pastakia, 1998; Choi and Gray, 2008a). Subsequently, however, two separate trends have emerged, one built around ecopreneurs and the other around sustainable entrepreneurs (Gibbs, 2009).

Ecopreneurs or sustainable entrepreneurs?[1]

The concepts of ecopreneur and green entrepreneur are similar and somewhat older than the concept of sustainable entrepreneur. Authors from the early 1990s who spoke of ecopreneurs usually focused their attention on case studies, including biographies or analyses of good practices (Pastakia, 1998; Dixon and Clifford, 2007), highlighting the entrepreneurs' ethical motivations and management techniques (Pastakia, 1998; Isaak, 2002; Schaltegger, 2002; Dixon and Clifford, 2007). Epistemologically speaking, these studies often took a normative approach, explicitly or implicitly presenting them as environmentally

Table 15.2 Ecopreneur and sustainable entrepreneur: major differences

Topics	Ecopreneur	Sustainable entrepreneur
Source discipline	Ethics/management	Economics
Historic origins and other keys	Sustainable development, United Nations Report on Development. Brundtland (1987) (See ref: World Commission … 1987)	Theory of entrepreneurship as a process of construction/ deconstruction (Schumpeter, 1954)
Trigger	Entrepreneur's motivations	Market failures
Perspective	Micro (biographies, case studies, etc.)	Macro (analysis of market trends)
Nature of the entrepreneur	Hero/an ideal to be achieved (Isaak, 2002)	Agents of innovation within the market (Filion, 1998; Dean and McMullen, 2007)
Effect on society	Double loop change (Argyris, 1993); the ecopreneur's aim is to change the system	Reactive or single loop (Argyris, 1993); sustainable entrepreneurs react to business opportunities and market opportunities in the environmental field, but do not wish to change the system

respectful heroes capable of transforming the economic system (Pastakia, 1998; Isaak, 2002; Schaltegger, 2002; Dixon and Clifford, 2007).

The terms *sustainable entrepreneur* and *sustainable entrepreneurship* have appeared more commonly in the literature since 2007 as growing numbers of researchers have taken an economic approach to the subject. Authors working on the connection between business opportunity and market failure clearly adopt an economic approach to entrepreneurship (Shepherd and Patzelt, 2011). Their definitions of sustainable entrepreneurship are viewed within the Schumpeterian framework of *destructive creation* in the way they explain the emergence of these new entrepreneurs and their unique relationship with the market (Albrecht, 2002; Pastakia, 1998; Cohen and Winn, 2007; Dean and McMullen 2007; Hockerts and Wüstenhagen, 2010), which differs from that of ecopreneurs (Pastakia, 1998; Isaak, 2002; Schaltegger, 2002; Dixon and Clifford, 2007). In many cases, their explanation for the surge in sustainable entrepreneurship is based on economic triggers, such as unmet needs in environmental protection and preservation. In some cases, sustainable entrepreneurs can act as agents of change: institutional entrepreneurs (to use a neo-institutional term) who upset the status quo and push their institutions towards sustainable development (Lindhult and Guizana, 2011).

The concept of sustainable entrepreneur presented above differs from the older notion of ecopreneur. Tenants of the ecopreneurship approach focus primarily on the need to consider ecological determinants, while authors who speak of sustainable entrepreneurs believe it is first and foremost about business opportunities related to sustainable development (Katsikis and Kyrgidou, 2007).

Anchoring the field in a broader debate

In 2007, Cohen and Winn called for the creation of a field of sustainable entrepreneurship. They argued that the same market failures that generated environmental and social problems were now conducive to radical technological and managerial innovations. Sustainable entrepreneurship would study a model of entrepreneurship within which actors could help address global and local environmental and social problems while receiving entrepreneurial economic rent, i.e. income generated between the time an innovation is launched and the time it is imitated (Collis and Montgomery, 2005). They identified two research avenues, namely the relationship between market failures and environmentally beneficial entrepreneurial opportunities, and sustainable entrepreneurship per se, and contended that sustainable entrepreneurship research differed from classical entrepreneurship research due to the emphasis on social and environmental goals, and aspirations to achieve a positive impact on the complex, global issues of sustainable development (Cohen and Winn, 2007).

Dean and McMullen, for their part, felt that the emerging field of sustainable entrepreneurship lay somewhere between welfare economics and classical entrepreneurship (Dean and McMullen, 2007). In their view, welfare economics pushes the idea that market failures are the roots of the social and environmental problems that prevent sustainable development goals from being achieved. On the other hand, the field of entrepreneurship regards these same failures as sources of business opportunities. The issue for sustainable entrepreneurship research is therefore to understand how sustainable entrepreneurs will exploit those failures in order to solve social and environmental problems while still generating profits. Dean and McMullen (2007) defined environmental entrepreneurship as a sub-field of sustainable entrepreneurship, between *environmental economics* and *entrepreneurship*.

It is reasonable to question the entrepreneurship-based theories from which the literature on sustainable entrepreneurship draws, and in which entrepreneurship-based theories sustainable entrepreneurship may be rooted. Sustainable entrepreneurship is an emerging field within the already emerging field of entrepreneurship, which is approached using standpoints from several disciplines with varying levels of paradigmatic consensus. Its conceptual foundations were laid by economists such as Schumpeter (1954), but the field is now addressed in almost all the humanities, especially management. The concepts of opportunity recognition and creation have become a central element of entrepreneurship, and some may see sustainable entrepreneurship as developing from there (e.g. the 'alert entrepreneur' (Kirzner, 1979)). However, sociologists engaged in entrepreneurship research expressed concern about ecological issues as early as the 1980s (Aldrich, 1986). Nowadays, there are some approaches in social renewal (Audretsch, 2007; Aldrich, 2012) that may offer promising paths for theorization of sustainable entrepreneurship.

The determinants of sustainable entrepreneurship

In all, researchers have identified seven determinants of sustainable entrepreneurship, namely (1) the scope and persistence of environmental problems (Dean, 2007), which trigger environment-related activities as business opportunities (Rose, 1990); (2) increasing raw material prices, which foster energy efficiency and renewable energy (Fiona, 2006; Doherty, 2007; Dale, 2008); (3) the emergence of new economic sectors attracting increasing interest from investors (Broad, 1991; Seabrook, 2004; Gangemi, 2006; Dean, 2007), especially in renewable energy; (4) public policies for sustainable development markets (Isaak, 2002); (5) greater public receptivity to sustainable development issues, thanks to education (Bonnet *et al.*, 2006; Tracey and Phillips, 2007; Nadim and Singh, 2011); (6) the quest for a better corporate image (Schaper, 2005; Clifton, 2008); and (7) the desire of some entrepreneurs to align their entrepreneurial intent with their values and their determination to change society (Kirkwood and Walton, 2010; Spence *et al.*, 2011).

Some studies proposed specific mappings of determinants. Hendrickson and Tuttle (1997) took a more straightforward approach, grouping sustainable entrepreneurship determinants into three categories: (1) values, i.e. the entrepreneur's personal ethics; (2) market opportunities; and (3) compliance, i.e. pressure to comply with what is socially acceptable. Kirkwood and Walton

(2010) analysed 14 New Zealand firms and identified five factors: (1) values; (2) the desire to earn a living; (3) passion; (4) the pleasure of working for themselves; (5) the identification of gaps in the market. Their study shows that, setting aside their environmental convictions, the motivations of ecopreneurs are similar to those of entrepreneurs in general. They also suggest that the financial motivations of ecopreneurs are less assertive than those of entrepreneurs in general.

The actors

Since 1992, research on 'sustainable entrepreneurs' can be divided into three main approaches, namely individual case studies, typologies or taxonomies of entrepreneurs, and research into common characteristics of sustainable entrepreneurs.

Intra-case: Individual case studies present sustainable entrepreneurs as complex and fascinating individuals with very high ethical standards (Choi and Gray, 2008a), driven by both idealism and pragmatism (Linnanen, 2002; Walley and Taylor, 2002; Schaper, 2005). These individuals reconcile these contradictory drives and create 'win-win-win' firms, i.e. firms that are profitable, socially beneficial and positive for the environment (Cathy and Edwyn, 1998). They are often portrayed as heroes, due to their values and actions (Broad, 1991; Dougherty, 2007; Waddock, 2008).

Inter-case: Taxonomic research focuses on the identification of different types of sustainable entrepreneurs and is often structured around the pull between idealism and opportunism (Linnanen, 2002; Walley and Taylor, 2002; Schaper, 2005; Kirkwood and Walton, 2010; Spence *et al.*, 2011). Dean and McMullen (2007) build a typology based on the types of market failures sustainable entrepreneurs seek to exploit. By contrast, Gerlach (2006) proposes a process-based approach to sustainable entrepreneurship, focusing on the existence of different promoters in organizations. While 'power' promoters intervene at policy level to promote rules associated with sustainable development, 'expert' promoters propose technical innovations, and 'process' promoters ensure that those innovations are implemented (Gerlach, 2006).

The following table presents these various typologies:

Understanding entrepreneurs' common characteristics

Choi and Gray (2008a) analysed 21 sustainable entrepreneurs – an unusually large sample for the field – and identified three common characteristics, namely: (1) they were experienced managers/entrepreneurs; (2) they could access unconventional financing, including loans from friends and relatives rather than from traditional investors which enabled them to maintain their flexibility; and (3) their management style was coherent, effective but somewhat unorthodox (Choi and Gray, 2008a).

Table 15.3 Typologies of sustainable entrepreneurs

Authors/year	Typology criteria	Types of entrepreneurs	Examples given
Walley and Taylor, 2002	Sustainable development or economic orientation	Innovative opportunist	Evan Connell (The Connell Group[1])
	Socio-economic environment favourable or unfavourable to sustainable development	Visionary champion	Anita Roddick (The Body Shop[2])
		Ethical maverick	Founder of The 8th Day Vegetarian Cafe[3] (Manchester)
		Adhoc enviropreneur	Tom Archer (The Archers[4])
Linnanen, 2002	Continuum between idealism and the desire to make a profit	Non-profit business	No example
		Successful idealist	No example
		Opportunist	No example
		Self-employed	No example
Schaltegger, 2002	Entrepreneur's impact on industry sector	Environmental administration	Systems: ISO[5] 14000, EMAS[6]
	Priority to environmental issues (ecopreneur seen as the last stage of sustainable entrepreneurship development)	Environmental management	Geberit Ltd.[7]
		Alternative actors	Ballard Power[8]
		Bioneer	Hess Nature[9]
		Ecopreneur	Landis & Staefa[10]
Gerlach, 2006	Area of expertise (political expertise, ability to innovate, management, network)	Power promoter	BP Group11 CEO Sir John Browne
		Expert promoter	Specific Commission
		Process promoter	No example
		Relationship promoter	No example
Dean and McMullen, 2007	A type of entrepreneur for each type of market failure	Coasian entrepreneurship (public property)	Private lighthouse keepers
		Institutional entrepreneurship (externalities)	Richard Sandor (Chicago Climate Exchange12)
		Market appropriating entrepreneurship (monopolistic power)	MCI Telecom13
		Political entrepreneurship (productive government intervention)	Privatization of the stamp industry in the USA

	Importance ascribed to market aims as opposed to non-market aims		
Spence et al., 2011	Informational entrepreneurship (imperfect information) Aware (aware of the issues but guided by economic rationality) Indifferent (identifies only the economic aspect of sustainable development) Committed (understands and tries to be sensitive to sustainability issues while exhibiting particular responsibility for the environment)		Clipper Wind14 No example No example No example
Pacheco et al., 2010	Sustainable entrepreneurship discovery opportunities (extant economic incentive and reward systems) Sustainable entrepreneurship creation opportunities (require the alteration or creation of economic incentive and reward systems)		
Hockerts and Wüstenhagen, 2010	Davids (small firms whose market shares are often small. Social and environmental aims are at least as important as economic aims.) Goliaths (large firms with equally large market shares. Social and environmental aims are secondary to profit and economic aims.)		

Notes

1 Consulted in June 2011 www.theconnellgroup.co.uk/
2 www.thebodyshop.ca/en/index.aspx
3 www.eighth-day.co.uk/
4 www.bbc.co.uk/radio4/features/the-archers/
5 www.iso.org/iso/home.html
6 http://ec.europa.eu/environment/emas/index_en.htm
7 www.geberit.co.uk/web/appl/uk/wcmsuk.nsf/pages/index
8 www.ballard.com/
9 http://de.hessnatur.com/shop/showCmsContent.action?contentID=home
10 www.landisandstaefa.co.za/
11 www.bpgroup.ca/
12 www.chicagoclimatex.com/
13 www.mci.com/
14 www.clipperwind.com/

Mapping processes in sustainable entrepreneurship

Sustainable entrepreneurship raises the question of entrepreneurship and the innovation process in a more acute way, in that entrepreneurs pursue several goals at the same time. According to some authors, it is the very nature of technology that is called into question (McDonough and Braungart, 2002; Wennersten, 2008). One response to this challenge would be to take nature as a source and model of innovation, via biomimicry, which consists of designing products whose structure and operation imitate processes observed in nature (Benyus, 1997; Larson, 2000).

Management processes

A recurrent theme in the field is that sustainable entrepreneurs' management processes have yet to be studied. In fact, as noted by Schaper (2002), the phenomenon has, so far, only been examined occasionally, on a case-by-case basis.

Parrish (2010) studied the organizational design of four sustainable enterprises (Native Energy, ForesTrade, Hill Holt Wood and Chumbe Island Coral Park) active in four industries (marketing and finance, wholesale food distribution, training and tourism). His analysis of these four cases led him to identify five rules that guided the entrepreneurs' organizational design process (justification of their existence, production of synergy, reconciliation of competing goals, prioritization of decision choices and allocation of profits). He also distinguished two types of reasoning: (1) perpetual reasoning, focused more on qualitative aspects, values and intuition; and (2) operational reasoning, focused on economic rationality, quantitative aspects and maximization of profits.

One of the most advanced studies seeking to understand sustainable entrepreneurial processes was published only recently (Belz and Binder, 2015). These authors tackle the lack of processual empirical studies within the nascent sustainable entrepreneurship literature. They aim to understand how entrepreneurs recognize, develop and exploit opportunities in the context of sustainable development. Using a multiple case study approach, they identified six phases of the sustainable entrepreneurial process: recognizing a social or ecological issue; recognizing a social or ecological opportunity; developing a double bottom line solution; developing a triple bottom line solution; funding and forming of a sustainable enterprise; and creating or entering a sustainable market. Interestingly, these authors determine that the triple bottom lines of ecological, social and economic goals are integrated sequentially, not simultaneously.

Although the idea of process is present in most definitions of sustainable and social entrepreneurship (Dacin *et al.*, 2010), there are very few studies that investigate the process of sustainable entrepreneurship. Those that exist rely on qualitative research designs involving single and multiple case studies. Belz and Binder (2015) found that only six empirical studies have examined entrepreneurs' recognition, development and exploitation of ecological and social opportunities. Two of these studies focus on opportunity development (Corner and

Ho, 2010; Keskin *et al.*, 2013), two on opportunity recognition (Robinson, 2006; Shaw and Carter, 2007), one on opportunity exploitation (Choi and Gray, 2008a) and one on all phases (Perrini *et al.*, 2010).

Conclusions and avenues for future research

This chapter has mapped the key definitions, actors and processes of sustainable entrepreneurship. This critical analysis of sustainable entrepreneurship research has attempted to identify avenues for future research. Clearly, despite early attempts, sustainable entrepreneurship has yet to be developed as a field, and some potential ways to achieve this are also outlined in the following paragraphs.

Mapping definitions

Although it is still too early to speak of knowledge integration, it may be interesting to attempt to reconcile the views of authors who have studied ecopreneurs with those of authors who have studied sustainable entrepreneurship. Are the two standpoints complementary only, and destined to develop alongside one another, or could they in fact be integrated? We believe there are many potential synergic effects that could result from integrated knowledge development. From an epistemological standpoint, work is also required on the very structure of sustainable entrepreneurship, to see whether this emerging field should be built around two standpoints each reflecting one of the two most commonly identified practices, namely: (1) ecopreneurial practice and (2) entrepreneurial practice that regards sustainable development as one of several sources of business opportunities.

Mapping actors: beyond case studies

The methodological approaches have relied primarily on small numbers of case studies focusing on (1) the tension between entrepreneurial idealism and pragmatism, and (2) the construction of typologies. Gibbs (2009) also mentions the empirical weakness of the literature on ecopreneurs, arguing that this is one of the major criticisms that can be levelled at a body of literature built on fairly weak empirical foundations, including classic studies based on only six cases (Pastakia, 1998), four cases (Schaltegger, 2002) or four cases per typology, mostly in anecdotal form (Walley and Taylor, 2002).

Recently, however, the situation has evolved somewhat, as researchers and research organizations have begun to work with larger samples (Kirkwood and Walton, 2010; Kuckertz and Wagner, 2010; Spence *et al.*, 2011). The typology proposed by Schaltegger and Wagner (2011), for example, is based on an analysis of more than 41 European firms, and in 2010 Québec's *Fondation de l'Entrepreneurship* produced a joint survey of sustainable entrepreneurship, in collaboration with Léger Marketing and the *Caisse de dépôt et placement du*

Québec, in which more than 7,300 Québecers took part. The survey found that entrepreneurs under 35 years of age were particularly sensitive to the subject of sustainable entrepreneurship.

We also propose several other avenues for research, focusing on the entrepreneurs themselves: for example, the thinking and design of activity systems of entrepreneurs engaged in sustainable development (Filion, 1999, 2004), the connection between social values and entrepreneurial practice for entrepreneurial actors engaged in sustainable development activities, the relations systems of entrepreneurs engaged in sustainable development, and the characteristics of their organizations and the resources around them. Another potential topic is the way these entrepreneurs identify, develop and exploit the entrepreneurial opportunities that will form the basis of their entrepreneurial systems. It would also be interesting to observe their everyday activities (Mintzberg, 1973; Hill, 1991) and identify their common characteristics, their past history, what the future holds for them, and the possibilities for reconversion of those who abandon the field.

Mapping processes

Most past research has taken a diachronic approach to the individuals concerned (i.e. it has studied the individual at a given moment in time). Sustainable entrepreneurs are presented as individuals who are able to reconcile business logic, social welfare and environmental protection or improvement. But are these entrepreneurs, within the business life cycle of a growing firm, also able to reconcile this business model, resulting from a 'virtuous circle', with that growth, which pushes them onto a more commercial path that may not necessarily reflect their social and environmental concerns? Future research could focus on the dilemma of 'mainstreaming' sustainable development initiatives.

The road ahead: implications for entrepreneurship education and mapping outcomes

Scaling up? – No single study is able to go beyond the isolated effects of a handful of specific cases to present the full impact of sustainable entrepreneurship. We know that some sustainable entrepreneurship initiatives have a single loop effect (i.e. they address market failures) while others have a double loop effect (i.e. they transform the market). But the question remains: To what extent are these entrepreneurs able to progress from making individual contributions to transforming the consumer system, either by reducing consumption or by instilling a more ecological form of consumption?

Implications for management education – Despite growing interest in ecological and sustainable entrepreneurship, education and training programmes designed to meet the needs of people motivated by sustainability are still rare (Richomme-Huet and De Freyman, 2011; Raufflet, 2013). Lastly, following on from the work of Nadim and Singh (2011), and from special issues of *Academy* *of Management Learning and Education* (2004 and 2010) on training for sustainable entrepreneurs and inclusion of sustainable development in university programmes, it may also be interesting to look in more depth at the training offered to sustainable entrepreneurs and ecopreneurs. What should be different about educational programs that lead to the learning of these forms of entrepreneurial practice? How could this be done within academic institutions? Should, or could, traditional entrepreneurship education, as it exists today, with its frequent focus on value and the creation of opportunity conducive to material wealth, be reconsidered in light of current social issues and sustainable development? It may also be interesting to perform more detailed comparisons of the backgrounds of ecopreneurs, sustainable entrepreneurs and classic entrepreneurs. These are all interesting, needed and promising avenues for future research.

Last but not least, this literature review shows that sustainable entrepreneurship has been studied from the perspective of determinants, actors and processes. Overall, this is very promising and novel. At the same time, our understanding of the multilevel, multifaceted outcomes of sustainable entrepreneurship for individuals, organizations, communities, economies and societies remains limited. Building evaluation tools and improving our understanding of these outcomes is a research endeavour that is both intellectually stimulating and relevant for practice and society.

Note

1 This chapter does not map concepts related to social entrepreneurship such as 'Base of the Pyramid', which seek to show how local entrepreneurship can promote development in the poorest regions of the world. See Fiona, 2006; Aaserud, 2007; Prahalad, 2010.

Bibliography

Aaserud K. (2007) 'A new kind of debt relief' *Profit Magazin*, 26 11–13.

Albrecht J. (2002) 'Environmental issue entrepreneurship: A Schumpeterian perspective' *Futures*, 34 649–661.

Aldrich H. (1986) 'Ecological theory: A critique of Hannan and Freeman' in Lindenberg S Coleman J Nowak S eds, *Approaches to Social Theory* Russell Sage and Basic Books, New York 173–175.

Aldrich H. (2012) 'The emergence of entrepreneurship as an academic field: A personal essay on institutional entrepreneurship' *Research Policy*, 41 1240–1248.

Anderson A. R. (1998) 'Cultivating the Garden of Eden: Environmental entrepreneuring' *Journal of Organizational Change Management*, 11 135.

Anonymous (2008) 'WIDE ANGLE looks at a green entrepreneur's carbon credit scheme to fight global warming – and turn a profit" *Business Wire*.

Argyris C. (1993) *Knowledge for action: A guide to overcoming barriers to organizational change* Jossey-Bass, San Francisco.

Audretsch D. B. (2007) *The entrepreneurial society* Oxford University Press, Oxford.

Belz F. M. and Binder J. K. (2015) 'Sustainable entrepreneurship: A convergent process model' *Business Strategy and the Environment*, Published online in Wiley Online Library (in press).

Benyus J. M. (1997) *Biomimicry: Innovation inspired by nature* William Morrow, New York.

Berchicci L. A. (2005) 'The green entrepreneur's challenge: The influence of environmental ambition in new product development' Unpublished PhD Technische Universiteit Delft, Netherlands.

Bonnet H., Quist J., Hoogwater D., Spaans J. and Wehrmann C. (2006) 'Teaching sustainable entrepreneurship to engineering students: The case of Delft University of Technology' *European Journal of Engineering Education*, 31 155.

Brès L., Raufflet E. and Filion L.J. (2011) Développement durable et entrepreneuriat. Published in the Proceedings: *Colloque de l'Association des Sciences Administratives du Canada/Administrative Sciences Association of Canada (ASAC)*, Université du Québec à Montréal (UQAM). Available: Working Paper 2011–05, Rogers – J.A. Bombardier Chair of Entrepreneurship, HEC Montréal.

Broad W. J. (1991) 'As biosphere is sealed, its patron reflects on life' *New York Times*, C1.

Choi D. Y. and Gray E. R. (2008a) 'Socially responsible entrepreneurs: What do they do to create and build their companies?' *Business Horizons*, 51 341–352.

Choi D. Y. and Gray E. R. (2008b) 'The venture development processes of "sustainable" entrepreneurs' *Management Research News*, 31 558.

Clifton R. (2008) 'In my opinion' *Management Today*, 12.

Cohen B. and Winn M. I. (2007) 'Market imperfections, opportunity and sustainable entrepreneurship' *Journal of Business Venturing*, 22 29–49.

Collis D. J. and Montgomery C. A. (2005) *Corporate strategy: A resource-based approach* McGraw-Hill/Irwin, Boston.

Corner P. A. and Ho M. (2010) 'How opportunities develop in social entrepreneurship' *Entrepreneurship Theory and Practice*, 34 635–659.

Dacin P. A., Dacin M. T. and Matear M. (2010) 'Social entrepreneurship: Why we don't need a new theory and how we move forward from here' *The Academy of Management Perspectives*, 24 37–57.

Dale A. (2008) 'Green products gain from new price equation' *Wall Street Journal – Eastern Edition*, 251 B7.

Dean T. J. and McMullen J. S. (2007) 'Toward a theory of sustainable entrepreneurship: Reducing environmental degradation through entrepreneurial action' *Journal of Business Venturing*, 22 50–76.

Dean V. (2007) 'Painting the town green' *ABA Bankers News*, 15 7.

Dixon S. E. A. and Clifford A. (2007) 'Ecopreneurship – A new approach to managing the triple bottom line' *Journal of Organizational Change Management*, 20 326–345.

Dougherty S. (2007) 'Helping cool off our planet' *The Gazette*, B2.

Filion L. J. (1998) 'From entrepreneurship to entreprenology: The emergence of a new discipline' *Journal of Enterprising Culture*, 6 1–23.

Filion L. J. (1999) 'Empirical systems modeling methodology (ESM): Applications to entrepreneurial actors' in Wagner J. A. III ed., *Advances in qualitative organization research volume 2* Jai Press, Stamford CT 201–220.

Filion L. J. (2004) 'Operators and visionaries: Differences in the entrepreneurial and managerial systems of two types of entrepreneurs' *International Journal of Entrepreneurship and Small Business*, 1 35–55.

Fiona H. A. (2006) 'A good time to be a green entrepreneur' *FT.com* 1.

Gangemi J. (2006) 'Green growth areas for entrepreneurs' *Business Week Online*, 1 1.

Garmhausen S., Johnson E. R. and Delaney T. (2008) 'Growing a green business' *Black Enterprise*, 38 108.

Gerlach A. (2006) 'Sustainability entrepreneurship in the context of emissions trading' *Emissions Trading and Business*, 73–87.

Gibbs D. (2009) 'Sustainability entrepreneurs, ecopreneurs and the development of a sustainable economy' *Greener Management International*, 55 63–78.

Hall J. K., Daneke G. A. and Lenox M. J. (2010) 'Sustainable development and entrepreneurship: Past contributions and future directions' *Journal of Business Venturing*, 25 439–448.

Hartmann, C. L. and Stafford, E. R. (1998) 'Crafting "enviropreneurial" value chain strategies through green alliances' *Business Horizons*, 41 62.

Hendrickson L. U. and Tuttle D. B. (1997) 'Dynamic management of the environmental enterprise: A qualitative analysis' *Journal of Organizational Change Management*, 10 363–382.

Hill T. (1991) *Production/operations management: Text and cases* Prentice Hall, New York.

Hockerts K. and Wüstenhagen R. (2010) 'Greening Goliaths versus emerging Davids – Theorizing about the role of incumbents and new entrants in sustainable entrepreneurship' *Journal of Business Venturing* 25 481–492.

Isaak R. (2002) 'The making of the ecopreneur' *Greener Management International*, 38 81.

Jekwa S. (2008) 'Fighting HIV/Aids one wrist at a time' *Finweek*, 42.

Katsikis I. N. and Kyrgidou L. P. (2007) 'The concept of sustainable entrepreneurship: A conceptual framework and empirical analysis' Paper presented in the Academy of Management Proceedings.

Keskin D., Carel D. J. and Molenaar N. (2013) 'Innovation process of new ventures driven by sustainability' *Journal of Cleaner Production*, 45 50–60.

Kirkwood J. and Walton S. (2010) 'What motivates ecopreneurs to start businesses?' *International Journal of Entrepreneurial Behaviour & Research*, 16 204–28.

Kirzner I. (1979) *Perception, opportunity and profit* University of Chicago Press, Chicago.

Kuckertz A. and Wagner M. (2010) 'The influence of sustainability orientation on entrepreneurial intentions – Investigating the role of business experience' *Journal of Business Venturing*, 25 524.

Larson A. L. (2000) 'Sustainable innovation through an entrepreneurship lens' *Business Strategy and the Environment*, 9 304–17.

Lee E. (2008) 'Do good, get rich' *Black Enterprise*, 38 72–75.

Lindhult E. and Guizana B. (2011) 'Entrepreneurship as driver of market and institutional change for sustainability' Paper to ICSB World Conference, Stockholm, 15–18 June.

Linnanen, L. (2002) 'An insider's experiences with environmental entrepreneurship' *Greener Management International*, 38 71.

Marsden T. and Smith E. (2005) 'Ecological entrepreneurship: Sustainable development in local communities through quality food production and local branding' *Geoforum*, 36 440–451.

McDonough W. and Braungart M. (2002) *Cradle to cradle: Remaking the way we make things* North Point Press, New York.

Mintzberg H. (1973) *The nature of managerial work* Harper & Row, New York.

Nadim A. and Singh P. (2011) 'A system's view of sustainable entrepreneurship education' *Journal of Strategic Innovation and Sustainability*, 7 105–114.

Pacheco D., Dean T. and Payne D. (2010) 'Escaping the green prison: Entrepreneurship and the creation of opportunities for sustainable development' *Journal of Business Venturing*, 25 464–480.

Parrish B. D. (2010) 'Sustainability-driven entrepreneurship: Principles of organization design' *Journal of Business Venturing*, 25 510–523.

Pastakia A. (1998) 'Grassroots ecopreneurs: Change agents for a sustainable society' *Journal of Organizational Change Management*, 11 157.

Perrini F., Vurro C. and Costanzo L. A. (2010) 'A process-based view of social entrepreneurship: From opportunity identification to scaling-up social change in the case of San Patrignano' *Entrepreneurship and Regional Development*, 22 515–534.

Potocan V. and Mulej M. (2003) 'Entrepreneurship: Between sustainable development and reality' *Public Finance and Management*, 3 241–262.

Prahalad C. K. (2010) *The fortune at the bottom of the pyramid: Eradicating poverty through profits* Wharton School Pub, Upper Saddle River NJ.

Raufflet E. (2013) 'Integrating sustainability in management education' *Humanities*, 2 439–448.

Richomme-Huet K. and De Freyman J. (2011) What sustainable entrepreneurship looks like: An exploratory study from a student perspective, *The 56th Annual International Council for Small Business World Conference* Stockholm, June 2011.

Robinson J. (2006) 'Navigating social and institutional barriers to markets: How social entrepreneurs identify and evaluate opportunities' in Mair J Robinson J and Hockerts K eds, *Social entrepreneurship* Palgrave Macmillan, Basingstoke 95–120.

Rose R. A. (1990) 'Ecopreneurs' *Success*, 37 51.

Schaltegger S. (2002) 'A framework for ecopreneurship' *Greener Management International*, 38 45–58.

Schaltegger S. and Wagner M. (2011) 'Sustainable entrepreneurship and sustainability innovation: Categories and interactions' *Business Strategy and the Environment*, 20 222–237.

Schaper M. (2002) 'The essence of ecopreneurship' *Greener Management International*, 38 26.

Schaper M. (2005) 'Being a green entrepreneur: Does it make business sense?' *Businessdate*, 13 5–7.

Schumpeter J. A. (1954) *History of economic analysis*, George Allen & Unwin, UK.

Seabrook C. (2004) 'Buckhead nonprofit tills green revolution Costa Rican school teaches care of Earth' *The Atlanta Journal – Constitution*, F1.

Shaw E. and Carter S. (2007) 'Social entrepreneurship: Theoretical antecedents and empirical analysis of entrepreneurial processes and outcomes' *Journal of Small Business and Enterprise Development*, 14 418–434.

Shepherd D. A. and Patzelt H. (2011) 'The new field of sustainable entrepreneurship: studying entrepreneurial action linking "What is to be sustained" with "What is to be developed"' *Entrepreneurship Theory and Practice*, 35 137–163.

Spence M., Ben Boubaker Gherib J. and Ondoua Biwolé V. (2011) 'Sustainable entrepreneurship: Is entrepreneurial will enough? A North-South comparison' *Journal of Business Ethics*, 99 335–367.

Surie, G. and Ashley, A. (2008) 'Integrating pragmatism and ethics in entrepreneurial leadership for sustainable value creation' *Journal of Business Ethics*, 81 235–246.

Tracey P. and Phillips N. (2007) 'The distinctive challenge of educating social entrepreneurs: A postscript and rejoinder to the special issue on entrepreneurship education' *Academy of Management Learning & Education*, 6 264–271.

Waddock S. A. (2008) *The difference makers: How social and institutional entrepreneurs created the corporate responsibility movement* Greenleaf Pub, Sheffield UK.

Walley E. E. and Taylor D. W. (2002) 'Opportunists, champions, mavericks...?' *Greener Management International*, 38 31.

Warnock J. (2008) 'Sustainability at the disco' *Contract*, 49 46.

Wennersten R. (2008) 'Sustainable technology' in Misra K ed. *Handbook of performability engineering* Springer, London 919–931.

World Commission on Environment and Development (1987) *Our common future* Oxford University Press, Oxford.

Young W. and Tilley F. (2006) 'Can businesses move beyond efficiency? The shift toward effectiveness and equity in the corporate sustainability debate' *Business Strategy and the Environment*, 15 402–415.

16 Public-private partnerships in Kazakhstan and Russia

The interplay between social value, entrepreneurship and sustainability

Nikolai Mouraviev and Nada K. Kakabadse

Introduction

Public-private partnerships (PPPs) are becoming an increasingly common method of delivering public services. A PPP arrangement exists when a government agency assigns a traditionally public responsibility to a private company in an attempt to improve delivery efficiency, lower costs, increase customer satisfaction and attract private funding (Hofmeister and Borchert 2004). Whilst governments in many nations (e.g. the UK, Australia, Germany, France, the Netherlands, Spain, USA and Canada) have implemented PPPs since 1990s and accumulated significant management experience, for other economies PPPs are fairly new (Osborne 2000; Akintoye *et al.* 2003; Grimsey and Lewis 2004; Urio 2010).

There is a critical link between sustainable entrepreneurship and PPPs owing to the latter's capacity to contribute to society's sustainability along three dimensions. First, partnerships demonstrate capacity to ensure sustainability of the natural environment (Shepherd and Patzelt 2011), for example, by expanding the use of renewable energy sources for power generation. Second, PPPs are able to build, maintain and enhance life support systems (Halkias and Thurman 2012), for example, by constructing and operating key elements of infrastructure – electrical grids, roads, airports and seaports, as well as urban infrastructure units including water supply facilities and trash recycling plants. Third, PPPs can effectively serve a community (Leiserowitz *et al.* 2006) by providing public services instead of the government. Examples of these public services include education, health care and recreation. To summarise, by contributing to all three dimensions of societal sustainability, the PPP work appears in the core of sustainable entrepreneurship (Peredo and Chrisman 2006; Hall *et al.* 2010), which explains the significance of this study. PPPs should be viewed as examples of sustainable entrepreneurship, i.e. the latter is a concept of creative business practices in society, whilst contractual PPPs are one of manifestations of creative business in collaboration with the government.

As this chapter aims to highlight the relations between PPP, entrepreneurship and sustainability, the term *interplay* accurately captures not only multiple links between these three categories, but also the influence that each element exerts on the other two and receives from the other two. This can be illustrated by partnerships' impact on environmental and social issues, whilst PPP success in solving certain problems drives further PPP deployment. For example, based on worldwide PPP experience to date, partnerships are particularly instrumental in effectively addressing a number of environmental problems, such as flood alleviation, water treatment, waste utilisation and the use of renewable energy sources (e.g. wind farms and waste-to-energy plants). In addition, PPPs are capable to provide effective solutions to certain social problems, such as child-care, by using private investment for building and operating kindergartens whilst parents and the government reimburse a private company over the long term. Other similar examples of where PPPs have a high success rate include construction and operation of hospitals, schools, stadiums and recreational facil-ities (spas, swimming pools, parks).

In the two ex-Soviet nations – Kazakhstan and Russia – PPP deployment is still in its infancy as it began only after 2005 (Mouraviev 2012). Nonetheless, in both economies PPP development is high on the government agenda and the governments are actively pushing for accelerated PPP formation. Why is it so? The chapter investigates the underpinnings of the government decision-making regarding PPP development through the prism of entrepreneurship that partner-ships foster. This research perspective is aligned with a view of sustainable entrepreneurship that entails not only preservation of nature, sources of life support and community, but also produces gains, both economic and non-economic, to the economy, individuals and society (Shepherd and Patzelt 2011). As PPPs are rarely studied from the sustainability perspective, the chapter addresses this knowledge gap by exploring the impact of partnerships on entrepreneurship. It is worth noting that, although a PPP is commonly viewed as an organisational arrangement that is inherently entrepreneurial because a private operator pursues the goal of profit maximisation and utilises creative tools to achieve this goal, the chapter focuses on how, in what ways PPPs con-tribute to sustainable entrepreneurship *beyond* the scope of entrepreneurial actions of a private operator that implements a partnership project. Hence, the policy and societal aspects of PPP impact on entrepreneurship and what makes the latter sustainable are highlighted in this chapter.

Kazakhstan and Russia have been selected for the study owing to a large number of commonalities in their economies and public policies. Having a common border (i.e. Russia is North of Kazakhstan), both nations are trans-itional economies and share many economic, political, business, social, educa-tional and cultural realities that stem from a common Soviet legacy. Although the two economies are different in size, the ways in which governments have shaped PPP development, created a legal and regulatory framework and selected sectors for partnership projects show considerable commonalities that allow for meaningful comparisons between Kazakhstan and Russia. An empirical exam-ination of dynamics underlying the PPP arrangements in Kazakhstan and Russia may thus contribute to a more comprehensive understanding of the role that the governments and other stakeholders attach to partnerships. More generally, the government approaches to PPPs may elucidate, at least in part, the partnerships' significance for the interplay between sustainability, entrepreneurship and innovation as this interplay increasingly becomes the driver of society's development and growth.

The chapter begins by elucidating a theoretical framework that links partnerships, entrepreneurship and sustainability. It then highlights the progress made in Kazakhstan and Russia to date in the PPP deployment. Next, internal and external PPP drivers in the two nations are discussed. Subsequently, the chapter demonstrates theoretical grounds based on which PPPs are typically launched (value for money and transaction cost economics) and discusses whether these two approaches are used in Kazakhstan and Russia. We then identify PPPs' social value that governments aim to promote, such as sustainable entrepreneurship, economic growth and innovation, which, if they materialise, outweigh limitations of the value-for-money concept and transaction cost economics.

Theoretical framework: PPP value creation and sustainable entrepreneurship

Partnerships are typically launched in the sectors where they sustain nature (e.g. solid waste utilisation plants), life support systems (e.g. water treatment) and community (e.g. kindergartens, schools and hospitals). These three areas are what, as literature suggests, sustainable entrepreneurship needs to focus on (Leiserowitz et al. 2006; Peredo and Chrisman 2006; Shepherd and Patzelt 2011). In the proposed theoretical framework, we link the three areas in which partnerships are deployed with the outcomes and argue that PPPs are instrumental for producing both economic and non-economic gains to the economy, individuals and society, which is also central to sustainable entrepreneurship (Pathak 2008; Hall et al. 2010; Halkias and Thurman 2012). Drawing on the concept of sustainable entrepreneurship that emphasises the link between *what is to be sustained* and *what is to be developed* (Shepherd and Patzelt 2011), the theoretical framework underpins the proposition that PPPs embrace both variables. This notion is supported by the government actions: despite the PPPs' controversial nature (i.e. many partnership advantages are often offset by high costs and risks, as this chapter shows), the governments continue to create favourable conditions for private investors and encourage them to engage in partnerships because the latter significantly contribute to sustainable entrepreneurship in a variety of ways.

This chapter's theoretical framework emphasises PPPs' capacity to create value. Whilst this value may have many manifestations, the focus is on the social dimension, and the critical component of social value refers to partnership ability to foster entrepreneurship *beyond* the scope of the core PPP activity, i.e. beyond the public service for the provision of which a partnership was deployed.

PPPs are entrepreneurial in their core due to the profit motive that drives creative and innovative actions of the private sector partners who actually implement projects (Grimsey and Lewis 2004; Hodge and Greve 2005). This PPP's nature conforms to conceptualisation of entrepreneurial action, which is described as the one that aims to bring into existence future goods and services (Venkataraman 1997). More importantly, partnerships also foster innovation and entrepreneurship beyond the private operator's scope: PPPs generate the supply chain and, hence, form an extensive competitive entrepreneurial environment that must satisfy the PPP needs. Additionally, PPPs create conditions for social entrepreneurship, further social cohesion and expand market relations by reducing the scope of the public sector. All these PPP benefits create social value that contributes to sustainability.

Social value can be understood as the outcome, rather than the process (van der Wal and Huberts 2008). Similarly to public value that lies in the satisfaction of those whom government programmes serve (Moore 2000; Stoker 2006), social value materialises in the satisfaction of society from the government services (Reynaers and De Graaf 2010). In a broad meaning, social value refers to benefits to society. As social value often overlaps economic value, it may take a form of a blend of intangible and tangible gains, such as expanded entrepreneurship beyond the scope of the PPP core activity.

As PPP social value is far from apparent, this chapter proceeds to the discussion of how PPP deployment evolved in Kazakhstan and Russia and then highlights internal and external PPP drivers, although the latter only in part explains why governments are interested in PPP proliferation. Subsequently, we highlight the contextual features in the social sphere in both nations, which shows the governments' pressing need to attract the private sector funding and deploy partnerships.

PPP development in Kazakhstan and Russia

PPP development in Kazakhstan began in 2006 when the government adopted the law on concessions. Subsequently, the government formed the National PPP Centre and two regional centres and approved seven PPP projects, although later some have shut down (Mouraviev 2012). The existing PPPs in the transportation sector include a railroad in Eastern Kazakhstan between Shar and Ust-Kamenogorsk and an airport in Aktau. In the energy sector, there is the construction and operation of an inter-regional electrical grid between Northern Kazakhstan and the Aktobe region. The widespread expectation is that in the coming few years many projects that have already been prepared by the PPP Centre will find their investors and one can see a much larger number of partnerships in a variety of sectors.

Compared to Kazakhstan, Russia's PPP deployment is faster and embraces more sectors (e.g. power and heat generation, water supply systems, waste utilisation facilities, sports objects and schools). Formation of contractual PPPs in Russia began after the federal government finally passed the law 'On Concessional Agreements' in 2005 and approved subsequent amendments to this law in 2008. From 2008, the number of partnerships, mostly concessions, has been rapidly growing. The Russian government aims for accelerated PPP development and its efforts in launching partnerships have been quite successful. As of April 2015, the total number of PPPs in the nation has reached 595 (www.pppi. ru), which vividly demonstrates the significant increase in the number of entrepreneurial firms that have chosen to become PPP investors and operators.

The PPP context in two nations: focus on the social sector

Why are governments in Kazakhstan and Russia so keen on extensive PPP deployment? There are two sets of underlying reasons. One includes PPP advantages that are relevant to most nations. These advantages stem from the partnership's nature and its principal characteristics that were discussed above. The other includes country-specific PPP drivers that are relevant exclusively to the context of Kazakhstan and Russia and stem from the needs that both economies experience.

Frequently identified advantages of PPPs include better risk allocation and burden-sharing; the use of private funds and know-how for the implementation of public tasks; insourcing private expertise in various fields including advancements in business as well as technology; economies of scale; and improvement of management capabilities of the public sector (Hofmeister and Borchert 2004). An overriding benefit is the 'value for money' perspective (Kakabadse *et al.* 2007). Furthermore, a critical argument in favour of PPPs is the use of private funds for construction and operation of public infrastructure. This allows the government to greatly reduce its own borrowing and move some projects off the books of the public sector. Thus, when PPPs are deployed, the cost of capital-intensive projects, such as those in infrastructure, will be borne by the private sector, and will not be counted as public spending.

Country-specific reasons of why governments in Kazakhstan and Russia are keen on PPP development include the following three significant internal drivers:

- a need to get private financing for utilities and housing infrastructure;
- a need to increase attractiveness of selected industries for private investors; and
- a need to give a stronger impetus to regional economic development.

Driven by a host of internal economic needs, governments in Kazakhstan and Russia increasingly resort to PPPs as a perceived effective and efficient solution. From the government perspective, powerful internal drivers complemented by widely publicised PPP advantages provide a strong and well justified impetus for accelerated partnership deployment that might embrace many industries.

In recent years governments in both Kazakhstan and Russia made substantial efforts to deploy PPPs in the social sector. There are two principal reasons for this. One is that in the time of economic downturn and low oil price government budgets reduced, which naturally resulted in the need to attract the private sector financing for upgrading social infrastructure, such as kindergartens, schools, hospitals, spas and stadiums. Another reason is that in the time of acute budget constraints the government wants to reduce the size and scope of the public sector, by involving private operators that essentially will be increasingly replacing the government organisations in the social sphere.

An example of this growing trend in Russia is a PPP project launched in 2011 in St Petersburg where the city government approved a partnership with a management company called *Peremena* for construction and subsequent maintenance of two schools and three kindergartens for a ten year period (GK *'Baltros' investiruyet 2.2 milliarda rublei v shkoly i detskiye sady* 2011). The private investment in construction was estimated at USD $70.9 million. To finance the project, the private sector partner used its own funds and bank loans whilst the city government will make all payments during the ten years, so that a private company recoups its investment and makes profit. An example from Kazakhstan includes a PPP contract that the government signed in 2011 with a Turkish company for construction and subsequent operation of 11 kindergartens over 14 years. Each of the 11 new kindergartens had to provide care for 320 children, with a total capacity of 3,520 children, whilst the construction cost was estimated at USD $39.12 million (*Stroitel'stvo i ekspluatatsiya kompleksa detskikh sadov v gorode Karagande po skheme kontsessii* 2011). Although the construction was later put on hold, the kindergartens' PPP served as a pilot social entrepreneurial project that could be a benchmark – in terms of effective operations and maintenance – for other similar projects that the government plans. Thus, its successful launch and performance may significantly accelerate the formation of many other partnerships in the social sphere.

To summarise, the government efforts aimed at extensive PPP deployment in the social sector aim to achieve four tasks: compensate the reduction of budget financing by the use of private funds; reduce the government scope in the social sphere and increase private entrepreneurship; ensure greater effectiveness of facilities' operations in the sector; and expand the volume and variety of services.

What is the basis for PPP formation in Kazakhstan and Russia?

Although the governments in Kazakhstan and Russia may have many compelling reasons to deploy partnerships, for practical purposes of PPP formation government agencies need a certain framework in order to conduct feasibility studies, determine revenue streams, assess risks and evaluate project costs. The theory provides two principal concepts that can be employed in the decision making process regarding whether to form a PPP: value for money (VfM) and transaction cost economics (TCE). Value for money, when applied to a PPP, means that a PPP is supposed to bring larger value for the money that the public sector spends, compared to when services are provided in-house (i.e. by public agencies) or when services are contracted out to a private company. The underlying logic is that using a PPP will make sense only if a partnership can deliver public sector services cheaper and/or better (i.e. at a lower cost and/or with improved quality) as opposed to other options. If value for money is not there, a PPP should not be formed.

The comprehensive definition of value for money is available in the UK's Her Majesty's Treasury *Value for Money Assessment Guide*:

> Value for money is defined as the optimum combination of whole-of-life costs and quality (or fitness for purpose) of the good or service to meet the user's requirement. The term whole-of-life is used to refer to the lifecycle of the good or service. VfM is not the choice of goods and services based on the lowest cost bid.
>
> (Her Majesty's Treasury 2006, 7)

The VfM concept allows public agencies to compare the costs of a planned PPP project with the cost of the same project, if it is going to be accomplished through traditional procurement. The definition above puts emphasis on the need to take into account the lifetime project costs, and also the quality of a good or service, making the output specification an important partnership feature. Hence, a trade-off between lifetime PPP project costs and service quality is in the core of the VfM concept.

Another concept that serves as a reference point for the government when it considers whether or not to form a PPP is derived from transaction cost economics. TCE uses total social costs and their minimisation as a criterion regarding which option for the public service provision to choose (Vining and Boardman 2008). Total social costs are defined as production costs incurred in service provision (including construction costs and payments to third parties), plus transaction costs (such as bidding costs and interest payments on loans), plus (net) negative externalities (such as cost of pollution less value of positive externalities such as reduced waiting time), holding quality constant (Vining and Boardman 2008, 149).

The TCE perspective argues that, if the employment of a PPP as opposed to the traditional public service delivery (via direct government provision or contracting out) minimises the sum of total social costs, a PPP should be preferred. Vining and Boardman (2008) emphasise that in assessment one should include all government transaction costs over the whole period of project time that derive from the project even if they do not appear in the project's budget. Also one should include all externalities and account for quality differences although these costs rarely show up in any budget (Vining and Boardman 2008).

The concept of using a PPP if and when it minimises total social cost has some similarities with looking at PPP from the value for money concept: both perspectives intend to compare the cost (or value) of a PPP project with some benchmark which is the cost (or value) of a traditional way of the public service provision. Also, in both perspectives not only the use of quantitative methods may be required, but also the application of qualitative methods, for example, for assessment of value of externalities in TCE, or for assessment of effect of PPP on wider access to public services in the VfM concept.

How often are VfM and/or TCE used in Kazakhstan and Russia as a basis for PPP formation? Are they used at all? Although both approaches may be to a certain extent in the background of government decision making, the realities of PPP formation show that governments provide extensive financing to partnership by paying part of capital cost, ensuring guaranteed revenue streams to a private operator, providing financial guarantees, extending low interest loans and granting tax exemptions. The Russian language literature is silent about TCE and PPP value for money as the governments in Kazakhstan and Russia do not explicitly use these concepts as a basis for deciding whether to form a partnership (Mouraviev 2012). This is in sharp contrast to Western literature that emphasises that a government should employ a PPP if and when a partnership incurs lower cost as opposed to the cost of the government's in-house provision (Sadka 2007; Hall 2008; Morallos and Amekudzi 2008). Although overall PPP costs may be higher due to extensive government financial support to a partnership, expensive technology and higher cost of private partner borrowing, the Russian language literature claims that PPPs are a preferred form for collaboration between the public sector and the private sector (Bazhenov 2011; Firsova 2012). This means that the Russian literature generally accepts a notion that a PPP incurs higher total project costs (compared to government in-house service delivery), although Western literature provides the opposite argument in support of PPPs (Mouraviev 2012, 49). According to KPMG data, the costs of contracting out in Russia are about 6 per cent less than the PPP costs (Shabashevich 2011, 3–4). This is exactly indicative of an evolving paradigm that provides taken-for-granted PPP acceptance, regardless of their costs. In other words, in Kazakhstan and Russia governments may approve a PPP with a total cost higher than that of traditional government procurement or the cost of in-house service provision. The academic literature and the government policy documents in Kazakhstan and Russia are silent about PPP efficiency, whilst there are no studies that aim to compare PPP costs with those of the public sector in-house service provision.

To summarise, empirical evidence shows that neither the value-for-money concept, nor the TCE approach are used for PPP deployment in Kazakhstan and Russia and, more generally, cannot serve as reference points for PPP development in these nations (Mouraviev 2012; Mouraviev and Kakabadse 2012, 2014).

PPP social value: entrepreneurship, social cohesion, innovation and sustainability

Whilst the theoretical foundation of PPP implementation in Kazakhstan and Russia appears controversial due to a clear reason – partnerships cost the government more than in-house public service provision – governments aim to maximise and publicise PPPs' positive impact on society. Hence, the PPP conundrum (i.e. PPPs' high cost versus societal benefit) is resolved in favour of societal gains when the government attaches certain benefits to partnerships and promotes them as social value. The latter attributes to society at large and include the following.

First, PPPs contribute to *entrepreneurship* by large-scale and long-term business projects that create demand for not only core activity but also for numerous goods and services that support this core activity. Many companies, existing and newly formed, support PPP business by acting as suppliers to a PPP, which generates competition (as many PPPs do purchasing by tenders) and also creates jobs. Specifically, PPPs aim to engage private investors in low-profit sectors (e.g. housing and utilities infrastructure) and create jobs in the core activity as well as supporting businesses (i.e. suppliers to partnerships). As partnership projects are lengthy (typically, no fewer than 10 years and can be as long as 50 years and even longer), this permits suppliers to a PPP to create sustainable operations, grow in size and also supply to other customers. Hence, partnerships generate a competitive entrepreneurial environment that they can enhance for a long time, thus making suppliers' businesses sustainable. More generally, by extensive PPP deployment, governments in both countries anticipate to boost sustainable economic growth, particularly at the regional and municipal levels, whilst mega projects at the national level are able to secure bank financing more easily and attract large established companies as PPP operators due to high economy-wide project significance. In summary, PPPs may play a significant role in sustainable regional economic development by contributing to economic growth via their own enterprise and related entrepreneurial activity.

A special note must be made in order to emphasise a connection between PPP-generated *entrepreneurship and sustainability*. As market failures detract society from sustainability (Dean and McMullen 2007), PPPs often serve as a critical tool that permits the government to render assistance to private firms in order to overcome a market failure in low-profit and/or heavily regulated sectors, such as utilities. Specifically, a PPP as entrepreneurial arrangement contributes to sustainability by overcoming market failures within the scope of its core business and also beyond the scope of its principal activity. Market failure is viewed as the failure to realise all possible gains from trade (Zerbe and McCurdy 2000). Hence, it is likely that in the PPP-generated competitive entrepreneurial environment firms and individual entrepreneurs will gain from enhanced commercial exchange with a partnership.

Second, the governments in both nations promote a strong association between PPPs and *innovation* in a variety of ways. One is that the private delivery of public services by partnerships (as opposed to traditional government delivery) is innovative as it never existed until a few years ago. The other, more important association, from the government perspective, establishes a direct link between PPPs and technological and managerial innovation. The governments claim that innovation is an intrinsic partnership's feature. This is due to the profit motive that drives a private partner to implement technologically advanced solutions aiming to provide services better and cheaper. Whilst in reality PPPs may or may not innovate, the governments promote partnerships as innovative business ventures that strongly contribute to both nations' strategy to modernise their economies. As the innovation strategy is undisputed in both Kazakhstan and Russia due to their current dependency on oil exports and the need to diversify the economy, PPPs fit into this strategy by possessing a powerful potential to innovate in technology, management and service delivery. Not surprisingly, the government presents this potential as a societal value.

Third, PPPs contribute to *social and economic cohesion* by overcoming distrust between the private and public sectors. Governments in Kazakhstan and Russia view PPPs not only as a tool to bypass the budgetary limitations for expanded provision of public services, but also as an instrument to overcome the historically formed distrust of private firms collaborating with the public sector. Hence, through cohesive networks of public and private actors PPPs increase societal sustainability.

Fourth, PPP's contribution to sustainable entrepreneurship can be viewed as a platform for *social entrepreneurship*. Whilst PPPs create social value, it is different from the meaning of social entrepreneurship when part of profit is spent for social purposes. In the case of a PPP, the government subsidises part of the total project cost and thus creates social value, which otherwise would not be created. Part of this social value may be focused on development of social entrepreneurship. As the subsidy is not related to any specific social purpose, PPPs can be used by governments to promote social entrepreneurship, which can make additional contributions to sustainability (e.g. by designing a business model for social entrepreneurship that would serve the needs of population in rural areas).

Fifth, PPPs enhance entrepreneurship and contribute to the market economy building through *replacing the government with private firms* in the provision of public services, which will result in the *reduced scope of the public sector*. Whilst this applies to all sectors in which PPPs are deployed, the most significant impact is expected in the social sector where partnerships provide health care, childcare and recreational services (e.g. swimming pools and spas). The significance is explained by the note that many services, such as health care and childcare, are private goods, rather than public goods. For example, whilst citizens in the two nations traditionally view childcare as a public good and the government responsibility, the private sector may replace the government in the provision of childcare. Hence, the private sector's extensive engagement in this field may foster societal sustainability by reducing dependence of the budget funds. The long-term government objective is to change the public perception in Kazakhstan and Russia and align it with the realities of a market-driven economy, i.e. that childcare as a private good should be provided privately, rather than by the government as it used to be in the Soviet past and still is in both nations, with an exception of a fairly small number of private kindergartens. Although this PPP value may not be appealing to the low-income population, it is significantly more appealing to all those with a higher income and those who call for reducing the scope of the public sector. Hence, overcoming the notorious dominance of the government (i.e. the Soviet legacy) may be viewed as a PPP social value, which is likely to be more commonly shared by younger generations.

Sixth, PPPs may substitute the government in its efforts to ensure *environmental sustainability*. Specifically, the governments deploy PPPs for solving certain environmental tasks, such as using private investment and technological innovation for building effective urban water treatment and water supply facilities or solid waste utilisation plants. Some examples of Russian PPPs include reconstruction of a water supply system in Perm (i.e. *Permskaya oblast'*); construction of water purification facilities in Petrozavodsk (the Republic of Karelia); and construction of a refuse recycling plant in Yanino (i.e. *Leningradskaya oblast'*). Similar PPP projects are being prepared in Kazakhstan. Hence, PPPs are increasingly substituting the government in its activities aimed at environmental sustainability.

To summarise, the set of elements that constitutes the PPPs' social value and that are likely to materialise over the long term outweigh limitations of the value-for-money concept and transaction cost economics. Pursuing long-term development objectives that focus on nations' transformation along multiple strategic dimensions (namely, innovation; sustainable economic growth; enhanced entrepreneurship; smaller government sector's scope; and greater environmental sustainability), the governments in Kazakhstan and Russia are keen on extensive deployment of public-private partnerships using them as one of the tools for achieving strategic objectives.

Conclusion

The gap between empirical evidence (i.e. PPPs' low value for money and high transaction costs) and government policy in Kazakhstan and Russia, which aims at accelerated PPP employment, can be bridged when one takes into account the social value that PPPs bring along and that the governments are keen on attaching to partnerships. At present, the governments attempt to overcome the lack of conceptual justification for PPP formation by the creation of a policy paradigm that provides readily available answers and solutions for fostering PPP development (Mouraviev and Kakabadse 2014). Whilst an emergent policy paradigm may be useful in praxis as it can significantly speed up the partnership formation, the PPP paradigm can only in part replace the need to promote social value that the government associates with PPPs. It is to the government advantage to pay special attention to promotion of PPP value that have broader significance to society. For example, emphasising the PPP snowball effect on development of entrepreneurship can help the government mitigate the perception that partnerships are launched in order to charge a fee for service that used to be free when it was provided publicly (e.g. a toll road).

The enhanced conceptualisation of PPPs suggests that partnerships should be viewed as a public management tool that promotes certain societal value and that calls for identification of an alternative PPP performance management framework. Rather than focusing on VfM or transaction costs, the principal elements of the framework may include the PPP impact on entrepreneurship, regional economic growth, social and economic cohesion, innovation and environmental sustainability. The societal value that is attached to PPPs in the context of Kazakhstan and Russia might be the core assessment criterion in this performance management framework.

The chapter contributes to the sustainable entrepreneurship research field by incorporating a new research sub-field that focuses on public-private collaboration and the government role in supporting PPP as a distinct form of entrepreneurial action. By linking the two streams – sustainability literature with the PPP literature – the chapter offers a new framework that emphasises the PPPs' ability to create social value, i.e. economic and non-economic gains to society. From the government perspective, the PPPs' capacity to create social value has proven more significant than each partnership's value for money. The reason for this stems from how a PPP generates, via its supply chain, a competitive and sustainable entrepreneurial environment. Theoretical implications of the study are, therefore, significant: whilst PPPs are often associated with monopolisation of public services (e.g. a toll road is often a monopoly) and ability to manipulate the price for a monopolised service, which serves as a strong factor against PPP deployment, a newly developed theoretical framework permits to reassess this criticism. The application of a different theoretical conceptual model that focuses on the PPP impact on sustainability and entrepreneurship permits to more fully capture PPP social value. Further research may contribute to more detailed PPP conceptualisation from the perspective of social value capture and highlight additional dimensions of how PPP, as one of the manifestations of sustainable entrepreneurship, creates social value.

Through the lens of PPP social value, transaction cost economics and value for money as decision tools for PPP deployment need to be revisited. Whilst both tools have been extensively discussed in the academic literature and have a certain degree of practical usefulness in decision making, a new framework calls for upgrading theoretical underpinnings and identifying robust conceptual foundations on which PPPs can be deployed. PPP social value, created by partnerships' engagement in sustainable entrepreneurship, may effectively serve as the core of a new set of PPP assessment criteria at the time of deployment and also at the time of performance evaluation.

As extensive PPP deployment and effective governance are likely to result in greater sustainability for economy, ecology, individuals and society at large, governments in Kazakhstan and Russia need to overcome multiple legal, institutional, regulatory and behavioural (i.e. distrust and/or partner's pursuit of self-interest) constraints and impediments. In particular, reducing the government overregulation of the private operators is likely to ensure greater PPP flexibility in innovation and management and may permit partnerships to more effectively address society's environmental, economic and social concerns.

References

Akintoye A., Beck M. and Hardcastle C. eds. (2003) *Public–private partnerships: managing risks and opportunities* Blackwell Science, Oxford.

Bazhenov, A. (2011) *Zadachi Vnesheconombanka po razvitiyu rynka proektov G.Ch.P. v 2011 godu* (in Russian). [Vnesheconombank tasks for the development of PPP projects in 2011]. In Annual meeting of the PPP Centre and representatives of regions of the Russian Federation regarding implementation of PPP projects. Moscow, 26–27 January: pp. 1–31. Available at: www.pppinrussia.ru/main/publications/articles [Accessed 3 June 2011].

Dean T.J. and McMullen J.S. (2007) 'Toward a theory of sustainable entrepreneurship: reducing environmental degradation through entrepreneurial action' *Journal of Business Venturing, 22 50–76.*

Firsova A.A. (2012) *Teoriya i metodologiya investirovaniya innovatsionnoy deyatelnosti na osnove gosudarstvenno-chastnogo partnerstva* (in Russian). [Theory and methodology for investment in innovation activity using public–private partnerships] Saratov State University Press, Saratov.

GK 'Baltros' investiruyet 2.2 milliarda rublei v shkoly i detskiye sady (2011) (in Russian). ['Baltros' holding invests 2.2 billion rubles in schools and kindergartens], 11 April. Available at: www.stateinvest.spb.ru [Accessed 12 July 2012].

Grimsey D. and Lewis M. (2004) *Public private partnerships: the worldwide revolution in infrastructure provision and project finance* Edward Elgar, Cheltenham.

Halkias D. and Thurman P. eds. (2012) *Entrepreneurship and sustainability: business solutions for poverty alleviation from around the world* Gower, London.

Hall D. (2008) 'Public-private partnerships (PPPs). Summary paper' Available at: www.psiru.org/publicationsindex.asp [Accessed 12 February 2011], 1–26.

Hall J.K., Daneke G. and Lenox M. (2010) 'Sustainable development and entrepreneurship: past contributions and future directions' *Journal of Business Venturing, 25(5) 439–448.*

Her Majesty's Treasury (2006) *Value for money assessment guidance* Author, London.

Hodge G. and Greve C. eds. (2005) *The challenge of public-private partnerships: learning from international experience* Edward Elgar, Cheltenham.

Hofmeister A. and Borchert H. (2004) 'Public-private partnership in Switzerland: crossing the bridge with the aid of a new governance approach' *International Review of Administrative Sciences, 70(2) 217–232.*

Kakabadse N., Kakabadse A. and Summers N. (2007) 'Effectiveness of private finance initiatives (PFI): study of private financing for the provision of capital assets for schools' *Public Administration and Development, 27 49–61.*

Leiserowitz A.A., Kates R.W. and Parris T.M. (2006) 'Sustainability values, attitudes, and behaviors: a review of multinational and global trends' *Annual Reviews of Environmental Resources, 31 413–444.*

Moore M. (2000) 'Managing for value: organizational strategy in for-profit, nonprofit, and governmental organizations' *Nonprofit and Voluntary Sector Quarterly, 29 183–204.*

Morallos D. and Amekudzi A. (2008) 'The state of the practice of value for money analysis in comparing public private partnerships to traditional procurements' *Public Works Management and Policy, 13(2) 114–125.*

Mouraviev N. (2012) 'What drives the employment of public-private partnerships in Kazakhstan and Russia: value for money?' *Organizations and Markets in Emerging Economies, 3(5) 32–57.*

Mouraviev N. and Kakabadse N.K. (2012) 'Conceptualising public-private partnerships: a critical appraisal of approaches to meanings and forms' *Society and Business Review*, *7(3)* 260–276.

Mouraviev N. and Kakabadse N. (2014) 'Public-private partnerships in Russia: dynamics contributing to an emerging policy paradigm' *Policy Studies*, *35(1)* 79–96.

Osborne S.P. ed. (2000) *Public-private partnerships: theory and practice in international perspective* Routledge, London.

Pathak R.D. (2008) 'Grass-root creativity, innovation, entrepreneurialism and poverty reduction' *International Journal of Entrepreneurship and Innovation Management*, *8(1)* 87–98.

Peredo A.M. and Chrisman J.J. (2006) 'Toward a theory of community-based enterprise' *Academy of Management Review*, *31* 309–328.

Reynaers A.-M. and de Graaf G. (2010) 'Public values in public–private partnerships' *International Journal of Public Administration*, *37* 120–132.

Sadka E. (2007) 'Public-private partnerships: a public economics perspective' *CESifo Economic Studies*, *53(3)* 466–490.

Shabashevich M. (2011) *Effektivnost' realizatsii infrastrukturnykh proektov GChP v Rossii* (in Russian). [Efficiency of PPP project implementation in infrastructure in Russia]. In Annual Meeting of the PPP Centre and Representatives of Regions of the Russian Federation Regarding Implementation of PPP Projects. Moscow, 26–27 January: 1–16. Available at: www.pppinrussia.ru/main/publications/articles [Accessed 3 June 2011].

Shepherd D.A. and Patzelt H. (2011) 'The new field of sustainable entrepreneurship: studying entrepreneurial action linking "What is to be sustained" with "What is to be developed"' *Entrepreneurship Theory and Practice*, *35(1)* 137–163.

Stoker G. (2006) 'Public value management: a new narrative for networked governance?' *American Review of Public Administration*, *36* 41–57.

Stroitel'stvo i ekspluatatsiya kompleksa detskikh sadov v Karagande po skheme kontsesii. Razyasneniya po povodu konkursnoi dokumentatsii (2011) (in Russian) [Construction and operation of kindergartens in the city of Karaganda in the form of a concession. Comments regarding tender documentation]. Regional Public–Private Partnership Centre of the *Karagandinskaya oblast'*. Available at: www.karaganda-ppp.kz [Accessed 12 January 2012].

Urio P. ed. (2010) *Public-private partnerships: success and failure factors for in-transition countries* University Press of America, Lanham, MD.

van der Wal Z. and Huberts L. (2008) 'Value solidity in government and business: results of an empirical study on public and private sector organizational values' *The American Review of Public Administration*, *38* 264–285.

Venkataraman S. (1997) 'The distinctive domain of entrepreneurship research'. In J. Katz, ed., *Advances in entrepreneurship, firm emergence, and growth* JAI Press, Greenwich, CT, *119–138*.

Vining A. and Boardman A. (2008) 'Public-private partnerships: eight rules for governments' *Public Works Management & Policy*, *13(2) 149–161* www.pppi.ru (2015) Web resource [Accessed 6 May 2015].

Zerbe R.O. and McCurdy H. (2000) 'The end of market failure' *Regulation*, *23 10–14*.

17 The everyday experiences of a sustainable entrepreneur

Brokering for social innovation at the intersection of networks of practice

Eeva Houtbeckers

Introduction

Sustainable entrepreneurship (SE) is suggested as one means to tackle contemporary sustainability challenges by focusing on 'the preservation of nature, life support, and community' while pursuing 'perceived opportunities to bring into existence future products, processes, and services for gain' (Shepherd and Patzelt 2011, 142). SE may also result in social innovation, which refers to 'new ideas that meet unmet needs' (Mulgan 2007, 4).

However, we know little of the process of entrepreneurs motivated by sustainability challenges (Poldner *et al.* 2015). Generally, entrepreneurs face a paradox of simultaneously fitting in and standing out in their respective fields (De Clercq and Voronov 2009). While they have to fit in and gain legitimacy in order to run their enterprise, they also need to stand out in order to create something new. Thus, standing out can be interpreted as creating social innovation in SE.

The aim of this chapter is to 'bring work in' (Barley and Kunda 2001) for examining one sustainable entrepreneur over time in her quest to create social innovation in the clothing sector, a sector often attached to sustainability challenges. This is done by adopting a process perspective (Steyaert 2007) to the entrepreneur's daily work and analysing the 'fitting in' and 'standing out' of the entrepreneur's activities observed in-situ and narrated in interviews during 2010–2014.

This study contributes to uncovering the everydayness (Karatas-Ozkan and Chell 2010; Steyaert and Katz 2004) of SE and examines how networks of practice (Brown and Duguid 2001) relate to the process of social innovation in SE. In addition, this study provides an empirical example of 'how their [entrepreneurs'] practices become classified along – two dimensions' (De Clercq and Voronov 2009, 410); namely fitting in and standing out. Moreover, the study shows that sustainable entrepreneurs need to work in several networks of practice in managing their venture.

The chapter is organised as follows. First, SE and social innovation are discussed in relation to fitting in and standing out in networks of practice from a processual perspective. Thereafter, the methodology based on narrative analysis is presented. The findings section presents how the studied sustainable entrepreneur took part in creating social innovation in the clothing sector. Finally, the findings are discussed with previous literature, and conclusions are drawn.

Creating social innovation in sustainable entrepreneurship

Sustainable entrepreneurship and social innovation

Sustainable entrepreneurship refers to entrepreneurial activities that enable sustainable development (Shepherd and Patzelt 2011). Sustainable entrepreneurs are considered as the catalysts for systemic change (Parrish and Foxon 2006). Moreover, they introduce future services because they work for a sustainable world that does not yet exist (Shepherd and Patzelt 2011).

In existing research, sustainability entrepreneurship has been introduced as a solution to market imperfections (Cohen and Winn 2007) and a means to realise sustainability innovation to the mass market (Schaltegger and Wagner 2011). The SE literature is characterised by the urgent need to take seriously the limited carrying capacity of our planet (Dean and McMullen 2007; Shepherd and Patzelt 2011). This casts a systemic perspective on SE, which is reinforced by various typologies of entrepreneurs (Schaltegger and Wagner 2011). Yet we know little of the process of SE (Poldner *et al.* 2015).

The notion of social innovation brings the focus on solutions to the contemporary problems with models explaining the different stages of social innovation (see for example Murray *et al.* 2010). Social innovation results are described as 'new ideas that meet unmet needs' in any sector (Mulgan 2007, 4). Social innovation may concern either the *process*, for instance individual creativity or organisational structure, or the *outcome*, for instance new products, features or methods (Phills *et al.* 2008). Regardless of the stance, entrepreneurs can be understood as agents of social innovation (Dees and Anderson 2006). Yet, there exists uncertainty as to how to define social innovation (DeBruin *et al.* 2014).

Sustainable entrepreneur in-between networks of practice

According to De Clercq and Voronov (2009), newcomers, such as entrepreneurs, need to build legitimacy in order to make an impact and 'fit in'. However, they are also expected to create new solutions and 'stand out'. This perspective highlights the essence of SE aiming to shift the way things are done and create social innovation.

De Clercq and Voronov described the 'entrepreneurship process as a combination of both purposeful and non-purposeful, socially embedded practices' (2009, 401). They drew from Bourdieu and used cultural and symbolic capital to explain entrepreneurship. While the use of capitals explains how newcomers affect established fields, the discussion lacks how newcomers know which field to relate to when sustainability challenges are dispersed among numerous fields of human and non-human activity. Moreover, while De Clercq and Voronov focused on institutional transformation, they are short on how knowledge sharing occurs within a field.

Networks of practice describes the sharing of knowledge in 'extended epistemic groups' (Brown and Duguid 2001, 204–206). Yet, the differences in practices between networks create barriers for sharing knowledge easily. In comparison to communities of practice (Lave and Wenger 1991), networks of practice may cross organisational boundaries and include competitors, while they also remain useful to the participants in the form of shared knowledge.

Thus, new ways of doing things emerge from in-between networks of practice when brokers introduce new ideas to them (Burt 2004). Brokers work at the borders of different communities by suppressing their other identities (Wenger 2000). Previous research has identified brokers of new ideas for example in professional open innovation communities (Fleming and Waguespack 2007).

According to Burt (2004), the best ideas are born from sharing knowledge between groups across structural holes, which represent differences in knowledge between actors. He introduced four levels of brokerage between the groups. First, the broker makes different actors familiar with each other's perspectives. Second, the broker introduces best practice to them. Third, the broker finds analogies between seemingly different groups and tries to enable learning, which is more demanding. Fourth, the broker creates a synthesis of the different groups.

In sum, like new ideas, social innovation is created across the borders of networks of practice by sustainable entrepreneurs working as brokers in-between networks of practice. In order to study the creation process, this study focuses on what actors do (Barley and Kunda 2001). This entails taking a processual perspective to entrepreneurship at the micro-level (Karatas-Ozkan and Chell 2010) and looking at entrepreneurs' everyday instances (Steyaert and Katz 2004).

Process perspective to sustainable entrepreneurship

This study uses a process perspective to SE. The interest in processes in entrepreneurship research calls for understanding ongoing processes instead of static categories (Steyaert 2012). One emphasis in processual research is to study entrepreneurs' experiences (Steyaert 2007), which are reflected in everyday instances and language use.

Increasingly, studies focus on the entrepreneurs' perspective, taking narratives as the starting point. According to Steyaert (2007), the narrative approach in entrepreneurship has been applied to understanding learning, legitimation and identity-construction. In their overview of methodologies, Larty and Hamilton (2011) concluded that there is a variety of approaches to study entrepreneurship from a narrative perspective, which makes it difficult to summarise existing research. However, the shared aim is to give alternative understandings of entrepreneurship (Gartner 2010).

Empirical context

The broad context for this study is the clothing sector, which employs 60 million people globally (International Labour Organization 2014). Producing and using clothing is a global complex socio-material network with economic, social, ecological and political effects. A single T-shirt requires a sophisticated web of activities from planting seeds, producing items from fabrics, using items and eventually getting rid of them (Rivoli 2009). Thus, the process of clothing includes activities from agriculture, manufacturing, logistics, wholesale, marketing, retail and waste management.

Clothing is accused of manifesting the harmful consumption culture including single-use and low-quality products combined with poor working conditions in developing countries. The sector has recent initiatives to make production and consumption more sustainable by, for example, introducing organic cotton, monitoring working conditions and improving recycling. Especially, the adoption of organic cotton reduces toxins generated in the production of virgin materials.

In addition to exploiting virgin materials, clothing waste recycling is an emerging issue due to the increasing amount of textile waste in Western societies. According to a Friends of the Earth Europe report (2013), from 5.8 million tons of annual clothing waste only one fourth is recycled. The recycled clothing is used as landfill, burned for energy, shipped to be sold in developing countries and reused for new clothing (Figure 17.1).

Although recycling is an emerging trend, the recycling of clothing is less developed than for instance paper and glass due to numerous different fabric fibres. Moreover, there are few asking what happens to the unused fabric cuts from industry or unsold clothing from retailing.

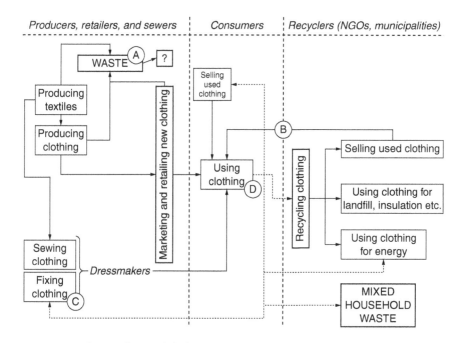

Figure 17.1 The circulation of clothing.

The clothing sector in Finland, like that in the majority of developed countries, suffers from a decline of jobs because manufacturing has been shifted to countries with lower levels of pay. Yet, institutions educate dressmakers consistently. Therefore, there are fewer jobs in the clothing sector and entrepreneurship is a viable choice for trained dressmakers.

Methodology

Data

I conducted an exploratory single case study, which enabled looking at the social innovation creation process comprehensively by focusing on one entrepreneur's work in terms of fitting in or standing out in emerging networks of practice. The sampling was purposeful (Marshall 1996). According to the first criterion, the activities should have existed beyond one year with evidence of turnover. Second, the business idea should have included an aim to contribute to sustainability. These criteria ensured that the chosen entrepreneur had experience on combining different aspects of sustainability, i.e. economic, social and ecological aspects, in everyday work. Yet despite purposeful sampling, it was not clear how the case would develop over time.

The entrepreneur, born in the early 1980s, established her enterprise in 2007 with a business partner. The data include seven interviews and three observation visits to shadow (Czarniawska 2007) the entrepreneur (Table 17.1).

In addition, I used various documents. The rich empirical material provides vivid in-situ and retrospective narratives of her entrepreneurial path.

Table 17.1 Research data

Type	Year (number)	Interviewee/location	Duration
Interview	2010 (1)* 2011 (1* + 1**) 2013 (3) 2014 (1)	Entrepreneur	30–150 minutes
Observation	2011 (1) 2013 (2)	Atelier	1–2 days
News articles	2009–2014 (10)	In various online and printed media	
Blog posts	2010–2014 (41)	Four blogs updated by the entrepreneur	
Photos	2013 (24)	During observation	

Notes
*   Another researcher generated the interview data for an independent research project (Haanpää and Tuppurainen 2012).
** Author and another researcher generated the interview data jointly.

It is important to ask how much narratives reflect how things are done in everyday situations, since retrospective narratives on past events are interpretations delivered by the narrator and influenced by the researcher. However, I understand that while the entrepreneur is largely capable of describing her everyday work (Hitchings 2012), using narratives from different times also provides material closer to the described events.

Data analysis

The strength of the narrative approach is to analyse text as longer entities for understanding one's position in the social world, and not break it into small categories whereby part of the meaning can be lost (Riessman 2008). This study looks at the connection between meaning and action (ibid.): What the entrepreneur made of her situation and what activities she undertook as an entrepreneur. Moreover, I adopt a *thematic analysis* to narratives, with a focus on *what* has been said instead of *how* or *why*, and rely more heavily on previous theory for the interpretation (ibid.).

I used qualitative data analysis software (NVivo) to organise the data. I carried out initial coding in two stages for organising the data (Saldaña 2013). First, I coded the data 'in vivo', using the entrepreneur's own words, which resulted in over 350 codes and revealed her narratives about different situations. Second, I grouped the narratives thematically (Attride-Stirling 2001), which exposed the different networks of practice (Table 17.2). Third, I captured the longitudinal aspect of the entrepreneurial path by developing timelines (Langley 1999) constructed from the narratives.

Findings

This section presents the networks of practice emerging from the entrepreneur's work in-between the initial networks (Figure 17.1). Thereafter, I describe her work, the 'fitting in' and 'standing out', and the emerging networks of practice. Finally, I discuss her brokering at the intersection of the networks of practice.

At the intersection of networks of practice

Based on the entrepreneur's narratives, the wasteful circulation of clothing was the starting point for initiating entrepreneurial activities. The early aim was to do *up-cycle design* using post-industry and post-consumer waste (A and B, Figure 17.1) as well as to make clothes from clothes (C). The latter is the most demanding form of up-cycle design since the process is unique. Additionally, the aim was to discuss the proper use of clothing with consumers, extending the lifecycle of clothing (D). All of these activities reduced the toxins and waste generated in the production of new fabrics from virgin materials.

Discussing these apparently simple positions reveals how the entrepreneur worked in a complex web of actors and activities. Here the main ones are

Table 17.2 Illustrative quotes

Networks of practice	Thematic grouping	Quotes
I Advancing up-cycle design		She aimed to make up-cycle design mundane compared to its marginal and elitist status (Observation 2013)
Higher degree of processing clothing waste	• Concerned about the future of clothing sector • Recycling clothing • Cooperating with clothing recyclers and manufacturers • Cooperating with up-cycle-designers • Organising recycling events	'It [environmental issues] is unknown overall – ecological and ethical thinking do not belong to the fashion business. They are two different worlds.' (Interview 2013)
Renewing the education of dressmakers	• Concerned about the future of dressmaking • Developing up-cycle designing • Including customers in the design process	'We teach younger people here and educate people who enter the door to think in novel ways and to realise that there exist alternatives nowadays.' (Interview 2010)
II Creating a seasonal employment model	• Concerned about youth unemployment • Coaching young professionals and interns • Gaining workforce	'We had no possibilities to employ anyone – so for almost three years I have run it [the developed employment model].' (Interview 2013)
III Promoting sustainable entrepreneurship	• Developing the system and pioneer structures • Developing her own activities • Developing sustainable entrepreneurship peer support • Educating others	'Sustainable entrepreneurship is an attitude to life. It is not abducted value-base from outside, so "now we have this set of criteria, this is how we work". But it is the activity itself.' (Interview 2010)

referred to broadly as (1) the clothing sector, (2) recycling, (3) entrepreneurship and (4) high youth unemployment. Initially, her professional knowledge was from the clothing sector. However, since the effects of clothing waste on the environment deeply concerned her, she started to get involved with recycling. Eventually, she established a venture in order to pursue a creative career in the clothing sector while using recycled materials. She also became involved with other entrepreneurs who were concerned about sustainability and aimed to catalyse systemic change. As typical in the clothing sector, her venture hosted one to three interns per semester. Thus, she came to experience the high degree of youth unemployment in the sector.

The described webs can be referred to as networks of practice (Brown and Duguid 2001) with their own means for knowledge sharing. What is more interesting for the purpose of this study is how she ended up working at the intersection of these networks of practice. Her knowledge from various existing networks enabled the emergence of new networks (Figure 17.2, p. 334).

During the studied years she (1) advanced up-cycle design, (2) created a seasonal employment model and (3) promoted sustainable[1] entrepreneurship. For people situated in the initial networks, her activities could have seemed partial – while for her it all made sense. Next, I describe her work in each emerging network of practice.

Advancing up-cycle design

Her passion for advancing up-cycle design dictated that she and her business partner refused to use new fabrics from virgin materials. At first, they were anxious about how their idealism would be greeted since it was not the standard approach in the clothing sector.

> Unfortunately I cannot touch that because I have principles. And if I once deviate from principles, I have sold out. And time after time the reaction has been appreciative. Instead of like 'bah' it is 'Well, it's great that someone still holds on to their principles. Can you suggest someplace else?'
>
> (Interview 2010)

In addition to her own atelier, her advancement of up-cycle design included influencing the clothing sector to reuse materials. The entrepreneur aimed to achieve a higher degree of processing clothing waste. She advanced this by participating in clothing sector trade shows, co-organising a popular annual recycling event, and cooperating with large clothing manufacturers. These seemingly different activities came together in her everyday work.

Another, albeit slower, way to influence the clothing sector was renewing the education.

> The [dressmaker] education drags behind – it has not been renewed since there's nowhere to renew. I have suggested up-cycle design. But also ateliers are dying away, no one knows what will happen.
>
> (Shadowing 2013)

She was appointed as the chair of an advisory board discussing dressmakers' education. Consequently, she promoted an up-cycle approach to design as a chair and while hosting interns.

Creating a seasonal employment model

Employment prospects were not optimistic for the hosted interns. Although she felt that she would like to engage them in up-cycle design as workers, she had no resources for employment. Eventually, she came up with a plan, which was inspired by the frustration toward the system allowing the over-education of dressmakers leading to unemployment. She described the job advertisement.

> Are you sick of employment policies and their ability to offer temporary work? Now we have something else for you!
>
> (Interview 2011)

The plan was to engage young graduate but unemployed dressmakers in up-cycle design. The activity started and they designed a collection, which was sold in the entrepreneur's store. By the end of the month, the financial commission received by 'crossways engaged' (interview 2013) young dressmakers was reported to the employment authorities who diminished the unemployment allowance accordingly. The innovative model enabled young professionals to keep their social security benefit while experimenting with entrepreneurship and developing their professional knowhow. In time, the majority were either employed elsewhere or accepted to continue their studies in highly sought after higher education institutions.

Promoting sustainable entrepreneurship

The entrepreneur had a holistic worldview that connected human awareness to the overall state of the planet. She brought up her perspective at various instances.

> No one is born here with an idea that my mission is to destroy this planet, cause suffering, – no one has this automatically inserted in their head. It is what our society feeds there, this contemporary model.
>
> (Interview 2010)

The entrepreneur did not initially label her venture as a sustainable enterprise. Yet, after a couple of years the enterprise was 'found' by activists and she became an advocate for SE.

> In our society, to put it rather bluntly, it is easier to work when you have a label under which you can go. In a way, the sustainable entrepreneurship concept makes it easier so that I don't have to be crazy alone. Instead I'm crazy with a label [laughs]. I have a diagnosis I can quote for this mental illness.
>
> (Interview 2013)

In addition to using the label, she also promoted it. She and other advocates arrived at establishing a peer-support organisation for sustainable entrepreneurs.

The 'fitting in' and 'standing out' of the entrepreneur

Next, I present a classification of the entrepreneur's activities in terms of 'fitting in' and 'standing out' (De Clercq and Voronov 2009) in the emerging networks of practice (Table 17.3). Some of her activities 'fitted in' and brought her benefits. For instance, the cooperation with large organisations in recycling provided a continuous flow of material for up-cycle designs. Getting involved with dressmakers' education gave her an opportunity to promote her views with sector representatives. By organising the recycling event, she noticed the new up-cycle designers.

In general, hosting interns enables organisations to gain inexpensive labour but interns have varying abilities. The entrepreneur's visible interest in up-cycle design attracted motivated interns. Moreover, after internships the employment model enabled her to engage skilful dressmakers to experiment with larger scale up-cycle design. Later, she implemented the learnings and set up her own up-cycle designer brand.

In addition to publicity, cooperation with other entrepreneurs in the same space saved her rental costs. Moreover, this hub of ecological service providers brought in more customers.

Inescapably, the standing out resulted in resistance and plans did not proceed; large organisations were suspicious of the advancement of up-cycle design. The large manufacturers were reluctant to let her use their industrial cuts.

> Two interior designers using recycled materials come to visit the entrepreneur to discuss cooperation. The designers are fascinated by the products being sold in the space. They stop in front of a rack full of colourful clothes from printed fabrics. Are they really materials someone considered waste? Yes. The entrepreneur explains that they came from a large Finnish clothes manufacturer. At first they were positive about her using their industrial cuts otherwise considered as waste. But when presenting the designs to the decision-makers, they became scared and wanted to protect the prints. The entrepreneur suggested they would use only the blank cuts. Still, they considered it too difficult to separate them from printed ones. The cooperation ceased and the cuts continued to go to waste. The visiting designers are shocked. She continues: I try to stab every potential place. This is a preaching job. But not to worry, [there exists] already six years of preaching.
>
> (Shadowing 2013)

The passage shows how the entrepreneur looked for places to source materials and promote up-cycle design. She engaged in a dialogue with manufacturers about the use of industrial cuts when she had the chance to discuss with them.

Concerning the other emerging networks of practice, the seasonal employment model gradually waned. She felt that the young professionals were slow to grasp entrepreneurial opportunities. Thus, she sought external funding to keep them engaged for longer periods. However, publicly funded youth employment

Table 17.3 Work in the emerging networks of practice

	Activities fitting in*	Benefits for the venture*	Activities standing out*	Potential effects of standing out
I Advancing up-cycle design	Own atelier (clothes-to-clothes designs) and second-hand shop	Space for creativity and experimentation	Unique designs are laborious and time-consuming	Consumers' awareness increases
Higher degree of processing clothing waste	Participating in clothing sector trade shows	Visibility	Ecological thinking does not belong to the fashion business; the entrepreneur feels like a freak	Sector awareness increases
	Co-organising an annual large recycling event for up-cycle designers	Opportunity to see newcomers and find new products to supply	Up-cycle designers are small and the field is scattered	Up-cycle designers cooperation increases
	Cooperation with large clothing recyclers	A continuous flow of material for up-cycle designing	Large organisations are reluctant to develop new models that require experimenting at the small scale	Large clothing recyclers develop their working methods
	Cooperation with large clothing manufacturers	A continuous flow of homogeneous material for up-cycle designing	Protecting the patterns prevents reuse of industrial cuts	Large clothing manufacturers start to use industrial cut
Renewing the education of dressmakers	Chairing an advisory group for dressmakers' education development	Opportunity to discuss with sector representatives	New material is easily available ('candyshop') so reuse of material seems irrelevant	Increase local production, dressmakers' employment and the use of clothing waste
	Hosting 1–3 interns per semester	Gaining inexpensive labour	Turnover of interns (every 3–12 weeks)	More up-cycle designers

II Creating a seasonal employment model	Coaching interns	Discussing with future professionals	Issues that prevent committing to employment	People find a meaningful career
	Communicating with employment authorities	Gaining inexpensive labour	Difficulties of forming cooperation with publicly funded employment projects	Moving between social security and entrepreneurship becomes less bureaucratic
	Own Reuse label: 'Community design and small serial production of clothing from clothing waste'	Larger-scale experiment with up-cycle design	Workers' reluctance to use entrepreneurial opportunities	More up-cycle designers
III Promoting sustainable entrepreneurship	Co-founding a peer-support organisation for sustainable entrepreneurs	Publicity	Peer-support organisation focused more on promoting the phenomenon than supporting entrepreneurs	Sustainable entrepreneurship becomes more common
	Hosting ecological services in the space	Financial synergies for splitting costs with subtenants	Managing the turnover of subtenants	The amount of ecological service providers increases
	Creating something 'new'	First-mover advantageous and psychological satisfaction	Difficulties in getting knowledgeable support	Changes in entrepreneurial practices

Note
* Themes below from narratives.

projects were suspicious towards her initiative since she was from the private sector. They also warned her not to get involved with employment bureaucracy.

> At the time when I built the employment model I went to present it to one project [funded by the European Union]. The main coordinator clapped her hands, stood up behind the table, went to get her colleague, and asked if she could hug me. I was like what the heck is happening here. [Coordinator said:] 'Do you understand you have access to something? If we could make a project out of it, it'd answer to everything we've hoped for. But for goodness sake, don't bring it here since your thing is so holistic that it'd be killed inside the bureaucracy. But yeah, try to hang on with your model.' And I was smiling like mmm [imitates a forced smile]. Well, someone else might have said right, I won't do it [alone]. But I did.
>
> (Interview 2013)

These experiences left her suspicious of publicly supported initiatives, and she turned further toward entrepreneurship. Later, she modified the model to engage professionals with more experience as entrepreneurs. These freelancers subleased space from her atelier and were involved with her up-cycle design team. According to her, these colleagues appreciated daily collaboration after the experiences of working in solitude as atelier keepers.

With regard to the established SE peer-support organisation, the entrepreneur reported that it did not bring the expected peer-support, although it brought her publicity. In her search for support she tried entrepreneurship associations and later a reality TV show.

> We [the team] attended [Finnish] Shark Tank last autumn. They are cold money investors, the judges. But they said that they wouldn't get on-board with something like this because it is such an unknown area. But in principle you speak convincingly and your idea surely works. I said that I'm searching for a business developer, a partner that starts to pace this firmly to become a business since I lack the experience. So far I've learned each step at a time. But I'd like to have someone who has already walked the path once.
>
> (Interview 2013)

Yet, her interest in novel solutions drove away people with business experience. Moreover, despite peer-support that existed in the established entrepreneurship associations, their hostile attitude toward SE made her feel uncomfortable.

Brokering at the intersection of networks of practice

Due to her work in various networks of practice, the entrepreneur was able to combine knowledge from these networks as a broker. Brokering in-between the networks of practice led to the creation of the emerging networks of practice discussed above.

The sustainable entrepreneur engaged in brokering on three levels (Burt 2004). First, she intermediated knowledge of different networks of practice, for example by connecting recycling and the clothing sector. Second, she introduced best practice to different networks; for example, by explaining what kinds of materials were the best for up-cycle designing. Third, she aimed at different networks of practice, learning about the analogies between them in terms of further applications; for example by engaging unemployed dressmakers with larger scale up-cycle designing. Finally, her long-term goal was to create a synthesis joining all the activities.

> This eco-dressmaking cannot be scaled easily. We could offer a service for people to come with their sacks. One of it clothes to be fixed and another [for us] to sort materials for reworking ... products to be sold in a store. Then we would look at what can be reused for energy. We would construct a recycling system based on a fortified cradle-to-cradle ideology in order to use the existing materials for as long as possible. Since at the moment this is not done efficiently.
>
> (Interview 2010)

However, her goals did not materialise during the fieldwork period. While in the course of time, she was able to construct emerging networks of practice that enabled her to work, she experienced conflicts. First, reusing materials is the norm in up-cycle design while in the fashion industry it is an emerging trend. Second, while interested in up-cycle design, young professionals were less enthusiastic about becoming entrepreneurs. Third, acting upon sustainability concerns is appreciated by some, while in the established views of entrepreneurship it is an oddity, or even considered as a threat.

Discussion and conclusions

Sustainable entrepreneurship refers to entrepreneurial activity that produces future goods for a more sustainable future (Shepherd and Patzelt 2011). Yet, we know little of the sustainable entrepreneurs' process (Poldner et al. 2015) or how the everyday work is done. This study aimed to examine how a sustainable entrepreneur created social innovation in the clothing sector over time by adopting the process perspective to entrepreneurship (Steyaert 2007, 2012).

By following the work of one sustainable entrepreneur during 2010–2014, this study examined how the entrepreneur worked in various networks of practice (Brown and Duguid 2001). She brokered knowledge between these networks (Burt 2004), in which she fitted in and stood out (De Clercq and Voronov 2009).

Interestingly, her work at the intersection of existing and emerging networks of practice resulted in the creation of potentially scalable activities, i.e. social innovation (Figure 17.2). The reuse of materials, educational development, employment model and peer-support are all potential activities in other sectors

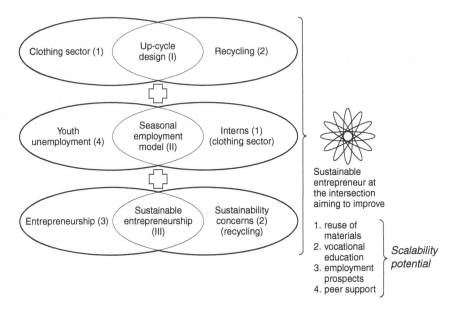

Figure 17.2 The combination of networks of practice.

as well. Yet, transferring knowledge is challenging since in one network of practice activity may be accepted, while in another it is not tolerated (Brown and
Duguid 2001). Due to the limited timeframe, this study cannot conclude
whether her venture led to the described potential effects. However, it is possible to form implications for theory and suggest avenues for future research.

Firstly, this study is a grounded longitudinal empirical example of introducing 'future services' (Shepherd and Patzelt 2011); namely reducing the use of
virgin materials while employing young professionals and enabling a socially
sustainable life. Furthermore, this study examines work (Barley and Kunda
2001), and answers calls to discuss the everydayness of entrepreneurship
(Karatas-Ozkan and Chell 2010; Steyaert and Katz 2004) in the context of SE.

Second, the study suggests how social innovation in SE is created via working
in several networks of practice. Instead of trying to transform one network, for
example an industrial sector (De Clercq and Voronov 2009), sustainable entrepreneurs can work in several networks. While the former is considered challenging, the latter is no easier. The entrepreneur's narratives confirmed the paradox
described by De Clercq and Voronov: While there was a need to transform institutions by standing out, i.e. create social innovation, the entrepreneur needed
existing networks of practice in order to function. However, fitting in was likely to
decrease the likelihood of social innovation, whereas standing out increased it. As
a result, there was a constant flux between fitting in and standing out.

By showing the importance of networks of practice for a sustainable entrepreneur, I suggest that it is not enough that sustainable entrepreneurs work

within close proximity to their passion; in this case reusing and recycling clothing. Instead, they benefit from acting as brokers in-between relevant networks of practice; addressing sustainability challenges requires versatile knowledge that is more likely to be gained from various networks. In addition, the everyday activities of the sustainable entrepreneur – here consisting of sewing, training and lobbying – bring together different networks of practice (Brown and Duguid 2001, 206), which previously were not considered together and may affect other networks. Thus, the studied entrepreneur can be interpreted as a broker (Burt 2004), who combined knowledge from various networks in order to build emerging networks of practice. Consequently, this study extends the use of brokering to sustainable entrepreneurs working in-between different networks of practice.

Third, while the promise of entrepreneurship for sustainability is to stand out, the existing research is short on the contextual differences, ethical and political aspects, and difficulties related to such work (Dey and Steyaert 2016). By applying the notion of networks of practice to sustainability entrepreneurship, this study shows how entrepreneurs are embedded in existing networks for learning how things are done. Thus, work for social innovation is embedded in specific contexts.

Altogether, this does not mean sustainable entrepreneurs should quit trying. On the contrary, by focusing on how things are done, the embedded SE processes can be further analysed. At its best, presenting the contextual everyday instances of SE increases understanding of the ways to address sustainability challenges via entrepreneurship.

Fourth, the study elaborates the process of building legitimacy described by De Clercq and Voronov (2009). While they suggested that entrepreneurs need to gain legitimacy in one network, this study shows that sustainable entrepreneurs need to be present in several networks of practice. In some networks sustainable entrepreneurs might be experts, fit in and reinforce institutions. Yet, with brokering knowledge between networks of practice they may be experienced as newcomers in others and stand out. Eventually, through their brokering they may transform the institutions and create social innovation.

Thus, it is not enough that the fitting in and standing out is analysed in one network of practice, but rather in several networks. This finding echoes the criticism of new venture legitimation theories that have collapsed different stakeholders (for example investors, consumers) into one assumed audience for entrepreneurs (Überbacher 2014). In practice, sustainable entrepreneurs participate in various networks of practice and accordingly they have to work in all of them. In regard to SE, the everyday work in various networks of practice explains why the creation of social innovation is complex.

Finally, this study opens up avenues for future research. The process approach can be applied to various themes in SE research, for instance venture failure. Moreover, future research could take into consideration the impact of the overall life situation of entrepreneurs with regard to social innovation process alongside work practices. Lastly, studying networks of practice in other sectors and including other actors' perspectives would enable SE research to provide deeper contextual understanding of the potential solutions to the complex array of sustainability challenges. The above mentioned directions for future research would increase our knowledge of the agentic and practice aspects of SE.

Acknowledgements

I wish to thank Simo Tuppurainen for the interviews generated in an independent research project by the Finnish Youth Research Network. Also, I thank the two anonymous reviewers, Hanna Timonen, Tiina Taipale and Ari Kuismin for their invaluable comments.

Note

1 Finnish practitioners use the concept 'societal entrepreneurship' ('yhteiskunnallinen yrittäjyys').

References

Attride-Stirling J. (2001) 'Thematic networks: An analytic tool for qualitative research' *Qualitative Research* 1 385–405.

Barley S. and Kunda G. (2001) 'Bringing work back in' *Organization Science* 12 76–95.

Brown J. S. and Duguid P. (2001) 'Knowledge and organization: A social-practice perspective' *Organization Science* 12 198–213.

Burt R. S. (2004) 'Structural holes and good ideas' *American Journal of Sociology* 110 349–399.

Cohen B. and Winn M. I. (2007) 'Market imperfections, opportunities, and sustainable entrepreneurship' *Journal of Business Venturing* 22 29–49.

Czarniawska B. (2007) *Shadowing: And other techniques for doing fieldwork in modern societies* Copenhagen Business School Press, Malmö, Oslo.

Dean T. J. and McMullen J. S. (2007) 'Toward a theory of sustainable entrepreneurship: Reducing environmental degradation through entrepreneurial action' *Journal of Business Venturing* 22 50–76.

DeBruin A., Shaw E. and Chalmers D. (2014) 'Social entrepreneurship: Looking back, moving ahead' in Chell E and Karatas-Ozkan M eds, *Handbook of research on small business and entrepreneurship* Edward Elgar, Cheltenham, 392–416.

De Clercq D. and Voronov M. (2009) 'Toward a practice perspective of entrepreneurship: Entrepreneurial legitimacy as habitus' *International Small Business Journal* 27 395–419.

Dees J. G. and Anderson B. B. (2006) 'Framing a theory of social entrepreneurship: Building on two schools of practice and thought' *Research on Social Entrepreneurship: Understanding and Contributing to an Emerging Field* 1 39–66.

Dey P. and Steyaert C. (2016) 'Rethinking the space of ethics in social entrepreneurship: Power, subjectivity, and practices of freedom' *Journal of Business Ethics* 133 627–641.

Fleming L. and Waguespack D. M. (2007) 'Brokerage, boundary spanning, and leadership in open innovation communities' *Organization Science* 18 165–180.

Friends of the Earth Europe (2013) *Less is more: Resource efficiency through waste collection, recycling and reuse.*

Gartner W. B. (2010) 'A new path to the waterfall: A narrative on a use of entrepreneurial narrative' *International Small Business Journal* 28 6–19.

Haanpää, L. and Tuppurainen, S. (2012) *Nuoret yrittävät. Vastuullisuus, joustavuus ja mahdollisuudet yrittäjyydessä. Nuorisotutkimusseura/Nuorisotutkimusverkosto julkaisuja* Hakapaino, Helsinki.

Hitchings R. (2012) 'People can talk about their practices' *Area* 44 61–67.

International Labour Organization (2014) *Textiles, clothing, leather and footwear sector* http://ilo.org/global/industries-and-sectors/textiles-clothing-leather-footwear/lang-en/index.htm Accessed 15 December 2014.

Karatas-Ozkan M. and Chell E. (2010) *Nascent entrepreneurship and learning* Edward Elgar, Cheltenham.

Langley A. (1999) 'Strategies for theorizing from process data' *Academy of Management Review* 24 691–710.

Larty J. and Hamilton E. (2011) 'Structural approaches to narrative analysis in entrepreneurship research: Exemplars from two researchers' *International Small Business Journal* 29 220–237.

Lave J. and Wenger E. (1991) *Situated learning: Legitimate peripheral participation* Cambridge University Press, Cambridge.

Marshall M. N. (1996) 'Sampling for qualitative research' *Family Practice* 13 522–526.

Mulgan G. (2007) *Social innovation: What it is, why it matters and how it can be accelerated* The Young Foundation.

Murray R., Caulier-Grice J. and Mulgan G. (2010) *The open book of social innovation* National Endowment for Science, Technology and the Art.

Parrish B. D. and Foxon T. J. (2006) 'Sustainability entrepreneurship and equitable transitions to a low-carbon economy' *Greener Management International* winter 47–62.

Phills J. A. J., Deiglmeier K. and Miller D. T. (2008) 'Rediscovering social innovation' *Stanford Social Innovation Review* 34–43.

Poldner K., Shrivastava P. and Branzei O. (2015) 'Embodied multi-discursivity: An aesthetic process approach to sustainable entrepreneurship' *Business & Society* 1–39.

Riessman K. K. (2008) *Narrative methods for the human sciences* Sage, Los Angeles.

Rivoli P. (2009) *The travels of a T-shirt in the global economy: An economist examines the markets, power, and politics of world trade* Second Edition Wiley, Hoboken, NJ.

Saldaña J. (2013) *The coding manual for qualitative researchers* Second Edition Sage, Los Angeles.

Schaltegger S. and Wagner M. (2011) 'Sustainable entrepreneurship and sustainability innovation: Categories and interactions' *Business Strategy and the Environment* 20 222–237.

Shepherd D. A. and Patzelt H. (2011) 'The new field of sustainable entrepreneurship: Studying entrepreneurial action linking "What is to be sustained" with "What is to be developed"' *Entrepreneurship Theory and Practice* 35 137–163.

Steyaert C. (2007) '"Entrepreneuring" as a conceptual attractor? A review of process theories in 20 years of entrepreneurship studies' *Entrepreneurship & Regional Development* 19 453–477.

Steyaert C. (2012) 'Making the multiple: Theorising processes of entrepreneurship and organisation' in Hjorth D. ed., *Handbook on organizational entrepreneurship* Edward Elgar, Cheltenham, 151–168.

Steyaert C. and Katz J. (2004) 'Reclaiming the space of entrepreneurship in society: Geographical, discursive and social dimensions' *Entrepreneurship & Regional Development* 16 179–196.

Überbacher F. (2014) 'Legitimation of new ventures: A review and research programme' *Journal of Management Studies* 51 667–698.

Wenger E. (2000) 'Communities of practice and social learning systems' *Organization* 7 225–246.

18 Employee energy cooperatives: employee entrepreneurial activities towards a more sustainable future

Anja Shadabi and Carsten Herbes

Funding

This chapter draws on research funded by the program "Socio-Ecological Research" (SÖF) of the German Federal Ministry of Education and Research (BMBF), reference number 01UN1202B. Financial support is gratefully acknowledged. The authors are solely responsible for the content of this text and the opinions expressed.

Introduction

In recent years, citizens have carried through many activities towards a more sustainable future through the use of renewable energy systems in their homes or the formation of cooperatives to produce electricity from renewable energy sources. Especially in the context of a change to more sustainable energy sources ("energy transition") citizens are ahead of many organizations in Germany. The number of citizen energy cooperatives rose significantly and close to 900 are operating today (Klaus Novy Institut, 2014). Besides, a large number of people have switched to green electricity tariffs. Many of the 1.5 million photovoltaic (PV) systems in Germany (Wirth, 2015) have been installed in private households (TrendResearch, 2013).

Companies' actions towards more sustainability are diverse, ranging from the introduction of environmental management systems such as EMAS or ISO 14001 to the adoption of the triple-bottom-line, CSR and other related concepts. Although a variety of instruments for the greening of organizations exists, research has found mixed results on the success of these programs (Jiang and Bansal, 2003; Boiral, 2007; Ones and Dilchert, 2012b). At the same time, research has pointed out that employees are a key to a successful contribution to sustainability in companies (Hanna *et al.*, 2000; del Brío *et al.*, 2007; Wolf, 2013). They not only have the interest and willingness to act more pro-environmentally at their workplace, but they can also bring in privately gained expertise, e.g., regarding renewable energy.

In considering these findings, a solution can be found in sustainable entrepreneurship. Sustainable entrepreneurship seems to not only contribute to the development of a sustainable economy (Gibbs, 2009; Parrish and Foxon, 2009) but can also be used to achieve institutional change (Thompson *et al.*, 2015). In following Shepherd and Patzelt's definition,

> sustainable entrepreneurship is focused on the preservation of nature, life support, and community in the pursuit of perceived opportunities to bring into existence future products, processes, and services for gain, where gain is broadly construed to include economic and non-economic gains to individuals, the economy, and society
>
> (Shepherd and Patzelt, 2011, p. 142)

we will provide an empirical example of employee driven sustainable entrepreneurship.

A considerable body of research on (sustainable) entrepreneurship focuses on individual entrepreneurs which seems to lack empirical evidence and which relies heavily on findings about individual motivations (Pastakia, 1998; Schaltegger, 2002; Gibbs, 2009). As a contribution to the field of sustainable entrepreneurship and in contrast to the focus of the research on single entrepreneurs and to also include the aspect of social interaction (Shepherd, 2015) we will show that the employee energy cooperatives (EECs) were implemented by groups of employees in the context of two different host companies. We further aim to demonstrate that EECs can address corporate inaction regarding sustainable entrepreneurial behaviors. The following research question will thereby guide our research: What influences the emergence of employee driven entrepreneurial action and what can be learned from the empirical example of EECs in this respect?

Corporate greening through entrepreneurial behavior

The greening of organizations cannot only be considered an important goal, but the more interesting aspect is how to achieve sustainable companies. Research found that employees can have a substantial impact in these change processes to more sustainable firms. Looking at corporate environmental programs, Klinkers and Nelissen (1996) found that their successful implementation depends on the inclusion of employees and a simple top-down process is described as having only limited success.

However, even if a company involves employees or allows them self-initiated pro-environmental activities, the employees' pro-environmental-activity-portfolio can still be small and limited. A way to enlarge that portfolio can be entrepreneurial actions by employees in the social and physical context of the company. Research in this field has strongly focused on the individual level characteristics and claims that successful entrepreneurs possess certain leadership characteristics and other "needed" qualities like risk taking, persistence and the courage to be able to overcome organizational inactivity (Hisrich and Peters, 1986; Ones and Dilchert, 2012a). A way to more substantial pro-environmental activities can thus come through employees being sustainable intrapreneurs, i.e., intrapreneurs, who turn environmental private interests into entrepreneurial ideas (Schrader and Harrach, 2013). A core influence on environmental entrepreneurship in organizations is further seen in the organizational commitment to environmental goals which is found to vary in dimension and also on how it impacts on individuals. Empowered by the offered opportunities and the concern for environmental issues, employees can act as entrepreneurial change agents in companies (Keogh and Polonsky, 1998).

Entrepreneurial activities have further been found to depend on supportive environments (Hostager et al., 1998) or a receiving organizational climate (Hisrich, 1990). Factors that have been recognized to foster entrepreneurship are the organizational structure and management support. Consequently, entrepreneurial activities are not only multidimensional but depend besides individual characteristics of the employees involved on organizational factors and precipitating events (Hornsby et al., 1993). These events can be changes in the company structure but can also come from environmental and organizational developments that have an impact on organizational or individual characteristics, e.g., the development of new technologies or a change in consumer demand.

Literature on corporate greening more and more embraces the idea of not only combining different fields of research but also different levels of analysis to understand sustainability issues and undergoing processes in organizations regarding economic, environmental and social aspects (Shrivastava and Hart, 1992; Starik and Rands, 1995; Siebenhüner and Arnold, 2007; Zollo et al., 2013). Individual characteristics and agency, support and enabling structures are found to foster pro-environmental behavior among employees. Ramus (2001) points out that pro-environmental behavior by employees needs to be explicitly encouraged by managers and supervisors. From all supportive behaviors she found in her study environmental communication to be the most important one (Ramus 2001). Besides communication, for successful environmental entrepreneurship, Schaltegger and Wagner (2011) see the need for an existing business case that enables sustainable innovations. In fact, in having prior knowledge about environmental issues, sustainable entrepreneurs follow not only own goals but act for the good of others (Patzelt and Shepherd, 2011).

EECs and the cooperative business form

EECs are employee driven businesses that are engaged in renewable energy projects. They operate PV installations on the organization's roof or hold shares in wind power projects. Although the EECs are founded by employees of diverse German organizations, they are legally independent from these organizations (which we will call "host companies" in the remainder of this chapter). Capital is raised among the EEC members and the produced electricity is fed into the grid based on German feed-in-tariff (FIT) regulation. Their intriguing promise is how these employee initiatives with their entrepreneurial activities possibly contribute to the greening of their host companies and thus impact in many ways on society and its ambition towards a more sustainable future.

Cooperatives are a legal business form. They are well known for their governance mechanism of "one member – one vote," i.e., regardless of the invested money all members of the cooperative have the same voting rights. In the General Assembly all cooperative members elect the supervisory board of the cooperative and the supervisory board appoints the board members. Supervisory board members and board members are themselves members of the cooperative. Cooperatives thus can be both – a collective where decisions are made by all members or a dual structure with a management in place where the appointed board is in charge (Cornforth *et al.*, 1988).

Cooperatives can also be regarded as hybrid organizations, following different, even competing logics (Foreman and Whetten, 2002, p. 623). Hybrid organizations are found to manage these different goals by combining and using them to their advantage (Pache and Santos, 2013). In following economic as well as environmental and social interests, the EECs are exemplary for hybrid organizations combining different logics. EECs, although being legally independent businesses, are embedded in their host organizations: The EEC members work together in the company and assume responsibility for the EECs and thereby combine different purposes, which result in synergies between the EECs and the host companies but also on an individual level among the EEC members who bring in different skills and expertise.

Study and methods

This study was conducted as part of a larger research project which looks into employee initiatives for pro-environmental activities in organizations. The overall research framework can be described as a multi-level approach looking at the individual as well as organizational level. Part of the study was the investigation of EECs in Germany. To our knowledge, there are currently around ten EECs in Germany. These EECs evolved in a variety of different organizations and therefore are not bound to a specific industry or to a particular business type. Among the host organizations we find small and middle sized companies as well as subsidiaries of MNCs and public organizations. We see a representation of very different operating fields, ranging from livestock transportation to an organization of higher education.

Data collection

With the aim to explore the phenomenon of EECs, we conducted ten semistructured interviews with one or two representatives of the different EECs between August 2013 and November 2015. All of the interviewees were members of the board or supervisory board of these EECs. The interview time ranged from 51 to 103 minutes. All interviews were recorded and transcribed. In addition to the interviews, further data were collected from publicly available documents, i.e., press reports, news from EECs' websites and other material (e.g., presentations). Quotes taken from the interview transcripts and all written documents were translated to English by the first author.

Case selection

For a more detailed investigation two of the studied cases were selected. First, these two cases can be considered exemplary for entrepreneurial activities of employees towards more sustainability in their companies. Second, both are formed in big industrial corporations, one in the field of car manufacturing, the other one is a German subsidiary of a multinational consumer goods manufacturer. And finally, in these two cases the idea of founding an employee energy cooperative was developed in a bottom-up manner.

Data analysis

Through a detailed description of "what" before analyzing the "how" and "why" (Miles *et al.* 2013; Patton 2015) we aim to provide a basis for more empirical research on employee driven initiatives. Including a rich context description (Dyer Jr. and Wilkins, 1991) of this ongoing phenomenon we attempt to provide empirical insights to the debate in the field of sustainable entrepreneurship. Before coding we viewed and read through the entire material, taking no notes at this stage (Corbin and Strauss, 2008). Using MAXQDA software, the data analysis was done in two steps to identify emerging themes and concepts. The first cycle of coding followed and was structured by the interview guideline and the codes were written closely to the interview material. In a second step codes were categorized and ordered around emerging themes (Miles *et al.*, 2013; Kuckartz, 2014). To provide a deeper understanding for employee activities in the field of sustainable entrepreneurship and to build a more holistic picture of central decisions, processes and activities that lead to the initiation and establishment we also looked into the context of these EECs and studied them in an exploratory way (Yin, 2003).

Cases

EEC 1 emerged in the context of an automobile manufacturer in Northern Germany to which we will refer as Carco[1] in this publication. Around 9,000 employees work on the site. Capital for the PV installations was raised from the EEC members and supplemented by a bank loan. EEC shares range from a minimum of 250 to a maximum of 10,000 euros. The EEC has 227 members, who are either company employees or relatives of employees. Carco rents several company owned roofs to the EEC with the rental contract running for 25 years with an option of an extension of 5 additional years. The EEC pays a symbolic fee of only one euro per year for using Carco's roofs.

EEC 2 evolved in a subsidiary of a multinational consumer goods manufacturer in Southern Germany (Foodco). Founded in 2010, the EEC also produces

Table 18.1 Description of EEC1 and EEC2

	EEC 1 (at Carco)	EEC 2 (at Foodco)
Number of members	227	60
Renewable energy investment	Photovoltaics	Photovoltaics
Members	Employees, family members of employees	Employees, former employees
Industry of host company	Automotive	Consumer goods
Year of foundation	2008	2010

Source: authors' research.

electricity from PV systems. The single investments ranged from 300 to 3,000 euros per member. Employees and former employees (having been employed in the company during the EEC emergence) were eligible to become members of the cooperative. The number of members is 60. Around 1,500 people work on the site. Similar to EEC1, EEC 2 has a rental contract with Foodco allowing them to install and run the PV installations on the company's roof. The rental contract is made for 25 years and an annual fee of 1,000 euros for the use of the roof is paid. However, the EEC has a sponsoring contract worth more than 1,000 euros, i.e., the rental payments are sponsored by the company and which allows Foodco to use the EEC for marketing purposes.

Findings

The data analysis revealed that the emergence of the EECs is driven by various factors, which are related to the respective host companies but also to developments that can be found in the societal context. In both cases, the EEC initiation was influenced by the German Renewable Energy Act (REA) which offered and partly still offers attractive feed-in-tariffs.[2] Apart from that, a change in the German cooperative law reduced the minimum number of members in a cooperative to three. This led to a boom of citizen energy cooperatives (TrendResearch, 2013), where individuals privately finance own renewable energy projects.

EEC initiation

EEC 1 was initiated by the members of the company's works council (employees' representatives according to German labor law). Some of the works council representatives are strong supporters of renewable energy and have promoted alternative energy production in their trade union. One of our interviewees who is also one of the EEC's board members is engaged in private activities for wind energy and has already founded several energy cooperatives. The original idea of having an environmental project was already developed around 1992, when the installation of wind power plants was discussed. It was considered important by the two interviewees that the cooperative law was eased which sparked the idea to start a new initiative for a renewable energy project. Before approaching the company they got the approval of their EEC idea by the trade union. To market the EEC idea in the company, flyers with the title "Carco's roofs for sunny times" were printed and distributed among the employees.

The site's warehouse manager was the project manager of EEC 2. In the EEC, he is the head of the board. In his own words, it was his "employees who actually always wanted to have that on the roof, such a PV installation." And in his position as warehouse manager, he says, he felt responsible for the EEC founding and was also the person in the company who ensured that the PV installation was implemented as a cooperative business. On its website, the EEC mentions that its role models are citizen energy cooperatives.

Both EECs successfully combine economic, social and environmental aspects. In considering that the EECs are hybrid organizations we find that different logics operate in these two cases: a business logic by being an economically sustainable business and an environmental protection logic because of their investment into a renewable energy project thus promoting a pro-environmental cause. Social aspects can also be found, regarding the mix of EEC members, the price of the shares and the positions in the management of the EECs. It is clear that as the EECs wanted to include as many employees as possible, share prices were kept low, starting from 250 euros in EEC 1 and 300 euros in EEC 2. That way, not only white collar employees and managers but also shop floor employees were able to join. Positions in board and supervisory board are filled with members from different departments, ensuring that all or most of the company departments are represented in the EECs. However, not all EEC members are equally involved in the decision-making (Cornforth et al., 1988, pp. 155–157). Both EECs gather for the annual General Assembly. In EEC 1, especially in the beginning, many questions were raised ("What's amortization? What are reserves?") and economic aspects discussed. A few core decisions, however, e.g., choosing a bank for a loan, are done by only a few board or supervisory board members. In both cases the company name was part of the EECs' name, e.g., "cooperative of the employees of Carco."

Societal and organizational context

The analysis further showed that the context was favorable for the emergence of the two EECs. Beside the societal influences which can be seen from the growing number of citizen energy cooperatives and the supportive climate which is mirrored in many different renewable energy projects all over the country the two EECs also met supportive organizational environments. In Carco, the aim is to grow into a green automobile manufacturer ("green factory") with a CO_2 neutral and energy-efficient car production. In Foodco, a sustainability plan had been developed a few years back, which made many activities regarding the energy consumption on the site possible. The company's CEO is seen as a great source of influence:

Our boss is one step ahead, I like that, he says, we cannot keep doing what we used to. We cannot always grow, grow, grow and the use of resources increases. No, this must stop. He clearly said, we want to grow, … but the use of resources must be stabilized. … And that's how it started, everybody was asked to think how the use of resources can be lowered.

Employees in Foodco are described as very active in looking for opportunities to save energy and they already managed to install other energy-saving devices in the company (e.g., solar thermal showers). We are informed that EEC members often possess their own PV installations at home. In EEC 2, the EEC activity is not regarded as a works council activity. However, the head of the works council is the head of the EEC supervisory board.

EEC management

Positions in the EEC board and supervisory board are filled with members from different company departments and thus positions are distributed to people with specific skills. The management of the EECs is done by the board and supervisory board members; however, positions are not assigned randomly. In EEC 2, posts in the board and supervisory board were chosen according to the department where the EEC members work (e.g., from HR, management accounting, technical department) and consequently according to the qualifications they possess. None of the two EECs has employed staff, and work for the EEC is done on a voluntary basis by elected members or even supported by retired EEC members (as in EEC 1). For the functioning of the EECs, team work is thus of high importance and none or only a few activities are outsourced. For example, in EEC 1, the accounting is done by a cooperative association.

Barriers

In the interviews, several barriers were mentioned that needed to be overcome before the EECs could be established. First, agreements with the companies had to be made. Prior to the founding of EEC 1, EEC supporters and the company had several meetings to discuss the EEC idea. The biggest barrier mentioned in our interview at EEC 1 was the middle management that was no longer supportive of the idea to create an EEC, because they did not believe in the EEC's financial success and talks between EEC supporters and the company were interrupted due to this:

The biggest hurdle – for me – was that at a certain point the middle management was not supportive any longer. And we had to decide, do we dare to do that now, alone, on our own, to run a business in the company itself, to get it going in the factory. Do we really do that without the support of the employer side, do we continue? That was, I believe, the biggest hurdle, which we had to clear emotionally and mentally.

Also in EEC 2, our interviewee was sure that a supportive atmosphere was needed. The new company strategy towards sustainability convinced his direct supervisor to support the EEC idea. Our interviewee is sure that without support from higher management, the EEC formation would not have been possible. The overall organizational support is also mirrored in the fact that higher Foodco managers are members of the EEC, for example the former head of HR or the factory manager.

One of the bigger barriers was to get a deed registration to have the right to access the PV installation on the company's roof for maintenance reasons or to be able to change damaged PV panels. And for Foodco a deed registration for a single person seemed at first impossible for such a small investment and the legal department was opposed. Our interviewee says it was difficult to convince them to do that as a "nobody compared to Foodco."

Contrary to common organizational logics, i.e., expecting short amortization times and far shorter time spans for contracts, long-term contracts were developed between the companies and the EECs. Both EECs got long-term rental contracts for the roofs on which the PV panels were installed. Additionally, also issues of insurance, change of ownership, technical factors (e.g., roof safety) and liability issues had to be settled between the company and the EECs. Especially these contracts were not easy to get, the legal departments were involved and in EEC 1 the contract had to be accepted and revised by the company's headquarters.

Similarities and differences of the two cases

In general, our findings show that the two EECs have many factors in common, having the very same business idea and therefore including similar legal and other demands. In both cases the overall societal context as well as an established pro-environmental policy in the host companies were important enablers. Most differences come from the different sizes of the EECs which can be explained by the different size of the projects and the investment opportunity. It is found that in both cases many people aimed to invest more into the EECs but they could not due to the limitations of the project sizes. In EEC 1 the aim is therefore to start new projects in the field of renewable energy.

Cooperatives are eager to fulfill a variety of benefits for its members (Cornforth et al., 1988). In case of the two EECs this means a rather safe investment based on fixed feed-in-tariffs, a contribution to the reduction of the environmental footprint and possibly also to the decision-making in their companies. EECs allow for employee involvement and networking between the members coming from different departments and levels of the company. Both of the EECs are so successful that follow-up projects are envisioned and many more employees would like to join.

Discussion

Our findings have several implications for research in the field of sustainable entrepreneurship. As has been identified in earlier studies, sustainable entrepreneurial behavior of the EECs contributes to the inclusion of environmental and social aspects in doing business. The interest of having returns on investment in this business model is not less important than in other businesses, but in the two investigated cases we found more than a purely financial interest: Analyses on the EEC members' level revealed that in both cases, groups of employees or members of the organization's management fostered the idea of having their own renewable energy project in the company. Members of the EECs are familiar with the renewable energy technology, e.g., by owning a PV installation themselves, or having invested in other PV projects. This study thus agrees with findings and propositions from entrepreneurship literature that it is of importance to know about the natural environment and to be able to recognize business opportunities (Patzelt and Shepherd, 2011).

Our research further points to and agrees with findings from (sustainable) entrepreneurship and corporate greening literature that it is important that the organization provides a supportive context with written communication on the company's environmental goals (Hisrich, 1990; Ramus and Steger, 2000). Both EECs met a favorable climate, in EEC 1 it was the target of the "green factory" and Carco's environmental declaration and in EEC 2 it was the clearly presented and implemented environmental goals by the CEO and the resulting Foodco sustainability plan. Besides, both EECs had important supporting structures: In EEC 1, the works council has a remarkable standing in the company and in EEC 2 the support by management was possible because of the EEC's fit to the company's new strategy. The organizational context was not only important for establishing the ground but also for the implementation of the EECs. In both cases the EEC supporters had to discuss and fight with the company management for their ideas. Not having regained the support of middle management (EEC 1) or having supportive supervisors (EEC 2), the emergence of the EECs would have been doubtful.

We further find that it is not only the entrepreneurial idea and economic viability that is needed for a successful implementation of these activities. Both EECs evolved from a supportive societal climate where installations of PV panels are common and the formation of citizen cooperatives is growing. We suggest that the EEC members bridged their role as employees and their privately gained knowledge regarding renewable energy technology.

Although entrepreneurship is often perceived to be based on the ability and motivation of single actors having certain personal characteristics (e.g., being visionary and flexible, having personal control) our research points to the importance of a supportive organizational climate (Hisrich, 1990; Hornsby *et al.*, 1993) and strategy. Rather than being initiated by single employees, the EECs are team projects, a group of employees established the idea, recruited members and tasks are divided among a group of people (from the board and supervisory board mainly). Our findings show that the sharing of tasks is a very important part in the EECs. Clearly, not all members are equally active in the formation and management of the EECs, but nevertheless shared work and management are essential for the functioning of the EECs.

Both EECs prove that it is possible to engage in entrepreneurial activities that are detached from their company's business environment. This is interesting because it points to the possibility of having other social or environmental projects which are financed and implemented by employees. Besides individual benefits for the employees that engage in the EECs' entrepreneurial activities, recent research confirms that employee pro-environmental initiatives provide an immense potential for environmental change in organizations (Boiral, 2009; Daily et al., 2009). EECs are a new phenomenon that can provide a good framework for these initiatives. Especially, the EECs' entrepreneurial character seems to have a rather strong influence on the greening of a company. However, research suggests that not only eco-initiatives as such provide clear benefits for an organization but also the underlying employee engagement has positive impacts on the host companies (Macey and Schneider, 2008) and might contribute to organizational effectiveness regarding the implementation of environmental actions.

Conclusion

In studying the question "What influences the emergence of employee driven entrepreneurial action and what can be learned from the empirical example of EECs in this respect?" we find that EECs as an example for employee entrepreneurial action increase sustainability in companies and thereby combine economic, social and environmental interests of employees. For being able to understand how the EEC evolved in the context of their host companies we aim to point to the fact that influences on several levels must be taken into account. As described earlier the REA with its feed-in tariffs made it easy to start businesses with fixed rates on return. Additionally, the fact that the new cooperative law made the founding of cooperatives easier has influenced the EEC developments.

Our analysis shows that even when societal changes are apparent, employee driven entrepreneurship needs an organizational context that is open or receptive for new developments and allows for this kind of innovation. We further see that it is not only the single employees' sustainable motivation and engagement but also privately gained knowledge and experience that impact on such a development. Nevertheless, it also shows that employees form or use established team or governance structures (e.g., the works council) to sell their idea in the company context and towards its management. Further sustainable development might be sparked through the existing cooperatives which is mirrored by the search for new projects (EEC 1) and the number of employees on the waiting list to join the EECs.

In response to Shepherd and Patzelt (2011) we find that EECs can be a great source of support for organizational greening processes. These cooperatives can also be regarded as a blueprint for other employee initiatives: EECs can become a role model for other sustainable entrepreneurial actions, not only in the field of renewable energy projects. For example, employee cooperatives could operate an electric car fleet or a company's own Kindergarten. Additionally, our study proves how employees can contribute their own ideas to companies and organizations. Engaging in an EEC means not only a personal growth potential for employees but also shows the impact of societal movements and actions on organizations. In summary, research on EECs opens opportunities to observe and analyze a social phenomenon in the making. Regarding their influence, future research might want to look at the impact of such entrepreneurial activities on the host companies and also look into the change processes that are sparked by such employee entrepreneurial initiatives since they might bring a change of organizational values and culture.

Notes

1 Both Carco and Foodco (in the next paragraph) are acronyms and have nothing in common with the real names of the host companies.
2 Recent changes to REA include considerable reductions in the feed-in tariffs which consequently lead to lower fixed payments.

References

Boiral, O. 2007. Corporate greening through ISO 14001: a rational myth? *Organization Science*, 18, 127–146.

Boiral, O. 2009. Greening the corporation through organizational citizenship behaviors. *Journal of Business Ethics*, 87, 221–236.

Corbin, J. and Strauss, A. 2008. *Basics of Qualitative Research: Techniques and Procedures for Developing Grounded Theory*, London, Sage.

Cornforth, C., Thomas, A., Spear, R. and Lewis, J. 1988. *Developing Successful Worker Co-operatives*, London, Sage.

Daily, B. F., Bishop, J. W. and Govindarajulu, N. 2009. A conceptual model for organizational citizenship behavior directed toward the environment. *Business & Society*, 48, 243–256.

Del Brío, J. Á., Fernández, E. and Junquera, B. 2007. Management and employee involvement in achieving an environmental action-based competitive advantage: an empirical study. *The International Journal of Human Resource Management*, 18, 491–522.

Dyer Jr., W. G. and Wilkins, A. L. 1991. Better stories, not better constructs, to generate better theory: a rejoinder to Eisenhardt. *Academy of Management Review*, 16(3), 613–619.

Foreman, P. and Whetten, D. A. 2002. Members' identification with multiple-identity organizations. *Organization Science*, 13, 618–635.

Gibbs, D. 2009. Sustainability entrepreneurs, ecopreneurs and the development of a sustainable economy. *Greener Management International*, 63–78.

Hanna, M. D., Newman, W. R. and Johnson, P. 2000. Linking operational and environmental improvement through employee involvement. *International Journal of Operations & Production Management*, 20, 148–165.

Hisrich, R. D. 1990. Entrepreneurship/intrapreneurship. *American Psychologist*, 45, 209–222.

Hisrich, R. D. and Peters, M. P. 1986. Establishing a new business venture unit within a firm. *Journal of Business Venturing*, 1, 307–322.

Hornsby, J. S., Naffziger, D. W., Kuratko, D. F. and Montagno, R. V. 1993. An interactive model of the corporate entrepreneurship process. *Entrepreneurship: Theory & Practice*, 17, 29–37.

Hostager, T. J., Neil, T. C., Decker, R. L. and Lorentz, R. D. 1998. Seeing environmental opportunities: effects of intrapreneurial ability, efficacy, motivation and desirability. *Journal of Organizational Change Management*, 11, 11–25.

Jiang, R. J. and Bansal, P. 2003. Seeing the need for ISO 14001. *Journal of Management Studies*, 40, 1047–1067.

Keogh, P. D. and Polonsky, M. J. 1998. Environmental commitment: a basis for environmental entrepreneurship? *Journal of Organizational Change Management*, 11(1), 38–49.

Klaus Novy Institut. 2014. *Wachstumstrend der Energiegenossenschaften ist ungebrochen* [Online]. Available: www.unendlich-viel-energie.de/wachstumstrend-der-energiegenossenschaften-ungebroche.

Klinkers, L. and Nelissen, N. 1996. Employees give business its green edge: employee participation in corporate environmental care. In: Wehrmeyer, W. (ed.) *Greening People – Human Resources and Environmental Management*, Sheffield, Greenleaf.

Kuckartz, U. 2014. *Qualitative Inhaltsanalyse. Methoden, Praxis, Computerunterstützung*, Weinheim, Beltz Juventa.

Macey, W. H. and Schneider, B. 2008. The meaning of employee engagement. *Industrial and Organizational Psychology*, 1, 3–30.

Miles, M. B., Huberman, A. M. and Saldana, J. 2013. *Qualitative Data Analysis: A Methods Sourcebook*, London, Sage.

Ones, D. S. and Dilchert, S. 2012a. Employee green behaviors. In: Jackson, S. E., Ones, D. S. and Dilchert, S. (eds.) *Managing Human Resource for Environmental Sustainability*, San Francisco, Jossey-Bass.

Ones, D. S. and Dilchert, S. 2012b. Environmental sustainability at work: a call to action. *Industrial and Organizational Psychology*, 5, 444–466.

Pache, A.-C. and Santos, F. 2013. Inside the hybrid organization: selective coupling as a response to competing institutional logics. *Academy of Management Journal*, 56, 972–1001.

Parrish, B. D. and Foxon, T. J. 2009. Sustainability entrepreneurship and equitable transitions to a low-carbon economy. *Greener Management International*, 47–62.

Pastakia, A. 1998. Grassroots ecopreneurs: change agents for a sustainable society. *Journal of Organizational Change Management*, 11, 157–173.

Patton, M. Q. 2015. *Qualitative Research & Evaluation Methods: Integrating Theory and Practice*, Thousand Oaks, CA, Sage.

Patzelt, H. and Shepherd, D. A. 2011. Recognizing opportunities for sustainable development. *Entrepreneurship Theory and Practice*, 35, 631–652.

Ramus, C. A. 2001. Organizational support for employees: encouraging creative ideas for environmental sustainability. *California Management Review*, 43(3), 85–105.

Ramus, C. A. and Steger, U. 2000. The roles of supervisory support behaviors and environmental policy in employee "ecoinitiatives" at leading-edge European companies. *Academy of Management Journal*, 43, 605–626.

Schaltegger, S. 2002. A framework for ecopreneurship. *Greener Management International*, 45–58.

Schaltegger, S. and Wagner, M. 2011. Sustainable entrepreneurship and sustainability innovation: categories and interactions. *Business Strategy and the Environment*, 20, 222–237.

Schrader, U. and Harrach, C. 2013. Empowering responsible consumers to be sustainable intrapreneurs. *In*: Schrader, U., Fricke, V., Doyle, D. and Thoresen, V.W. (eds.) *Enabling Responsible Living*, Berlin, Heidelberg, Springer.

Shepherd, D. A. 2015. Party on! A call for entrepreneurship research that is more interactive, activity based, cognitively hot, compassionate, and prosocial. *Journal of Business Venturing*, 30, 489–507.

Shepherd, D. A. and Patzelt, H. 2011. The new field of sustainable entrepreneurship: studying entrepreneurial action linking "what is to be sustained" with "what is to be developed." *Entrepreneurship Theory and Practice*, 35, 137–163.

Shrivastava, P. and Hart, S. 1992. Greening organizations. *Academy of Management*, 185–189.

Siebenhüner, B. and Arnold, M. 2007. Organizational learning to manage sustainable development. *Business Strategy and the Environment*, 16, 339–353.

Starik, M. and Rands, G. P. 1995. Weaving an integrated web: multilevel and multisystem perspectives of ecologically sustainable organizations. *Academy of Management Review*, 20, 908–935.

Thompson, N. A., Herrmann, A. M. and Hekkert, M. P. 2015. How sustainable entrepreneurs engage in institutional change: insights from biomass torrefaction in the Netherlands. *Journal of Cleaner Production*, 106, 608–618.

TrendResearch. 2013. Kurzstudie – Anteile einzelner Marktakteure an Erneuerbare Energien-Anlagen in Deutschland. [Accessed 10.9.2013.]

Wirth, H. 2015. *Aktuelle Fakten zur Photovoltaik in Deutschland*, Freiburg, Fraunhofer ISE.

Wolf, J. 2013. Improving the sustainable development of firms: the role of employees. *Business Strategy and the Environment*, 22, 92–108.

Yin, R. K. 2003. *Case Study Research: Design and Methods*, Oaks, UK, New Delhi.

Zollo, M., Cennamo, C. and Neumann, K. 2013. Beyond what and why: understanding organizational evolution towards sustainable enterprise models. *Organization & Environment*, 26, 241–259.

19 Building sustainable social enterprises

Combining multiple institutional logics

Olivia Kyriakidou

Introduction

The sustainable management and development of any venture is challenging under any conditions. When the venture is a social enterprise incorporating elements from different institutional logics, it is especially so (Scott and Meyer 1991). By using market-based methods to solve social problems, social enterprises are by nature areas of contradiction as they attempt to marry two distinct and ostensibly competing organizational objectives: creating social value and creating economic value (Austin *et al.* 2006). Social enterprises seek to create social value (Peredo and McLean 2006), but they employ a market-based organizational form to sustain this value creation (Mair and Marti 2006). They also seek to create value for customers, but instead of full remuneration posing to investors, the surplus benefits of organizational activity accrue primarily to targeted beneficiaries (Austin *et al.* 2006). In this sense, social enterprises are caught between the competing demands of the market logic and the welfare logic that they combine. As the degree of incompatibility between logics increases, social enterprises face heightened challenges that may threaten their sustainable development (Tracey *et al.* 2011). Moreover, this evidence suggests that social enterprises may be highly unstable and unlikely to retain both logics over time. As a result, social enterprises need to find ways to deal with the multiple demands to which they are exposed. The purpose of this chapter is to explore how they may do so.

The existence and functioning of social enterprises poses interesting conceptual questions for institutional theory because social enterprises challenge the conceptualization of organizations as entities reproducing a single coherent institutional template in order to gain legitimacy and secure support from external institutional referents (DiMaggio and Powell 1983). A central feature of social enterprises is that the institutional logics that they embody are not always compatible (Greenwood *et al.* 2011). They may have to incorporate antagonistic practices that may not easily work together (Tracey *et al.* 2011). In addition, because adopting elements prescribed by a given logic often requires defying demands of the other logics, social enterprises may potentially jeopardize their legitimacy vis-à-vis important institutional referents (D'Aunno *et al.* 1991).

Finally social enterprises incorporating incompatible logics often see coalitions representing these logics emerge inside themselves (Pache and Santos 2010). These coalitions are likely to fight against each other to make the template they favor prevail, thus bringing the institutional conflict inside (Glynn 2000; Zilber 2002). These challenges are particularly acute for social enterprises that are exposed to long-term institutional pluralism, which requires them to incorporate competing logics over the long run, rather than in a temporary fashion.

Social enterprises must contend with competing external demands (Pache and Santos 2010) and internal identities (Kraatz and Block 2008). As a result, excessive turbulence may characterize the life of organizations that grapple with these multiple influences. Such instability could deplete organizations' capability to solve complex problems, particularly if the development of the organization leads to the collapse of institutional plurality and the dominance of one logic (Kraatz and Block 2008).

Research suggests that social enterprises try to address these challenges either by keeping logics separate or by attempting to reconcile them internally (Besharov and Smith 2012; Greenwood *et al.* 2011; Murray 2010). This literature provides a useful framework for starting to explore the functioning of social enterprises. Yet, by providing mainly an organizational-level perspective, it reveals little about how the incorporation of logics is actually achieved inside organizations. Specifically, entrepreneurship literature has yet to explore the processes deployed by individual social entrepreneurs as they try to navigate competing institutional logics. A few studies have identified situations where competing logics continued to co-exist for a lengthy period of time (Marquis and Lounsbury 2007; Reay and Hinings 2005). Although these studies recognize such situations, they do not provide insights into how the co-existing logics are sustained. Since competing logics create countervailing determinants of power and bring rivalry to the fore (Thornton 2004), it is not clear how the existence of multiple field-level logics can translate into stability for actors and the work they accomplish in their day-to-day activities. Social entrepreneurs need to address these tensions to operate sustainably and find ways to deal with the multiple demands to which they are exposed over the long run, rather than in a temporary fashion. This gap is important to address because attempting to manage the contradictory yet interrelated elements that exist in competing institutional logics allows us to conceptualize sustainability not simply as involving tensions and tradeoffs between logics that are meant to be separate, but importantly in terms of developing organizational responses and capabilities that can embrace or synthesize these tensions.

We address this gap by exploring how social enterprises internally incorporate elements of the competing logics that they embody. We propose that the conceptual lens of paradox can take us beyond economic and social value separation as a way to accomplish sustainability in social enterprises, towards potential synthesis of poles forming a duality, or transcendence of tensions, as well as emphasizing a longitudinal dynamic and productive interrelationship between poles. Sensemaking and organizational paradoxes (Smith and Lewis 2011) can be an important mechanism of sustainability in social enterprises. This mechanism complements prior mechanisms put forth in empirical work, such as power struggle and negotiation among competing internal and external institutional logics (Ashforth *et al.* 2009).

We first provide a review of social entrepreneurship, addressing market-based and social-based organizing. We then engage with the literature on paradox management, discussing the nature of organizational paradoxes as a constitutive organizational feature, and suggest ways of dealing with paradoxes. Subsequently, we describe our research setting and methods, and present our findings and analyses. We finally address how a paradox lens can help us advance research on sustainability in social enterprises. We argue that viewing economic and social value creation not as necessarily opposing but as dynamically interrelated or even complementary activities, enables us to conceive prescriptions that move beyond structural separation towards synthesis or transcendence. A paradox view also encourages longitudinal approaches that can track the dynamic interrelationship between the two poles of the paradox enabling us to move closely and pragmatically track practice. Overall, our study contributes to an emergent theory of social enterprises. We clarify how social enterprises operate and explain how they are capable of taking advantage of the wide repertoire of organizing elements available to them in pluralistic institutional environments.

Sustainability as a means of realizing competing institutional logics in social entrepreneurship

The successful management of sustainability requires managing the rivalry of competing logics. Several scholars have advocated that companies should aim to balance features that are considered contradictory, incompatible or in tension. For example, Abell (1999) recommended that firms should balance competing for the present, with developing competencies for the future, mirroring March's (1991) suggestion to balance exploitation of current organizational arrangements with exploration, the search for new ways of competing and new offerings. Abell (1999) recommended that firms should have two planning horizons, short term and long term, that would be in an iterative relationship with each other. He also suggested that firms should balance financial controls (present performance) with strategic controls (whether the organization effectively develops competencies for future success).

Social entrepreneurship presents very distinct and poignant challenges (Elkington and Hartigan 2008) as it "demands that entrepreneurs fuse together key elements of different logics that may have little in common and may even be in conflict" (Tracey *et al.* 2011, p. 60). Specifically, social entrepreneurship combines market-based organizing, where resources are acquired by promising direct financial returns that are achieved by realizing the organizational goal of creating economic value, with welfare-based organizing, where resources are acquired by promising donors indirect social returns that are achieved by realizing the organizational goal of creating social value (Battilana and Dorado 2010).

As broad belief systems that shape cognition and guide decision making in a field (Friedland and Alford 1991; Ocasio 1997; Suddaby and Greenwood 2005; Thornton 2004), institutional logics are taken-for-granted social prescriptions that represent shared understandings of what constitutes legitimate goals and how they may be pursued (Scott 1994). Over the past two decades, research in institutional theory has studied the role logics play in shaping actors' beliefs and practices as well as how these logics emerge, rise and fall (Dobbin 1994; Thornton and Ocasio 1999).

Research has also shown that multiple institutional logics often co-exist in organizational fields (e.g., Marquis and Lounsbury 2007; Reay and Hinings 2005), where they may impose different, and potentially conflicting, demands on organizations (D'Aunno *et al.* 1991; Goodrick and Salancik 1996; Oliver 1991). These studies have contributed to explaining variance in organizational practices within and across organizational fields (Lounsbury 2007). They have rarely, however, examined how organizations can deal internally with institutional pluralism – that is, with demands imposed by multiple institutional logics within the same organizational set-up (Kraatz and Block 2008; Pache and Santos 2010).

Dealing with multiple institutional logics is challenging for social entrepreneurs and organizations because it is likely to trigger tensions that should be addressed by the entrepreneurs, who are ultimately the ones who enact institutional logics (Glynn 2000; Zilber 2002). It is particularly challenging for social enterprises because, in contrast with organizations that incarnate existing organizational archetypes, social enterprises can rely neither on an existing model for handling the tension between the logics they combine nor on a pool of individuals with experience in doing so.

Focusing more specifically on responses to competing logics, a recent stream of research recognizes that the availability of multiple institutional models of action creates opportunities for social enterprises to draw from the broader repertoire of behaviors prescribed by competing logics (Battilana and Dorado 2010; Binder 2007; Greenwood *et al.* 2010; Greenwood *et al.* 2011; Lounsbury 2007; Reay and Hinings 2009). These studies suggest that social enterprises may reconcile competing logics by enacting a combination of activities drawn from each logic in an attempt to secure endorsement from a wide range of field-level actors (Greenwood *et al.* 2011). For example, Battilana and Dorado's (2010) study on commercial microfinance organizations in Bolivia highlights how these organizations combined development and banking logics to fight poverty.

Yet these examples also illustrate the internal challenges associated with the combination of competing logics. Social entrepreneurs might not be able to simultaneously satisfy the competing demands from important external constituents, such as commercial clients and beneficiaries and secure the required external support to survive. Likewise, Battilana and Dorado (2010) highlighted that one of the two microfinance organizations that they studied was unable to grow because of internal rifts created by an adherence to competing norms and values. Interestingly, their study also reveals that the other organization was able to downplay these rifts by hiring personnel free from attachments to either logic, by fostering members' commitment to operational excellence, and by developing a strong identity that reduced the perceived competition between logics.

Overall, these studies emphasize the challenges associated with logic combination, but also identify some of the factors that may allow social enterprises to address the continued and competing pressures from institutional referents. However, they reveal little about the way in which social entrepreneurs manage to marry ostensibly contradictory organizational goals in environments where even basic institutional infrastructure may not be in place. Understanding this process in detail is important for unpacking the internal functioning of social enterprises and for understanding how they may survive and thrive in the midst of pluralistic environments.

To summarize, the existing body of research on social entrepreneurs' responses to competing institutional logics leaves unanswered questions when it comes to explaining the functioning of social enterprises (McPherson and Sauder 2013). To understand more clearly how social entrepreneurs deal with persistently competing logics, it is important to understand which elements of the logics they enact, because these are the key linkages between institutional logics and sustainability processes at the organizational level of analysis (Smets et al. 2012; Thornton et al. 2012). Our purpose in this study was to explore these issues empirically by addressing the following research question:

Research Question 1: How do social entrepreneurs deal with enduring competing institutional logics in the context of sustainable social enterprises?

In the following section, we argue for a paradoxical management of institutional pluralism that focuses on the dynamic relationship of the demands imposed by multiple and competing institutional logics. A paradox approach to the management of institutional tensions explores the relationship between the poles of a duality and proposes synthesis and transcendence as further ways of managing tensions that move beyond separation (Chen 2002).

Paradox theory

Paradox theory can offer a valuable lens in the study of multiple institutional models of action not only in offering a more holistic approach to organizational tensions across a range of phenomena and levels of analysis but also in terms of offering avenues for how tensions can be managed, that is, by going beyond the separation thesis, and move towards integrating rigid dualities into flexible polarities.

At the core of paradox theory lies the acceptance of dualities of co-existing tensions where no compromise or singular choice between them has to be made (Eisenhardt 2000; Westenholz 1993). The effective management of these tensions is based therefore on finding creative ways to engage both poles capitalizing on the inherent pluralism within the duality (Eisenhardt 2000, p. 703). This process of managing paradox by shifting rigid dualities into more workable entities has often been referred to in the literature as synthesis or transcendence (Chahrazad *et al.* 2011; Chen 2002; Lewis 2000; Poole and Van de Ven 1989). Such processes make sustainable social entrepreneurship more likely by enabling the reconciliation of ostensibly competing organizational objectives (i.e., creating economic value versus creating social value). That is, social entrepreneurship rests on a distinctive version of paradoxical thinking that results in an organization that simultaneously creates economic and social value.

So far research on organizational tensions has followed Poole and Van de Ven's (1989) view of taking paradoxes as a given and trying to deal with them through temporal or spatial separation. However, "synthesis" could be a valuable approach for research on how tensions created by competing logics are perceived and managed simultaneously at the individual level. For example, Bloodgood and Bongsug (2010) argue that exploring competition without simultaneously considering cooperation offers an incomplete view of competition as competitors do not always act on the same level of competitiveness and at times they can work together towards a common goal. In a similar vein the concept of duality assumes both contradictory but also complementary relationships between the poles of a paradox. In an exploration of the paradox of stability and change, Farjoun (2010, p. 202) notes that "the apparent paradox of stability and change arises because the concepts are usually defined as opposites and by implication separate." Adopting a more dynamic conceptualization of stability, Farjoun identifies stability with continuity and low variance, but instead of taking this to imply fixity or rigidity, it is seen as adaptation. In this sense, we have the paradoxical situation that variable practices can contribute to stability in outcomes, and stable practices can enable variable outcomes. Paradox theory therefore, through its assumptions of duality (rather than dualism) between poles, encourages more holistic studies of distinct institutional logics in social entrepreneurship that can combine economic and social value elements.

Paradoxical thinking is a critical antecedent of social entrepreneurship because it enables an individual to combine social and economic goals (Emerson and Tversky 1996; Tracey *et al.* 2011). Traditionally, social value creation has been considered inconsistent with or even diametrically opposed to profit maximization (Dart 2004; Eikenberry and Kluver 2004), yet paradoxical thinking suggests the possibility of using one objective (i.e., profit) as a means of furthering the other objective (i.e., social value creation). As a result, economic and social value creation can be viewed as mutually reinforcing, as opposed to mutually exclusive, processes (Cho 2006; Harding 2004; Hartigan 2006; Hibbert *et al.* 2005; Lasprogata and Cotton 2003). Thus, paradoxical thinking enables the reconciliation of seemingly competing objectives in the form of a "double bottom line" that tightly couples and accounts for financial and social objectives (Austin *et al.* 2006).

Moreover, a paradox perspective emphasizes the embedded and constitutive nature of paradoxes in organizations, thus encourages a longitudinal perspective which can explore the dynamic relationship between the poles of a paradox, and on how paradoxes evolve over time and interact with each other (Blood-good and Bongsug 2010). Current research on social entrepreneurship has offered a more static view of managing tensions; however, paradox-inspired research over longer time frames, might explore to what extent and how organizations manage tensions over time, and potentially assume a more dynamic balance (Burgelman and Grove 2007). Such management could involve for example reframing the situation (Westenholz 1993), developing paradoxical cognition in managers as a behavioral capability (Eisenhardt *et al.* 2010) or a mind-set and attendant organizational processes that can address both poles of a paradox dynamically over time (Heracleous and Wirtz 2014).

A paradoxical lens therefore enables us to use paradox as a guiding framework that can enrich our research and understanding of complex organizational phenomena such as the need for innovation and efficiency, economic and social value by replacing the notion of conflicting, independent opposites with that of interdependent, dynamically interrelated poles of a duality (Chen 2002; Farjoun 2010). Paradox theory extends our conceptual arsenal by offering the assumption that the poles can be complementary and dynamically interrelated over time, and assuming that they are in a state of duality rather than a dualism, preserving the option of integration. Paradox theory also proposes that synthesis of the poles, or transcendence via re-framing can take place; and fosters the pursuit of organizational processes that can contribute to both poles of the paradox.

The root cause of the paradox in the present study is social enterprises' combining institutional logics and therefore multiple ways of acting and making sense of organizational outcomes. Scholars have noted that institutional logics constrain sensemaking by providing scripts for action and schemata through which organizational phenomena get interpreted. What happens when those schemata generate contradictory interpretations – for example, defining the same organizational outcome as both success and failure? We build on these concepts through our empirical study of sustainable social enterprises in Greece to develop our understanding of how actors manage the rivalry of competing logics.

Method

A qualitative approach was deployed to remain sufficiently open-ended to allow unforeseen themes to emerge from proximity to the individual entrepreneurs studied. Following scholars in sustainable entrepreneurship (Parrish 2010), we deploy a multiple case studies approach, seeking to build evidence through comparing cases with similar features (Yin 1994).

Our research participants were social entrepreneurs leading sustainable social enterprises in Greece. They were all recipients of social enterprise awards in Greece as well as finalists of social entrepreneurship competitions for the social enterprise of the year in 2014 and 2015. This process revealed several individuals involved in founding sustainable social enterprises. We recruited 11 case study participants using theoretical sampling (Eisenhardt 1989) representing 11 social enterprises and focusing on the characteristics of the individual social entrepreneurs rather than the industry in which they are located. Each person was interviewed in 2015 after the end of the competition. The ages of participants ranged from 27 to 60 years and were the founding partners of award-winning social enterprises. The group included 6 women and 5 men. Of the 11 participants, 7 were married, 3 were living with a partner and 1 was single. The recruitment process undoubtedly generated a selective sampling of social entrepreneurs and social enterprises. However, there was no intention in working with this small, purposive sample to arrive at generalized conclusions about sustainable social enterprises; rather, the aim was to develop a group of information-rich cases to describe the paradoxical management of institutional pluralism in enough detail and depth that readers can "connect to that experience, learn how it is constituted, and deepen their understanding of the issues it reflects" (Seidman 1991, p. 41).

Semi-structured interviews were conducted loosely framed around key themes (e.g., reasons for setting up the social enterprise; their role in the social venture; their views on sustainability; how they manage growth). All participants talked freely and openly, and the discussions were allowed to develop spontaneously at the participants' will. All interviews were conducted at the participants' place of work and each interview lasted approximately two hours. They were tape recorded with the consent of the participants and later transcribed verbatim by the authors.

Data analysis

Our data analysis progressed through an iterative "back and forth" process (Miles and Huberman 1984). Transcripts were examined and comments were categorized on a case by case basis to begin with, enabling a condensation of meaning whilst remaining close to the participants' comments (Kvale 1996). Following Eisenhardt (1989), the next stage was a cross case comparison, which resulted in clusters of first order codes (Pratt 2009) relating to the participants' statements for example, "profit as a necessary evil." Van Maanen *et al.* (2007) stress the importance of returning to the literature to gain additional insights for assistance with data analysis. This led to a consolidation of first order codes into second order themes (e.g., social impact cost-benefit analysis) that emerged through comparison with extant literature. Four of these themes represent the processes used by social entrepreneurs to combine competing logics in a sustainable way. In light of the restricted space, our findings section presents evidence using power quotes (Pratt 2009) that succinctly exemplify the participants' perspectives.

Findings

The following section highlights the processes and strategies sustainable entrepreneurs deploy to address the complexities of their social ventures where competing institutional logics prevail. These processes include: 1) reconstructing profit as a means of increasing the sustainability of social value creation; 2) performing social impact judgments regarding the costs and benefits of entrepreneurial value creation; 3) reframing social entrepreneurship as a research and development lab; and 4) balancing innovation and scale through complex networks.

Profit as a means of increasing the sustainability of social value creation

Traditional businesses find a path to financial sustainability by growing their revenues, improving their gross and operating margins, increasing their free cash flow, efficiently managing both capital expenditures and working capital, and building their asset base. Achieving these financial performance indicators typically results in access to financing and higher stock prices. High impact social enterprises are also built and managed to achieve these financial goals, except that social businesses value social impact over profit, and unlike a traditional business, they use profit as a tool for making a meaningful social impact. Sustainable social businesses create foundations to which they can contribute their profits to further their mission.

Sustainable social enterprises consider service delivery contracts or other forms of earned income streams. At the same time, social entrepreneurs refer to their venture as a social enterprise not because of its legal structure but because of its ability to deliver a social return on their investments.

> Profit is a necessary "evil." How can I increase the viability and sustainability of my social venture without stabilizing my revenues and managing my exposure to various risks?

> Without profit we would never be able to achieve our mission and even further our mission and our social impact. We continuously try to find ways to increase our profits in order to grow our business and develop an ecosystem to target our social problem from multiple perspectives.

For social enterprises, income generating activities enhance financial sustainability by reducing dependence on the generosity of donors or the budgets of grant giving foundations and government agencies.

> I was never fond of charitable donations as it feels like always standing with your right hand open in front of the donators asking for money. I strongly believe that in this way you are always dependent from the strategy and the pockets of your donors. And such dependency may threaten over the long turn the continuity, predictability and controllability of your funds. I want our social venture to be self-sustaining by trying to generate revenues from our services.

Social entrepreneurs in sustainable social enterprises try to clearly and forcefully make the case to all their stakeholders why their enterprise deserves their continued financial support. Stakeholders in these high impact social businesses include investors and lenders, donors and grant providers, clients and customers, impacted communities and employees.

> Financial sustainability is what makes our mission and social impact both meaningful and lasting for all our stakeholders.

Sustainability therefore is enhanced through developing the soundness of the social enterprise's financial footing. The people who pay for a social enterprise's services are not always the same as those who use them. Revenue-generating models have become the ideal and the sustainable social enterprises have established ways to survive and grow without perpetual philanthropic infusions. Moreover, all social enterprises of our sample were social cooperatives and had gained numerous awards for delivering high social impact. In this sense, their legitimacy was enough to please their social constituents. They were able to gain local political support, mobilize public funds, secure the sourcing of social employees and guarantee mentoring by partner social organizations. Their ability to display compliance with the commercial logic in addition allowed them to gain credibility with their commercial constituents. They were able to interact on a more equal footing with partners, and as a result, they were able to negotiate more favorable conditions to sustain their commercial activity.

Social impact cost-benefit analysis

Social entrepreneurship is exceptionally challenging, since the entrepreneur not only must attempt the founding of an organization but also must work to establish an infrastructure that supports the organization (Mair and Marti 2009). Often, new markets and new distribution channels must be erected, old cultural stereotypes must be challenged, and innovative revenue streams must be uncovered in the context of minimal disposable income (Mair and Marti 2009). In purely cost-benefit terms, the personal risks of such an approach are high and the benefits unknown, rendering necessary the social impact distortion of cost-benefit analysis as a precondition to engaging in the challenging process of creating and sustainably growing a social enterprise.

> We do not really care about what sector our organization sits in, but we only care about the long-term results that we produce, and how much it costs to deliver those. We continuously demand from ourselves higher and higher standards of proof of a social return on our investment. We do not waste our resources on ineffective programs that only deliver superficial or short-term results.

Simply claiming to be doing good is not enough. We are not a label behind which we try to hide poor businesses. Instead, we try to deliver a better social return on investment than the best for-profit, public or charitable associations. By generating an income and yet prioritizing social over financial returns we believe that we provide a sustainable example of what positive social impact really means.

Social impact cost-benefit analysis leads entrepreneurs to weight more heavily the benefits associated with the delivery of social impact and the costs of failing to act. The pressure for accountability heightens entrepreneurs' attention on the social impact of their endeavors that might satisfy their stakeholders' concerns by simultaneously providing market based accountability and a focus on solving social problems. At the same time, it also increases the perceived costliness of forms that fail to account for their effectiveness in delivering social impact.

Social enterprise as a research and development lab

Social enterprise has never been about a sector, about legal structures or models of governance. It is about working at the margins; pushing the boundaries of what is possible, working with the people and problems failed by for-profit business, government or traditional charity.

The role of social enterprises is to take risks and push the boundaries.

In the future, we are going to have great competition and we must be ready for this. Charities and private businesses will be carrying much of the work we are currently doing. But our job is to innovate and challenge. We act as a research and development lab, inventing and testing better ways to make a better society, and we will continue to do so.

Recognizing that social enterprise provides a research and development function changes social entrepreneurs' attitude towards failure. Social enterprises that fail for trying something new are no longer seen as something to be ashamed of, but as undertaking important steps on the way to success. Moreover, considering social enterprise as a research and development lab also changes the conversation around competition and collaboration.

We are not working on our own. We actively work with for-profit, public and charitable sectors to develop more effective solutions to social problems and roll-out those innovations into the mainstream.

In this sense, the social entrepreneurs of sustainable social ventures, the disrupters, the change-makers, always find a way of working within the confines of whatever environment and whatever market they are in to find a better solution to any given social problem.

We exist not simply to sell into markets but to make and shape markets, not to commercialize social problems but to revolutionize our approach to them.

Balancing innovation and scale through complex networks

Sustainable social enterprises understand scale in a very sophisticated way and try to balance it with innovation. Social entrepreneurs in sustainable social ventures do not consider scale in blunt terms of turnover, profit or numbers of beneficiaries reached; neither do they measure success by longevity. Instead, they are more concerned with, and more conscious of, the scale of their impact.

> Success for me is inextricably and tightly linked to impact. Impact through changing the business practices of others, through changing government policies, through spreading solutions that work. Success for us is when we will do ourselves out of a job.

Scale is also achieved through the increasing interconnectivity of social entrepreneurs who create and take part in highly networked micro-social enterprises, collaborating across international boundaries.

> We highly value our approach of making strong connections to tackle a specific, every time, social issue, which are then dissolved for new connections to be made: crowdsourcing expertise and capacity as well as funding. For our young volunteers in particular, our "digital natives," this direct, collaborative approach to solve local and global problems is an attractive alternative to organized political participation.

Social enterprises trying to solve similar problems, or carving out a niche in a particular market are able to share learning. Effective social enterprise models spread through this informal sharing even more rapidly than through more formal mechanisms like licensing or social franchising.

Discussion and conclusion

Our study seeks a better understanding of the functioning of sustainable social enterprises, approached as ventures that incorporate contradictory institutional logics (Battilana and Dorado 2010; Greenwood *et al.* 2011). It focuses specifically on the processes social entrepreneurs use in order to enact multiple institutional logics within the boundaries of organizations, identifying specific patterns of logic combinations, thereby providing clues about how social enterprises can become sustainable. An exploration of the main actors of sustainable social enterprises in Greece allowed us to describe how social enterprises that are persistently embedded in competing institutional logics combined elements of the social impact and commercial logics through selecting practices from each logic as they tried to solve specific problems and reassure the durability of the social benefit.

Our research suggests that social entrepreneurs reconstruct as compatible practices previously constructed as contradictory based on the clashes of the logics these practices enact. They perceive that the practices do not fully support each other, but they can accommodate them. This significant shift from contradictory to compatible logics produces an expanded practice repertoire which supports their growth and sustainability.

The reconstruction of previously considered contradictory practices as compatible allows social entrepreneurs to satisfy both practical and symbolic concerns. Such processes do not require actors to come up with alternative ways of doing things. The social entrepreneurs of our sample used institutional logics in different ways to solve different kinds of problems. A strength of sustainable social enterprises is that they have access to a much broader repertoire of institutionalized practices that they combine in unique ways. This places them at an advantage if they are able to craft a combination of elements that fits well with the demands of their environment and helps them leverage a wider range of support. Our study thus suggests that sustainable social enterprises are characterized by a certain degree of reflexivity, motivated by the contradictions in which they are embedded (Seo and Creed 2002). We provide evidence to the fact that, in the face of institutional logics that are competing over the long term, social enterprises do not just comply with institutional prescriptions (DiMaggio and Powell 1983) or with the cognitive frames into which their leading actors have been socialized (Hwang and Powell 2009). The social enterprises of our sample with social origins as social cooperatives were not trapped into replicating just social practices. In contrast, our data suggest that our social enterprises chose contradictory institutional logics which they reconstructed as compatible. Overall, our findings suggest that crafting various logic combinations, sustainable social enterprises show their ability to work around institutional constraints and use them to their advantage, thus demonstrating a fair amount of agency.

Discussions of how social enterprises can achieve sustainability are very much dependent on how sustainability is conceptualized and most importantly whether the economic and social values are considered competing or complementary aspects of the organizational phenomena in question. Following a paradoxical view of sustainability in social enterprises as an organization's ability to equally pursue different and often conflicting areas, aiming to synthesize or transcend polarities, enables us to move beyond the dominant separation-oriented prescriptions of the current literature. Paradox offers a more pragmatic perspective on the ongoing need to accept paradox as an embedded feature of organizations, and as a potentially productive source of creative tensions that can support organizational effectiveness (Lewis 2000; Smith and Lewis 2011).

Viewing economic and social activities not as mutually exclusive but as interwoven polarities shifts thinking from an either/or to a both/and mindset. By viewing the sustainability of social enterprises literature from a paradox perspective, we move one step further from using paradox as a generic description of seemingly contradictory demands to a lens that explores the tensions and their dynamic potential for ongoing integration across organizational phenomena. Following a paradox perspective on sustainability research in social enterprises can inform a broader spectrum of the complexity of organizational life in social enterprises.

References

Abell D. F. (1999) "Competing today while preparing for tomorrow" *Sloan Management Review*, Spring, 73–81.

Ashforth B. E., Reingen P. H. and Ward J. C. (2009) *Friend and foe? The dynamics of duality in a cooperative* Working paper, Arizona State University, Tempe.

Austin J., Stevenson H. and Skillern W. (2006) "Social and commercial entrepreneurship: Same, different, or both?" *Entrepreneurship Theory and Practice*, 30 1–22.

Battilana J. and Dorado S. (2010) "Building sustainable hybrid organizations: The case of commercial microfinance organizations" *Academy of Management Journal*, 53 1419–1440.

Besharov M. and Smith W. (2012) *Paradoxes of social enterprises: Sustaining utilitarian and normative identities simultaneously* Cornell University Press, Ithaca.

Binder A. (2007) "For love and money: Organizations' creative responses to multiple organizational logics" *Theory and Society*, 36 547–571.

Bloodgood J. M. and Bongsug C. (2010) "Organizational paradoxes: Dynamic shifting and integrative management" *Management Decision*, 48 85–104.

Burgelman R. A. and Grove A. S. (2007) "Let chaos reign, then rein in chaos – repeatedly: Managing strategic dynamic for corporate longevity" *Strategic Management Journal*, 28 965–979.

Chahrazad A., Denis J. L. and Langley A. (2011) "Having your cake and eating it too: Discourses of transcendence and their role in organizational change dynamics" *Journal of Organizational Change Management*, 24 333–348.

Chen M. J. (2002) "Transcending paradox: The Chinese 'middle way' perspective" *Asia Pacific Journal of Management*, 19 179–187.

Cho A. H. (2006) "Politics, values and social entrepreneurship: A critical appraisal" in Mair J., Robinson J. and Hockerts K. eds, *Social entrepreneurship* Palgrave Macmillan, London.

D'Aunno T., Sutton R. I. and Price R. H. (1991) "Isomorphism and external support in conflicting institutional environments: A study of drug abuse treatment units" *Academy of Management Journal*, 34 636–661.

Dart R. (2004) "The legitimacy of social enterprise" *Nonprofit Management and Leadership*, 14 411–424.

DiMaggio P. and Powell W. W. (1983) "The iron cage revisited: Institutional isomorphism and collective rationality in organizational fields" *American Sociological Review*, 48 147–160.

Dobbin F. (1994) *Forging industrial policy: The United States, Britain, and France in the railway age* Cambridge University Press, Cambridge.

Eikenberry A. M. and Kluver J. D. (2004) "The marketization of the nonprofit sector: Civil society at risk?" *Public Administration Review*, 64 132–140.

Eisenhardt K. M. (1989) "Building theories from case study research" *Academy of Management Review*, 14 532–550.

Eisenhardt K. (2000) "Paradox, spirals, ambivalence: The new language of change and pluralism" *Academy of Management Review*, 25 703–705.

Eisenhardt K., Furr N. and Bingham C. B. (2010) "Crossroads – microfoundations of performance: Balancing efficiency and flexibility in dynamic environments" *Organization Science*, 21 1263–1273.

Elkington J. and Hartigan P. (2008) *The power of unreasonable people: How social entrepreneurs create markets that change the world* Harvard Business School Press, Boston.

Emerson J. and Tversky F. (1996) *New social entrepreneurs: The success, challenge and lessons of non-profit enterprise creation* Roberts Foundation, Homeless Economic Development Fund, San Francisco.

Farjoun M. (2010) "Beyond dualism: Stability and change as a duality" *Academy of Management Review*, 35 202–225.

Friedland R. and Alford R. R. (1991) "Bringing society back in: Symbols, practices, and institutional contradictions" in Powell W. W. and DiMaggio P. J. eds., *The new institutionalism in organizational analysis* University of Chicago Press, Chicago.

Glynn M. A. (2000) "When cymbals become symbols: Conflict over organizational identity within a symphony orchestra" *Organization Science*, 11 285–298.

Goodrick E. and Salancik G. R. (1996) "Organizational discretion in responding to institutional practices: Hospitals and Cesarean births" *Administrative Science Quarterly*, 41 1–28.

Greenwood R., Diaz A. M., Li S. X. and Lorente J. C. (2010) "The multiplicity of institutional logics and the heterogeneity of organizational responses" *Organization Science*, 21 521–539.

Greenwood R., Raynard M., Kodeih F., Micellota E. and Lounsbury M. (2011) "Institutional complexity and organizational responses" *Academy of Management Annals*, 5 1–55.

Harding R. (2004) "Social enterprise: The new economic engine?" *Business Strategy Review*, 15 39–43.

Hartigan P. (2006) "It's about people, not profits" *Business Strategy Review*, 17 42–45.

Heracleous L. and Wirtz J. (2014) "Sustainable competitive advantage at Singapore Airlines: Dual strategy as mastering paradox" *Journal of Applied Behavioral Science*, 1–22.

Hibbert S. A., Hogg G. and Quinn T. (2005) "Social entrepreneurship: Understanding consumer motives for buying The Big Issue" *Journal of Consumer Behaviour*, 4 159–172.

Hwang H. and Powell W. W. (2009) "The rationalization of charity: The influences of professionalism in the nonprofit sector" *Administrative Science Quarterly*, 54 268–298.

Kraatz M. and Block E. (2008) "Organizational implications of institutional pluralism" in Greenwood R., Oliver, C., Suddaby R. and Sahlin-Andersson K. eds., *The Sage handbook of organizational institutionalism* Sage, Thousand Oaks, CA.

Kvale S. (1996) *InterViews – An introduction to qualitative research interviewing* Sage, Thousand Oaks, CA.

Lasprogata G. A. and Cotton M. N. (2003) "Contemplating 'enterprise': The business and legal challenges of social entrepreneurship" *American Business Law Journal*, 41 567–595.

Lewis M. W. (2000) "Exploring paradox: Toward a more comprehensive guide" *Academy of Management Review*, 25 760–776.

Lounsbury M. (2007) "A tale of two cities: Competing logics and practice variation in the professionalization of mutual funds" *Academy of Management Journal*, 50 289–307.

Mair J. and Marti I. (2006) "Social entrepreneurship research: A source of explanation, prediction, and delight" *Journal of World Business*, 41 36–44.

Mair J. and Marti I. (2009) "Entrepreneurship in and around institutional voids: A case study from Bangladesh" *Journal of Business Venturing*, 24 419–435.

March J. G. (1991) "Exploration and exploitation in organizational learning" *Organization Science*, 2 71–87.

Marquis C. and Lounsbury M. (2007) "Vive la resistance: Competing logics and the consolidation of U.S. community banking" *Academy of Management Journal*, 50 799–820.

McPherson C. M. and Sauder M. (2013) "Logics in action: Managing institutional complexity in a drug court" *Administrative Science Quarterly*, 58 165–196.

Miles M. B. and Huberman A. M. (1984) *Qualitative data analysis: a sourcebook of new methods* Sage, Thousand Oaks, CA.

Murray F. (2010) "The oncomouse that roared: Hybrid exchange strategies as a source of distinction at the boundary of overlapping institutions" *American Journal of Sociology*, 116 341–388.

Ocasio W. (1997) "Towards an attention-based view of the firm" *Strategic Management Journal*, 18 187–206.

Oliver C. (1991) "Strategic responses to institutional processes" *Academy of Management Review*, 16 145–179.

Pache A. C. and Santos F. (2010) "When worlds collide: The internal dynamics of organizational responses to conflicting institutional demands" *Academy of Management Review*, 35 455–476.

Parrish B. (2010) "Sustainability-driven entrepreneurship: Principles of organization design" *Journal of Business Venturing* 25 510–523.

Peredo A. M. and McLean M. (2006) "Social entrepreneurship: A critical review of the concept" *Journal of World Business*, 41 56–65.

Poole M. S. and Van de Ven A. H. (1989) "Using paradox to build management and organization theories" *Academy of Management Review*, 14 562–578.

Pratt M. G. (2009) "For the lack of a boilerplate: Tips on writing up (and reviewing) qualitative research" *Academy of Management Journal*, 52 856–862.

Reay T. and Hinings C. R. (2005) "The recomposition of an organizational field: Health care in Alberta" *Organization Studies*, 26 351–384.

Reay T. and Hinings C. R. (2009) "Managing the rivalry of competing institutional logics" *Organization Studies*, 30 629–652.

Scott W. R. (1994) "Institutions and organizations: Toward a theoretical synthesis" in Scott W. R. and Meyer J. W. eds., *Institutional environments and organizations: Structural complexity and individualism* Sage, Thousand Oaks, CA.

Scott W. R. and Meyer J. (1991) "The organization of societal sectors: Propositions and early evidence" in DiMaggio P. J. and Powell W. eds., *The new institutionalism in organizational analysis* University of Chicago Press, Chicago.

Seidman I. E. (1991) *Interviewing as qualitative research* Teachers College Press, New York.

Seo M. and Creed W. E. D. (2002) "Institutional contradictions, praxis and institutional change: A dialectical perspective" *Academy of Management Review*, 27 222–247.

Smets M., Morris T. and Greenwood R. (2012) "From practice to field: A multilevel model of practice-driven institutional change" *Academy of Management Journal*, 55 877–904.

Smith W. K. and Lewis M. W. (2011) "Toward a theory of paradox: A dynamic equilibrium model of organizing" *Academy of Management Review*, 36 381–403.

Suddaby R. and Greenwood R. (2005) "Rhetorical strategies of legitimacy" *Administrative Science Quarterly*, 50 35–76.

Thornton P. H. (2004) *Markets from culture* Stanford University Press, Stanford, CA.

Thornton P. H. and Ocasio W. (1999) "Institutional logics and the historical contingency of power in organizations: Executive succession in the higher education publishing industry, 1958–1990" *American Journal of Sociology*, 105 801–843.

Thornton P. H., Ocasio W. and Lounsbury M. (2012) *The institutional logics perspective: A new approach to culture, structure and process* Oxford University Press, Oxford.

Tracey P., Phillips N. and Jarvis O. (2011) "Bridging institutional entrepreneurship and the creation of new organizational forms: A multilevel model" *Organization Science*, 22 60–80.

Van Maanen J., Sorensen J. B. and Mitchell T. R. (2007) "The interplay between theory and method" *Academy of Management Review*, 32 1145–1154.

Westenholz A. (1993) "Paradoxical thinking and change in the frames of reference" *Organization Studies*, 14 37–58.

Yin R. K. (1994) *Case study research: Design and methods* Sage Publications, Los Angeles, CA.

Zilber T. (2002) "Institutionalization as an interplay between actions, meanings, and actors: The case of a rape crisis center in Israel" *Academy of Management Journal*, 45 234–254.

20 Social entrepreneurship in an INGO

Exploring the challenges of innovation and hybridization

Jamie Newth

Introduction

The emergence of entrepreneurship as an activity which addresses enduring social or environmental challenges has been a source of innovation, promise and insight for practitioners and scholars alike. While researchers have contributed to understandings of social entrepreneurship and social enterprise in many contexts, it is a curious anomaly of social entrepreneurship scholarship that so little consideration has been given to its application within international humanitarian non-government organizations (INGOs) and aid agencies. The lack of research is notable because these development organizations have tremendous potential to realize the benefits of social entrepreneurship due to their capability and capacity that has been developed through the provision of community and economic development programs in the world's most vulnerable communities. We therefore lack relevant theory to explain and guide action in this sector.

As INGOs pursue or facilitate social entrepreneurship to increase their impact and/or make their activities more financially sustainable, they are forced to contend with the competing logics (social and commercial) of this activity itself, but also with the ways in which this conflicts with their own dominant development (social) logic. These logics are based on the institutional parameters of the category in which the organization operates, i.e., private, public or non-profit sector (Doherty *et al.*, 2014). Billis (2010) provides us with the following organizational templates to explicate category logics (Table 20.1). This is a useful framework for illustrating not only how social entrepreneurs and social enterprises combine competing logics but how this can be problematic in terms of governance and resourcing (cf. Doherty *et al.*, 2014; Newth and Woods, 2014).

International development agencies are being forced to respond to many geopolitical, economic and technological environment changes. The threats and opportunities these changes create will likely necessitate a degree of hybridization. Hybrid organizations are those that combine institutional logics (Battilana and Dorado, 2010; Doherty *et al.*, 2014; Pache and Santos, 2013). Examples of such organizations include social enterprises which combine commercial and social logics (Doherty *et al.*, 2014); microfinance organizations which combine

Table 20.1 Organizational templates

	Institutional guide	Governorship	Owners	Business model/ revenue
Private	Market forces	Share of ownership	Shareholders	Sales
Public	Public benefit and collective choice	Elected representatives	Citizens and state	Taxation
Non-profit	Social and environmental goals	Elected representatives or appointed trustees	Members	Donations, membership fees and legacies

Source: adapted from Billis, 2010.

development and banking logics (Battilana et al., 2015), public-private partnerships which combine state, market and civil society logics (Jay, 2013), and research centers and education institutions which combine scientific or academic with market logics (cf. Pache and Santos, 2013). These organizations also bridge, or blur, institutional fields (Tracey et al., 2011). Institutional logics are understood to be the "taken for granted social prescriptions that represent shared understandings of what constitutes legitimate goals and how they may be pursued" (Battilana and Dorado, 2010, 1420). Hybrid organization research in social entrepreneurship is particularly concerned with organizations that combine logics that would otherwise be considered incompatible.

This chapter uses Shepherd and Patzelt (2011) as an organizing framework to illustrate the opportunities that social entrepreneurship offers INGOs, all of which are relevant to the organization under examination here. The points within an INGO that are challenged by the pursuit of social entrepreneurship are then identified and discussed in terms of how changes at these points force, or require, hybridity. This discussion seeks to contribute to the literature around hybridization in social entrepreneurship and enterprise by drawing out the specific aspects of a particular non-profit that are challenged by the hybrid logic of social entrepreneurship strategies and initiatives. Drawing on Newth and Woods' (2014) development of Schumpeter's (1934) notion of resistance as it applies to social entrepreneurship and institutional theory, the micro-level institutional bases for tension and resistance to social entrepreneurship are considered via an in-depth case study.

This chapter's empirical application of Shepherd and Patzelt's (2011) framework and its combination with institutional theory, specifically institutional logics, contributes to social and sustainable entrepreneurship theory. It also provides specific insight into the application of this theory in the international development sector. This represents an initial step in addressing the lack of research into social entrepreneurship in this sector in general, and towards building theory which explains and informs the contextual bases that enable and constrain entrepreneurial action in established development organizations.

The social entrepreneurship opportunity of the INGO

Shepherd and Patzelt's (2011) sustainable entrepreneurship is a conceptualization of entrepreneurship that draws together the fields of entrepreneurship and sustainable development. It has the potential to spur greater entrepreneurship research amongst the development sector. Their framework gives broad consideration to entrepreneurship for economic, environmental and community benefit, as well as delineating the activities and processes for sustaining versus developing our planet's states of nature, sources of life support, and communities. In conceptualizing social (sustainable) entrepreneurship in this way, they furnish researchers with a theoretical framework which is directly applicable to the many entrepreneurs and agencies who are working to fight poverty and humanitarian injustices around the world. Importantly, this framework makes this phenomena more amendable to analysis from an entrepreneurship perspective and provides a bridge between the literatures of entrepreneurship and development respectively. Entrepreneurship researchers (of all flavors) could find sophisticated development work in developing country contexts particularly fertile research sites and may discover they have many insightful contributions that explain and inform the innovation and entrepreneurship behavior that occurs there. Likewise, development scholars and practitioners may find entrepreneurship theory, and in particular social entrepreneurship and social enterprise research, useful for explaining what they see 'out in the field' and for advancing the practice of development agencies and NGOs.

Shepherd and Patzelt (2011) argue that sustainable entrepreneurship differs from social entrepreneurship in that it incorporates not only entrepreneurship that *develops*, but also that which *sustains* our social and natural world.

> Sustainable entrepreneurship is focused on the preservation of nature, life support, and community in the pursuit of perceived opportunities to bring into existence future products, processes, and services for gain, where gain is broadly construed to include economic and non-economic gains to individuals, the economy, and society.
>
> (Shepherd and Patzelt, 2011, 142)

This chapter contends that, in fact, extant definitions of social entrepreneurship do account for such activity (e.g., de Mendiguren Castresana, 2013; McMullen, 2011; Yunus, 2008; Zahra *et al.*, 2009). Indeed, the breadth of activity that can be included under current definitions of social entrepreneurship is already a source of contention and subsuming it within another broader term is unhelpful. Rather, the more nuanced understanding their framework enables is a significant contribution to social entrepreneurship research, in particular to how it intersects with humanitarian development. This chapter therefore builds upon their framework, but maintains the social entrepreneurship moniker.

When the Shepherd and Patzelt (2011) framework is applied to humanitarian INGOs, it reveals the scale of the opportunity for social entrepreneurship in working in developing nations. For such organizations, social entrepreneurship as an activity which creates economic and non-economic gains for the purposes of sustaining our natural world, securing its life giving properties, and building resilient, thriving communities frames a compelling strategic imperative.

Such NGOs, particularly large INGOs, represent a severely under-researched organizational sector by social entrepreneurship scholars. And despite debate around their efficacy they remain important global players in the efforts to sustain and develop our natural and social world. This is true, at the very least, because of the sheer quantity of financial, human, social and brand capital, and other resources that are being mobilized by such organizations. To social entrepreneurship researchers this makes such organizations important.

However, they are also very relevant to social entrepreneurship researchers because of their mission, their opportunity and the risk they face. Their mission is to address extreme poverty and social injustice in sustainable ways to achieve enduring change – the purpose aligns with that of many social entrepreneurs and of the field more generally. And indeed they seek revenue generation for social impact and are experimenting with ways to combine these activities into enterprises. They are also relevant because such organizations have a significant opportunity to use social entrepreneurship to achieve this mission, be it as catalysts, advisors, investors or as entrepreneurs themselves. In the same vein INGOs are at risk of disintermediation or obsolescence from the activities of social entrepreneurs and the rise of the social enterprise sector generally. This will be most acutely felt from the disruption to their funding sources as social enterprises and entrepreneurs attract the resources that have previously been acquired by NGOs. But this speaks to a less tangible shift – that of decreasing relevance to funders, policy-makers and private donors (and to public discourse) in terms of theory of change and a wavering belief in the efficacy of international aid.

After decades of developing community development methodologies which integrate education, health, food security and economic development programs, many INGOs are uniquely placed to pursue social entrepreneurship strategies to achieve their goals, or to at least incorporate its principles into program design. In particular, the use of social entrepreneurial approaches, and social enterprises specifically, show potential for complementing traditional NGO delivered community development programs in highly impactful ways. The complementarity also allows these organizations to leverage the personnel, social capital and organizational capacity that is deployed among the most vulnerable in developing nations and developing markets. This leaves them well positioned to implement and support the business models and organizational structures (and governance) that harness the enterprising potential of local populations. They are also well equipped to facilitate the creation of value-adding market mecha-nisms to protect and empower vulnerable market participants in instances of institutional voids (Mair and Marti, 2009). This capability stems from their understanding of the idiosyncratic market machinations and social structures of developing country contexts and the ways in which they result in enduring social problems, and how this systemically ensures that certain populations remain vulnerable. They are also not bound by the strict commercial logic of the private sector that would require higher financial returns from any market-based approach than INGOs and hybrid organizations such as social enterprises. This changes the feasibility profile of social entrepreneurship initiatives and leaves space for ensuring social value creation remains primary.

Notwithstanding the problematics of the involvement of business in the development agenda (Arora and Romijn, 2009; de Mendiguren Castresana, 2013) and the ethical challenges of social entrepreneurship (cf. Zahra *et al.*, 2009), from a humanitarian perspective INGOs arguably are ideal agents to catalyze social entrepreneurship in developing country contexts. This is because their community-led, social mission could provide a degree of surety of the 'social' in social entrepreneurship or the catalyzing of market based approaches that social entrepreneurial individuals and businesses will utilize. Moreover, social entrepreneurship seems to have the potential to create the institutional change in less developed countries required for economic growth but has been largely inaccessible to INGOs (McMullen, 2011).

However, research has outlined the many challenges social entrepreneurship can present for non-profit organizations because of the institutional logics which underpin such organizations. This includes organizational identity (Alvord *et al.*, 2004; Moss *et al.*, 2011; Smith *et al.*, 2010), legitimacy (Dart, 2004; Nicholls and Cho, 2006) and the appropriateness of entrepreneurial intervention amongst vulnerable populations (Mair and Marti, 2009).

Research method

The research project was guided by overarching research questions which explored, broadly, how social entrepreneurship innovation happens within INGOs and what forces shape an innovation as it is developed within that context. One of the purposes was to understand the specific aspects of the organ-ization that need to shift to accommodate social entrepreneurship innovations. The ways in which the tensions, resistance and conflicts manifest are varied and subtle. An immersive research approach using participant-observation made these manifestations amenable to the researcher as he was able to observe and experience the actions and omissions, the decisions and prevarications, and the attitudes and thinking behind them. The research aims to elaborate upon the application of hybrid organization theory in social entrepreneurship. While the consideration of social enterprises as hybrid organizations has proven fruitful, the consideration of hybridity as opportunity for NGOs – and the aspects of such organizations that are challenged by shifts towards hybridity – has been limited (e.g., Battilana *et al.*, 2015; Greenwood *et al.*, 2011; Pache and Santos, 2013).

Data were collected primarily through participant-observation to generate rich, subtle insights and were complemented by organizational document analysis and 17 interviews with senior staff and those involved in the innovation processes under investigation (Watson, 2011, 2012). Interviews lasted from 60 to 90 minutes and were semi-structured to allow interesting and valuable lines of enquiry to be followed as they emerged.

As an embedded actor working under the job title of Social Enterprise Consultant full-time for 24 months, the author was 'hands-on' in the construction, evaluation and implementation of social entrepreneurship initiatives. This enabled deep insight into both the opportunities and organizational challenges therein. This allowed the researcher to get beyond arm's-length observation to experience and reflect upon the phenomena first-hand to complement that experience with the perspectives of other internal stakeholders. Reconciling the participant-observation data with that collected via interviews and document analysis revealed interesting discrepancies between the espoused intentions of the organization and the lived reality of staff. It highlighted the cultural, identity and capability challenges of pursuing social entrepreneurship beyond the more easily identified tensions of strategy and structure.

Reflections on observations, interview transcripts and organizational documents were analyzed and coded thematically using NVivo 10 data analysis software. This led to first order findings around resistance, institutional misalignment with the type of innovation strategies that were espoused in interviews and codified in organizational documents, and the resources that the organization believed to be available fuel innovation processes. With these concepts identified, the data then were parsed for findings that evidenced institutional logic tension, resistance and instances of hybridity. From this analysis the framework of findings emerged as the themes were crystalized into aspects of the organization where it was apparent that hybridization would need to occur to implement and embed social entrepreneurship innovations.

This particular organizational context was chosen for investigation for three main reasons. First, the pursuit of social entrepreneurship by INGOs is presently underresearched. Second, the pursuit of social entrepreneurship by the INGO sector would be significant in terms of the financial, human and social capital that may be mobilized. This makes understanding social entrepreneurship within and around such organizations important. Third, World Vision NZ (WVNZ) is an established organization with a strongly embedded social logic with corresponding business models and management approaches. Its initial steps into social entrepreneurship represent a clear and significant challenge to this. The projects and innovations which force hybridization therefore force very clear and observable outcomes. This combination of a rich research site with clearly manifesting phenomena present a compelling research context.

Shepherd and Patzelt's (2011) framework aims to encompass a field of activities undertaken by a range of actors. However, as illustrated in Table 20.3, it also maps across the activities of World Vision, a global humanitarian INGO with operations in over 100 countries, employing 50,000 people, and revenue exceeding US$2 billion. Outside of its emergency relief work, World Vision runs integrated, long-term development programs with communities comprising 100 million people. These programs comprise health, water and sanitation, education and life skills, child rights and equity, agriculture and food security, economic development, disaster risk reduction and climate change, peacebuilding, and microfinance (www.wvi.org). This work is funded by 10 million donors as well as various government grants.

This chapter is based on a 24 month study in the New Zealand office (WVNZ) of the World Vision International federated partnership. National offices of the partnership are independent entities but are bound to the partnership by a declaration of federation, a brand license, and access to other intellectual property and global support services. WVNZ funds, monitors and evaluates more than 55 development programs in over 17 countries. As a 'support office,' WVNZ's primary responsibility is the engagement of New Zealanders in the plight of those living in extreme poverty overseas. The purpose is two-fold: the raising of funds for development projects and relief initiatives in these countries, and to mobilize New Zealanders through education and advocacy.

Two sets of findings are presented here. The first, outlined in Table 20.3, was generated from the understanding of the organization's range of development activities that was enabled by the researcher's immersion in organizational life and access to documents and staff, and visits to various sites of activity around the world. The second set is outlined in Table 20.4. This outlines the points at which the institutional logics of the organization would hinge, should hybridization occur. These findings in particular were able to be generated through participant-observation and the nuanced understanding of embedded organizational attitudes and norms that would not be accessible through interviews and document analysis alone. They are however further evidenced by representative interview quotes in the Appendix.

The rationale for social entrepreneurship at World Vision New Zealand

The primary driver for innovation at WVNZ, including social entrepreneurship and enterprise, is its declining relevance to its donors. This pertains primarily to its 55,000 child sponsors and other ad hoc donors, but includes the New Zealand government and its international aid policy. This has caused a decline in revenue and threatens future income to a deeply concerning degree. Similarly the rise of the alternative theories of change that social entrepreneurship provides creates a strategic threat as it has the potential to disrupt sources of income in fundamental ways.

One of the perennial innovation challenges of WVNZ, like many nonprofits, in terms of innovating its community development programs is the restrictions created by its established funding sources. Specifically, donations solicited on a particular premise, or from a particular marketing construct such as child sponsorship, must be used to fund the corresponding program to fulfil the donor promise. This leaves little resource or mandate for innovation. The global World Vision partnership that it operates within provides the immense 'on-the-ground' capacity that is required to deliver the long-term integrated programs it funds. However, the requirement to operate within this partnership further restricts innovation in program design or use of non-traditional development methodologies or partners. The lack of revenue streams, reserves or sources of capital over which WVNZ has complete discretion as to their use, prevents the strategic independence necessary to determine where, how or with whom they work outside of the global World Vision partnership. For these reasons income from social enterprise (or venture philanthropy for social enterprise) presents itself as an attractive alternative to the traditional donation proposition.

Beyond increased income and/or more flexible income from social enterprise which can increase the volume of existing programs that WVNZ could fund or offset the decline in traditional income streams, there is an opportunity to utilize social enterprise models to increase the impact of the organizational capacity deployed in developing country contexts. These opportunities are many and vary across geographical, economic, political and social contexts but are generically mapped across Shepherd and Patzelt's (2011) framework in Table 20.3 below. This illustrates both how the opportunities that the organization faces fit with the framework and how they are a natural extension of their extant capabilities and logic models of impact (cf. Ebrahim and Rangan, 2014), albeit via different business models. Previous programming that drew on an enterprise approach has been limited to micro-finance and economic development programs such as facilitating livelihoods training. The creation or support of enterprises for development had not previously been pursued in earnest.

Social entrepreneurship as a strategy is also given impetus by the organization's understanding of the future role of INGOs amid a shifting geopolitical, economic and technological environment, as outlined in Table 20.2. Overall, there is an expectation that the days of rich countries sending money to poor countries as a basis for addressing global poverty are waning.

These strategic threats, the decline of traditional funding models and the input of internal actors has compelled the organization to consider, and increasingly pursue, social entrepreneurship strategies. While this is because of the promise they hold, explicit hybridization was not part of the change agenda. Rather it is the source of the difficulty in achieving the desired outcomes.

Forays in social entrepreneurship at World Vision New Zealand

The social entrepreneurship initiatives that WVNZ is pursuing fall predominantly under a strategic program whereby the organization seeks partnerships with businesses, social entrepreneurs or other organizations or enterprising

Table 20.2 WVNZ interpretation of the future of development

Macro-level changes	• Urbanization of global poverty with low income countries having very young populations and 90% of population growth occurring in less developed regions. • Increased oil, water and food scarcity through climate change and competition for resources. • Shifting power structures ('West' to 'East') disrupting multilateral agendas. • Most economic growth occurring in developing nations with increased 'South'–'South' trade and investment. • Pervasive penetration of low-cost mobile ICT amongst the poor.
Development field level changes	• Direct access to the poor via mobile devices to deliver services (e.g., cash transfers; micro-finance; social welfare; education; market information). • Local citizen sector organizations become more important as partners and delivery agents for INGOs. • Development models will need to be less standardized leading to specialization and/or differentiated models based on context. • Cross-sector collaboration and integration – social enterprise and investment, public-private-NGO partnerships, trade-aid-investment blends. • 'Aid Exit' – aid programs designed to end the need for further aid and to enhance growth. • Increase in emergencies.
Change to the role of INGOs	• 'Aid' no longer simply about rich to poor transfers – increased domestic self-sufficiency. • INGOs to catalyze capital for positive 'development friendly' outcomes, not just transfer of aid. • INGO impact occurs through facilitating blended aid: official development assistance, cross sector partnerships, catalyzing private sector growth and FDI, impact investment and development impact bonds.

Source: adapted from World Vision New Zealand internal documents.

young people. The basis for the partnerships is alignment between the vision of the partner and the mission of WVNZ. Ideal outcomes from such partnerships include the generation of funds from new sources, greater public engagement (particularly youth) in issues of poverty and social justice, and enabling novel business models without complicating the organization's central operations. This strategy is a key reason for the tendency towards structural decoupling outlined below.

An example of this is a joint venture social enterprise which provides a marketplace for volunteers to donate their time and talent to fundraise for a worthy cause. In partnership with a university student social entrepreneur, the enterprise monetizes the latent resource that is the volunteer energy of supporters who may be unwilling or unable to donate cash. The enterprise creates an online marketplace where volunteers create a profile outlining the service they are willing to provide and select a cause to which 100 percent of the funds raised will go. The website connects the volunteers to customers seeking that service and manages the financial transaction and enables feedback on the impact the funds are having.

Another is a spin-out impact investment organization which was co-created with a small group of existing supporters. This venture seeks to attract venture philanthropy and investment capital to invest in social enterprises and other impact investment vehicles globally. This is an attempt to create a vehicle that can mobilize investment capital towards WVNZ's humanitarian agenda, diversify its revenue streams, and take advantage of the rise of the impact investment movement. The rationale for this diversification is not only the alignment to its humanitarian mission but the potential to utilize the network of complementary capability that has been established in likely markets to facilitate the identification of impact investment opportunities. There is also some potential, as indicated in Table 20.3 below, for the creation or curation of investable social enterprises. One example of this involves the creation of a wholly owned enterprise which connects the produce of smallholder farmer co-operatives in East Africa with local markets and those in North Africa, Middle East and Europe. This enables the development of improved agricultural techniques and infrastructure and generates higher prices for the otherwise vulnerable smallholder farmers. Notwithstanding the risks of financial investments and appropriateness of an enterprise approach to humanitarianism, an initiative such as this has significant market and engagement potential with New Zealand supporters. There is potential to use the brand capital and legitimacy of WVNZ to legitimize this approach to poverty alleviation while also using the spin-out venture brand to signify the innovation and progressiveness of the approach. This could appeal to existing high net-worth donors looking for an alternative to further traditional donations, or new supporters who would not normally be attracted to WVNZ or traditional aid appeals.

Other social entrepreneurship opportunities outlined in Table 20.3 draw their appropriateness and strategic rationale from both their complementarity of impact potential and mission, and the ability to utilize both extant resources deployed in the developing country contexts and donor (and investor) market legitimacy. While this rationale and the strategic imperative to innovate compels future social entrepreneurship action, such action in the past has not brought institutional hybridity due to intentional structural decoupling. The decoupling of the microfinance unit (VisionFund) has limited the financial risk for World Vision itself from such activities but it likewise prevented its hybrid logic from embedding in the founding organization. It also prevented microfinance from being as integrated into humanitarian development programming as it otherwise would have been if the global World Vision partnership had continued on a journey of hybridization.

Kistruck and Beamish (2010) found that such structural decoupling mitigated the cultural, network and cognitive embeddedness of the non-profit form. To

Table 20.3 Applying sustainable entrepreneurship to World Vision

Sustainable entrepreneurship framework (Shepherd and Patzelt, 2011)	World vision – illustration of relevance	Opportunity through hybridization
What is to be sustained:		
Nature	• Farmer Managed Natural Regeneration (FMNR)	• Sale of carbon credits (under Clean Development Mechanism of the Kyoto Protocol)
Sources of life support	• Climate change advocacy • FMNR • Sustainable food production • Food security • Water and sanitation	• Sale of carbon credits
Communities	• Community development programs • Social capital building in youth programs and savings and loans schemes • Microfinance	• Integrated microfinance in community development programs
What is to be developed:		
Economic gain	• Savings and loans programs • Microfinance • Value chain facilitation • Economic citizenship programs • Cooperatives and other market institution facilitation	• Social enterprise investment and support • Market access • Employment • Livelihoods • Private sector partnerships • Micro-franchising • Social enterprise venturing
Non-economic gains to individuals	• Health programs • Education programs • Emergency relief	• Private sector Joint Ventures/partnerships • Development impact bonds
Non-economic gains to society	• Health programs • Education programs • Emergency relief	• Development impact bonds

this end WVNZ's approach to achieving the initiatives outlined above is by keeping them at the edge of the organization through partnerships or the creation of spin-out ventures. This was a way of navigating the opportunity without stifling it within the incompatible logic that governs behavior within the organization, and mitigating the tension between social and commercial dimensions of the organization (Austin *et al.*, 2006). In many ways this approach de-risks the innovation process in terms of brand association and decreases the level of resourcing required as it leverages the time, energy and capital of other parties. It is a useful strategy for bringing innovations to market, creating new value, and leveraging the salient resources and legitimacy the organization does have.

However, this approach limits the value that is captured by WVNZ and may not create the organizational renewal, financial resilience or strategic independence it seeks. And although the new ventures and joint ventures may ultimately be highly successful, their position outside the core of the organization does limit the support they receive, both in resources and in strategic patience. This is an outcome of the operating plan and corresponding budget decisions and staff allocations.

Hybrid organizing in an INGO

Evidence from this research project suggests that the social logic of social entrepreneurship aligns directly with the development logic of WVNZ and can be considered synonymous. However, the commercial logic does conflict and is the source of the challenges in pivoting to such an approach, despite an acceptance of its merits. Furthermore, the ongoing innovation required in such an approach also presents a stumbling block. The conflict between the purely social logic of WVNZ as a traditional charity and the hybrid logic of social enterprise manifests through the challenges of shifting norms around risk, business model innovation, novel value propositions, financial and institutional compliance, and governance. While WVNZ has realized the strategic imperative of utilizing more entrepreneurial approaches in its development work, the development of a commercial logic lags behind. The charity logic still dominates the organization and creates resistance to the entrepreneurial initiatives that are attempted (Newth and Woods, 2014) and jeopardizes the development of a genuinely hybrid organization. This resonates with the findings of Kistruck and Beamish (2010) who found that in organizations that pursued social entrepreneurship, the non-profit identity in non-profit organizations was more resilient than the for-profit identity in for-profits.

This resistance to social entrepreneurship, social enterprise and hybridity is not without merit. There remains a strong need and clear mandate to continue with much of the status quo in terms of where and how the organization achieves its humanitarian ends. Nonetheless, the organization must now make, and continue to make, strategic choices about the paths it will take in the face of antagonistic demands.

WVNZ is beginning to adopt the hybrid logic required to realize the benefit of a social entrepreneurship approach to humanitarian development. However,

Table 20.4 Comparing extant/previous social logic versus required hybridized social entrepreneurship logic

	Established social/development logic	*Hybridized social entrepreneurship logic*
Finance and institutional compliance	Revenue used as proxy for impact. Cost to revenue ratio seen as proxy for efficiency and stewardship. A focus on maximizing financial throughput.	Focus on maximizing impact. Mobilize capital to be brought to bear on development agenda using World Vison's capability and insight, not just through its 'books.' Prioritize reporting impact over throughput.
Risk appetite	Little mandate for financial risk and fear of alienating existing donors.	Acceptance that failure is a necessary part of innovation.
Business model	Donations and government grants to deliver development programs.	Relevant to many classes of capital – donations, grants, venture philanthropy and impact investment – to deliver programs and facilitate social entrepreneurship. Impact is leveraged by social entrepreneurs.
Value proposition	Trustworthy child-focused humanitarian charity. Development practice communicated via the 'child sponsorship' marketing construct.	Market-leading development agency employing sophisticated impact measurement methods, engages supporters transparently in their work, catalyzing social entrepreneurs as well as delivering humanitarian programs.
Governance	As a support office, fundraising donations is of primary importance. Focus is on marketing and 'sales' to increase efficacy of extant business model and value proposition, while minimizing costs.	Stewardship mandate includes pursuit of innovative business models (improved capital raising), value propositions (relevance to new supporters) and development practices (social entrepreneurship).

the process of embedding the hybrid logic significantly lags behind its attempts to implement entrepreneurial initiatives. This means practice is advancing more quickly than the organization is able to shift (hybridize) its logics. This conflict in logics creates many embedded points of resistance to the initiatives as outlined in Table 20.4.

Increased and/or diversified revenue was, like for many non-profits, a primary motivator for pursuing social enterprise (Morris *et al.*, 2007; Smith *et al.*, 2010). Nonetheless, organizational attitudes towards revenue and expenditure form the basis of a particularly sticky institutional logic and are also the driver of other bases of resistance. Because the primary function of WVNZ is fundraising, the stewardship and efficacy of the organization in doing so is of primary importance. This places a focus on maximizing through-put – maximizing revenue and minimizing expenditure. However, because the organization is an INGO, its impact on its mission is also central to the organizational consciousness. Revenue therefore becomes a crude proxy for impact in the field and relevance to the donor market. This attitude is driven by a desire to comply with the institutional expectations of stakeholders (Newth and Woods, 2014). It constrains entrepreneurship in two particularly salient ways. First, it leaves few resources for experimentation and finding new ways to increase impact, marketability, or financial efficiency. Second, it causes a narrow focus on the type of financial capital that the organization attracts, i.e., only donations and only for the purpose of funding World Vision programs. This means other forms of finance, such as various forms of investment capital, are institutionally excluded because the in-field offices (National Offices) of the World Vision partnership are not organized to deploy such capital. Furthermore, because of the lack of resources for innovation, the organization has not had a mandate to find a way to become relevant to this form of capital. A focus on complying with the institutionalized attitudes of supporters and the 'through-put' understanding of stewardship has meant organizational prioritization of monitoring of income and expenditure, not innovation.

Attracting other forms of capital, however, may not increase income as it would be accounted for as debt or equity, for example, or not pass through the organization at all. In other words, this capital may be catalyzed or mobilized to have an impact in ways complementary to World Vision's programs, but may not have a positive influence on the finances of WVNZ in ways which fit with the income versus expenditure priorities of the organization. Without a way to capture, or at least communicate, the value of catalyzing complementary forms of financial capital to the field, innovations in non-donation business models will be a challenge and a basis of resistance from a finance and institutional compliance perspective.

The institutional compliance also forces a low appetite for risk as the desire to comply with donor expectations, the through-put attitude towards finance and the resultant lack of risk capital leaves little mandate for risk-taking. In particular, the fear of failure and the perception that this would be an unacceptable waste of resources ensures the organizational inertia. It is powered by its social logic and inhibits the entrepreneurial initiatives that could provide the organizational renewal that is required.

It is in the change or addition of business model(s) that hybridization would be most conspicuous as it would entail an expansion beyond donations to include trading revenue, private sector partnerships or investment management. An initial challenge in this shift is the understanding and acceptance by key gatekeeper staff of how alternative business models can achieve the social ends that the organization's mission prescribes. However, this challenge is exacerbated by the organization's position in the value chain within the World Vision partnership. Not only has the organization's donor market oriented operations and structure developed around the donation business model, its partnership with National Offices of the World Vision partnership, and the 'middle-ware' support provided by World Vision International is built around the donation business model. The development programs that National Offices deliver with funds from Support Offices such as WVNZ are designed, like most INGOs, to make use of grants. They therefore have not needed to develop the capabilities or capacity to provide the 'in-field' structures necessary to make alternative business models, such as impact investment, feasible for WVNZ.

Business models are animated by the value proposition that an organization can provide. And it is in the inertia of their value proposition that makes hybridization and the animation of alternative revenue models pertinent and, seemingly, necessary for organizational vitality. The organization has grown, very successfully, on the basis that it is a trustworthy child-focused humanitarian charity. The success came from the market penetration of its child sponsorship 'product.' In particular, the pledge nature of the product which ensured ongoing income and a high lifetime customer (donor) value enabled the growth of WVNZ and the rest of the World Vision global partnership. However, child sponsorship became the marketing construct that communicated the practice of humanitarian development and solicited donor support and its success lay in its simplicity – sponsor a child and save that child's life. However, this oversimplification of how community development is achieved has, to some extent, pushed the organization into a corner in terms of its relationship with donors as it does not engage them in the complex, integrated, long-term, community-wide program of activity in which organization has developed significant capability. This value proposition, therefore, does not adequately communicate its source of competitive advantage (to the extent this term is appropriate in humanitarian endeavors).

The simple, emotional value proposition does not compel the organization to develop sophisticated impact measurement methods to communicate value to donors or to position itself as market leading in its practice. And in particular it does not position it to leverage the rise of alternative methods of achieving impact in less-developed country contexts, such as social entrepreneurship, venture philanthropy and impact investment.

Concluding remarks

Drawing on Newth and Woods' (2014) work on resistance, Kistruck and Beamish's (2010) embeddedness, and the rapidly growing body of work on organizational hybridity and novel blends of institutional logics (Battilana and Dorado, 2010; Doherty et al., 2014; Pache and Santos, 2010), this chapter applies Shepherd and Patzelt's (2011) framework for sustainable entrepreneurship to the present activities and potential innovations of WVNZ, a humanitarian INGO. Their framework provides a useful basis for understanding those entrepreneurship opportunities and the nature of the impact they can have. In order to sustainably undertake social entrepreneurship activities such as the founding or facilitation of social enterprise or the mobilization of social impact investment, the organization must combine institutional logics that would otherwise be considered incompatible – in other words they must, to some extent, hybridize the organization. This involves an intentional shift along the value creation spectrum from a sole focus on social value creation to the simultaneous pursuit of social and financial value.

To remain relevant to changing donor expectations and shifting global humanitarian landscape, and increase income and impact, WVNZ has undertaken a program of innovation that can be characterized as social entrepreneurship. This includes the collaboration on a revenue generating social enterprise, the founding of a spin-out impact investment start-up, and an ongoing program of exploring partnerships with social entrepreneurs. This chapter has discussed the institutional challenges to achieving this at the organizational (micro) level.

In the case presented here, the aspects of the organization in which the logics needed to blend effectively for the desired innovations to be achieved were identified to be finance and institutional compliance, risk appetite, business model, value proposition and governance. Hybridization of these aspects of the organization would embed principles of innovation and entrepreneurship that are typically eschewed at a deep institutional level and shift governing priorities from fundraising for program delivery to catalyzing capital for development impact. Those principles include an impact orientation rather than a financial through-put one. This necessitates an openness to multiple business models based on a more sophisticated value proposition that engages donors and customers more authentically in the organization's theory of change. Embedded innovativeness and a degree of commercial logic will also require a tolerance to failure and a willingness to experiment with new offerings. While the approach thus far has been to structurally decouple social entrepreneurship initiatives, questions remain whether this approach provides the ventures with the freedom from stifling the non-profit logic, or whether this unnecessarily starves them of organizational support. It is also questionable as to whether this limits the value that is captured for WVNZ in terms of finance, brand capital and organizational renewal.

If we continue to see growth in organizations and policies that break down or transcend sectoral boundaries – between public, private and civil society sectors

– then we will see greater hybridization of existing organizations, and many that are 'born hybrid.' Researchers will need therefore a more nuanced understanding of the opportunities and challenges that hybridity creates in organizational contexts, in particular where the hybridity comes from combining institutional logics that were previously considered incompatible (Greenwood *et al.*, 2011; Pache and Santos, 2010). Social innovation and entrepreneurship acts as a crucible for investigating the potential and the consequences of such combinations. Research in this context will not only build our understanding of the field, but may provide insights into the management and governance of organizations that seek to blend other logics in entrepreneurial ways.

This chapter has specifically argued that INGOs represent an under-researched context for social entrepreneurship but one with significant potential for improving our understanding of how social entrepreneurship can play a role in the alleviation of poverty in the world's least developed countries. Moreover the role that INGOs could play in this presents a rich vein of research in terms of how large non-profit organizations approach hybridization in order to innovate both their practice and their funding models.

In providing an empirical application of Shepherd and Patzelt's (2011) framework in concert with institutional theory, an exploration of the micro-level institutional bases of tension and resistance was possible. This proved a fruitful theoretical lens for elucidating the challenges of social entrepreneurship in an INGO and informing our understanding of how innovation of this kind is compelled or constrained by institutional contexts. In particular, financial and institutional compliance, attitudes and perspectives of risk, governance, and the embedded systems associated with existing value propositions and business models are presented as hybridization hinge points within organizations operating solely, or primarily, on social value creation logics. There is significant potential for research that extends on these contributions to unpack and explore the nuanced, micro-institutional bases of resistance to social entrepreneurship and the inherent hybridity this approach brings to organizations.

Appendix

Table A20.1 Representative data of extant institutional logic

	Established social/development logic	Representative data
Finance and institutional compliance	Revenue used as proxy for impact. Cost to revenue ratio seen as proxy for efficiency and stewardship. A focus on maximizing financial throughput.	But I think it's actually more to do with the concept of stewardship here, so which is basically, don't stuff up, save money on the paperclips, you know, stay in the crappiest hotel we can find and that's good stewardship. So I think that's the ingrained view of what we're supposed to be doing as employees … Whereas I would actually argue that if you're spending all of your efforts on something other than what's most strategically important, that's actually not good stewardship. But again, people don't understand that so much.
		I don't think there's anything malicious in it at all. I don't even think it's intentional. It's just the way we're set up, you know, with budget cycles and planning cycles and all these sorts of things. There's no room in any of that to do a lot of innovation. And so people could be genuinely supportive of an idea but then if it doesn't fit the process it just bounces off. So again, there's nothing malicious in that part of the culture. It's really just sort of a, it's as much process driven as anything.
		Senior Executive A
		We exist because actually we want to see life in all its forms for a whole bunch of children in communities who would otherwise not see that kind of life. And that's a pretty compelling 'why.' For us maybe it's the 'what.' And particularly in terms of 'what do we do and what is the organizational form' that we struggle with. So we still measure so much of our impact in terms of the bottom line. But I know from … common sense that if it was just about money we would have solved world poverty because actually it would be in the interest of the superpowers to solve it because a stable world is much a much safer world than an unstable world. So clearly it's about more than money so what we're looking at is a really complex interaction of government policy of international policies, of the trading world, of structural reform – all those kind of poverty trap issues that sit in there. So I think for us, its the 'what we do' question, and what's the organizational form to handle that – is just more complex than how we've portrayed in the past.
		Senior Executive B

Risk appetite	Little mandate for financial risk and fear of alienating existing donors.	Because by nature the organization doesn't do well with risk because it's a charity, and also we've been so stuck in this controlling, making sure that it's perfect, and we deliver only the perfect story to the supporter.
		… I think the underlying inherent aversion to risk is still very strong, and I think when push comes to shove I think that at the moment my gut feel is that we'll still override [an innovation].
		Mid-level Manager A
		I guess the one that always comes in any survey of staff etcetera, it always comes to the top of the pile, is risk aversion in terms of culture. So it's very risk averse. That's been sort of built into us for a number of reasons I suppose …
		Senior Executive A
		And it's about what our risk appetite is, and at what point does the board need to get involved in that. And they could potentially call the risk card on anything that we do because it's related to reputation and that's in the governance mandate.
		Senior Executive D
Business model	Donations and government grants to deliver development programs.	I think that we do welcome innovation if it's inside the box so to speak. So we all love the story from the field where they've come up with some clever way of solving a problem etcetera. Those sorts of things we love and we celebrate that. But that's all innovation within our current business model. The thing that's very difficult is anything that challenges our current business model. We find it very hard to adapt. Much of the organization globally is built around the child sponsorship and ADP model. And that, that's good; it's needed. You know, we've two million, whatever it is, or four million sponsored kids around the world and 3000 projects in so many countries; you need standardized processes to make that thing work.
		But the challenge for us often is if we need to do something outside of that model it bounces off, yeah. So in many ways, the process and the structure is really informed to that culture. So part of the conservatism is really around if it doesn't fit this model. There's the underlying … it's the body rejecting the transplant almost.
		Senior Executive A

continued

Table A20.1 Continued

	Established social/development logic	Representative data
Value proposition	Trustworthy child-focused humanitarian charity. Development practice communicated via the 'child sponsorship' marketing construct.	When we started we didn't say we are a child sponsorship agency. It was Bob Pierce trying to work out how to solve a problem and it organically grew. And then the marketers found the most effective way of working was to create this child sponsorship construct which, as we know, isn't exactly what happens anyway. *Senior Executive C*
Governance	As a support office, fundraising donations is of primary importance. Focus is on marketing and 'sales' to increase efficacy of extant business model and value proposition, while minimizing costs.	And so I think a lot of the problem for innovation for us is almost our understanding of World Vision as historically a … it's almost our DNA, we do everything end-to-end. We control it tightly. You know, we're all conservative and risk averse in how we do all these things. And so I guess it's an open question whether we'll ever be able to do any serious business model innovation under that governance model. It's not doing that maliciously or willingly. It's just, "I can't make this fit. And at the end of the day I have to report to a board and the board's going to be asking me about my revenue numbers, which you've got to talk about. It sounds really interesting, I can be generally supportive but if it's not actually fitting my process and not supporting the things that I'm going to be held accountable for then you'll only get so much help in trying to get something out." *Senior Executive A*

References

Alvord, S. H., Brown, D. L. and Letts, C. W. 2004. Social entrepreneurship and societal transformation: An exploratory study. *Journal of Applied Behavioural Science*, 40, 260–282.

Arora, S. and Romijn, H. 2009. *Innovation for the base of the pyramid: Critical perspectives from development studies on heterogeneity and participation*, United Nations Univ., Maastricht Economic and Social Research and training centre on Innovation and Techn.

Austin, J., Stevenson, H. and Wei-Skillern, J. 2006. Social and commercial entrepreneurship: Same, different, or both? *Entrepreneurship Theory and Practice*, 30, 1–22.

Battilana, J. and Dorado, S. 2010. Building sustainable hybrid organisations: The case of commercial microfinance organizations. *Academy of Management Journal*, 53, 1419–1440.

Battilana, J., Sengul, M., Pache, A.-C. and Model, J. 2015. Harnessing productive tensions in hybrid organizations: The case of work integration social enterprises. *Academy of Management Journal*, 58(6), 1658–1685.

Billis, D. 2010. *Hybrid organizations and the third sector: Challenges for practice, theory and policy*, Basingstoke, Palgrave Macmillan.

Dart, R. 2004. The legitimacy of social enterprise. *Nonprofit Management and Leadership*, 14, 411–424.

De Mendiguren Castresana, J. C. P. 2013. Social enterprise in the development agenda: Opening a new road map or just a new vehicle to travel the same route? *Social Enterprise Journal*, 9, 247–268.

Doherty, B., Haugh, H. and Lyon, F. 2014. Social enterprises as hybrid organizations: A review and research agenda. *International Journal of Management Reviews*, 16(4), 417–436.

Ebrahim, A. and Rangan, V. K. 2014. What impact? *California Management Review*, 56, 118–141.

Greenwood, R., Raynard, M., Kodeih, F., Micelotta, E. R. and Lounsbury, M. 2011. Institutional complexity and organizational responses. *The Academy of Management Annals*, 5, 317–371.

Jay, J. 2013. Navigating paradox as a mechanism of change and innovation in hybrid organizations. *Academy of Management Journal*, 56, 137–159.

Kistruck, G. M. and Beamish, P. 2010. The interplay of form, structure, and embeddedness in social intrapreneurship. *Entrepreneurship Theory and Practice*, 34, 735–761.

Mair, J. and Marti, I. 2009. Entrepreneurship in and around institutional voids: A case study from Bangladesh. *Journal of Business Venturing*, 24, 419–435.

McMullen, J. S. 2011. Delineating the domain of development entrepreneurship: A market-based approach to facilitating inclusive economic growth. *Entrepreneurship Theory and Practice*, 35, 185–193.

Morris, M. H., Coombes, S. M. T., Schindehutte, M. and Allen, J. A. 2007. Antecedents and outcomes of entrepreneurial and market orientations in a non-profit context: Theoretical and empirical insights. *Journal of Leadership & Organizational Studies*, 13, 12–39.

Moss, T. W., Short, J. C., Payne, G. T. and Lumpkin, G. 2011. Dual identities in social ventures: An exploratory study. *Entrepreneurship Theory and Practice*, 35, 805–830.

Newth, J. and Woods, C. 2014. Resistance to social entrepreneurship: How context shapes innovation. *Journal of Social Entrepreneurship*, 5, 192–213.

Nicholls, A. and Cho, A. 2006. Social entrepreneurship: The structuration of the field. In: Nicholls, A. (ed.) *Social entrepreneurship: New models of sustainable social change*, New York, Oxford University Press.

Pache, A.-C. and Santos, F. 2010. When worlds collide: The internal dynamics of organizational responses to conflicting institutional demands. *Academy of Management Review*, 35, 455–476.

Pache, A.-C. and Santos, F. 2013. Inside the hybrid organization: Selective coupling as a response to competing institutional logics. *Academy of Management Journal*, 56, 972–1001.

Schumpeter, J. A. 1934. *The theory of economic development*, Cambridge, MA, Harvard University Press.

Shepherd, D. A. and Patzelt, H. 2011. The new field of sustainable entrepreneurship: Studying entrepreneurial action linking "what is to be sustained" with "what is to be developed." *Entrepreneurship Theory and Practice*, 35, 137–163.

Smith, B. R., Knapp, J., Barr, T. F. and Cannatelli, B. L. 2010. Social enterprises and the timing of conception. *Journal of Nonprofit & Public Sector Marketing*, 22, 208–134.

Tracey, P., Phillips, N. and Jarvis, O. 2011. Bridging institutional entrepreneurship and the creation of new organizational forms: A multilevel model. *Organization Science*, 22, 60–80.

Watson, T. J. 2011. Ethnography, reality, and truth: The vital need for studies of 'how things work in organizations and management. *Journal of Management Studies*, 48(1), 202–217.

Watson, T. J. 2012. Making organisational ethnography. *Journal of Organizational Ethnography*, 1, 15–22.

World Vision International. 2014. *www.wvi.org* [Online]. [Accessed 27 October 2014].

Yunus, M. 2008. *Creating a world without poverty: Social business and the future of capitalism*, New York, Public Affairs Books.

Zahra, S. A., Gedajlovic, E., Neubaum, D. O. and Shulman, J. M. 2009. A typology of social entrepreneurs: Motives, search processes and ethical challenges. *Journal of Business Venturing*, 24, 519–532.

Index

Page numbers in *italics* denote tables, those in **bold** denote figures. End of chapter notes are denoted by a letter n between page number and note number.

50+20 responsible management education framework 230–1, *232*

Abell, D. F. 354
Adams, Paula 188
Adnan Menderes University, Turkey 248
Advance Exhaust Purification Systems 278
Africa: entrepreneurial marine protected area, Tanzania 128–9, 133, *134*, 135; entrepreneurship education 236–41; farmer cooperatives 378
agribusiness software solutions 239–40
agriculture 244–5; *see also* Turkish agricultural sector
aid agencies *see* international humanitarian non-government organizations (INGOs)
air pollution, cruise shipping 277, 278, 279, *280*, 281
Ajzen, I. 235
ALTIS (Alta Scuola Impresa e Società) 236–41
Amann, W. 229–30
ambidexterity theoretical perspective 102, 107–17
Anderson, B. S. 105
Andriopoulous, C. 111
anti-nuclear movement 82–3, 86, 88
Aotearoa-New Zealand *see* Māori sustainable innovation
architectural ambidexterity 108–9
Ashoka 237, 238
Auckland, New Zealand *see* Māori sustainable innovation

Baba, K. 77
Bali, Indonesia 129–31, 133, *134*, 135

Bangladesh 43
Barefoot College, Rajasthan 230
Baregheh, A. 43
Battilana, J. 355–6, 370
Beamish, P. 378, 382
Belize 131–3, *134*, 135, 276
Belize Barrier Reef Reserve System 132
Belz, F. M. 211, 212, 298
Berger, I. E. 77
Billis, D. 369, *370*
Binder, J. K. 211, 212, 298
bio-diesel fuel 279
bioclimatic architectural design 159–60
biomimicry 158, 298
bioneers *75*, 76, 92
biophilia 145, 150–2, 159–60
Biorock coral nurseries 130
Birkinshaw, J. 109
Bloodgood, J. M. 357
Boardman, A. 312
Bongsug, C. 357
Bonilla-Priego, M. J. 282
Bornstein, D. 16, 17
Boschee, J. 19, 20
Bourdieu, Pierre 321
British Council 248
brokerage 322, 332–3
Burdge, R. 275
Burt, R. S. 322
business models, international humanitarian NGOs *381*, 383, *387*
business schools 228–41, **231**, **232**, **234**, **236**
Butt, N. 275

Cantillon, Richard 13
Cao, Q. 111

capability building, Singapore 26, 27, 28, 31, 37
Capability Development Grants programme, Singapore 28
carbon dioxide emissions, cruise shipping 277, 278, 279, 280, 281
Cardiff University 151
Caribbean 276
Carnival Corporation & PLC 273, 277–8
Center of Ecotourism and Sustainable Development 276
Chang, Y. Y. 111
change agents 65, 75, 76, 92, 340
change-oriented sustainable intrapreneurs 75–7, 75, 83–7, 92–3, 94
Chernobyl nuclear disaster 86
CHICOP see Chumbe Island Coral Park, Tanzania
Chilala, Tessa 196
childcare, public-private partnerships (PPPs) 311, 315
Chin, M. K. 214
China 211, 213; solar PV industry 216–24, 219, 220, **222**
China Democratic National Construction Association (CDNCA) 219, 220, 221
Chinese Communist Party 219, 224
Chinese People's Political Consultative Conference (CPPCC) 219, 220, 221
Choi, D. Y. 291, 295
chronic diseases 154
Chumbe Island Coral Park, Tanzania 128–9, 133, 134, 135
classic entrepreneurship 13
climate mentors 79, 91
Closed Forest Reserve Agreement, Zanzibar 129
clothing sector 322–34, **323**, 326, 330–1, **334**
co-management 127, 132–3, 135
coastal ecotourism 281
coastal zone management approach 132
coffee 237–8
Cohen, B. 104, 246, 290, 293
collaboration 247; in management of tensions 177–80, **177**
collaboration based education process 232–3, **232**
Colwell, S. 126
committed activists 76, 92
community engagement, cruise shipping 275–7, 279, 280, 280, 281–2
compartmentalization strategies 65
compliance strategies 65

Confucian values 212, 213, 221
connected difference 181–2
conservation see entrepreneurial marine protected areas (EMPAs)
consolidation of conservation-based entrepreneurial activity 127, **127**, 128–9, 130–1, 132, 133, 134, 135
consultancy, university-industry collaboration 259, 260
contextual ambidexterity 108, 109, 111, 113–15
Convention on Biodiversity 125
cooperatives: business form 341; employee energy 338–49, 343; farmer cooperatives, Africa 378
coral reefs, protection of 128–33
coral restoration 130, 132
corporate culture, and pro-environmental behavior life-work spillover 84–5, 86–7, 340, 344, 345–6
corporate environmental programs 339–40; see also employee energy cooperatives (EECs); pro-environmental behavior life-work spillover
corporate giving activities, cruise shipping 278–9, 280, 282
corporate political activity (CPA) perspective 210–24, **213**, **215**; solar PV industry, China 219, 220, **222**
Corporate Social Responsibility (CSR) 42, 215, 282
Costa Concordia accident 281
cost-benefit analysis, social impact 361–2
CPA see corporate political activity (CPA) perspective
creative destruction 16, 17, 20, 293
creativity, double spiral of 194–5, **195**, 203, 204
Crete see European Sustainability Academy (ESA), Crete
Cruise Line International Association 274
cruise ship size 273
cruise tourism sector 272–83, 280
CSCP 235
CSR see Corporate Social Responsibility (CSR)

Dacin, P. A. 65
dairy industry: Ghana 239; Turkey 251
Daniel, L. 43–4, 45
Davis, S. 16, 17
Davis, Wade 202–3
De Clercq, D. 63, 321, 334, 335

Dean, T. J. 104, *290*, 293–4, *295*, *296*
Dearing, J. 272
Dearing, J. A. 190, 191, 201–2
Dees, Greg 14, 16, 19–20
defiance strategies 65, 66
Dess, G. G. 105
destructive creation 16, 17, 20, 293
development agencies *see* international
   humanitarian non-government
   organizations (INGOs)
Dimov, D. 65
dive shops 130
Divine Chocolate *49*
donations 17, 360; cruise shipping 278–9,
   280, 282; international humanitarian
   NGOs 375–6, 378, *381*, 383, *387*;
   SCOPE Plus, India 176, 178, 179, 182
Dorado, S. 355–6, 370
Dostoyevsky, Fyodor 22
double spiral of creativity 194–5, **195**,
   203, 204
doughnut economics model 191, 200–3,
   201
Drayton, Bill 18
dried fruit industry, Turkey *250*
Drucker, Peter 21
dual mission management 112–13
dualities of tensions 356–8
durability of conservation-based
   entrepreneurial activity 127–8, **127**,
   129, 131, 132–3, *134*, 135
Dyllic, T. 245

Eckhardt, J. T. 126
eco-building *see* green building design
ECO-Exhaust Gas Cleaning 277, 283n1
eco-innovation 76, 150, 153, 164
eco-socio innovation (ESI) 40–54, **47**, *49*
Economic and Social Research Council
   (ESRC) 149
Economic Development Board (EDB),
   Singapore 27
economic effects, cruise shipping 274,
   281–2
economic gains 13, 15–17, 21–2
ecopreneurship 42, *290*, 292–3, *292*, *295*
education: entrepreneurship 228–41, **231**,
   232, **234**, **236**, 300–1; Turkish
   agricultural sector 259, *260*; *see also*
   environmental education
EECs *see* employee energy cooperatives
   (EECs)
Eisenhardt, K. M. 359
Eku, Stephen 239

Elkington, John 146
embeddedness 57, 58–9, 60–8, **61**, 378, 382
Emigoh Ghana Limited, Ghana 239
EMPAs *see* entrepreneurial marine
   protected areas (EMPAs)
employee energy cooperatives (EECs)
   338–49, *343*
employees: absenteeism and green building
   design 152; *see also* pro-environmental
   behavior life-work spillover
energy consumption, cruise shipping
   277–8, 279
energy cooperatives, employee 338–49,
   343
energy efficiency 81, 90–1
Energy Efficiency National Partnership,
   Singapore 28
entrepreneurial behaviours 105–6, 112
entrepreneurial knowledge 114
entrepreneurial marine protected areas
   (EMPAs) 124–36, **125**, **127**, *134*
entrepreneurial orientation 101, 104,
   105–7
entrepreneurship education 228–41, **231**,
   232, **234**, **236**, 300–1
environmental activism, and pro-
   environmental behavior life-work
   spillover 78, **78**
environmental concerns, cruise shipping
   274–5
environmental education: cruise shipping
   280, 282; Zanzibar 128
environmental entrepreneurship 58–9, 60,
   294
Environmental Protection Agency (EPA),
   US 159, *159*
environmental self-identity 77, 78
environmentalism 40; and pro-
   environmental behavior life-work
   spillover 76–8, **78**
environment-values-resources (EVR)
   framework 41, 45–8, **46**, **47**, *49*
EO *see* entrepreneurial orientation
ESA *see* European Sustainability Academy
   (ESA), Crete
ESI *see* eco-socio innovation (ESI)
ethically oriented sustainable entre- and
   intrapreneurs 75, 76–7
ethics, spiral of 193–4, **193**, 203, 204
European Sustainability Academy (ESA),
   Crete 144–5, 156–63, **163**, 165–6
European Union 129, 238
EVR *see* environment-values-resources
   (EVR) framework

exploitation-exploration tensions 107–10, 112–15
eye hospital, Kenya 238

Farjoun, M. 357
farmer cooperatives, Africa 378
farming 244–5; *see also* Turkish agricultural sector
feed-in-tariffs (FIT), Germany 340, 343, 349n2
finances, international humanitarian NGOs 375–6, 378, 381, 382, 386
financial self-reliance 20
financial sustainability 360–1
financially oriented sustainable entre- and intrapreneurs 75, 76
Finland 153; clothing sector 323, 324–34, 326, 330–1, 334
Fishbein, M. 235
fishing, and marine protected areas 128–33
FIT *see* feed-in-tariffs (FIT), Germany
fitting in and standing out of sustainable entrepreneurs 329–32, 330–1, 334, 335
Fleishman, Joel L. 19
Fondation de l'Entrepreneurship, Québec 299–300
food sourcing, cruise shipping 278, 280
Forbes 240
foreign labour, Singapore 25–6, 31–2, 32, 33, 34
Fragments of Hope, Belize 132
frames 189–90
Freeman, R. E. 59
Freitag 49
Friends of Laughing Bird Caye Committee 131
Friends of the Earth 323
fruit and vegetable processing: Ghana 239; Turkey 251
Fukushima nuclear disaster 82–3, 86, 88

Galapagos 279
game theory 61–2
GEF 132
Gerlach, A. 295, 296
Germany, employee energy cooperatives (EECs) 338–43, 343
Ghana 236, 239
Ghina, A. 235
Gibbs, D. 299
Gibson, C. 109
Global Coral Reef Alliance (GCRA) 130
Google 150

governance, international humanitarian NGOs 381, 387
Grameen Bank 149
Granovetter, M. 58
Gray, B. J. 63, 104–5
Gray, E. R. 291, 295
Greece *see* European Sustainability Academy (ESA), Crete
Green, J. F. 136
green activities and green positioning of employees 87–90, 93, 95
Green and Black's 49
green building design 143–5, 150–2, 155–64; biomimicry 158; biophilia 145, 150–2, 159–60; European Sustainability Academy (ESA), Crete 144–5, 156–63, 163, 165–6; and health 143, 145, 150–2, 158–9; and healthcare sector 144, 145, 152, 162–3, 163; triple bottom line 159, 163, 164
green energy 82, 83, 84, 85, 87; *see also* renewable energies
green entrepreneurship 58–9
green prison concept 62
greenhouse gas emissions, cruise shipping 277, 278, 279, 280, 281
Groot, K. 104, 213

Hall, J. K. 211
Hamilton, E. 322
Hansen, E. G. 246
Harrach, C. 74–5, 97
Haynie, J. M. 62, 214
He Korunga a Ng Tikanga 193–4, 193, 203, 204
health, and green building design 143, 145, 150–2, 158–9
healthcare sector 152–5, 162–3, 163; and green building design 144, 145, 152
Healy, A. M. 105
Heidegger, Martin 22
Hendrickson, L. U. 294
Hockerts, K. 245, 297
Hond, F. 214
Hondo, H. 77
hospitals, and green building design 144, 145, 152
Hostager, T. J. 97
Huberman, A. M. 29
human capital development, Singapore 26, 27–8, 35, 37
hybridization 65, 66, 341; international humanitarian NGOs 369–70, 373–4, 379, 380–3, 381, 384–5

ideology of entrepreneurs 211, 214, 215, **215**, 217, 221, 223
IEQ *see* Indoor Environmental Quality (IEQ) metrics
ignorance strategies 65, 66
IKEA 150
IMO *see* International Maritime Organization
India 230; Program Nav Kria 172–82, *173*, *174*, **177**
indigenous entrepreneurship *see* M ori sustainable innovation
indigenous management theory 214
Indonesia 129–31, 133, *134*, 135
Indoor Environmental Quality (IEQ) metrics 152, 161, 162
informal economy, Turkey 252–3, *265*
INGOs *see* international humanitarian non-government organizations (INGOs)
Innocent Smoothies 49
innovation: double spiral of 194–5, **195**, 203, 204; eco-innovation 76, 150, 153, 164; eco-socio innovation (ESI) 40–54, **47**, *49*; open innovation model 161, **162**, 247; *see also* social innovation
Innovation and Capability Voucher (ICV) scheme, Singapore 28
Innovation Eye Center, Kenya 238
innovation-oriented sustainable entre- and intrapreneurs *75*, 76
innovativeness 105–6
institutional compliance, international humanitarian NGOs *381*, 382–3, 386
institutional logics 352–65, 369–70, 380–3, *381*
institutional theory 48–50, 65, 245, 353, 355; *see also* Turkish agricultural sector
insurgent sustainable entrepreneurs 65
intention 16
Inter-Ministerial Committee on Sustainable Development (IMCSD), Singapore 26
International Convention for the Prevention of Pollution from Ships 281
international humanitarian non-government organizations (INGOs) 369–85, *370*; hybridization 369–70, 373–4, *379*, 380–3, *381*, 384–5; World Vision New Zealand (WVNZ) 374–83, *377*, *379*, *381*, 386–8
International Maritime Organization 275, 281
International Union for the Conservation of Nature 128

intrapreneurship, sustainable 73, 74–7, *75*, 83–7, 92–3, *94*, 97, 340
Investment Protection Act, Zanzibar 128, 129
IPPP *see* Oruarangi Industry Pollution Prevention Programme (IPPP)
Isaak, R. 92, *290*

Jansen, J. J. P. 109–10
Jerneck, A. 190
Johnson, D. 274, 275, 281
Junni, P. 108

Kashima, Y. 78
Katsikis, I. N. *291*
Kazakhstan, public-private partnerships (PPPs) 307–8, 309–17
Kenya 236, 238
Kiage, Jacqueline 238
kindergartens, public-private partnerships (PPPs) 311, 315
Kirkwood, J. *290*, 294–5
Kistruck, G. M. 378, 382
Klein, R. A. 275, 276, 281
Klewitz, J. 246
Klinkers, L. 339
Knight, Craig 151
knowledge exchanges 115
Kuckertz, A. 229, 234–5
Kyrgidou, L. P. *291*

Lakoff, G. 189–90
Lambooy, T. 133
Lamers, M. 133
Larson, D. 253–4
Larson, F. D. 257
Larty, J. 322
Laughing Bird Caye, Belize 131–3, *134*, 135
leadership: ambidextrous 109–10; social 19, 20
Levashova, Y. 133
Levinsohn, D. 58
Lewis, M. W. 111
Li, X. H. 210, 212, 213
Liang, X. Y. 210, 212, 213
life-work spillover effects *see* pro-environmental behavior life-work spillover
Light, P. C. 20, 21
Linnanen, L. 91, *296*
livestock related business, Turkey *251*
Loomis, T. M. 190
Lubatkin, M. H. 110

Lumpkin, G. T. 105

Maathai, Wangari 149
McAdam, M. 247
McGrall, S. 189–90
McKenna, M. 257
McMullen, J. S. 104, *290*, 293–4, *295*, *296*
Mair, J. 171
Makaurau Marae 204
Makaurau Marae, Aotearoa-New Zealand
    187–8, 202–3; Oruarangi Industry
    Pollution Prevention Programme
    188–9, **188**, 195–200, **199**, 204
management barriers or support, for pro-
    environmental activities 84–5, 86–7,
    340, 344, 345–6
management education 228–41, **231**, **232**,
    234, **236**, 300–1
management of tensions 170–83;
    exploitation-exploration tensions
    107–10, 112–15; multiple institutional
    logics 352–65, 369–70, 380–3, *381*;
    Program Nav Kria, India 172–82, *173*,
    174, **177**
management processes 298–9, 300
managers, ambidextrous 109–10
M ori sustainable innovation 187–204;
    doughnut economics model 191, 200–3,
    201; He Korunga a Ng Tikanga 193–4,
    193, 203, 204; Oruarangi Industry
    Pollution Prevention Programme
    188–9, **188**, 195–200, **199**, 204;
    Takarangi framework 194–5, **195**, 203,
    204
March, J. G. 107, 108, 354
marine protected areas 124–36, **125**, **127**,
    134
maritime tourism 272–83, *280*
market failures 126, 293–4, *295*; and
    public-private partnerships (PPPs) 314
Markusson, N. 77
Marti, I. 171
Martin, R. 20
matrix of ethics 193–4, **193**, 203, 204
Meek, W. R. 58–9
Messina 276
Mexico 276
M-Farm Limited, Kenya 239–40
Miami 278, 279, 283
microcredit 43, 149
Miles, M. B. 29
Miller, D. 105
Mintzberg, H. 229
motivations 18, 40, 50, 61, 294–5; and

Confucian values 212, 213, 221;
    corporate political activity (CPA)
    perspective 212–13, **213**, 214; pro-
    environmental behavior life-work
    spillover 76, 77, 78, 81, 82–3, 90–2
Muff, K. 232–3
Mulgan, G. 149, 181–2
multiple institutional logics 352–65,
    369–70, 380–3, *381*
Muñoz, P. 65

Nadim, A. 300–1
National Coffee Policy, Uganda 238
National Geographic 129
national parks, Belize 131–3
National Protected Areas System Plan
    (NPASP), Belize 132–3
National Union of Coffee (NUCAFE),
    Uganda 237–8
nature based designed buildings *see* green
    building design
Nature Conservancy 129, 132
NCL 279–80
Nelissen, N. 339
networks: of practice 320–36, *326*, *330–1*,
    334; stakeholder 59, 60–8, **61**
New Public Management 25
New Zealand *see* M ori sustainable
    innovation
NGOs *see* international humanitarian
    non-government organizations
    (INGOs)
Nieuwenhuis, Marlon 151
Nkandu, Joseph 237–8
"No Navi Grandi" social initiative, Venice
    282
No Take Zones (NTZs) 130, 131–3
Nobel Prizes 43, 149
non-economic gains 13, 15–17, 21–2
non-government organizations *see*
    international humanitarian non-
    government organizations (INGOs)
Nowak, A. 148
NTZs *see* No Take Zones (NTZs)
NUCAFE *see* National Union of Coffee
    (NUCAFE), Uganda

Oguya, Susan 239–40
oligopolization 273
olive industry, Turkey 250, 253, 254, 255,
    256
Olsson, L. 190
One Foundation 49
open innovation model 161, **162**, 247

Open University 149
operational reasoning 298
opportunity creation 61–2, 63, 294; *see also* corporate political activity (CPA) perspective
opportunity evaluation 62, 63
opportunity exploitation 61–2, 63, 104, 107–10; marine protected areas 126–7, **127**, 128, 130, 131–2, 133, *134*
opportunity exploration 107–10
opportunity recognition 61–2, 63, 104, 112, 114, 294
O'Reilly, C. A., III 108, 109, 110
organizational ambidexterity 102, 107–17
organizational barriers or support, for pro-environmental activities 84–5, 86–7, 340, 344, 345–6
organizational learning theory 235
organizational tensions *see* management of tensions
Oruarangi Industry Pollution Prevention Programme (IPPP) 188–9, **188**, 195–200, **199**, 204
Osberg, S. 20

Pacheco, D. F. 61–2, *297*
Papachroni, A. 110
paradox of stability and change 357
paradox theory 356–8
paradoxical thinking 357
Parrish, B. D. 298
Pastakia, A. *290*
Patzelt, H. 1, 13, 14–15, 19, 61, 101, 102, 103–4, 112, 114, 171, 189, *291*, 339, 371–2
PEB *see* pro-environmental behavior life-work spillover
peer support organization 328, *331*, 332
Pemuteran, Indonesia 129–31, 133, *134*, 135
perpetual reasoning 298
personal values of entrepreneurs 114, 210, 212, 214, 215, **215**, 216, 220–1, 224
pesticides, Turkey 253
Phills, J. A., Jr 149
photovoltaic systems 82, 84, 158; solar PV industry, China 216–24, *219*, 220, **222**; *see also* employee energy cooperatives (EECs)
Pinkse, J. 104, 213
Placencia, Belize 131–3, *134*, 135
planetary boundaries 200–2, **201**
plants, and wellbeing 151–2
political activity *see* corporate political activity (CPA) perspective

politically oriented sustainable entrepreneurship 82–3, 91–2, 94
pollution: cruise shipping 277, 278, 279, 280, 281; Oruarangi Industry Pollution Prevention Programme 188–9, **188**, 195–200, **199**, 204
Poole, M. S. 357
Praszkzier, R. 148
Preskill, H. 235
prison collaboration, India 177–9, **177**
private sphere pro-environmental behavior 77–8, **78**, 83, 85, 86, 89, 90–1, 92, 93, 96
proactiveness 105–6
process perspective 104, 322
processes of sustainable entrepreneurship 298–9, 300
Productivity and Innovation Credit scheme, Singapore 36
pro-environmental behavior life-work spillover 73–98; green activities and green positioning of employees 87–90, 93, 95; politically oriented sustainable entrepreneurship 82–3, 91–2, 94; private sphere pro-environmental behavior 77–8, **78**, 83, 85, 86, 89, 90–1, 92, 93, 96; public sphere pro-environmental behavior 77–8, **78**, 82–3, 86, 88, 90, 91–2, 93, 96; sustainable intrapreneurs 73, 74–7, *75*, 83–7, 92–3, 94, 97, 340; task-oriented pro-environmental behavior 90–1, 93, 95; thrifty sustainable entrepreneurship 81–2, 91, 94; *see also* employee energy cooperatives (EECs)
profit motive 13, 14–15, 20; public-private partnerships (PPPs) 308–9, 314
Program Nav Kria, India 172–82, *173*, *174*, **177**
project management, university-industry collaboration 259, *261*
psychological wellbeing, and green building design 145
public sphere pro-environmental behavior 77–8, **78**, 82–3, 86, 88, 90, 91–2, 93, 96
public-private partnerships (PPPs) 306–17

quadruple helix innovation **162**
Québec 299–300

raddi-exchange project, India **177**, 179–80
radio station, Ghana 239
Raisch, S. 110
Ramus, C. A. 75, 76, 340

Rapata, Maryanne 187, 196, 204
rational manager 76, 93
Raworth, Kate 191, 200–2, **201**
Ray, Bola 239
recursive negotiation model 44
recycling, clothing 323, **323**, 325, *326*,
    327, 329, *330*, 333, **334**
Reef Sanctuary Agreement, Zanzibar 129
reefs, protection of 128–33
reform and rehabilitation initiatives, India
    177–9, **177**
reframing 189–90, 191, 203, 357
Reinstaller, A. 212
renewable energies 81, 82, 84, 85, 90–1,
    158, 280; employee energy cooperatives
    (EECs) 338–49, *343*; solar PV industry,
    China 216–24, *219*, *220*, **222**
Renewable Energy Act (REA), Germany
    343, 349n2
Research, Innovation and Enterprise
    (RIE) plan, Singapore 27
research and development function 362–3
resilience 105
resistance 370, 380–2
resource efficiency, Singapore 26, 27, 31,
    37
resources 20; tensions with access to
    175–6; *see also* environment-values-
    resources (EVR) framework
responsible leadership development 230–1
restorative perspective 21
Rio + 20 Summit 200
risk appetite, international humanitarian
    NGOs *381*, 382–3, *387*
risk-taking 105, 106
Rockström, Johan 200
Rosenstie School of Marine and
    Atmospheric Science 278
Rowley, T. J. 65
Royal Caribbean International 273, 278–9
Rural Development Support Programme,
    Turkey 254
Russ-Eft, D. 235
Russia, public-private partnerships (PPPs)
    307–8, 309–17

Santorini 276
Saul, J. 44
Saveriades, A. 275
Say, Jean-Baptiste 16
scale 363
Schaltegger, S. 92, *290*, *291*, *296*, 299, 340
Schaper, M. 298
Schlange, L. E. 60

schools, public-private partnerships (PPPs)
    311, 315
Schrader, U. 74–5, 97
Schumpeter, Joseph 16, 20, 293, 294, 370
scientism, risk of 22
SCOPE Plus, India 172–82, *173*, *174*, **177**
scrubber technology, cruise shipping 279
seasonal employment model, clothing
    sector *326*, 328, 329–32, *331*, 333, **334**
Seghezzo, L. 171
sequential ambidexterity 110
Shane, S. A. 126
Shepherd, D. A. 1, 13, 14–15, 19, 61, 101,
    102, 103–4, 112, 114, 171, 189, *291*,
    339, 371–2
Sheridan, L. 276
Sierra Leone 236
Siggelkow, N. 183, 216
Singapore, state-led social innovation
    25–38, **32**, **33**, **35**, **36**, **37**
Singapore Certified Energy Manager
    (SCEM) grants 28
Singapore Innovation and Productivity
    Institute (SiPi) 28, *29*, **30**
Singh, P. 300–1
SMEs 244–5; ambidexterity 111, 112–15;
    approach to sustainable
    entrepreneurship 245–7, **246**; state-led
    social innovation, Singapore 25–38, **32**,
    33, **35**, **36**, **37**; *see also* Turkish
    agricultural sector
Smith, Adam 13
Smith, W. K. 112
social cohesion 144–5; and public-private
    partnerships (PPPs) 309, 315
social contracts **61**, 63–4, 65–6, 67, 68
social entrepreneurship 13, 14–21, 59,
    102–3, 147–8, 371–2; management of
    tensions 112–13, 170–83; multiple
    institutional logics 352–65, 369–70,
    380–3, *381*; Program Nav Kria, India
    172–82, *173*, *174*, **177**; *see also*
    international humanitarian non-
    government organizations (INGOs)
social gains 13, 15–17, 21–2
social impact cost-benefit analysis 361–2
social impacts, cruise shipping 275–7, 279,
    280, *280*, 281–2
social innovation 43–4, 45, 321;
    definitions 148–9; state-led in Singapore
    25–38, **32**, **33**, **35**, **36**, **37**; workplace
    innovation 150–2
social leadership 19, 20
social network theory 247

social sector, public-private partnerships (PPPs) 310–11, 315
social value 14; public-private partnerships (PPPs) 308, 309, 313–16, 317
solar energy 81, 82, 84, 85, 158, 280; photovoltaic industry, China 216–24, *219*, *220*, **222**; *see also* employee energy cooperatives (EECs)
Sole Rebels 49
Southern Environmental Association 132
Spence, M. *297*
spiral of ethics 193–4, **193**, 203, 204
stability and change, paradox of 357
stakeholder networks 59, 60–8, **61**
stakeholder theory 57, 59–60
Standard Industrial Classification (SIC) 42
Standards, Productivity and Innovation Board (SPRING), Singapore 28
standing out and fitting in of sustainable entrepreneurs 329–32, *330–1*, *334*, *335*
Stanford Social Innovation Review 149
Starr Radio 103.5, Ghana 239
state-led social innovation, Singapore 25–38, **32**, **33**, **35**, **36**, **37**
Steffen, W. 190, 204
Steyaert, C. 322
strategic agricultural planning 254–6, *266*
student internships 260
subjectivist theory of entrepreneurship 106
sustainability, definitions 146, **147**
sustainability conveyors 65
sustainability perspective 21
sustainable development 1, 101; Singapore 26–8
sustainable entrepreneurship: characteristics of sustainable entrepreneurs 295; dangers of 19–21; definitions 13, 101, 102–4, 171, 211–12, 289–94, *290–1*, *292*, 299; determinants of 294–5; versus ecopreneurship *292*, *293*; processes of 298–9, *300*; temporal and context issues 104–5, 106–7; typologies of sustainable entrepreneurs 295, 296–7, 299–300
sustainable intrapreneurship 73, 74–7, *75*, 83–7, 92–3, *94*, 97, 340
Sustainable Shore Excursion Standard 278, 280
Sustainable Singapore Blueprint (SSB) 26, 27, 37
Sweeting, J. E. N 275
systemic social change 20–1

T Group, China 217–24, *219*, *220*, **222**
Takarangi framework 194–5, **195**, 203, 204
Tanzania 128–9, 133, *134*, 135
Tapsell, P. 194
task-oriented pro-environmental behavior 90–1, 93, 95
Taylor, D. W. 91, 92, *290*, *296*
TBL *see* triple bottom line (TBL)
TCE *see* transaction cost economics (TCE)
Te Ao Hurihuri 189, **193**, 195, 202, 204
Teal, G. 276
tensions *see* management of tensions
territorial based conservation *see* entrepreneurial marine protected areas (EMPAs)
Thøgersen, J. 77
thrifty sustainable entrepreneurship 81–2, 91, 94
TOBB (The Union of Chambers and Stock Markets of Turkey) 248, 257
tourism: coastal ecotourism 281; cruise shipping 272–83, *280*; marine protected areas 129–31, 132
Tracey, P. 354
training 300–1; *see also* entrepreneurship education
transaction cost economics (TCE) 311, 312–13
transformational change 1–2
Tripathi, S. 231
triple bottom line (TBL) 60, 101, 146, 148, 298; and green building design *159*, **163**, 164
Turkish agricultural sector 247–59, *250–1*, *263–4*; effectiveness of governmental policies 253–8, *258*, *265–6*; state monitoring mechanisms 252–3, *258*, *265*; university-industry collaboration 258–9, *260–1*
Tushman, M. L. 108, 109, 110
TUSIAD (Turkish Industry and Business Association) 248, 253, 257, 260
Tuttle, D. B. 294
typologies of sustainable entrepreneurs 295, 296–7, 299–300

Uganda 237–8
UK-TURKEY Higher Education Partnership Programme 248
UNDP 132
UNESCO World Heritage Site 132
United Nations 129

University of Exeter 151
University of Miami 278
University of Oregon 152
University of Southampton 248
up-cycle design 325, *326*, 327, 329, *330*, 333, **334**

value creation 60, 64
Value for Money Assessment Guide, UK 312
value for money (VfM) concept 310, 311–13
value propositions, international humanitarian NGOs 381, 383, *387*
value-based business 214
values 41; Confucian 212, 213, 221; personal values of entrepreneurs 114, 210, 212, 214, 215, **215**, 216, 220–1, 224; *see also* environment-values-resources (EVR) framework; social value
Van de Ven, A. H. 357
Van den Hazel, P. 155
Van der Werff, E. 77, 78
Van Maanen, J. 359
Vanclay, F. 275
Venice 277, 282
Venkataraman, S. 61, 104
venture philanthropy 19, 378
VfM *see* value for money (VfM) concept
Vining, A. 312
volunteers 377–8
Voronov, M. 63, 321, 334, 335

Wagner, M. 229, 234–5, *291*, 299, 340
Walley, E. E. 91, 92, 290, 296
Walton, S. 290, 294–5
waste management, cruise shipping 278, 280, 281

waste-exchange project, India **177**, 179–80
water consumption, cruise shipping 278
Wayne, S. L. 275
wellbeing, and green building design 143, 145, 150–2, 158–9
Wild, P. 272
Wilkinson, P. 276
Wilkinson, S. 200
wind energy 82, 280; *see also* employee energy cooperatives (EECs)
Winn, M. I. 104, 246, 290, 293
Woods, C. R. 194
workplace innovation 150–2; *see also* employee energy cooperatives (EECs); pro-environmental behavior life-work spillover
World Bank 132, 257
World Economic Forum 148, 155
World Heritage Site 132
World Vision New Zealand (WVNZ) 374–83, *377*, *379*, 381, 386–8
World Wide Fund for Nature (WWF) 132
Wright, C. 75, 76, 92, 93
Wüstenhagen, R. 297
WVNZ *see* World Vision New Zealand (WVNZ)

York, J. G. 61
Young, Michael 149
Young Foundation 149
youth employment, clothing sector 326, *326*, 328, 329–32, *331*, 333, **334**
Yunus, Mohammad 43, 149

Zahra, S. A. 102
Zanzibar 128–9, 133, *134*, 135
Zolli, A. 105